ELEMENTARY ALGEBRA
Part 2

About the Cover

The design on the cover, which is repeated in black and white on the title page, is a collage of symbols, formulas, instruments, and other devices indicating modern everyday uses of mathematics. The pairs of pictures which open chapters are designed to continue the same theme. They show achievements which have come about with the aid of mathematics in various fields such as science, communication, and transportation.

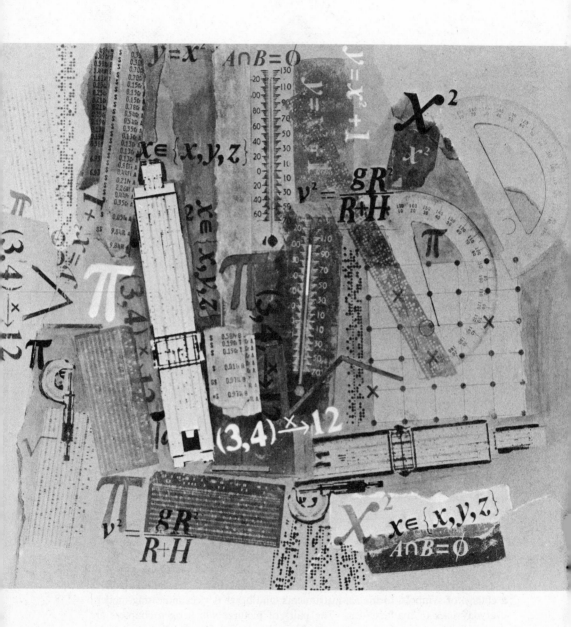

Elementary Algebra

Part 2

RICHARD A. DENHOLM

MARY P. DOLCIANI

EDITORIAL ADVISERS ANDREW M. GLEASON

ALBERT E. MEDER, JR.

HOUGHTON MIFFLIN COMPANY · BOSTON

NEW YORK   ATLANTA   GENEVA, ILLINOIS   DALLAS   PALO ALTO

ABOUT THE AUTHORS

Richard A. Denholm, Associate Director, Computer-Oriented Mathematics Project for Grades 4–12, University of California, Irvine. Dr. Denholm directs the preparation of mathematics and science teachers through the University's Department of Mathematics and Office of Teacher Education. Previously Director of Curriculum and Instruction, Orange County, California, Department of Education, he has been actively concerned with the improvement of mathematics education for several years.

Mary P. Dolciani, Professor and Chairman, Department of Mathematics, Hunter College of the City University of New York. Dr. Dolciani has been a member of the School Mathematics Study Group (SMSG) and a director and teacher in numerous National Science Foundation and New York State Education Department institutes for mathematics teachers.

EDITORIAL ADVISERS

Andrew M. Gleason, Professor of Mathematics, Harvard University. Professor Gleason is prominently associated with curriculum changes in mathematics. He was chairman of the Advisory Board for SMSG as well as co-chairman of the Cambridge Conference which wrote the influential report, *Goals for School Mathematics.*

Albert E. Meder, Jr., Dean and Vice Provost and Professor of Mathematics, Emeritus, Rutgers University, the State University of New Jersey. Dr. Meder was Executive Director of the Commission on Mathematics of the College Entrance Examination Board, and has been an advisory member of SMSG.

STUDENT'S EDITION	ISBN: 0–395–14250–4
STUDENT'S EDITION W/ODD ANSWERS	ISBN: 0–395–14228–8
TEACHER'S EDITION	ISBN: 0–395–14251–2

Contents

7 Multiplication and Division with Fractions   219

8 Addition and Subtraction with Fractions   247

9 Solving Equations and Graphing   285

10 Solving Inequalities and Graphing   321

11 Systems of Open Sentences   357

12 The Real Number System   391

13 Products, Roots, and Quadratic Equations   431

14 Polygons and Circles   453

15 Ratios and Similar Right Triangles 489

PICTURE CREDITS

Page xii / *top*, Courtesy of United Nations — *bottom*, Magnum, Werner Bischof; Page 36 / *top*, Massachusetts General Hospital — *bottom*, Elizabeth Wilcox; Page 71 / The Associated Publishers; Page 72 / *top*, Bibliothèque Nationale, Diderot — *bottom*, Courtesy of Wolf Composition, photo by Marnie Weeks; Page 112 / *top*, Courtesy of the Science Museum, London, photo by Douglas R. G. Sellick — *bottom*, Courtesy of Radio Corporation of America; Page 142 / *top*, Museum of Fine Arts, Boston — *bottom*, Courtesy of R. A. Moog, Inc., Trumansburg, N. Y.; Page 182 / *top*, F. Botts, Grimoldi — *bottom*, Courtesy of Metcalf & Eddy, Inc., photo by Marnie Weeks; Page 217 / Courtesy of Esther C. Goddard; Page 218 / *top*, U.S. Dept. of Agriculture — *bottom*, U.S. Dept. of Agriculture, photo by Murray Lemmon; Page 246 / *top*, Courtesy of Ford Motor Company — *bottom*, Magnum, Burk Uzzle; Page 283 / Wide World Photos; Page 284 / *top*, Science Museum, London — *bottom*, Courtesy of The Aluminum Association; Page 320 / *top*, The Smithsonian Institution — *bottom*, Courtesy of American Textile Manufacturer's Institute; Page 356 / *top*, Courtesy of the Bell Family, © National Geographic Society — *bottom*, Courtesy of Grumman Aerospace Corporation; Page 390 / *top*, Courtesy of Henry Ford Museum, Dearborn, Michigan — *bottom*, Courtesy of Corning Glass Company; Page 430 / *top*, Culver Pictures, Inc. — *bottom*, Thomas J. Croke; Page 451 / Courtesy of Columbia University Library, D. E. Smith Collection; Page 452 / *top*, photo by Werner Forman. Reprinted with permission of The Macmillan Company and George Weidenfeld & Nicholson, Ltd., from *Africa: History of a Continent* by Basil Davidson. © 1966 by Basil Davidson — *bottom*, Marnie Weeks; Page 487 / Courtesy of Royal Greek Embassy; Page 488 / *top*, Courtesy of International Harvester — *bottom*, Erik Anderson; Page 284 / *top*, British Crown Copyright, Science Museum, London.

$=$	is equal to (*p. 4*)	$0.\overline{36}$	the repeating decimal 0.363636 ... (*p. 192*)
$\neq$	is not equal to (*p. 4*)		
$\doteq$	is approximately equal to (*p. 408*)	$\%$	percent; hundredths (*p. 203*)
		$\sqrt{}$	radical sign (*p. 397*)
$<$	is less than (*p. 4*)	$\sqrt{a}$	the positive square root of a (*p. 397*)
$>$	is greater than (*p. 4*)		
$\leq$	is less than or equal to (*p. 4*)	$\sqrt[n]{r}$	the principal nth root of r (*p. 402*)
$\geq$	is greater than or equal to (*p. 4*)		
		± 3	plus or minus 3 (*p. 397*)
$-r$	the opposite (additive inverse) of r (*p. 7*)	$\overline{AB}$	segment AB (*p. 224*)
		$\angle DCF$	angle DCF (*p. 454*)
$\dfrac{1}{r}$	the reciprocal (multiplicative inverse) of r (*p. 23*)	$\triangle BOC$	triangle BOC (*p. 462*)
		$\overparen{ADB}$	arc ADB (*p. 465*)
$\lvert r \rvert$	the absolute value of r (*p. 10*)	$180°$	180 degrees (*p. 459*)
$r \cdot s$	the product of r and s (*p. 21*)	$m\,\overline{AB}$	the length of segment AB (*p. 461*)
$\{\ \}$	set (*p. 38*)		
$\emptyset$	the empty set (*p. 38*)	$m\angle BAC$	the measure of angle BAC (*p. 461*)
$\cap$	intersection of sets (*p. 119*)		
$\cup$	union of sets (*p. 392*)	$m\,\overparen{PQN}$	the measure of arc PQN (*p. 466*)
$\ldots$	and so on (*p. 38*)		
π	(pi) the ratio of the circumference of a circle to its diameter (*p. 55*)	A'	A-prime (*p. 489*)
		$\sim$	is similar to (*p. 490*)
		$\cong$	is congruent to (*p. 490*)
(x, y)	an ordered pair (*p. 59*)	$\sin r°$	the sine of r degrees (*p. 498*)
$f(x)$	value of the function f for a specified value of x (*p. 60*)	$\cos r°$	the cosine of r degrees (*p. 502*)
3^5	$3 \cdot 3 \cdot 3 \cdot 3 \cdot 3$; 3 is called the base, 5 is called the exponent (*p. 82*)	$\tan r°$	the tangent of r degrees (*p. 507*)
		$\oplus$	addition in a modular system (*p. 387*)
G.C.F.	Greatest Common Factor (*p. 118*)	$\ominus$	subtraction in a modular system (*p. 387*)
L.C.D.	Least Common Denominator (*p. 262*)	$\otimes$	multiplication in a modular system (*p. 428*)
$\dfrac{a}{b}$	a fraction (*p. 183*); the ratio of a to b (*p. 199*)	$\oplus$	division in a modular system (*p. 428*)
$a{:}b$	the ratio of a to b (*p. 199*)		

xi

A primitive bridge in rural Nepal . . .

A modern suspension bridge across the Golden Gate . . .

Directed Numbers
and Operations

Primitive bridges were often made by laying vines or fallen trees across streams. The perilous Nepalese bridge pictured is an example of such a structure in use today in an isolated section of the country. A quarter of the way around the world, the Golden Gate Bridge spans the Golden Gate, entrance to San Francisco Bay. Completed in 1937, it is still an impressive monument to modern architecture and engineering. Rising 220 feet above the water, it is 6451 feet long, one of the largest suspension bridges in the world. Its huge towers, 746 feet high, support the two steel cables, each $36\frac{1}{2}$ inches in diameter, from which the bridge hangs. The designer, Joseph B. Strauss, used precise mathematical calculations in designing it.

Working with Directed Numbers; Absolute Value

1–1   The Number Line and Directed Numbers

Such ideas as "10 degrees below zero" and "a profit of $185" can be represented by directed numbers. For 10 degrees below zero we can write **−10,** which we read *negative 10.* The profit of $185 can be written **185,** which represents *positive 185.* The set of directed numbers is made up of the positive numbers, the negative numbers, and zero. The picture of the number line in Figure 1–1 shows some of the directed numbers assigned to the line. The point marked **0** is called the **origin.** Positive numbers name points to the **right** of zero, while points to the **left** are named by negative numbers.

Figure 1–1

A number assigned to a point on the number line is the coordinate

1

of the point; the point is the graph of the number. On the number line in Figure 1–1, the number $-\frac{2}{3}$, read "negative two thirds," is the *coordinate* of point *A*, while point *A*, lying $\frac{2}{3}$ units to the left of the origin, is the *graph* of the number $-\frac{2}{3}$. The *coordinate* of point *B* is the number **2** (positive 2); point *B* lies 2 units to the right of the origin and is the *graph* of the number **2**.

You have probably noted that in the case of directed numbers the idea of **direction** is important: the graphs of positive numbers lie in a **positive** direction from the zero point, while the graphs of negative numbers lie in a **negative** direction. Every directed number also has a "size" or magnitude, represented by a nonnegative number which states the distance between the origin and the graph of the directed number. From the number line pictured in Figure 1–2, verify that the magnitude of -2 is **2**, and that the magnitude of $2\frac{1}{2}$ is $2\frac{1}{2}$. Note that, for any given magnitude except zero, there are associated *exactly two* directed numbers, one positive and one negative. For example, with a magnitude of 3 we associate the numbers **3** and -3.

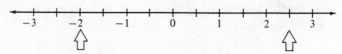

Figure 1–2

ORAL EXERCISES

Tell whether each directed number names a point to the *left* or to the *right* of zero.

SAMPLE: $-10\frac{1}{8}$ *What you say:* Left of zero

1. $-3\frac{1}{5}$	**4.** -5.75	**7.** $-\frac{1}{2}$	**10.** $(3.2 + 5)$
2. 14	**5.** 6^2	**8.** -16.25	**11.** $\frac{10}{75}$
3. $2\frac{1}{8}$	**6.** 0.00001	**9.** -0.0025	**12.** $\frac{1}{6758}$

Match each item in Column 1 with the corresponding item in Column 2.

COLUMN 1	COLUMN 2
13. 40	**A.** Positive two and three tenths
14. -8	**B.** Negative three and one-half
15. 2.3	**C.** Positive forty
16. $-\pi$	**D.** Negative pi
17. $-3\frac{1}{2}$	**E.** Negative eight

For each of the following, name the directed number whose graph is described.

18. 3.4 units to the left of 0   **21.** 6.2 units to the right of 0

19. 25 units to the left of 0   **22.** $1\frac{7}{8}$ units to the right of 0

20. $\frac{10}{3}$ units to the right of 0   **23.** π units to the left of 0

24. Name the positive number whose magnitude is 14.

25. Name the negative number whose magnitude is 10.

WRITTEN EXERCISES

Complete each statement to make it true.

SAMPLE: -10 is the coordinate of the point __?__ units to the __?__ of the origin.

Solution: -10 is the coordinate of the point *10* units to the *left* of the origin.

 1. $-6\frac{1}{5}$ is the coordinate of the point __?__ units to the __?__ of the origin.

2. $10\frac{1}{3}$ is the coordinate of the point __?__ units to the __?__ of the origin.

3. The graph of $4\frac{1}{2}$ is __?__ units to the __?__ of the origin.

4. The graph of $-\frac{5}{8}$ is __?__ units to the __?__ of the origin.

5. The point 16 units to the left of the origin is the graph of __?__.

6. The point $2\frac{1}{5}$ units to the left of the origin is the graph of __?__.

7. The point 1.6 units to the right of the origin is the graph of __?__.

8. The graph of $3\frac{1}{7}$ is __?__ units to the __?__ of the graph of 0.

9. The graph of $-1\frac{1}{8}$ is __?__ units to the __?__ of the graph of 0.

10. __?__ is the coordinate of the point 26 units to the right of the origin.

For each of the following, tell the coordinate of the point on the number line at which you would finish.

11. Start at the origin; move 3 units in the positive direction.

12. Start at the origin; move 2 units in the positive direction, then 3 units in the positive direction.

13. Start at the origin; move 4 units in the negative direction, then move another 4 units in the negative direction.

14. Start at the origin; move 6 units in the positive direction, then 5 units in the negative direction.

For each number, give the distance between the origin and the graph of the number; then give the magnitude of the number.

SAMPLE: $-6\frac{3}{4}$ *Solution:* Distance, $6\frac{3}{4}$ units; magnitude, $6\frac{3}{4}$.

B   **15.** 10.3   **18.** $4\frac{1}{3}$ **21.** $\frac{5}{2}$ **24.** -1

16. -24 **19.** $-6\frac{1}{2}$ **22.** -0.75 **25.** 36.25

17. -30 **20.** 12.4   **23.** 0.005   **26.** $-\frac{7}{5}$

Name a second directed number that has the same magnitude as the given number.

27. -17 **29.** 96   **31.** $8\frac{1}{4}$ **33.** $-5\frac{1}{8}$

28. 62   **30.** -1.05 **32.** -0.01 **34.** 2.08

1–2   Order Relationships and the Number Line

In describing how two numbers are related, we often make order relationship statements about them. You will recall that "5 is less than 9" can be written $5 < 9$. Notice, on the number line shown below, that the graph of **5** is to the *left* of the graph of **9**. To save unnecessary words, we agree to use the number coordinate of a point on the number line to name the point; this makes it possible for us to say, briefly, "5 is to the left of 9." The statement $4 > -6$ is read "4 is greater than negative 6." Verify on the number line that **4** is to the *right* of -6.

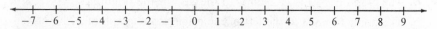

Do you see why we say that the directed numbers are ordered? The number line illustrates the fact that each directed number is less than any directed number to its right. Similarly, each directed number is greater than any directed number to its left.

For any directed numbers **r** and **s**,
if **r** is to the right of **s** on the number line, then **r** > **s**;
if **r** is to the left of **s** on the number line, then **r** < **s**.

Other number relationships with which you are probably familiar include:

Symbol	Meaning
=	**is equal to**
$\neq$	**is not equal to**
$\geq$	**is greater than or equal to**
$\leq$	**is less than or equal to**

ORAL EXERCISES

Use *is greater than* or *is less than* to make each statement true.

SAMPLE: -10 __?__ $3\frac{1}{2}$ *What you say:* -10 is less than $3\frac{1}{2}$.

1. 7 __?__ 12   **5.** 0 __?__ 2   **9.** -0.3 __?__ 0.3
2. -5 __?__ -3 **6.** 0 __?__ 8   **10.** $\frac{1}{2}$ __?__ $-\frac{1}{2}$
3. -4 __?__ 2   **7.** 14 __?__ 0   **11.** 1.07 __?__ 1.60
4. 6 __?__ 1.5   **8.** -3 __?__ 0   **12.** -0.5 __?__ -0.1

Use *is equal to* or *is not equal* to make each statement true.

13. -10 __?__ 10   **16.** 0 __?__ -2 **19.** $(3 + 5)$ __?__ 8
14. 3^2 __?__ 9   **17.** -1.5 __?__ $-1\frac{1}{2}$ **20.** -0.5 __?__ 0.05
15. 8 __?__ 4^2 **18.** 10^2 __?__ -100 **21.** $\frac{3}{2}$ __?__ $\frac{2}{3}$

WRITTEN EXERCISES

State the meaning of each number statement in two different ways.

SAMPLE 1: $3 < 7$ *Solution:* 3 is less than 7;
                      3 lies to the left of 7 on the number
                      line.

SAMPLE 2: $4 \geq -6$ *Solution:* 4 is greater than or equal to -6;
                        4 names the same point as -6 or a
                        point to the right of -6.

1. $8 < 15$ **5.** $2 \leq 5$ **9.** $-3 \geq -3$
2. $-40 < 16$ **6.** $0 > -10$ **10.** $2 \geq -5$
3. $10 > 4$ **7.** $9 \geq -3$ **11.** $-1 < 0$
4. $3 > -6$ **8.** $-4 \leq 2$ **12.** $-16 < 0$

Tell which statements are true and which are false.

13. $-15 < -5$ **17.** $-\frac{3}{5} < -\frac{4}{5}$ **21.** $-1.9 \neq 1.9$
14. $-1 < -\frac{1}{3}$ **18.** $-3 \geq 0$ **22.** $-3 \leq -6$
15. $6 \geq -21$ **19.** $5 \leq 5.01$ **23.** $0 \geq -0.15$
16. $0.05 \neq 0.50$ **20.** $0.03 \neq 0.0003$ **24.** $-10 \leq 0$

B **25.** $3\frac{1}{2} = \pi$ **27.** $0 \leq 0.0001$ **29.** $-\frac{3}{10} \geq -\frac{3}{100}$
26. $-0.002 < -0.0002$ **28.** $-6 \neq 3^2$ **30.** $-\frac{1}{2} > \frac{1}{10}$

If *R, M, K,* and *T* are directed numbers, tell which of the following statements are true and which are false.

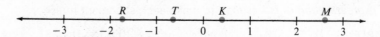

31. *R* and *T* are negative numbers.   **35.** $K \geq 0$

32. *K* is a negative number.   **36.** $-2 < R$

33. *R* is less than zero.   **37.** $R > K$

34. *M* is a positive number.   **38.** $M \geq T$

39. The magnitude of *R* is less than the magnitude of *K*.

40. The magnitude of *T* is less than the magnitude of *R*.

For each of the following statements about the directed number *r*, indicate which word, *positive* or *negative*, will make the statement true.

C **41.** If $r > 0$, then *r* is a __?__ number.

42. If $r < 0$, then *r* is a __?__ number.

43. If $r \geq 0$, then *r* is not a __?__ number.

44. If $r \leq 0$, then *r* is not a __?__ number.

45. If $r \neq 0$, then *r* is either a __?__ or a __?__ number.

46. If $r = 0$, then *r* is neither a __?__ nor a __?__ number.

1–3   Directed Numbers and Opposites

In the illustration below, notice how pairs of directed numbers have been formed. The two numbers in each pair have the same magnitude, since they are equally distant from 0. For example, 3 is 3 units from 0 and −3 is 3 units from 0; each has the magnitude **3**. Any directed

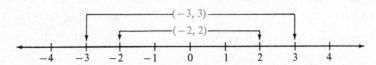

number can be paired with another directed number which has the same magnitude but lies in the opposite direction from zero. For this reason, two numbers like 2 and −2 are called opposites of each other; 0 is its own opposite. Thus we see that the symbol −3 can be read either "**the opposite of 3**" or "**negative 3.**" The opposite of 8 is **−8.** The opposite of −5 is **5** (*positive* 5).

You should recall that, if two numbers are opposites of each other, then their **sum** is **0.** We often describe such numbers as additive inverses of each other. Thus **2** is the additive inverse of -2, and -2 is the additive inverse of **2**. Do you agree that each of the following statements is true?

$$6 + (-6) = 0 \qquad (-12) + 12 = 0 \qquad 3\tfrac{1}{2} + (-3\tfrac{1}{2}) = 0$$

  For every directed number **r** there is a number **−r** such that

$$r + (-r) = (-r) + r = 0.$$

Let us see what we know about values of **r** and **−r**:

1. If r is a **positive** number, then $-r$ is negative; in symbols, if $r > 0$, then $-r < 0$.
2. If r is a **negative** number, then $-r$ is positive; in symbols, if $r < 0$, then $-r > 0$.
3. If r is **zero**, then $-r$ is zero; in symbols, if $r = 0$, then $-r = 0$.
4. The opposite of $-r$ is r; in symbols, $-(-r) = r$.

EXAMPLES: If $r = 7$, then $-r = -7$.
If $r = -5$, then $-r = -(-5) = 5$.
If $r = 3$, $-r = -3$;
so $-(-r) = -(-3) = 3 = r$.
If $r = -3$, $-r = -(-3) = 3$;
so $-(-r) = -3 = r$.

Another useful property concerning opposites (additive inverses) is the following:

  The opposite (additive inverse) of the sum of two numbers is the sum of their opposites:

$$-(r + s) = -r + (-s)$$

Study the examples below showing how this property is applied.

EXAMPLE 1. $-(2 + 5) = -2 + (-5)$
$= -7$

EXAMPLE 2. $-(-3 + 4) = 3 + (-4)$
$= -1$

EXAMPLE 3. $-[(-6) + 2] = 6 + (-2)$
$= 4$

EXAMPLE 4. $-[5 + (-2)] = -5 + 2$
$$= -3$$

ORAL EXERCISES

State the opposite of each of the following, and express it as a directed number.

SAMPLE: A $10.00 increase in price

What you say: A $10.00 decrease in price; -10.

1. 85 feet below sea level

2. Depositing $25.00 in the bank

3. A 5% decrease in cost

4. 16° above zero

5. Withdrawing $10.00 from the bank

6. 3000 feet above sea level

7. 40° below freezing

8. A 10 yard gain in football

9. A profit of $9.00

10. A 4 yard loss in football

11. 50¢ earned

12. A loss of $30.00

Name the additive inverse of each number.

13. -6

14. $3.5m$

15. $-4\frac{1}{5}$

16. -10

17. 0.35

18. 1.06

19. 0

20. $1\frac{1}{3}$

21. $-4t$

22. $-0.03h$

23. 0.03

24. $2\frac{1}{8}$

WRITTEN EXERCISES

Express each of the following in symbols.

SAMPLE 1: Negative 7   *Solution:* -7

SAMPLE 2: The opposite of -9 *Solution:* $-(-9)$ or 9

 1. Positive 65

2. The opposite of -12

3. The opposite of 8.5

4. Negative 19.4

5. The opposite of negative 2

6. The additive inverse of 16

7. The additive inverse of $5x$

8. The opposite of 0

9. The additive inverse of -6.1

10. The opposite of -10.5

11. Negative 8.3

12. The opposite of π

13. The additive inverse of the opposite of 2

14. The additive inverse of the opposite of -7.

Tell whether each statement is true or false.

15. $(-9) + 9 = 0$ **18.** $0 = -(\frac{1}{2}) + \frac{1}{2}$ **21.** $-1.7 + 1.7 = 0$

16. $4b + (-4b) = 0$ **19.** $-7x + 7x = 0$ **22.** $-5 + (-5) = 0$

17. $(-15) + (-15) = 0$ **20.** $\frac{2}{3} + [-(\frac{2}{3})] = 0$ **23.** $0 = 2.3 + (-2.3)$

Simplify each of the following expressions.

SAMPLE: $-(4 + 10)$ *Solution:* $-(4 + 10) = -4 + (-10)$
$$= -14$$

24. $-(12 + 7)$ **27.** $-(-5 + 7)$ **30.** $-[-(4)]$

25. $-(10 + 1)$ **28.** $-(-9 + 6)$ **31.** $-(-5\frac{1}{3} + 2)$

26. $-(-35)$ **29.** $-[-(-6)]$ **32.** $-(3\frac{1}{2} + 4)$

Show that each statement is true.

SAMPLE: $-(4 + 8) = -4 + (-8)$ *Solution:* $\underline{-(4 + 8) = -4 + (-8)}$

$$\begin{array}{c|c} -(12) & -12 \\ -12 & -12 \end{array}$$

$\boxed{\text{B}}$ **33.** $-(12 + 10) = -12 + (-10)$ **36.** $-(12 + 8) = -12 + (-8)$

34. $-15 + (-7) = -(15 + 7)$ **37.** $-[(-5) + 3] = 5 + (-3)$

35. $-8 + (-9) = -(8 + 9)$ **38.** $8 + (-7) = -[(-8) + 7]$

Use the symbol $<, >$ or $=$ to make each statement true.

$\boxed{\text{C}}$ **39.** When $9 < k$, we know that $-9 \underline{\ ?\ } k$.

40. When $-9 = k$, we know that $-(-9) \underline{\ ?\ } k$.

41. When $9 = k$, we know that $-9 \underline{\ ?\ } k$.

42. When $-(-9) > k$, we know that $9 \underline{\ ?\ } k$.

43. When $-(-9) = k$, we know that $-9 \underline{\ ?\ } k$.

44. When $-(9) = k$, we know that $9 \underline{\ ?\ } k$.

1–4   Absolute Value and Directed Numbers

In our earlier work with directed numbers and the number line we said that the magnitude of a number is the distance between the number and 0. The magnitude of a number is called its **absolute value**. Since the magnitude of -3 is **3**, the **absolute value** of -3 is **3**. The magnitude of 6 is **6**, and the **absolute value** of 6 is **6**. The **absolute value** of 0 is **0**. For nonzero numbers, the absolute value is often defined as "the positive number of any pair of opposite directed numbers."

The symbol "| |" is used to stand for the words "the absolute value of." For example,

Words		Symbols
The **absolute value** of **16**	can be written	$\lvert 16 \rvert$.
The **absolute value** of **−2**	can be written	$\lvert -2 \rvert$.
The **absolute value** of **5$\frac{1}{3}$**	can be written	$\lvert 5\frac{1}{3} \rvert$.
The **absolute value** of **−2$\frac{3}{4}$**	can be written	$\lvert -2\frac{3}{4} \rvert$.

By using the absolute value symbol, we can express statements about absolute value quite simply. Here are some examples:

$$\underbrace{\text{The absolute value of } -10}_{\lvert -10 \rvert} \quad \underbrace{\text{is}}_{=} \quad \underbrace{10}_{10}$$

$$\underbrace{\text{The absolute value of } 2\tfrac{1}{3}}_{\lvert 2\frac{1}{3} \rvert} \quad \underbrace{\text{is}}_{=} \quad \underbrace{2\tfrac{1}{3}}_{2\frac{1}{3}}$$

Since the absolute value of any directed number r is equal to the distance between r and 0, we can use symbols to summarize $\lvert r \rvert$ as follows:

For every directed number **r**

if $r \geq 0$, then $\lvert r \rvert = r$,

if $r < 0$, then $\lvert r \rvert = -r$.

ORAL EXERCISES

Use words to translate the meaning of each symbol.

SAMPLE 1: $\lvert -12 \rvert$ *What you say:* The absolute value of −12.

SAMPLE 2: $-\lvert 2 \rvert$ *What you say:* The opposite of the absolute value of 2.

1. $\lvert 35 \rvert$	**4.** $\lvert -1 \rvert$	**7.** $\lvert -3.5 \rvert$	**10.** $-\lvert -3 \rvert$
2. $\lvert -16\frac{1}{2} \rvert$	**5.** $\lvert 0 \rvert$	**8.** $-\lvert 6 \rvert$	**11.** $-\lvert 19 \rvert$
3. $\lvert 4\frac{1}{8} \rvert$	**6.** $\lvert 2.6 \rvert$	**9.** $-\lvert -6 \rvert$	**12.** $-\lvert 10.1 \rvert$

For each number, indicate its distance from 0 (magnitude) and state its absolute value. Refer to the number line if necessary.

SAMPLE: −3   *What you say:* −3 is 3 units from 0;
                              the absolute value of −3 is 3.

13. −4   **15.** 3   **17.** −1⅓   **19.** 3⅔

14. −2⅔   **16.** 1   **18.** 2   **20.** −1

WRITTEN EXERCISES

Express each of the following in symbols.

SAMPLE: The absolute value of 6 is 6.   *Solution:* |6| = 6

1. The absolute value of −9 is 9.

2. The absolute value of 20 is 20.

3. The absolute value of 3¼ is 3¼.

4. The absolute value of −245 is 245.

5. The absolute value of 9.4 is 9.4.

6. The absolute value of 4.3 is 4.3.

Tell which of these statements are true and which are false.

7. |10| = 10   **11.** −4.2 = |4.2| **15.** |−3| > 0

8. |−76| = −76   **12.** 165 = |−165| **16.** |−26| > |10|

9. |−12| = 12   **13.** |25| = |−25| **17.** |−4.9| < |−3.4|

10. |3⅕| = 3⅕   **14.** |8| > |−8| **18.** |−17| ≠ |17|

Simplify each expression.

SAMPLE: |4| + |−15| *Solution:* |4| + |−15|
                                                = 4 + 15 = 19

19. |2| + 17   **23.** |4.2| + |1.5| **27.** |−8| − |−4|

20. |−3| + |12| **24.** 104 + |25| **28.** −|35|

21. |30| + |−7| **25.** |−18| + |6| **29.** −|−35|

22. |−14| + 62   **26.** |−9| − |−3| **30.** |−3| + |7| + 4

31. |−(−8)| **34.** −|10| + |−10| **37.** |−10| · |4|

32. −|−3| + 3   **35.** −|7| + |7| **38.** |−3| + |6 + 8|

33. −35 + |35| **36.** −(5|−2|)   **39.** −|3.4 + 7| − |−2|

Find the value of each expression if $a = 4$, $b = -7$, $c = -5$, and $d = 10$.

SAMPLE: $(|b| + |c|) + d$

Solution: $(|-7| + |-5|) = (7 + 5) + 10$
$$= \quad 12 \quad + 10 = 22$$

C **40.** $|a| + |b| + |c|$ **43.** $|a| \cdot |b| \cdot |c|$ **46.** $|b + c| + a$
41. $(|a| + |b|) - |c|$ **44.** $|d| \cdot |a| \cdot |b|$ **47.** $d + |a + c|$
42. $-(a + |c|) + d$ **45.** $a + d + |b|$ **48.** $d - |a + c|$

Addition and Subtraction of Directed Numbers

1–5 Addition of Directed Numbers

The following list shows the properties that are assumed to hold true for addition with directed numbers.

When r, s, and t are directed numbers:

$r + s$ is a unique directed number   **Closure property**
$$r + s = s + r \quad \textbf{Commutative property}$$
$$(r + s) + t = r + (s + t) \quad \textbf{Associative property}$$
$$0 + r = r + 0 = r \quad \textbf{Additive property of zero}$$
$$-r + r = r + (-r) = 0 \quad \textbf{Additive property of opposites}$$
$$-(r + s) = -r + (-s) \quad \textbf{Property of the opposite of a sum}$$

ORAL EXERCISES

Tell which statements are true and which are false.

1. $3 + (-4) = (-4) + 3$ **6.** $-10 + (-8) = -8 + 10$
2. $-(5 + 9) = -5 + 9$ **7.** $-6b + (-9b) = -(6b - 9b)$
3. $(-6 + 2) + 3 = -6 + (2 + 3)$ **8.** $3.5 + (-3.5) = 0$
4. $-6 + 6 \neq 0$ **9.** $4\frac{1}{8} + 10 = -10 + (-4\frac{1}{8})$
5. $-3m + 3m = 0$ **10.** $2.1k + 4.3k = 4.3k + 2.1k$

Name the property of addition illustrated by each statement.

11. $-4 + (2 + 9) = (-4 + 2) + 9$ **14.** $0 = -7.3 + 7.3$
12. $-14 + 14 = 0$ **15.** $-19 + 0 = -19$
13. $0 + (-35) = -35$ **16.** $6 + (-12) = -12 + 6$

WRITTEN EXERCISES

Show that each of the following gives a true statement when $a = 3$, $b = 6$, $c = -5$, and $d = 1$.

SAMPLE: $b + c = c + b$ *Solution:*

$$\begin{array}{c|c} b + c = c + b \\ 6 + (-5) & -5 + 6 \\ 1 & 1 \end{array}$$

1. $(a + b) + d = a + (b + d)$ **6.** $-a + 0 = -a$

2. $b + (-b) = 0$ **7.** $-b + (-c) = -(b + c)$

3. $-(b + d) = -b + (-d)$ **8.** $c + (d + a) = (c + d) + a$

4. $c + b = b + c$ **9.** $-c + c = 0$

5. $0 + c = c$ **10.** $-(a + d) = -a + (-d)$

Show that each statement is true.

SAMPLE: $-6 + (3 + 10) = (-6 + 3) + 10$

Solution: $-6 + (3 + 10) = (-6 + 3) + 10$

$$\begin{array}{c|c} -6 + 13 & -3 + 10 \\ 7 & 7 \end{array}$$

11. $-12 + 12 = -9 + 9$ **15.** $-20 + (8 + 16) = (-20 + 8) + 16$

12. $-18 + 40 = 40 + (-18)$ **16.** $(-34 + 5) + 6 = -34 + (5 + 6)$

13. $-(14 + 8) = -14 + (-8)$ **17.** $(-9 + 7) + 3 = (-9 + 3) + 7$

14. $(-6 + 6) + 19 = 19$ **18.** $(-5 + 5) + (-11 + 11) = 0$

Simplify each expression completely and justify each step.

SAMPLE: $b + [3 + (-b)]$

Solution: $b + [3 + (-b)] = b + [(-b) + 3]$ Commutative property of addition

$= [b + (-b)] + 3$ Associative property of addition

$= 0 + 3$ Addition property of opposites

$= 3$ Additive property of zero

19. $(m + 2) + (-m)$ **23.** $40 + (-40 + w)$

20. $(-10 + k) + 10$ **24.** $b + [a + (-b)]$

21. $r + [s + (-r)]$ **25.** $[x + (-y)] + [y + (-x)]$

22. $-t + (s + t)$ **26.** $[b + d] + [(-b) + (-c)]$

1–6 Absolute Value and Rules for Addition

The addition of directed numbers can be stated in terms of absolute value. For example, we can add the positive numbers 3 and 4 in either of these ways:

$$(1) \quad 3 + 4 = 7 \quad \text{or} \quad (2) \quad |3| + |4| = 7.$$

Do you see that the result is the same in each case? Study these examples.

$$6 + 9 = 15 \quad \text{or} \quad |6| + |9| = 15$$
$$1.2 + 6 = 7.2 \quad \text{or} \quad |1.2| + |6| = 7.2$$
$$10 + 24 = 34 \quad \text{or} \quad |10| + |24| = 34$$

For the addition of two negative numbers we can write either of these:

$$(1) \quad -5 + (-4) = -9 \quad \text{or} \quad (2) \quad -(|-5| + |-4|) = -9.$$

Again the result is the same in each case. Here are some other examples.

$$-12 + (-7) = -19 \quad \text{or} \quad -(|-12| + |-7|) = -19$$
$$-15 + (-13) = -28 \quad \text{or} \quad -(|-15| + |-13|) = -28$$

Thus we can use the idea of absolute value to make the following statements about adding directed numbers:

---

1. The sum of two **positive** numbers is the sum of their **absolute values**.

2. The sum of two **negative** numbers is the **opposite** of the sum of their **absolute values**.

Now let's consider the sum of the *positive* number **8** and the *negative* number **−3**. Do you agree that the simplified form of 8 + (−3) is 5? We can write:

$$(1) \quad 8 + (-3) = 5 \quad \text{or} \quad (2) \quad |8| - |-3| = 5.$$

Here are some other examples:

$$10 + (-6) = 4 \quad \text{or} \quad |10| - |-6| = 4$$
$$15 + (-6) = 9 \quad \text{or} \quad |15| - |-6| = 9$$

Suppose we are to add −10 and 3. We can write:

$$(1) \quad -10 + 3 = -7 \quad \text{or} \quad (2) \quad -(|-10| - |3|) = -7$$

Consider these further examples.

$$-18 + 6 = -12 \quad \text{or} \quad -(|-18| - |6|) = -12$$
$$-10.8 + 3.2 = -7.6 \quad \text{or} \quad -(|-10.8| - |3.2|) = -7.6$$

On the basis of our observations, we can add a third statement about the sum of two directed numbers:

3. The absolute value of the sum of two numbers, of which one is **positive** and one is **negative**, is the **difference** of their **absolute values**, and
   a. if the **positive** number has the greater absolute value, the sum of the given numbers is **positive**;
   b. if the **negative** number has the greater absolute value, the sum of the given numbers is **negative**.

The following examples show how the rules for finding the sum of two directed numbers can be used in adding several directed numbers.

EXAMPLE 1. Add $10 + (-16) + 8 + (-6)$

   Solution: $10 + (-16) + 8 + (-6)$

   Step 1: $-6 \quad + 8 + (-6)$

   Step 2: $2 \quad + (-6)$

   Step 3: -4, Answer

EXAMPLE 2. Add   *Solution:*   Step 1:   Step 2:   Step 3:

15	15	−38	−57
−38	25	−19	40
25	40	−57	−17, Answer
−19			

ORAL EXERCISES

Complete each of the following.

SAMPLE: $-3 + 10 = ?$ *What you say:* $-3 + 10 = 7$

1. $4 + 9 = ?$ 3. $\frac{1}{5} + (-\frac{4}{5}) = ?$ 5. $-6.2 + 4.1 = ?$
2. $-3 + (-2) = ?$ 4. $-\frac{1}{7} + \frac{4}{7} = ?$ 6. $3 + (-8) + 8 = ?$

7. $-6 + 8 = ?$ **10.** $-4 + (-10) = ?$ **13.** $-10 + 5 = ?$
8. $10 + (-5) = ?$ **11.** $6 + (-6) = ?$ **14.** $-6 + (-3) + 6 = ?$
9. $-8 + 6 = ?$ **12.** $-5 + (-3) = ?$ **15.** $7 + (9) + (-7) = ?$

Add.

16. 5
8
___

18. $-2w$
$10w$
_____

20.   7
-9
___

22. $12rs$
$-12rs$
_____

17. $-5b$
$-2b$
_____

19.   2
-10
____

21. -15
5
___

23.   4.8
-2.5
____

WRITTEN EXERCISES

Add these directed numbers.

 1.   9
10
-3
___

3. -6
-3
2
5
___

5. -7
8
4
-2
___

7. -3.8
-1.1
6.3
1.5
___

2. -9
-3
9
14
___

4.   14
5
-6
-9
___

6. -5
-6
-2
10
___

8.   16.2
-10.1
-15.3
2.4
____

9. $-7 + 6 + 8$
10. $5 + (-7) + 2$
11. $-10 + (-3) + 8$
12. $-6 + 4 + (-2)$
13. $9 + (-6) + 4$

14. $(-4) + (-5) + (-10)$
15. $12 + (-8) + (-4)$
16. $30 + (-20) + (-10)$
17. $-3 + 4 + 2 + (-2)$

B **18.** $-13 + 108 + (-35) + 5$
19. $-21 + 64 + (-10) + 6$
20. $5.3 + (-1.6) + 4.2 + 1.1$
21. $4.8 + (-2.7) + (-5.6) + 1.6$
22. $-1.8 + (-2.4) + 1 + (-7.2)$
23. $2.5 + (-0.5) + 3.1 + 2.4 + (-2.6)$
24. $0.4 + (-1.3) + (-3) + (-0.7) + (-1.4)$
25. $-0.5 + (-10.3) + 0.7 + (-1.2) + (-3)$

PROBLEMS

Solve each of the following problems by adding directed numbers.

SAMPLE: A store owner's records showed these financial gains and losses over the first three months the store was open: a profit of $105.40; a profit of $395.50; a loss of $209.00. What was his financial position at the end of three months?

Solution: 105.40 + 395.50 + (−209.00) = 291.90

The storeowner had a profit of $291.90.

1. Mr. Dent opened a savings account at the bank and made these deposits and withdrawals: $18.00 deposit; $12.00 withdrawal; $30.00 deposit. Find the amount of money left in his account.

2. Mrs. Washington's doctor put her on a diet for six weeks. The following list shows how much she had gained or lost each week: 3 pounds lost; 2 pounds lost; $1\frac{1}{2}$ pounds gained; $2\frac{1}{2}$ pounds lost; 2 pounds lost; $3\frac{1}{2}$ pounds gained. How much weight had Mrs. Washington gained or lost at the end of six weeks?

3. The girls' athletic club had $12.00 in its treasury and then collected $22.50 in dues. The following amounts were spent for a party: $6.40 refreshments; $1.60 for paper plates and cups. What was the financial position of the club?

4. An undersea research vessel is at a depth of 480 feet. It goes down another 60 feet and then rises 180 feet. What is the final position of the vessel?

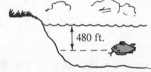

480 ft.

5. The fullback of a football team made these gains and losses in four plays: 3 yard loss; 4 yard gain; $1\frac{1}{2}$ yard loss; 8 yard gain. What was his net gain or loss?

6. A hiker was at the peak of Mt. Whitney, 14,495 feet above sea level. After climbing down for one hour he had descended 840 feet; an hour later he had descended another 650 feet. How many feet above sea level was the hiker at the end of the second hour?

7. The foundation of a large building is 34 feet below the ground level. The top of the building is 198 feet above the foundation level. How far above ground level is the top of the building?

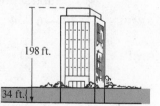

198 ft.

34 ft.

8. A football player made the following gains and losses on five plays: 12, −2, 6, −5, −8. Altogether, how many yards did he gain? How many yards did he lose? What was his total net gain or loss?

1–7   **Subtraction of Directed Numbers**

You probably recall that subtraction and addition are related operations, that is, they are inverse operations. Suppose you are to find the *difference* between 18 and 6. If the problem is written as **18 − 6 = ?** you see at once that the solution is **12**. However, do you see that the problem could have been stated: "What number must be added to 6 to make 18?" In this case the problem is written as **? + 6 = 18.** Do you agree that again the solution is **12**?

The inverse relationship between addition and subtraction is used in the subtraction of directed numbers. For example, to answer the question "What is the difference between 9 and −5?" we can write either of two *equivalent sentences.* (Remember: sentences are **equivalent** if they have the same solution.)

$$9 - (-5) = ? \quad \text{or} \quad ? + (-5) = 9$$

Do you agree that **14** is the solution in each case? We can replace each **?** with **14** to verify this.

$9 - (-5) = ?$		$? + (-5) = 9$	
$9 - (-5)$	14	$14 + (-5)$	9
$9 + 5$	14	$14 - 5$	9
14	14	9	9

 If **r** and **s** are directed numbers, their difference **r − s** is the same as the sum **r + (−s)**.

$$r - s = r + (-s)$$

Study these pairs of examples of equivalent sentences. Can you give the solution for Examples 4 and 5?

	Subtraction		Addition
EXAMPLE 1.	$10 - 6 = 4$	is equivalent to	$10 + (-6) = 4$
EXAMPLE 2.	$7 - (-2) = 9$	is equivalent to	$7 + 2 = 9$
EXAMPLE 3.	$-8 - 3 = -11$	is equivalent to	$-8 + (-3) = -11$
EXAMPLE 4.	$7 - 10 = ?$	is equivalent to	$7 + (-10) = ?$
EXAMPLE 5.	$-8 - (-2) = ?$	is equivalent to	$-8 + 2 = ?$

ORAL EXERCISES

For each subtraction expression in Column 1 tell which addition expression in Column 2 names the same number.

COLUMN 1	COLUMN 2
1. $5 - 4$	**A.** $-5 + (-4)$
2. $3 - (-6)$	**B.** $6 + 10$
3. $-5 - 4$	**C.** $3 + 6$
4. $6 - 10$	**D.** $5 + (-4)$
5. $-4 - 6$	**E.** $6 + 4$
6. $6 - (-10)$	**F.** $3 + (-6)$
7. $6 - (-4)$	**G.** $-4 + (-6)$
8. $3 - 6$	**H.** $6 + (-10)$

Tell what number is named by each expression.

9. $12 - 7$	**12.** $2 - (-8)$	**15.** $-9 - 5$	**18.** $-3 + 6$
10. $10 + (-8)$	**13.** $5 - (-17)$	**16.** $-14 - 7$	**19.** $-0.6 + 0.5$
11. $6 - 15$	**14.** $-5 + (-10)$	**17.** $-2 - 6$	**20.** $-3.5 - 2.4$

WRITTEN EXERCISES

Subtract each lower number from the number above it.

1. $\quad 25$ $\underline{-10}$	**5.** $\quad -56a$ $\underline{-24a}$	**9.** $\quad -108$ $\underline{-108}$	**13.** $\quad -62mn$ $\underline{45mn}$
2. -17 $\underline{-15}$	**6.** $\quad 42$ $\underline{-18}$	**10.** $-75t$ $\underline{75t}$	**14.** -62 $\underline{-62}$
3. $\quad 31$ $\underline{-65}$	**7.** $\quad 24x$ $\underline{67x}$	**11.** -165 $\underline{-104}$	**15.** -6.25 $\underline{1.34}$
4. $\quad 20$ $\underline{30}$	**8.** $\quad 15$ $\underline{-36}$	**12.** $-31k$ $\underline{31k}$	**16.** $-10.74r$ $\underline{-2.31r}$

Complete each subtraction. Check by addition.

SAMPLE: $12 - (-20)$

Solution: $12 - (-20) = 12 + 20$ *Check:* $-20 + 32 = 12$
$$= 32$$

17. $19 - 6$ **22.** $18y - 28y$ **27.** $(-2.4ab) - (3.5ab)$

18. $(-30) - 24$ **23.** $2.3 - 2.0$ **28.** $(-10) - (-10)$

19. $(-10) - 9$ **24.** $5.8 - (-3.0)$ **29.** $365 - (-365)$

20. $22 - 7$ **25.** $(-0.2a) - 0.7a$ **30.** $(-184) - (239)$

21. $25x - 29x$ **26.** $(-0.8s) - 0.4s$ **31.** $(-63t) - 54t$

Write an equation for each question, and then answer the question.

SAMPLE: What number is 4 less than -8?

Solution: $? = (-8) - 4$; the number is -12.

B **32.** What number is 8 less than 15?

33. What number is 10 less than 9?

34. What number is 5 less than 0?

35. What number is 6 less than -3?

36. What number is $4\frac{1}{2}$ less than $-1\frac{1}{2}$?

37. How much greater than -10 is 4?

38. What number, when added to 12, gives the result -4?

39. How much greater than -7 is $-(4 + 9)$?

40. What number, when added to $-3 + (-4)$, gives the result -9?

Multiplication and Division of Directed Numbers

1–8 Multiplication and Directed Numbers

You will probably recall the following ideas from your earlier work dealing with factors and products of directed numbers. Be sure that you understand the pairs of examples that are given.

(1) **Positive** number $\times$ **positive** number = **positive** number.

$$(12)(10) = 120 \qquad\qquad (3.5)(6.7) = 23.45$$
$$|12| \cdot |10| = 120 \qquad\qquad |3.5| \cdot |6.7| = 23.45$$

(2) **Negative** number $\times$ **negative** number = **positive** number

$$(-6)(-8) = 48 \qquad\qquad (-2\tfrac{1}{2})(-3) = 7\tfrac{1}{2}$$
$$|-6| \cdot |-8| = 48 \qquad\qquad |-2\tfrac{1}{2}| \cdot |-3| = 7\tfrac{1}{2}$$

(3) **Positive** number $\times$ **negative** number = **negative** number

$$(10)(-15) = -150 \qquad\qquad (2)(-5\tfrac{1}{4}) = -10\tfrac{1}{2}$$
$$-(|10| \cdot |-15|) = -150 \qquad -(|2| \cdot |-5\tfrac{1}{4}|) = -10\tfrac{1}{2}$$

From the above examples, do you see that the rules for multiplying two directed numbers can be stated in terms of absolute value as follows?

1. The product of two **positive** numbers is the **product** of their **absolute values**.
2. The product of two **negative** numbers is the **product** of their **absolute values**.
3. The product of a **positive** number and a **negative** number is the **opposite of the product** of their **absolute values**.

When the factors in an indicated product include variables, the rules for multiplication of directed numbers are applied in a similar way.

$$(-3)(m) = -3m \qquad\qquad (w)(w) = w^2$$
$$(-k)(k) = -k^2 \qquad\qquad (2x^2)(-x) = -2x^3$$

The following list gives the familiar properties we assume to hold true for multiplication of all directed numbers.

For all directed numbers r, s, and t,

$r \cdot s$ is a unique directed number	**Closure property**
$r \cdot s = s \cdot r$	**Commutative property**
$(r \cdot s)t = r(s \cdot t)$	**Associative property**
$r \cdot 0 = 0 \cdot r = 0$	**Multiplicative property of zero**
$r \cdot 1 = 1 \cdot r = r$	**Multiplicative property of one**
$r(s + t) = r \cdot s + r \cdot t$	**Distributive property**

An indicated product often consists of several factors, as shown in these examples. Check to see if you agree that each statement is true.

$$(-4)(2)(6)(-10) = 480 \qquad\qquad (-5x)(-2)(-3)(6) = -180x$$
$$(-1)(3t)(9)(-2)(8t) = 432t^2 \qquad\qquad (-8)(2)(5)(4) = -320$$

So the rule for multiplying directed numbers can be extended to:

> The absolute value of a product is the **product of the absolute values** of the factors, and
>
> a. if there is an **odd** number of **negative** factors, the product is **negative**;
> b. if there is an **even** number of **negative** factors, the product is **positive**.

ORAL EXERCISES

Simplify each expression.

SAMPLE: $(-6)(m)$ *What you say:* $-6m$

1. $(9)(7)$ **5.** $(-12)(5)$ **9.** $(21)(-d)$
2. $(-3)(-8)$ **6.** $(4)(-k)$ **10.** $(-2)(3a)$
3. $(10)(-6)$ **7.** $(19)(y)$ **11.** $(-3)(2a)(0)$
4. $(7)(-4)$ **8.** $(-m)(-3)$ **12.** $(-2)^3$

13. $(-4)(-3)(-1)(2)$ **14.** $(-4)(0)(-5)(-3)$ **15.** $(-3)^3$

Name the property of multiplication illustrated by each sentence.

16. $(-3)(k) = (k)(-3)$ **20.** $0(-4t) = 0$
17. $4(a + b) = 4a + 4b$ **21.** $(-m)(-r) = (-r)(-m)$
18. $(-10)(1) = -10$ **22.** $[(-3)(-8)]9 = -3[(-8)(9)]$
19. $3(xy) = 3x(y)$ **23.** $[(-b)(5)]0 = 0$

WRITTEN EXERCISES

Perform each indicated multiplication.

1. $(-18)(5)$ **6.** $(0)(-1.8)$ **11.** $-3[6(-5)]$
2. $(-24)(-3)$ **7.** $48(-29)(-1)$ **12.** $(-t)^3$
3. $-(9 \cdot 5)$ **8.** $-[48(-29)]$ **13.** $|-6| \cdot |-7| \cdot |-1|$
4. $-25(4)$ **9.** $(5)(-5)(-5)$ **14.** $-[(-1)(4) - 3]$
5. $-(-4 \cdot 18)$ **10.** $(-2)^4$ **15.** $-(6 \cdot 7)(-2)$

16. $(3)(4)(-5)$ **19.** $|-2| \cdot |45|$ **22.** $(-1)(-1)(-1)(-1)$

17. $(4)(-2)(6)$ **20.** $(-8)^2$ **23.** $(-4x)^3$

18. $-3.2 \cdot 0$ **21.** $-10[2(-4)]$ **24.** $-6(-7)(-8)(0)$

Complete each of the following to make a true statement.

SAMPLE: $(8)(?) = -48$ *Solution:* $(8)(-6) = -48$

B

25. $(-9)(?) = 36$ **29.** $(?)(-12) = 24$ **33.** $(-402)(?) = -402$

26. $(10)(?) = 70$ **30.** $(k)(?) = -\frac{1}{2}k$ **34.** $(327)(?) = -327$

27. $(-7)(?) = -35$ **31.** $(-2b)(?) = 6b$ **35.** $(?)(-m) = -m$

28. $(6)(?) = -6x$ **32.** $(?)(-t) = 0$ **36.** $(-3)(6)(?) = 54$

C

37. $[5(-7)](?) = 105$ **40.** $(-14)[(?)(-3.5)](-5) = 0$

38. $-[7(?)](-4) = -84$ **41.** $-[2(-2)(-2)](?) = 16$

39. $(?)[(-4)(-15)] = -60$ **42.** $(?)[|-4| \cdot |-17|] = -68$

Which sets of numbers are closed under multiplication?

43. $\{-1, 0, 1\}$ **45.** $\{0, -1, -2, -3, \ldots\}$

44. $\{\ldots, -3, -2, -1, 0, 1, 2, 3, \ldots\}$

1–9 Division of Directed Numbers

The division operation is simple to understand once you have mastered multiplication of directed numbers. You will probably recall that division is related to multiplication. For example, $5 \cdot 3 = 15$ and $15 \div 3 = 5$.

At this time it is important that you have the following ideas about division well in mind:

(1) **Division by zero** is not possible.

(2) **Division** is the **inverse** operation of **multiplication**. $r \cdot s = t$ is equivalent to $r = t \div s, s \neq 0$, or to $s = t \div r, r \neq 0$.

(3) If the product of two numbers is **1**, the numbers are **reciprocals** of each other. Every nonzero directed number has a reciprocal, also called its **multiplicative inverse**.

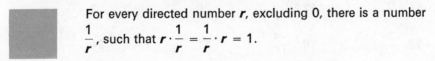

For every directed number *r*, excluding 0, there is a number $\frac{1}{r}$, such that $r \cdot \frac{1}{r} = \frac{1}{r} \cdot r = 1$.

EXAMPLES: 5 and $\frac{1}{5}$ are reciprocals of each other, since $5 \cdot \frac{1}{5} = 1$;

$-\frac{1}{3}$ and -3 are reciprocals of each other, since $(-\frac{1}{3})(-3) = 1$.

By using reciprocals (multiplicative inverses), we can write any indicated division as an indicated product.

For each directed number *r*, and each directed number *s* except 0,

$$r \div s = r \cdot \frac{1}{s}.$$

EXAMPLES:

$10 \div 2 = 5$	and	$10 \cdot \frac{1}{2} = 5$
$8 \div -\frac{1}{4} = -32$	and	$8 \cdot (-4) = -32$
$-6 \div 3 = -2$	and	$-6 \cdot \frac{1}{3} = -2$
$-12 \div -3 = 4$	and	$-12 \cdot -\frac{1}{3} = 4$

ORAL EXERCISES

Name the multiplicative inverse (reciprocal) of each number.

SAMPLE: $-\frac{2}{3}$ *What you say:* $-\frac{3}{2}$

1. 5   **4.** $\frac{2}{5}$ **7.** $\frac{1}{m} \ (m \neq 0)$ **10.** $-a, a \neq 0$

2. -7 **5.** $-\frac{1}{2}$ **8.** $\frac{3}{k} \ (k \neq 0)$ **11.** $\frac{1}{3.5}$

3. $\frac{1}{4}$ **6.** $-\frac{1}{8}$ **9.** $-\frac{2}{a} \ (a \neq 0)$ **12.** $\frac{1}{4.8}$

Complete each indicated division.

SAMPLE: $\frac{-15}{5}$ *What you say:* -3

13. $\frac{18}{6}$ **16.** $\frac{0}{9}$ **19.** $\frac{-15}{-15}$ **22.** $\frac{w}{-w}, w \neq 0$

14. $\frac{10}{-5}$ **17.** $\frac{6}{-6}$ **20.** $\frac{m}{1}$ **23.** $\frac{0}{-5}$

15. $\frac{28}{-4}$ **18.** $\frac{-4}{1}$ **21.** $\frac{k}{-1}$ **24.** $\frac{15}{-1}$

WRITTEN EXERCISES

Write an equivalent multiplication expression for each of the following.

SAMPLE 1: $-8 \div 4$ *Solution:* $-8 \cdot \frac{1}{4}$

SAMPLE 2: $-\frac{2}{3}$ *Solution:* $-2 \cdot \frac{1}{3}$

$\boxed{A}$

1. $10 \div \frac{1}{2}$ **5.** $14 \div (-\frac{1}{2})$ **9.** $(-12) \div (-\frac{1}{2})$ **13.** $\frac{4}{-1}$

2. $-4 \div 3$ **6.** $20 \div (-\frac{1}{4})$ **10.** $\frac{m}{-3}$ **14.** $\frac{13}{-1}$

3. $36 \div (-6)$ **7.** $-10 \div 5$ **11.** $\frac{13}{b}, b \neq 0$ **15.** $\frac{9}{4}$

4. $\frac{25}{-5}$ **8.** $\frac{19}{a}, a \neq 0$ **12.** $b \div (-2)$ **16.** $-50 \div (-10)$

Complete each of the following to make true statements.

SAMPLE 1: $-9 \cdot ? = 1$ *Solution:* $-9 \cdot (-\frac{1}{9}) = 1$

SAMPLE 2: $\frac{-5}{-8} = (-5) \cdot ?$ *Solution:* $\frac{-5}{-8} = (-5)(-\frac{1}{8})$

17. $4 \cdot ? = 1$ **22.** $1 = (-\frac{1}{2}) \cdot ?$ **27.** $1 = a \cdot ?, a \neq 0$

18. $19 \cdot ? = 1$ **23.** $1 = (-\frac{2}{3}) \cdot ?$ **28.** $1 = (-b) \cdot ?, b \neq 0$

19. $(-5) \cdot ? = 1$ **24.** $? = (-\frac{1}{8})(-8)$ **29.** $\frac{-5}{2} = -5 \cdot ?$

20. $? \cdot (-3) = 1$ **25.** $1 = 3 \cdot ?$ **30.** $\frac{3}{2} = ? \cdot \frac{1}{2}$

21. $\frac{6}{2} = 6 \cdot ?$ **26.** $\frac{-9}{10} = ? \cdot \frac{1}{10}$ **31.** $? \cdot \frac{1}{3} = \frac{-2}{3}$

Find the value of each expression if $a = 2, b = -1, c = -3$, and $d = 10$.

SAMPLE: $\frac{bd}{a}$ *Solution:* $\frac{(-1)(10)}{2} = \frac{-10}{2} = -5$

32. $\frac{cd}{a}$ **35.** $\frac{-c}{-b}$ **38.** $\frac{c^2}{-b}$ **41.** $\frac{cd}{ab}$

33. $\frac{bc}{ad}$ **36.** $\frac{(a^2 + b)}{c}$ **39.** $\frac{(a + d)}{-c}$ **42.** $\frac{ac}{b}$

34. $\frac{bc}{a}$ **37.** $\frac{b^2}{a}$ **40.** $d \cdot \frac{1}{a}$ **43.** $\frac{bcd}{a}$

B **44.** $b \cdot \dfrac{1}{ac}$ **46.** $\dfrac{1}{a} \cdot \dfrac{1}{b} \cdot \dfrac{1}{c}$ **48.** $\dfrac{c^2 \cdot b}{a}$ **50.** $\dfrac{(b+2)^4}{d^2}$

45. $\dfrac{c^3}{b^3}$ **47.** $\dfrac{-(bcd)}{a}$ **49.** $\dfrac{(5+c)^3}{b}$ **51.** $\dfrac{c^3 \cdot b^3}{3b}$

C **52.** 1 divided by what number gives -2?

53. 1 divided by what number gives $-\frac{1}{3}$?

54. -3 divided by what number gives 9?

55. $-\frac{1}{2}$ divided by what number gives $-\frac{1}{4}$?

CHAPTER SUMMARY

Inventory of Structure and Concepts

1. **Directed numbers** correspond to points on the number line. Zero is included in the set of directed numbers and the zero point is called the **origin.**

2. **Positive** numbers correspond to points to the **right** of the origin. **Negative** numbers correspond to points to the **left** of the origin. **Zero** is neither positive nor negative.

3. A directed number is the **coordinate** of the point to which it corresponds on the number line. The point itself is the **graph** of the number.

4. The **magnitude** of a directed number is equal to the distance of its graph from the origin.

5. A move on the number line from the origin to the **right** is a move in the **positive** direction; a move from the origin to the **left** is in the **negative** direction.

6. For any directed numbers r and s, if r is to the right of s on the number line, then r **is greater than** s; if r is to the left of s, then r **is less than** s.

7. The common relationship symbols and their meanings are:

$=$	is equal to	$\leq$	is less than or equal to
$\neq$	is not equal to	$>$	is greater than
$<$	is less than	$\geq$	is greater than or equal to

8. Every directed number can be paired with another directed number such that both are equally distant from 0 on the number line. These numbers are called **opposites** (or **additive inverses**) of each other. For every directed number r, there is a number $-r$ (read "the opposite of r") such that $r + (-r) = (-r) + r = 0$.

9. The **opposite of the sum** of two numbers is the same as the sum of their opposites. That is, $-(r + s) = (-r) + (-s)$.

10. The magnitude of a number is the **absolute value** of the number, which is indicated by the symbol "$| \ |$." The absolute value is the **positive** number of any pair of directed numbers; the absolute value of 0 is 0. Thus, for every directed number r, if $r \geq 0$, then $|r| = r$,

$$\text{if } r < 0, \text{ then } |r| = -r.$$

11. The following properties are assumed for addition of directed numbers r, s, and t.
    Closure property: $r + s$ is a unique directed number
    Commutative property: $r + s = s + r$
    Associative property: $(r + s) + t = r + (s + t)$
    Additive property of zero: $0 + r = r + 0 = r$
    Additive property of opposites: $-r + r = r + (-r) = 0$
    Property of the opposite of a sum: $-(r + s) = -r + (-s)$

12. The rules for adding two directed numbers can be stated in terms of absolute value:
    (1) The sum of two **positive** numbers is the **sum** of their **absolute values**.
    (2) The sum of two **negative** numbers is the **opposite** of the **sum** of their **absolute values**.
    (3) The absolute value of the sum of two numbers, of which one is **positive** and one is **negative**, is the **difference** of their **absolute values**, and
       a. if the **positive** number has the greater absolute value, the sum of the given numbers is **positive**;
       b. if the **negative** number has the greater absolute value, the sum of the given numbers is **negative**.

13. Addition and subtraction are **inverse** operations. For directed numbers r and s, $r - s = r + (-s)$.

14. The following properties are assumed for multiplication of directed numbers r, s, and t.
    Closure property: rs is a unique directed number
    Commutative property: $rs = sr$
    Associative property: $r(st) = (rs)t$
    Distributive property: $r(s + t) = rs + rt$
    Multiplicative property of 0: $r \cdot 0 = 0 \cdot r = 0$
    Multiplicative property of 1: $r \cdot 1 = 1 \cdot r = r$

15. The rules for multiplying directed numbers can be stated in terms of absolute value:
    (1) The product of two **positive** numbers is the **product** of their **absolute values**.

(2) The product of two **negative** numbers is the **product** of their **absolute values**.

(3) The product of a **positive** number and a **negative** number is the **opposite of the product** of their **absolute values**.

(4) The absolute value of the product of several factors is the **product** of the **absolute values** of the factors, and

    a. if there is an **odd** number of **negative** factors, the product is **negative**;

    b. if there is an **even** number of **negative** factors, the product is **positive**.

16. Multiplication and division are **inverse** operations. For every directed number r (except 0) there is a number $\dfrac{1}{r}$ such that $r \cdot \dfrac{1}{r} = \dfrac{1}{r} \cdot r = 1$;

and, for all directed numbers r and s, $s \neq 0$, $r \div s = r \cdot \dfrac{1}{s}$.

Vocabulary and Spelling

directed numbers (*p. 1*)

origin (*p. 1*)

coordinate (*p. 1*)

graph (*p. 2*)

positive direction (*p. 2*)

negative direction (*p. 2*)

magnitude (*p. 2*)

order relationship (*p. 4*)

opposites (*p. 6*)

additive inverses (*p. 6*)

absolute value (*p. 9*)

additive property of zero (*p. 12*)

closure property (*p. 12*)

commutative property (*p. 12*)

associative property (*p. 12*)

inverse operations (*p. 18*)

equivalent sentences (*p. 18*)

distributive property (*p. 21*)

multiplicative property of zero (*p. 21*)

multiplicative property of one (*p. 21*)

reciprocals (*p. 23*)

multiplicative inverses (*p. 23*)

Chapter Test

1. Name the coordinate of the point $4\frac{1}{10}$ units to the left of the origin.

2. Name two directed numbers whose magnitude is 8.

3. Name the coordinate of the point at which you would finish if you start at the origin, move $2\frac{1}{2}$ units in the positive direction, and then move 6 units in the negative direction.

Make each of the following a true statement by using $=$, $<$, or $>$.

4. $-5 \underline{\ ?\ } -6.4$ **6.** $(-3)(-12) \underline{\ ?\ } 6^2$ **8.** $4 + (-6) \underline{\ ?\ } -1$

5. $10 \underline{\ ?\ } -2 + 15$ **7.** $4 - 19 \underline{\ ?\ } -10$ **9.** $8 \div (-2) \underline{\ ?\ } -4$

10. If k is a positive number, then $k \underline{\ ?\ } 0$.

11. If k is a negative number, then $k \underline{\ ?\ } 0$.

12. If k is a directed number that is neither positive nor negative, then $k \underline{\ ?\ } 0$.

Complete each of the following to make a true statement.

13. $|-17| = ?$ **15.** $|-2| + |10| = ?$ **17.** $|-9| \cdot |-3| = ?$

14. $|3.9| = ?$ **16.** $|7| - |-3| = ?$ **18.** $-(|-5| + |-8|) = ?$

Add.

19. $\begin{array}{r} -15 \\ 74 \\ 35 \\ -19 \\ \hline \end{array}$ **20.** $\begin{array}{r} 1\frac{1}{2} \\ -3\frac{1}{4} \\ -5\frac{1}{4} \\ 6 \\ \hline \end{array}$ **21.** $\begin{array}{r} -2.80 \\ -1.03 \\ -7.15 \\ -1.23 \\ \hline \end{array}$

Subtract each lower number from the one above it.

22. $\begin{array}{r} -48 \\ 26 \\ \hline \end{array}$ **23.** $\begin{array}{r} -9.27 \\ -1.05 \\ \hline \end{array}$ **24.** $\begin{array}{r} 96 \\ -24 \\ \hline \end{array}$

Complete each of the following to make a true statement.

25. $(-9)(-10) = ?$ **27.** $(3)(4)(-2) = ?$ **29.** $(6)(-9)(0) = ?$

26. $-2[(3)(-5)] = ?$ **28.** $18 \div (-9) = ?$ **30.** $(-42) \div (-6) = ?$

Chapter Review

1–1 The Number Line and Directed Numbers

Complete each statement by using the word *positive* or the word *negative*.

1. The number -6 is in a $\underline{\ ?\ }$ direction from the origin.

2. The number 15 is in a $\underline{\ ?\ }$ direction from the origin.

3. The number -1 is in a $\underline{\ ?\ }$ direction from -10.

Name these directed numbers.

4. 6.8 units to the left of 0   **5.** $19\frac{1}{2}$ units to the right of 0

6. The point whose graph is $6\frac{1}{2}$ units to the left of the origin

Give the magnitude of each directed number.

7. -27 **8.** 27   **9.** 3.8   **10.** -16.5

1–2   Order Relationships and the Number Line

Give the meaning of each symbol in words.

11. $\neq$ **12.** $<$ **13.** $\leq$ **14.** $>$ **15.** $\geq$

Write a number sentence for each of the following.

16. -8 is to the left of 4.   **19.** 3 is equal to or greater than -8.

17. 0 is to the right of -9.   **20.** -14 is equal to or less than -3.

18. -2 is greater than -2.3.   **21.** -1.6 is not the same as 1.6.

1–3   Directed Numbers and Opposites

Write a directed number for each expression.

22. The opposite of 34   **25.** The opposite of x

23. The opposite of -45 **26.** The additive inverse of -10

24. The opposite of $\frac{2}{3}$ **27.** The additive inverse of $3m$

Complete each of the following to make a true statement.

28. $5 + (-5) = \,?$ **30.** $-(8 + 9) = \,?$ **32.** $-19 + 9 = \,?$

29. $-3t + 3t = \,?$ **31.** $-(-68) = \,?$ **33.** $-(-3 + 8) = \,?$

1–4   Absolute Value and Directed Numbers

Write a number statement for each of the following.

34. The absolute value of -3 is 3.   **35.** The absolute value of $\frac{1}{3}$ is $\frac{1}{3}$.

Name these directed numbers.

36. Two different numbers each having an absolute value of 13

37. A number whose absolute value is zero

Give the value of each expression.

38. $|-30| + 4$ **40.** $|-4.1| + |-2|$ **42.** $|-5| + |7| + |2|$

39. $|10| + |-3|$ **41.** $|14| - |-3|$ **43.** $-|10 - 35|$

1–5 Addition of Directed Numbers

Name the addition property suggested by each sentence.

44. $t + m = m + t$ **47.** $-w + w = w + (-w)$

45. $0 + x = x + 0 = x$ **48.** $a + (b + c) = (a + b) + c$

46. $-(b + d) = -b + (-d)$

Show whether each of the following gives a true or a false statement, when $r = 2$, $s = -5$, and $t = -1$.

49. $r + (s + t) = (r + s) + t$ **51.** $-(r + s) = -r + s$

50. $0 + (s + t) = (s + t)$ **52.** $-s + (-t) = -(s + t)$

1–6 Absolute Value and Rules for Addition

Use the words *always*, *sometimes*, or *never* to make true statements.

53. The sum of two positive numbers is __?__ a positive number.

54. The sum of two negative numbers is __?__ a positive number.

55. The sum of a positive number and a negative number is __?__ positive.

56. The sum of 0 and a negative number is __?__ a negative number.

Add.

57. -35 **58.** -16 **59.** 85 **60.** 2.31

     48 -10 103 -8.75

61. $6 + (-8)$ **62.** $10 + (-15) + 3$ **63.** $-3 + 6 + 8 + (-8)$

1–7 Subtraction of Directed Numbers

Subtract each lower number from the number above it.

64. -35 **65.** $40k$ **66.** -10.8 **67.** $-4.6t$

     17 $-5k$ -15.9 $-3.2t$

Complete each indicated subtraction.

68. $6 - 14$ **69.** $(-3) - 5$ **70.** $6.5 - (-4)$ **71.** $(-6t) - 4t$

1-8 Multiplication of Directed Numbers

Use the word *positive* or the word *negative* to make each statement true.

72. The absolute value of a positive number is __?__.

73. The absolute value of a negative number is __?__.

74. The absolute value of a number is never __?__.

Match each item in Column 1 with the related item in Column 2.

COLUMN 1	COLUMN 2
75. $x(y + w) = xy + xw$	**A.** Commutative property
76. $m \cdot 0 = 0 \cdot m = 0$	**B.** Multiplicative property of 1
77. $ab = ba$	**C.** Distributive property
78. $t \cdot 1 = 1 \cdot t = t$	**D.** Multiplicative property of 0
79. $a(bc) = (ab)c$	**E.** Associative property

Simplify each expression.

80. $(-15)(4)$

82. $(18)(-14)$

84. $(-t)(15)(4)$

81. $(35)(19)$

83. $(-9)(-8)$

85. $(-7)(-3)(b)$

1-9 Division of Directed Numbers

Name the reciprocal (multiplicative inverse) of each number.

86. 3

87. -5

88. $-\frac{2}{5}$

89. $\frac{m}{3}, m \neq 0$

Complete each indicated division.

90. $-40 \div 8$

91. $-35 \div (-7)$

92. $27 \div (-3)$

93. $\frac{-16k}{8}$

Complete each of the following to make a true statement.

94. $7 \cdot (?) = 1$

95. $(-\frac{2}{3})(-\frac{3}{2}) = ?$

96. $(?)(-t) = 1$

Review of Skills

Write each of the following in exponential notation.

1. $2 \cdot 2 \cdot 2 \cdot 2 \cdot 2$

2. $ab \cdot ab \cdot ab$

3. $(-5)(-5)(-5)$

4. $x \cdot x \cdot x \cdot x$

5. $\frac{1}{3} \cdot \frac{1}{3} \cdot \frac{1}{3}$

6. $\frac{m}{2} \cdot \frac{m}{2} \cdot \frac{m}{2}$

Match each set of numbers in Column 1 with the related item in Column 2.

COLUMN 1

7. $\{0, 1, 2, 3, 4, \ldots\}$

8. $\{\ldots, -3, -2, -1, 0, 1, 2, 3, \ldots\}$

9. $\{0, 2, 4, 6, 8, \ldots\}$

10. $\{-1, -2, -3, -4, \ldots\}$

11. $\{1, 2, 3, 4, 5, \ldots\}$

12. $\{1, 3, 5, 7, 9, \ldots\}$

COLUMN 2

A. Set of positive integers

B. Set of nonnegative even numbers

C. Set of whole numbers

D. {integers}

E. {negative integers}

F. Set of positive odd numbers

Name the number whose graph is indicated by each letter.

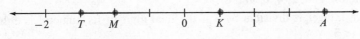

13. T **14.** K **15.** A **16.** M

Write the set of numbers graphed on each number line

17.  **19.**

18.  **20.**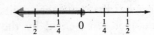

Simplify each expression.

21. $3x + 5x$

22. $ab + 8ab$

23. $7x + 3y + 6y$

24. $13t - 6t + t$

25. $(-1)(x) + 5x$

26. $2m^2 + m^2 - 5m^2$

Match each item in Column 1 with the related item in Column 2.

COLUMN 1

27. area of a rectangle

28. circumference of a circle

29. area of a square

30. area of a circle

31. area of a triangle

32. perimeter of a square

33. perimeter of a rectangle

COLUMN 2

A. s^2

B. $\frac{1}{2} \cdot b \cdot h$

C. $4s$

D. $\pi \cdot d$

E. $l \cdot w$

F. $2l + 2w$

G. πr^2

■ ■

CHECK POINT
FOR EXPERTS

Seven Rules for Divisibility

There are some simple rules for divisibility that are often useful when you are working with the set of integers. Recall that when we say that one number is **divisible** by another we mean that division of the first number by the second has a **zero remainder**.

We can state the rules for divisibility by 2 and by 5 as follows:

---

1. An integer is divisible by **2** if the **final digit** of its numeral is one of the digits **0, 2, 4, 6**, and **8**.

2. An integer is divisible by **5** if the **final digit** of its numeral is either **0** or **5**.

Now notice that **10 = 2 × 5**, so any integer that is divisible by **10** must be divisible by both **2** and **5**. This gives us a third rule:

---

3. An integer is divisible by **10** if the **final digit** of its numeral is **0**.

To decide when a number is divisible by **4**, we first note that all multiples of **100**, such as 100 and 200, are divisible by **4**. So if the numeral for a number has three or more digits, do you see that we need only think about the number represented by the final two digits? For example, **3516 = 3500 + 16**; we know that **3500** is divisible by **4**, and that **16 = 4 × 4**, so we can write

$$3516 = 3500 + 16 = 4(\text{some integer}) + 4(4)$$
$$= 4[(\text{some integer}) + 4].$$

Thus we know that **3516** is divisible by **4** because **16** is divisible by **4**. So we state a fourth divisibility rule:

---

4. An integer is divisible by **4** if the **last two digits** of its numeral represent a number divisible by **4**.

A similar rule for divisibility by **8** follows from the fact that every multiple of **1000** is divisible by **8**. For example

$$75,336 = 75000 + 336 = 8(\text{some integer}) + 8(42)$$
$$= 8[(\text{some integer}) + 42].$$

Thus **75336** is divisible by **8** because **336** is divisible by **8**. The rule can be stated as follows:

5. An integer is divisible by **8** if the **last three digits** of its numeral represent a number divisible by **8**.

To decide when a number is divisible by **3** and when it is divisible by **9**, we find the sum of the digits of its numeral. For example, consider the number **6312**. The sum of the digits is $6 + 3 + 1 + 2 = 12$. Now note that **12** is divisible by **3**, and so is the number **6312**, which equals 3×2104. It can be shown that it is always true that when the sum of the digits of a numeral is divisible by 3 the number the numeral represents is also divisible by 3. This gives us a sixth rule:

6. An integer is divisible by **3** if the **sum of the digits** of its numeral is divisible by **3**.

There is a similar rule for divisibility by **9**. For example, consider the number **2484**, and the sum of its digits. $2 + 4 + 8 + 4 = 18 = 9 \times 2$ and $2484 = 9 \times 276$. Both the number and the sum of the digits of its numeral are divisible by **9**.

7. An integer is divisible by **9** if the **sum of the digits** of its numeral is divisible by **9**.

Do you agree that any number that is divisible by 9 is also divisible by 3? Is every number that is divisible by 3 also divisible by 9?

Questions

For each of the following numerals, find a digit to replace the letter *a* so that the resulting numeral will name a number that is divisible by 9.

1. $71a$ **2.** $304a6$ **3.** $a05$

In each of the following numerals, which of the three digits 1, 3, and 5 must be used to replace the letter *d* so that the resulting numeral will name a number divisible by 3?

4. $48d2$ **6.** $-4d$ **8.** $1,001,00d$

5. $3d0$ **7.** $d37$ **9.** $-99,99d$

10. Is 36 divisible by 4? Is 736 divisible by 4?

11. Is 18 divisible by 4? Is 1418 divisible by 4?

12. Is 44 divisible by 4? Is 19,744 divisible by 4?

13. Is 488 divisible by 8? Is $-5,488$ divisible by 8?

14. Is 344 divisible by 8? Is 427, 344 divisible by 8?

15. Is 036 divisible by 8? Is $-19,036$ divisible by 8?

An early ether inhaler . . .

Modern aids to surgery . . .

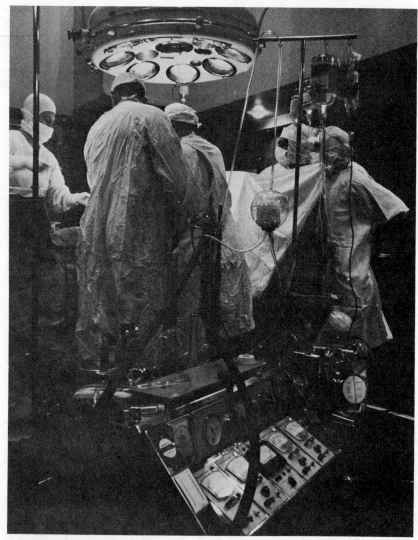

Solving Open Sentences

A significant event in medical history took place in Boston in 1846, when ether was first used in performing an operation. The ether inhaler was a glass vessel containing a sponge, and provided with valves to control the mixture of ether and air to be inhaled; the valves were so arranged that the pressure of expired air closed one and opened another, allowing vapor that had been breathed to pass into the room instead of returning to the inhaler. In the modern surgery team, anesthesiologists, at the right in the picture, play a vitally important role. The instrument panel shows the controls of a pump designed by modern technologists to oxygenate and recirculate blood during open heart surgery. In medicine, as in other fields, mathematics is important in the development of new techniques.

Solution Sets of Open Sentences

2–1 Open Sentences, Expressions, and Variables

Each of the following sentences might be described as **open** because some information is missing. The blank stands for whatever needs to be supplied to make a complete and accurate statement.

Bill is ——— inches taller than Louis.

My brother's first name is ———.

There are ——— books in the school library.

It is not possible to tell whether an open sentence is true or false until some replacement is given for the blank. Mathematical sentences like the following are called open sentences.

$$m + 6 > 9 \qquad 3 + 2.5 = ? \qquad k - 0 = k$$

An open sentence may be an equation or an inequality. The missing information may be indicated by a letter, a question mark, or a blank. Such a symbol is called a variable. Every open sentence contains at least one variable.

To solve an open sentence it is necessary to know from what set of numbers replacements for the variable may be taken. This set is called the replacement set or the domain of the variable. Each member of the domain that can replace the variable and cause the open sentence to become a **true** statement is a solution of the equation or the inequality. The set of all those members of the domain that produce true statements is the solution set. Normally, there are some members of the domain that do not belong to the solution set.

The domain of a variable may be stated either in roster form or by a rule. For example:

Roster	Rule
$\{-1, -2, -3, -4, \ldots\}$	{the negative integers}
$\{1, 3, 5, 7, 9\}$	{the first five positive odd numbers}

If the domain of the variable of an open sentence is not indicated, we shall assume it to be {the directed numbers}.

Suppose that you are to find the solution set for $n + 5 = 7$, and that the domain of the variable is $\{0, 1, 2, 3, 4, \ldots\}$. Do you see that **2** is the only number in the domain that can replace the variable and result in a true statement? Thus the solution set is $\{2\}$.

$$0 + 5 = 7 \quad \textbf{false}$$
$$1 + 5 = 7 \quad \textbf{false}$$
$$2 + 5 = 7 \quad \textbf{true}$$
$$3 + 5 = 7 \quad \textbf{false}$$
$$\vdots \qquad \vdots$$

Consider the open sentence $n + 1 > 5$ when the domain of the variable is $\{0, 2, 4, 6, 8, \ldots\}$. Notice which members of the domain result in true statements. The solution set is $\{6, 8, 10, 12, \ldots\}$.

$$0 + 1 > 5 \quad \textbf{false}$$
$$2 + 1 > 5 \quad \textbf{false}$$
$$4 + 1 > 5 \quad \textbf{false}$$
$$6 + 1 > 5 \quad \textbf{true}$$
$$8 + 1 > 5 \quad \textbf{true}$$
$$\vdots \qquad \vdots$$

You may already know that some sentences do not have solutions. Let's look at the sentence $\dfrac{x}{2} = 3\dfrac{1}{3}$ when the domain of the variable is {the integers}. Do you see that you could continue replacing x with integers without ever getting a true statement? Thus, the solution set is the empty set, which is written { } or $\emptyset$.

$$\vdots \qquad \vdots$$
$$\frac{-2}{2} = 3\tfrac{1}{3} \quad \textbf{false}$$
$$\frac{-1}{2} = 3\tfrac{1}{3} \quad \textbf{false}$$
$$\frac{0}{2} = 3\tfrac{1}{3} \quad \textbf{false}$$
$$\frac{1}{2} = 3\tfrac{1}{3} \quad \textbf{false}$$
$$\vdots \qquad \vdots$$

ORAL EXERCISES

Give a rule that describes each set.

SAMPLE: {2, 3, 5, 7}   *What you say:* {the first four prime numbers}

1. {a, b, c, d, e}

2. {1, 2, 3, 4, ...}

3. {0, 2, 4, 6, 8}

4. {November, December}

5. {101, 102, 103}

6. {... −2, −1, 0, 1, 2 ...}

7. {10, 20, 30, 40, 50}

8. {−3, −4, −5, −6, ...}

9. {1, 3, 5, 7, 9, ...}

Use the roster method to state each set.

10. {the first four months of the year}

11. {the positive integers less than 3}

12. {the integers between −2 and −3}

13. {the whole numbers}

14. {the prime numbers}

15. {the even prime numbers}

16. {the whole numbers equal to or greater than 3}

17. {the integers equal to or less than −5}

WRITTEN EXERCISES

Find all the values for each expression when the domain of *t* is {10, 20, 30} and the domain of *s* is {−1, 0, 1}.

SAMPLE: $3s$ *Solution:* (3)(−1) = −3
(3)(0) = 0
(3)(1) = 3

[A]

1. $7s$

2. $5t$

3. $3s^2$

4. $1 + 4s$

5. $8t + 15$

6. $3 + 6s$

7. $9 − 2s$

8. $510 − 2t$

9. $\dfrac{8s}{2}$

10. $4(t + 5)$

11. $3 − 10s$

12. $\dfrac{2t}{5}$

13. $\dfrac{-6t}{12}$

14. $2.3t + 1$

15. $\dfrac{s}{-2}$

Write the solution set for each open sentence if the domain of the variable is {the integers}.

SAMPLE 1: $n + 15 = 20$ *Solution:* {5}

SAMPLE 2: $k > -4$ *Solution:* {−3, −2, −1, 0, 1, . . .}

16. $9 + a = 17$	**23.** $c - 3 = 14$	**30.** $\frac{1}{2}h = 16$
17. $3 + m = 11$	**24.** $5r = -15$	**31.** $k \div 3 = -5$
18. $19 - w = 4$	**25.** $t + 2 = 15$	**32.** $10 \div r = -1$
19. $8 + x = 5$	**26.** $2m = 5\frac{1}{2}$	**33.** $\frac{1}{2}m = 5$
20. $3 + y = -6$	**27.** $8w = -40$	**34.** $b \cdot b \cdot b = -8$
21. $n > 7$	**28.** $-3 < b$	**35.** $z \cdot z = 4$
22. $d < 2$	**29.** $3y = 14$	**36.** $n + 0 = n$

Give the solution set for each sentence if the domain of the variable is {the directed numbers}.

SAMPLE 1: $t = t + 0$ *Solution:* {the directed numbers}

SAMPLE 2: $r + 1 > 7$ *Solution:* {the directed numbers greater than 6}

B
37. $(m)(1) = m$	**40.** $-10 > t$	**43.** $\dfrac{n}{n} = 1$
38. $y + 2 > 5$	**41.** $-3 < w$	**44.** $m^2 + 1 = 26$
39. $r - 0 = r$	**42.** $s^2 + 1 = 10$	**45.** $\dfrac{x}{x} = 0$

C
46. $\dfrac{m}{m} = -1$	**47.** $(s^3)(-1) = 27$	**48.** $m^2 > 4$

PROBLEMS

1. The formula $A = lw$ is used to calculate the area of a rectangle. In this rectangle the length is given as 15 inches. Suppose the domain of the variable w is {10, 20}. That is, 10 and 20 are numbers of inches that are replacements for w in $A = 15 \cdot w$. Give all the possible values for the area of the rectangle. Hint: If $w = 10$, then $A = 15 \cdot 10$ (sq. in.).

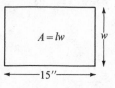

2. The area A of the square given here can be found by using the formula $A = s^2$. Find all the values for the area if the domain of the variable s, in feet, is {2, 4, 8}.

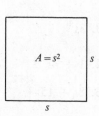

3. The total surface area A of a cube-shaped box can be found by using the formula $A = 6s^2$. Members of the domain are numbers of inches. Find all the values for the total surface area of the box if the domain of s is $\{1, 2, 4, 5\}$.

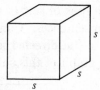

4. The volume V of the box shown here can be found by using the formula $V = 4 \cdot 9 \cdot h$. Find all the possible values for the volume of the box when the domain of the variable h, in inches, is $\{2, 4, 6\}$.

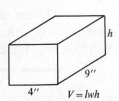

5. The volume V of a cylinder-shaped chemical storage tank can be calculated with the formula $V = Bh$ where B is the area of the base and h is the height. What are the possible values for the volume of the tank if the area of the base is 192 square feet and the domain of h, in feet, is $\{5, 10, 20\}$?

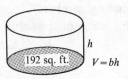

2–2 Graphs of Sets of Numbers

A directed number can be thought of as the coordinate of a point on the number line. The point is then called the graph of that directed number. To draw a graph of the set $\{-1, -\frac{1}{2}, 0, \frac{1}{2}, 1\}$ we simply make large dots at the corresponding points on the number line in this manner.

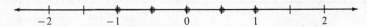

The number line graph below illustrates the set described by the rule {**the directed numbers greater than 2**}.

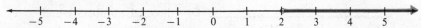

Notice that the open dot at 2 indicates that the graph does not include 2. The red arrow shows that all numbers to the right of 2 are in the graph.

The graph of the set described by the rule {**the directed numbers between and including** $-\frac{1}{2}$ **and** $\frac{1}{2}$} must have solid dots at $-\frac{1}{2}$ and $\frac{1}{2}$ to show that those points are included in the graph.

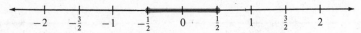

Graphs of sets of numbers are used to represent the solution sets of open sentences. Consider the equation $y + 1 = -1$ when the domain of y is {**the directed numbers**}. Do you see that the solution set is $\{-2\}$? The graph of this solution set is shown below.

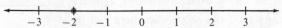

How is the solution set of $k \leq 1$ graphed? If the domain of k is {**the directed numbers**}, then 1 and all numbers less than 1 are members of the solution set. We can graph this solution set as follows:

Now consider the inequality $x \leq 4$ when the domain of x is {**the counting numbers**}. Do you agree that the solution set is $\{1, 2, 3, 4\}$? The graph of the solution set is shown below.

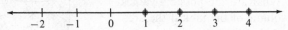

ORAL EXERCISES

Match each graph in Column 1 with the correct set in Column 2.

COLUMN 1   COLUMN 2

1. 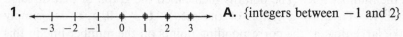   **A.** {integers between -1 and 2}

2. 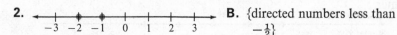   **B.** {directed numbers less than $-\frac{1}{2}$}

3. 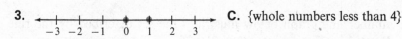   **C.** {whole numbers less than 4}

4. 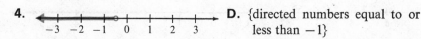   **D.** {directed numbers equal to or less than -1}

5. 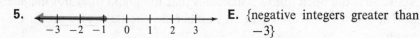   **E.** {negative integers greater than -3}

Describe the set of numbers graphed in each of the following.

6. 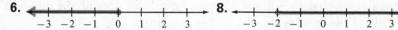   **8.**

7. 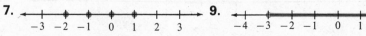   **9.**

WRITTEN EXERCISES

Write an open sentence for each solution set that is graphed. The domain is {the directed numbers}.

SAMPLE 1:

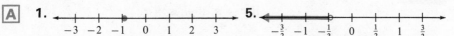

Solution: $x = 2$ (Many other answers are possible.)

SAMPLE 2:

Solution: $x \leq 1$

 1.

2.

3.

4.

5.

6.

7.

8.

Graph the solution set for each open sentence. The domain of the variable is {the directed numbers}.

9. $t > 4$ **13.** $k < \frac{1}{2}$ **17.** $\frac{c}{2} = -1$

10. $m \leq 1\frac{1}{2}$ **14.** $n - 10 = -8$ **18.** $m \geq -4$

11. $x - 3 = 1$ **15.** $r \leq 4$ **19.** $w \geq -\frac{1}{2}$

12. $a + 1 = 1$ **16.** $y \geq 0$ **20.** $r + 1 < 2$

Match each open sentence in Column 1 with a related graph in Column 2. The domain of the variable is {the directed numbers}.

COLUMN 1   COLUMN 2

B **21.** $|t| = 2$

22. $|y| \geq 1$

23. $|m| < 3$

24. $|k| \leq \frac{1}{2}$

A.

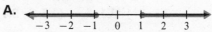

B.

C.

D.

Graph the solution set of each sentence if the domain of the variable is {the directed numbers}.

C **25.** $|x| > 1.5$ **27.** $|m| \leq 1\frac{1}{2}$ **29.** $|k| + 1 = 3$

26. $|n| = \frac{1}{3}$ **28.** $|b| < \pi$ **30.** $|r| \geq 2\frac{1}{2}$

2–3 Basic Properties of Number Sentences

Earlier in this book you solved simple number sentences and wrote and graphed their solution sets. Of course more complicated number sentences require that we use systematic methods to solve them. These methods are based on an understanding of the properties of equality and inequality.

You will probably recall these basic properties of equality.

Reflexive property: For any number r, $r = r$.

Symmetric property: For any numbers r and s,

$$\text{if } r = s, \text{ then } s = r.$$

The transitive property applies to both equality and inequality and is stated in the following way.

Transitive property of equality: For any numbers r, s, and t,

$$\text{if } r = s \text{ and } s = t, \text{ then } r = t.$$

Transitive property of inequality: For any numbers r, s, and t:

$$\text{if } r > s \text{ and } s > t, \text{ then } r > t;$$
$$\text{if } r < s \text{ and } s < t, \text{ then } r < t.$$

We often make use of the familiar distributive property and the substitution principle to combine **similar terms** and thus simplify the work of solving open sentences. For example, you know that $2.5x^2 + 3.1x^2$ is the same as $5.6x^2$. Here is how that conclusion is justified.

$$\mathbf{2.5x^2 + 3.1x^2 = (2.5 + 3.1)x^2} \qquad \text{Distributive property}$$

$$= \mathbf{5.6x^2} \qquad \text{Substitution principle}$$

ORAL EXERCISES

Name the property of equality or the property of inequality suggested by each sentence.

1. $5 < 9$ and $9 < 15$, so $5 < 15$.

2. $10 = 6 + 4$ and $6 + 4 = 3 + 7$, so $10 = 3 + 7$.

3. $6 \div 3 = 2$, so $2 = 6 \div 3$.

4. If $x < -5$ and $-5 < t$, then $x < t$.

5. If $3 + (-5) = k$ and $k = (-2)(1)$, then $3 + (-5) = (-2)(1)$.

6. If $t > |-3|$ and $|-3| > y$, then $t > y$.

WRITTEN EXERCISES

Apply the transitive property of equality or the transitive property of inequality to complete each sentence.

SAMPLE 1: $-3 = -6 \cdot \frac{1}{2}$ and $-6 \cdot \frac{1}{2} = (-1)(3)$, so ___?___.

Solution: $-3 = -6 \cdot \frac{1}{2}$ and $-6 \cdot \frac{1}{2} = (-1)(3)$, so $-3 = (-1)(3)$.

SAMPLE 2: $-8 < 3$ and $3 < 10$, so ___?___.

Solution: $-8 < 3$ and $3 < 10$, so $-8 < 10$.

1. $3(-8) = -4 \cdot 6$ and $-4 \cdot 6 = 12(-2)$, so ___?___.

2. $(-2)(-3)1 = 6$ and $6 = -12 \div -2$, so ___?___.

3. $-4 < 19$ and $19 < 30$, so ___?___.

4. $-12 > -18$ and $-18 > -26$, so ___?___.

5. If $m + n = y$ and $y = m - n$, then ___?___.

6. If $k < w$ and $w < b$, then ___?___.

7. $|-19| > |8|$ and $|8| > |-2|$, so ___?___.

8. $|-3| = 10 - 7$ and $10 - 7 = |3|$, so ___?___.

9. $-3.2 \cdot 0 = 0$ and $0 = 12 \cdot 0$, so ___?___.

10. $|4| < |-9|$ and $|-9| < 10$, so ___?___.

Rewrite each expression by applying the distributive property.

11. $b(16 + 7)$ **15.** $x^2(2.5 + 1.8)$ **19.** $n(5 + 7) + n(3 + 4)$

12. $w(-3 + 8)$ **16.** $ab(3 + 9 + 5)$ **20.** $k(3 + 4 + 6 + 9)$

13. $xy(15 + 4)$ **17.** $r^2s(12 - 2)$ **21.** $2m(9 + 10 + 18)$

14. $t(5 + 9 + 3)$ **18.** $y(-3 + 7 + 1)$ **22.** $abc(2 + 5 + 10 + 6)$

Simplify each of the following by combining similar terms. In Exercises 23–31, give a reason for each step.

SAMPLE: $-3n + 9n$

Solution: $-3n + 9n = (-3 + 9)n$ Distributive property

$\qquad\qquad = 6n$ Substitution principle

23. $4x + 6.5x$ **24.** $-10m + 3m$ **25.** $3a + 9a - 5a$

26. $10t + 3t$ **28.** $4.2x^2 + 5.4x^2$ **30.** $14xy + 10xy + 3xy$

27. $-8y + 10y$ **29.** $16k - 9k$ **31.** $18a^2 + 5a^2 + 6$

SAMPLE: $14(a + b) + 2(a - b)$

Solution: $14(a + b) + 2(a - b) = 14a + 14b + 2a + (-2b)$
$$= 14a + 2a + 14b + (-2b)$$
$$= 16a + 12b$$

B   **32.** $5r + 2r + 3s + 4s$ **37.** $6(k + 2) + (3)(2k)$

33. $13m + (5m - 2m)$ **38.** $3(9c + d) + 5(5c - d)$

34. $18k + (-9k + k)$ **39.** $2(4a + c + 3) + 2(c + 5)$

35. $7t + t + 8 + 10 + 3$ **40.** $-3(4n^2 - 2) + 2(5n^2 + 3)$

36. $2mn + 8m + 7mn - 2m$ **41.** $3[8a + 4(3 - a)] + 10$

PROBLEMS

1. Find the perimeter of the square in the illustration, if the length of each side is represented by the expression $3m + n$. Use the formula $P = 4s$ and give the answer in simplest form.

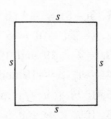

2. The five-sided figure shown here is a regular pentagon, so all of the sides are of equal length. Find the perimeter of the figure if the length of one side is represented by the expression $\frac{2}{5}a + a$.

3. Find the perimeter of the given rectangle. Use the formula $P = 2l + 2w$.

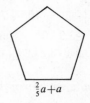

4. The formula $A = lw$ is used to find the area of a rectangle. What is the area of the rectangle shown at the right?

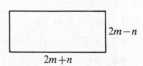

5. Use the formula $A = \frac{1}{2}bh$ to find the area of the given triangle, if the length of b is 10 inches and the length of h is $n - 3$ inches.

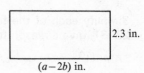

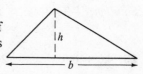

Transformations of Open Sentences

2–4   The Addition Properties of Equality and Inequality

Do you agree with the statement "If two numbers are equal and the same number is added to each, the resulting sums are equal?" This idea is illustrated in the following examples.

EXAMPLE 1.

$10x = 10x$	**Given**
$10x + 3x = 10x + 3x$	**Add 3x to each**
$13x = 13x$	**Sums are equal**

EXAMPLE 2.

$9a = 9a$	**Given**
$9a + (-2a) = 9a + (-2a)$	**Add −2a to each**
$7a = 7a$	**Sums are equal**

The addition properties of equality and inequality can be stated in this manner:

Addition property of equality: For any numbers *r*, *s*, and *t*,

$$\text{if } r = s, \text{ then } r + t = s + t.$$

Addition property of inequality: For any numbers *r*, *s*, and *t*,

$$\text{if } r < s, \text{ then } r + t < s + t;$$
$$\text{if } r > s, \text{ then } r + t > s + t.$$

The process of adding the same number to each member of a given number sentence is called transformation by addition. The solution set of the given sentence is the same as the solution set of the sentence that results from the transformation. Sentences that have the same solution set are equivalent sentences.

An important idea to keep in mind as a part of your equation-solving strategy is that the solution is easy once the variable stands alone as one member of the equation. The use of transformations by addition to accomplish this is illustrated in the following examples. In each, the domain of the variable is {the directed numbers}.

EXAMPLE 1. Solve the equation $y + 8 = 20$, and check your solution.

$y + 8 = 20$	**Given equation**
$y + 8 + (-8) = 20 + (-8)$	**Add -8 to each member**
$y + 0 = 20 + (-8)$	**Property of additive inverses**
$y = 12$	**Additive property of 0**

Check: $y + 8 = 20$

$12 + 8$	20
20	20

The solution set is $\{12\}$.

EXAMPLE 2. Solve the inequality $y + 6 < -4$.

$y + 6 < -4$	**Given inequality**
$y + 6 + (-6) < -4 + (-6)$	**Add -6 to both members**
$y + 0 < -4 + (-6)$	**Property of additive inverses**
$y < -10$	**Additive property of 0**

The solution set is {**the directed numbers less than -10**}.

In Examples 3 and 4 it is important to recall that our definition of subtraction enables us to write an expression that indicates subtraction as an addition expression. For example, $n - 5 = n + (-5)$, and $-3 - t = -3 + (-t)$.

EXAMPLE 3. Solve the equation $b - 7 = -2$ and check.

$b - 7 = -2$	**Given equation**
$b + (-7) = -2$	**Definition of subtraction**
$b + (-7) + 7 = -2 + 7$	**Add 7 to both members**
$b + 0 = -2 + 7$	**Property of additive inverses**
$b = 5$	**Additive property of 0**

Check: $b - 7 = -2$

$5 - 7$	-2
$5 + (-7)$	-2
-2	-2

The solution set is $\{5\}$.

EXAMPLE 4.   Solve the inequality $m - 2 > -9$.

$m - 2 > -9$	**Given inequality**
$m + (-2) > -9$	**Definition of subtraction**
$m + (-2) + 2 > -9 + 2$	**Add 2 to both members**
$m + 0 > -9 + 2$	**Property of additive inverses**
$m > -7$	**Additive property of 0**

The solution set is {the directed numbers greater than -7}.

ORAL EXERCISES

In each of the following tell whether or not the two sentences are equivalent. The domain of the variable is {the directed numbers}.

SAMPLE: $x + 3 = 12$ and $x + 1 = 10$

What you say: The solution set for each sentence is {9}; the sentences are equivalent.

1. $t + 4 = 24$ and $t = (2)(10)$
2. $r + 2 = 5$ and $r = 2 + 1$
3. $k + 3 = -6$ and $k + 3 = 6$
4. $x > 5$ and $x > 3 + 2$
5. $s \leq 1$ and $s \leq 7 - 6$

6. $10 = x + 2$ and $x = 8$
7. $m = 1 + 4^2$ and $m = 20 - 3$
8. $n + 1 < 4$ and $n + 2 < 5$
9. $b - 3 = 5$ and $b + 3 = 11$
10. $q + 4 = 12$ and $q + 1 = 15$

State a reason to justify each step in the solutions of these sentences.

11.
$x + 4 = 19$	Given
$x + 4 + (-4) = 19 + (-4)$	?
$x + 0 = 19 + (-4)$	?
$x = 15$	?

12.
$r - 6 < 8$	Given
$r + (-6) < 8$	?
$r + (-6) + 6 < 8 + 6$	?
$r + 0 < 8 + 6$	?
$r < 14$	?

13.
$n - 12 = -15$	Given
$n + (-12) = -15$	?
$n + (-12) + 12 = -15 + 12$	?
$n + 0 = -15 + 12$	?
$n = -3$	?

WRITTEN EXERCISES

Solve each equation, check your solution, and write the solution set. The domain of the variable is {the directed numbers}.

SAMPLE: $q + 2 = -3$

Solution:
$$q + 2 = -3$$
$$q + 2 + (-2) = -3 + (-2)$$
$$q + 0 = -3 + (-2)$$
$$= -5$$

Check:
$$\frac{q + 2 = -3}{-5 + 2 \quad | \quad -3}$$
$$-3 \quad | \quad -3$$

The solution set is {−5}.

A

1. $y + 3 = 14$
2. $n + 2 = 8$
3. $t + 5 = -4$
4. $b - 7 = 3$
5. $12 + x = 17$

6. $k + \frac{1}{2} = 4\frac{1}{2}$
7. $r - 8 = 10$
8. $w - 2 = -5$
9. $a + 1.4 = 5.9$
10. $22 = z + 20$

11. $p + 18 = 0$
12. $m - 3 = 0$
13. $t - 0 = 6$
14. $-5.3 + x = 4.6$
15. $n - \frac{1}{4} = \frac{1}{2}$

Solve each inequality and write the solution set. The domain of the variable is {the integers}.

SAMPLE: $r + 6 < -9$

Solution:
$$r + 6 < -9$$
$$r + 6 + (-6) < -9 + (-6)$$
$$r + 0 < -9 + (-6)$$
$$r < -15$$

The solution set is
{−16, −17, −18, −19, ...}.

16. $y + 2 > 5$
17. $m + 3 > 4$
18. $t + 9 > 16$
19. $x + 7 < 3$
20. $a + 2 < -1$

21. $3 + x > 0$
22. $n - 6 \geq 7$
23. $r - 10 < 13$
24. $b - 3 > -2$
25. $x - 5 \leq 0$

26. $r + \frac{1}{2} < -2\frac{1}{2}$
27. $y - 3 > -9$
28. $-4 + k > 1$
29. $0 + t \leq 0$
30. $(-1)(-r) \geq 4$

Solve each sentence for x.

SAMPLE: $x + r = k$

Solution:
$$x + r = k$$
$$x + r + (-r) = k + (-r)$$
$$x + 0 = k + (-r)$$
$$x = k - r$$

B

31. $x + m = a$
32. $x - rs = t$
33. $x + t \geq m$

34. $d = k + x$
35. $c + x = -y$
36. $x - k < s$

37. $x + 3 = ab$
38. $z + x > m$
39. $x + (-c) = -h$

2–5 The Multiplication Properties of Equality and Inequality

Suppose that both the left and right members of a given equation are multiplied by the same number. This is called transformation by multiplication. Do you agree that the resulting equation is **equivalent** to the given equation? Your answer to this question should be "Yes." The following example illustrates this idea.

EXAMPLE. $2x = 8$ **Given**

$3(2x) = 3(8)$ **Each is multiplied by 3**

$6x = 24$ **Substitution principle**

Check that the solution set of each equation is $\{4\}$.

Thus we can state the multiplication property of equality:

For each *r*, *s*, and *t*,

if *r* = *s*, then *rt* = *st*.

The numerical parts of expressions like $-4k$, $\frac{1}{3}x$, and $0.5t$ are called the coefficients of the variables.

In $-4k$ the coefficient of k is **−4**.

In $\frac{1}{3}x$ the coefficient of x is $\frac{1}{3}$.

In **0.5t** the coefficient of t is **0.5**.

In m the coefficient of m is **1**, since m is the same as $1m$.

A key idea in equation-solving strategy is to carry out multiplication transformations such that the coefficient of the variable becomes **1**. You will recall that this is accomplished by multiplying the coefficient of the variable by its reciprocal. Follow each step in the example below.

EXAMPLE. $\dfrac{2x}{3} = 12$ **Given equation**

$\frac{2}{3} \cdot x = 12$ **Substitution principle**

$\frac{3}{2} \cdot \frac{2}{3} \cdot x = \frac{3}{2} \cdot 12$ **Multiply both members by $\frac{3}{2}$**

$1 \cdot x = \frac{3}{2} \cdot 12$ **Multiplication property of reciprocals**

$x = 18$ **Multiplicative property of 1**

There is a multiplication property for inequality that is very similar to the one for equality. Notice that both members of each inequality below are multiplied by the same **positive number.**

$$-3 < 5 \qquad \text{and} \qquad (2)(-3) < (2)(5)$$
$$-6 \le -2 \qquad \text{and} \qquad (8)(-6) \le (8)(-2)$$
$$8 > -1 \qquad \text{and} \qquad (4)(8) > (4)(-1)$$

Do you agree that the sense of an inequality remains the same if each member is multiplied by the same positive number?

 For any numbers *r*, *s*, and *t*, with *t* > 0,

if *r* < *s*, then *rt* < *st*;

if *r* > *s*, then *rt* > *st*.

It is important to note what occurs when both members of an inequality are multiplied by the same **negative** number.

$$-2 < 10 \qquad \text{but} \qquad (-4)(-2) > (-4)(10)$$
$$3 \le 4\tfrac{1}{2} \qquad \text{but} \qquad (-2)(3) \ge (-2)(4\tfrac{1}{2})$$
$$6 > -8 \qquad \text{but} \qquad (-5)(6) < (-5)(-8)$$
$$9 \ge 5 \qquad \text{but} \qquad (-2)(9) \le (-2)(5)$$

If you are a sharp observer you noticed that multiplying both members of an inequality by a negative number **reverses** the sense of the sentence. Thus it is necessary to reverse the inequality symbol if the inequality statement is to be correct.

 For any numbers *r*, *s*, and *t*, with *t* < 0,

if *r* < *s*, then *rt* > *st* ;

if *r* > *s*, then *rt* < *st*.

Follow each step in the solutions of the inequalities that follow.

EXAMPLE 1.

$-3x < -24$	**Given**
$-\tfrac{1}{3} \cdot -3 \cdot x > -\tfrac{1}{3} \cdot -24$	**Multiply each member by** $-\tfrac{1}{3}$
$1 \cdot x > 8$	**Multiplication property of reciprocals**
$x > 8$	**Multiplicative property of 1**

The solution set is {directed numbers greater than 8}.

EXAMPLE 2.

$$-7n > 35 \qquad \textbf{Given}$$
$$(-\tfrac{1}{7})(-7)n < (-\tfrac{1}{7})(35) \qquad \textbf{Multiply each member by } -\tfrac{1}{7}$$
$$1 \cdot n < -5 \qquad \textbf{Multiplication property of reciprocals}$$
$$n < -5 \qquad \textbf{Multiplicative property of 1}$$

The solution set is {directed numbers less than -5}.

ORAL EXERCISES

Name the coefficient of the variable in each expression. Then give the reciprocal (multiplicative inverse) of the coefficient.

SAMPLE 1: $16y$ *What you say:* The coefficient of y is 16; the reciprocal of 16 is $\tfrac{1}{16}$.

SAMPLE 2: $-\dfrac{n}{3}$ *What you say:* The coefficient of n is $-\tfrac{1}{3}$; the reciprocal of $-\tfrac{1}{3}$ is -3.

1. $8b$ **4.** $-t$ **7.** $\tfrac{2}{3}d$ **10.** $\dfrac{5x}{9}$

2. $12k$ **5.** $\tfrac{1}{2}n$ **8.** $-\dfrac{2r}{5}$ **11.** $1\tfrac{1}{2}r$

3. $-5a$ **6.** $-\tfrac{1}{5}r$ **9.** $-2m$ **12.** $-\dfrac{t}{5}$

Tell what number is needed to complete each sentence.

SAMPLE 1: $(?)5t = t$ *What you say:* $(\tfrac{1}{5})5t = t$

SAMPLE 2: $(?)(-2n) = n$ *What you say:* $(-\tfrac{1}{2})(-2n) = n$

13. $(?)4k = k$ **15.** $(?)(-3s) = s$ **17.** $(?)\dfrac{2b}{5} = b$

14. $(?)7m = m$ **16.** $(?)(-2b) = b$ **18.** $(?)(0.1r) = r$

WRITTEN EXERCISES

Solve each open sentence and write the solution set. The domain of the variable is the {directed numbers}.

SAMPLE 1: $4t = -20$ *Solution:*
$$4t = -20$$
$$\tfrac{1}{4} \cdot 4t = \tfrac{1}{4} \cdot -20$$
$$t = -5 \qquad \{-5\}$$

SAMPLE 2: $3n > 4.5$ *Solution:* $3n > 4.5$
$$\tfrac{1}{3} \cdot 3n > \tfrac{1}{3} \cdot 4.5$$
$$n > 1.5$$

{directed numbers greater than 1.5}

A

1. $8s = 72$ **9.** $-4t = 20$ **17.** $\tfrac{2}{5} \cdot s = -4$

2. $15y = 240$ **10.** $-\tfrac{2}{3}m = 10$ **18.** $\dfrac{2h}{5} = -10.5$

3. $3.7w = 14.8$ **11.** $4r = -27$ **19.** $y(-4) > 8$

4. $\dfrac{m}{4} = -6$ **12.** $\dfrac{c}{5} \leq -9$ **20.** $\dfrac{m}{7} < \dfrac{1}{10}$

5. $3x > 21$ **13.** $-\tfrac{1}{4}k > 2$ **21.** $-5b \geq 30$

6. $11.1 = 3a$ **14.** $-\dfrac{b}{3} < 1.2$ **22.** $\dfrac{-3k}{5} \leq -9$

7. $10w \geq -500$ **15.** $-7n = 63$ **23.** $(2)(4m) = 136$

8. $\tfrac{1}{2}s < 45$ **16.** $x \cdot \tfrac{1}{2} = 6$ **24.** $1\tfrac{1}{10}b = -132$

Solve each sentence; graph the solution set.

SAMPLE: $\dfrac{r}{3} \geq -1$ *Solution:* $\dfrac{r}{3} \geq -1$
$$3 \cdot \dfrac{r}{3} \geq 3 \cdot -1$$
$$r \geq -3$$

Graph: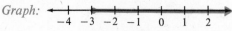

25. $4t > 6$ **29.** $-\dfrac{n}{5} < 0$ **33.** $3k \leq 13$

26. $\dfrac{3b}{2} \leq 3$ **30.** $\dfrac{2k}{3} = 2$ **34.** $14m = -35$

27. $18y < -36$ **31.** $2\tfrac{1}{2} \cdot r > -10$ **35.** $10 \leq \tfrac{2}{5}n$

28. $\dfrac{s}{3} \geq -1$ **32.** $(s)(-6) < 18$ **36.** $-7 > 3h$

Solve and check each equation. Write the solution set.

SAMPLE: $\tfrac{1}{4}t = 3.5$

Solution: $\tfrac{1}{4}t = 3.5$ *Check:* $\tfrac{1}{4}t = 3.5$
$$4 \cdot \tfrac{1}{4}t = 4(3.5)$$ $\tfrac{1}{4} \cdot 14 \;\big|\; 3.5$
$$t = 14$$ $3.5 \;\big|\; 3.5$ {14}

37. $4b = -10$ **39.** $x \cdot \tfrac{1}{4} = \tfrac{1}{2}$ **41.** $15b = -12$

38. $-3n = 7$ **40.** $-\dfrac{5r}{2} = 25$ **42.** $\dfrac{3n}{12} = 24$

Solve each formula for the variable in red. Assume that no divisor is equal to 0.

SAMPLE: $A = lw$

$\quad\quad\quad$ *Solution:* $\quad A = lw$

$$\frac{1}{w} \cdot A = \frac{1}{w} \cdot l \cdot w$$

$$\frac{A}{w} = l$$

B **43.** $v = at$ $\quad\quad\quad$ **46.** $d = 2r$ $\quad\quad\quad$ **49.** $V = s^2 h$

44. $c = \pi d$ $\quad\quad\quad$ **47.** $p = 4s$ $\quad\quad\quad$ **50.** $V = lwh$

45. $V = Bh$ $\quad\quad\quad$ **48.** $A = \frac{1}{2}bh$ $\quad\quad\quad$ **51.** $V = lwh$

2–6 Solving More Complex Open Sentences

The solution of a number sentence can often require the use of such ideas as combining similar terms and the addition and multiplication properties. If you size up a problem and then plan your work with care, even very complex sentences are easily solved. Observe the strategy used in this example. First similar terms are combined. Then the addition property of equality is used so the term containing the variable will stand alone as one member of the equation. Finally the multiplication property of equality is used so that the coefficient of the variable becomes 1.

EXAMPLE.

$3t + t + 3 = 15 + 4$	**Given equation**
$4t + 3 = 19$	**Combine similar terms**
$4t + 3 + (-3) = 19 + (-3)$	**Addition property of equality**
$4t + 0 = 19 + (-3)$	**Property of additive inverses**
$4t = 16$	**Additive property of 0**
$\frac{1}{4} \cdot 4 \cdot t = \frac{1}{4} \cdot 16$	**Multiplication property of equality**
$1 \cdot t = \frac{1}{4} \cdot 16$	**Multiplication property of reciprocals**
$t = 4$	**Multiplicative property of 1**

Check:

$3t + t + 3 = 15 + 4$	
$(3)(4) + 4 + 3$	$15 + 4$
$12 + 7$	19
19	19

The solution set is $\{4\}$.

Very similar techniques can be applied in solving complex inequalities. Observe the strategy used to solve the inequality in this example.

EXAMPLE.

$-n + 3n + 4 \geq -9$	**Given inequality**
$2n + 4 \geq -9$	**Combine similar terms**
$2n + 4 + (-4) \geq -9 + (-4)$	**Addition property of inequality**
$2n + 0 \geq -13$	**Property of additive inverses**
$2n \geq -13$	**Additive property of 0**
$\frac{1}{2} \cdot 2 \cdot n \geq \frac{1}{2} \cdot -13$	**Multiplication property of inequality**
$1 \cdot n \geq -6\frac{1}{2}$	**Multiplication property of reciprocals**
$n \geq -6\frac{1}{2}$	**Multiplicative property of 1**

The solution set is {**directed numbers greater than or equal to** $-6\frac{1}{2}$}.

ORAL EXERCISES

Match each expression in Column 1 with its simplified form in Column 2.

COLUMN 1	COLUMN 2
1. $6 + 3k - 1 + k$	**A.** $n - 2$
2. $3n + 10 - 2n - 8$	**B.** $2k + 7$
3. $\frac{4b}{7} - 10 + \frac{b}{7} - 1$	**C.** $b + 11$
4. $2k + (10 - 3)$	**D.** $4k + 5$
5. $-5b + 7 + 4 + 6b$	**E.** $\frac{5b}{7} - 11$
6. $\frac{n}{2} + 5 + \frac{n}{2} - 7$	**F.** $n + 2$

Give a simpler name for each expression.

SAMPLE: $\frac{2n}{5} + \frac{n}{5}$ *What you say:* $\frac{2}{5}n + \frac{1}{5}n = \frac{3}{5}n = \frac{3n}{5}$

7. $8t + 2t$	**11.** $3w + 10 + 4w$	**15.** $-a + 3a + 2$
8. $5y - y$	**12.** $4 - 2r + 5r$	**16.** $4x^2 + 2 - x^2$
9. $2.3k + 1.9k$	**13.** $4 + x - 5\frac{1}{2}$	**17.** $8c - c + 4 + 3$
10. $2m - 10m$	**14.** $\frac{n}{4} + \frac{n}{2}$	**18.** $\frac{2n}{5} + 6 + \frac{n}{5} - 3$

WRITTEN EXERCISES

Solve each equation. Check your answer and write the solution set.

SAMPLE: $5b + 3 = -12$

Solution:
$$5b + 3 = -12$$
$$5b + 3 + (-3) = -12 + (-3)$$
$$5b = -15$$
$$\tfrac{1}{5} \cdot 5b = \tfrac{1}{5} \cdot -15$$

Check:

$5b + 3 = -12$	
$5(-3) + 3$	-12
$-15 + 3$	-12
-12	-12

The solution set is $\{-3\}$.

A

1. $2s + 7 = 19$

2. $9a - 2 = 25$

3. $39 = 4a + 3$

4. $10b - 5b = 45$

5. $8x + 9 - 2x = 33$

6. $-3 + 7t + 4 = 64$

7. $\dfrac{r}{5} - 10 + \dfrac{2r}{5} = 5$

8. $-2k + k - 5k = -42$

9. $-a + 3a = -8$

10. $9 + \dfrac{c}{5} = -1$

11. $19 = 11 - \dfrac{z}{5}$

12. $\dfrac{2x}{3} + 7 = 5$

13. $40 + 13w = -47w$

14. $30y = 36y + 360$

15. $-20 = 1 - \dfrac{7y}{2}$

16. $\tfrac{1}{2}(4n - 10) = 7$

17. $-3(r + 2) = 0$

18. $a(3 + a) - a^2 = 39$

Solve each inequality and graph the solution set.

SAMPLE: $6t + 10 \geq 13$

Solution:
$$6t + 10 \geq 13$$
$$6t + 10 + (-10) \geq 13 + (-10)$$
$$6t \geq 3$$
$$\tfrac{1}{6} \cdot 6t \geq \tfrac{1}{6} \cdot 3$$
$$t \geq \tfrac{1}{2}$$

Graph: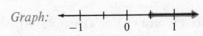

19. $5a - 1 \leq 9$

20. $3n + 2 > 11$

21. $9r + 1 < 4$

22. $y + 3y - 6 \leq 6$

23. $\dfrac{m}{2} - 2 \geq -3$

24. $-14 \leq 3b - 2$

25. $-12\left(\dfrac{t}{6} - \dfrac{1}{3}\right) < 2t$

26. $\tfrac{2}{3}d - 1 \leq -3$

27. $-6x + 5 + x > -(13 + x)$

28. $-w + 2(9 - w) < 0$

29. $\frac{3}{4} + \frac{r}{4} \le 0$ **32.** $-68 \ge -17(6k - 2)$

30. $-3t + 4 > 7$ **33.** $15\left(\frac{1}{5} - \frac{w}{3}\right) \ge -2w$

31. $3n + 5 < n - 5$

Solve each sentence and write the solution set.

B **34.** $-20y = 221 + 6y$ **37.** $39a = 171 + a$ **40.** $3(1 + d) > 3d$

35. $-5b + 2 \ge 12$ **38.** $y - 1 > 9 - 4y$ **41.** $\frac{1}{2}(3n - 6) = n + 2$

36. $-47x = 40 + 13x$ **39.** $2(s - 1) \le 2s$ **42.** $5(x + 1) = 4(x + 2)$

SAMPLE: $3|x| - 2 = 7$ *Solution:* $3|x| - 2 = 7$
$$3|x| - 2 + 2 = 7 + 2$$
$$3|x| = 9$$
$$\tfrac{1}{3} \cdot 3|x| = \tfrac{1}{3} \cdot 9$$
$$|x| = 3$$
$$\{-3, 3\}$$

C **43.** $|y| + 2 = 3$ **45.** $3(|a| + 1) \le 3 - |a|$

44. $5|t| + 9 = 34$ **46.** $\frac{1}{2}(4 - 6|n|) \le -2(2|n| - 1)$

PROBLEMS

1. Write an expression for the sum of three consecutive whole numbers if the least number is represented by w.

2. Write an expression for the sum of three consecutive even integers if the least number is represented by x.

3. The sum of three consecutive odd integers is 63. Find the integers.

4. Find the dimensions of a rectangular rug whose perimeter is 48 feet if its length is twice its width. (Use $P = 2l + 2w$).

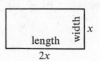

5. Bill's bedroom measures 18 feet long and 10 feet wide. Its area is twice the area of Ken's room, which is 12 feet long. How wide is Ken's room?

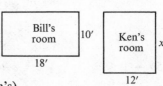

Hint: Area of Bill's = 2(Area of Ken's)
$$18 \cdot 10 = 2(12 \cdot x)$$

6. The length of a rectangle exceeds three times the width by 6 yards. The perimeter of the rectangle is 188 yards. Find the dimensions of the rectangle.

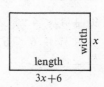

7. The area of a fifteen-foot square is the same as the area of a rectangle that is 9 feet wide. What is the length of the rectangle?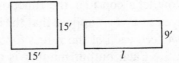

8. Kim has a collection of L.P. records. If she adds 5 more records to her collection, she will then have more than 24. How many records are in Kim's collection? Hint: If the number in Kim's collection is x, then $x + 5 > 24$.

9. The numbers of degrees in the three angles of a given triangle are consecutive whole numbers. What is the measure of each angle? (The sum of the degree measures of the angles of a triangle is 180.)

10. Find the measure of each angle of a triangle, if the numbers of degrees in the angles are consecutive even numbers.

2-7 Functions and Function Equations

Do you recall what a "function machine" is and how it works? Such a machine is shown here. Numbers are fed into the machine at the place marked **input**. Then, according to a rule, a certain thing is done to each input number and the result appears at the place marked **output**. Can you predict what the output will be as each number in the set $\{5, 10, 15, 20\}$ is fed into the machine?

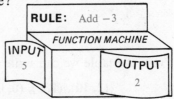

When 5 is the input, the machine adds -3 to 5; the output is **2**.

We can record each input and the resulting output of a function machine as an **ordered number pair**. The **first** number in the pair is the **input** number and the **second** is the **output** number.

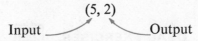

$$(5, 2)$$
Input ———— Output

Check that after all four of the input numbers have been fed into the machine the following set of number pairs will result: $\{(5, 2), (10, 7), (15, 12), (20, 17)\}$. This set of number pairs is a **function**.

 A function is a set of ordered pairs, in which no two pairs have the same first number.

Now let's consider the function machine shown below, whose rule is given as $x \cdot 5$. Suppose that the domain of x is $\{2, 1, 0, -1, -2, \ldots\}$. As we feed each of the values for x into the machine an output number results. Each output number is a **value of the function for** x and this fact is indicated by the symbol $f(x)$. We can express this idea by writing the **function equation** $f(x) = x \cdot 5$.

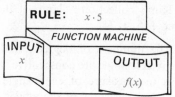

When the value of x is **2** the value of $f(x)$ is $2 \cdot 5$ or **10**. This is recorded as the ordered pair **(2, 10)**.

$$(2, 10)$$
$$x \overset{\nearrow}{} \overset{\nwarrow}{f(x)}$$

Some of the values for x and $f(x)$, when $x \cdot 5 = f(x)$, are recorded in in this table. Can you tell what numbers should replace each question mark?

Function Equation: $x \cdot 5 = f(x)$

x	$f(x)$	$(x, f(x))$
2	10	(2, 10)
1	5	(1, 5)
0	0	(0, 0)
−1	−5	(?, ?)
−2	?	(?, ?)
⋮	⋮	⋮

From the table we can write the set of ordered number pairs

$$\{(2, 10), (1, 5), (0, 0), (-1, -5), (-2, -10), \ldots\}.$$

Of course it is not possible to write every ordered number pair, but do you see from the pattern that no two pairs will have the same first number? Thus this set of ordered pairs is a function.

ORAL EXERCISES

For each of the following sets tell whether any two pairs have the same first member. Then state whether or not the set of pairs is a function.

SAMPLE: $\{(1, 10), (2, 20), (3, 30), (4, 40), (5, 50), \ldots\}$

What you say: No two number pairs have the same first number; the set of number pairs is a function.

1. $\{(0, 7), (2, 5), (4, 3), (6, 1)\}$
2. $\{(-1, 0), (-2, 1), (-3, 2), \ldots\}$
3. $\{(1, 3), (2, 3), (3, 4), (4, 4), (5, 5), (6, 5)\}$
4. $\{(1, 2), (1, 3), (2, 2), (2, 3)\}$
5. $\{(1, 5), (2, 5), (3, 5), (4, 5), \ldots\}$
6. $\{(\frac{1}{2}, 1), (\frac{1}{3}, 2), (\frac{1}{4}, 3), (\frac{1}{5}, 4), (\frac{1}{6}, 5)\}$
7. $\{(0, 1), (1, 2), (0, 3), (1, 4), (0, 5), \ldots\}$
8. $\{(0, 0), (1, 1), (2, 2), (3, 3), \ldots\}$
9. $\{(a, 1), (b, 3), (c, 5), (d, 7), (e, 8)\}$
10. $\{(1, -1), (2, -2), (3, -3), \ldots (40, -40)\}$

Give a function equation suggested by each rule.

SAMPLE 1: $x + 8$ *What you say:* $f(x) = x + 8$

SAMPLE 2: $n \cdot \frac{1}{2}$ *What you say:* $f(n) = n \cdot \frac{1}{2}$

11. $t \cdot 5$ 14. $n \div 10$ 17. $n + 6$
12. $3m + 2$ 15. $x + 1$ 18. $t \div -4$
13. x^2 16. $-t + 5$ 19. $a - 1.5$

WRITTEN EXERCISES

Make a table of values for each function equation for the given domain of the variable. Then write the function as a set of ordered pairs.

SAMPLE: *Solution:*

$f(m) = 3m + 2$;
domain of m: $\{2, 3, 4, 5, \ldots\}$

m	$f(m)$	$(m, f(m))$
2	8	(2, 8)
3	11	(3, 11)
4	14	(4, 14)
5	17	(5, 17)
⋮	⋮	⋮

The function is $\{(2, 8), (3, 11), (4, 14), (5, 17), \ldots\}$.

A

1. $f(x) = x + 1$; domain of x: $\{0, 1, 2, 3, 4\}$
2. $f(r) = 2 + r^2$; domain of r: $\{0, 2, 4, 6, \ldots\}$
3. $f(m) = m - 3$; domain of m: $\{5, 7, 9, 11, 13\}$
4. $f(a) = 3(a + 1)$; domain of a: $\{10, 20, 30, \ldots\}$
5. $f(t) = 4t \div 6$; domain of t: $\{6, 8, 12, 15\}$
6. $f(h) = h \cdot \frac{1}{h}$; domain of h: $\{2, 3, 5, 7, 11, 13\}$

7. $f(n) = (-1)(n);$ domain of n: $\{1, 2, -1, -2\}$

8. $f(y) = 10 - 2y;$ domain of y: $\{\frac{1}{2}, 1, 1\frac{1}{2}, 2, 2\frac{1}{2}\}$

9. $f(b) = 3b - 1;$ domain of b: $\{1, 2, 3, 4, \ldots\}$

10. $\dfrac{5n}{2} = f(n);$ domain of n: $\{2, 4, 6, 8, 10, 12\}$

11. $12w - 2 = f(w);$ domain of w: $\{\frac{1}{2}, \frac{1}{3}, \frac{1}{4}, \frac{1}{6}\}$

12. $f(m) = m^3;$ domain of m: $\{-2, -1, 0, 2, 1\}$

13. $f(z) = z^2;$ domain of z: $\{-10, -8, -6, -4, -1, 0\}$

14. $f(r) = 36 \div r;$ domain of r: $\{3, 6, 9, 12, 18\}$

Match each function equation in Column 1 with a related set of ordered pairs in Column 2. The domain of the variable is $\{0, 2, 4, 6\}$.

COLUMN 1	COLUMN 2
15. $f(n) = n^2 + 1$	**A.** $\{(0, 10), (2, 13), (4, 16), (6, 19)\}$
16. $f(t) = 3t \div 3$	**B.** $\{(0, 1), (2, 5), (4, 17), (6, 37)\}$
17. $f(x) = (-3)(x)$	**C.** $\{(0, 5), (2, 1), (4, -3), (6, -7)\}$
18. $f(m) = 5 - 2m$	**D.** $\{(0, 0), (2, -2), (4, -4), (6, -6)\}$
19. $f(y) = 1.5y + 10$	**E.** $\{(0, 0), (2, -6), (4, -12), (6, -18)\}$
20. $f(a) = -a$	**F.** $\{(0, 0), (2, 2), (4, 4), (6, 6)\}$

Complete each set of ordered pairs for the given function equation.

SAMPLE: $f(m) = 4 + 2m$: $\{(-2, 0), (-1, ?), (0, ?), (1, ?), (2, ?)\}$

Solution: $\{(-2, 0), (-1, 2), (0, 4), (1, 6), (2, 8)\}$

B **21.** $f(t) = \frac{1}{2}(t + 4)$: $\{(-1, \frac{3}{2}), (-2, 1), (-3, ?), (-4, ?)\}$

22. $f(r) = \dfrac{2r}{5} + 1$: $\{(0, 1), (2, 1\frac{4}{5}), (4, ?), (6, ?), (8, ?), \ldots\}$

23. $f(g) = \frac{1}{2}(g^2)$: $\{(-3, \frac{9}{2}), (-2, ?), (-1, ?), (0, ?), (1, ?), (2, ?)\}$

24. $f(n) = n^2 - n$: $\{(1, ?), (2, ?), (3, ?), (-1, ?), (-2, ?), (-3, ?)\}$

25. $f(a) = 3a + 1$: $\{(\frac{1}{2}, 2\frac{1}{2}), (\frac{1}{3}, ?), (\frac{1}{4}, ?), (-\frac{1}{2}, ?), (-\frac{1}{3}, ?), (-\frac{1}{4}, ?)\}$

26. $f(m) = 2m - 5$: $\{(\frac{1}{2}, -4), (1, ?), (1\frac{1}{2}, ?), (2, ?), (2\frac{1}{2}, ?), (3, ?), \ldots\}$

C **27.** $f(x) = x + 3$: $\{(-4, ?), (-3, ?), (-2, ?), (-1, ?), (0, ?)\}$

28. $f(h) = -h - 4$: $\{(2, -6), (4, ?), (6, ?), (-2, ?), (-4, ?), (-6, ?)\}$

29. $f(y) = y^2 + 3y + 1$: $\{(0, ?), (1, ?), (2, ?), (-3, ?), (-5, ?), \ldots\}$

30. $f(t) = 3t^2 + 2t + 4$: $\{(-1, ?), (-2, ?), (-3, ?), (-5, ?), \ldots\}$

CHAPTER SUMMARY

Inventory of Structure and Concepts

1. The **substitution principle** states that for any numbers r and s, if $r = s$, then r and s may be substituted for each other.

2. The **reflexive property of equality** states that for any number r, $r = r$.

3. The **symmetric property of equality** states that for any numbers r and s, if $r = s$, then $s = r$.

4. The **transitive property of equality** states that for any numbers r, s, and t, if $r = s$ and $s = t$, then $r = t$.

5. The **transitive property of inequality** states that for any numbers r, s, and t:
   (a) if $r > s$ and $s > t$, then $r > t$;
   (b) if $r < s$ and $s < t$, then $r < t$.

6. The **addition property for equality** states that for any numbers r, s, and t, if $r = s$, then $r + t = s + t$.

7. The **addition property for inequality** states that for any numbers r, s, and t:
   (a) if $r > s$, then $r + t > s + t$;
   (b) if $r < s$, then $r + t < s + t$.

8. **Equivalent** number sentences are sentences that have the same solution set.

9. The **multiplication property for equality** states that for any numbers r, s, and t, if $r = s$, then $rt = st$.

10. The **multiplication property for inequality** states that for any numbers r, s, and t,
    (a) when $t > 0$: if $r > s$, then $rt > st$;
                      if $r < s$, then $rt < st$.
    (b) when $t < 0$: if $r > s$, then $rt < st$;
                      if $r < s$, then $rt > st$.

11. A **function** is a set of ordered pairs in which no two pairs have the same first number.

Vocabulary and Spelling

open sentence (*p. 37*)   substitution principle (*p. 44*)

variable (*p. 37*)   distributive property (*p. 44*) replacement set (*p. 38*)

domain of a variable (*p. 38*)

solution (*p. 38*)

solution set (*p. 38*)

empty set (*p. 38*)

graph of a solution set (*p. 42*)

reflexive property (*p. 44*)

symmetric property (*p. 44*)

transitive property for equality

  (*p. 44*)

transitive property for inequality

  (*p. 44*)

similar terms (*p. 44*)

addition property for equality (*p. 47*)

addition property for inequality

  (*p. 47*)

equivalent sentences (*p. 47*)

coefficient (*p. 51*)

multiplication property for equality

  (*p. 51*)

multiplication property for inequality

  (*p. 52*)

function (*p. 59*)

function equation (*p. 60*)

ordered pairs (*p. 60*)

Chapter Test

Give the additive inverse and the multiplicative inverse for each number. Assume that no variable has the value zero.

1. 15   **3.** $\frac{2}{5}$ **5.** x

2. -3 **4.** $-\frac{3}{2}$ **6.** $3k$

Find the solution set for each open sentence.

7. $x - 4 = 8$; domain: {the whole numbers}.

8. $t + 4 = 4 + t$; domain: {the directed numbers}.

9. $x + 5 = 12$; domain: {the negative numbers}.

10. $y - 1 > 5$; domain: {the integers}.

11. $7 \geq r - 2$; domain: {the counting numbers}.

12. $m + 1 \leq -1$; domain: {the directed numbers}.

13. $t < 4$; domain: {the integers}.

Tell whether or not both expressions name the same number when the replacement for the variable is 3.

14. $3 \cdot n$ and $n \cdot 3$ **17.** $(4t)^2$ and $4 \cdot t \cdot t$

15. $t(3 + 4)$ and $3t + 4$ **18.** $-(4 + b)$ and $-4 + b$

16. y^3 and $3y$ **19.** $2(r \cdot r)$ and $r(2r)$

Indicate whether each of the following sentences is *true*, or *false*, or *neither* true nor false.

20. $9 + 2 \geq 5$ **22.** $(3 \cdot 3)2 = 2 \cdot 3^2$ **24.** $4 + b = 4b$

21. $3x + 1 \neq 10$ **23.** $8 - 5 < 12$ **25.** $(5 + 7)3 = (3 \cdot 5) + (3 \cdot 7)$

Arrange the numbers in each exercise in order, beginning with the smallest and ending with the largest.

26. $-3, \frac{1}{2}, -10, 1\frac{1}{2}, 5, 0$ **27.** $-\frac{3}{8}, -\frac{3}{5}, -\frac{3}{7}, \frac{3}{8}, \frac{3}{5}, \frac{3}{7}$

Graph the solution set for each sentence. The domain for each is {the directed numbers}.

28. $x - 5 \geq 1$ **30.** $2r - 12 = -16$

29. $t + 2 < 3$ **31.** $\frac{1}{4}(8k + 12) = -4$

Write a set of ordered pairs for each of the following according to the function equation and specified domain.

32. $f(n) = \frac{n}{2} + 1$; domain: $\{-2, -1, 0, 1, 2\}$

33. $f(m) = 2m^2 - m$; domain: $\{-6, -4, -2, 0, 1, 2, 4, 6\}$

Chapter Review

2–1 Open Sentences, Expressions, and Variables

Give the values for each expression.

1. $5n - 2$; domain: $\{\frac{1}{2}, 1, 1\frac{1}{2}, 2\}$

2. $4t^2 + 1$; domain: $\{-4, -3, -2, -1\}$

3. $(5 - k)2$; domain: $\{-4, -2, 0, 2, 4\}$

4. $\frac{3b}{2}$; domain: $\{-20, -10, 0, 10, 20\}$

5. $8y + 3$; domain: $\{-\frac{1}{2}, -\frac{1}{4}, 0, \frac{1}{4}, \frac{1}{2}\}$

6. $2x^3 - 2$; domain: $\{-3, -2, -1, 0, 1, 2\}$

Write the solution set for each sentence.

7. $10 + b = 14$; domain: {the directed numbers}

8. $n + 2 \leq 6$; domain: {the whole numbers}

9. $s^2 + 1 > 9$; domain: {the negative integers}

Solve each problem.

10. The area of this triangle can be computed by using the formula $A = \frac{1}{2}bh$. Find all the values for the area of the triangle if the base is 16 centimeters long and the domain of the height, h, in centimeters, is $\{9, 18, 27\}$.

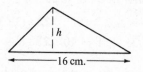

11. Use the distance formula $d = rt$ (distance = rate of speed $\times$ time) to find all of the values for the distances traveled by an auto whose rate of speed is 55 miles per hour. The domain of the time variable t, in hours, is $\{2, 3, 4\frac{1}{2}, 5, 6\}$.

2–2   Graphs of Sets of Numbers

Graph the solution set of each sentence. The domain of the variable is {the directed numbers}.

12. $r \geq -2$ **14.** $s \leq 2.5$ **16.** $k + 2 < 1$

13. $n - 2 = n$ **15.** $w > 2$ **17.** $y \neq -1$

2–3   Basic Properties of Number Sentences

Match each sentence in Column 1 with the related property in Column 2.

COLUMN 1

18. $10 = 3^2 + 1$, so $3^2 + 1 = 10$

19. $4 > 2$ and $2 > -1$, so $4 > -1$

20. $\frac{10}{2} = 5$ and $5 = 4 + 1$, so $\frac{10}{2} = 4 + 1$

COLUMN 2

A. Transitive property of inequality

B. Symmetric property of equality

C. Transitive property of equality

Simplify each expression.

21. $k(-2 + 5)$ **24.** $4x^2 - x^2 + 9x^2$ **26.** $3rs + 16rs - 7rs$

22. $3t(9 + 4) + t$ **25.** $(2b - 7b) + 2$ **27.** $4z + 9z^2 - z + 5z^2$

23. $2ab - 3a + 7ab$

2–4   The Addition Properties of Equality and Inequality

Name the additive inverse of each number.

28. 6   **29.** -9 **30.** $2a$ **31.** $-5t$

Solve each sentence and give a reason to justify each step.

32. $b + 3 = -10$　　　**33.** $s - 2.5 < 8$　　　**34.** $w + 2 \geq 5$

Solve each sentence for *m*.

35. $m + a = 2b$　　　**36.** $m - 2ab = 3$　　　**37.** $k + m \leq s$

2–5　The Multiplication Properties of Equality and Inequality

Name the multiplicative inverse of each number.

38. $\frac{4}{5}$　　　　**39.** -1　　　　**40.** $-\frac{3}{2}$　　　　**41.** $\frac{2a}{5}$, $a \neq 0$

Use the symbols $=$, $<$, and $>$ to make each of the following a true statement.

42. 6 ? $10 - 4$, so $6 \cdot 5$? $(10 - 4)5$

43. -3 ? 2, so $(-3)(4)$? $(2)(4)$

44. 2.1 ? 1.5, so $(2.1)(-3)$? $(1.5)(-3)$

If the domain of the variable is {the directed numbers}, solve each sentence and graph the solution set.

45. $\frac{2n}{5} \geq -6$　　　　　**46.** $-5t = 35$　　　　　**47.** $-\frac{s}{5} \leq \frac{2}{5}$

2–6　Solving More Complex Open Sentences

Solve each equation and check. Then write the solution set.

48. $3y + 9 + y = 33$　**50.** $\frac{2}{3}(6n + 9) = 26$　**52.** $6 = 10 + \frac{y}{3}$

49. $5t - 7 - t = 41$　**51.** $-5(k + 5) = 0$　**53.** $15a = 25a - 100$

Solve each inequality and graph the solution set.

54. $7n + 2 \geq 23$　　　**55.** $4t - 5 \leq 1$　　　**56.** $-5a + 2 > -7$

2–7　Functions and Function Equations

Write a set of ordered pairs that is a function for each of the following.

57. $f(x) = 3x - 1$; domain of x: $\{-4, -2, 0, 2, 4\}$

58. $f(r) = \frac{2r}{5} - 2$;　domain of r: $\{-10, -5, 5, 10, 15\}$

59. $m^2 + 2 = f(m)$;　domain of m: {the even numbers}

60. $|t| = f(t)$;　domain of t: {the negative integers}

Review of Skills

Simplify each expression.

1. $3x^2 + x^2$ **4.** $-5t^3 + t^3$ **7.** $t(3 + 6)$

2. $4b + 7b$ **5.** $10ab + 6ab$ **8.** $(2 + 9)xy$

3. $3y^3 + 5y^3$ **6.** $7x^2 - 3x^2$ **9.** $m^2(4 - 1)$

Add.

10. $-8y$ **11.** $-4x^2$ **12.** $-3xy$ **13.** t^2

      $3y$ $10x^2$ $-4xy$ $4t^2$

       y $9x^2$ $-xy$ $-7t^2$

Subtract each lower number from the number above it.

14. 4.6   **16.**   4.5   **18.** $9y$ **20.** $-6m$

    1.8 -2.2 $25y$ $-8m$

15. 12   **17.** $15x$ **19.** $-3t$ **21.** $-86w^2$

    19         $4x$ $10t$ $-24w^2$

Complete each of the following to make a true statement.

22. $3x(?) = 18x$ **25.** $n \cdot n \cdot n \cdot (?) = n^4$ **28.** $(?) - 6xy = 2xy$

23. $4(?) = 20y$ **26.** $3b \cdot b \cdot (?) = 6b^3$ **29.** $(?) - 8ab = -3ab$

24. $2t^2(?) = 6t^2$ **27.** $4x^2 + (?) = x^2$ **30.** $8x(?) = 2x^2$

Add.

31. $2.01 + 10.25 + 6.39$ **33.** $2\frac{1}{2} + 5\frac{1}{8} + 16 + 1\frac{7}{8}$

32. $75.2 + 3.1 + 850.1$ **34.** $\frac{1}{2} + \frac{3}{8} + \frac{3}{4} + \frac{1}{8} + \frac{1}{4}$

Multiply; use the distributive property.

SAMPLE: $3 \cdot 4\frac{1}{5}$ *Solution:* $3 \cdot 4\frac{1}{5} = 3(4 + \frac{1}{5})$

$$= (3 \cdot 4) + (3 \cdot \tfrac{1}{5})$$
$$= 12 + \tfrac{3}{5}$$
$$= 12\tfrac{3}{5}$$

35. $7 \cdot 8\frac{1}{9}$ **37.** $3\frac{2}{3} \cdot 6$ **39.** $10 \cdot 6.3$

36. $5 \cdot 6\frac{1}{5}$ **38.** $4 \cdot 1.25$ **40.** $8 \cdot 9\frac{3}{4}$

Graph each set of number pairs on a 6 × 6 lattice of points.

SAMPLE: {(1, 0), (2, 1), (3, 0), (4, 5)}   *Solution:*

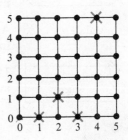

41. {(0, 1), (1, 3), (3, 4), (4, 4)}

42. {(5, 5), (4, 4), (3, 3), (2, 2), (1, 1), (0, 0)}

43. {(0, 5), (1, 4), (2, 3), (4, 3), (3, 5), (5, 0)}

■ ■

CHECK POINT
FOR EXPERTS

Introduction to Flow Charts

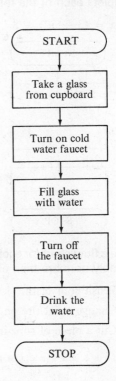

When you are faced with a particular task to be done or an objective to be reached, you are often guided by a set of directions, a recipe, or a map.

In many situations, a **flow chart** can be helpful in planning the work and in finding the easiest way to solve the problem. For example, the flow chart shown at the right gives steps that you might follow in getting a drink of water. Study the diagram and see that three different flow-chart symbols have been used.

The oval box is called a **terminal** symbol. It indicates the start and the stop of the list of steps.

 Arrows are **flow** symbols, and are used to show direction from one step to another.

 The rectangle has been used as an **operation** symbol, to indicate an action or an operation to be carried out.

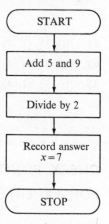

Study the flow chart at the right, which gives the steps for finding the value of x in $x = \dfrac{5 + 9}{2}$.

For any given problem, the number of operations listed in the flow chart will depend on whether it seems necessary to show a great deal of detail. If a general outline is satisfactory, the flow chart may be fairly brief.

Questions

Complete each of the following flow charts for finding the value of *x*.

1. $x = (3 + 12) - 8$ **2.** $x = 3(10 + 9)$

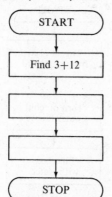 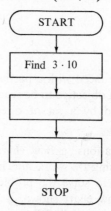

Make a flow chart for each "problem." Use as few operations as possible — probably no more than eight will be needed for each of these.

3. Brush your teeth.   **5.** Take out the garbage.

4. Change a flat tire on a car.   **6.** Shine your shoes.

7. Cut a piece of rope into two equal lengths.

Benjamin Banneker

Benjamin Banneker was a mathematician who lived during the early period of American history. He was born in Maryland and attended a school near Baltimore. While he was at school Banneker developed an interest in science and mathematics. At the age of 22 he constructed a wooden clock, believed to have been the first clock made in America.

Later, the young man borrowed books on mathematics and astronomy from George Ellicott, a Quaker who operated a flour mill. Banneker soon mastered the contents of these books and even discovered mathematical errors that the authors had made. His skill in the field of astronomy was further demonstrated in 1789, when he accurately predicted an eclipse of the sun.

Benjamin Banneker's first almanac was published in 1791 and attracted much attention. It was praised by Thomas Jefferson, who sent a copy to the Academy of Sciences in Paris. Banneker's almanacs contained astronomical calculations and weather predictions, tables of interest, numbers, and money, lists of the laws and judicial officers of the United States, and extracts of prose and verse.

Perhaps Banneker's most distinguished honor was his appointment to the commission which planned the layout of the streets for the District of Columbia. His name was submitted to President Washington by Thomas Jefferson, probably at the suggestion of Banneker's old friend George Ellicott, who was also a member of the commission. After serving on the commission, Banneker returned to his home in Maryland and resumed work on his astronomical investigations and on his almanacs, which he continued to publish until 1802.

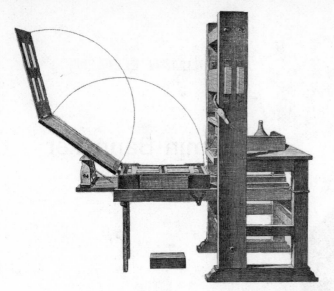

An eighteenth-century printing press . . .

A phototypesetter producing punched tape . . .

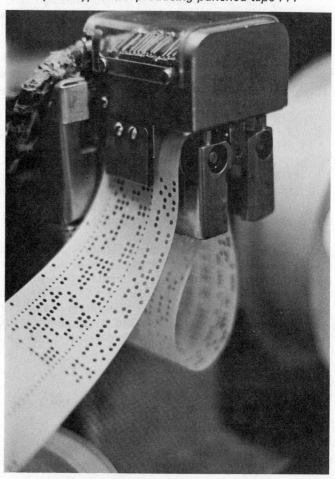

Operations with Polynomials

Gutenberg's printing press of the fifteenth century saw few changes until the advent of steam-powered presses, about 1815. Early presses were very similar to the eighteenth-century one shown, with type set by hand. Hand composition continued to be the only method of typesetting until the 1880's, when the first machine for the purpose, the linotype, was patented. Since the 1930's, advances have been many, especially in the field of phototypesetting, in which high-speed machines produce punched tape, coded to produce negatives on photographic film. The images on the developed film are transferred to the plates for printing. In a computerized typesetting system, copy typed on a special keyboard produces tape which is fed into a computer programmed to "justify" lines and to hyphenate words. The tape turned out by the computer is the final tape which is fed into the typesetting machine.

Addition and Subtraction

3–1 . Addition of Polynomials

Each of the expressions in Examples 1 and 2 is a polynomial. In general, a polynomial is either a single term or a sum of terms. Since the variable in each expression is x we say that these expressions are polynomials in x. They are called polynomials in one variable, since only the single variable x is used.

EXAMPLE 1. Polynomials in One Variable:

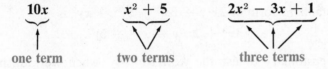

Notice that in each of the following polynomials there is more than one variable.

73

EXAMPLE 2.   Polynomials in More than One Variable:

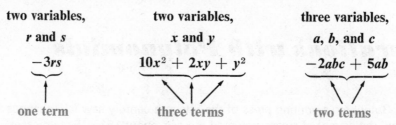

two variables, r and s	two variables, x and y	three variables, a, b, and c
$-3rs$	$10x^2 + 2xy + y^2$	$-2abc + 5ab$
one term	three terms	two terms

In this course we shall agree that replacements for variables are always directed numbers, so polynomials are, in fact, names for directed numbers. This leads us to the logical conclusion that the basic assumptions established for operations on directed numbers also apply to operations on polynomials.

Some polynomials are named according to the number of their terms: a one-term polynomial is a **monomial**; a two-term polynomial is a **binomial**; a three-term polynomial is a **trinomial**.

You should recall that the numerical part of a polynomial such as $-5x$ or $12x^2$ is called the **coefficient**.

The coefficient of $-x$ is -1.

The coefficient of $2xy$ is 2.

The coefficient of $\dfrac{2x}{3}$ is $\dfrac{2}{3}$.

A term without a variable, such as $\frac{1}{2}$, **15**, or -1.5, is also a monomial and is called a **constant**.

You may recall that it is customary in the study of algebra to write polynomials in a **standard form**. That is, for a polynomial in one variable the first term on the left has the largest exponent, the second term has the next largest exponent, and so on. A polynomial in more than one variable is written in standard form by ordering the terms according to the exponents of one variable.

The standard form of $-10x + 7x^2 + 5$ is $7x^2 - 10x + 5$.

The standard form of $2 - 8x^3 + x$ is $-8x^3 + x + 2$.

The standard form of $2x^2y + 3x^3 + 5y^3 - xy^2$ is

$$3x^3 + 2x^2y - xy^2 + 5y^3.$$

It is customary to use the word **simplify** when working problems involving polynomials. To simplify the indicated addition $10x^2 + 26x^2$ we write $36x^2$; the simplified form of $(9x^2 + 6) + (3x^2 - 2)$ is written as $12x^2 + 4$. Of course each problem could be arranged in vertical form, as shown below.

$$10x^2 \qquad 9x^2 + 6y$$
$$\underline{26x^2} \qquad \underline{3x^2 - 2y}$$
$$36x^2 \qquad 12x^2 + 4y$$

Thus, in order to **add two polynomials** you **combine their similar terms**.

Notice that the terms of the polynomials in the addition below are first arranged in standard form, then the similar terms are combined.

$$(2x^2 + 5x^4 - 3) + (2 - x^3) \qquad 5x^4 \qquad + 2x^2 - 3$$
$$\underline{\qquad - x^3 \qquad + 2}$$
$$5x^4 - x^3 + 2x^2 - 1$$

It is usually possible to check the sum of two polynomials by assigning nonzero values to the variables.

Add and check, using **2** as the value of *x*.

$$-10x^2 + \ x + 5 \rightarrow -10(4) + 2 + 5 \ = -33$$
$$\underline{6x^2 + 2x - 3 \rightarrow 6(4) + 2(2) - 3 \quad = \quad 25}$$
$$-4x^2 + 3x + 2 \rightarrow -4(4) + 3(2) + 2 = \ -8$$

Note that we have checked that the sum $-4x^2 + 3x + 2$ is correct when $x = 2$. This does not assure us that the sum is correct for *all* values of the variable, but it gives us reason to feel fairly certain that it is. If it had *not* checked for $x = 2$, we would know that some careless error had been made. Why is **2** a better choice than **1** as a checking value?

ORAL EXERCISES

Name the coefficient of each polynomial.

1. $5x^2$
2. $3rt$
3. $\dfrac{2k}{5}$

4. $-xy$
5. $\dfrac{n}{2}$
6. $-\dfrac{t}{3}$

7. $10.6y$
8. s
9. $-7w$

10. $(x^2)(5)$
11. $(b)(-\frac{1}{2})$
12. $-t$

State the number of terms in each expression, and classify it as a monomial, a binomial, or a trinomial.

SAMPLE: $15m^3 - 4m + 12$ *What you say:* 3 terms; trinomial

13. $\dfrac{3t}{2}$ **16.** $(5)(y^2)$ **19.** $3s^4 + 10t$

14. $12 + 5x^2$ **17.** $4k^3 - 10m$ **20.** $4 + 6w^2 + w$

15. $x + 4y$ **18.** $n^2 + (-3)$ **21.** $\dfrac{n^2}{3} + 2n - \tfrac{1}{2}$

WRITTEN EXERCISES

Write each of the following in simplified standard form.

SAMPLE: $(-6 + x) + 10$ *Solution:* $x + 4$

A   **1.** $(6n + 8n)$ **6.** $(2m + 3n) + 5m$

2. $(4x^2) + (12x^2)$ **7.** $(6 + 4k) + 2$

3. $(7ab) + (-4ab)$ **8.** $(10x^2 - 3) + 5x$

4. $(-8b) + (5b)$ **9.** $2c^2 + (10 - 8c^2)$

5. $(2y^2) + (8y) + (7y^2) + (-y)$ **10.** $(5w^3 + 2w + 6w^2 + 10) + 15w$

Add these polynomials.

11. $3x - 2y$ **15.** $9s^5 + 16t$ **19.** $3t^3 - 4t$
$\underline{9x + 3y}$ $\underline{-4s^5\qquad}$ $\underline{\qquad t - 6}$

12. $3t^2 + 10s^2$ **16.** $6x^2 - 4x + 7$ **20.** $4y^3 - 2y^2 \qquad + 1$
$\underline{2t^2 + \ 4s^2}$ $\underline{2x^2 - 6x + 7}$ $\underline{-6y^3 \qquad\quad + 4y - 9}$

13. $-5k + 5$ **17.** $\ \ x^2 + 8x + 9$ **21.** $\ \ w^2 + 3w + 2$
$\underline{\ \ 3k - 2}$ $\underline{-6x^2 \qquad\ \ - 4}$ $\underline{-w^2 + \ w - 5}$

14. $3b^2 + 2c$ **18.** $\ \ x^2 - 3x + 2$ **22.** $6n^3 - 4n^2 - 5n$
$-b^2 + 6c$ $-4x^2 \qquad\ - 5$ $\underline{\qquad 3n^2 + 2n - 4}$
$\underline{10b^2 - 5c}$ $\underline{\qquad\quad 4x + 3}$

Check the sum in each of the following exercises by letting $x = 2$, $y = 3$, and $z = 5$. Correct any errors you find.

23. $4y - \ 7$ **25.** $\ \ 3x - 2y$ **27.** $2y^2 + 5y$
$\underline{2y + 10}$ $\underline{-4x + 8y}$ $\underline{\qquad 2y - 10}$
$6y + \ 3$ $-x + 6y$ $2y^2 + 7y - 10$

24. $\ \ 9z + 5$ **26.** $2xy + 5z$ **28.** $\ \ x^3 + 2x^2 - 9$
$\underline{-2z + 8}$ $xy - 2z$ $3x^3 \qquad\quad - 4$
$7z + 13$ $\underline{-xy + 6z}$ $\underline{\qquad\quad x^2 + 4}$
     $6xy + 13z$ $4x^3 - 3x^2 - 9$

Solve each equation. The domain of the variable is {directed numbers}.

SAMPLE: $2x + (3x + 2) = 32$ Solution: $2x + (3x + 2) = 32$
$$(2x + 3x) + 2 = 32$$
$$5x = 30$$
$$x = 6$$

29. $3y + (7y - 5) = 45$ **31.** $(4m - 2) - m = -9$
30. $(4k + 2) - 3k = 9$ **32.** $-2t + (4 - 3t) = -24$

Simplify each of the following expressions.

33. $(2b + 8) + (10b + 4)$ **35.** $(2x^2 + 3xy - 5x) + (xy - 3x)$
34. $(1.5x + 2) + (3.7x + 10)$ **36.** $(3z - z^2 + 2) + (6 + 5z^2)$

B **37.** $(\frac{1}{2}y - \frac{3}{2}) + (\frac{1}{2}y + \frac{1}{2})$
38. $(3m^3 - n^2) + (m^3 - 6n^2)$
39. $(8 + \frac{2}{3}k) + (-\frac{1}{3}k - 7)$
40. $(2.5x^2 - 9.1) + (1.8x^2 - 3x)$
41. $(6a^4 + 3a^2) + (a^3 - 2a - 3a^2)$
42. $(-2x^2 + 3x + 1) + (3x^2 - 5x - 1)$

C **43.** $(y^3 + 3y^2 - 5y - 1) + (4y^3 - 2y^2 + 3y + 6)$
44. $(-2n^3 + n^2 + 4n - 3) + (4n^3 - n^2 - 5n + 2)$
45. $(2w^4 - w^3 + w^2 - 2w - 2) + (-w^4 + 3w^2 + 2w - 4)$
46. $(4x^5 + x^4 - 2xy + 3) + (2x^4 + 3x^3 - x^2 + 2xy - 10)$

PROBLEMS

Write each answer as a polynomial in standard form.

1. Find the perimeter of the figure shown, if the lengths of the sides are represented by the given polynomials.

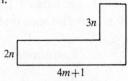

2. The area of each region is represented by the given polynomial.
   a. Find the total area of the three regions.
   b. What is the combined area of regions I and II?
   c. Find the combined area of regions II and III; of regions I and III.

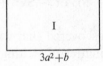

3. The area of the shaded part of the rectangle is given by the polynomial $3x^2 + y^2$. What is the area of the rectangle? What is the area of the rectangle when x is 8 (inches) and y is 2.5 (inches)?

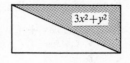

4. The volume of each cylinder-shaped tank is given by a polynomial.
   a. What is the combined volume of the three tanks?
   b. Find the combined volume of tanks II and III.
   c. Which is greater, the volume of tank I or the combined volume of tanks II and III?

$$4t^3 + 5st^2 + 10 \qquad t^3 + 2st^2 \qquad 3t^3 + 3st^2 + 10$$

5. Find the total area of the given figure. Each polynomial represents the area of the region in which it is located.

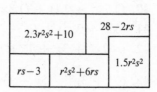

3–2 Subtraction of Polynomials

You will recall that addition and subtraction are **inverse** operations, and that subtracting one directed number from another is the same as **adding the opposite,** or additive inverse, of the number subtracted. For example, **10 − 3** is the same as **10 + (−3)**. This idea is useful in the subtraction of polynomials.

The opposite of the polynomial $x - 5$ is written as $-(x - 5)$, or $-x + 5$. Be sure that you fully understand the examples shown below.

Polynomial:	Opposite:
$8x^3$	$-(8x^3)$, or $-8x^3$
$x^2 + 6y$	$-(x^2 + 6y)$, or $-x^2 - 6y$
$-3x^2 + 2x - 1$	$-(-3x^2 + 2x - 1)$, or $3x^2 - 2x + 1$
$5x^2 - xy + 5$	$-(5x^2 - xy + 5)$, or $-5x^2 + xy - 5$

If you studied the examples with care you discovered that writing the opposite of a given polynomial is simply a matter of writing the sum of the opposites of the terms.

How do you suppose we apply the definition of subtraction to polynomials? Subtracting one polynomial from another is the same as adding the opposite of the polynomial to be subtracted.

$$(5x + 3y) - (2x + y) = (5x + 3y) + [-(2x + y)]$$
$$= (5x + 3y) + (-2x - y)$$
$$= 3x + 2y$$

The following examples further illustrate this idea.

$$7ab^2 - 3ab^2 = 7ab^2 + (-3ab^2) = 4ab^2$$

$$(10x - 5y) - (3x - y) = (10x - 5y) + (-3x + y) = 7x - 4y$$

$$(3x^2 + 8) - (-4x^2 - x + 2) = (3x^2 + 8) + (4x^2 + x - 2)$$
$$= 7x^2 + x + 6$$

Of course, the same subtraction problems could be arranged in vertical form, as shown below.

$7ab^2$	$10x - 5y$	$3x^2 \quad\ + 8$
$3ab^2$	$3x - \ y$	$-4x^2 - x + 2$
$4ab^2$	$7x - 4y$	$7x^2 + x + 6$

The accuracy of an answer to a subtraction problem can be checked in the same way as in the case of addition, by assigning nonzero values to the variables. Thus in checking the second answer above, we might let $x = 2$ and $y = 3$ and write:

$$10x - 5y \rightarrow 10(2) - 5(3) = 5$$
$$3x - \ y \rightarrow 3(2) - \ 3 \ = 3$$
$$7x - 4y \rightarrow 7(2) - 4(3) = 2$$

In the case of subtraction, an even more convenient check is to apply the inverse relation of addition and subtraction. Thus to check the first answer in the example we note that $3ab^2 + 4ab^2 = 7ab^2$ and $7ab^2 - 3ab^2 = 4ab^2$ are equivalent statements. Since the first is a true statement, we see that the answer of $4ab^2$ for the subtraction is correct. Using the same sort of reasoning for the last part of the example, we can write:

$3x^2 \quad\ + 8$	*Check:* $-4x^2 - x + 2$
$-4x^2 - x + 2$	$7x^2 + x + 6$
$7x^2 + x + 6$	$3x^2 \quad\ + 8$

ORAL EXERCISES

Name the opposite of each polynomial.

1. $15x^2y^2$ **5.** $-\dfrac{5w}{3}$ **9.** $-(-3x)$

2. $4y$ **6.** $3.5y$ **10.** $-\frac{5}{8}b$

3. $\dfrac{3t}{2}$ **7.** $-13x^2$ **11.** $4x - 2y$

4. $-12rst$ **8.** $-(5n)$ **12.** $-t + 5$

Tell how to express each of the following without parentheses.

SAMPLE: $-(3x^2 + 5x - 9)$ *What you say:* $-3x^2 - 5x + 9$

13. $-(5x + 2)$ **17.** $-(4y^3 - 7y^2 + 1)$

14. $-(-4s + 6t)$ **18.** $-(10 + 13x^2)$

15. $-(2m^2 - 3n)$ **19.** $-(4ab - 6 + 3b^3)$

16. $-(-10w - 7)$ **20.** $-(-5b - 10c^2 + 8)$

WRITTEN EXERCISES

Simplify each of the following expressions.

SAMPLE: $3mn^2 - 8mn^2$ *Solution:* $-5mn^2$

1. $5x^2 - 2x^2$ **6.** $2ab - (-5ab)$ **11.** $(r + s) - (r + s)$

2. $3mn - mn$ **7.** $8xy - (-xy)$ **12.** $(a - b) - (a + b)$

3. $10abc - 15abc$ **8.** $1.5t - 1.1t$ **13.** $2.7xyz - (-1.1xyz)$

4. $-2x - 3x$ **9.** $-3.6k - 4.2k$ **14.** $(3m + 2) - 3m$

5. $4r^2 - 9r^2$ **10.** $-m - (-5m)$ **15.** $8w - (w + 1)$

Subtract each lower polynomial from the one above. Check your answer by addition.

SAMPLE: $\begin{array}{r} 8x^2 - 3xy \\ x^2 + 6xy \\ \hline \end{array}$ *Solution:* $\begin{array}{r} 8x^2 - 3xy \\ x^2 + 6xy \\ \hline 7x^2 - 9xy \end{array}$ *Check:* $\begin{array}{r} x^2 + 6xy \\ 7x^2 - 9xy \\ \hline 8x^2 - 3xy \end{array}$

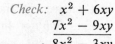

16. $\begin{array}{r} 3x + 5 \\ x + 2 \\ \hline \end{array}$ **18.** $\begin{array}{r} 10a + b \\ -a + 2b \\ \hline \end{array}$ **20.** $\begin{array}{r} 8a^2 - 5a + 2 \\ a^2 \qquad - 2 \\ \hline \end{array}$

17. $\begin{array}{r} 5x^2 + 3y \\ 2x^2 - y \\ \hline \end{array}$ **19.** $\begin{array}{r} x^2 - 3x + 1 \\ x^2 - 2x - 4 \\ \hline \end{array}$ **21.** $\begin{array}{r} 5b^2 + 2b - 5 \\ 3b^2 - 4b \\ \hline \end{array}$

22. $8ab + 5b$
$\underline{6ab + 9b}$

23. $2y^2 - 4y + 5$
$\underline{-y^2 + \ y + 2}$

24. $-10r^2 - 6rs + 10$
$\underline{4r^2 + 2rs - \ 3}$

Simplify each expression.

SAMPLE: $(4b + 2c) - (b + c)$

Solution: $(4b + 2c) - (b + c) = 4b + 2c - b - c$
$\qquad\qquad\qquad\qquad = (4b - b) + (2c - c) = 3b + c$

25. $(8m + 3) - (m + 12)$

28. $(-x + 3y) - (-5x - y)$

26. $(4x^4 + 9) - (5 + 2x^4)$

29. $(-5y + z) - (-4y - z)$

27. $(9rs + s) - (4rs - 3s)$

30. $(a^2 - 3a + 2) - (-a^2 - 2a + 2)$

Solve each equation. The domain of the variable is {directed numbers}.

31. $6x - (3x + 1) = 16$

34. $(4h - 2) - h = -20$

32. $(4a + 3) - 3a = 5\frac{1}{2}$

35. $(4 - 3k) - 2k = -21$

33. $-3r - (7 - 5r) = 11$

36. $(2s - 5) - (3s + 2) = 5$

Simplify each expression.

B **37.** $2t - [3 - (t + 2)]$

39. $-2a - [3a - (14 - a)]$

38. $5y - [y - (6 + 2y)]$

40. $-[3x - (5 - 2x) + 3]$

C **41.** $(-2y - 22) - [8 - (y + 24)]$

43. $(2s^2 - 5s - 2) - (-2 - 5s - 2s^2)$

42. $(23 - 2x) - [3x - (5 - 6x)]$

44. $18 + 3z + [(-3z - 5) - 17]$

PROBLEMS

Write each answer as a polynomial in standard form.

1. A man walks along the perimeter of this rectangular field to get from point A to point B. How far did he walk? How much farther did he walk than would have been required had he walked diagonally across the field?

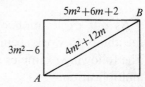

2. What is the combined area of the two unshaded rectangles in the figure? Find the area of the shaded portion of the figure if the area of the large rectangle is represented by $9.5x^2 + 3xy - y^2$.

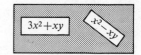

3. The fuel consumed per hour by a large jet aircraft is given by $4.03g^2 + 3t + 1.02$. The fuel consumed per hour by a small aircraft is given by $1.85g^2 - 2.3t$. How much more fuel is consumed per hour by the larger aircraft?

4. The volume of liquid in the storage tank is represented by $m^2 + 2m - 3$. The total volume of the tank is $4.3m^3 - 2m^2 + 7m$. What is the volume of the empty part of the tank?

5. The thrust of a J-12 jet engine is indicated by the polynomial $1.4k^3 + 3.9k - 1.04$. When a supercharger device is installed in the engine the thrust is increased to $1.48k^3 - 0.5k + 3.25$. By how much did the supercharger increase the thrust of the engine?

Multiplication

3–3 Powers of Monomials

You should have the following basic ideas about exponents well in mind:

In 3^5, the base is **3** and the exponent is **5**.

If an exponent is not indicated, we understand that it is **1**.
For example, $x = x^1$ and $10 = 10^1$.

The **exponent** indicates the number of times the **base** is used as a **factor** in a product.

As our exploration of algebraic ideas and polynomials continues, the ability to work accurately with exponents becomes very important. The following examples serve to illustrate a basic rule of exponents for multiplication.

$$\overset{\textbf{4 factors}}{\overbrace{\qquad\quad}}\ \overset{\textbf{2 factors}}{\overbrace{\quad}}$$

EXAMPLE 1. $3^4 \cdot 3^2 = (3 \cdot 3 \cdot 3 \cdot 3) \cdot (3 \cdot 3)$

$$\overset{\textbf{6 factors}}{\overbrace{\qquad\qquad\quad}}$$

$$= 3 \cdot 3 \cdot 3 \cdot 3 \cdot 3 \cdot 3 = 3^6$$

EXAMPLE 2. $t^2 \cdot t^3 = \overbrace{(t \cdot t)}^{\text{2 factors}} \cdot \overbrace{(t \cdot t \cdot t)}^{\text{3 factors}}$

$= \overbrace{t \cdot t \cdot t \cdot t \cdot t}^{\text{5 factors}} = t^5$

EXAMPLE 3. $(xy)^3 \cdot (xy) = \overbrace{(xy)(xy)(xy)}^{\text{3 factors}} \cdot \overbrace{(xy)}^{\text{1 factor}}$

$= \overbrace{(xy)(xy)(xy)(xy)}^{\text{4 factors}} = (xy)^4$

Thus we can arrive at the following general rule of exponents.

For any directed number **a** and positive integers **p** and **q**:

$$a^p \cdot a^q = a^{p+q}.$$

We make use of this rule of exponents, together with the properties of multiplication, to simplify indicated products of monomials. Be certain that you understand each step in this example:

EXAMPLE 1. $(3ab^2) \cdot (-5a^3b) = (3 \cdot -5)(a \cdot a^3)(b^2 \cdot b)$
$$= (-15)(a^{1+3})(b^{2+1}) = -15a^4b^3$$

It is very important that you understand the meaning of such symbols as $(4x)^3$ and $(m^4)^2$.

EXAMPLE 2.   EXAMPLE 3.

$(4x)^3 = 4x \cdot 4x \cdot 4x$ $(m^4)^2 = m^4 \cdot m^4$
$\quad = (4 \cdot 4 \cdot 4)(x \cdot x \cdot x)$ $\quad = m^{4+4}$
$\quad = 4^3 \cdot x^3 = 64x^3$ $\quad = m^{4 \cdot 2}$
$\qquad\qquad\qquad\qquad\qquad = m^8$

For all directed numbers **a** and **b** and every positive integer **p**,
$$(ab)^p = a^p \cdot b^p.$$

For every directed number **a**, and all positive integers **p** and **q**,
$$(a^p)^q = a^{pq}.$$

ORAL EXERCISES

Match each expression in Column 1 with an expression that has the same meaning in Column 2.

COLUMN 1

1. $a^3 \cdot a^5$

2. $x^2 \cdot x^2 \cdot y^3$

3. $(a^2b^2)^3$

4. $(a^5)^3$

5. $-3(xy)^3$

6. $(3x^2y^2)(5y^3)$

7. $(-3xy)^3$

8. $(xy^3)^4$

COLUMN 2

A. $15 \cdot x \cdot x \cdot y \cdot y \cdot y \cdot y \cdot y$

B. $xy^3 \cdot xy^3 \cdot xy^3 \cdot xy^3$

C. $a^5 \cdot a^5 \cdot a^5$

D. x^4y^3

E. $(-3xy)(-3xy)(-3xy)$

F. $(a \cdot a \cdot b \cdot b)(a \cdot a \cdot b \cdot b)(a \cdot a \cdot b \cdot b)$

G. $(a \cdot a \cdot a)(a \cdot a \cdot a \cdot a \cdot a)$

H. $-3 \cdot xy \cdot xy \cdot xy$

Use exponential notation to give a simpler name for each expression.

SAMPLE: $7 \cdot a \cdot a \cdot b \cdot b \cdot a \cdot a$ *What you say:* $7a^4b^2$

9. $3(x \cdot x \cdot x)(y \cdot y \cdot y)$

10. $2(x \cdot x)(x \cdot y)(y \cdot y)$

11. $5(m \cdot m \cdot m)(m \cdot m)$

12. $-[(mn)(mn)(mn)(mn)]$

13. $\left(\dfrac{a}{5} \cdot \dfrac{a}{5} \cdot \dfrac{a}{5}\right) - \left(\dfrac{r}{3} \cdot \dfrac{r}{3} \cdot \dfrac{r}{3}\right)$

14. $[(x \cdot x \cdot x) + (r \cdot r)] + (y \cdot y \cdot y)$

WRITTEN EXERCISES

Write each expression in a form such that no exponent is greater than 1.

SAMPLE: $(5n^2)^3$ *Solution:* $(5n^2)^3 = (5n^2)(5n^2)(5n^2)$
$$= (5 \cdot 5 \cdot 5)(n^2 \cdot n^2 \cdot n^2)$$
$$= (5 \cdot 5 \cdot 5 \cdot n \cdot n \cdot n \cdot n \cdot n \cdot n)$$

1. $(ab^2)(b)$

2. $(rs)^2(rs)^2$

3. $k^2 \cdot k^2 \cdot k^2$

4. $(2ab)(3ab)^2$

5. $(10n)^{3+1}$

6. $(3w^2)^2 \cdot w^2$

7. $(-3)^3(n)^3$

8. $(m^2n^2)(mn)^3$

9. $(xy)^3(xy)(3y^2)$

10. $4(m^3)^2 \cdot n^2$

11. $(rs)(r^2s)(-rs^2)$

12. $(m^{3+1})(n^{2+1})(r^2)$

Copy and complete each of the following.

SAMPLE: $(6xy^2)(8xy^3)$
$$= (6 \cdot 8)(x \cdot x)(y^2 \cdot y^3)$$
$$= (\ ?\ )(\ ?\ )(\ ?\ )$$
$$= ?$$

Solution: $(6xy^2)(8xy^3)$
$$= (6 \cdot 8)(x \cdot x)(y^2 \cdot y^3)$$
$$= 48(x^{1+1})(y^{2+3})$$
$$= 48x^2y^5$$

13. $(2mn^2)(5m^2n^2)$
$\quad = (2 \cdot 5)(m \cdot m^2)(n^2 \cdot n^2)$
$\quad = (\ ? \ )(\ ? \ )(\ ? \ )$
$\quad = \ ?$

15. $(-3rs)(2rs^2)(7r^3)$
$\quad = (-3 \cdot 2 \cdot 7)(r \cdot r \cdot r^3)(s \cdot s^2)$
$\quad = (\ ? \ )(\ ? \ )(\ ? \ )$
$\quad = \ ?$

14. $(-4a^2b)(2ab^4)$
$\quad = (-4 \cdot 2)(a^2 \cdot a)(b \cdot b^4)$
$\quad = (\ ? \ )(\ ? \ )(\ ? \ )$
$\quad = \ ?$

16. $(-\frac{2}{3}xy^3)(\frac{1}{2}xy)(9x^3y^2)$
$\quad = (-\frac{2}{3} \cdot \frac{1}{2} \cdot 9)(x \cdot x \cdot x^3)(y^3 \cdot y \cdot y^2)$
$\quad = (\ ? \ )(\ ? \ )(\ ? \ )$
$\quad = \ ?$

Find the integer named by each numeral.

SAMPLE: $(-2^3)(10)^2$ $\qquad$ *Solution:* $(-2)^3(10)^2 = (-8)(100) = -800$

17. $(-3)^2(3)^3$

18. $(2^{3+1}) + 5^2$

19. $(-10)^2(10)^2$

20. $(2^3)^2$

21. $(-1)(3^2)^2$

22. $-\frac{1}{2} \cdot (4^3)$

23. $\frac{1}{2} \cdot \frac{1}{2} \cdot (-8)^2$

24. $-(3^{1+2})(10)^2$

25. $(-2)^5(3)^2(-5)^2$

Complete the table of values for each expression.

SAMPLE: $pq^2 - p^3$ $\qquad$ *Solution:*

p	q	$pq^2 - p^3$
2	2	?
1	3	?
0	−2	?

p	q	$pq^2 - p^3$
2	2	0
1	3	8
0	−2	0

B **26.** $(2m)^2 - 3n^2$

m	n	$(2m)^2 - 3n^2$
4	3	?
5	−2	?
1	0	?

28. $\frac{1}{2}(x^2y^3)(xy^2)$

x	y	$\frac{1}{2}(x^2y^3)(xy^2)$
−2	1	?
0	0	?
3	−3	?

27. $(ab)^2 \cdot (ab^2)$

a	b	$(ab)^2 \cdot (ab^2)$
−2	−1	?
−3	0	?
0	5	?
10	1	?

29. $m(m^2 + 1) + (mn)^2$

m	n	$m(m^2 + 1) + (mn)^2$
3	0	?
4	0	?
−3	0	?
−4	0	?

Simplify each expression.

C **30.** $(cd)^3(0.5c^2d) + (c^2d)^2(2c^2)$ **32.** $(2k)^2(-10k^4) + (6k)(-k^2)$

31. $(3mn)^2 + 5(-6m^2n^2) + (mn)^2$ **33.** $(ar)^5(2ar^2) + (0.3a^2r^2)(100r^3)$

3–4   The Number Plane and Integer Pairs

You are already familiar with the idea of graphing ordered pairs of numbers on a lattice. The graph of each number pair, (1, 3), (2, 2), (3, 1), and (4, 0) is indicated by the symbol × in Figure 3–1. Notice that both numbers in each pair are **positive** integers.

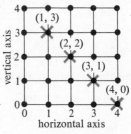

Figure 3–1

Now let us consider how we can extend our ideas of graphing to ordered number pairs that include both positive and negative integers. First it is necessary to broaden our thinking about lattice points as suggested by Figure 3–2. Notice that the lattice is divided into four parts by the two number lines. One number line is called the **horizontal axis** and the other is called the **vertical axis**. Each of the four parts of the lattice is called a **quadrant**. The graph of each of the following integer pairs is shown on the lattice in Figure 3–3. $A(0, 3)$, $B(-3, 1)$, $C(2, -2)$, $D(-4, -2)$, $E(-2, 0)$, $F(-3, -5)$. The integer pair **(0, 0)** corresponds with the point of intersection of the axes (plural of *axis*) and is called the **origin**. If neither integer in an integer pair is zero, the integer pair corresponds with a point in one of the quadrants. However, if either integer in an integer pair is zero, the integer pair corresponds with a point on one of the axes.

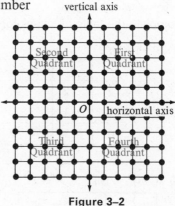

Figure 3–2

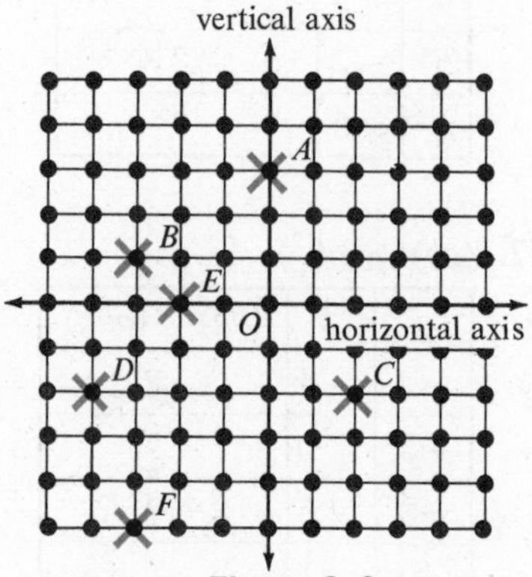

Figure 3–3

ORAL EXERCISES

Name the ordered integer pair that corresponds with each point labeled with a letter.

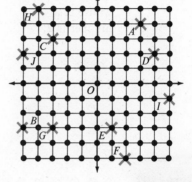

1. *A*	**6.** *F*
2. *B*	**7.** *G*
3. *C*	**8.** *H*
4. *D*	**9.** *I*
5. *E*	**10.** *J*

Tell whether the graph of each integer pair is in quadrant 1, 2, 3, or 4 or on an axis. Refer to the lattice for Exercises 1–10, if necessary.

11. $(-2, 1)$ **14.** $(-1, -3)$ **17.** $(0, 3)$ **20.** $(1, 4)$

12. $(4, -2)$ **15.** $(-1, -5)$ **18.** $(2, 2)$ **21.** $(-5, 0)$

13. $(4, 0)$ **16.** $(-4, 4)$ **19.** $(0, -5)$ **22.** $(-2, 3)$

WRITTEN EXERCISES

Draw a four-quadrant lattice like the one shown here. On the lattice, indicate the graph of each integer pair with X, and label the point with the letter named.

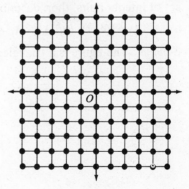

A

1. $(0, 4)$; *A*	**5.** $(-3, -3)$; *X*	**9.** $(0, -4)$; *W*
2. $(-2, 5)$; *K*	**6.** $(5, -2)$; *B*	**10.** $(4, -3)$; *C*
3. $(3, 4)$; *M*	**7.** $(1, -4)$; *H*	**11.** $(-3, 0)$; *Y*
4. $(0, 0)$; *T*	**8.** $(-5, -4)$; *E*	**12.** $(2, 5)$; *N*

For each of the following, draw a four-quadrant lattice like the one used in Exercises 1–12. Use a curve to enclose all points of the lattice that are graphs of members of the set of integer pairs described; then write the set in roster form.

SAMPLE: {the integer pairs whose first number is 2}   *Solution:*

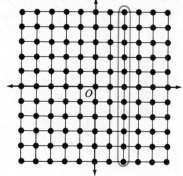

The set is: {(2, 5), (2, 4), (2, 3), (2, 2), (2, 1), (2, 0), (2, −1), (2, −2), (2, −3), (2, −4), (2, −5)}.

13. {the integer pairs whose first number is 4}

14. {the integer pairs whose first number is 0}

15. {the integer pairs whose second number is 0}

16. {the integer pairs whose first number is −3}

17. {the integer pairs whose second number is 2}

18. {the integer pairs whose first number and second number are the same positive number}

On a lattice, draw the polygon whose vertices are determined by the given set of integer pairs, then describe the figure.

SAMPLE: {(4, 1), (0, 3), (−1, −1)}

Solution: The figure is a triangle.

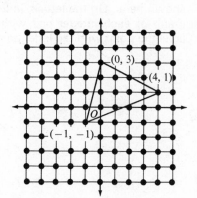

19. {(−4, 3), (−4, −3), (3, 2)}

20. {(0, 0), (3, 0), (3, 3), (0, 3)}

21. {(−3, 2), (−4, 0), (−2, −3), (2, −2), (2, 4)}

22. {(−4, 2), (1, 2), (1, −3)}

For each of the following, draw a four-quadrant lattice like the one used in Exercises 1–12. Use a curve to enclose all points of the lattice that are graphs of members of the set of integer pairs described; then write the set in roster form.

SAMPLE: {the integer pairs whose first number is negative and whose second number is the opposite of the first}

Solution:

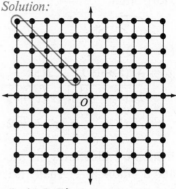

The set is: $\{(-1, 1), (-2, 2), (-3, 3), (-4, 4), (-5, 5)\}$.

B

23. {the integer pairs whose first number is positive and whose second number is the opposite of the first}

24. {the integer pairs whose first number and second number are the same but neither is negative}

25. {the number pairs whose first number is a non-negative integer and whose second number is the opposite of the first}

26. {the integer pairs whose first number and second number are the same but neither is positive}

3–5 Multiplication of Polynomials

The familiar idea of the distributive property and the rules of exponents are applied when you multiply polynomials. In Example 1, we show a polynomial multiplied by a monomial, first in the horizontal form and then in the vertical form.

EXAMPLE 1. Horizontal:

$$2x(3x^2 - 4x + 1) = 6x^3 - 8x^2 + 2x$$

Vertical:

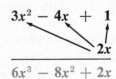

$$3x^2 - 4x + 1$$
$$2x$$
$$\overline{6x^3 - 8x^2 + 2x}$$

Many problems in algebra involve the multiplication of one binomial by another. To accomplish this, each term of one binomial is multiplied by each term of the other; then the products are added. Example 2 illustrates this process in both the horizontal and vertical forms.

EXAMPLE 2.

Horizontal:

$(4x + 2)(5x + 1)$

$= 4x(5x + 1) + 2(5x + 1)$

$= 20x^2 + 4x + 10x + 2$

$= 20x^2 + \qquad 14x \qquad + 2$

Vertical:

$$
\begin{array}{r}
5x + 1 \\
4x + 2 \\
\hline
10x + 2 \quad \leftarrow 2(5x + 1) \\
20x^2 + 4x \qquad \leftarrow 4x(5x + 1) \\
\hline
20x^2 + 14x + 2
\end{array}
$$

Example 3 illustrates the process for finding the product of a trinomial and a binomial. Usually it is simpler to set up this type of problem in the vertical form.

EXAMPLE 3.

$$
\begin{array}{r}
3x^2 - 5x + 2 \\
2x - 7 \\
\hline
-21x^2 + 35x - 14 \quad \leftarrow -7(3x^2 - 5x + 2) \\
6x^3 - 10x^2 + 4x \qquad \leftarrow 2x(3x^2 - 5x + 2) \\
\hline
6x^3 - 31x^2 + 39x - 14
\end{array}
$$

ORAL EXERCISES

Name the missing term in each of the following.

SAMPLE: $5t(3t^2 + 2) = 15t^3 + ?$ *What you say:* $10t$

1. $-2n(3n^2 - 1) = -6n^3 + ?$ **5.** $-1(3z^5 - 6z^2 - 7z) = -3z^5 + ? + ?$

2. $6(-a + b) = ? + 6b$ **6.** $(3 - 2a - 3a^2)(-5) = -15 + 10a + ?$

3. $(2a - 4)3 = ? - 12$ **7.** $2ab(5a^2 + b) = 10a^3b + ?$

4. $\frac{1}{2}(8x - 10y) = ? - 5y$ **8.** $-st(-s^2 + 3t) = ? - 3st^2$

Use the distributive property to simplify each expression.

SAMPLE: $-2x(3x + 6)$ *What you say:* $-6x^2 - 12x$

9. $5(3x - 1)$ **13.** $-b(2b + 7)$ **17.** $(3x^2 - x)(-1)$

10. $-4(2 - 3y)$ **14.** $10(r + s)$ **18.** $-2w(4w^3 + 3w^2)$

11. $2t(t + 4)$ **15.** $9(m - n)$ **19.** $d^3(d + d^2)$

12. $-m(4 - m)$ **16.** $(3w - 5)6$ **20.** $3a(a + b + c)$

WRITTEN EXERCISES

Complete each indicated multiplication.

A

1. $8t^3 - 4t + 2$
$\underline{ 3t}$

3. $4a + 2b^2 - 3$
$\underline{ ab}$

5. $7a^2 + 3ab + 2b^2$
$\underline{ -5a}$

2. $5m^2 - 2m + 6$
$\underline{ -4m}$

4. $x^2y - 10xy + 2y$
$\underline{ 3xy}$

6. $6r^2 - 4rs + 3s^2$
$\underline{ -2rs}$

7. $-2ab(-a^2 - b^2)$

8. $6(m^2 + 2mn + 6)$

9. $-3(4 - 2x - 7x^2)$

10. $2x^2(x + xy - 5y^2)$

11. $(6m^2 - 4mn + 3n^2)(-2mn)$

12. $(4b^2 + 3bc + 2c^2)(-5b)$

13. $(r + 1)(r + 2)$

14. $(m + 4)(m + 3)$

15. $(a - 2)(a + 2)$

16. $(h - 3)(h + 5)$

17. $(t - 5)(t - 5)$

18. $(2r + 1)(r + 3)$

19. $3n - 1$
$\underline{ n + 2}$

21. $6d + 5$
$\underline{ 3d - 3}$

23. $7y - 6$
$\underline{ 2y - 5}$

20. $5x - 2$
$\underline{ 3x + 1}$

22. $5w + 2$
$\underline{ 3w - 4}$

24. $x^2 + y$
$\underline{ x^2 - y}$

Solve each equation and check your answer. The domain of the variable is {the directed numbers}.

25. $2r + 5(6 - r) = 3$

26. $3b + 2(b - 5) = 35$

27. $5(2x - 3) - 7x = -39$

28. $3(a - 4) - 9a = 42$

29. $7 = (2y + 5) - 3(y - 4)$

30. $5(2n - 3) = -7 + 2(5 - n)$

Complete each indicated multiplication.

B

31. $(2x - 1)(x + 3)$

32. $(4z - 3)(z + 5)$

33. $(2n + 3)(n - 5)$

34. $(2x + 7t)(2x - 7t)$

35. $(m^2 - n^2)(m^2 + n^2)$

36. $(2r^2 + 4)(r^2 - 3)$

37. $(2x - 3y)(2x - 10y)$

38. $(a^2 + b^2)(a^2 + b^2)$

C

39. $(s + 1)(s^2 + 3s - 5)$

40. $(2n - 1)(n^2 + 3n + 5)$

41. $(x + 1)(2x + 3) + (x + 1)(3x - 2)$

42. $(2r + s)(3r - s) - (r - s)(2r - s)$

PROBLEMS

Write each answer as a polynomial in standard form.

1. Find the area of each of regions *A, B, C,* and *D* in the accompanying figure. Then find the total area of the figure.

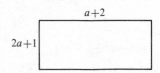

2. Find the area of this rectangle if the polynomials represent the length and width. What is the perimeter?

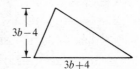

3. What is the area of this triangle in terms of the given polynomials? (Use $A = \frac{1}{2}bh$)

4. The figure shows the floor of a room partly covered by a carpet. What is the area of the floor? Find the area of the carpet. What is the area of that part of the floor that is not covered?

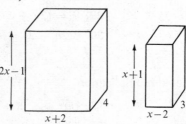

5. Calculate the volumes of the two box-shaped figures. Then find out by how much the volume of the large box exceeds the volume of the small box. (Use $V = lwh$).

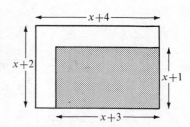

6. Find the area of the shaded triangular region. (Use $A = \frac{1}{2}bh$). What is the area of the square region formed by the two triangles?

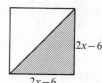

3–6 Polynomials Raised to a Power

The expression x^2 means "x squared" or "x raised to the second power." In a similar manner $(2x + 1)^3$ means "the quantity $2x + 1$ cubed" or "the quantity $2x + 1$ raised to the third power." Do you see that an exponent can be used to tell how many times a polynomial is used as a factor? That is,

$$(x + 2y)^2 \text{ means } (x + 2y)(x + 2y)$$
$$(2t - 3)^3 \text{ means } (2t - 3)(2t - 3)(2t - 3)$$
$$(m + 1)^4 \text{ means } (m + 1)(m + 1)(m + 1)(m + 1).$$

The process of finding a power of a polynomial factor is called **expanding** the expression. For example,

$$(3x + 2)^2 = (3x + 2)(3x + 2) = 9x^2 + 12x + 4,$$

so the expanded form of $(3x + 2)^2$ is $9x^2 + 12x + 4$.

Be certain that you understand how each of these polynomials is expanded.

EXAMPLE 1. $(4t - 2)^2$

$$
\begin{array}{r}
4t - 2 \\
4t - 2 \\
\hline
-8t + 4 \\
16t^2 - 8t \\
\hline
16t^2 - 16t + 4
\end{array}
$$

$(4t - 2)^2 = 16t^2 - 16t + 4$

EXAMPLE 2. $(2x + 1)^3$

$$
\begin{array}{ll}
2x + 1 & \longrightarrow 4x^2 + 4x + 1 \\
2x + 1 & \qquad\qquad 2x + 1 \\
\hline
2x + 1 & \qquad 4x^2 + 4x + 1 \\
4x^2 + 2x & \quad 8x^3 + 8x^2 + 2x \\
\hline
4x^2 + 4x + 1 & 8x^3 + 12x^2 + 6x + 1
\end{array}
$$

$(2x + 1)^3 = 8x^3 + 12x^2 + 6x + 1$

ORAL EXERCISES

Tell how to express each product as a polynomial raised to a power.

SAMPLE: $(x + y)(x + y)(x + y)$ *What you say:* $(x + y)^3$

1. $(n + 1)(n + 1)$
2. $(2 + a)(2 + a)(2 + a)(2 + a)$
3. $(xy)(xy)(xy)(xy)(xy)$
4. $(3n - m)(3n - m)(3n - m)$
5. $(a + b)(a + b)$
6. $(3y - 2x)(3y - 2x)(3y - 2x)$
7. $(x - 1)^2(x - 1)(x - 1)$
8. $(r + 2s)(r + 2s)^2(r + 2s)^3$

94   Chapter 3

WRITTEN EXERCISES

Expand each expression as indicated. In Exercises 1–12, check your answers by letting $x = 3$, $y = 4$, and $m = 2$.

SAMPLE: $(x + 1)^2$ *Solution:* $(x + 1)^2 = x^2 + 2x + 1$

Check:

$(x + 1)^2$	$= x^2 + 2x + 1$
$(3 + 1)^2$	$(3 \cdot 3) + (2 \cdot 3) + 1$
4^2	$9 \ + \ 6 \ + 1$
16	16

A
1. $(m + 3)^2$ 7. $(x - y)^2$ 13. $(x + y)^3$

2. $(x + 2)^2$ 8. $(5y + 1)^2$ 14. $(m + x)^3$

3. $(x - 1)^2$ 9. $(2x + 3)^2$ 15. $(2x - 2)^3$

4. $(2y - 1)^2$ 10. $(2 - 3y)^2$ 16. $2x(x + 5)^2$

5. $(y - 4)^2$ 11. $(3x - 4y)^2$ 17. $-3y(y + 2)^2$

6. $(x + y)^2$ 12. $(2m + x)^2$ 18. $(x - y)(x + y)^2$

B
19. $(y + \frac{1}{2})^2$ 22. $(y - \frac{1}{2})^2$

20. $2x^2 + (x - 1)^2$ 23. $(x + \frac{1}{3})^2$

21. $3m^2 - (m + 2)^2$ 24. $(x + 2y)(x - 2y)^2$

C
25. $(x + y + m)^2$ 28. $(x + y)^3$ 31. $(x + y)^4$

26. $(x + y - m)^2$ 29. $(2x - 3y)^3$ 32. $(x - y)^2(x + y)^2$

27. $(m - x + y)^2$ 30. $(y - m)^4$ 33. $(2x^2 - 3xy + y^2)^2$

PROBLEMS

Write each answer as a polynomial in standard form.

1. Calculate the area of this square. Use $A = s^2$.

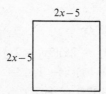

2. Find the volume of the given cube. Use $V = e^3$.

3. Find the volume of the cylindrical tank shown here. Use $V = Bh$, where B stands for the area of the bottom of the tank and h stands for the height of the tank.

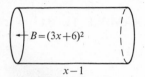

4. The box shown here has a square base. Find its volume. Use $V = Bh$, where B stands for the area of the base and h stands for the height of the box.

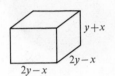

Division

3–7   Division of Monomials

Suppose you were asked to supply the missing information in each of these sentences:

$$7^4 = 7 \cdot (?) \qquad m^3 = m \cdot (?) \qquad 8x^5 = 4x^2 \cdot (?)$$

As you probably know, the inverse relationship between multiplication and division allows us to replace each sentence by an equivalent division sentence:

$7^4 = 7 \cdot 7^3$ is equivalent to both $\dfrac{7^4}{7} = 7^3$ and $\dfrac{7^4}{7^3} = 7$;

$m^3 = m \cdot m^2$ is equivalent to both $\dfrac{m^3}{m} = m^2$ and $\dfrac{m^3}{m^2} = m$;

$8x^5 = 4x^2 \cdot 2x^3$ is equivalent to both $\dfrac{8x^5}{4x^2} = 2x^3$ and $\dfrac{8x^5}{2x^3} = 4x^2$.

These examples suggest the following rule of exponents that will be used frequently in our work dealing with division of polynomials.

For any directed number **a** not equal to **0**, and for all positive integers **p** and **q** where **p** > **q**,

$$\frac{a^p}{a^q} = a^{p-q}.$$

At first glance it may not be easy to supply the missing information in sentences like $5^3 = 5^8 \cdot (?)$ and $3x^4 = x^7 \cdot (?)$. But do you see that $5^3 = 5^8 \cdot \dfrac{1}{5^5}$ and $3x^4 = x^7 \cdot \dfrac{3}{x^3}$? Follow each step in the following examples.

EXAMPLE 1. $3x^4 = x^7 \cdot$ (?) is equivalent to $\dfrac{3x^4}{x^7} = $?

$$\frac{3x^4}{x^7} = \frac{3}{x^3} \cdot \frac{x^4}{x^4}$$

$$= \frac{3}{x^3} \cdot 1 = \frac{3}{x^3}$$

So $\qquad 3x^4 = x^7 \cdot \dfrac{3}{x^3} \cdot$

EXAMPLE 2. $5^3 = 5^8 \cdot$ (?) is equivalent to $\dfrac{5^3}{5^8} = $?

$$\frac{5^3}{5^8} = \frac{1}{5^5} \cdot \frac{5^3}{5^3}$$

$$= \frac{1}{5^5} \cdot 1 = \frac{1}{5^5}$$

So $\qquad 5^3 = 5^8 \cdot \dfrac{1}{5^5} \cdot$

Notice that we have used the idea that expressions like $\dfrac{x^4}{x^4}$ equal 1. Of course, we are assuming that x is not **0**. Thus we arrive at the following rule of exponents for division:

> For any directed number **a** not equal to **0**, and for all positive integers **p** and **q** where **p** < **q**,
>
> $$\frac{a^p}{a^q} = \frac{1}{a^{q-p}} \cdot$$

Here are more examples to help you verify the rules of exponents for division.

EXAMPLE 3.

$$\frac{m^9}{m^2} = \frac{m^7}{1} \cdot \frac{m^2}{m^2}$$

$$= m^7 \cdot 1 = m^7$$

EXAMPLE 4.

$$\frac{t^5}{t^7} = \frac{1}{t^2} \cdot \frac{t^5}{t^5}$$

$$= \frac{1}{t^2} \cdot 1 = \frac{1}{t^2}$$

EXAMPLE 5.

$$\frac{7x^8}{-2x^3} = \frac{7x^5}{-2} \cdot \frac{x^3}{x^3}$$

$$= \frac{7x^5}{-2} \cdot 1 = \frac{7x^5}{-2}$$

EXAMPLE 6.

$$\frac{18y^2}{3y^6} = \frac{6}{y^4} \cdot \frac{3y^2}{3y^2}$$

$$= \frac{6}{y^4} \cdot 1 = \frac{6}{y^4}$$

WRITTEN EXERCISES

Complete each of the following sentences. Assume that no divisor is equal to 0.

SAMPLE 1: $\dfrac{3w^2}{5w^6} = (?) \cdot \dfrac{w^2}{w^2}$ *Solution:* $\dfrac{3w^2}{5w^6} = \dfrac{3}{5w^4} \cdot \dfrac{w^2}{w^2}$

SAMPLE 2: $\dfrac{6y^8}{9y^5} = (?) \cdot \dfrac{3y^5}{3y^5}$ *Solution:* $\dfrac{6y^8}{9y^5} = \dfrac{2y^3}{3} \cdot \dfrac{3y^5}{3y^5}$

1. $\dfrac{x^{10}}{x^3} = (?) \cdot \dfrac{x^3}{x^3}$

2. $\dfrac{5m}{m} = (?) \cdot \dfrac{m}{m}$

3. $\dfrac{2y^2}{y^5} = (?) \cdot \dfrac{y^2}{y^2}$

4. $\dfrac{t^6}{t^3} = (?) \cdot \dfrac{t^3}{t^3}$

5. $\dfrac{7n^2}{5n^8} = (?) \cdot \dfrac{n^2}{n^2}$

6. $\dfrac{3k^5}{5k^2} = (?) \cdot \dfrac{k^2}{k^2}$

7. $\dfrac{x^3y^5}{x^2y^2} = (?) \cdot \dfrac{x^2y^2}{x^2y^2}$

8. $\dfrac{-6z^5}{2z^2} = (?) \cdot \dfrac{2z^2}{2z^2}$

9. $\dfrac{11m^{10}}{-3m^7} = (?) \cdot \dfrac{m^7}{m^7}$

SAMPLE 3: $\dfrac{15x^7}{3x^5} = \dfrac{15}{3} \cdot x^{7-5} = ?$ *Solution:* $\dfrac{15x^7}{3x^5} = \dfrac{15}{3} \cdot x^{7-5} = 5x^2$

10. $\dfrac{3a^5}{a^3} = 3a^{5-3} = ?$

11. $\dfrac{12m^8}{3m^3} = \dfrac{12}{3} \cdot m^{8-3} = ?$

12. $\dfrac{4k^5}{10k^9} = \dfrac{4}{10} \cdot \dfrac{1}{k^{9-5}} = ?$

13. $\dfrac{m^4}{3m^7} = \dfrac{1}{3} \cdot \dfrac{1}{m^{7-4}} = ?$

14. $\dfrac{10y^6}{-2y^2} = \dfrac{10}{-2} \cdot y^{6-2} = ?$

15. $\dfrac{-12x^9}{3x^2} = \dfrac{-12}{3} \cdot x^{9-2} = ?$

Simplify each expression.

16. $\dfrac{5k^2}{k}$

17. $\dfrac{c^8}{c^6}$

18. $\dfrac{4xy^2}{2x}$

19. $\dfrac{x^2}{x^6}$

20. $\dfrac{-18r^3}{-2r}$

21. $\dfrac{9x^2y^2}{6xy^3}$

22. $\dfrac{-20a^4}{-4a^2}$

23. $\dfrac{5m}{35m^3}$

24. $\dfrac{4c^3}{-2c}$

25. $\dfrac{12t^7}{4t^6}$

26. $\dfrac{3a}{6a^2}$

27. $\dfrac{-27r^5s^5}{3r^5s^5}$

Complete each sentence. Assume no denominator is equal to 0.

B **28.** $\dfrac{8x^5y^4}{4x^3y^3} = \dfrac{8}{4} \cdot x^{5-3} \cdot y^{4-3} = \,?$

29. $\dfrac{16t^9s^8}{4t^7s^3} = \dfrac{16}{4} \cdot t^{9-7} \cdot s^{8-3} = \,?$

30. $\dfrac{-7x^8y^6}{56x^6y^8} = \dfrac{-7}{56} \cdot x^{8-6} \cdot \dfrac{1}{y^{8-6}} = \,?$

Simplify each expression, assuming that no divisor is equal to 0.

31. $\dfrac{-24t^7s^8}{6t^7s^3}$ **33.** $\dfrac{64r^5s^7}{8r^{10}s^{10}}$ **35.** $\dfrac{(4ab)^2}{12ab^3}$

32. $\dfrac{18m^5n^4}{-6m^3n^3}$ **34.** $\dfrac{14t^{11}s^5}{-42t^{12}s^4}$ **36.** $\dfrac{-16a^5b^2}{(2ab)^3}$

C **37.** $\dfrac{(4c^5d^2)^2}{-(2c^2d^2)^3}$ **38.** $\dfrac{-(3x^3y^2)^3}{9(x^2y^3)^3}$ **39.** $\dfrac{-(9m^5n^2)^2}{-27m^6n^6}$

3–8   Division of Polynomials

The expression $\dfrac{6x + 10}{2}$ can be simplified without difficulty by applying the distributive property. That is, $6x$ is divided by 2 and 10 is divided by 2, and the two results are added together.

$$\frac{6x + 10}{2} = \frac{6x}{2} + \frac{10}{2} = 3x + 5$$

Sometimes an indicated division is easier to simplify if you write it with the division bracket.

EXAMPLE. $\dfrac{12x^2 - 15x + 9}{3}$ is the same as $3\overline{)12x^2 - 15x + 9}$,

so $\dfrac{12x^2 - 15x + 9}{3} = 4x^2 - 5x + 3.$

The following two examples further illustrate the application of the distributive property. Assume that no denominator is equal to 0.

EXAMPLE 1.

$$\frac{10m^5 - 6m^3}{2m^2} = \frac{10m^5}{2m^2} - \frac{6m^3}{2m^2} = 5m^3 - 3m$$

EXAMPLE 2.

$$\frac{28r^7 + 16r^5 - 20r^3}{-4r^2} = \frac{28r^7}{-4r^2} + \frac{16r^5}{-4r^2} - \frac{20r^3}{-4r^2} = -7r^5 - 4r^3 + 5r$$

Our work with polynomials and the division operation will not be complete until we consider indicated divisions like $\frac{x^2 + 4x + 3}{x + 1}$ and $\frac{x^2 + 5x + 8}{x + 3}$. To carry out these indicated divisions the work is organized much like a long division problem in arithmetic. Follow each step in Example 1.

EXAMPLE 1. Step 1. Check to be sure that both the dividend and the divisor are written in standard form.

$$
\begin{array}{r}
\boxed{\text{quotient}} \searrow x + 3 \\
x + 1\overline{)x^2 + 4x + 3} \\
\boxed{\text{divisor}} \quad x^2 + x \boxed{\text{dividend}} \\
\hline
3x + 3 \\
3x + 3 \\
\hline
0
\end{array}
$$

Step 2. Divide x^2 by x. The result, x, is recorded as the first term of the quotient.

Step 3. Multiply $x(x + 1)$. The result, $x^2 + x$, is recorded below the dividend.

Step 4. Subtract $(x^2 + 4x + 3) - (x^2 + x)$. The result, $3x + 3$, is recorded.

Step 5. Divide $3x$ by x. The result, 3, is recorded as the second term of the quotient.

Step 6. Multiply $3(x + 1)$. The result, $3x + 3$, is recorded below the dividend.

Step 7. Subtract $(3x + 3) - (3x + 3) = 0$.

Since the remainder is **0**, we say that the division "came out even." We can check the accuracy of our work by finding the product of the quotient and the divisor and verifying that it is the same as the dividend.

Check:

dividend	= quotient × divisor
$x^2 + 4x + 3$	$(x + 3)(x + 1)$
$x^2 + 4x + 3$	$x^2 + 4x + 3$

As you have probably guessed it is not always the case that the division "comes out even." There may be a nonzero remainder. Follow the steps described in Example 2.

EXAMPLE 2. Step 1. Check to be sure that both polynomials are in standard form.

$$
\begin{array}{r}
x + 2 \\
x + 3 \overline{\smash{)}x^2 + 5x + 8} \\
x^2 + 3x \\
\hline
2x + 8 \\
2x + 6 \\
\hline
2
\end{array}
$$

quotient — $x + 2$

divisor — $x + 3$

dividend — $x^2 + 3x$

Step 2. Divide x^2 by x. The result, x, is recorded as the first term of the quotient.

Step 3. Multiply $x(x + 3)$. The result, $x^2 + 3x$, is recorded below the dividend.

Step 4. Subtract $(x^2 + 5x + 8) - (x^2 + 3x)$. The result, $2x + 8$, is recorded.

Step 5. Divide $2x$ by x. The result, 2, is recorded as the second term of the quotient.

Step 6. Multiply $2(x + 3)$. The result, $2x + 6$, is recorded below the dividend.

Step 7. Subtract $(2x + 8) - (2x + 6)$. The remainder is 2.

This time, the check must take the remainder into consideration.

Check: dividend = (quotient × divisor) + remainder

$x^2 + 5x + 8$	$(x + 2) \times (x + 3) + 2$
$x^2 + 5x + 8$	$(x^2 + 5x + 6) + 2$
$x^2 + 5x + 8$	$x^2 + 5x + 8$

ORAL EXERCISES

Tell how to complete each sentence.

SAMPLE: $x(\underline{\ ?\ }) = 5x^2 + 3x$

What you say: $x(5x + 3) = 5x^2 + 3x$

1. $t(\underline{\ ?\ }) = 3t^7 + 5t^2$

2. $6y^2 - 10y = 2y(\underline{\ ?\ })$

3. $m(\underline{}) = 8m^{10} - 3m^5$ **6.** $15a^3 + 5a^2 - 25a = 5a(\underline{})$

4. $2b(\underline{}) = 6b^3 + 4b$ **7.** $-2x(\underline{}) = (-8x^3 + 10x^2 - 6x)$

5. $(\underline{})3x = 12x^4 - 9x^2$ **8.** $3xy(\underline{}) = 15x^3y^2 - 12x^2y^3$

Give the quotient for each indicated division.

9. $\dfrac{18x^3 - 14x}{2}$ **12.** $\dfrac{28t^3 - 36t^2}{4t}$ **15.** $\dfrac{27x^2 - 15y^2}{3}$

10. $\dfrac{27n^5 + 15n^2}{3n}$ **13.** $\dfrac{8m^3 - 11m^2}{m^2}$ **16.** $\dfrac{16c^5 + 34c^3}{-2c}$

11. $\dfrac{32k^9 - 28k^5}{4k}$ **14.** $\dfrac{30y^{10} - 20y^6}{2y^3}$ **17.** $\dfrac{-8s^{12} - 32w^{10}}{4w^3}$

WRITTEN EXERCISES

Find each indicated quotient.

A

1. $\dfrac{30x^5 - 24x^4 + 9x^2}{3x}$ **5.** $\dfrac{-48a^6b^5 + 54a^4b^5}{-6a^2b^2}$

2. $\dfrac{28k^7 + 14k^3 - 35k^2}{7k^2}$ **6.** $\dfrac{10x^4y^3 - 15x^3y^5}{2.5xy}$

3. $\dfrac{-21m^5 + 36m^3 - 15m}{-3m}$ **7.** $\dfrac{60a^6b^5 - 72a^4b^3}{-12a^2b^2}$

4. $\dfrac{4x^6y^5 - 10x^4y^4 + 6x^3y^3}{2xy}$ **8.** $\dfrac{6r^7s^8 - 4r^5s^6}{-0.5r^3s}$

Complete each indicated division and check each answer. Begin by making sure that each polynomial is in standard form.

SAMPLE: $\dfrac{x^2 + 5x + 9}{2 + x}$

Solution:
$$
\begin{array}{r}
x + 3 \\
x + 2\overline{)x^2 + 5x + 9} \\
\underline{x^2 + 2x} \\
3x + 9 \\
\underline{3x + 6} \\
3
\end{array}
$$

Check: $x^2 + 5x + 9 \overset{?}{=} (x + 3)(x + 2) + 3$

$x^2 + 5x + 9$	$(x^2 + 5x + 6) + 3$
$x^2 + 5x + 9$	$x^2 + 5x + 9$

9. $\dfrac{y^2 + 6y + 8}{y + 2}$ **10.** $\dfrac{a^2 + 42 - 13a}{a - 7}$ **11.** $\dfrac{32x^2 + 28x + 3}{4x + 3}$

12. $\dfrac{7x + x^2 + 14}{x + 4}$

13. $\dfrac{24 + x^2 + 10x}{6 + x}$

14. $\dfrac{t^2 - 11t + 29}{t - 4}$

15. $\dfrac{-19x + 10x^2 - 15}{2x - 5}$

16. $\dfrac{x^2 + 8x - 5}{x - 2}$

17. $\dfrac{-5r + r^2 - 9}{r + 3}$

18. $\dfrac{6b^2 + 19b + 10}{2b + 5}$

19. $\dfrac{14s^2 - 12 + 22s}{7s - 3}$

20. $\dfrac{2n^2 - 3 + n}{n - 1}$

21. $\dfrac{4z^2 - 8}{2z + 3}$

22. $\dfrac{2a^2 - 4a + 5}{a - 3}$

23. $\dfrac{2x - 6 + 3x^2}{3x + 5}$

Complete each indicated division.

B **24.** $\dfrac{x^2 + 5.5x + 6}{x + 4}$

25. $\dfrac{6r^2 + 6.4r - 6}{3r + 5}$

26. $\dfrac{2.5a^2 + 14.5a - 3}{5a - 1}$

27. $\dfrac{a^2 - 6ab - 27b^2}{a + 3b}$

28. $\dfrac{c^2 - 11cd - 102d^2}{c + 6d}$

29. $\dfrac{4x^2 + 12xy + 10y^2}{2x + 3y}$

30. $\dfrac{100 - 81w^2}{9w + 10}$

31. $\dfrac{10 - 4x^2}{-2x + 3}$

32. $\dfrac{9r^2 + 15s^2 - 48rs}{3s - 9r}$

C **33.** $\dfrac{x^3 + 3x^2 - 4x - 15}{x - 2}$

34. $\dfrac{4x^3 + 12x^2 - 16x - 47}{x + 3}$

PROBLEMS

Write each answer as a polynomial in standard form.

1. The area of this rectangular region is given by the polynomial $18m^2 - 17m + 4$. If $9m - 4$ represents the length, find the width.

$18m^2 - 17m + 4$ | ?

$9m - 4$

2. The width and area for the rectangle at the right. Find the length.

$8x^2 + 10x + 3$ | $2x + 1$

?

3. The volume and height of a storage tank are shown in the figure at the right. Find the area of the base.
Hint: Use $V = Bh$, where B is the area of the base and h is the height.

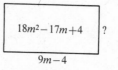

$x - 3$ | $x^3 - 3x^2 - 14x + 42$

?

4. The product of the polynomial $(x - 5)$ and some other polynomial is $x^2 + x - 30$. What is the other polynomial?

5. A supersonic aircraft travels for a period of time represented by $(2x - 5)$. The distance traveled is $10x^2 - 41x + 40$. Find the speed.

Hint: Speed $= \dfrac{\text{distance}}{\text{time}}$.

CHAPTER SUMMARY

Inventory of Structure and Concepts

1. A **polynomial** is a single term or a sum of terms.

2. A polynomial that consists of one term is called a **monomial**; if it consists of two terms it is called a **binomial**; if it consists of three terms it is called a **trinomial**.

3. A polynomial in **one variable** is in **standard form** when the variable of the first term on the left has the largest exponent, the variable of the second term has the second largest exponent, the variable of the third term has the third largest exponent, and so on.

4. A polynomial in **more than one variable** is in **standard form** when the terms are ordered according to the exponents of one of the variables.

5. For any directed number a and positive integers p and q,
$$a^p \cdot a^q = a^{p+q}.$$

6. For all directed numbers a and b and every positive integer p,
$$(ab)^p = a^p \cdot b^p.$$

7. For every directed number a and all positive integers p and q,
$$(a^p)^q = a^{pq}.$$

8. For any directed number a not equal to 0 and all positive integers p and q where $p > q$,
$$\frac{a^p}{a^q} = a^{p-q}.$$

9. For any directed number a not equal to 0 and all positive integers p and q where $p < q$,
$$\frac{a^p}{a^q} = \frac{1}{a^{q-p}}.$$

Vocabulary and Spelling

polynomial (*p. 73*)

monomial (*p. 74*)

trinomial (*p. 74*)

constant (*p. 74*)

standard form (*p. 74*)

horizontal axis (*p. 86*)

vertical axis (*p. 86*)

quadrant (*p. 86*)

origin (*p. 86*)

expand an expression (*p. 93*)

quotient (*p. 99*)

divisor (*p. 99*)

dividend (*p. 99*)

remainder (*p. 100*)

Chapter Test

Write each polynomial in standard form.

1. $4m - 3m^3 + 10 + m^2$ **3.** $-3y^2 + 12y^4 - 2y^5 + 5$

2. $6x^2 - 3x - 2x^4 + 7$ **4.** $-5 + 9k^2 - 2k + 5k^3$

Simplify each of the following by carrying out the indicated operation.

5. $(3x^2 + 9) + (x^2 + 2x)$ **9.** $(3t - 5)(8t + 7)$

6. $(4a^2 - 6a + 5) + (-3a + 7)$ **10.** $(x + y)^2 - (x^2 - y^2)$

7. $(5w^2 - 3w + 2) - (w^2 + 8w)$ **11.** $(10m^2 - 6m - 28) \div (2m - 4)$

8. $(5m^3 + 2m^2 - m - 2)(-3m^5)$ **12.** $\dfrac{3m^2 + 14mn - 5n^2}{5n + m}$

Expand each of the following.

13. $(2ab)^3$ **16.** $(x - y)^2$ **19.** $(a + c)^3$

14. $(2mk^2)^2$ **17.** $(\frac{1}{2}r^2s^2)^2$ **20.** $(2 - x^2)^2$

15. $(2x - 3)^2$ **18.** $(a + b)^2$ **21.** $(3a + 2b)^2$

Give the ordered pair of integers that corresponds with each labeled point in the lattice and tell in which quadrant the point is located.

22. A

23. T

24. M

25. B

26. R

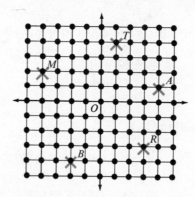

Solve each equation. The domain of the variable is $\{$ the directed numbers $\}$.

27. $3x + (x - 1) = 19$ **29.** $(3x + 1)^2 - 9x^2 = 31$

28. $2(x + 5) - 3(x - 4) = 7$ **30.** $(x + 2)^2 = (x - 1)^2$

Chapter Review

3–1   Addition of Polynomials

Simplify each of the following.

1. $4m + (2 - 9m)$

2. $10a^2 + (10 - 8a^2)$

3. $(6x^2 - 7) + (4x^2 + x)$

4. $(2m^3 - 4m^2 + 1) + (-6m^3 - 9)$

Add.

5. $\begin{array}{r} 8x^2 + x - 3 \\ -6x^2 + 4 \\ \hline \end{array}$

6. $\begin{array}{r} -5x + 2y \\ 9x - 3y \\ \hline \end{array}$

7. $\begin{array}{r} 4a^3 - 9a^2 - 5a \\ 6a^2 + 2a + 3 \\ \hline \end{array}$

Write each answer as a polynomial in standard form.

8. Find the sum of the lengths of the three line segments shown here, if the length of each is represented by the given polynomial.

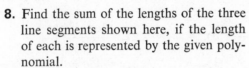

9. The length of each side of this polygon is as indicated by a polynomial. What is the perimeter of the polygon?

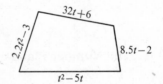

3–2   Subtraction of Polynomials

Rewrite each expression in standard form without parentheses.

10. $-(15 + 32t^3)$

11. $-(10rs - 4r^2 + 6)$

12. $-(9k^3 + k^2 - 4k + 5)$

13. $(-1)(-4c^2 - 7c + 13)$

Subtract each lower polynomial from the one above it.

14. $\begin{array}{r} 9cd + 5d \\ 2cd - 9d \\ \hline \end{array}$

15. $\begin{array}{r} 3z^2 - 7y + 5 \\ -z^2 + y + 2 \\ \hline \end{array}$

16. $\begin{array}{r} -15r^2 - 12rs + 20s^2 \\ 4r^2 + 7rs - 7s^2 \\ \hline \end{array}$

Write each answer as a polynomial in standard form.

17. What is the length of segment *KM* in this figure?

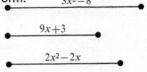

18. The area of the rectangle-shaped region in this figure is represented by the polynomial $7d^2 - 15cd - 3c^2$. The area of the triangle-shaped region is $d^2 + c^2$. Find the area of the shaded region.

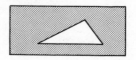

3–3   Powers of Monomials

Use exponential notation to simplify each expression.

19. $(3 \cdot 3 \cdot 3)(t \cdot t \cdot t \cdot t)$

20. $(x \cdot x \cdot x)(xy)(xy)(xy)$

21. $(a^2)(a^3)(a \cdot a \cdot a \cdot a)$

22. $\dfrac{(r \cdot r \cdot r \cdot r)(s \cdot s)}{r \cdot r \cdot s}$

Simplify each expression.

23. $(xy^2)(5x^3y^3)$

24. $(2r^2s^5)(-14r^3s^4)$

25. $(-2c^2d)^3$

26. $(-5abc)^2$

27. $\dfrac{18m^3n^{10}}{-3mn^2}$

28. $\dfrac{-45a^2bc^3}{5abc}$

3–4   The Number Plane and Integer Pairs

Write the integer pair that corresponds with each point labeled with a letter.

29. S

30. T

31. W

32. K

33. M

34. A

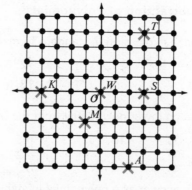

Name the quadrant in which each point is located.

35. $(-3, -5)$

36. $(2, -4)$

37. $(-5, 1)$

38. $(3, 4)$

39. $(-2, 2)$

40. $(4, -1)$

41. $(5, -5)$

42. $(-2, -4)$

3–5 Multiplication of Polynomials

Complete each indicated multiplication.

43. $4k(6k^3 - 2k + 5)$ **46.** $(m + 7)(m + 2)$

44. $-8rs(r^2 - 2rs - s^2)$ **47.** $(2b + 3a)(b - 5a)$

45. $(2w + 1)(w^2 + 3w + 7)$ **48.** $(-6n + n^2 + 5)(n + 1)$

Write each answer as a polynomial in standard form.

49. Find the area of this rectangle if the polynomials represent the length and width.

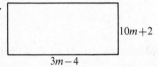

50. Find the volume of this cone. Use the formula $V = \frac{1}{3}Bh$ where B is the area of the base, and h is the height.

3–6 Polynomials Raised to a Power

Expand each of the following.

51. $(t + 5)^2$ **53.** $(4n + t)^2$ **55.** $(a + b)(a - b)^2$

52. $(3y + 1)^2$ **54.** $(a + \frac{1}{2})^2$ **56.** $3m(m - 4)^2$

3–7 Division of Monomials

Simplify each expression by completing the indicated division.

57. $\dfrac{19m^5}{m^2}$ **59.** $\dfrac{-75x^8}{-3x^3}$ **61.** $\dfrac{-10r^2s^2}{5r^7s^5}$

58. $\dfrac{-35t^3}{t^7}$ **60.** $\dfrac{36a^4b^5}{-3a^3b^2}$ **62.** $\dfrac{3m^3n^2}{-15m^5n}$

3–8 Division of Polynomials

Complete each indicated division.

63. $(72m^{10} - 48m^7) \div (8m^3)$ **65.** $\dfrac{6x^2 - 13x - 28}{3x + 4}$

64. $\dfrac{-36x^5 + 16x^3 - 8x}{-4x}$ **66.** $\dfrac{13n + 10n^2 - 32}{5n - 6}$

Review of Skills

Name the largest whole number that will divide evenly into both numbers of each pair.

SAMPLE: 18, 24   *Solution:* 6

1. 6, 9   **4.** 5, 10   **7.** 30, 15

2. 10, 15   **5.** 12, 33   **8.** −14, 35

3. 34, 14   **6.** 90, 100   **9.** −12, −28

Match each set in Column 1 with the corresponding set of numbers in Column 2.

COLUMN 1	COLUMN 2
10. {prime numbers}	**A.** {1, 2, 3, 4, 6, 12}
11. {multiples of 8}	**B.** {2, 3, 5, 7, 11, 13, . . .}
12. {divisors of 12}	**C.** {2}
13. {even prime numbers}	**D.** {7, 14, 21, 28, 35, 42, . . .}
14. {multiples of 7}	**E.** {8, 16, 24, 32, 40, . . .}

Write each of the following in three different ways as the product of two monomial factors.

SAMPLE: $10ab$ *Solution:* $(10)(ab)$; $(2a)(5b)$; $(10a)(b)$

15. $12xy^2$ **17.** $-10a$ **19.** $-6ay$ **21.** $4a^3b$

16. $9rs$ **18.** $-4w$ **20.** b^2x **22.** $-27c^3$

Multiply. Write your answers in simplest form.

23. $\frac{2}{3} \times \frac{9}{10}$ **25.** $1\frac{1}{2} \times 2\frac{2}{3}$ **27.** $\frac{5}{3} \times \frac{3}{10}$

24. $\frac{3}{4} \times \frac{2}{5}$ **26.** $2\frac{3}{4} \times 1\frac{1}{8}$ **28.** $\frac{1}{2} \times \frac{1}{8} \times \frac{2}{3}$

Add.

29. $6\frac{2}{3}$ **30.** $17\frac{5}{8}$ **31.** $26\frac{1}{4}$

  $\underline{1\frac{3}{4}}$ $\underline{36\frac{1}{2}}$ $\underline{17\frac{5}{16}}$

Write the two sets asked for in each of the following.

SAMPLE: *Solution:*

$A \cap B = \{2, 9\}$

$A \cup B = \{2, 3, 4, 6, 7, 8, 9\}$

$A \cap B = ?$ $A \cup B = ?$

32.

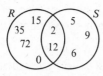

$R \cup S = ?$ $R \cap S = ?$

33.

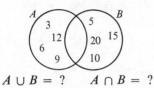

$A \cup B = ?$ $A \cap B = ?$

34. $X = \{2, 3, 5, 7, 11, 13\}$
$Y = \{0, 2, 4, 6\}$
$X \cup Y = ?$ $X \cap Y = ?$

35. $M = \{1, 3, 5, 7, 9\}$
$N = \{2, 4, 6, 8\}$
$M \cup N = ?$ $M \cap N = ?$

36. $K = \{3, 12, 19, 6, 4, 21\}$
$B = \{4, 10, 6, 3, 19\}$
$K \cup B = ?$ $K \cap B = ?$

■ ■

CHECK POINT
FOR EXPERTS

Flow Charts and a Mini-Calculator

You have probably seen simple adding machines and desk calculators. A flow chart can be helpful in planning the steps needed for solving a problem on such a computer. You will find that different models of desk computers vary in the number of keys provided, and in the way the keys are to be used, so we shall invent one of our own to use as an illustration of preparing a flow chart for a machine.

Pictured on the right is the keyboard of our imaginary "mini-calculator" with which we can add, subtract, multiply, and divide numbers. Study the keyboard and note the location of the ten keys that are marked with the digits **0** through **9**, as well as the four operation keys $\boxplus$, $\boxminus$, $\boxtimes$, and $\boxdiv$.

The key **GT** we shall call the **grand total** key, and use it to instruct the calculator to find the final answer. The **ON-OFF** switch is used to turn the machine on and off. The **CLEAR** key is to remove any information

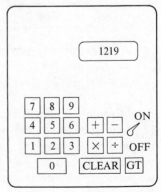

that may be in the machine; it should always be pressed as soon as the mini-calculator is switched on.

At the top of the keyboard, do you see the display register screen? In the picture it shows the number 1219. This screen shows numbers as they are entered, and the results of operations.

Study the following charts, which show the steps to be taken in solving addition and subtraction problems on our imaginary calculator.

EXAMPLE 1. 394 + 825   **EXAMPLE 2.** 5638 − 965

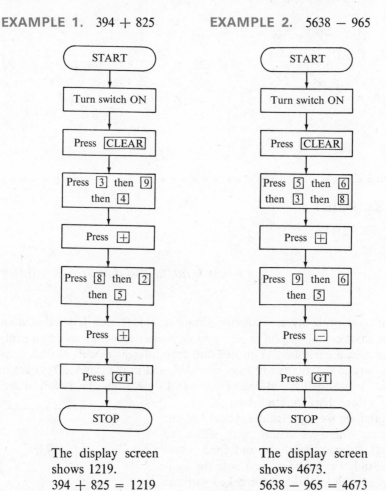

The display screen
shows 1219.
394 + 825 = 1219

The display screen
shows 4673.
5638 − 965 = 4673

In Example 2, the subtraction problem, after keys 5, 6, 3, and 8 were pressed for the first number, that number was entered into the machine by pressing the + key. Then the keys for the second number were pressed, and the key − was pressed for subtraction. This entered the number 965 into the machine. Finally, pressing the GT key caused the answer to be displayed. For multiplication and division, the procedure is similar to that for subtraction.

Questions

For each of the following flow charts, tell what problem has been programmed, and give the answer to the problem.

1.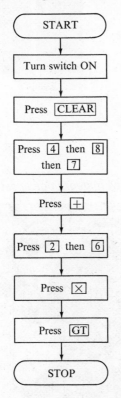

2.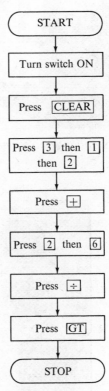

For each of the following, design a flow chart for using the mini-calculator in the solution.

3. 4025
  +3797

4.   38
   125
   400
  + 16

5. 5963
  −4015

6. 387
  × 25

7. $x = (13^2)(5)$

8. $r = \frac{493}{29}$

9. $y = (20^2)(7^2)$

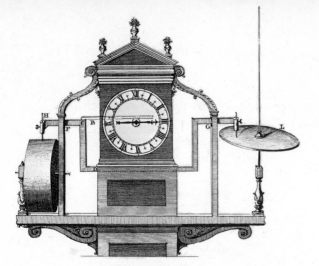

Sir Christopher Wren's weather-clock . . .

Tiros M meteorological satellite . . .

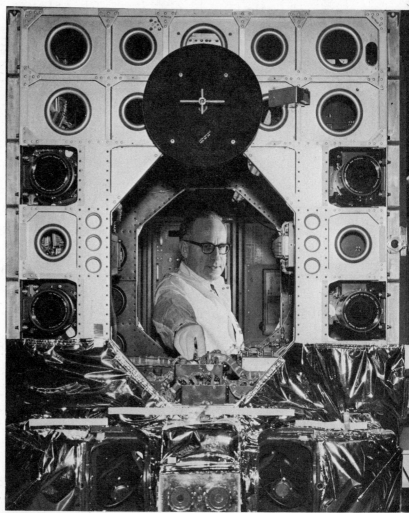

Products and Factors

The weather, its causes, and its changes, have long been of interest to man. An early instrument for measuring weather changes, called the weather-clock, was invented in 1663 by Sir Christopher Wren. Attached to an ordinary clock were a simple barometer and a wind vane. This intricately delicate device could record atmospheric pressure and wind velocity over a 12-hour period. Through the centuries, man's ingenuity has led him to construct increasingly complex equipment for precise weather observation. The Tiros M meteorological satellite, launched in January, 1970, provides world-wide weather reporting. Equipped with two cameras and two radiometers, this weather-watcher sends back to earth information on weather conditions around the world, day and night. Although man still has little control over the weather, such modern equipment supplies accurate information, making it possible to prepare for changes.

Factors of Numbers

4–1   Integral Factors

When two or more numbers are multiplied, the result is called the product of the numbers; the numbers are called factors of the product.

EXAMPLE 1. $\underbrace{9 \cdot 5}_{\text{factors of 45}} = \overbrace{45}^{\text{product of 9 and 5}}$

EXAMPLE 2. $\overbrace{45}^{\text{product of 3, 5, and 3}} = \underbrace{3 \cdot 5 \cdot 3}_{\text{factors of 45}}$

Since 9 is an integer, and since it *divides evenly* into 45 (that is, there is no remainder), we say that 9 is an integral factor of 45. As you might guess, 1 is an integral factor of *every* integer. Look at the pairs of statements on the next page and see how the two statements in each pair are related.

9 is an integral factor of **45**; 9 is a divisor of **45**.
3 is an integral factor of **45**; 3 is a divisor of **45**.
5 is an integral factor of **45**; 5 is a divisor of **45**.

For the present our work with integral factors will usually be with **positive** integral factors.

Suppose that you divide **45** by **8**. Since the result is $5\frac{5}{8}$, which is not an integer, we say that **8** is *not* an integral factor of **45**. Do you see how the two statements in each of the following pairs of statements are related?

8 is *not* an integral factor of **45**;   **8** is *not* a divisor of **45**.
7 is *not* an integral factor of **45**;   **7** is *not* a divisor of **45**.
10 is *not* an integral factor of **45**; **10** is *not* a divisor of **45**.

 For any positive integers **r**, **s**, and **t**, if **r · s = t**, then **r** and **s** are integral factors of **t**.

It is often helpful to know the set of all the different integral factors of a number. For example, to find the integral factors of **12**, you can begin by dividing **12** by **1**, then by **2**, then by **3**, and so on until you are certain you have found all the different integral factors.

$\frac{12}{1}$ = **12** and $\frac{12}{12}$ = **1**; **1** and **12** are integral factors of **12**.
$\frac{12}{2}$ = **6** and $\frac{12}{6}$ = **2**; **2** and **6** are integral factors of **12**.
$\frac{12}{3}$ = **4** and $\frac{12}{4}$ = **3**; **3** and **4** are integral factors of **12**.

The set of integral factors of **12** is $\{1, 2, 3, 4, 6, 12\}$.

As we said earlier, **1** is an integral factor of every integer. Also, do you see that every integer is an integral factor of itself? Let us agree to drop the word "integral" when possible, and understand that when we talk about the **factors** of a positive integer we mean its **positive integral factors**.

ORAL EXERCISES

Answer each question with *yes* or *no*.

1. Is 8 a factor of 40?   **4.** Is 13 a factor of 52?

2. Is 10 a factor of 120?   **5.** Is 9 a divisor of 75?

3. Is 1 a factor of 13?   **6.** Is 6 a factor of 3?

7. Is 6 a divisor of 24?   **9.** Is 19 a divisor of 19?

8. Is 7 a factor of 25?   **10.** Is 495 a factor of 495?

Match each number in Column 1 with its set of factors in Column 2.

COLUMN 1	COLUMN 2
11. 20	**A.** $\{1, 2, 4, 5, \ldots, 50, 100\}$
12. 35	**B.** $\{1, 5, 65, 13\}$
13. 100	**C.** $\{1, 57, 19, 3\}$
14. 37	**D.** $\{35, 7, 5, 1\}$
15. 2	**E.** $\{2, 1\}$
16. 57	**F.** $\{1, 2, 4, 5, 20, 10\}$
17. 65	**G.** $\{1, 37\}$

WRITTEN EXERCISES

Name the number represented by each indicated product.

A

1. $3 \cdot 5 \cdot 6 \cdot 10$ **7.** $2 \cdot 2 \cdot 3 \cdot 1$

2. $4 \cdot 9 \cdot 2 \cdot 2$ **8.** $5 \cdot 7 \cdot 11 \cdot 3$

3. $5 \cdot 5 \cdot 5 \cdot 4$ **9.** $5^2 \cdot 3^2 \cdot 2$

4. $10 \cdot 10 \cdot 10 \cdot 2 \cdot 3$ **10.** $2^2 \cdot 3^2 \cdot 4$

5. $2 \cdot 2 \cdot 2 \cdot 10 \cdot 10$ **11.** $10 \cdot 9 \cdot 8$

6. $5 \cdot 5 \cdot 3 \cdot 2$ **12.** $1 \cdot 2 \cdot 3 \cdot 4 \cdot 5$

Write the complete set of integral factors of each number.

SAMPLE: 36   *Solution:* $\{1, 2, 3, 4, 6, 9, 12, 18, 36\}$

13. 18	**16.** 19	**19.** 111
14. 42	**17.** 35	**20.** 105
15. 27	**18.** 41	**21.** 72

Copy each sentence and supply the missing factors. Do not use **1** as replacement for any missing factor.

SAMPLE: $10 = 1 \cdot (?) \cdot (?)$ *Solution:* $10 = 1 \cdot 2 \cdot 5$

22. $15 = (?)(?)1$ **26.** $57 = 1 \cdot (?) \cdot (?)$

23. $27 = 3 \cdot 1 \cdot (?) \cdot (?)$ **27.** $24 = 2^2(?)(?)$

24. $42 = 1 \cdot (?)(?)$ **28.** $72 = 2 \cdot (?)(4)(?)$

25. $42 = 3 \cdot (?)(?)$ **29.** $30 = 5 \cdot (?) \cdot (?) \cdot 1$

PROBLEMS

Indicate each nonempty set in roster form; if a set is empty, use the symbol ∅.

SAMPLE: {positive integers that have 3 as a factor}

Solution: {3, 6, 9, 12, . . .}

1. {positive integers that have 2 as a factor}

2. {positive integers that have 5 as a divisor}

3. {positive integers that have 17 as a factor}

For each of the following, express the first number as the product of two integral factors of which one factor is the second number; if it cannot be done, write "impossible."

SAMPLE: 138; 6   *Solution:* 138 = 6 · 23

4. 144; 4   **5.** 119; 17   **6.** 144; 7   **7.** 216; 12

8. The volume of a box-shaped container is 42 cubic inches. The measure of each dimension, *l*, *w*, and *h*, is an integer greater than 1. What are the dimensions of the container?

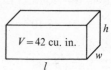

4–2   Prime Factors

Now let us consider the use of members of the set of **prime numbers** as integral factors. It is important to recall that each prime number has these two basic properties:

(1) Each is a **positive integer** greater than **1**.

(2) Each has **exactly two** different integral factors, **1** and the **number itself**.

The following table will help you identify the first four prime numbers.

Number	Set of Factors	Prime/Not Prime
2	{1, 2}	Prime
3	{1, 3}	Prime
4	{1, 2, 4}	Not Prime
5	{1, 5}	Prime
6	{1, 2, 3, 6}	Not Prime
7	{1, 7}	Prime

We often indicate the set of prime numbers in this way:

$$\{2, 3, 5, 7, 11, 13, 17, 19, 23, 29, 31, \ldots\}$$

Consider the factored forms of **24** and of **18** shown in Example 1.

EXAMPLE 1. $24 = 2 \cdot 2 \cdot 2 \cdot 3$ $18 = 2 \cdot 3 \cdot 3$

Do you see that each factored form contains only **prime** numbers? Thus we can say that $2 \cdot 2 \cdot 2 \cdot 3$ is a **prime factored** form of **24** and $2 \cdot 3 \cdot 3$ is a **prime factored** form of **18**. A prime factored form of a number can often be written more briefly by using exponential notation, as shown in Example 2.

EXAMPLE 2. $40 = 2 \cdot 2 \cdot 2 \cdot 5$ $36 = 2 \cdot 2 \cdot 3 \cdot 3$
$$= 2^3 \cdot 5 \qquad\qquad = 2^2 \cdot 3^2$$

Any number, other than 1, that is not itself prime can be expressed in **one** and **only one** way as the product of two or more prime numbers. Such a number is called a **composite** number.

ORAL EXERCISES

Tell which numbers are *prime* and which are *composite*.

1. 18	**4.** 16	**7.** 2	**10.** 57
2. 23	**5.** 19	**8.** 5	**11.** 31
3. 100	**6.** 45	**9.** 9	**12.** 33

For each of the following, tell whether or not the factored form given is the *prime* factored form.

13. $16 = 2 \cdot 8$	**16.** $70 = 2 \cdot 5 \cdot 7$
14. $15 = 5 \cdot 3$	**17.** $32 = 2 \cdot 2 \cdot 2 \cdot 4$
15. $18 = 3 \cdot 3 \cdot 2$	**18.** $84 = 3 \cdot 4 \cdot 7$

WRITTEN EXERCISES

For each of the following, show a series of equations arriving at the prime factored form of the number.

SAMPLE: $60 = (4)(15)$ *Solution:* $60 = (4)(15)$
$$60 = (2 \cdot 2)(3 \cdot 5)$$
$$60 = 2 \cdot 2 \cdot 3 \cdot 5 = 2^2 \cdot 3 \cdot 5$$

A
1. $50 = (5)(10)$
2. $70 = (10)(7)$
3. $42 = (2)(21)$
4. $36 = (4)(9)$
5. $48 = (2)(4)(6)$

6. $48 = (12)(4)$
7. $48 = (4)(4)(3)$
8. $120 = (15)(8)$
9. $120 = (2)(10)(6)$
10. $75 = (25)(3)$

Express each number in prime factored form, using exponential notation to show repeated factors.

SAMPLE: 24   *Solution:* $24 = 2 \cdot 2 \cdot 2 \cdot 3$
$= 2^3 \cdot 3$

11. 40
12. 27
13. 72
14. 50

15. 300
16. 108
17. 144
18. 100

19. 54
20. 110
21. 32
22. 128

Write each number as the sum of two different prime numbers.

SAMPLE: 20   *Solution:* $20 = 3 + 17$, or $20 = 7 + 13$

23. 8
24. 22
25. 18

26. 28
27. 26
28. 34

29. 32
30. 12
31. 30

Write each nonempty set in roster form; if a set is empty, use the symbol ∅.

B
32. {even prime numbers}
33. {prime numbers between 1 and 30}

34. {prime numbers less than 2}
35. {prime numbers less than 50}

C
36. {the prime numbers} ∩ {the even numbers}
37. {the prime numbers} ∩ {the multiples of 8}
38. {the prime numbers} ∩ {the multiples of 13}

4–3 Greatest Common Factor (G.C.F.)

There are many times in the study of algebra when we find it helpful to know the greatest common factor of two or more numbers. In the following example, note that if we write the set of factors of each of the numbers **12** and **18**, it is a simple matter to identify their greatest common factor.

EXAMPLE.   Set of factors of **12**: {**1, 2, 3, 4, 6,   12   **}
Set of factors of **18**: {**1, 2, 3,   6, 9,   18**}

Since the greatest factor that is common to *both* sets is **6**, we see that the greatest common factor, abbreviated **G.C.F.**, of **12** and **18** is **6**.

The Venn diagram in the figure at the right illustrates the intersection of the two sets of factors.

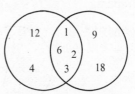

Factors of 12   Factors of 18

Using set notation, we could show the same idea as follows:

Factors of 12　　　Factors of 18　　　Common Factors

{1, 2, 3, 4, 6, 12} ∩ **{1, 2, 3, 6, 9, 18}** = 　**{1, 2, 3, 6}**

From either illustration, we can see readily that the **G.C.F.** of **12** and **18** is **6**.

The greatest common factor of two numbers can also be identified by writing each in prime factored form.

EXAMPLE.　　$40 = \boxed{2 \cdot 2 \cdot 2 \cdot \quad \boxed{5}}$
　　　　　　$60 = \boxed{2 \cdot 2 \cdot \quad 3 \cdot \boxed{5}}$

Notice that the prime numbers **2** and **5** are common factors of *both* numbers, 40 and 60, with the factor **2** appearing at least *twice* in the prime factored form of each number. Do you see that the **G.C.F.** of **40** and **60** is **2 · 2 · 5**, or **20**?

What do you suppose is the G.C.F. of two **prime** numbers, like **5** and **13**, or **17** and **29**?

EXAMPLE 1.

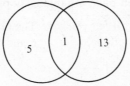

Factors of 5　Factors of 13

{1, 5} ∩ **{1, 13}** = **{1}**, so the **G.C.F.** of **5** and **13** is **1**.

EXAMPLE 2.

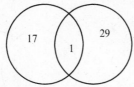

Factors of 17　Factors of 29

{1, 17} ∩ **{1, 29}** = **{1}**, so the **G.C.F.** of **17** and **29** is **1**.

Do you see why the G.C.F. of *any* two prime numbers will be **1**?

Next consider two **consecutive** numbers like **6** and **7** or **15** and **16**. Study these Venn diagrams and identify the **G.C.F.** of each pair of numbers.

EXAMPLE 3.

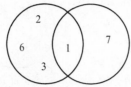

$$\{1, 2, 3, 6\} \cap \{1, 7\} = \{1\}$$

Factors of 6   Factors of 7

EXAMPLE 4.

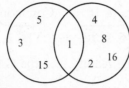

$$\{1, 3, 5, 15\} \cap \{1, 2, 4, 8, 16\} = \{1\}$$

Factors of 15   Factors of 16

Do you see that for each pair the **G.C.F.** is **1**? If you were to consider many other pairs of consecutive integers, you would find that in every case the **G.C.F.** is **1**.

Are there any pairs of integers other than prime integers and consecutive integers whose G.C.F. is 1? Consider the pairs **8** and **15**, **7** and **12**, **16** and **21**, and you will see that the answer is "yes." Any pair of integers whose G.C.F. is 1 are called relatively prime integers.

ORAL EXERCISES

Use the given information to name the G.C.F. of the two numbers whose set of factors is given; indicate which pairs are relatively prime.

SAMPLE:

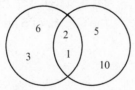

Factors of 6   Factors of 10

What you say: The G.C.F. of 6 and 10 is 2.

1.

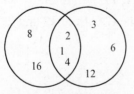

Factors of 16   Factors of 12

2.

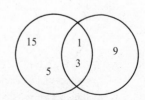

Factors of 15   Factors of 9

3.

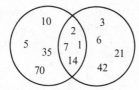

Factors of 70   Factors of 42

6.

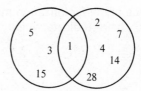

Factors of 15   Factors of 28

4.

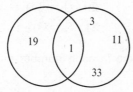

Factors of 19   Factors of 33

7.

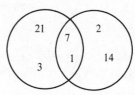

Factors of 21   Factors of 14

5. 20: {1, 2, 4, 5, 10, 20}
24: {1, 2, 3, 4, 6, 8, 12, 24}

8. 32: {1, 2, 4, 8, 16, 32}
52: {1, 2, 4, 13, 26, 52}

Name the number that will make the statement true; give a supporting reason for your answer.

SAMPLE: The G.C.F. of 7 and 19 is __?__.

What you say: 1; 7 and 19 are prime numbers.

9. The G.C.F. of 3 and 5 is __?__.
10. The G.C.F. of 9 and 10 is __?__. ·
11. The G.C.F. of 25 and 24 is __?__.
12. The G.C.F. of 17 and 23 is __?__.
13. The G.C.F. of 10 and 21 is __?__.

WRITTEN EXERCISES

For each number in the given pair, write its set of factors; then tell the G.C.F. of the two numbers.

SAMPLE: (27, 30)   *Solution:* 27: {1, 3, 9, 27}
30: {1, 2, 3, 5, 6, 15, 30}
The G.C.F. of 27 and 30 is 3.

A

1. (14, 18)	**5.** (18, 38)	**9.** (42, 54)
2. (50, 35)	**6.** (20, 28)	**10.** (50, 30)
3. (44, 33)	**7.** (4, 11)	**11.** (15, 28)
4. (29, 37)	**8.** (26, 39)	**12.** (33, 34)

Use the prime factorization method to find the G.C.F. of the two numbers in each pair. Indicate which pairs are relatively prime.

SAMPLE: (8, 20)   *Solution:* $8 = 2 \cdot 2 \cdot 2$
                                               $20 = 2 \cdot 2 \cdot 5$
                                    The G.C.F. of 8 and 20 is $2 \cdot 2$, or 4.

13. (14, 24)   **16.** (20, 35)   **19.** (42, 70)
14. (15, 45)   **17.** (50, 49)   **20.** (104, 54)
15. (60, 12)   **18.** (21, 15)   **21.** (18, 75)

Write the set of factors for the two numbers in each number pair; then show that they are relatively prime.

SAMPLE: (8, 15)   *Solution:*   8: $\{1, 2, 4, 8\}$; 15: $\{1, 3, 5, 15\}$
                                Since $\{1, 2, 4, 8\} \cap \{1, 3, 5, 15\} = \{1\}$,
                                8 and 15 are relatively prime.

B **22.** (20, 21)   **25.** (15, 16)   **28.** (16, 21)
       23. (35, 26)   **26.** (4, 9)   **29.** (15, 28)
       24. (24, 55)   **27.** (25, 27)   **30.** (36, 55)

Complete each statement with one of the words **always**, **sometimes**, or **never**.

C **31.** The G.C.F. of two even numbers is __?__ greater than 1.
       32. The G.C.F. of two prime numbers is __?__ 1.
       33. The G.C.F. of two composite numbers is __?__ 1.
       34. The G.C.F. of a prime number and a composite number is __?__ 1.
       35. The G.C.F. of two even numbers is __?__ 1.

Factors of Polynomials

4–4   Factoring Monomials

What you have learned so far about factors of numbers can be applied in finding the G.C.F. of two monomials that involve variables. First recall that a monomial can often be expressed as the product of two or more factors in several ways. For example, what are some of the ways in which you might write the monomial $10y^3$ as a product?

$$10y^3 = 10 \cdot y^3 = 2 \cdot 5 \cdot y^3 = 2y^3 \cdot 5 = (-2y)(-5y^2)$$
$$= 2 \cdot 5 \cdot y \cdot y \cdot y = 2 \cdot 5 \cdot y^2 \cdot y = 10 \cdot y \cdot y \cdot y$$

Can you think of other ways of expressing $10y^3$ as a product? Notice that in one case we used negative integers as coefficients of the factors.

Remember also that the **degree** of a variable in a monomial is indicated by the **exponent** of the variable. For example, in $10y^3$ the degree of y is **three**; in $-2m^2n$ the degree of m is **two** and the degree of n is **one**.

Suppose that we need to know the G.C.F. of $6x^2y$ and $9x^3y^2$. If we write the two monomials in factored form, we have

$$6x^2y = 2 \cdot \boxed{3} \cdot \boxed{x \cdot x} \cdot \boxed{y}$$
$$9x^3y^2 = \boxed{3} \cdot 3 \cdot \boxed{x \cdot x} \cdot x \cdot \boxed{y} \cdot y$$

So the G.C.F. is $3 \cdot x \cdot x \cdot y = 3x^2y$.

Notice that $3x^2y$, the G.C.F. of $6x^2y$ and $9x^3y^2$, consists of the G.C.F. of the coefficients 6 and 9, multiplied by each variable to the greatest degree to which it is found in both monomials.

To find the G.C.F. of the pair of monomials $12m^2n$ and $-15mn$, where one of the coefficients is a negative integer, the procedure is similar.

$$12m^2n = 2 \cdot 2 \cdot \boxed{3} \cdot \boxed{m \cdot m} \cdot \boxed{n}$$
$$-15mn = -1 \cdot \boxed{3} \cdot 5 \cdot \boxed{m} \cdot \boxed{n}$$

So the G.C.F. is $3 \cdot m \cdot n = 3mn$. Notice that when a coefficient is a negative integer, we begin by writing it as -1 times its opposite, thus

$$-15 = -1 \cdot 15 = -1 \cdot 3 \cdot 5.$$

Check again to see that $3mn$, the G.C.F. of $12m^2n$ and $-15mn$, is the G.C.F. of coefficients 12 and -15 times the greatest degree of each of the variables m and n that is common to both monomials.

ORAL EXERCISES

Answer each question *yes* or *no*.

1. Is $6x^2$ a factor of $24x^2y^2$?

2. Is $3b$ a factor of $9b^5c^2$?

3. Is 10 a divisor of $32mn$?

4. Is xyz a factor of $8x^2y^2$?

5. Is a^2b^2 a factor of $-5a^2b^5$?

6. Is $3rs^2$ a factor of $-21r^2s$?

7. Is $2k^3$ a divisor of $10k^3t^2$?

Name each missing factor.

8. $-10 = 5 \cdot (?)$

9. $8 = (-2) \cdot (2) \cdot (?)$

10. $-6ab = 3 \cdot (?) \cdot a \cdot b$

11. $49x^2y^3 = -7 \cdot (?) \cdot x^2y^3$

WRITTEN EXERCISES

Complete each of these sentences.

A
1. $15r^2 = 3r(\underline{\ ?\ })$

2. $32m^4 = 4m(\underline{\ ?\ })$

3. $12rs^2 = 3rs(\underline{\ ?\ })$

4. $60x^5y^5 = (12x^3y^2)(\underline{\ ?\ })$

5. $35m^3n^2 = (-5mn)(\underline{\ ?\ })$

6. $54y^7z^4 = (3y^3z^3)(\underline{\ ?\ })$

7. $42a^2b^2 = 6ab(\underline{\ ?\ })$

8. $-10p^5q^3 = (-2pq)(\underline{\ ?\ })$

9. $-35st^2 = 5 \cdot (?) \cdot s \cdot t^2$

10. $-18a^3b^3c = (6abc)(\underline{\ ?\ })$

11. $45m^5n^3t^4 = (-15m^2n^2t^2)(\underline{\ ?\ })$

12. $-57r^2s^2t = (19r^2s^2)(\underline{\ ?\ })$

Write three different factorizations of each polynomial.

SAMPLE: $20a^2b$ *Solution:* $(4a^2)(5b); 20(a^2b); (20a^2)(b)$
(There are other possible answers.)

13. $24t$

14. $42u$

15. $10mn$

16. $-32xy$

17. $-15a^2b^2$

18. $60a^2b^2$

19. $19c^2d^2$

20. $56n^2p^3$

21. $-12c^2w^2$

Show a complete factorization of each monomial, and name the G.C.F. of the two monomials.

SAMPLE 1: $6x^2, 15xy$ *Solution:* $6x^2 = 2 \cdot 3 \cdot \quad x \cdot x$
$15xy = \quad 3 \cdot 5 \cdot x \cdot \quad y$
The G.C.F. of $6x^2$ and $15xy$ is $3x$.

SAMPLE 2: $8m^2n^2, 14mn^2, 10m^2n$

Solution: $8m^2n^2 = 2 \cdot 2 \cdot 2 \cdot m \cdot m \cdot n \cdot n$
$\quad 14mn^2 = \quad 2 \cdot 7 \cdot m \cdot n \cdot n$
$\quad 10m^2n = \quad 2 \cdot 5 \cdot m \cdot m \cdot n$
The G.C.F. of $8m^2n^2$, $14mn^2$, and $10m^2n$ is $2mn$.

22. $10x^2, 2x^3$

23. $3xy, 10xy$

24. $8a^2b, 4ab^2$

25. $15x, 10y$

26. $24, 18x^3$

27. $12abc^2, 10a^2b^2c$

28. $4axy, 2xy$

29. $9st^3, 9s^3t$

30. $-2a^2, 6ab^5c$

31. $4ax, 18ax^2y$

32. $21r^2s^3t^4, -35r^2s^2t$

33. $-x^5y^4z^2, x^2y$

In each of the following, name the G.C.F. of the given monomials.

SAMPLE: $-100x^5y^3, -75x^3y, 50xy^2$ *Solution:* $25xy$

B
34. $-105m^3n, -70m^4$

35. $12a^4, 72a^8, -60a^2$

36. $-18w^5, 12w^4, -6w^3$

37. $84rs^2t, 7r^2st, -28r^4s^2t^3$

38. $14h^2n, -7h^2n^2, -56h^4n^3$

39. $-102x^2y^4, -42x^7y^3, -x^2y^2$

4–5 Polynomial Factoring

Transforming a given polynomial into a product of other polynomials is called **polynomial factoring**. A common form of polynomial factoring is one in which we apply the distributive property to write a polynomial as the product of two factors of which one factor is the monomial that is the greatest common factor of the terms of the given polynomial. For example, consider the polynomial $10a^2 + 10b$. Since **10** is the G.C.F. of $10a^2$ and $10b$, we can use the distributive property and write

$$10a^2 + 10b = 10(a^2 + b).$$

The following examples illustrate in more detail this kind of polynomial factoring.

EXAMPLE 1. $\begin{aligned} 4t^3 + 6t &= (2t \cdot 2t^2) + (2t \cdot 3) \\ &= 2t(2t^2 + 3) \end{aligned}$

EXAMPLE 2. $\begin{aligned} 15x^2 - 10xy &= (5x \cdot 3x) - (5x \cdot 2y) \\ &= 5x(3x - 2y) \end{aligned}$

EXAMPLE 3. $\begin{aligned} 6m^3 - 18m^2 + 10m \\ &= (2m \cdot 3m^2) - (2m \cdot 9m) + (2m \cdot 5) \\ &= 2m(3m^2 - 9m + 5) \end{aligned}$

After you factor a polynomial, it is a good idea to check your work by multiplying the factors and comparing the result with the original polynomial.

EXAMPLE.

$$\underbrace{34y^5 + 17y^3 - 51y^2}_{\text{given polynomial}} = 17y^2(2y^3 + y - 3) \quad Check: \quad \begin{array}{r} 2y^3 + y - 3 \\ 17y^2 \\ \hline 34y^5 + 17y^3 - 51y^2 \end{array}$$

Sometimes you will need to apply the distributive property more than once in factoring a given polynomial.

EXAMPLE. Factor $2ab + 3bc - 10ad - 15cd$

Step 1. Rearrange terms, using the commutative property of addition. $\qquad 2ab - 10ad + 3bc - 15cd$

Step 2. Use the associative property to group the terms as the sum of two binomials. $(2ab - 10ad) + (3bc - 15cd)$

Step 3. Apply the distributive property to factor each binomial. $2a(b - 5d) + 3c(b - 5d)$

Step 4. Treat $(b - 5d)$ as a common factor and apply the distributive property again. $(2a + 3c)(b - 5d)$

$$2ab + 3bc - 10ad - 15cd = (2a + 3c)(b - 5d)$$

Check: Multiply: $2a \ + \ 3c$

$\qquad\qquad\qquad\qquad b \ - \ 5d$

$\qquad\qquad\qquad\quad \overline{- \ 10ad - 15cd}$

$\qquad\qquad 2ab + 3bc$

$\qquad\qquad \overline{2ab + 3bc - 10ad - 15cd}$, which is the given polynomial.

ORAL EXERCISES

Name the G.C.F. of the terms in each polynomial.

SAMPLE: $8m^2 + 6m$ *What you say:* $2m$

1. $8r^2 + 16r$ **6.** $9t^2 - 45b$ **11.** $a^4b^3 + a^2b^2$

2. $2x^2 + 12x$ **7.** $3d^2 + 18c^2$ **12.** $x^5y^3 - x^3y^4$

3. $12a^2 + 6$ **8.** $6x^2 - 24x$ **13.** $a^3b^3c + b^2$

4. $16y^3 + 24$ **9.** $3k^2 + 5$ **14.** $m^2 + 10$

5. $8s^2 - 24s$ **10.** $5m^3 - 15n^3$ **15.** $60m^3n + 48m^2n$

Match each polynomial in Column 1 with an equivalent factored form in Column 2.

COLUMN 1

16. $12x^2 - 3y^2$

17. $x^2y^5 + x^3y^2$

18. $6x^2 - 21x^3$

19. $3x^2 + 12y^2$

20. $x^2y + xy^2$

COLUMN 2

A. $3(x^2 + 4y^2)$

B. $xy(x + y)$

C. $(4x^2 - y^2)3$

D. $x^2y^2(y^3 + x)$

E. $3x^2(2 - 7x)$

WRITTEN EXERCISES

Find each product by using the distributive property.

A
1. $5r(3r + 4)$ **5.** $abc(ab - bc)$ **9.** $3a(2 + 7a + a^2)$

2. $2b^2(6b + 4)$ **6.** $2n^3(1 + n^2)$ **10.** $ab(3ab - 3a + 2b)$

3. $(-2n)(5n + 1)$ **7.** $5m(4m^2 - 3m)$ **11.** $5r^2(6r^2 - r + 2)$

4. $xy(3x + y)$ **8.** $3t^2(4rt + t)$ **12.** $-4(-3x^3 + x - y)$

Write each of the following expressions in factored form. Check your work by multiplication.

SAMPLE: $25y - 10y^2$ *Solution:* $5y(5 - 2y)$ *Check:* $\begin{array}{r} 5 - 2y \\ 5y \\ \hline 25y - 10y^2 \end{array}$

13. $4r + 6$ **17.** $4x^2 - 6$ **21.** $4x^2 + 8x - 6$

14. $3n - 9$ **18.** $8m^2 + 12t^3$ **22.** $5 - 15y - 25y^2$

15. $ab^2 + a$ **19.** $6b^2 + 7b$ **23.** $6a^2b + 3ab^2$

16. $4x^2 - 8$ **20.** $15ab + 30a^2b^2$ **24.** $5n^2 - 15n + 20$

Write each expression in factored form.

SAMPLE: $3a(b + 2) + 5(b + 2)$ *Solution:* $(3a + 5)(b + 2)$

25. $x(y + 2) + 3(y + 2)$ **27.** $t^2(t - 2) + 3(t - 2)$

26. $m(m - 3) + 6(m - 3)$ **28.** $2x(c + 2d) - 4(c + 2d)$

B
29. $(4r + 5s)k - (4r + 5s)h$ **31.** $3b^2 + 2b + 12b + 8$

30. $k^2 + 2k + kt + 2t$ **32.** $2b(b - c) - mn(b - c)$

C
33. $3x^2 - 2x + 6x - 4$ **35.** $2s^2 + 2t + 4st + s$

34. $10y^2 + 15y - 2y - 3$ **36.** $r^3 - s^3 - sr^2 + rs^2$

PROBLEMS

The area of each region is represented by a polynomial. Express it in factored form.

1.   **2.**   **3.**

$28x^2 - 20x$ $\pi x^2 - \pi y^2$ $12 - 14x + 2x^2$

4. The area of the rectangular region shown here is $6x^2 + 12x$. Complete each of the following statements.

$6x^2+12x$

If the width is x, the length is __?__.
If the width is $2x$, the length is __?__.
If the length is $6x$, the width is __?__.

5. Find the length of one side of the square shown in this figure.

$36x^4y^2$

6. Write the area of the shaded portion of this figure as a polynomial, and then write it in factored form.
Hint: Area of circle $= \pi r^2$.

$4r$

$7r$

4–6   Polynomials, Functions, and the Number Plane

You will recall that we described a function machine that would develop a set of number pairs called a **function**. According to the machine shown here, every input number, **x**, is to be multiplied by **−2**. The result is a set of values of $f(x)$, called output numbers,

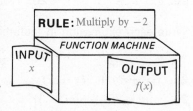

that are the values of the function for the given values of **x**. The function is the set of all ordered pairs of the form $(x, f(x))$.

The rule of a function machine can often be expressed as a polynomial. For the machine shown here, the rule is given by the polynomial **2x + 1**, which means "multiply x by **2** and then add **1**." If the domain of x is given as $\{-2, -1, 0, 1, 2\}$, we replace the x in $(2x + 1)$ with elements of the given set. Thus for each member of the domain (input) we will have a corresponding value for $f(x)$ (output), as recorded in the table at the right.

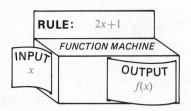

x	$f(x)$	$(x, f(x))$
-2	-3	$(-2, -3)$
-1	-1	$(-1, -1)$
0	1	$(0, 1)$
1	3	$(1, 3)$
2	5	$(2, 5)$

Finally, we can write the set of ordered number pairs

$$\{(-2, -3), (-1, -1), (0, 1), (1, 3), (2, 5)\}.$$

Do you see why this set of ordered number pairs is a function?

We can represent the function that the machine has developed by drawing the graph of the set of ordered pairs. Thus the four-quadrant lattice at the right shows the graph of the function

$$\{(-2, -3), (-1, -1), (0, 1), \\ (1, 3), (2, 5)\}.$$

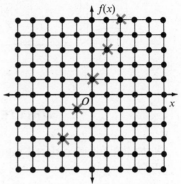

Notice that the horizontal axis is called the *x*-axis, while the vertical axis is the *f(x)*-axis.

ORAL EXERCISES

Complete each table according to the polynomial function rule shown on the machine. Use as the domain of the variable the set of numbers listed in the first column of the table.

1.

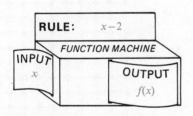

x	$f(x)$	$(x, f(x))$
-2	-4	$(-2, -4)$
-1	-3	?
0	-2	?
1	-1	?
2	0	?

2.

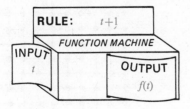

t	$f(t)$	$(t, f(t))$
4	5	$(4, 5)$
2	3	?
0	1	?
-2	?	?
-4	?	?

3.

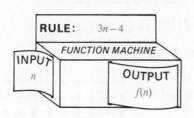

n	$f(n)$	$(n, f(n))$
3	?	(3, 5)
2	?	?
1	−1	?
0	−4	?
−1	−7	?
−2	?	(−2, −10)

WRITTEN EXERCISES

Write the set of ordered number pairs that is the function shown on the graph.

SAMPLE:

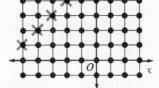

Solution:

$\{(-5, 1), (-4, 2), (-3, 3), (-2, 4), (-1, 5)\}$

A **1.**

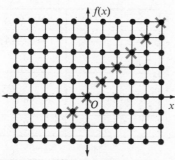

3.

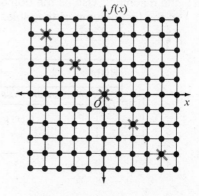

2.

4.

Complete each table by using the given polynomial as the function rule; then write the function as a set of ordered pairs.

SAMPLE: $3t + 2$ *Solution:*

t	$f(t)$	$(t, f(t))$
-4	-10	?
-2	?	?
0	?	?
2	?	?

t	$f(t)$	$(t, f(t))$
-4	-10	$(-4, -10)$
-2	-4	$(-2, -4)$
0	2	$(0, 2)$
2	8	$(2, 8)$

$$\{(-4, -10), (-2, -4), (0, 2), (2, 8)\}$$

5. $5y - 1$

y	$f(y)$	$(y, f(y))$
8	39	?
4	?	?
0	?	?
-4	?	?
-8	?	?

8. $4a - 1$

a	$f(a)$	$(a, f(a))$
$\frac{1}{4}$	?	?
$\frac{1}{2}$	?	?
0	?	?
$-\frac{1}{2}$	?	?
$-\frac{1}{4}$	?	?

6. $y^2 + 2$

y	$f(y)$	$(y, f(y))$
-3	11	?
-2	?	?
-1	?	?
0	?	?
1	?	?
2	?	?

9. $3m^2 - 4$

m	$f(m)$	$(m, f(m))$
-6	104	?
-4	?	?
-2	?	?
0	?	?
2	?	?
4	?	?

7. $\dfrac{b}{2} + \dfrac{1}{2}$

b	$f(b)$	$(b, f(b))$
-5	?	?
-3	?	?
-1	?	?
0	?	?
1	?	?

10. $x^2 + 2x - 10$

x	$f(x)$	$(x, f(x))$
0	?	?
1	?	?
2	?	?
3	?	?
4	?	?

Using the given polynomial as the function rule, write each function as a set of ordered pairs for the specified domain of the variable. Then graph the function.

SAMPLE: $\dfrac{x^2}{2} - 3$; domain: $\{-4, -2, 0, 2, 4\}$

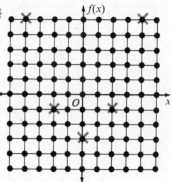

Solution:

$\{(-4, 5), (-2, -1), (0, -3), (2, -1), (4, 5)\}$

B **11.** $-2n + 5$; domain: $\{0, 1, 2, 3, 4, 5\}$

12. $\dfrac{s^2}{2} - 3$; domain: $\{-4, -2, 2, 4\}$

13. $4 - t^2$; domain: $\{3, 2, 1, 0, -1, -2, -3\}$

14. $t^2 - 3t + 1$; domain: $\{-1, 0, 1, 2, 3, 4\}$

15. $\dfrac{n}{2} + 1.5$; domain: $\{-5, -3, -1, 1, 3, 5\}$

16. $\dfrac{m}{3} + \dfrac{2}{3}$; domain: $\{1, 4, 7, -2, -5\}$

CHAPTER SUMMARY

Inventory of Structure and Concepts

1. For any positive integers r, s, and t, if $r \cdot s = t$, then r and s are **factors** of t.
   A **factor** of an integer is also a **divisor** of the integer.

2. Every positive integer has **at least two** factors, 1 and the number itself.
   A **prime number** is a positive integer greater than 1 that has **exactly two** different factors, 1 and the number itself.

3. An integer greater than 1 that is not prime is a **composite number.**

4. A composite number can be expressed in one and only one way as a **product** of **prime numbers.** When it is so expressed, it is said to be in **prime factored form.**

5. The **greatest common factor (G.C.F.)** of two or more numbers is the greatest integral factor, or divisor, that is common to the numbers.

6. Numbers are **relatively prime** if their greatest common factor is 1.

7. The horizontal axis of a four-quadrant lattice is called the **x-axis**; the the vertical axis is called the $f(x)$**-axis**.

Vocabulary and Spelling

factor (*p. 113*)

product (*p. 113*)

integral factor (*p. 113*)

set of factors (*p. 114*)

prime number (*p. 116*)

prime factored form (*p. 117*)

composite number (*p. 117*)

greatest common factor (G.C.F.) (*p. 118*)

Venn diagram (*p. 119*)

consecutive integers (*p. 120*)

relatively prime integers (*p. 120*)

degree of a variable (*p. 123*)

polynomial factoring (*p. 125*)

Chapter Test

Write in roster form the following subsets of {1, 2, 3, 4, 5, . . ., 15}; if any answer is the empty set, use the symbol ∅.

1. {prime numbers equal to or less than 15}

2. {composite numbers equal to or less than 15}

3. {numbers equal to or less than 15, but neither prime nor composite}

Write each number as a product of two integral factors in as many ways as you can.

4. 45   5. 70   6. 56

Tell whether each statement is true or false.

7. The product of two prime numbers can never be a prime number.

8. Every even number greater than 2 is a composite number.

9. The set of factors of any composite number has more than two members.

10. The product of two prime numbers is never an even number.

11. The G.C.F. of any two relatively prime numbers is 1.

Name the number whose set of factors is given in set A and the number whose set of factors is given in set B. Then, state the G.C.F. of the two numbers.

12.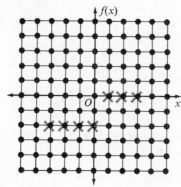

13.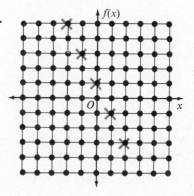

Write as a set of ordered pairs the function specified by the given polynomial for the domain of the variable indicated.

14. $5m - 8$; domain: $\{-1, -2, -3, -4, -5, -6\}$

15. $\frac{2}{3}x + 7$; domain: $\{0, 3, 6, 9, 12, 15\}$

16. $y^2 - y$; domain: $\{-2, -1, 0, 1, 2, \ldots\}$

Write as a set of ordered pairs the function represented by the graph on each lattice.

17.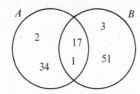

18.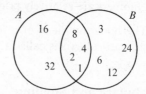

Name the greatest common factor for the two monomials in each of the following.

19. $10m^3$; $7m^2$ **20.** $-12a^2bx$; $10a^2by$ **21.** $\frac{1}{3}k^2t^5$; $-\frac{1}{3}k^3t^3$

Write each polynomial in factored form.

22. $27r^2s + 6rs$ **23.** $-35s^3t^4 + 7s^2t^7$ **24.** $15a^2b^2c^2 - 3ab^2 + 6ac^2$

Write each answer as a polynomial in standard form.

25. The area of triangle ABC is $16x^3y^4$. Find the height of the triangle.

26. The length of the rectangle is $6y$. If the area is $18y^3 - 12y$, what is the width?

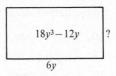

Write each number in prime factored form.

27. 72   **28.** 250

Write the set of integral factors for each number.

29. 63   **30.** 122

Chapter Review

4–1 Integral Factors

Write the set of integral factors of each number.

1. 15	**4.** 30	**7.** 64
2. 24	**5.** 44	**8.** 57
3. 63	**6.** 33	**9.** 41

Solve each problem.

10. The volume of this box is 350 cubic inches. The measure of each of the unknown dimensions is an integral number of inches greater than 1. What are the unknown dimensions?

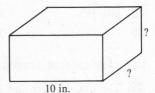

11. The area of a rectangle is 30 square feet. The measure of each dimension, length and width, is an integral number of feet. Name three possible pairs of integers that could name the length and the width.

4–2 Prime Factors

Write each of the following numbers in prime factored form.

12. 38	**14.** 49	**16.** 85
13. 26	**15.** 61	**17.** 111

Tell whether each statement is true or false.

18. The number 1 is not a prime number.

19. All prime numbers are also odd numbers.

20. If *n* is a prime number, its only integral factors are *n* and 1.

4–3   **Greatest Common Factor (G.C.F.)**

Match each number in Column 1 with its set of factors in Column 2.

COLUMN 1	COLUMN 2
21. 28	**A.** $\{1, 62, 31, 2\}$
22. 90	**B.** $\{1, 4, 28, 7\}$
23. 62	**C.** $\{1, 2, 23, 46\}$
24. 55	**D.** $\{1, 55, 11, 5\}$
25. 46	**E.** $\{1, 2, 3, 5, 6, 10, 15, 18, 30, 45, 90\}$

Complete each of the following to make a true statement.

26. Since $\{1, 3, 5, 15\} \cap \{1, 2, 4, 5, 10, 20\}$ = ?, the G.C.F. of 15 and 20 is _?_.

27. Since $\{1, 7\} \cap \{1, 3, 9\}$ = ?, the G.C.F. of _?_ and _?_ is _?_.

28. Since $\{1, 2, 4, 8\} \cap \{1, 3, 7, 21\}$ = ?, the G.C.F. of _?_ and _?_ is _?_.

Find the G.C.F. of the two numbers in each number pair.

29. (10, 16)	**31.** (20, 60)	**33.** (14, 15)
30. (17, 29)	**32.** (275, 100)	**34.** (80, 24)

Complete each statement.

35. The G.C.F. of 9 and 16 is _?_; 9 and 16 _____?_____ relatively prime.
(are/are not)

36. The G.C.F. of 7 and 12 is _?_; 7 and 12 _____?_____ relatively prime.
(are/are not)

37. The G.C.F. of 19 and 57 is _?_; 19 and 57 _____?_____ relatively prime.
(are/are not)

4–4   **Factoring Monomials**

For each of the following, name the greatest degree of the variable *x* that is common to both monomials.

38. $3mx^2$; x^3y

39. $-9tx^5$; $-4tx^5$

40. $\frac{1}{2}x^3y$; $-xy$

41. $5ax^5$; $25ax^8$

42. $12x^{10}y^{10}$; $-2x^{10}y^4$

43. $13rx$; $8r^8x$

Find the missing monomial factor in each equation.

44. $15m^3n^2 = 3m^3(\underline{\ ?\ })$

45. $-18r^2s = -2s(\underline{\ ?\ })$

46. $-11a^2b^2c(\underline{\ ?\ }) = 44a^5b^5c^2$

47. $7xyz^3(\underline{\ ?\ }) = -42xy^3z^4$

Name the G.C.F. for the two monomials in each exercise.

48. $3a^2b$; $12a^3b$

49. $8x^2y^3$; $15xy^2$

50. $-26st^3$; $10s^3t$

51. $2a^2b^2c^3$; $-4a^3bc^2$

4–5   Polynomial Factoring

Write each expression in factored form.

52. $24b^3 + 8b^2$

53. $30x^2y + 18xy^2$

54. $15mns - 14mnt$

55. $6a^2 + 30a - 18$

56. $10 - 15w + 25w^2$

57. $21a^2b^2c^2 - 12ab^2 + 6a^2bc$

4–6   Polynomials, Functions, and the Number Plane

Using the given polynomial as a function rule, complete each function table, write the function as a set of ordered pairs, and show its graph on a lattice.

58. $2b + 1$

59. $\dfrac{h}{2} - 1$

b	$f(b)$	$(b, f(b))$
-3	?	?
-2	?	?
-1	?	?
0	?	?
1	?	?
2	?	?

h	$f(h)$	$(h, f(h))$
-8	?	?
-6	?	?
-4	?	?
-2	?	?
0	?	?
2	?	?

Write the set of number pairs shown on the lattice. Then tell whether or not the set of number pairs is a function.

60. 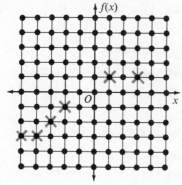 **61.**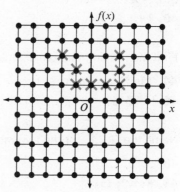

Review of Skills

Find the value of each expression if $r = 3$, $s = -2$, and $t = 5$.

1. $5r^2s$ **4.** $-st^2 + 10$ **7.** $r^3 + s^3 - t^2$

2. $-3rst$ **5.** $\dfrac{1}{r} \cdot \dfrac{1}{t}$ **8.** $(r + t)^2$

3. $\dfrac{4rt}{s}$ **6.** $\dfrac{r^2 - s^2}{t}$ **9.** $(t - s)^2$

Write each set of numbers in roster form.

10. {the whole numbers less than 10}

11. {the first ten prime numbers}

12. {the negative integers greater than -10}

13. {the integers between 5 and -5}

Find the solution set of each equation and check your answer. The domain of the variable is {the integers}.

14. $8 + k = 17$ **17.** $3a = -19$ **20.** $-1.5 + w = 6.5$

15. $15 - x = 3$ **18.** $\frac{1}{2}y + 3 = 10$ **21.** $3x - 7 + x = 21$

16. $12 + m = -14$ **19.** $n \cdot 1 = n$ **22.** $-2 + 5a + 6 = -26$

Solve each inequality and graph the solution set on the number line. The domain of the variable is {the directed numbers}.

23. $t + 1 > 3$ **24.** $x - 3 \leq 0$ **25.** $k \geq -1.5$

Solve each equation for the variable in red. Assume that no divisor is zero.

26. $A = lw$

27. $r = dt$

28. $c = 2\pi r$

29. $v = at$

30. $v = lwh$

31. $i = pr$

Find each indicated product.

32. $(m + 3)(m - 1)$

33. $(2t + 5)(t + 7)$

34. $(3x - 4)(4x - 2)$

35. $(a + b)(a^2 + 3ab + 2b^2)$

Complete each indicated division. Check your answer by multiplication.

36. $m + 2\overline{)m^2 - m - 6}$

37. $3a + 4\overline{)12a^2 + a - 20}$

Add; express each answer in standard form.

38. $\begin{aligned} -8y^2 + y + 5 \\ \underline{3y^2 + 6y - 1} \end{aligned}$

39. $\begin{aligned} 7m^4 \qquad\quad + 3m^2 - 5 \\ \underline{\quad - 2m^3 \qquad\quad + 2} \end{aligned}$

40. $(6b^2 - 7) + (3 + 2b^2)$

41. $(3x^3 - 5x) + (x + 10)$

42. $(4a^4 - 2a^3 + 1) + (6a^2 + 3)$

43. $(2b + 7 - 3b^2) + (-5 + 8b + 9b^2)$

Subtract each lower polynomial from the one above it.

44. $\begin{aligned} 9x - 2y \\ \underline{3x + 3y} \end{aligned}$

45. $\begin{aligned} 6x^2 - 4x + 9 \\ \underline{2x^2 - 6x + 9} \end{aligned}$

■ ■

CHECK POINT
FOR EXPERTS

Flow Charts and Storage Registers

Compare the mini-calculator keyboard shown here with the one pictured on page 109. What features does this one have that did not appear on the other?

You probably note that there are three new keys and a **storage register**. The function of the $\boxed{x^2}$ key is to square the number that has just been entered into the machine. The keys $\boxed{\textbf{TO STOR}}$ and $\boxed{\textbf{FROM STOR}}$ are used in connection with the storage register. When you

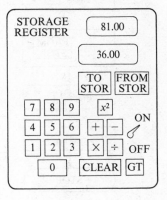

press $\boxed{\begin{array}{c}\text{TO}\\\text{STOR}\end{array}}$, the number that is then in the display register is moved into the storage register, where it is displayed until needed. When the stored number is to be used, it can be retrieved by pressing the key $\boxed{\begin{array}{c}\text{FROM}\\\text{STOR}\end{array}}$.

The following example illustrates the use of the new keys and the storage register in simplifying the expression $9^2 + 6^2$. The flow chart shows the steps of the process. The two columns at the right of the flow chart show the numbers that appear on the display and the storage register screens at each step of the flow chart.

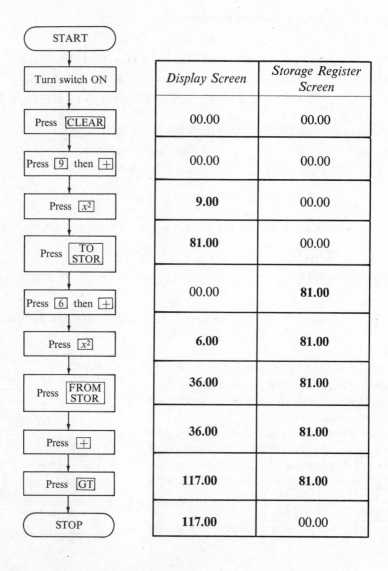

	Display Screen	Storage Register Screen
START		
Turn switch ON		
Press CLEAR	00.00	00.00
Press 9 then +	00.00	00.00
Press x^2	9.00	00.00
Press TO STOR	81.00	00.00
Press 6 then +	00.00	81.00
Press x^2	6.00	81.00
Press FROM STOR	36.00	81.00
Press +	36.00	81.00
Press GT	117.00	81.00
STOP	117.00	00.00

Questions

Copy and complete each of the following flow charts. In each case, assume that the machine is "on" and has been "cleared."

1. Simplify $(5^2)(3^2)$.

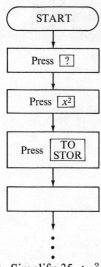

3. Simplify $7^2 + 4^2$.

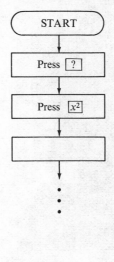

2. Simplify $35 \div \frac{28}{4}$.

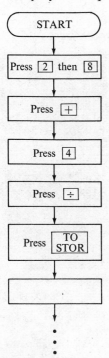

4. Simplify $8^2 - 3^2$.

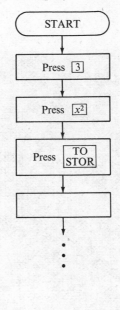

An ancient water organ . . .

An electronic synthesizer . . .

Quadratic Polynomials and Factoring

That many mathematicians are also skilled musicians is not strange, for mathematics plays an important part in composing music and in constructing musical instruments. The hydraulos, or water organ, first developed in the third century B.C., was an organ whose wind supply was provided by pumps and a reservoir; the theory of hydraulic pressure involved is an application of physics. The Moog electronic synthesizer is probably the most modern application of mathematics and physics to music. It is presently used more for composing and for recording than for use before live audiences. Robert Moog describes his synthesizer as "a system of instruments," each with its own role in shaping a given sound. It employs all sorts of electronic devices, such as amplifiers, oscillators, and tape recorders, with the final sound controlled by the performer at the keyboard and instrument panel.

Multiplying Binomials

5–1 Products of Binomials

It is now important that you become quite efficient at multiplying binomials at sight. With a little practice you can easily accomplish this by using the short cut indicated in these examples.

EXAMPLE 1. $(x + 4)(x + 6)$

Think: *Write:*

$(x + 4)(x + 6); x \cdot x = x^2$ $x^2 +$

$(x + 4)(x + 6); 6x + 4x = 10x$ $x^2 + 10x +$

$(x + 4)(x + 6); 4 \cdot 6 = 24$ $x^2 + 10x + 24$

So $(x + 4)(x + 6) = x^2 + 10x + 24$.

143

EXAMPLE 2. $(2n + 3)(n - 5)$

Think:	*Write:*
$(2n + 3)(n - 5); 2n \cdot n = 2n^2$	$2n^2 +$
$(2n + 3)(n - 5); -10n + 3n = -7n$	$2n^2 + (-7n) +$
$(2n + 3)(n - 5); 3 \cdot -5 = -15$	$2n^2 + (-7n) + (-15)$

So $(2n + 3)(n - 5) = 2n^2 - 7n - 15$.

You will probably recall that we have said that the **degree** of a monomial in one variable is indicated by the **exponent** of the variable. Thus

$$10x^3 \text{ is of degree three in } x;$$
$$3x^2 \text{ is of degree two in } x.$$

The degree of a **polynomial** in one variable is the **greatest degree** of any term of the polynomial.

$$3x^2 - x - 16 \text{ is of degree two};$$
$$x^2 - 25 \text{ is of degree two}.$$

A polynomial of degree two is called a quadratic polynomial. Do you see that each of the following polynomials is of degree two, and thus is a quadratic polynomial?

$$y^2 + 3y + 1 \qquad\qquad t^2 - 4t$$
$$\frac{2n^2}{3} + 7n - 10 \qquad\qquad 5 - 3x + 6x^2$$

ORAL EXERCISES

Name the degree of each polynomial.

SAMPLE: $45x^4$ *What you say:* $45x^4$ is of degree four.

1. $6x^3 + 1$ **3.** $14 - x^2$ **5.** $-12x - 6x^4$

2. $-10x$ **4.** $\dfrac{x^2}{2} + x$ **6.** $125 + x^{10}$

Tell which of these polynomials are quadratics and which are not.

7. $2x - 3$ **9.** $40 + x + x^2$ **11.** $\dfrac{x^2}{5} + 1$

8. $16 - x^2$ **10.** $2x + x + 3$ **12.** $-18x^2$

WRITTEN EXERCISES

Supply the missing first term in each quadratic expression.

SAMPLE: $(2x + 5)(x - 1) = (?) + 3x - 5$

Solution: $(2x + 5)(x - 1) = (2x)(x) + 3x - 5$; the missing term is $2x^2$.

 1. $(x + 1)(x + 4) = (?) + 5x + 4$
2. $(n + 2)(n + 5) = (?) + 7n + 10$
3. $(2x + 3)(x + 1) = (?) + 5x + 3$
4. $(4 + y)(2 - y) = (?) - 2y - y^2$

Supply the missing middle term in each quadratic expression.

SAMPLE: $(y + 3)(y + 4) = y^2 + (?) + 12$

Solution: $(y + 3)(y + 4) = y^2 + (4y + 3y) + 12$; the missing term is $7y$.

5. $(m + 7)(m + 2) = m^2 + (?) + 14$
6. $(2t + 5)(3t + 2) = 6t^2 + (?) + 10$
7. $(3k + 1)(k - 6) = 3k^2 + (?) - 6$
8. $(3 + s)(6 - s) = 18 + (?) - s^2$

Supply the missing last term in each quadratic expression.

SAMPLE: $(3r + 8)(4r - 3) = 12r^2 + 23r + (?)$

Solution: $(3r + 8)(4r - 3) = 12r^2 + 23r + (8)(-3)$; the missing term is -24.

9. $(2x + 5)(x + 2) = 2x^2 + 9x + (?)$
10. $(8a - 6)(a - 4) = 8a^2 - 38a + (?)$
11. $(-x + 5)(4x - 1) = -4x^2 + 21x + (?)$
12. $(2 - y)(5 + 6y) = 10 + 7y + (?)$
13. $(-2b - 8)(b - 1) = -2b^2 - 6b + (?)$

Complete each indicated multiplication in the four steps shown by the numbering in the sample. Then simplify the result if possible.

SAMPLE:

Solution: $\overset{①}{x^2} + \overset{②}{3x} + \overset{③}{6x} + \overset{④}{18}$
$= x^2 + 9x + 18$

14. $(x + 5)(x + 2)$
15. $(n + 4)(n + 6)$
16. $(a - 2)(a + 3)$

17. $(5 + t)(4 + t)$
18. $(y - 6)(y - 10)$
19. $(2x + 1)(4x + 3)$

Complete each indicated multiplication mentally.

20. $(x + 6)(x + 7)$ **24.** $(n + 9)(2n - 5)$

21. $(m + 10)(m + 8)$ **25.** $(3k + 6)(5k - 10)$

22. $(2a + 5)(a + 3)$ **26.** $(8 + b)(5 - b)$

23. $(y - 3)(y - 8)$ **27.** $(2a + 3)(a - 2)$

B **28.** $(-3x + 4)(x - 1)$ **32.** $(-2 + n)(9 + 3n)$

29. $(2y + 5)(-y + 2)$ **33.** $(-1 + r)(1 - r)$

30. $\left(\dfrac{t}{2} + 1\right)(t + 4)$ **34.** $(0.2w - 0.1)(0.4w + 0.2)$

31. $(-9m - 1)(-3m + 7)$ **35.** $(-5 + 2b)(-7 + b)$

5–2 Product of the Sum and the Difference of Two Numbers

You have worked with indicated products like $(x + 5)(x - 1)$, for which the final product, $x^2 + 4x - 5$, contains *three* terms. Now notice, in Examples 1–3 which follow, that the simplified form of each of these products contains only *two* terms. Also look at the two binomials that are multiplied and note that their **first** terms are the **same**, while the **last** term of one binomial is the **opposite** of the last term of the other.

EXAMPLE 1. $(x + 3)(x - 3) = x^2 - 3x + 3x - 9$
$$= x^2 - 9$$

EXAMPLE 2. $(2x + 5)(2x - 5) = 4x^2 - 10x + 10x - 25$
$$= 4x^2 - 25$$

EXAMPLE 3. $(4 - x)(4 + x) = 16 + 4x - 4x - x^2$
$$= 16 - x^2$$

If you are a good observer, you have probably found a pattern that always occurs in this kind of problem. Each final product is a two-termed quadratic polynomial, and is the **difference** of **two squares**. We can use the pattern to simplify the work of multiplying the sum and the difference of the same two numbers. We make the following general statement about such products:

The product of the sum and the difference of the same two numbers is the square of the first number minus the square of the second number; for any two numbers **r** and **s**,

$$(r + s)(r - s) = r^2 - s^2.$$

ORAL EXERCISES

Tell whether each polynomial is or is not the difference of two squares.

1. $x^2 - 4$ **5.** $4n^2 + 36$ **9.** $x^2 - 1$

2. $t^2 - 10$ **6.** $16 - r^2$ **10.** $64 - z^2$

3. $36 - y^2$ **7.** $y^2 + 45$ **11.** $1000 - s^2$

4. $r^2 - s^2$ **8.** $4r^2 - 1$ **12.** $4a^2 - 16$

Match each indicated product in Column 1 with the correct polynomial in Column 2.

COLUMN 1	COLUMN 2
13. $(x - 6)(x + 6)$	**A.** $4x^2 - 25$
14. $(x - 10)(x + 10)$	**B.** $a^2 - b^2$
15. $(x + 8)(x - 8)$	**C.** $x^2 - 100$
16. $(3 + x)(3 - x)$	**D.** $x^2 - 36$
17. $(2x - 5)(2x + 5)$	**E.** $x^2 - 64$
18. $(a + b)(a - b)$	**F.** $9 - x^2$

WRITTEN EXERCISES

Copy and complete each sentence.

SAMPLE 1: $(8 + 3)(8 - 3) = (8)^2 - (?)^2 = ?$

Solution: $(8 + 3)(8 - 3) = (8)^2 - (3)^2 = 64 - 9 = 55$

SAMPLE 2: $(2n - 5)(2n + 5) = (2n)^2 - (?)^2 = ?$

Solution: $(2n - 5)(2n + 5) = (2n)^2 - (5)^2 = 4n^2 - 25$

1. $(x + 8)(x - 8) = (x)^2 - (?)^2 = ?$

2. $(r - 6)(r + 6) = (?)^2 - (6)^2 = ?$

3. $(5 + 2)(5 - 2) = (5)^2 - (?)^2 = ?$

4. $(6 - 3)(6 + 3) = (6)^2 - (?)^2 = ?$

5. $(4 + t)(4 - t) = (4)^2 - (?)^2 = ?$

6. $(9 - y)(9 + y) = (?)^2 - (y)^2 = ?$

7. $(2c + 4)(2c - 4) = (?)^2 - (4)^2 = ?$

8. $(c - d)(c + d) = (?)^2 - (d)^2 = ?$

9. $(5 - 3a)(5 + 3a) = (?)^2 - (?)^2 = ?$

10. $(2x - 3y)(2x + 3y) = (?)^2 - (?)^2 = ?$

Complete each indicated product mentally. Check your answers for Exercises 11, 15, 19, and 21 by writing out the solution in vertical form.

SAMPLE: $(2x - 1)(2x + 1)$ *Solution:* $4x^2 - 1$ *Check:*

$$\begin{array}{r} 2x - 1 \\ 2x + 1 \\ \hline 2x - 1 \\ 4x^2 - 2x \\ \hline 4x^2 - 1 \end{array}$$

11. $(m + 1)(m - 1)$ **16.** $(5 + k)(5 - k)$ **21.** $(3t - s)(3t + s)$

12. $(a - 6)(a + 6)$ **17.** $(10 - 3s)(10 + 3s)$ **22.** $(x - \frac{1}{2})(x + \frac{1}{2})$

13. $(3 + t)(3 - t)$ **18.** $(m - n)(m + n)$ **23.** $(m + \frac{1}{4})(m - \frac{1}{4})$

14. $(5 - 2y)(5 + 2y)$ **19.** $(6x + 7)(6x - 7)$ **24.** $(2y + \frac{1}{3})(2y - \frac{1}{3})$

15. $(x + y)(x - y)$ **20.** $(a + 2b)(a - 2b)$ **25.** $(a + 3c)(a - 3c)$

$\boxed{\text{B}}$ **26.** $(ab + 3bc)(ab - 3bc)$ **30.** $(20x - 0.7)(20x + 0.7)$

27. $(15xy + 2)(15xy - 2)$ **31.** $(0.9 + d)(0.9 - d)$

28. $(-2 + 4x)(2 + 4x)$ **32.** $(0.3t - \frac{1}{3})(0.3t + \frac{1}{3})$

29. $(m + 0.2)(m - 0.2)$ **33.** $(\frac{1}{2}ab - \frac{1}{5}cd)(\frac{1}{2}ab + \frac{1}{5}cd)$

$\boxed{\text{C}}$ **34.** $(2\pi + c)(2\pi - c)$ **36.** $[a + (b + c)][a - (b + c)]$

35. $\left(\dfrac{2a}{3} + \dfrac{b}{5}\right)\left(\dfrac{2a}{3} - \dfrac{b}{5}\right)$ **37.** $\left(-\dfrac{c}{2} + 3\right)\left(\dfrac{c}{2} + 3\right)$

PROBLEMS

Write each answer as a polynomial in standard form.

1. Find the area of this parallelogram in terms of the given polynomials.
Hint: Use Area = base · height.

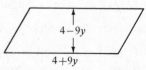

2. Find the area of the pictured rectangle if its dimensions are represented by the given polynomials.

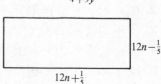

3. The area, B, of the base of a cylinder is represented by $16\pi + 3$, and its height, h, is represented by $16\pi - 3$. Find the volume of the cylinder. Hint: the volume of a cylinder is given by the formula $V = Bh$.

4. The length of each side of square $ABCD$ shown at the right is represented by x. The shaded rectangle $DEFG$ is formed by increasing the length of one side by 13 units and decreasing the length of an adjacent side by 13 units. Express the area of the rectangle.

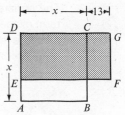

5–3   Squaring a Binomial

The squares of the binomials $x + 5$ and $n - 7$ may be indicated by $(x + 5)^2$ and $(n - 7)^2$, respectively. You will recall that $(x + 5)^2$ means $(x + 5)(x + 5)$ and that $(n - 7)^2$ means $(n - 7)(n - 7)$. Once again it is important for you to become skillful in doing such multiplications at sight. The process is the same as that used in finding the product of any two binomials. Study the following examples carefully and look for a pattern that can lead to a short cut for squaring a binomial.

EXAMPLE 1. $(x + 3)^2$

Think: *Write:*

$(x + 3)(x + 3)$; $x \cdot x = x^2$ $x^2 +$

$(x + 3)(x + 3)$; $3x + 3x = 6x$ $x^2 + 6x +$

$(x + 3)(x + 3)$; $3 \cdot 3 = 9$ $x^2 + 6x + 9$

So $(x + 3)^2 = x^2 + 6x + 9$.

EXAMPLE 2. $(3y - 5)^2$

Think: *Write:*

$(3y - 5)(3y - 5)$; $3y \cdot 3y = 9y^2$ $9y^2 +$

$(3y - 5)(3y - 5)$; $-15y + (-15y) = -30y$ $9y^2 + (-30y) +$

$(3y - 5)(3y - 5)$; $(-5)(-5) = 25$ $9y^2 + (-30y) + 25$

So $(3y - 5)^2 = 9y^2 - 30y + 25$.

Study Examples 1 and 2 and see that we can summarize our results as follows:

The square of a binomial is equal to the square of the first term of the binomial, plus twice the product of the two terms, plus the square of the second term; for any two positive numbers **r** and **s**,

$$(\boldsymbol{r} + \boldsymbol{s})^2 = \boldsymbol{r}^2 + 2\boldsymbol{r}\boldsymbol{s} + \boldsymbol{s}^2$$
$$(\boldsymbol{r} - \boldsymbol{s})^2 = \boldsymbol{r}^2 - 2\boldsymbol{r}\boldsymbol{s} + \boldsymbol{s}^2.$$

The result of squaring a binomial is a three-termed quadratic polynomial called a **trinomial square**.

ORAL EXERCISES

Fill in this table to illustrate the steps for squaring a binomial.

		Square of first term	Twice the product of the terms	Square of second term
1.	$(a + b)^2$	a^2	$2ab$	?
2.	$(m - n)^2$	m^2	$-2mn$	?
3.	$(y + 9)^2$	y^2	?	81
4.	$(b - c)^2$	b^2	?	c^2
5.	$(x - 7)^2$	?	$-14x$	?
6.	$(2a + 3)^2$	?	?	9
7.	$(4 + 5t)^2$	?	$40t$	?
8.	$(2 - 3k)^2$	?	?	?

WRITTEN EXERCISES

Complete each indicated multiplication mentally. Verify the answers for Exercises 1–15 by vertical multiplication.

SAMPLE: $(3y + 8)^2$ *Solution:* $9y^2 + 48y + 64$ *Check:*
$$
\begin{array}{r}
3y + 8 \\
3y + 8 \\
\hline
24y + 64 \\
9y^2 + 24y \\
\hline
9y^2 + 48y + 64
\end{array}
$$

 1. $(1 + 5b)^2$ **2.** $(ab + 3)^2$ **3.** $(15 - b)^2$

4. $(2n + 4)^2$ **8.** $(6 - 6z)^2$ **12.** $(x + \frac{1}{2})^2$

5. $(2m - 3)^2$ **9.** $(1 - 7d)^2$ **13.** $(r + 20)^2$

6. $(y - 4)^2$ **10.** $(p + q)^2$ **14.** $(2t - s)^2$

7. $(7t + 8)^2$ **11.** $(3a + b)^2$ **15.** $(10k - 12)^2$

B **16.** $(-x + 1)^2$ **19.** $(0.4c - 0.5)^2$ **22.** $(-12 + 4mn)^2$

17. $(rs + t)^2$ **20.** $(\frac{1}{2}y + 10)^2$ **23.** $(25 - \frac{1}{5}r)^2$

18. $(3ab - c)^2$ **21.** $(x^2 - 15)^2$ **24.** $(\frac{1}{3} + 9abc)^2$

PROBLEMS

Express the area of each square as a polynomial in standard form.

1. 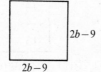   **2.**   **3.**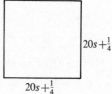

Express the area of each shaded square as a polynomial.

4. 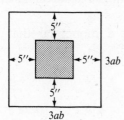   **5.** 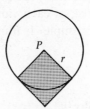   **6.**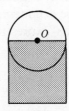

The radius of circle *P* is $(12 + 9k)$.   The radius of circle *O* is $(12 + 9k)$.

Factoring Quadratic Polynomials

5–4 Factors and Square Monomials

You will probably recall that numbers like **36** and **64** are called **square numbers**; $36 = 6^2$ and $64 = 8^2$. Do you know whether or not the number **169** is a square number? You may use a table of square numbers to answer such a question if you are not sure.

A portion of a table of squares is shown at the right. If you look in the column headed n^2, you will find the number **169**; to its left, in the *n* column, is the number **13**. Thus 169 is a square number, and **169** $= 13^2$.

Can you find the number **75** in the column headed n^2? What about the number **40**? Since neither is in the n^2 column, do you see that we conclude that neither **75** nor **40** is a square number?

It is not difficult to decide whether a monomial like $16x^2$ or $100x^4y^6$ is a square monomial. Do you see that $16x^2 = 4x \cdot 4x$ and $100x^4y^6 = 10x^2y^3 \cdot 10x^2y^3$? Therefore, $16x^2 = (4x)^2$ and $100x^4y^6 = (10x^2y^3)^2$.

n	n^2
1	1
2	4
3	9
4	16
5	25
6	36
7	49
8	64
9	81
10	100
11	121
12	144
13	169
14	196
15	225

Notice that in the case of $16x^2$, the coefficient, **16**, is a square and x^2 is a square; in $100x^4y^6$ the coefficient, **100**, is a square and the exponent, or degree, of each variable is an even number. Thus we say that a monomial is a square if (1) the coefficient is a square number and (2) the exponent, or degree, of each variable is even.

Each expression in Example 1 illustrates a monomial that **is** a **square**.

EXAMPLE 1.

$$4r^4s^4 = (2r^2s^2)^2 \qquad 36x^2y^8 = (6xy^4)^2 \qquad a^2b^2c^6 = (abc^3)^2$$

Do you see why each monomial in Example 2 **is not** a **square**?

EXAMPLE 2. $13a^4b^4 \qquad 25m^2n^3 \qquad -16x^4y^6$

ORAL EXERCISES

Complete each of the following to make a true statement.

SAMPLE: $400 = (20)(?) = (?)^2$

What you say: $400 = (20)(20) = 20^2$

1. $81 = (9)(?) = (?)^2$ **2.** $1 = (?)(1) = (?)^2$

3. $49 = (7)(?) = (?)^2$ **6.** $25 = (5)(?) = (?)^2$

4. $64 = (?)(8) = (?)^2$ **7.** $121 = (11)(?) = (?)^2$

5. $144 = (?)(12) = (?)^2$ **8.** $10,000 = (100)(?) = (?)^2$

Tell whether or not each monomial is a square, and justify your answer.

SAMPLE 1: $9t^4$ *What you say:* $9t^4$ is a square because 9 is a square and the exponent of the variable t is an even number.

SAMPLE 2: $5m^6n^2$ *What you say:* $5m^6n^2$ is not a square because 5 is not a square.

9. $25m^2$ **13.** $-9a^2b^2$ **17.** $3a^4b^2$

10. $4a^2b^2$ **14.** $81s^6t^8$ **18.** $16r^8s^4t^6$

11. $64x$ **15.** m^4x^2 **19.** $25w^4x^2y$

12. $100r^4$ **16.** $85x^2y$ **20.** $144k^4r^4t^{10}$

WRITTEN EXERCISES

Complete the following tables of squares.

 1.

n	n^2
1	1
2	4
3	9
4	?
5	?
6	?
7	?
8	?
9	?
10	?

n	n^2
11	?
12	?
13	?
14	?
15	?
16	?
17	?
18	?
19	?
20	?

n	n^2
21	?
22	?
23	?
24	?
25	?
26	?
27	?
28	?
29	?
30	?

Complete each equation.

SAMPLE: $25m^6 = (?)(5m^3) = (?)^2$

Solution: $25m^6 = (5m^3)(5m^3) = (5m^3)^2$

2. $49t^2 = (7t)(?) = (?)^2$

3. $9m^4n^6 = (3m^2n^3)(?) = (?)^2$

4. $36a^2b^4 = (?)(6ab^2) = (?)^2$

5. $121x^{10}y^8z^2 = (?)(11x^5y^4z) = (?)^2$

6. $81m^6n^2r^2 = (?)(9m^3nr) = (?)^2$

7. $64k^{10}m^8 = (?)(8k^5m^4) = (?)^2$

8. $100a^2b^2c^2 = (10abc)(?) = (?)^2$

9. $144m^{12}n^{10}t^4 = (12m^6n^5t^2)(?) = (?)^2$

Use the tables of squares from Exercise 1 to complete each of the following.

SAMPLE 1: $(26)^2 = ?$ *Solution:* $(26)^2 = 676$

SAMPLE 2: $841 = (?)^2$ *Solution:* $841 = (29)^2$

10. $64 = (?)^2$	**14.** $169 = (?)^2$	**18.** $144 = (?)^2$
11. $(15)^2 = ?$	**15.** $484 = (?)^2$	**19.** $361 = (?)^2$
12. $324 = (?)^2$	**16.** $(13)^2 = ?$	**20.** $(30)^2 = ?$
13. $676 = (?)^2$	**17.** $(17)^2 = ?$	**21.** $729 = (?)^2$

Complete each equation. Use the table from Exercise 1 if necessary.

SAMPLE: $529r^4t^{10} = (?)^2$ *Solution:* $(23r^2t^5)^2$

22. $196x^8y^2 = (?)^2$	**27.** $(23m^3z^5)^2 = (?)$
23. $400r^4s^6 = (?)^2$	**28.** $(8ab^7)^2 = (?)$
24. $625y^{10}z^4 = (?)^2$	**29.** $(16w^3x^2y)^2 = (?)$
25. $289k^2m^{14} = (?)^2$	**30.** $(22a^2b^3c^4)^2 = (?)$
26. $441v^4h^4 = (?)^2$	**31.** $(28xy^3z)(28xy^3z) = (?)$

B

32. $25b^{2n} = (?)^2$	**35.** $(19ax^{2n})^2 = (?)$
33. $36t^{2y} = (?)^2$	**36.** $225a^{2m}b^{2n} = (?)^2$
34. $(4x^k)^2 = (?)$	**37.** $289x^2y^{2n} = (?)^2$

PROBLEMS

For each square, write a monomial representing either its area or the length of its side, using the information given. The area, A, of a square of side s is given by the formula $A = s^2$.

1.

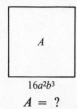

$16a^2b^3$

$A = ?$

2.

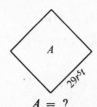

$29r^5t$

$A = ?$

3.

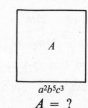

$a^2b^5c^3$

$A = ?$

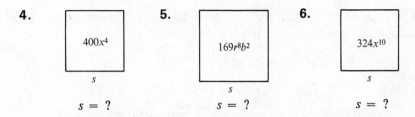

4. $400x^4$ s $s = ?$

5. $169r^8b^2$ s $s = ?$

6. $324x^{10}$ s $s = ?$

For each circle, write a monomial representing either its area or the length of its radius, using the information given. The area, A, of a circle of radius r is given by the formula $A = \pi r^2$.

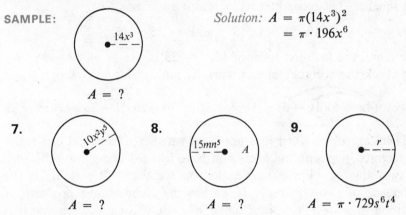

SAMPLE: $14x^3$ $A = ?$

Solution: $A = \pi(14x^3)^2$
$= \pi \cdot 196x^6$

7. $10x^2y^5$ $A = ?$

8. $15mn^5$ A $A = ?$

9. r $A = \pi \cdot 729s^6t^4$

5–5 Factoring the Difference of Two Squares

Earlier in this chapter you worked on problems and exercises that involved your finding the product of the sum and the difference of the same two numbers. For example, the product of the two binomials $(n + 3)$ and $(n - 3)$ is the quadratic binomial $n^2 - 9$, which is the **difference of two squares**, the square of n and the square of **3**.

Now let us investigate the idea of **factoring** an expression that is the difference of two squares. This may be thought of as the **reverse** of the process of finding the product of the sum and the difference of two numbers. For example, since we know that

$$(n + 3)(n - 3) = n^2 - 9,$$

it must also be true that

$$n^2 - 9 = (n + 3)(n - 3),$$

because of the symmetric property of equality.

The process of factoring a binomial that is the difference of two squares may be summarized like this:

For all numbers **r** and **s**,

$$r^2 - s^2 = (r + s)(r - s).$$

Let us apply this in factoring the polynomial $16x^2 - 25$. First we check that $16x^2 - 25$ is in fact the difference of two squares. Do you see that in the first term, $16x^2$, the coefficient **16** is a square and x^2 is a square? The second term, 25, is also a square.

$$16x^2 = (4x)^2 \quad \text{and} \quad 25 = (5)^2$$

Therefore, the factored form of $16x^2 - 25$ is $(4x + 5)(4x - 5)$. We can check the accuracy of our work by multiplying the factors.

Check: $(4x + 5)(4x - 5) = 16x^2 + [20x + (-20x)] - 25 = 16x^2 - 25$

There are times when it is not clear whether a binomial can really be factored by using the ideas you have learned about the difference of two squares. For example, do you see that $-9 + 4c^2d^4$ is the difference of two squares? If we use the commutative property of addition to write $-9 + 4c^2d^4$ as $4c^2d^4 - 9$, it is easy to see that it is the difference of the squares of $2cd^2$ and **3**. We can factor it as follows:

$$4c^2d^4 - 9 = (2cd^2 + 3)(2cd^2 - 3)$$

Now consider the binomial $5x^2 - 45$. Notice that, since **5** is the greatest common factor of each term, we can write $5x^2 - 45 = 5(x^2 - 9)$. Because $x^2 - 9$ is a difference of squares, we can write

$$5x^2 - 45 = 5(x^2 - 9) = 5(x + 3)(x - 3).$$

ORAL EXERCISES

Tell whether or not each binomial is the difference of two squares.

1. $m^2 - 9$	**7.** $64 + t^2$	**13.** $-25 + d^2$
2. $x^2 - 4$	**8.** $1 - b^2$	**14.** $4k^2 - 64$
3. $4t^2 - 16$	**9.** $16 - x^2$	**15.** $4r^2s^2 - 1$
4. $d^2 + 25$	**10.** $n^2 + 100$	**16.** $15 - 18c^2d^2$
5. $r^2 - s^2$	**11.** $4y^2 - 25$	**17.** $121t^2 - s^2$
6. $49 - q^2$	**12.** $36z^4 - 144$	**18.** $-9x^2 + 36$

WRITTEN EXERCISES

Factor each binomial and check your work by multiplication.

A
1. $r^2 - 16$ **7.** $225 - n^2$ **13.** $49a^2 - 100b^2$

2. $t^2 - 4$ **8.** $r^2 - 64s^2$ **14.** $a^2b^4 - d^2$

3. $4m^2 - 1$ **9.** $25w^2 - 49$ **15.** $9 - 16t^2$

4. $16y^2 - 1$ **10.** $64 - 9x^2$ **16.** $36y^2 - 169z^4$

5. $25x^2 - 1$ **11.** $100 - 81s^2$ **17.** $121x^2 - 400$

6. $36 - x^2$ **12.** $81t^2 - 25$ **18.** $9p^2 - 625$

Copy and complete each of the following.

SAMPLE: $3x^2 - 48 = (?)(x^2 - 16)$
                      $= (\underline{?})(\underline{\ ?\ })(\underline{\ ?\ })$

Solution: $3x^2 - 48 = 3(x^2 - 16)$
                      $= 3(x + 4)(x - 4)$

19. $2n^2 - 18 = (?)(n^2 - 9)$ **22.** $12y^6 - 75 = 3(\underline{\ ?\ })$
            $= (\underline{?})(\underline{\ ?\ })(\underline{\ ?\ })$ $= 3(\underline{\ ?\ })(\underline{\ ?\ })$

20. $7a^2 - 7b^2 = (?)(a^2 - b^2)$ **23.** $10y^2 - 40 = (?)(y^2 - 4)$
            $= (\underline{?})(\underline{\ ?\ })(\underline{\ ?\ })$ $= (\underline{?})(\underline{\ ?\ })(\underline{\ ?\ })$

21. $32s^2 - 2 = 2(\underline{\ ?\ })$ **24.** $13 - 13k^2 = (?)(1 - k^2)$
            $= 2(\underline{\ ?\ })(\underline{\ ?\ })$ $= (\underline{?})(\underline{\ ?\ })(\underline{\ ?\ })$

Factor each binomial completely.

SAMPLE: $5ab^2 - 45a$ *Solution:* $5ab^2 - 45a = 5a(b^2 - 9)$
                                          $= 5a(b + 3)(b - 3)$

B
25. $3x^2 - 27$ **29.** $4a^2 - 625$ **33.** $2abc^2 - 8ab$

26. $5s^2 - 20$ **30.** $100 - 4y^2$ **34.** $10st^2 - 10sr^2$

27. $3r^6 - 3$ **31.** $4xy^2 - 16x$ **35.** $5ak^2 - 80a$

28. $-b^2 + 25$ **32.** $5t^2 - 5$ **36.** $-75 + 3d^2$

C
37. $-n + n^7$ **39.** $-3b^2 + 27$ **41.** $2y^6 - 32y^4$

38. $147yz^2 - 75y$ **40.** $x^5 - 25x^3$ **42.** $-63a + 112at^2$

5–6   Factoring a Trinomial Square of the Form $a^2 + 2ab + b^2$

In an earlier section of this chapter, we pointed out that

$$(x + 5)^2 = (x + 5)(x + 5)$$

and that, applying the skills we had developed for multiplying two binomials, we know that

$$(x + 5)(x + 5) = x^2 + 10x + 25.$$

This led us to the observation that the square of a binomial is equal to the square of the first term of the binomial, plus twice the product of the two terms, plus the square of the second term. Thus we see that the result of squaring a binomial is a quadratic polynomial containing three terms, and is called a **trinomial square**.

We can summarize this by writing

For all numbers *a* and *b*,

$$(a + b)^2 = a^2 + 2ab + b^2.$$

Applying the symmetric property of equality, we can also write

For all numbers *a* and *b*,

$$a^2 + 2ab + b^2 = (a + b)^2.$$

Thus, in order to factor a polynomial as a **trinomial square** of this kind, we must first make sure it can be written in the form $a^2 + 2ab + b^2$. Study the following examples to see how this is applied.

EXAMPLE 1.   Factor $n^2 + 2n + 1$.

Solution: $n^2 + 2n + 1 = (n)^2 + 2(n)(1) + (1)^2$
$$= (n + 1)^2$$

EXAMPLE 2.   Factor $r^2 + 8r + 16$.

Solution: $r^2 + 8r + 16 = (r)^2 + 2(r)(4) + (4)^2$
$$= (r + 4)^2$$

EXAMPLE 3.   Factor $4a^2 + 12a + 9$.

Solution: $4a^2 + 12a + 9 = (2a)^2 + 2(2a)(3) + (3)^2$
$$= (2a + 3)^2$$

EXAMPLE 4.   Factor $9b^2 + 6bc + c^2$.

Solution: $9b^2 + 6bc + c^2 = (3b)^2 + 2(3b)(c) + (c)^2$
$$= (3b + c)^2$$

ORAL EXERCISES

Match each trinomial square in Column 1 with its factored form in Column 2.

COLUMN 1

1. $9b^2 + 6b + 1$

2. $4b^2 + 8b + 4$

3. $b^2 + 2bc + c^2$

4. $25b^2 + 20b + 4$

5. $4b^2 + 8bc + 4c^2$

COLUMN 2

A. $(b + c)^2$

B. $(2b + 2c)^2$

C. $(3b + 1)^2$

D. $(5b + 2)^2$

E. $(2b + 2)^2$

Tell whether or not each trinomial is the square of a binomial of the form $(a + b)$. Justify your answer.

SAMPLE 1: $x^2 + 6x + 10$

What you say: No; the last term is not a square.

SAMPLE 2: $n^2 + 6n + 9$

What you say: Yes; $n^2 + 6n + 9 = (n)^2 + 2(n)(3) + (3)^2$

6. $x^2 + 3x + 1$

7. $5x^2 + 4x + 4$

8. $xy + 3y + 9$

9. $x^2 + 4x + 4$

10. $9t^2 + 6t + 1$

11. $x^2 - 3x - 12$

12. $25x^2 + 20x + 4$

13. $4 + 8y + 4y^2$

WRITTEN EXERCISES

Show that each of the following is true when $a = 2$, $b = 5$, and $c = 3$.

SAMPLE: $a^2 + 2a + 1 = (a + 1)^2$

Solution:

$$
\begin{array}{c|c}
a^2 + 2a + 1 = & (a + 1)^2 \\
\hline
2^2 + 2 \cdot 2 + 1 & (2 + 1)^2 \\
4 \ + \ 4 \ + 1 & 3^2 \\
9 & 9
\end{array}
$$

1. $b^2 + 10b + 25 = (b + 5)^2$

2. $c^2 + 12c + 36 = (c + 6)^2$

3. $81 + 18a + a^2 = (9 + a)^2$

4. $4c^2 + 4c + 1 = (2c + 1)^2$

5. $4a^2 + 4ab + b^2 = (2a + b)^2$

6. $(b + 2c)^2 = b^2 + 4bc + 4c^2$

7. $(3 + 4c)^2 = 9 + 24c + 16c^2$

8. $(2a + 2c)^2 = 4a^2 + 8ac + 4c^2$

9. $(a + 15)^2 = a^2 + 30a + 225$

10. $(3c + 5a)^2 = 9c^2 + 30ac + 25a^2$

Complete each equation, then simplify the right member.

SAMPLE: $(2a + 3)^2 = (?)^2 + 2(?) + (?)^2$

Solution: $(2a + 3)^2 = (2a)^2 + 2(6a) + (3)^2$
$$= 4a^2 + 12a + 9$$

11. $(n + 7)(n + 7) = (?)^2 + 2(?) + (?)^2$
12. $(3 + x)(3 + x) = (?)^2 + 2(?) + (?)^2$
13. $(y + 10)^2 = (?)^2 + 2(?) + (?)^2$
14. $(t + 8)^2 = (?)^2 + 2(?) + (?)^2$
15. $(2n + 3) = (?)^2 + 2(?) + (?)^2$
16. $(4 + 3y)^2 = (?)^2 + 2(?) + (?)^2$
17. $(2x + y)^2 = (?)^2 + 2(?) + (?)^2$
18. $(2a + 5b)^2 = (?)^2 + 2(?) + (?)^2$
19. $(3n + 2m)^2 = (?)^2 + 2(?) + (?)^2$
20. $(5r + 3)^2 = (?)^2 + 2(?) + (?)^2$

Write each expression as a trinomial square.

21. $(y + 6)^2$ **25.** $(2x + 1)^2$ **29.** $(2a + b)^2$
22. $(n + 9)^2$ **26.** $(2y + 3)^2$ **30.** $(3m + n)^2$
23. $(5 + y)^2$ **27.** $(3n + 1)^2$ **31.** $(2x + 3y)^2$
24. $(7 + x)^2$ **28.** $(b + c)^2$ **32.** $(6k + 3m)^2$

Factor each trinomial square and check by multiplication.

SAMPLE: $r^2 + 6rs + 9s^2$ *Solution:* $(r + 3s)^2$

Check: $(r + 3s)^2 = (r)^2 + 2(r)(3s) + (3s)^2$
$$= r^2 + 6rs + 9s^2$$

33. $r^2 + 8r + 16$ **38.** $s^2 + 12s + 36$
34. $z^2 + 4z + 4$ **39.** $9w^2 + 6w + 1$
35. $n^2 + 2n + 1$ **40.** $16a^2 + 8a + 1$
36. $a^2 + 2ab + b^2$ **41.** $25 + 10k + k^2$
37. $m^2 + 2m + 1$ **42.** $9 + 12t + 4t^2$

B **43.** $4t^2 + 12t + 9$ **46.** $16y^2 + 24yz + 9z^2$
44. $25v^2 + 60v + 36$ **47.** $16m^2 + 40mn + 25n^2$
45. $4x^2y^2 + 12xy + 9$ **48.** $36r^2 + 24rt + 4t^2$

SAMPLE: $4x^2 + 8x + 4$ *Solution:* $4x^2 + 8x + 4 = 4(x^2 + 2x + 1)$
$$= 4(x + 1)^2$$

C **49.** $6m^2 + 12m + 6$

50. $12p^2 + 12p + 3$

51. $x^3 + 10x^2 + 25x$

52. $7a^3 + 14a^2 + 7a$

5–7   Factoring a Trinomial Square of the Form $a^2 - 2ab + b^2$

When we square a binomial that is the **difference** of two numbers, the result is also a quadratic *trinomial square*. For example

$$(x - 3)^2 = (x - 3)(x - 3)$$
$$= x^2 - 6x + 9.$$

Do you see that this result differs from the square of a binomial **sum** in just one respect, the **sign** of the **middle term**? Thus we can write

For all numbers **a** and **b**,

$$(a - b)^2 = a^2 - 2ab + b^2.$$

Once again we can apply the symmetric property of equality and write

For all numbers **a** and **b**,

$$a^2 - 2ab + b^2 = (a - b)^2.$$

Study the following examples to see how this is applied.

EXAMPLE 1.   Factor $x^2 - 4x + 4$.

Solution: $x^2 - 4x + 4 = (x)^2 - 2(x)(2) + (2)^2$
$$= (x - 2)^2$$

EXAMPLE 2.   Factor $k^2 - 12k + 36$.

Solution: $k^2 - 12k + 36 = (k)^2 - 2(k)(6) + (6)^2$
$$= (k - 6)^2$$

EXAMPLE 3.   Factor $4x^2 - 12x + 9$.

Solution: $4x^2 - 12x + 9 = (2x)^2 - 2(2x)(3) + (3)^2$
$$= (2x - 3)^2$$

EXAMPLE 4.   Factor $49 - 14b + b^2$.

Solution: $49 - 14b + b^2 = (7)^2 - 2(7)(b) + (b)^2$
$$= (7 - b)^2$$

ORAL EXERCISES

Tell whether or not each trinomial is the square of a binomial of the form $(a - b)$. Justify your answer.

SAMPLE 1: $s^2 - 6s + 8$

What you say: No; the last term is not a square.

SAMPLE 2: $x^2 + 6x + 9$

What you say: No; the coefficient of the middle term is not negative.

1. $x^2 + x + 1$
2. $2y^2 - 2y + 1$
3. $z^2 + 4z + 4$
4. $m^2 - 4m - 4$

5. $r^2 - 8r + 16$
6. $25y^2 + 10y - 9$
7. $k^2 - 6k + 9$
8. $9 - 6t + t^2$

Match each trinomial square in Column 1 with its factored form in Column 2.

COLUMN 1
9. $4b^2 - 4b + 1$
10. $b^2 - 2bc + c^2$
11. $9b^2 - 6b + 1$
12. $4b^2 - 4bc + c^2$

COLUMN 2
A. $(3b - 1)^2$
B. $(2b - 1)^2$
C. $(2b - c)^2$
D. $(b - c)^2$

WRITTEN EXERCISES

Show that each of the following is true if $r = 4$, $s = 6$, and $t = 10$.

SAMPLE: $s^2 - 2s + 1 = (s - 1)^2$ *Solution:*

$$\begin{array}{c|c}
s^2 - 2s + 1 & (s - 1)^2 \\
\hline
36 - 12 + 1 & (6 - 1)^2 \\
24 + 1 & 5^2 \\
25 & 25
\end{array}$$

A

1. $r^2 - 10r + 25 = (r - 5)^2$
2. $t^2 - 16t + 64 = (t - 8)^2$
3. $36 - 12s + s^2 = (6 - s)^2$
4. $4r^2 - 12r + 9 = (2r - 3)^2$

5. $9s^2 - 6s + 1 = (3s - 1)^2$
6. $1 - 10t + 25t^2 = (1 - 5t)^2$
7. $4r^2 - 4rs + s^2 = (2r - s)^2$
8. $4t^2 - 12st + 9s^2 = (2t - 3s)^2$

Complete each equation and simplify.

SAMPLE: $(3b - 2)^2 = (?)^2 - 2(?) + (?)^2$

Solution: $(3b - 2)^2 = (3b)^2 - 2(6b) + (2)^2$
$$= 9b^2 - 12b + 4$$

9. $(4k - 1)^2 = (?)^2 - 2(?) + (?)^2$ **13.** $(3a - 2b)^2 = (?)^2 - 2(?) + (?)^2$
10. $(m - 5)^2 = (?)^2 - 2(?) + (?)^2$ **14.** $(5x - 1)^2 = (?)^2 - 2(?) + (?)^2$
11. $(2y - 3)^2 = (?)^2 - 2(?) + (?)^2$ **15.** $(4 - 3m)^2 = (?)^2 - 2(?) + (?)^2$
12. $(3x - 2)^2 = (?)^2 - 2(?) + (?)^2$ **16.** $(4r - 5s)^2 = (?)^2 - 2(?) + (?)^2$

Write each of the following as a trinomial square.

17. $(c - 2)^2$ **21.** $(3 - y)^2$ **25.** $(t - 8r)^2$
18. $(2a - 1)^2$ **22.** $(2 - k)^2$ **26.** $(x - 3y)^2$
19. $(y - 5)^2$ **23.** $(2n - 3m)^2$ **27.** $(4m - 3n)^2$
20. $(t - 10)^2$ **24.** $(4b - 2c)^2$ **28.** $(6 - 4b)^2$

Factor each trinomial square and check by multiplication.

SAMPLE: $9t^2 - 6st + s^2$ *Solution:* $(3t - s)^2$

                  Check: $(3t - s)^2 = (3t)^2 - 2(3t)(s) + (s)^2$
$$= 9t^2 - 6st + s^2$$

29. $r^2 - 4r + 4$ **35.** $a^2 - 12a + 36$ **41.** $1 - 4t + 4t^2$
30. $m^2 - 2m + 1$ **36.** $x^2 - 2xy + y^2$ **42.** $25 - 10y + y^2$
31. $s^2 - 8s + 16$ **37.** $4s^2 - 4s + 1$ **43.** $64x^2 - 16xy + y^2$
32. $y^2 - 6y + 9$ **38.** $9a^2 - 6a + 1$ **44.** $9 - 12z + 4z^2$
33. $r^2 - 10r + 25$ **39.** $25t^2 - 10t + 1$ **45.** $36 - 60m + 25m^2$
34. $b^2 - 14b + 49$ **40.** $4r^2 - 12r + 9$ **46.** $4x^2 - 12xy + 9y^2$

B   **47.** $4x^2y^2 - 12xyz + 9z^2$ **50.** $a^2 - 18abc + 81b^2c^2$
     48. $r^4 - 2r^2 + 1$ **51.** $16t^2 - 24txy + 9x^2y^2$
     49. $25x^4 - 10x^2y + y^2$ **52.** $y^4 - 10y^2 + 25$

Factor each trinomial completely.

SAMPLE: $3x^3 - 6x^2 + 3x$

Solution: $3x^3 - 6x^2 + 3x = 3x(x^2 - 2x + 1)$
$$= 3x(x - 1)^2$$

C   **53.** $18x^2 - 12x + 2$ **56.** $z^3 + 25z - 10z^2$
     54. $7a^3 - 14a^2 + 7a$ **57.** $3a - 42a^2 + 147a^3$
     55. $20rs^2 - 60rs + 45r$ **58.** $6x^4 - 12x^2y^2 + 6y^4$

5–8   **Factoring a Product of Two Binomial Sums or Two Binomial Differences**

By now you should be fairly proficient in performing, at sight, multiplications like those in the examples below. Example 1 shows a product of two **binomial sums.** Note that all three terms of the resulting quadratic polynomial are positive. Example 2 shows a product of two **binomial differences.** Do you see why the middle term of such a product will always be negative?

EXAMPLE 1. $(x + 3)(x + 7) = x^2 + 10x + 21$

EXAMPLE 2. $(x - 5)(x - 7) = x^2 - 12x + 35$

We are now ready to investigate reversing the process in order to factor quadratic trinomials like $x^2 + 7x + 10$ and $x^2 - 8x + 15$.

Suppose that you needed to factor the quadratic trinomial $x^2 + 7x + 10$. How would you decide at the start that it must be the product of two binomial **sums?** What factors were probably multiplied to give x^2? The third term, **10,** could be the product of **2** and **5,** or of **10** and **1;** which pair of factors would give **7** as the coefficient of the middle term? The process is summarized in Example 3.

EXAMPLE 3.

$$x^2 + 7x + 10 = (x \quad)(x \quad) \qquad x^2 \text{ is factored as } x \cdot x.$$
$$= (x + \quad)(x + \quad) \qquad \text{The factors are binomial sums.}$$
$$= (x + 2)(x + 5) \qquad \text{The product of 2 and 5 is 10, and the sum of 2 and 5 is 7.}$$

A similar process applies in the factoring of the quadratic trinomial $x^2 - 6x + 8$. Notice that the coefficient of the **middle** term is **negative,** while the **third** term is a **positive** number. Do you see how this tells us that the trinomial is the product of two binomial **differences?** Two possible pairs of negative factors of the third term, **8,** are $(-1)(-8)$ and $(-2)(-4)$; since the coefficient of the middle term is -6, which pair of factors should we use? This is summarized in Example 4.

EXAMPLE 4.

$$x^2 - 6x + 8 = (x \quad)(x \quad) \qquad x^2 \text{ is factored as } x \cdot x.$$
$$= (x - \quad)(x - \quad) \qquad \text{The factors are binomial differences.}$$
$$= (x - 2)(x - 4) \qquad \text{The product of } -2 \text{ and } -4 \text{ is 8, and the sum of } -2 \text{ and } -4 \text{ is } -6.$$

ORAL EXERCISES

Complete each first statement with a pair of factors which may be used as addends to complete the second statement.

SAMPLE: $15 = (?) \cdot (?)$ *What you say:* $15 = 3 \cdot 5$
$\ 8 = (?) + (?)$ $8 = 3 + 5$

1. $12 = (?) \cdot (?)$ **4.** $8 = (?) \cdot (?)$ **7.** $50 = (?) \cdot (?)$
$\ 7 = (?) + (?)$ $-9 = (?) + (?)$ $15 = (?) + (?)$

2. $4 = (?) \cdot (?)$ **5.** $20 = (?) \cdot (?)$ **8.** $50 = (?) \cdot (?)$
$\ 5 = (?) + (?)$ $12 = (?) + (?)$ $27 = (?) + (?)$

3. $20 = (?) \cdot (?)$ **6.** $33 = (?) \cdot (?)$ **9.** $18 = (?) \cdot (?)$
$-9 = (?) + (?)$ $-14 = (?) + (?)$ $-11 = (?) + (?)$

For each trinomial, name a pair of factors of the third term whose sum equals the coefficient of the middle term.

SAMPLE: $x^2 - 9x + 18$ *What you say:* $18 = (-6)(-3)$ and
$(-6) + (-3) = -9$

10. $x^2 + 3x + 2$ **14.** $y^2 - 6y + 8$ **18.** $n^2 - 9n + 8$
11. $m^2 + 5m + 4$ **15.** $z^2 - 5z + 6$ **19.** $x^2 + 12x + 20$
12. $t^2 - 5t + 4$ **16.** $y^2 + 5y + 6$ **20.** $b^2 + 12b + 32$
13. $y^2 + 7y + 12$ **17.** $a^2 - 9a + 20$ **21.** $s^2 - 14s + 24$

WRITTEN EXERCISES

Write each number as the product of two positive integers or of two negative integers in all the possible ways.

SAMPLE: 20   *Solution:* $20 = (1)(20) = (2)(10) = (4)(5)$
$= (-1)(-20) = (-2)(-10) = (-4)(-5)$

1. 10	**5.** 16	**9.** 14	**13.** 7
2. 18	**6.** 9	**10.** 8	**14.** 4
3. 15	**7.** 21	**11.** 33	**15.** 1
4. 12	**8.** 24	**12.** 50	**16.** 3

Complete the factoring of each trinomial and check by multiplication.

SAMPLE: $x^2 - 7x + 12 = (x - ?)(x - 4)$

Solution: $(x - 3)(x - 4)$ *Check:* $(x - 3)(x - 4) = x^2 - 7x + 12$

17. $r^2 + 11r + 24 = (r + ?)(r + 3)$

18. $x^2 + 9x + 20 = (x + 4)(x + \;?)$
19. $t^2 + 13t + 30 = (t + 3)(t + \;?)$
20. $r^2 - 9r + 20 = (r - \;?)(r - 5)$
21. $m^2 + 12m + 20 = (m + \;?)(m + 2)$
22. $z^2 - 17z + 30 = (z - 15)(z - \;?)$
23. $w^2 - 11w + 18 = (w - \;?)(w - 9)$
24. $n^2 + 15n + 50 = (n + 5)(n + \;?)$
25. $k^2 + 7k + 12 = (k + \;?)(k + \;?)$
26. $12 + 13x + x^2 = (\;? + x)(1 + x)$
27. $s^2 - 14s + 33 = (s - \;?)(s - \;?)$

Factor each trinomial and check by multiplication.

28. $x^2 + 5x + 6$ **33.** $r^2 - 8r + 7$ **38.** $s^2 + 17s + 30$
29. $y^2 + 8y + 7$ **34.** $s^2 - 10s + 24$ **39.** $k^2 + 6k + 8$
30. $n^2 - 7n + 6$ **35.** $b^2 + 12b + 20$ **40.** $a^2 - 9a + 8$
31. $b^2 - 6b + 8$ **36.** $x^2 - 13x + 30$ **41.** $21 + 10c + c^2$
32. $x^2 + 10x + 24$ **37.** $c^2 + 11c + 30$ **42.** $t^2 - 11t + 30$

B **43.** $48 - 14y + y^2$ **45.** $x^2 - 18xy + 32y^2$ **47.** $s^2 - 11st + 24t^2$
44. $m^2 + 8mn + 7n^2$ **46.** $b^2 + 9bc + 14c^2$ **48.** $p^2 + 14pq + 24q^2$

5–9   Factoring a Product of a Binomial Sum and a Binomial Difference

We have also seen how to find the product of two binomials of which one was a **sum** and the other was a **difference**. For example:

$$(x + 3)(x - 5) = x^2 - 2x - 15$$
$$(x - 2)(x + 6) = x^2 + 4x - 12$$

Now let us consider how we can reverse the process in order to find the binomial factors of such a quadratic trinomial. Study the examples above and you will see that in each of the trinomials the third term is a negative number. The coefficient of the middle term in one case is positive and in the other case is negative.

Suppose that we need to factor the quadratic trinomial $x^2 + 3x - 10$ into a pair of binomial factors. The first term, x^2, has factors $x \cdot x$. What pairs of factors of the third term, -10, can we find? There are these four possibilities:

$$(1)(-10) \qquad (-1)(10) \qquad (2)(-5) \qquad (-2)(5)$$

Which of the pairs should we use so that their **sum** will equal **3**, the coefficient of the middle term?

If your answer is $(-2)(5)$ you are thinking correctly. We can summarize the procedure for factoring $x^2 + 3x - 10$ as follows:

EXAMPLE 1.

$$x^2 + 3x - 10 = (x \quad)(x \quad) \qquad x^2 \text{ is factored as } x \cdot x.$$
$$= (x - \quad)(x + \quad) \qquad \text{One factor of } -10 \text{ is positive}$$
$$\text{and the other factor is negative.}$$
$$= (x - 2)(x + 5) \qquad \text{The product of } -2 \text{ and } 5 \text{ is}$$
$$-10, \text{ and the sum of } -2 \text{ and}$$
$$5 \text{ is } 3.$$

Check: $(x - 2)(x + 5) = x^2 + 3x - 10$

The method for factoring the quadratic trinomial $x^2 - 2x - 24$ is similar to the method used in Example 1. We factor x^2 as $x \cdot x$. The last term, -24, must be the product of a negative factor and a positive factor. The coefficient of the middle term tells us that the **sum** of the numbers that are the factors of -24 must be -2. Example 2 gives a summary of the steps for factoring $x^2 - 2x - 24$:

EXAMPLE 2.

$$x^2 - 2x - 24 = (x \quad)(x \quad) \qquad x^2 \text{ is factored as } x \cdot x.$$
$$= (x - \quad)(x + \quad) \qquad \text{One factor of } -24 \text{ is positive}$$
$$\text{and the other factor is negative}$$
$$= (x - 6)(x + 4) \qquad \text{The product of } -6 \text{ and } 4 \text{ is}$$
$$-24, \text{ and the sum of } -6 \text{ and}$$
$$4 \text{ is } -2.$$

Check: $(x - 6)(x + 4) = x^2 - 2x - 24$

ORAL EXERCISES

Complete each first statement with a pair of factors which may be used as addends to complete the second statement.

SAMPLE: $-12 = (?) \cdot (?)$ *What you say:* $-12 = (2) \cdot (-6)$
$ -4 = (?) + (?)$ $-4 = (2) + (-6)$

1. $-6 = (?) \cdot (?)$ **2.** $-12 = (?) \cdot (?)$ **3.** $-20 = (?) \cdot (?)$
$ \ 5 = (?) + (?)$ $1 = (?) + (?)$ $8 = (?) + (?)$

4. $-10 = (?) \cdot (?)$ **6.** $-20 = (?) \cdot (?)$ **8.** $-18 = (?) \cdot (?)$
$\quad\ 3 = (?) + (?)$ $\qquad 1 = (?) + (?)$ $\qquad -3 = (?) + (?)$

5. $-10 = (?) \cdot (?)$ **7.** $-20 = (?) \cdot (?)$ **9.** $-25 = (?) \cdot (?)$
$\quad -3 = (?) + (?)$ $\qquad -8 = (?) + (?)$ $\qquad\ 0 = (?) + (?)$

For each trinomial name a pair of factors of the third term whose sum equals the coefficient of the middle term.

SAMPLE: $x^2 + 2x - 15$ *What you say:* $-15 = (-3)(5)$
$\qquad\qquad\qquad\qquad\qquad\qquad\qquad (-3) + (5) = 2$

10. $x^2 - 4x - 5$ **13.** $x^2 - 2x - 3$ **16.** $k^2 + k - 42$

11. $n^2 + 5n - 6$ **14.** $m^2 - 3m - 10$ **17.** $r^2 + 5r - 14$

12. $y^2 + y - 6$ **15.** $t^2 - 3t - 18$ **18.** $x^2 + 3xy - 10y^2$

WRITTEN EXERCISES

Factor each trinomial and check by multiplication.

SAMPLE: $x^2 - 2x - 3$ *Solution:* $(x + 1)(x - 3)$

$\qquad\qquad\qquad\qquad\qquad$ *Check:* $(x + 1)(x - 3) = x^2 - 2x - 3$

A

1. $s^2 + s - 12$ **11.** $c^2 + c - 20$ **21.** $a^2 + a - 56$

2. $t^2 + 7t - 18$ **12.** $x^2 - x - 42$ **22.** $t^2 + 5t - 14$

3. $x^2 + 2x - 3$ **13.** $y^2 - 3y - 28$ **23.** $y^2 - 2y - 63$

4. $a^2 - 4a - 5$ **14.** $m^2 + 2m - 24$ **24.** $x^2 - 4x - 60$

5. $b^2 - 3b - 10$ **15.** $a^2 - 4a - 32$ **25.** $r^2 + 17r - 60$

6. $b^2 + 3b - 10$ **16.** $x^2 + 7x - 30$ **26.** $m^2 - 7m - 60$

7. $x^2 + x - 6$ **17.** $w^2 + 10w - 11$ **27.** $z^2 + 5x - 50$

8. $r^2 + 5r - 6$ **18.** $z^2 - 6z - 7$ **28.** $n^2 + 6n - 16$

9. $n^2 - 3n - 18$ **19.** $x^2 + 11x - 26$ **29.** $k^2 - 5k - 14$

10. $k^2 - 4k - 21$ **20.** $b^2 - 2b - 15$ **30.** $y^2 - 6y - 27$

SAMPLE: $x^2 - 3xy - 10y^2$

Solution: $(x + 2y)(x - 5y)$

Check: $(x + 2y)(x - 5y) = x^2 - 3xy - 10y^2$

31. $m^2 - 5mn - 24n^2$ **34.** $x^2 + 6xy - 55y^2$

32. $r^2 - 2rs - 8s^2$ **35.** $b^2 + 10bc - 24c^2$

33. $a^2 + 3ab - 10b^2$ **36.** $c^2 - 5cd - 24d^2$

B

37. $x^2 - 16xz - 57z^2$ **39.** $a^2 - 24ac - 81c^2$

38. $u^2 + 13uv - 68v^2$ **40.** $r^2 + 14rt - 72t^2$

Extension of Factoring

5–10 More Ideas about Factoring Quadratic Trinomials

The same factoring skills that we have developed so far can be applied in factoring more complicated quadratic trinomials. In fact, if a quadratic trinomial has resulted from multiplying one binomial by another, it should be possible for us to begin with the trinomial and reverse the process to discover the two binomial factors.

EXAMPLE 1. Factor $5a^2 + 13a + 6$.

(1) How can we factor the first term, $5a^2$. Since $5a^2 = (5a)(a)$, we write

$$(5a \quad)(a \quad).$$

(2) Since all of the terms are *positive*, we know we have a product of binomial sums, so we write

$$(5a + \ )(a + \ ).$$

(3) What are the pairs of *positive* factors of the third term?

$6 = (1)(6) = (2)(3)$, so we examine the following possibilities:

Possible factors	Middle term
$(5a + 6)(a + 1)$	$5a + 6a = 11a$
$(5a + 1)(a + 6)$	$30a + 1a = 31a$
$(5a + 2)(a + 3)$	$15a + 2a = 17a$
$(5a + 3)(a + 2)$	$10a + 3a = \boxed{13a}$

(4) The last possibility listed gives the correct middle term, $13a$, so we write

$$5a^2 + 13a + 6 = (5a + 3)(a + 2).$$

EXAMPLE 2. Factor $3x^2 - 10x + 8$.

(1) The first term must be factored $(3x)(x)$, so we write

$$(3x \quad)(x \quad).$$

(2) Since the middle term is *negative* and the last term is *positive*, we have a product of binomial differences, so we write

$$(3x - \ )(x - \ ).$$

(3) What are the pairs of *negative* factors of the third term? $8 = (-1)(-8) = (-2)(-4)$, so we examine the following possibilities:

Possible factors	Middle term
$(3x - 1)(x - 8)$	$-24x + (-1x) = -25x$
$(3x - 8)(x - 1)$	$-3x + (-8x) = -11x$
$(3x - 2)(x - 4)$	$-12x + (-2x) = -14x$
$(3x - 4)(x - 2)$	$-6x + (-4x) = \boxed{-10x}$

(4) The last possibility listed gives the correct middle term, $-10x$, so we write

$$3x^2 - 10x + 8 = (3x - 4)(x - 2).$$

EXAMPLE 3.   Factor $6a^2 - 7a - 3$.

(1) The first term, $6a$, can be factored either as $(a)(6a)$ or as $(2a)(3a)$, so we begin with these two possibilities:

$$(a \quad)(6a \quad) \quad \text{and} \quad (2a \quad)(3a \quad)$$

(2) The third term is *negative*, so we know that one of its factors is positive and the other is negative.

(3) The third term, -3, can be factored either as $(-1)(3)$ or as $(1)(-3)$. We look at all eight possible arrangements of these factor pairs in the two possibilities named in the first step, to see which leads to $-7a$ as the middle term.

Possible factors	Middle term
$(a + 1)(6a - 3)$	$-3a + 6a = 3a$
$(a - 3)(6a + 1)$	$a + (-18a) = -17a$
$(a - 1)(6a + 3)$	$3a + (-6a) = -3a$
$(a + 3)(6a - 1)$	$-a + 18a = 17a$
$(2a + 1)(3a - 3)$	$-6a + 3a = -3a$
$(2a - 3)(3a + 1)$	$2a + (-9a) = \boxed{-7a}$
$(2a - 1)(3a + 3)$	$6a + (-3a) = 3a$
$(2a + 3)(3a - 1)$	$-2a + 9a = 7a$

(4) Since the sixth possibility in the list gives the correct middle term, $-7a$, we write

$$6a^2 - 7a - 3 = (2a - 3)(3a + 1).$$

At first you may find it necessary to list all the possible combinations, as we have done, in order to determine the correct factoring of a quadratic trinomial. However, with practice you will often be able to complete the work mentally.

ORAL EXERCISES

Name the missing term in each quadratic trinomial.

1. $(x + 2)(3x - 5) = 3x^2 + (?) - 10$
2. $(4n + 3)(n + 1) = 4n^2 + (?) + 3$
3. $(10b + 4)(b - 1) = 10b^2 + (?) - 4$
4. $(2y + 6)(y + 3) = 2y^2 + (?) + 18$
5. $(3k - 4)(k + 1) = 3k^2 + (?) - 4$
6. $(2n + 9)(n - 2) = 2n^2 + (?) - 18$

For each of the following trinomials, decide whether the factors of the third term are *both positive*, *both negative*, or *one positive* and *one negative*; justify your answer.

SAMPLE: $2x^2 - 11x + 15$

What you say: Both negative; the third term is positive and the middle term is negative.

7. $2a^2 + 13a + 18$ **11.** $9y^2 - 2y - 7$
8. $4x^2 + x - 3$ **12.** $3w^2 + 5w - 8$
9. $4b^2 - 7b + 3$ **13.** $15x^2 - 31x + 10$
10. $5r^2 - 17r - 12$ **14.** $6t^2 - 7t - 3$

WRITTEN EXERCISES

Copy and complete the factoring of each quadratic trinomial.

SAMPLE: $5x^2 + 2x - 7 = (5x + ?)(x - ?)$

Solution: $5x^2 + 2x - 7 = (5x + 7)(x - 1)$

 1. $2x^2 + 3x + 1 = (2x + ?)(x + ?)$
2. $2k^2 + 5k + 3 = (2k + ?)(k + ?)$
3. $5a^2 - 7a + 2 = (5a - ?)(a - ?)$
4. $7y^2 - 10y + 3 = (7y - ?)(y - ?)$
5. $8t^2 + 2t - 3 = (4t + ?)(2t - ?)$
6. $2n^2 + n - 6 = (2n - ?)(n + ?)$

Factor each trinomial and check by multiplication.

SAMPLE: $2a^2 + 3a - 14$ *Solution:* $(2a + 7)(a - 2)$

Check: $(2a + 7)(a - 2) = 2a^2 + 3a - 14$

7. $3x^2 + 4x + 1$ **12.** $3n^2 + 7n - 6$ **17.** $2y^2 - 9y - 5$

8. $t^2 - 4t + 3$ **13.** $4c^2 - 11c - 3$ **18.** $5x^2 - 2x - 7$

9. $2y^2 - 3y + 1$ **14.** $7x^2 - 10x + 3$ **19.** $8t^2 + 2t - 3$

10. $2a^2 + 5a + 3$ **15.** $4y^2 + 4y - 15$ **20.** $5d^2 - 17d - 12$

11. $3m^2 + 8m + 5$ **16.** $5s^2 - 3s - 2$ **21.** $3a^2 + 5a - 8$

Factor each trinomial.

SAMPLE: $2x^2 + xy - 6y^2$ *Solution:* $(2x - 3y)(x + 2y)$

22. $3a^2 - 17ab - 6b^2$ **24.** $5x^2 + 8xy + 3y^2$ **26.** $6c^2 + 11cd - 7d^2$

23. $5r^2 - 8rs + 3s^2$ **25.** $7a^2 + 3ab - 4b^2$ **27.** $2u^2 - 9uv - 5v^2$

B   **28.** $8x^2 - 22x + 15$ **31.** $15x^2 - 2x - 8$

29. $6k^2 + 25k + 14$ **32.** $18y^2 - 19y - 12$

30. $8n^2 - 27n - 20$ **33.** $6z^2 - z - 12$

C   **34.** $24a^2 + 5a - 36$ **36.** $6x^2 - 47xy - 63y^2$

35. $10t^2 + 11st - 18s^2$ **37.** $8c^2 + 26cd - 15d^2$

5–11   Combining Several Types of Factoring

At first glance it may not be obvious that a given polynomial can be factored. However, if you take time to examine the polynomial you may be surprised to find that you can factor it very easily. A basic rule to follow when factoring a polynomial is to look first for a monomial factor common to all of its terms. If there is one, apply the distributive property to write the polynomial as the product of the greatest common monomial factor and a polynomial factor. Then look at the polynomial factor to see if it can be factored as a product of two binomials.

Study the following examples carefully. Notice that in Example 1, the polynomial factor in each case is the difference of two squares. In Example 2, it is a trinomial square, while in Example 3, it is a factorable quadratic trinomial, but not a square.

EXAMPLE 1.   **$5x^2 - 45$**   **$2a^2b - 8b$**

$= 5(x^2 - 9)$ $= 2b(a^2 - 4)$

$= 5(x + 3)(x - 3)$ $= 2b(a + 2)(a - 2)$

EXAMPLE 2.　$-x^2 + 6x - 9$　　　　$2st^2 + 16st + 32s$

$\qquad = -1(x^2 - 6x + 9)$　　　$= 2s(t^2 + 8t + 16)$

$\qquad = -1(x - 3)^2$　　　　　$= 2s(t + 4)^2$

EXAMPLE 3.　$nx^2 - 7nx + 12n$　　　$2abc^3 + 3abc^2 + abc$

$\qquad = n(x^2 - 7x + 12)$　　　$= abc(2c^2 + 3c + 1)$

$\qquad = n(x - 3)(x - 4)$　　　$= abc(2c + 1)(c + 1)$

It is wise to make a practice of always checking the results of factoring by multiplying the factors and comparing the product with the original polynomial.

WRITTEN EXERCISES

Factor each of the following. Begin by using the distributive property to factor out the greatest common monomial factor; then notice that the polynomial factor is the difference of two squares.

SAMPLE:　$3a^2 - 75$　　　　　*Solution:* $3(a^2 - 25) = 3(a + 5)(a - 5)$

1. $5x^2 - 5$　　　　**6.** $10r^2 - 40$　　　　**11.** $20 - 5n^2$

2. $3t^2 - 12$　　　　**7.** $2b^2 - 50$　　　　**12.** $3ab^2 - 27a$

3. $4a^2 - 4$　　　　**8.** $18a^2 - 8$　　　　**13.** $rs^2 - 36r$

4. $2m^2 - 18$　　　　**9.** $75 - 27x^2$　　　　**14.** $x^2y - 4y$

5. $4n^2 - 36$　　　　**10.** $7 - 7m^2$　　　　**15.** $xyz^2 - 81xy$

Factor each of the following. First factor out the greatest common monomial factor, as before; then notice that the polynomial factor is a trinomial square.

SAMPLE:　$xy^2 - 16xy + 64y$

Solution: $x(y^2 - 16y + 64) = x(y - 8)^2$

16. $3x^2 + 18x + 27$　　　　　**22.** $9m^2n^2 - 6m^2n + m^2$

17. $x^2y - 4xy + 4y$　　　　　**23.** $8ax^2 - 8ax + 2a$

18. $2a^2 + 20a + 50$　　　　　**24.** $8n^2 + 24n + 18$

19. $-t^2 + 12t - 36$　　　　　**25.** $4rn^2 - 20rn + 25r$

20. $5n^2 + 20n + 20$　　　　　**26.** $3 - 12z + 12z^2$

21. $abc^2 - 6abc + 9ab$　　　　**27.** $-8b^2 - 8b - 2$

Factor each trinomial product and check by multiplication.

SAMPLE: $10a^2b - 32ab + 6b$

Solution: $2b(5a^2 - 16a + 3) = 2b(5a - 1)(a - 3)$

28. $30s^2 + 3s - 9$

29. $10x^2 + 42x + 36$

30. $4bc^2 + bc - 18b$

31. $4rs^2 + 16rs + 7r$

32. $-4n^2 + 17n - 18$

33. $20a^2 + 22a - 12$

34. $4s^2t^2 - 18s^2t + 18s^2$

35. $25w^2 + 10w - 15$

36. $8xy^2 - 37xy - 15x$

37. $10x^2y + 16xy + 6y$

38. $12a^2 - 2ab - 24b^2$

39. $10b^2c^2 - 38b^2c + 28b^2$

Factor each polynomial.

B **40.** $50x^2 - 20x + 2$

41. $n^3 + 5n^2 + 4n$

42. $12k^2 - 24k - 15$

43. $144a^2 - 49b^4$

44. $-15 + t + 6t^2$

45. $-4y - y^2 + 21$

46. $3x^2 - 300$

47. $12s^2t^2 - 24s^2t + 12s^2$

48. $xyz^2 - 14xyz + 49xy$

49. $-42a - 27ab - 3ab^2$

50. $6x^3y - 26x^2y^2 - 20xy^3$

51. $30h^2 + 4hk - 2k^2$

CHAPTER SUMMARY

Inventory of Structure and Concepts

1. The general form of the **product** of the **sum** of two numbers, r and s, and their **difference** is:

$$(r + s)(r - s) = r^2 - s^2.$$

The product, $r^2 - s^2$, is the difference of two squares. Similarly, a quadratic polynomial that is the **difference** of **two squares** is factored by the application of the reflexive property of equality to the same generalized form.

$$r^2 - s^2 = (r + s)(r - s)$$

2. The general form for the **square** of a **binomial sum** is:

$$(r + s)^2 = r^2 + 2rs + s^2$$

The general form for the **square** of a **binomial difference** is:

$$(r - s)^2 = r^2 - 2rs + s^2$$

Similarly, a quadratic polynomial that is the **square** of a **binomial** is factored by the application of the reflexive property of equality to the same generalized forms:

$$r^2 + 2rs + s^2 = (r + s)^2$$
$$r^2 - 2rs + s^2 = (r - s)^2$$

3. A **monomial** is a **square** if the coefficient is a square and the degree of each variable is even.

4. To factor a **quadratic trinomial** of the form $ax^2 + bx + c$, where a, b, and c are numbers, with a positive, we recognize that
   a. if both b and c are positive, the binomial factors are sums;
   b. if b is negative and c is positive, the binomial factors are differences;
   c. if c is negative, one binomial factor is a sum and the other is a difference.

5. In **factoring** a **polynomial**, the first step should be to determine if there is a monomial factor (other than 1) that is a common factor of each term of the polynomial.

Vocabulary and Spelling

quadratic polynomial (*p. 144*)
difference of two squares (*p. 146*)
trinomial square (*p. 150*)
square number (*p. 151*)
table of squares (*p. 152*)
square monomial (*p. 152*)

symmetric property of equality (*p. 155*)
binomial sum (*p. 164*)
binomial difference (*p. 164*)
monomial factor (*p. 172*)
greatest monomial factor (*p. 172*)

Chapter Test

Find each product.

1. $(x + 5)(x + 3)$ **4.** $(3a + 2)(a - 3)$ **7.** $(x - 9)(2x - 3)$

2. $(t - 8)(t + 8)$ **5.** $(5 - 4y)(5 + 4y)$ **8.** $(3a - 6)(2a + 7)$

3. $(b - 4)(b - 5)$ **6.** $(2a + 5b)(a + 3b)$ **9.** $(2n + 7)(2n - 7)$

Write each of the following as a trinomial square.

10. $(x + 8)^2$ **11.** $(2b - 3)^2$ **12.** $(2r - 5s)^2$

Complete each of the following to make it a trinomial square.

13. $x^2 + (?) + 9$ **14.** $4x^2 - 4xy + (?)$ **15.** $(?) - 18m + 81$

Complete each equation.

16. $64m^2n^2 = (?)^2$ **17.** $324r^{10}s^2 = (?)^2$ **18.** $169x^6y^8z^4 = (?)^2$

Factor each polynomial as completely as possible.

19. $x^2 + 7x + 10$ **23.** $b^2 + 11b - 42$ **27.** $2x^2 - 12x + 18$
20. $a^2 - a - 56$ **24.** $5t^2 + 17t + 14$ **28.** $50a^2 - 20a - 30$
21. $r^2 - 26r + 48$ **25.** $6k^2 - 13k + 7$ **29.** $10r^2s - 32rs + 6s$
22. $x^2 - 25$ **26.** $3x^2 - 48$ **30.** $-3t^2 - 18t - 27$

Chapter Review

5–1   Products of Binomials

Find the missing term to complete each trinomial.

1. $(t + 8)(t + 2) = t^2 + (?) + 16$
2. $(3n + 7)(4n - 3) = (?) + 19n - 21$
3. $(x - 9)(x - 2) = x^2 - 11x + (?)$
4. $(4 + y)(7 - y) = 28 + (?) - y^2$

Write each indicated product as a trinomial.

5. $(9 + y)(5 - y)$ **7.** $(2a - 5)(a - 2)$ **9.** $(-5 + 4x)(1 + x)$
6. $(x - 7)(x + 5)$ **8.** $(3k + 10)(2k - 5)$ **10.** $(b + 6)(2b - 7)$

5–2   Product of the Sum and the Difference of Two Numbers

Write each indicated product as the difference of two squares.

11. $(x + 12)(x - 12)$ **13.** $(7 - 3b)(7 + 3b)$
12. $(15 + k)(15 - k)$ **14.** $(4a - 3x)(4a + 3x)$

5–3   Squaring a Binomial

Write each indicated product as a trinomial square.

15. $(5y - 3)(5y - 3)$ **17.** $(3b + 6)^2$ **19.** $(2a + b)^2$
16. $(m + 7)(m + 7)$ **18.** $(10 - y)^2$ **20.** $(r - 3s)^2$

5–4   Factors and Square Monomials

Name the correct replacement for n in each equation.

21. $n \cdot n = 196$ **23.** $n \cdot n = 144$ **25.** $n^2 = 169$

22. $n \cdot n = 81$ **24.** $n \cdot n = 225$ **26.** $n^2 = 625$

Complete each equation.

27. $400a^2 = (?)^2$ **29.** $576r^4s^2 = (?)^2$ **31.** $(28x^2y)^2 = ?$

28. $324x^2y^2 = (?)^2$ **30.** $m^8n^{10}r^4 = (?)^2$ **32.** $(21r^3s^5)^2 = ?$

5–5   Factoring the Difference of Two Squares

Factor each of these expressions.

33. $k^2 - 49$ **35.** $64x^2 - 1$ **37.** $100 - m^2$

34. $9r^2 - 16$ **36.** $3a^2 - 3b^2$ **38.** $64 - 9z^2$

5–6   Factoring a Trinomial Square of the Form $a^2 + 2ab + b^2$

Factor each trinomial square.

39. $x^2 + 10x + 25$ **41.** $4r^2 + 4r + 1$ **43.** $25n^2 + 30n + 9$

40. $m^2 + 4m + 4$ **42.** $9 + 6x + x^2$ **44.** $9x^2 + 12xy + 4y^2$

5–7   Factoring a Trinomial Square of the Form $a^2 - 2ab + b^2$

Factor each trinomial square.

45. $m^2 - 16m + 64$ **47.** $1 - 12y + 36y^2$ **49.** $16 - 24m + 9m^2$

46. $4x^2 - 12x + 9$ **48.** $9t^2 - 12st + 4s^2$ **50.** $x^2 - 14xy + 49y^2$

5–8   Factoring a Product of Two Binomial Sums or Two Binomial Differences

Factor each trinomial.

51. $x^2 + 9x + 20$ **53.** $x^2 - 9x + 18$ **55.** $z^2 + 13z + 30$

52. $m^2 - 12m + 20$ **54.** $a^2 - 4a + 3$ **56.** $t^2 + 11t + 28$

5–9 Factoring a Product of a Binomial Sum and a Binomial Difference

Factor each trinomial.

57. $n^2 - 2n - 24$ **60.** $m^2 + 5m - 24$ **63.** $y^2 + 15y - 54$

58. $r^2 + 6r - 7$ **61.** $x^2 - x - 20$ **64.** $b^2 - 6b - 27$

59. $t^2 - 7t - 30$ **62.** $a^2 + 2ab - 3b^2$ **65.** $r^2 - 5rs - 14s^2$

5–10 More Ideas about Factoring Quadratic Trinomials

Factor each trinomial.

66. $8m^2 + 2m - 3$ **69.** $8z^2 - 2z - 15$ **72.** $3b^2 + 5bc - 8c^2$

67. $7y^2 + 50y + 7$ **70.** $4x^2 - 21x - 18$ **73.** $6n^2 + 11n - 7$

68. $5a^2 - 12a + 7$ **71.** $20y^2 - 31y + 12$ **74.** $2k^2 - 9k - 5$

5–11 Combining Several Types of Factoring

Factor each expression completely.

75. $7b^2 - 63$ **78.** $10r^2 - 16r + 6$ **81.** $8x^2 - 2x - 36$

76. $36 - 4m^2$ **79.** $ab^2 - 16ab + 64a$ **82.** $-5n^2 - 19n - 14$

77. $5x^2 - 5y^2$ **80.** $3m^2n^2 + 30m^2n + 75m^2$ **83.** $5t^2 - 30t + 45$

Review of Skills

For each figure write the ratio of the number of shaded squares to the total number of squares.

SAMPLE: *Solution:* $\dfrac{\text{shaded squares}}{\text{total squares}} = \dfrac{6}{16}$

1.   **2.** 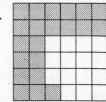   **3.**

4.   **5.**   **6.**

Complete each set of fractions according to the pattern.

7. $\{\frac{1}{4}, \frac{2}{8}, \frac{3}{12}, (?), (?), (?), (?), \frac{8}{32}, \frac{9}{36}\}$

8. $\{\frac{1}{3}, \frac{2}{6}, \frac{3}{9}, (?), (?), (?), (?), (?), \frac{9}{27}, \frac{10}{30}\}$

9. $\{\frac{2}{5}, \frac{4}{10}, \frac{6}{15}, (?), (?), (?), (?), \frac{18}{45}\}$

Complete each of the following to make a true statement.

10. $\frac{1}{2} = \frac{?}{10}$

13. $\frac{2}{3} = \frac{?}{21}$

16. $\frac{1}{4} = \frac{5}{?}$

11. $\frac{1}{?} = \frac{4}{20}$

14. $\frac{3}{4} = \frac{?}{8}$

17. $\frac{5}{2} = \frac{?}{6}$

12. $\frac{7}{8} = \frac{?}{24}$

15. $\frac{3}{10} = \frac{24}{?}$

18. $\frac{6}{1} = \frac{?}{4}$

Use one of the symbols =, >, or < to complete each of the following.

19. $\frac{1}{2} \; ? \; \frac{7}{10}$

21. $\frac{2}{3} \; ? \; \frac{3}{4}$

23. $\frac{7}{4} \; ? \; \frac{11}{4}$

20. $\frac{4}{5} \; ? \; \frac{8}{10}$

22. $\frac{5}{8} \; ? \; \frac{5}{10}$

24. $\frac{4}{7} \; ? \; \frac{4}{11}$

Show that each statement is true.

SAMPLE: $\frac{1}{2} = \frac{5}{10}$ *Solution:* $\frac{1}{2} = \frac{1}{2} \cdot \frac{5}{5} = \frac{5}{10}.$

25. $\frac{5}{8} = \frac{15}{24}$

27. $\frac{5}{3} = \frac{35}{21}$

29. $\frac{25}{75} = \frac{1}{3}$

26. $\frac{1}{3} = \frac{7}{21}$

28. $\frac{4}{10} = \frac{2}{5}$

30. $\frac{7}{2} = \frac{28}{8}$

Write each percent as a fraction and as a decimal.

SAMPLE: 35%   *Solution:* $\frac{35}{100}$; 0.35

31. 29%   **33.** 45%   **35.** 9%   **37.** 15%

32. 73%   **34.** 150%   **36.** 68%   **38.** 98%

Draw a number line like the one shown and on it mark points *A − H*, the graphs of the following numbers.

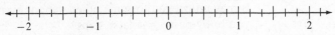

39. $A; \frac{1}{3}$

41. $C; \frac{7}{6}$

43. $E; -1\frac{2}{3}$

45. $G; -\frac{12}{6}$

40. $B; -\frac{3}{2}$

42. $D; -\frac{2}{3}$

44. $F; 2\frac{1}{3}$

46. $H; \frac{3}{6}$

CHECK POINT
FOR EXPERTS

Flow Charts with Decisions and Loops

A most important use of a flow chart is in planning the steps of a problem that involves **making a decision**.

The flow chart shown here lists the basic steps used in sharpening a pencil. At one point a decision must be made, as indicated by the question in the **diamond-shaped box**. If the answer to the question is "Yes," the program stops. If the answer is "No," a **loop** built into the chart takes you back to the first step. This looping procedure may be repeated.

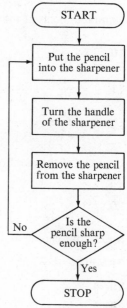

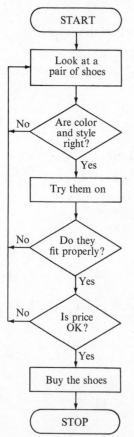

The next flow chart shows the steps for solving a problem in which decision-making is needed at more than one point.

The problem involves the buying of a pair of shoes. Study the chart and see that if the response is "No" at any of the three decision points indicated by the diamond-shaped boxes, there is a loop which takes you back to the start of the program. Of course, a loop need not always take you back to the *first* step. It may return you to some other step, or even cause you to by-pass some later steps.

Questions

1. Suggest suitable entries for completing the flow chart for starting a car.
2. Copy and complete the other flow chart, for finding the solution set of the sentence $x + 1 > 3$, if the domain of the variable is $\{0, 2, 4, 6, 8\}$. Use the program to find the solution set.

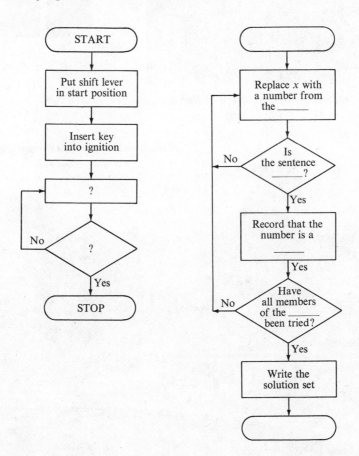

3. Design a flow chart that will give the solution set of the sentence $n - 1 < 5$ if the domain of the variable is $\{1, 3, 5, 7, 9\}$. Then use the program to find the solution set.
4. Design a flow chart that will give the set of principal values for $\sqrt{t}$ if the domain of t is $\{-4, -1, 1, 4\}$.
5. Design a flow chart that will indicate which members of this set are even numbers: $\{10, 7, 36, 5, 0\}$. Use the fact that a number is even if division by 2 gives a remainder of 0.

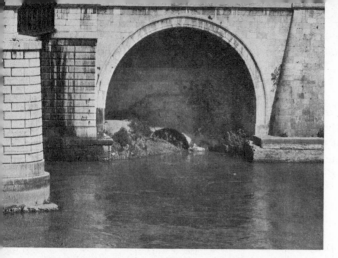

The Cloaca Maxima, a sewer of ancient Rome . . .

A modern sewage-treatment plant . . .

Working with Fractions

When man first found removal of wastes and drainage necessary, he discharged these liquids directly into nearby streams. Since water can assimilate a certain amount of natural pollution without harm to water quality, this was not serious in ancient times; in the sixth century, B.C., the Cloaca Maxima was built to drain the marsh on which the Roman Forum was situated. With today's rapidly expanding populations and discharge of large quantities of wastes from industries, the assimilation capacities of many bodies of water are being exceeded, so waste treatment is necessary to reduce pollutants to acceptable limits. Modern sewage-treatment plants often occupy many acres of land and treat thousands of gallons of water, employing highly complex chemical and biological research in the process. Solving water pollution control problems involves modern science and technology to an ever increasing degree.

Simplifying Fractions

6–1 Algebraic Fractions

If a numeral is written in the form $\dfrac{a}{b}$, where a represents any integer and b represents a nonzero integer, we call the numeral a fraction. The upper number, a, is called the numerator of the fraction and the lower number, b, is called its denominator.

$$\text{numerator} \rightarrow \quad \dfrac{a}{b} \quad \leftarrow \text{denominator}$$

In this chapter we shall work with familiar fractions like

$$\tfrac{2}{3}, \ -\tfrac{7}{8}, \ -\tfrac{3}{4}, \quad \text{and} \quad \tfrac{5}{2},$$

as well as with fractions which involve variables, such as

$$\frac{n}{2}, \frac{5}{y}, \quad \text{and} \quad \frac{x+2}{x^2+5x+6}.$$

Just as **5** can be written in fractional form as $\frac{5}{1}$, so **5n** can be written $\frac{5n}{1}$. In general, we shall refer to all of these various forms as **algebraic fractions**.

When a fraction involves a variable, the number represented by the fraction depends, of course, upon the number by which the variable is replaced. Since the fractional form indicates division, and division by zero is not defined, we agree that a fraction represents a number only when its denominator is not zero. Thus the replacement set for each variable in a fraction must be restricted by excluding any numbers which result in a value of zero for the denominator. For example, $\frac{15}{x}$ means **15** divided by **x**, so we must state the restriction $x \neq 0$. Study the following table showing the restrictions needed on the replacement sets of the variables in the fractions given.

Fractions	Restrictions on the variables
$\dfrac{15}{x-3}$	$x \neq 3$
$\dfrac{x-2}{7}$	no restriction
$\dfrac{5}{ab}$	$a \neq 0,\ b \neq 0$
$\dfrac{x+3}{x^2-1} = \dfrac{x+3}{(x-1)(x+1)}$	$x \neq 1,\ x \neq -1$
$\dfrac{5m+2}{m^2-m-6} = \dfrac{5m+2}{(m-3)(m+2)}$	$m \neq 3,\ m \neq -2$

In the last two of the examples, notice that we have factored each denominator, and then examined each factor to see what value of the variable gives that factor a value of 0.

ORAL EXERCISES

Name any restrictions on the variable in each fraction.

SAMPLE: $\dfrac{10}{k+3}$ *What you say:* $k \neq -3$.

1. $\dfrac{3}{5b}$ **2.** $\dfrac{-2}{y-5}$ **3.** $\dfrac{5x+3}{x+4}$

4. $\dfrac{10 + 7}{x}$ **6.** $\dfrac{4 + 5}{2z}$ **8.** $\dfrac{-6}{4 - t^2}$

5. $\dfrac{3m}{4 - m}$ **7.** $\dfrac{10}{a^2}$ **9.** $\dfrac{5n + 6}{10 - 2n}$

WRITTEN EXERCISES

Write each of the following as a fraction, and name any restrictions on the variables.

1. $10 \div y$ **5.** 10 **9.** $a \div b$

2. $-18 \div 7$ **6.** $3x$ **10.** $x \div 3y$

3. $-25 \div b$ **7.** $m \div (m - 2)$ **11.** $t \div (3n + 15)$

4. $(x + 3) \div 10$ **8.** $(y + 3) \div y$ **12.** $(x + 10) \div 2b$

Write each of the following so it is not in fractional form.

SAMPLE: $\dfrac{12x}{3}$ *Solution:* $4x$

13. $\dfrac{15}{3}$ **16.** $\dfrac{-18k}{6}$ **19.** $\dfrac{6x + 10y}{2}$

14. $\dfrac{100 + 6}{53}$ **17.** $\dfrac{7x + 9x}{-2}$ **20.** $\dfrac{-b^2 + 11b^2}{-5}$

15. $\dfrac{10y}{2}$ **18.** $\dfrac{24t}{8 - 2}$ **21.** $\dfrac{21}{x^2 + 7 - x^2}$

Find the number represented by each algebraic fraction if $a = 3$, $x = 2$, and $y = 5$.

22. $\dfrac{a + 4}{y}$ **26.** $\dfrac{xy}{-a}$ **30.** $\dfrac{5a}{a + x + y}$

23. $\dfrac{2x + y}{3}$ **27.** $\dfrac{a^2 + 10}{3y}$ **31.** $\dfrac{a^2 + x}{6 + y}$

24. $\dfrac{-2a}{5}$ **28.** $\dfrac{x - 2y}{-1}$ **32.** $\dfrac{a^2 - x^2}{y^2}$

25. $\dfrac{ax}{y}$ **29.** $\dfrac{1}{a + x}$ **33.** $\dfrac{y^2 - x^2}{a^2 - x^2}$

Factor the denominator of each fraction. Then write the set of excluded values of the variable.

SAMPLE: $\dfrac{2x + 5}{x^2 - 8x + 15}$ *Solution:* $\dfrac{2x + 5}{(x - 5)(x - 3)}$

Excluded values: $\{5, 3\}$

B 34. $\dfrac{5k}{k^2 - 9}$ 37. $\dfrac{7t - 8}{t^2 + 8t + 12}$ 40. $\dfrac{10s}{3s^2 - 5s - 2}$

35. $\dfrac{4b + 3}{b^2 + 5b + 6}$ 38. $\dfrac{-5}{x^2 - 3x - 28}$ 41. $\dfrac{-3k + 10}{k^2 - 8k + 15}$

36. $\dfrac{5 - 4n}{n^2 - 4n - 21}$ 39. $\dfrac{y + 3}{y^2 + 5y - 14}$ 42. $\dfrac{t^2 + 5}{64 - t^2}$

6–2 Equivalent Fractions

Notice that the figures that follow are all the same size. Do you see that the same portion of each figure is shaded but that three different fractions are used to indicate the shaded portions?

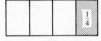   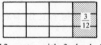

4 parts, with 1 shaded   12 parts, with 3 shaded   8 parts, with 2 shaded

We say that $\frac{1}{4}$, $\frac{3}{12}$, and $\frac{2}{8}$ are **equivalent fractions**. That is, each one of these fractions represents the same number. One way of demonstrating this fact is to carry out each indicated division, and then compare the resulting **decimal fractions**.

$$\tfrac{1}{4} = 1.00 \div 4 = 0.25; \qquad \tfrac{3}{12} = 3.00 \div 12 = 0.25;$$

$$\tfrac{2}{8} = 2.00 \div 8 = 0.25$$

Thus we conclude that $\frac{1}{4} = \frac{3}{12} = \frac{2}{8}$.

Another way to decide would be to use the **multiplicative property of one** to change the three fractions into equivalent fractions with a common denominator and then compare.

$$\tfrac{1}{4} = \tfrac{1}{4} \cdot 1 = \tfrac{1}{4} \cdot \tfrac{6}{6} = \tfrac{6}{24}; \qquad \tfrac{3}{12} = \tfrac{3}{12} \cdot 1 = \tfrac{3}{12} \cdot \tfrac{2}{2} = \tfrac{6}{24};$$

$$\tfrac{2}{8} = \tfrac{2}{8} \cdot 1 = \tfrac{2}{8} \cdot \tfrac{3}{3} = \tfrac{6}{24}.$$

Since each number equals $\frac{6}{24}$, we see that $\frac{1}{4} = \frac{3}{12} = \frac{2}{8}$.

In comparing two fractions, we can also use a method that we call the **cross-product method**, illustrated in the following examples.

EXAMPLE 1.   Are $\frac{1}{2}$ and $\frac{4}{8}$ equivalent fractions?

We multiply the numerator of one fraction by the denominator of the other, as suggested by the arrows in the diagram, and compare the cross-products.

$$\frac{1}{2} \diagdown \frac{4}{8}$$

$1 \cdot 8$	$2 \cdot 4$
8	8

The **cross-products** are **equal**.

Also, since $\frac{1}{2} = \frac{1}{2} \cdot \frac{4}{4} = \frac{4}{8}$, the **fractions** are **equivalent**.

EXAMPLE 2. Are $\frac{3}{8}$ and $\frac{4}{12}$ equivalent fractions?

Finding the cross-products, we have:

$$\frac{3}{8} \diagdown \frac{4}{12}$$

$3 \cdot 12$	$8 \cdot 4$
36	32

Since $36 > 32$, the **cross-products** are **not equal**.

Now notice that

$$\frac{3}{8} = \frac{3}{8} \cdot \frac{3}{3} = \frac{9}{24} \quad \text{and} \quad \frac{4}{12} = \frac{4}{12} \cdot \frac{2}{2} = \frac{8}{24}.$$

Since $\frac{9}{24} > \frac{8}{24}$, the **fractions** are **not equivalent**, and $\frac{3}{8} > \frac{4}{12}$.

EXAMPLE 3. Are $\dfrac{-7}{8}$ and $\dfrac{6}{-7}$ equivalent fractions?

We note that $\dfrac{6}{-7} = \dfrac{-6}{7}$, so we compare the cross-products of $\dfrac{-7}{8}$ and $\dfrac{-6}{7}$.

$$\frac{-7}{8} \diagdown \frac{-6}{7}$$

$-7 \cdot 7$	$8 \cdot -6$
-49	-48

Since $-49 < -48$, the **cross-products** are **not equal**.

Changing the fractions to equivalent ones with the common denominator **56**,

$$\frac{-7}{8} = \frac{-7}{8} \cdot \frac{7}{7} = \frac{-49}{56} \quad \text{and} \quad \frac{-6}{7} = \frac{-6}{7} \cdot \frac{8}{8} = \frac{-48}{56}.$$

Since $\dfrac{-49}{56} < \dfrac{-48}{56}$ the **fractions** are **not equivalent**, and $\dfrac{-7}{8} < \dfrac{6}{-7}$.

From Examples 1–3, we make the following assumptions:

Given two fractions $\dfrac{a}{b}$ and $\dfrac{c}{d}$, where *a* and *c* are any integers and *b* and *d* are both positive integers,

$$\text{if } a \cdot d < b \cdot c, \text{ then } \frac{a}{b} < \frac{c}{d},$$

$$\text{if } a \cdot d = b \cdot c, \text{ then } \frac{a}{b} = \frac{c}{d},$$

$$\text{if } a \cdot d > b \cdot c, \text{ then } \frac{a}{b} > \frac{c}{d}.$$

Are the fractions $\dfrac{-3x}{8}$ and $\dfrac{9x}{-24}$ equivalent? We can answer this question by writing $\dfrac{9x}{-24}$ as $\dfrac{-9x}{24}$ and comparing the cross products.

$$\frac{-3x}{8} \diagdown\diagup \frac{-9x}{24}$$

$-3x \cdot 24$	$8 \cdot -9x$
$-72x$	$-72x$

Do you agree that the cross-products are equal? So $\dfrac{-3x}{8} = \dfrac{9x}{-24}$.

ORAL EXERCISES

For each of the following, replace *x* so that the fraction describes the shaded portion of the figure.

SAMPLE: $\dfrac{2}{x}$ *What you say:* Since $\frac{2}{5}$ of the figure is shaded, replace *x* by 5.

1. $\dfrac{2}{x}$    4. $\dfrac{6}{x}$ 7. $\dfrac{11}{x}$

2. $\dfrac{5}{x}$ 5. $\dfrac{x}{18}$ 8. $\dfrac{x}{4}$

3. $\dfrac{x}{8}$ 6. $\dfrac{x}{6}$ 9. $\dfrac{x}{35}$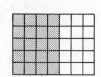

10. $\frac{x}{6}$ **11.** $\frac{3}{x}$ **12.** $\frac{5}{x}$

WRITTEN EXERCISES

Complete each set of equivalent fractions according to the pattern shown; assume that no denominator equals zero.

SAMPLE: $\left\{\dfrac{t}{4}, \dfrac{2t}{8}, \dfrac{3t}{12}, (?), (?), (?)\dfrac{7t}{28}\right\}$

Solution: $\left\{\dfrac{t}{4}, \dfrac{2t}{8}, \dfrac{3t}{12}, \dfrac{4t}{16}, \dfrac{5t}{20}, \dfrac{6t}{24}, \dfrac{7t}{28}\right\}$

 1. $\left\{\dfrac{1}{2}, \dfrac{2}{4}, \dfrac{3}{6}, (?), (?), (?), (?), (?), \dfrac{9}{18}\right\}$

2. $\left\{\dfrac{1}{5}, \dfrac{2}{10}, \dfrac{3}{15}, (?), (?), (?), (?), (?), (?), \dfrac{10}{50}\right\}$

3. $\left\{\dfrac{x}{3}, \dfrac{2x}{6}, \dfrac{3x}{9}, (?), (?), (?), (?), (?), \dfrac{9x}{27}\right\}$

4. $\left\{\dfrac{2}{3n}, \dfrac{4}{6n}, \dfrac{6}{9n}, (?), (?), (?), (?), (?), (?), \dfrac{20}{30n}\right\}$

5. $\left\{\dfrac{-3}{5}, \dfrac{-6}{10}, \dfrac{-9}{15}, \dfrac{-12}{20}, (?), (?), (?), (?), (?), \dfrac{-30}{50}\right\}$

6. $\left\{\dfrac{-5}{y}, \dfrac{-10}{2y}, \dfrac{-15}{3y}, (?), (?), (?), (?), (?), (?), \dfrac{-50}{10y}\right\}$

7. $\left\{\dfrac{2a}{-3}, \dfrac{4a}{-6}, \dfrac{6a}{-9}, (?), (?), (?), (?), (?), \dfrac{18a}{-27}\right\}$

For each of the two figures, write a fraction to indicate the portion that is shaded; then tell whether or not the two fractions you have written are equivalent.

SAMPLE: 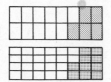   *Solution:* $\frac{5}{16}$ and $\frac{10}{32}$; they are equivalent.

8.

9.

10.

11.   **12.**   **13.**

Use the cross-product method to show that the fractions in each pair are equivalent. Assume that no denominator is equal to zero.

SAMPLE: $\dfrac{-5}{k}, \dfrac{25}{-5k}$ *Solution:*

$$\begin{array}{c|c} -5 \cdot 5k & k \cdot -25 \\ -25k & -25k \end{array} \qquad \dfrac{-5}{k} = \dfrac{25}{-5k}$$

14. $\frac{4}{7}, \frac{20}{35}$ **18.** $\dfrac{-10x}{15}, \dfrac{-2x}{3}$ **22.** $\dfrac{n+1}{5}, \dfrac{3(n+1)}{15}$

15. $\dfrac{-2}{3}, \dfrac{-18}{27}$ **19.** $\dfrac{-6k}{45}, \dfrac{2k}{-15}$ **23.** $\dfrac{x^2}{2}, \dfrac{23x^2}{46}$

16. $\dfrac{7}{-8}, \dfrac{-21}{24}$ **20.** $\dfrac{7r}{-n}, \dfrac{-42r}{6n}$ **24.** $\dfrac{-3ab}{2}, \dfrac{9ab}{-6}$

17. $\dfrac{8b}{36}, \dfrac{2b}{9}$ **21.** $\dfrac{-9z}{21}, \dfrac{3z}{-7}$ **25.** $\dfrac{4y^2}{1}, \dfrac{76y^2}{19}$

In each exercise, express both fractions either in decimal form or as equivalent fractions with a common denominator; then use one of the symbols =, >, <, to indicate the relationship between the two numbers that the fractions represent, assuming that each variable represents a positive integer.

SAMPLE: $\frac{4}{5}, \frac{14}{20}$ *Solution:* $4 \div 5 = 0.8;\ 14 \div 20 = 0.7$
$$\frac{4}{5} > \frac{14}{20}$$

26. $\frac{18}{24}, \frac{3}{4}$ **29.** $\dfrac{28k}{40}, \dfrac{7k}{10}$ **32.** $\dfrac{-6ab}{8}, \dfrac{3ab}{-4}$

27. $\dfrac{5x}{2}, \dfrac{20x}{8}$ **30.** $\dfrac{9z^2}{10}, \dfrac{45z^2}{-50}$ **33.** $\dfrac{5r^2}{-8}, \dfrac{-15r^2}{24}$

28. $\dfrac{-2y}{5}, \dfrac{-14y}{35}$ **31.** $\dfrac{8xy}{16}, \dfrac{6xy}{12}$ **34.** $\dfrac{12ab^2}{35}, \dfrac{3ab^2}{8}$

Use the cross-product method to decide which symbol, =, >, or <, will make each of the following a true statement.

SAMPLE: $\frac{3}{8} ? \frac{9}{20}$ *Solution:*

$$\begin{array}{c|c} 3 \cdot 20 & 8 \cdot 9 \\ 60 & 72 \end{array} \qquad \frac{3}{8} < \frac{9}{20}$$

B **35.** $\dfrac{-3}{5}$? $\dfrac{-8}{24}$ **38.** $\dfrac{-4}{18}$? $\dfrac{-5}{7}$ **41.** $\dfrac{-9}{8}$? $\dfrac{8}{-7}$

36. $\dfrac{-5}{10}$? $\dfrac{5}{-10}$ **39.** $\dfrac{3}{8}$? $\dfrac{3}{7}$ **42.** $\dfrac{10}{6}$? $\dfrac{10}{4}$

37. $\dfrac{-7}{7}$? $\dfrac{-10}{3}$ **40.** $\dfrac{-4}{10}$? $\dfrac{40}{100}$ **43.** $\dfrac{6}{10}$? $\dfrac{4}{10}$

6–3 Using Decimal Fractions

Earlier we said that fractions like $\dfrac{7}{8}$ and $\dfrac{-3}{4}$ can be written as decimal fractions. This is accomplished simply by completing the indicated division. Do you see that in Examples 1 and 2 each division has a zero remainder?

EXAMPLE 1. $\dfrac{7}{8}$:

$$
\begin{array}{r}
0.875 \\
8\overline{)7.000} \\
6\,4 \\
\hline
60 \\
56 \\
\hline
40 \\
40 \\
\hline
0
\end{array}
$$

$$\dfrac{7}{8} = 0.875$$

EXAMPLE 2. $\dfrac{-3}{4}$:

$$
\begin{array}{r}
-0.75 \\
4\overline{)-3.0} \\
2\,8 \\
\hline
20 \\
20 \\
\hline
0
\end{array}
$$

$$\dfrac{-3}{4} = -0.75$$

We say that the **decimal equivalent** of $\frac{7}{8}$ is **0.875**; the **decimal equivalent** of $\dfrac{-3}{4}$ is **−0.75** Numbers like 0.875 and −0.75 are called **terminating decimals,** since each division finally ended.

You will recall that **0.875** is read **eight hundred seventy-five thousandths,** and **−0.75** is read **negative seventy-five hundredths.** The chart below shows the **place value system** for decimal notation. The value of each place to the right of the decimal point is given in both fractional and decimal form.

Hundreds	*Tens*	*Ones*	·	*Tenths*	*Hundredths*	*Thousandths*	*Ten-thousandths*
100	10	1		$\dfrac{1}{10}$	$\dfrac{1}{100}$	$\dfrac{1}{1000}$	$\dfrac{1}{10,000}$
100	10	1		0.1	0.01	0.001	0.0001

You can use this chart to write decimal numerals in **expanded form**, and thus understand better the meaning of such decimal fractions as **0.734** and **48.25**.

EXAMPLE 3. $0.734 = \frac{7}{10} + \frac{3}{100} + \frac{4}{1000} = \frac{734}{1000}$

$\qquad\qquad\ \ 0.734 = 0.7 + 0.03 + 0.004 = 0.734$

EXAMPLE 4. $48.25 = 40 + 8 + \frac{2}{10} + \frac{5}{100} = 48\frac{25}{100}$

$\qquad\qquad\ \ 48.25 = 40 + 8 + 0.2 + 0.05 = 48.25$

Do you see from Examples 1–4 that fractions and decimal fractions are simply different ways of expressing the same numbers?

$$\tfrac{1}{4} = 0.25 = \tfrac{25}{100} \qquad \tfrac{3}{8} = 0.375 = \tfrac{375}{1000}$$

You will recall from previous experience that the divisions indicated by some fractions do *not* have zero remainders.

EXAMPLE 5. $\tfrac{2}{3}$:

$$\begin{array}{r} 0.666\ldots \\ 3\overline{)2.000} \\ \underline{1\,8} \\ 20 \\ \underline{18} \\ 20 \\ \underline{18} \\ 2 \end{array}$$

The three dots indicate that the digits in the quotient repeat on and on in the same way. Instead of using the three dots, we usually write **0.666 . . .** as **0.6̄**, with the bar indicating that the **6** is the repeating digit.

EXAMPLE 6. $\tfrac{12}{33}$:

$$\begin{array}{r} .3636\ldots \\ 33\overline{)12.0000} \\ \underline{9\,9} \\ 2\,10 \\ \underline{1\,98} \\ 120 \\ \underline{99} \\ 210 \\ \underline{198} \\ 12 \end{array}$$

The three dots indicate that the pair of digits **3** and **6**, repeat on and on in the same way, so we write **0.3636 . . .** as **0.3̄6̄**, with the bar indicating that the **36** keeps repeating.

A decimal fraction such as **0.6̄** or **0.3̄6̄**, that has a repeating digit or sequence of digits, is called a **repeating decimal**.

ORAL EXERCISES

Read each of the following numerals to show its meaning.

SAMPLE: 0.47   *What you say:* Forty-seven hundredths

1. 0.63	**5.** 0.08	**9.** -6.75
2. 0.96	**6.** -0.76	**10.** 0.40
3. 2.7	**7.** 0.3615	**11.** 0.008
4. 0.694	**8.** 0.309	**12.** 134.275

Tell whether each decimal fraction is terminating or repeating.

13. 0.12563	**16.** $0.\overline{3}$	**19.** 0.111 . . .
14. $0.\overline{14}$	**17.** 0.025	**20.** 0.0808
15. 0.632 . . .	**18.** 0.637	**21.** 0.33333

Give the meaning of the red digit in each decimal fraction.

SAMPLE: 35.075   *What you say:* Seven hundredths

22. 0.962	**25.** 147.01	**28.** 0.8752
23. 0.0476	**26.** 4.896	**29.** 0.9381
24. 63.09	**27.** 9.074	**30.** 0.0027

WRITTEN EXERCISES

Complete the following table for each fraction.

	Fraction	Decimal Equivalent	Expanded Fractional Form	Expanded Decimal Form
SAMPLE:	$\frac{9}{20}$	0.45	$\frac{4}{10} + \frac{5}{100} = \frac{45}{100}$	$0.4 + 0.05 = 0.45$
1.	$\frac{3}{8}$	?	?	?
2.	$\frac{7}{20}$	?	?	?
3.	$\frac{1}{4}$	?	?	?
4.	$\frac{1}{2}$	?	?	?
5.	$\frac{3}{4}$	?	?	?
6.	$\frac{5}{8}$	?	?	?
7.	$\frac{1}{8}$	?	?	?
8.	$\frac{12}{25}$	?	?	?

A

Express each fraction as a repeating decimal.

SAMPLE: $\frac{10}{33}$

$$
\begin{array}{r}
0.3030\ldots \\
33\overline{)10.0000} \\
9\;9 \\
\hline
100 \\
99 \\
\hline
100 \\
99 \\
\hline
1
\end{array}
$$

$\frac{10}{33} = 0.\overline{30}$

9. $\frac{1}{3}$ **12.** $\frac{3}{11}$ **15.** $\frac{8}{6}$

10. $\frac{2}{9}$ **13.** $\frac{1}{9}$ **16.** $\frac{7}{11}$

11. $\frac{-2}{3}$ **14.** $\frac{5}{3}$ **17.** $\frac{1}{7}$

Simplify each of the following. Write your answer both in fractional and in decimal form.

SAMPLE 1: $\frac{3}{10} + \frac{6}{100} + \frac{1}{1000}$ *Solution:* $\frac{361}{1000}$; 0.361

SAMPLE 2: $0.2 + 0.05 + 0.003$ *Solution:* 0.253; $\frac{253}{1000}$

18. $\frac{7}{10} + \frac{9}{100} + \frac{4}{1000}$ **22.** $\frac{4}{10} + \frac{0}{100} + \frac{9}{1000}$

19. $0.3 + 0.08 + 0.006$ **23.** $0.6 + 0.007 + 0.0004$

20. $0.9 + 0.08 + 0.001$ **24.** $0.1 + 0.02 + 0.003 + 0.0005$

21. $\frac{5}{10} + \frac{6}{100} + \frac{7}{1000} + \frac{2}{10,000}$ **25.** $\frac{-8}{10} + \frac{-2}{100} + \frac{-7}{1000}$

Draw a number line like the one shown, and on it mark points $A - L$, the graphs of the numbers paired with those letters.

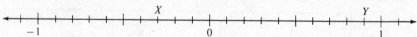

SAMPLE 1: $X: \frac{-3}{10}$ *Solution:* See the number line.

SAMPLE 2: $Y: 0.9$ *Solution:* See the number line.

26. $A: -\frac{1}{2}$ **29.** $D: -\frac{3}{5}$ **32.** $G: \frac{-9}{10}$ **35.** $J: -0.3$

27. $B: -0.6$ **30.** $E: \frac{5}{10}$ **33.** $H: 0.3$ **36.** $K: \frac{9}{10}$

28. $C: \frac{1}{2}$ **31.** $F: -0.5$ **34.** $I: \frac{-3}{10}$ **37.** $L: \frac{0}{10}$

Rewrite each expression so that the numerical portion is a decimal numeral.

SAMPLE: $\dfrac{4ab}{5}$ *Solution:* $\dfrac{4ab}{5} = \dfrac{4}{5}ab = 0.8ab$

38. $\dfrac{3xy}{10}$ **41.** $\dfrac{a^2b^2}{4}$ **44.** $\dfrac{7w}{100}$

39. $\frac{5}{8}r^2s^2$ **42.** $\dfrac{-5yz}{4}$ **45.** $-\dfrac{39xy}{1000}$

40. $\dfrac{6mn}{4}$ **43.** $\dfrac{3ab}{5}$ **46.** $\dfrac{wx}{8}$

Express as a decimal numeral the value of each expression when the variable is replaced by 10.

SAMPLE: $\dfrac{9}{x} + \dfrac{6}{x^2} + \dfrac{3}{x^3}$ *Solution:* $\dfrac{9}{10} + \dfrac{6}{10^2} + \dfrac{3}{10^3} = 0.963$

B   **47.** $\dfrac{2}{y} + \dfrac{5}{y^2} + \dfrac{7}{y^3}$ **49.** $\dfrac{-4}{c} + \dfrac{-8}{c^2} + \dfrac{-7}{c^3}$

48. $\dfrac{3}{b} + \dfrac{8}{b^2} + \dfrac{2}{b^3} + \dfrac{5}{b^4}$ **50.** $5b^2 + 6b + \dfrac{2}{b} + \dfrac{8}{b^2}$

6–4   Reducing Algebraic Fractions to Lowest Terms

You have used the idea that equivalent fractions are simply different ways for naming the same number. For example, the two fractions $\frac{1}{2}$ and $\frac{5}{10}$ are equivalent; so are the fractions $\dfrac{2xy}{3}$ and $\dfrac{6xy}{9}$. To verify these, we can use the familiar multiplicative property of one, together with the idea that any fraction having the same nonzero numerator and denominator represents the number 1.

EXAMPLE 1. $\frac{1}{2} = \frac{1}{2} \cdot 1 = \frac{1}{2} \cdot \frac{5}{5} = \frac{5}{10}$.

EXAMPLE 2. $\dfrac{2xy}{3} = \dfrac{2xy}{3} \cdot 1 = \dfrac{2xy}{3} \cdot \dfrac{3}{3} = \dfrac{6xy}{9}$.

We can state this idea as the following property of fractions:

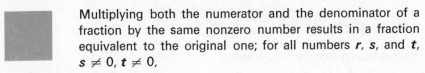

Multiplying both the numerator and the denominator of a fraction by the same nonzero number results in a fraction equivalent to the original one; for all numbers *r*, *s*, and *t*, $s \neq 0, t \neq 0,$

$$\frac{r}{s} = \frac{rt}{st}.$$

By a similar process we can use division to simplify fractions like $\dfrac{9}{15}$ and $\dfrac{5m}{7m}$ as follows:

EXAMPLE 3. $\dfrac{9}{15} = \dfrac{3 \cdot 3}{5 \cdot 3} = \dfrac{3}{5} \cdot \dfrac{3}{3} = \dfrac{3}{5} \cdot 1 = \dfrac{3}{5}$

Notice that we can think of this same process as dividing both the numerator and the denominator by the common factor, 3. Thus,

$$\frac{9}{15} = \frac{9 \div 3}{15 \div 3} = \frac{3}{5}.$$

EXAMPLE 4. $\dfrac{5m}{7m} = \dfrac{5 \cdot m}{7 \cdot m} = \dfrac{5}{7} \cdot \dfrac{m}{m} = \dfrac{5}{7} \cdot 1 = \dfrac{5}{7}$

Do you agree that the result is the same when both the numerator and the denominator are divided by m, where $m \neq 0$? Thus,

$$\frac{5m}{7m} = \frac{5m \div m}{7m \div m} = \frac{5}{7}.$$

We can now state this property of fractions:

Dividing the numerator and the denominator of a fraction by the same nonzero number results in a fraction equivalent to the original one; for all integers r, s, and t, $s \neq 0$, $t \neq 0$,

$$\frac{rt}{st} = \frac{rt \div t}{st \div t} = \frac{r}{s}.$$

We are now ready to use the preceeding properties in reducing algebraic fractions to lowest terms. A fraction is in **lowest terms when** the numerator and the denominator have only **1** and -1 as common factors. We accomplish this by dividing both numerator and denominator by their **greatest common factor** (G.C.F.)

The following examples illustrate the basic processes for reducing algebraic fractions to lowest terms.

EXAMPLE 5.   Reduce $\dfrac{15ab}{35a}$ to lowest terms.

Factor numerator and denominator to show their G.C.F.
$$\frac{15ab}{35a} = \frac{3b \cdot 5a}{7 \cdot 5a}$$

Divide both numerator and denominator by the G.C.F., $5a$.
$$= \frac{(3b \cdot 5a) \div 5a}{(7 \cdot 5a) \div 5a} = \frac{3b}{7}$$

The result is a fraction in lowest terms and equivalent to the original fraction.

EXAMPLE 6. Reduce $\dfrac{3m + 6}{m^2 + 6m + 8}$ to lowest terms.

Factor numerator and denominator to determine their G.C.F.

$$\frac{3m + 6}{m^2 + 6m + 8} = \frac{3(m + 2)}{(m + 4)(m + 2)}$$

Divide numerator and denominator by the G.C.F., $(m + 2)$.

$$= \frac{3(m + 2) \div (m + 2)}{(m + 4)(m + 2) \div (m + 2)}$$

$$= \frac{3}{m + 4}$$

The result is a fraction in lowest terms and equivalent to the original fraction.

ORAL EXERCISES

Tell how to complete the following table, assuming no zero denominators.

	Fraction	G.C.F. of numerator and denominator	Divide numerator and denominator by G.C.F.	Fraction in lowest terms
SAMPLE:	$\dfrac{15x}{-20xy}$	$5x$	$\dfrac{15x \div 5x}{-20xy \div 5x}$	$\dfrac{3}{-4y}$
1.	$\dfrac{24x}{8}$	8	$\dfrac{24x \div 8}{8 \div 8}$	?
2.	$\dfrac{5a}{9a}$	a	$\dfrac{5a \div a}{9a \div a}$	?
3.	$\dfrac{18ab^2}{-15ab}$	$3ab$	?	?
4.	$\dfrac{3(a + b)}{5(a + b)}$	$(a + b)$	?	?
5.	$\dfrac{2x - 2y}{7x - 7y}$	$(x - y)$	?	?
6.	$\dfrac{6rs + 3st}{12s}$	$3s$	?	?

WRITTEN EXERCISES

Write each fraction in lowest terms. Assume that no denominator equals zero.

A

1. $\dfrac{15x}{6}$

2. $\dfrac{35m^2}{7}$

3. $\dfrac{24a}{3}$

4. $\dfrac{15x^2}{10x}$

5. $\dfrac{4(x-y)}{7(x-y)}$

6. $\dfrac{-3(a+b)}{10(a+b)}$

7. $\dfrac{8xy}{24xy}$

8. $\dfrac{18}{6y}$

9. $\dfrac{24a^2b}{36ab}$

10. $\dfrac{9st^2}{-36st}$

11. $\dfrac{6(a-b)}{10(s+t)}$

12. $\dfrac{15(x-y)}{3(x+y)}$

13. $\dfrac{21xy}{28y}$

14. $\dfrac{-8cd^2}{24cd}$

15. $\dfrac{33x^2y^2}{55xy}$

16. $\dfrac{19a^2b^2}{57a^2c}$

17. $\dfrac{(a+c)(a-b)}{(a-c)(a-b)}$

18. $\dfrac{4(a^2+b^2+c^2)}{10}$

Reduce each fraction to lowest terms, using the factored form indicated.

19. $\dfrac{2r+2s}{7r+7s} = \dfrac{2(r+s)}{7(r+s)}$
$= ?$

20. $\dfrac{4a-4b}{20} = \dfrac{4(a-b)}{4 \cdot 5}$
$= ?$

21. $\dfrac{6x+6y}{15x-15y} = \dfrac{3(2x+2y)}{3(5x-5y)}$
$= ?$

22. $\dfrac{x-y}{x^2-y^2} = \dfrac{x-y}{(x+y)(x-y)}$
$= ?$

23. $\dfrac{4a^2-b^2}{2a+b} = \dfrac{(2a+b)(2a-b)}{2a+b}$
$= ?$

24. $\dfrac{(x-2)^2}{x^2-4} = \dfrac{(x-2)(x-2)}{(x+2)(x-2)}$
$= ?$

Write each fraction in lowest terms. Assume that no denominator equals zero.

25. $\dfrac{9a+9b}{12a-12b}$

26. $\dfrac{3x+3y}{5x+5y}$

27. $\dfrac{15r+15s}{25r-25s}$

28. $\dfrac{3a-3b}{a^2-b^2}$

29. $\dfrac{y^2-9}{y+3}$

30. $\dfrac{x^2-16}{x-4}$

31. $\dfrac{k-3}{k^2-9}$

32. $\dfrac{4-r^2}{2+r}$

33. $\dfrac{10r^2s}{15rs^2+25r}$

34. $\dfrac{3x+3y}{(x+y)^2}$

35. $\dfrac{a-a^2b}{b-ab^2}$

36. $\dfrac{x^2-9}{x^2-6x+9}$

B **37.** $\dfrac{x^2 - 3x}{x^2 - 2x - 3}$ **39.** $\dfrac{3x^2 + 15x + 18}{3x^2 - 12}$ **41.** $\dfrac{x^2 + 6xy + 9y^2}{x^2 - 9y^2}$

38. $\dfrac{s^2 + s - 6}{3s^2 - 27}$ **40.** $\dfrac{(x - 3)^2}{x^2 - 9}$ **42.** $\dfrac{a^2 + ab - 6b^2}{a^2 - 4b^2}$

C **43.** $\dfrac{m^2 - 5m + 6}{m^2 - 4m + 4}$ **45.** $\dfrac{2x^3 - x^2 - 10x}{x^3 - 2x^2 - 8x}$

44. $\dfrac{y^2 - 8y + 15}{y^2 + 4y - 21}$ **46.** $\dfrac{4t^4 + 2t^3 - 6t^2}{4t^4 + 26t^3 + 30t^2}$

Ratio and Percent

6–5   Ratio and Rate

In Figure 6–1 are several square and triangular shapes. If we want to compare the number of squares to the number of triangles we can write the fraction

Figure 6–1

$$\frac{\text{number of squares}}{\text{number of triangles}}.$$

Counting, we find that there are **10** squares and **8** triangles, so we have the fraction $\frac{10}{8}$, which is the same as $\frac{5}{4}$ when it is reduced to lowest terms.

Another way to state the relationship is to say that the number of squares and the number of triangles are in a **ratio** of **10** to **8**, or **5** to **4**. Such a ratio is often written **5 : 4**.

If we want to compare the number of red triangles to the number of red squares in Figure 6–1, we can write, in fraction form,

$$\frac{\text{number of red triangles}}{\text{number of red squares}} = \frac{2}{4} = \frac{1}{2}.$$

Expressed in ratio form, we write **2** to **4**, or **1** to **2**. As before, **1** to **2** can also be written **1 : 2**.

The ratio of any number r to any nonzero number s is the quotient of r and s, and can be written $\dfrac{r}{s}$, or $r : s$.

Suppose that the pay for an after-school job is **90¢** per hour. This means that the employee has a rate of pay of **90¢** for each hour he works. Expressions like **90¢ per hour**, **29¢ per pound**, and **35 miles per hour** are often called rate expressions, or rates. A rate can easily be written as a ratio. Do you see that "90¢ per hour" is really "90 cents for 1 hour", or a ratio of 90 cents : 1 hour? Likewise, "per pound" means "for 1 pound," etc. The following table shows examples of rate expressions.

Observation	*Ratio*	*Rate Expression*
A car travels **280** miles in **5** hours.	$\dfrac{280 \text{ miles}}{5 \text{ hours}}$	**56** miles per hour
10 oranges weigh **1** pound.	$\dfrac{10 \text{ oranges}}{1 \text{ pound}}$	**10** oranges per pound
360 gallons of water run from a pipe in **one** hour.	$\dfrac{360 \text{ gallons}}{1 \text{ hour}}$	**360** gallons per hour
22 inches of rain fell in **three** months.	$\dfrac{22 \text{ inches}}{3 \text{ months}}$	$7\frac{1}{3}$ inches per month

Do you see why we could conclude from the first observation that the car traveled an average of **56** miles an hour? How far would you expect it to travel in **3** hours?

Based on the second observation, how much would **five dozen** oranges weigh? How many gallons of water would run from the pipe described in the third observation in a **4-hour** period?

ORAL EXERCISES

Match each ratio in Column 1 with an equal ratio in Column 2.

COLUMN 1

1. 35 to 100

2. 10 : 100

3. 60 : 40

4. $\dfrac{-19}{35}$

5. $(3x + y)$ to 17

6. $\dfrac{14}{-6}$

COLUMN 2

A. −19 to 35

B. 14 : −6

C. 7 to 20

D. 3 : 2

E. 1 : 10

F. $\dfrac{3x + y}{17}$

Give the rate expression implied in each statement.

SAMPLE: The weight of a cubic foot of ocean water is 64 pounds.

What you say: 64 pounds per cubic foot

7. Light travels 186,000 miles in one second.

8. In one hour the car traveled 53 miles.

9. Tom worked six hours and earned $9.00

10. Over a three hour period the temperature rose 45 degrees.

WRITTEN EXERCISES

Write each ratio in lowest terms. Assume that no variable equals zero.

SAMPLE 1:   8 to 72   *Solution:* 1 : 9

SAMPLE 2: $\dfrac{xyz}{3x}$ *Solution:* $yz : 3$

A **1.** 5 to 10   **5.** $\dfrac{5k}{7k}$ **9.** $\dfrac{90}{40}$

2. 8 to 32   **6.** $\dfrac{3m}{3n}$ **10.** -6 to 10

3. 7 : 70   **7.** $12x$ to $12y$ **11.** $x^2 : 3x^2$

4. $\dfrac{ab}{ac}$ **8.** $3r : 5r$ **12.** $\dfrac{8bc}{40bd}$

Write a ratio in lowest terms to compare the length of each longer segment to the length of the shorter one.

SAMPLE: 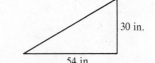   *Solution:* $\dfrac{40 \text{ in.}}{3 \text{ ft.}} = \dfrac{40 \text{ in.}}{36 \text{ in.}} ; \dfrac{40}{36} = \dfrac{10}{9}$

13.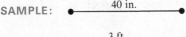

16.

30 in.

54 in.

14. $2\frac{1}{2}$ ft.

20 in.

17.   1.5 ft.

4.5 ft.

15.

4 ft.

18 ft.

18.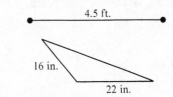

16 in.

22 in.

Write a ratio in lowest terms to compare the area of each smaller rectangular region to the area of the larger one.

SAMPLE: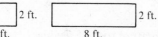

Solution: $\dfrac{(6 \cdot 7) \text{ sq. in.}}{(6 \cdot 8) \text{ sq. in.}}$; $\dfrac{6 \cdot 7}{6 \cdot 8} = \dfrac{7}{8}$

19. 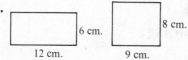 **21.**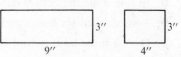

20. **22.**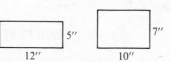

Replace each variable so that the two ratios in the pair are equal. Use the cross-product method to check your work.

SAMPLE: $2 : 5$ and $6 : x$

Solution: $2 : 5$ and $6 : 15$

Check: $\dfrac{2}{5} \times \dfrac{6}{15}$

$2 \cdot 15$	$5 \cdot 6$
30	30

23. $\dfrac{7}{10}$ and $\dfrac{x}{60}$ **27.** $\dfrac{x}{4}$ and $\dfrac{75}{100}$

24. $n : 12$ and $10 : 24$ **28.** $50 : 40$ and $y : 120$

25. $5 : 9$ and $t : 27$ **29.** $-3 : 5$ and $k : 55$

26. $8 : x$ and $80 : 10$ **30.** $18 : 45$ and $2 : z$

Find the value of the ratio $a : b$ according to each equation.

SAMPLE: $3a = 5b$

Solution: $3a = 5b$

$$\dfrac{3a}{3b} = \dfrac{5b}{3b}$$

$$\dfrac{a}{b} = \dfrac{5}{3}$$

The ratio $a : b$ is $5 : 3$.

B **31.** $2a = 7b$ **34.** $5b = 9a$ **37.** $a = 5b$

32. $9a = 4b$ **35.** $7a = 14b$ **38.** $10a = b$

33. $7a = 7b$ **36.** $3b = 12a$ **39.** $\dfrac{a}{2} = 6b$

C **40.** $4a - 7b = 0$ **42.** $-5b + 12a = 2b$

41. $3a - 4b = 0$ **43.** $-6a + 7b = -3a$

PROBLEMS

 1. A car travels a distance of 58 miles in 2 hours. At this rate how far will the car travel in 1 hour? in 4 hours? in $2\frac{1}{2}$ hours?

2. The gasoline used by a car in traveling 56 miles is 4 gallons. How many miles did the car travel per gallon? How many gallons are needed to travel 84 miles?

3. A 1-carat diamond sells for $500. At this rate, what is the cost of a $\frac{3}{4}$-carat diamond?

4. The price of hamburger was changed from 1 pound for $0.59 to three pounds for $1.79. Was the price raised or lowered and how much?

5. Under certain weather conditions sound travels at the rate of 1000 feet per second. Under such conditions how long will it take for the sound of a cannon shot to travel 3000 feet? 4500 feet?

6. A filler pipe allows cleaning fluid to flow into a 1500 gallon tank at the rate of 75 gallons per hour. At this rate how much time is needed to half-fill the tank? How long will it take to completely fill the tank?

 7. There are 27 members on the student council. The ratio of girls to boys is 4 to 5. How many boys are on the council? How many girls?

8. A rope 90 feet long is cut into two pieces. Their lengths are in the ratio of 4 to 5. How long are the pieces of rope?

9. Carol typed a 1000 word assignment in 25 minutes. Judy typed 798 words in 19 minutes. Who typed at the faster rate?

10. A banker recommends that Mr. Smith invest in bonds and stocks at the ratio of 7 to 3. If Mr. Smith has $3400 to invest how much should go into bonds?

6–6 The Meaning of Percent

Both the word "percent" and the symbol "%" imply "hundredths." Numerals like **15%** and **4%** look different from other numerals, but only because of the symbol %. However, we can write

$$15\% = \tfrac{15}{100} = 0.15 \qquad \text{and} \qquad 4\% = \tfrac{4}{100} = 0.04.$$

To illustrate this further, consider the large square in Figure 6–2, which has been marked off into **100** small squares, all the same size. Count the number of squares that have been shaded; there are **20** shaded squares, or twenty times $\frac{1}{100}$ of the large square.

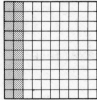

Figure 6–2

The shaded portion of the square can also be expressed as the ratio of the number of shaded squares to the total number of squares.

$$\frac{\textbf{number of shaded squares}}{\textbf{total number of squares}} = \frac{20}{100} = 20 \textbf{ percent} = 20\%$$

The meaning of **percent** can be defined as follows:

For any number **r**,

$$r\% = r \cdot \tfrac{1}{100} = r \cdot 0.01.$$

Let us see how we can apply this definition in order to express a fraction or a decimal as a percent.

EXAMPLE 1.   Write $\frac{3}{5}$ as a percent.

$$\tfrac{3}{5} = \tfrac{60}{100} = 60 \cdot \tfrac{1}{100} = 60\%$$

EXAMPLE 2.   Write **0.29** as a percent.

$$\textbf{0.29} = \textbf{29} \cdot \textbf{0.01} = 29\%$$

There may be times when it will help to write a fraction as a decimal first, before writing it as a percent.

EXAMPLE 3.   Write $\frac{3}{8}$ as a percent.

$$\tfrac{3}{8} = \textbf{0.375} = \textbf{37.5} \cdot \textbf{0.01} = 37.5\%$$

We can also use the definition of percent to express percents as fractions or as decimals.

EXAMPLE 4.   Write **30%** both as a fraction and as a decimal.

$$30\% = 30 \cdot \tfrac{1}{100} = \tfrac{30}{100} = \tfrac{3}{10}$$
$$30\% = 30 \cdot 0.01 = 0.30$$

EXAMPLE 5.   Write $8\tfrac{1}{2}\%$ both as a fraction and as a decimal.

$$8\tfrac{1}{2}\% = \tfrac{17}{2} \cdot \tfrac{1}{100} = \tfrac{17}{200}$$
$$8\tfrac{1}{2}\% = 8.5\% = 8.5 \cdot 0.01 = 0.085$$

ORAL EXERCISES

Name the correct replacement for each question mark.

SAMPLE: $\dfrac{2}{5} = \dfrac{(?)}{100} = (?) \cdot \dfrac{1}{100} = 40\%$

What you say: $\frac{2}{5} = \frac{40}{100} = 40 \cdot \frac{1}{100} = 40\%$

1. $\frac{3}{4} = \frac{75}{100} = (?) \cdot \frac{1}{100} = (?)\%$ 5. $15\% = 15 \cdot 0.01 = \ ?$

2. $\dfrac{1}{2} = \dfrac{(?)}{100} = (?) \cdot \dfrac{1}{100} = 50\%$ 6. $47\% = 47 \cdot 0.01 = \ ?$

3. $\frac{3}{5} = \frac{60}{100} = (?) \cdot \frac{1}{100} = (?)\%$ 7. $(?)\% = 78 \cdot 0.01 = \ ?$

4. $\frac{7}{10} = \frac{70}{100} = (?) \cdot \frac{1}{100} = (?)\%$ 8. $(?)\% = 25 \cdot 0.01 = \ ?$

WRITTEN EXERCISES

Show what percent of the small squares are shaded in each exercise.

SAMPLE:

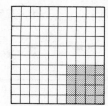

Solution: $\dfrac{\text{number of shaded squares}}{\text{total number of squares}} = \dfrac{16}{100}$

$$= 16 \cdot \tfrac{1}{100} = 16\%$$

[A] 1.

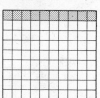

3.

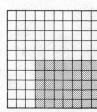

2.

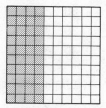

4.

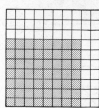

5. 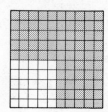   **6.**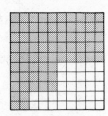

Express each decimal first as a fraction with the denominator 100, and then as a percent.

SAMPLE: 0.36   *Solution:* $0.36 = \frac{36}{100} = 36\%$

7. 0.47   **10.** 0.23   **13.** 0.375   **16.** 0.01

8. 0.25   **11.** 0.38   **14.** 0.03   **17.** 0.46

9. 0.95   **12.** 0.65   **15.** 0.875   **18.** 0.59

Express each percent as a fraction in lowest terms.

SAMPLE: 16%   *Solution:* $16\% = \frac{16}{100} = \frac{4}{25}$

19. 30%   **22.** 100%   **25.** 99%   **28.** 150%

20. 54%   **23.** 5%   **26.** 1%   **29.** 10%

21. 75%   **24.** 90%   **27.** 200%   **30.** 275%

31. Copy and complete the following number line.

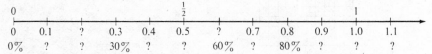

In each of the following, replace the question mark with one of the symbols =, >, < to make the statement true. Use the number line completed in Exercise 31 to help you decide.

32. 10% ? 15%   **35.** 0.25 ? 30%   **38.** $\frac{45}{100}$? 50%

33. 0.7 ? 70%   **36.** 70% ? 80%   **39.** $\frac{1}{2}$? $\frac{1}{2}\%$

34. $\frac{90}{100}$? 9%   **37.** 85% ? $\frac{8}{100}$ **40.** $\frac{50}{100}$? 50%

Tell what fractional part and what percent of each figure is shaded.

SAMPLE: *Solution:* $\frac{3}{4}$; 75%

41.   **42.**   **43.**

44.   **46.**   **48.**

45.   **47.**   **49.**

Write each of these percents both as a decimal and as a fraction in simplest form.

SAMPLE: $\frac{1}{15}\%$ *Solution:* $\frac{1}{15}\% = \frac{1}{15} \cdot \frac{1}{100} = \frac{1}{1500}$
$= 0.000\overline{6}$

B **50.** $\frac{1}{12}\%$ **52.** 0.8% **54.** $\frac{2}{3}\%$
   51. $\frac{1}{5}\%$ **53.** 0.75% **55.** 0.05%

6–7   Using Percent

There are times when we carry out mathematical operations with numbers expressed in percent notation. For example, consider the information shown here about the ages of the students in the sophomore class of a high school.

> **Sophomore Class**
> 25% are 15 years old.
> 60% are 16 years old.
> 15% are 17 years old.

EXAMPLE 1.   What percent of the students in the class are **16** years old or older?

$$60\% + 15\% = 75\%$$

75% of the students are **16** years old or older.

In most cases, however, it is necessary to write a percent as either a fraction or a decimal before computing.

EXAMPLE 2.   In the sophomore class described, suppose there are **420** students in all. How many of them are **15** years old?

$$25\% \text{ of } 420 \text{ is how many?}$$
$$\tfrac{1}{4} \quad \cdot \quad 420 = \qquad x$$
$$x = \tfrac{420}{4} = 105$$

105 sophomores are **15** years old.

EXAMPLE 3. Of the **420** sophomores, **252** are enrolled in a mathematics class of some sort. What percent of the sophomores are taking mathematics?

$$\underbrace{252}\ \underbrace{\text{is}}\ \underbrace{\text{what percent}}\ \underbrace{\text{of}}\ \underbrace{420?}$$

$$252 = \qquad x\% \qquad \cdot \quad 420$$

$$252 = \frac{x}{100} \cdot 420$$

$$\frac{252}{420} = \frac{x}{100}$$

$$x = \frac{252 \cdot 100}{420} = 60$$

60% of the sophomores are taking mathematics.

EXAMPLE 4. In the same school, **20%** of the junior class is enrolled in mathematics classes. If there are **96** juniors in mathematics classes, how many juniors are there in all?

$$\underbrace{96}\ \underbrace{\text{is}}\ \underbrace{20\%}\ \underbrace{\text{of}}\ \underbrace{\text{how many?}}$$

$$96 = \quad \tfrac{1}{5} \quad \cdot \qquad x$$

$$5 \cdot 96 = (5 \cdot \tfrac{1}{5}) \cdot \qquad x$$

$$480 = x$$

There are 480 juniors in the school.

If you have followed the work in Examples 1–4 closely you should have detected a rather simple strategy for solving a percent problem.

1. Write a sentence stating the problem briefly.
2. Translate the word statement into a number statement with a variable.
3. If a number in the statement is in percent notation, express it as either a fraction or a decimal.
4. Solve the equation.

ORAL EXERCISES

Tell how to complete each series of statements.

SAMPLE: $\tfrac{1}{2}$ of 48 is __?__   *What you say:* $\tfrac{1}{2}$ of 48 is 24.
          0.50 of 48 is __?__   0.50 of 48 is 24.
          50% of 48 is __?__   50% of 48 is 24.

1. $\frac{1}{4}$ of 36 is ___?___ .
   0.25 of 36 is ___?___ .
   25% of 36 is ___?___ .

2. $\frac{1}{10}$ of 850 is ___?___ .
   0.10 of 850 is ___?___ .
   10% of 850 is ___?___ .

3. 6 is $\frac{1}{2}$ of ___?___ .
   6 is 0.50 of ___?___ .
   6 is 50% of ___?___ .

4. 9 is $\frac{2}{5}$ of ___?___ .
   9 is 0.40 of ___?___ .
   9 is 40% of ___?___ .

5. 4 is ___?___ of 16.
   4 is ___?___ % of 16.

6. 8 is ___?___ of 10.
   8 is ___?___ % of 10.

7. 15 is ___?___ of 40.
   15 is ___?___ % of 40.

WRITTEN EXERCISES

Evaluate each of the following.

SAMPLE: 65% of 35   *Solution:* $(0.65)(35) = 22.75$

A

1. 30% of 150
2. 6% of 175
3. 24% of 390
4. 3% of 61
5. 60% of 1000

6. 25% of 100
7. 100% of 96.3
8. 7% of 15.2
9. 150% of 35
10. 300% of 19

11. 1.5% of 50
12. $3\frac{1}{2}$% of 200
13. 2% of 61.5
14. 0.75% of 100
15. 75% of 100

Write an equation for each of these statements; then find a replacement for the variable that makes the statement true.

SAMPLE 1: x is 14% of 32   *Solution:* $x = (0.14)(32) = 4.48$
Replace x with 4.48.

SAMPLE 2: y is 7% of $500.   *Solution:* $y = \frac{7}{100} \cdot 500 = 35$
Replace y with $35.

16. k is 25% of 76.
17. m is 10% of 960.
18. x is 3% of 350.
19. n is 75% of 100.
20. z is 1% of 7600.
21. b is 7% of 3200.

22. 15% of 80 is t.
23. 20% of $65 is y.
24. 37.5% of 56 is x.
25. 100% of 64 is c.
26. z is 200% of $590.
27. k is 150% of 42.

Write an equation for each question. Then find the number that is the correct answer for each question.

SAMPLE: 18 is 60% of what number?   *Solution:* $18 = 60\% \cdot x$
$$= \tfrac{3}{5} \cdot x$$
$$x = \tfrac{5}{3} \cdot 18 = 30$$
The number is 30.

28. 45 is 25% of what number?　　**33.** 67.3 is 100% of what number?

29. 28 is 40% of what number?　　**34.** 25% of what number is 96?

30. 53 is 50% of what number?　　**35.** 75% of what number is 300?

31. 21 is 75% of what number?　　**36.** 30% of what number is 150?

32. 19 is 80% of what number?　　**37.** 6% of what number is 42?

Find the percent that answers each question correctly.

SAMPLE:　48 is what percent of 96?　　*Solution:* $48 = \dfrac{x}{100} \cdot 96$

$$\tfrac{48}{96} = \tfrac{1}{2} = \dfrac{x}{100}$$

$$x = 50$$

48 is 50% of 96.

38. 24 is what percent of 56?　　**42.** What percent of 60 is 12?

39. 18 is what percent of 40?　　**43.** What percent of 90 is 45?

40. 12 is what percent of 40?　　**44.** What percent of 35 is 27?

41. What percent of 100 is 69?　　**45.** 330 is what percent of 30?

Find the number that is the answer for each question.

Ⓑ **46.** 75% of what number is 11.4?　　**49.** 34 is $1\tfrac{1}{2}$% of what number?

47. 150% of what number is 3.9?　　**50.** 31.06 is 18% of what number?

48. 1.23 is 3% of what number?　　**51.** 4.8% of what number is 230?

PROBLEMS

1. There are 165 boys in the sophomore class at Lincoln High School. 40% of the boys have after-school jobs. How many boys have jobs?

2. The Garden City weatherman said that he recorded some rainfall on 20% of the 365 days last year. On how many days was rainfall recorded? On what percent of the days was no rainfall recorded?

3. The library in Central High School contains 14,000 books. There are reference books, fiction books, and non-fiction books. If 27% of the books are reference and 35% are fiction, what percent are non-fiction? How many books are there of each kind?

4. William earned $290 on his summer vacation job. He saved 60% of his earnings toward the purchase of a car. How much money did he save?

5. Carson High School has a total of 2600 students. On a certain day 7% of the students are absent. How many students are absent? What percent are present?

6. Ken worked 34 problems correctly on a test of 40 problems. What percent did he work correctly? What percent were not correct?

7. Mr. Carson purchased a used car for $1395. If the sales tax in his state is 5% of the purchase price, how much sales tax did he pay?

8. Diane bought a coat on sale. It was regularly priced at $12.50, but had been marked down 10%. How much did she pay for the coat?

9. A large passenger jet aircraft has a seating capacity of 340 persons. If there are 238 passengers aboard on a certain flight, what percent of the seats are filled?

10. A stereo tape deck regularly sells for $50. If it is on sale for $35, by what percent has the regular price been reduced?

CHAPTER SUMMARY

Inventory of Structure and Concepts

1. An **algebraic fraction** is a symbol for a number. It is written in the form $\frac{a}{b}$, where a and b are numbers, with b not zero. The number a is called the **numerator** of the fraction, and the number b is called its **denominator**. The reason that b cannot be zero is that the fraction form indicates division, and division by zero is not defined.

2. Fractions that name the same number are **equivalent fractions**.

3. For the fractions $\frac{a}{b}$ and $\frac{c}{d}$, where a and c are any integers and b and d are both positive integers,

$$\text{if } a \cdot d < b \cdot c, \quad \text{then} \quad \frac{a}{b} < \frac{c}{d},$$
$$\text{if } a \cdot d = b \cdot c, \quad \text{then} \quad \frac{a}{b} = \frac{c}{d},$$
$$\text{if } a \cdot d > b \cdot c, \quad \text{then} \quad \frac{a}{b} > \frac{c}{d}.$$

4. If a decimal numeral names the same number as a fraction, the decimal numeral is the **decimal equivalent** of the fraction.

5. Some decimal equivalents of fractions are **terminating** decimals; others are **repeating** decimals. For example:

These terminate: $\frac{1}{2} = 0.50$; $\frac{5}{8} = 0.625$; $-\frac{3}{4} = -0.75$.

These repeat: $\frac{1}{3} = 0.3\overline{3}$; $-\frac{1}{9} = -0.1\overline{1}$; $\frac{2}{3} = 0.6\overline{6}$.

6. When both the numerator and the denominator of a fraction are multiplied or divided by the same nonzero number the resulting fraction is equivalent to the original one.

$$\text{For } s \neq 0, t \neq 0, \frac{r}{s} = \frac{rt}{st}, \quad \text{and} \quad \frac{rt \div t}{st \div t} = \frac{r}{s}.$$

7. When the numerator and the denominator of a fraction have only 1 as their greatest common factor, the fraction is in **lowest terms**.

8. A **ratio** is a quotient of two numbers. If r is any number and s is any nonzero number, the ratio of r to s can be written $\frac{r}{s}$ or $r : s$.

9. A comparison of two related values or quantities, such as **35 miles per hour**, or **10 inches** of rainfall **per year**, is called a **rate expression**.

10. The word **percent** and the symbol **%** imply **hundredths**. For a number r, $r\% = r \cdot \frac{1}{100} = r \cdot 0.01$.

Vocabulary and Spelling

numerator (*p. 183*)

denominator (*p. 183*)

algebraic fraction (*p. 184*)

equivalent fractions (*p. 186*)

decimal fractions (*p. 186*)

cross-product (*p. 186*)

decimal equivalent (*p. 191*)

terminating decimal (*p. 191*)

place value system (*p. 191*)

expanded form (*p. 192*)

repeating decimals (*p. 192*)

reduce to lowest terms (*p. 196*)

ratio (*p. 199*)

rate (*p. 200*)

rate expression (*p. 200*)

percent (%) (*p. 203*)

Chapter Test

In each exercise arrange the numerals according to the values of the numbers represented, beginning with the one of least value.

1. $\frac{3}{5}, \frac{5}{5}, \frac{1}{2}, \frac{2}{3}$

2. $8\%, 40\%, 1\%, 3\%$

3. $10\%, \frac{1}{4}, 0.13, 4.2, 100\%, \frac{10}{3}$

4. $\frac{8}{10}, \frac{90}{100}, \frac{70}{100}, \frac{3}{5}, \frac{3}{10}, \frac{6}{12}$

Write each fraction both as a decimal and as a percent.

5. $\frac{3}{5}$

6. $\frac{3}{8}$

7. $\frac{5}{6}$

Match each fraction with its corresponding repeating decimal.

COLUMN 1	COLUMN 2
8. $\frac{3}{7}$	**A.** $0.3\overline{3}$
9. $\frac{2}{9}$	**B.** $0.\overline{428571}$
10. $\frac{1}{3}$	**C.** $0.2\overline{2}$
11. $\frac{1}{11}$	**D.** $0.0\overline{909}$

Complete each set of equivalent fractions according to the existing pattern.

12. $\{\frac{3}{8}, \frac{6}{16}, \frac{9}{24}, (?), (?), (?), (?), (?), \frac{27}{72}\}$

13. $\left\{\frac{7}{5k}, \frac{14}{10k}, \frac{21}{15k}, (?), (?), (?), (?), (?), \frac{63}{45k}\right\}, k \neq 0.$

Use the symbol $=$, $>$, or $<$ to make each a true statement. Let $x = 3$, $y = 2$, and $a = -1$.

14. $\frac{5}{2}$? $1\frac{1}{3}$ **16.** 0.04 ? 40% **18.** $\frac{x}{a}$? $\frac{y}{a}$

15. $-\frac{a}{5}$? 20% **17.** $\frac{4xy}{3}$? $\frac{6y}{x}$

Reduce each fraction to lowest terms. Assume no denominator equals zero.

19. $\frac{14t^3}{42st}$ **20.** $\frac{-8x^2y}{12xy^2}$ **21.** $\frac{5m + 5n}{20m - 20n}$ **22.** $\frac{r + r^2s}{s + rs^2}$

Tell which ratio in each exercise is the greater.

23. $\frac{5}{9}; \frac{3}{7}$ **24.** 3 to 4; 1 to 10

Solve each problem.

25. The pressure exerted by compressed gas on the walls of a storage tank is 85 pounds per square inch. What is the total pressure exerted on a rectangular surface that is 9 inches long and 4 inches wide?

26. Mr. Norton earns $600 per month. He spends $120 per month for rent. What percent of his income is for rent?

27. Mr. Watkins earns $670 per month. His payroll deduction for taxes is 12% of his pay. How much is deducted for taxes?

Complete each statement.

28. 35% of 600 is __?__.   **30.** 15 is 60% of __?__.

29. 12 is __?__% of 20.

Chapter Review

6–1 Algebraic Fractions

Write each of the following as a fraction. Name any values of the variable for which the fraction is not defined.

1. $15 \div (3a - 6)$ **4.** $3a \div (2 + a)$ **7.** $3b \div (b + 8)$

2. $-17 \div 2k$ **5.** $(10 + y) \div 3y$ **8.** $25 \div -4t$

3. $(n + 3)$ divided by n **6.** $19x^2 \div (4x - 6)$ **9.** $(7 + 9n) \div (n + 10)$

6–2 Equivalent Fractions

Complete each set of equivalent fractions according to the existing pattern.

10. $\{\frac{3}{8}, \frac{6}{16}, \frac{9}{24}, (?), (?), (?)\}$ **11.** $\{\frac{-x}{5}, \frac{-2x}{10}, \frac{-3x}{15}, (?), (?), (?)\}$

12. $\{\frac{3x^2}{2}, \frac{6x^2}{4}, \frac{9x^2}{6}, (?), (?), (?)\}$

13. $\{\frac{2ab}{7}, \frac{4ab}{14}, \frac{6ab}{21}, (?), (?), (?)\}$

Name a fraction that indicates the shaded portion of each figure.

14.

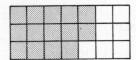

16.

15.

17.

Use the symbol $=$, $>$, or $<$ to make each statement true.

18. $\frac{-2}{3} \; ? \; \frac{-30}{45}$ **19.** $\frac{3}{7} \; ? \; \frac{20}{35}$ **20.** $\frac{10}{3} \; ? \; \frac{51}{20}$

6–3 Using Decimal Fractions

Write the decimal equivalent for each fraction.

21. $\frac{7}{8}$ **22.** $\frac{4}{5}$ **23.** $\frac{-6}{10}$ **24.** $\frac{2}{3}$

25. $\frac{3}{4}$ **26.** $\frac{1}{3}$ **27.** $\frac{5}{2}$ **28.** $\frac{-10}{8}$

Express each of the following as a single decimal numeral.

29. $0.7 + 0.01 + 0.009 + 0.0005$ **31.** $30 + 6 + 0.1 + 0.05 + 0.007$

30. $\frac{2}{10} + \frac{6}{100} + \frac{3}{1000} + \frac{8}{10,000}$ **32.** $0.8 + 0.003 + 0.0005$

6–4   Reducing Algebraic Fractions to Lowest Terms

Write each of the following in lowest terms. Assume that no denominator equals zero.

33. $\frac{15a^2b}{75ab}$ **36.** $\frac{72a^2b}{48ab^2}$ **39.** $\frac{9(x-y)}{5(x-y)}$

34. $\frac{-9cd^2}{54cd}$ **37.** $\frac{-3mn^2}{57mn}$ **40.** $\frac{7r+7s}{21r+21s}$

35. $\frac{n-5}{n^2-25}$ **38.** $\frac{5a+5b}{(a+b)^2}$ **41.** $\frac{x^2-4}{x^2-4x+4}$

6–5   Ratio and Rate

Write each ratio as a fraction in lowest terms.

42. 22 to 50   **44.** 18 : 10   **46.** 315 : 500

43. 146 to 64   **45.** 80 : 50   **47.** $6ab$ to $34ab^2$

Complete each of the following so that the two ratios are equal.

48. 3 : 10 and 12 : (?)   **50.** −5 to 3 and 50 to (?)

49. 4 : (?) and 40 : 70   **51.** 70 to 5 and (?) to 1

6–6   The Meaning of Percent

Complete each of the following to make a true statement.

52. $\frac{4}{5} = \frac{(?)}{100} = (?)\%$ **54.** $\frac{9}{20} = \frac{(?)}{100} = (?)\%$

53. $\frac{3}{10} = \frac{(?)}{100} = (?)\%$ **55.** $\frac{15}{10} = \frac{(?)}{100} = (?)\%$

Write each fraction both as a decimal and as a percent.

56. $\frac{5}{8}$ **58.** $\frac{18}{12}$ **60.** $\frac{7}{10}$

57. $\frac{1}{4}$ **59.** $\frac{95}{100}$ **61.** $\frac{120}{100}$

6–7 Using Percent

Complete each statement.

62. 20% of 90 is __?__.

64. 75% of __?__ is 60.

63. 4% of 38 is __?__.

65. 21 is 25% of __?__.

Solve each problem.

66. Susan has $280 in her savings account. She is planning to spend 15% of her savings for new clothes. What percent of her money will remain in the bank account? How much does she plan to spend for clothes?

67. At a sale, Tom bought a sport coat that was originally priced at $18.50. The original price had been reduced 20% for the sale. How much did Tom pay for the coat?

Review of Skills

Simplify each indicated product or quotient.

1. $(3ab)(5ab^2)$

4. $(-3xy)(-5y)(2x^2)$

2. $(18x^2y) \div (3xy)$

5. $(56s^2t^3) \div (-7st^2)$

3. $(-6cd)(2bc)$

6. $(-72mnq^2) \div (-6nq)$

Name each missing factor.

7. $(3r^2s)(?) = 27r^3st^2$

9. $-35x^2yz^2 = (5xyz)(?)$

8. $(-ab)(?) = 10ab^5$

10. Complete the following table.

$x + y$	7				4	0	1		−9		12	
x	3	−3	−5	−6			5	−8		0		
y	4	5	−5	2					−12	−2	7	
xy	12				−21	−16	−24					18

Factor each polynomial completely.

11. $x^2 - 49$

14. $10abc + 8ab^2c + 2a^2b$

17. $x^2 - 3x - 10$

12. $4t^2 - 1$

15. $m^2 + 4m + 4$

18. $9x^2 - y^2$

13. $9 - 16r^2$

16. $y^2 + 5y + 6$

19. $2r^2 - 3r - 20$

Robert H. Goddard

The Space Age is sometimes thought of as beginning in 1957 with the launching of the Russian satellite, Sputnik I. However, the man who actually launched the world into rocketry and space flight began his far-reaching lifework nearly fifty years earlier. That man was Robert H. Goddard (1882–1945) who had a vision of the future when, at the age of 17, he climbed a tree. As he looked across the landscape, he thought how wonderful it would be to make a device which might ascend to Mars, and tried to imagine what such a device might look like.

After making wooden models of his first crude ideas, he came to realize that a knowledge of physics and mathematics was absolutely necessary, so he attacked those subjects in high school with a real purpose. In 1904 he went on to Worcester Polytechnic Institute, where he began to fill notebooks with his ideas on rocket propulsion and space exploration.

By 1909 he had developed the idea of multiple, or step, rockets, and had worked on a plan for using liquid hydrogen and oxygen as fuels. After graduate work at Clark University, from which he obtained his Ph.D. degree in mathematical physics, he began, in 1915, to experiment with jet propulsion. In 1919 the Smithsonian Institution published his mathematical theory and experimental results under the title "A Method of Reaching Extremely High Altitudes," in which he showed that a rather modest rocket could go as far as the moon.

His historic first liquid-propellant rocket was launched on March 16, 1926, at a farm in Auburn, Massachusetts. In this first rocket, the motor was placed ahead of the tanks, because Dr. Goddard felt that the flight would be more stable if pulled instead of pushed. But in this first flight he discovered that the jet was more powerful than he had expected, and he promptly placed the fuel tanks *above* the jet rather than below it. He continued to work on rockets until his death in 1945. In all, he patented more than two hundred rocket ideas.

Although Dr. Goddard did not live to see the space explorations of the 1960's, it can truly be said that the most fitting memorials to this quiet, persistent, and dauntless man are the giant rockets that rise from the launching pads, the outcome of the dream of a 17-year-old boy.

217

George Washington Carver in his laboratory . . .

Research chemists sampling a new beverage . . .

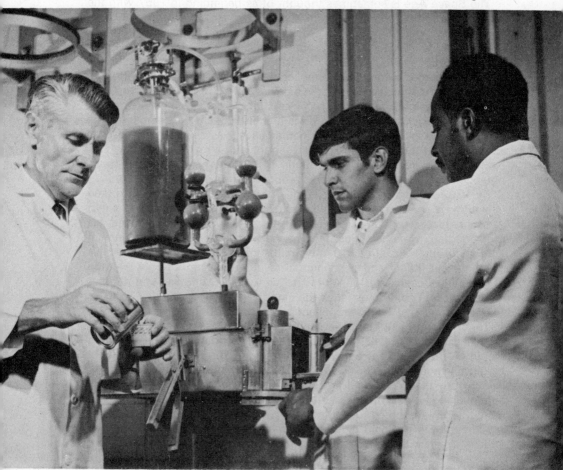

Multiplication and Division with Fractions

Chemurgy, the application of chemistry to the development of industrial raw materials from farm and forest products, is a relatively new science. An early contributor was George Washington Carver, who won international fame for agricultural research through his work at Tuskegee Institute from 1896 to 1943. He found more than 300 products that could be made from the peanut, and 118 from the sweet potato, as well as uses for clays, cotton, and soy beans. His research expanded the economy of the South, while laying a firm basis for research carried on today by the United States Department of Agriculture. In the picture, research chemists are sampling a whey-cream beverage, an experimental food with high nutritional value and low cost.

Multiplication

7–1 Basic Ideas about Multiplication with Fractions

You are already familiar with number sentences like $3(\frac{1}{2}) = x$ and $2(-\frac{2}{3}) = y$, each of which calls for the product of an integer and a number in fractional form. A number line illustration of each can serve as a model for the solution.

EXAMPLE 1. $3(\frac{1}{2}) = x$

Since the tip of the third arrow is at $\frac{3}{2}$, we see that $x = \frac{3}{2}$. Thus $3(\frac{1}{2}) = \frac{3}{2}$.

EXAMPLE 2. $2(-\frac{2}{3}) = y$

$y = -\frac{4}{3}$, so $2(-\frac{2}{3}) = -\frac{4}{3}$.

219

To solve a sentence like $\frac{1}{4} \cdot \frac{1}{2} = x$ or $\frac{1}{5} \cdot \frac{2}{3} = y$, each of which calls for the product of two numbers both in fractional form, we can use a rectangular region as a model.

EXAMPLE 3. $\frac{1}{4} \cdot \frac{1}{2} = x$

If we divide a rectangular region into two equal parts, do you see that each part is $\frac{1}{2}$ of the whole region?

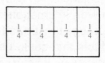

Next, the region is divided into four equal parts, as shown by the red vertical lines. Each of the four parts is $\frac{1}{4}$ of the whole region.

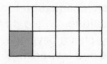

Finally, we see that each small rectangle, of which one is shaded, is $\frac{1}{4}$ of $\frac{1}{2}$ of the whole region; it is also $\frac{1}{8}$ of the region. Thus $\frac{1}{4} \cdot \frac{1}{2} = \frac{1}{8}$, and $x = \frac{1}{8}$.

EXAMPLE 4. $\frac{1}{5} \cdot \frac{2}{3} = y$

If a rectangular region is divided into three equal parts, then two of those parts represent $\frac{2}{3}$ of the whole region.

The red lines show the region divided into five equal parts, each of which is $\frac{1}{5}$ of the whole region.

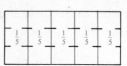

The red shaded portion shows $\frac{1}{5}$ of $\frac{2}{3}$ of the region. Check the diagram to see that it is also $\frac{2}{15}$ of the whole region.
Thus $\frac{1}{5} \cdot \frac{2}{3} = \frac{2}{15}$, and $y = \frac{2}{15}$.

From the models in Examples 3 and 4, verify the following statement about multiplying numbers expressed in fractional form.

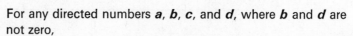

For any directed numbers **a**, **b**, **c**, and **d**, where **b** and **d** are not zero,

$$\frac{a}{b} \cdot \frac{c}{d} = \frac{a \cdot c}{b \cdot d}.$$

The following examples apply this definition. Note that each product is expressed in lowest terms.

EXAMPLE 5.

$$\frac{3}{4} \cdot \frac{-5}{8} = \frac{(3)(-5)}{(4)(8)}$$

$$= \frac{-15}{32} = -\frac{15}{32}$$

EXAMPLE 6.

$$\frac{7a}{3} \cdot \frac{5ab}{10} = \frac{(7a)(5ab)}{(3)(10)}$$

$$= \frac{35a^2b}{30} = \frac{7a^2b}{6}$$

Now let us use the definition of multiplication of numbers in fractional form to write each of the products $\frac{5x^2}{9} \cdot \frac{-3}{4}$ and $\frac{-3}{4} \cdot \frac{5x^2}{9}$ as a single fraction.

EXAMPLE 7.

$$\frac{5x^2}{9} \cdot \frac{-3}{4} = \frac{(5x^2)(-3)}{(9)(4)}$$

$$= \frac{-15x^2}{36} = -\frac{5x^2}{12}$$

EXAMPLE 8.

$$\frac{-3}{4} \cdot \frac{5x^2}{9} = \frac{(-3)(5x^2)}{(4)(9)}$$

$$= \frac{-15x^2}{36} = -\frac{5x^2}{12}$$

Do you see that the results in Examples 7 and 8 indicate that the familiar **commutative property** for multiplication applies to multiplication with fractions?

For any directed numbers **a**, **b**, **c**, and **d**, where **b** and **d** are not zero,

$$\frac{a}{b} \cdot \frac{c}{d} = \frac{c}{d} \cdot \frac{a}{b}.$$

Study the examples below. Assume that no denominator equals zero.

EXAMPLE 9.

$$\left(\frac{2a}{3} \cdot \frac{4a}{5b}\right) \cdot \frac{-5}{2} = \frac{2a \cdot 4a}{3 \cdot 5b} \cdot \frac{-5}{2}$$

$$= \frac{8a^2}{15b} \cdot \frac{-5}{2} = \frac{-40a^2}{30b} = -\frac{4a^2}{3b}$$

EXAMPLE 10.

$$\frac{2a}{3} \cdot \left(\frac{4a}{5b} \cdot \frac{-5}{2}\right) = \frac{2a}{3} \cdot \frac{4a \cdot -5}{5b \cdot 2}$$

$$= \frac{2a}{3} \cdot \frac{-20a}{10b} = \frac{-40a^2}{30b} = -\frac{4a^2}{3b}$$

The products shown in Examples 9 and 10 indicate that the associative property for multiplication also holds for multiplication with fractions.

For any directed numbers **a**, **b**, **c**, **d**, **e**, and **f**, where **b**, **d** and **f** are not zero,

$$\left(\frac{a}{b} \cdot \frac{c}{d}\right) \cdot \frac{e}{f} = \frac{a}{b} \cdot \left(\frac{c}{d} \cdot \frac{e}{f}\right).$$

In our work with algebraic fractions, we also assume that the multiplicative property of one holds true.

For any directed numbers **a** and **b**, with **b** $\neq$ 0,

$$\frac{a}{b} \cdot 1 = 1 \cdot \frac{a}{b} = \frac{a}{b}.$$

Recall that we have seen that any fraction for which the numerator and the denominator are the same represents the number **1**. We know, of course, that no replacement for a variable can be used which gives a zero denominator. With that restriction, then, we can say:

$$\frac{6}{6} = 1 \qquad \frac{b}{b} = 1 \qquad \frac{2x}{2x} = 1 \qquad \frac{-5b}{-5b} = 1$$

ORAL EXERCISES

Give the multiplication statement suggested by each number line picture.

SAMPLE:

What you say: $2 \cdot \left(-\frac{2}{5}\right) = -\frac{4}{5}$

1.
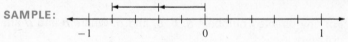

2.

3.

4.
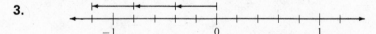

Express each of the following as a single fraction.

5. $\frac{1}{3} \cdot \frac{1}{2}$ **6.** $4 \cdot \frac{1}{5}$ **7.** $\frac{10}{2} \cdot \frac{2}{3}$

8. $\frac{2}{5} \cdot \frac{2}{3}$

11. $(-\frac{1}{3}) \cdot (-\frac{1}{3})$

14. $(-\frac{1}{2}) \cdot -\frac{1}{2}$

9. $\left(\frac{-4}{5}\right) \cdot \frac{1}{5}$

12. $\frac{r}{3} \cdot \frac{1}{2}$

15. $-\frac{3}{8} \cdot \frac{a}{b}$

10. $\frac{x}{y} \cdot \frac{5}{7}$

13. $\frac{4}{1} \cdot \frac{n}{1}$

16. $\frac{xy}{6} \cdot 52$

Tell which symbols represent the number 1 and which do not. Remember that no denominator can be zero.

17. $\frac{3b}{3b}$

19. $\frac{10xy^2}{10xy^2}$

21. $7mn \div 7mn$

18. $\frac{-4rs}{4rs}$

20. $-\frac{2t}{2t}$

22. $-5a \div (-5a)$

WRITTEN EXERCISES

For each sentence, tell which property of multiplication applies.

SAMPLE: $\frac{-3x}{t} \cdot \frac{5y}{10} = \frac{5y}{10} \cdot \frac{-3x}{t}$ *Solution:* Commutative property.

1. $\left(\frac{2b}{c} \cdot \frac{3}{5}\right) \cdot \frac{1}{7} = \frac{2b}{c} \cdot \left(\frac{3}{5} \cdot \frac{1}{7}\right)$

5. $\frac{8}{8} \cdot \frac{3abc}{d} = \frac{3abc}{d}$

2. $\frac{-5a}{b} \cdot \frac{a}{6b} = \frac{a}{6b} \cdot \frac{-5a}{b}$

6. $\frac{-6xy}{15z} \cdot \frac{7x}{10} = \frac{7x}{10} \cdot \frac{-6xy}{15z}$

3. $\frac{2k}{10} \cdot \left(5 \cdot \frac{2}{3}\right) = \left(\frac{2k}{10} \cdot 5\right) \cdot \frac{2}{3}$

7. $\frac{n+3}{t} \cdot \frac{5}{8} = \frac{5}{8} \cdot \frac{n+3}{t}$

4. $\frac{xy}{3} \cdot \frac{mn}{10} = \frac{mn}{10} \cdot \frac{xy}{3}$

8. $1 \cdot \frac{4x^2y^2}{9z^3} = \frac{4x^2y^2}{9z^3}$

For each of the following, draw a rectangular region as a model of the indicated product, then write an equation stating the product.

SAMPLE: $\frac{2}{5}$ of $\frac{1}{3}$ *Solution:*  $\frac{2}{5} \cdot \frac{1}{3} = \frac{2}{15}$

9. $\frac{1}{4}$ of $\frac{1}{3}$

12. $\frac{5}{8}$ of $\frac{1}{2}$

15. $\frac{1}{3}$ of $\frac{7}{10}$

10. $\frac{1}{2}$ of $\frac{5}{8}$

13. $\frac{3}{8}$ of $\frac{1}{3}$

16. $\frac{2}{5}$ of $\frac{3}{8}$

11. $\frac{2}{3}$ of $\frac{1}{4}$

14. $\frac{1}{7}$ of $\frac{7}{8}$

17. $\frac{1}{2}$ of $\frac{5}{6}$

Write each product as a single fraction in lowest terms.

18. $\left(-\frac{1}{w}\right) \cdot \frac{2}{x}$

19. $\frac{2}{32} \cdot \frac{10}{42}$

20. $18a^2b \cdot \frac{4}{3a^2}$

21. $\dfrac{3a}{2} \cdot \dfrac{b}{6a}$ **23.** $\dfrac{6s}{13t} \cdot \dfrac{26st}{3s}$ **25.** $\frac{3}{8} \cdot \frac{2}{3} \cdot \frac{5}{10}$

22. $\dfrac{5x}{6y} \cdot \dfrac{2x}{3}$ **24.** $\dfrac{9x}{4} \cdot \dfrac{2m}{2m}$ **26.** $\left(-\dfrac{5}{x}\right)\left(\dfrac{1}{2x}\right)\left(\dfrac{1}{3}\right)$

Show that each sentence is correct.

SAMPLE: $\dfrac{-10b^2}{3} \cdot \dfrac{2c}{6} = \dfrac{2c}{6} \cdot \dfrac{-10b^2}{3}$

Solution: $\dfrac{-10b^2}{3} \cdot \dfrac{2c}{6} = \dfrac{2c}{6} \cdot \dfrac{-10b^2}{3}$

$\dfrac{(-10b^2)2c}{3 \cdot 6}$	$\dfrac{2c(-10b^2)}{6 \cdot 3}$
$\dfrac{-20b^2c}{18}$	$\dfrac{-20b^2c}{18}$

27. $\dfrac{2c^2}{7} \cdot \left(\dfrac{3c}{a} \cdot \dfrac{4}{3a}\right) = \left(\dfrac{2c^2}{7} \cdot \dfrac{3c}{a}\right) \cdot \dfrac{4}{3a}$

28. $\dfrac{-4abc}{15b^2} \cdot \dfrac{-10ac}{5} = \dfrac{-10ac}{5} \cdot \dfrac{-4abc}{15b^2}$

29. $\dfrac{-6rs}{10s} \cdot \dfrac{-3t}{-3t} = \dfrac{(-3)(-6)(rs)(t)}{(10)(-3)(s)(t)}$

 30. $\dfrac{10ab}{10ab} \cdot \dfrac{21a^2b}{8c} = \dfrac{(10 \cdot 21)(ab)(a^2b)}{10 \cdot 8 \cdot ab \cdot c}$

31. $\dfrac{10rs}{3r^2s} \cdot \left(-\dfrac{6rs}{5}\right) = \left(-\dfrac{6rs}{5}\right) \cdot \dfrac{10rs}{3r^2s}$

32. $\dfrac{-8a^2b}{13b} \cdot \left(\dfrac{15ab}{6a} \cdot \dfrac{4}{9bc}\right) = \left(\dfrac{-8a^2b}{13b} \cdot \dfrac{15ab}{6a}\right) \cdot \dfrac{4}{9bc}$

33. $\left(\dfrac{3m}{5} \cdot \dfrac{9mn^2}{4}\right) \cdot \dfrac{7}{8} = \dfrac{7 \cdot 9mn^2 \cdot 3m}{5 \cdot 4 \cdot 8}$

PROBLEMS

 1. A given number is 6 times as large as $\frac{5}{12}$. What is the number?

2. A given number is $\frac{7}{2}$ times as large as $\frac{3}{4}$. What is the number?

3. Name the number that is $\frac{1}{4}$ as large as $\frac{11}{8}$.

On the line segment below, the points named with letters are equally spaced; complete each statement.

4. If the length of $\overline{AB}$ is $\frac{9}{2}$ units, the length of $\overline{AD}$ is __?__ units.

5. If the length of $\overline{BD}$ is $\frac{9}{5}$ units, the length of $\overline{BH}$ is __?__ units.

6. If the length of $\overline{AC}$ is $\frac{7}{8}$ units, the length of $\overline{DE}$ is __?__ units.

7. If the length of $\overline{AD}$ is $\frac{5}{8}$ units, the length of $\overline{AC}$ is __?__ units.

8. If the length of $\overline{CH}$ is $\frac{2}{3}$ units, the length of $\overline{CF}$ is __?__ units.

B **9.** The fraction $\dfrac{x}{9}$ represents a number less than 1. What is the largest integer that can replace x?

10. The fraction $\dfrac{x}{9}$ represents a number greater than 1. What is the smallest integer that can replace x?

11. The volume in gallons of an oil storage tank is represented by the expression $\dfrac{25\pi h}{9}$. If the tank is 60% full, how many gallons of oil are are in it?

12. The number of cubic yards in the total volume of the iceberg pictured here is given by the expression $\dfrac{3600hd^2}{49}$. About $\frac{1}{8}$ of the iceberg is above the surface of the water. How would you represent the volume of the part above the surface? of the part below the surface?

7–2   Using Factoring in Multiplication with Fractions

The rule that we have stated for multiplying two numbers expressed as fractions can be extended to simplifying an indicated product of any two algebraic fractions. That is, if a, b, c, and d represent polynomials, then for all values of the variables for which $b \neq 0$ and $d \neq 0$,

$$\frac{a}{b} \cdot \frac{c}{d} = \frac{a \cdot c}{b \cdot d}.$$

In the following examples, notice how the ideas developed in earlier chapters for multiplying and factoring polynomials are applied. In each case, the product is finally expressed as a single fraction in lowest terms.

EXAMPLE 1. $\dfrac{r+s}{5} \cdot \dfrac{r-s}{2t} = \dfrac{(r+s)(r-s)}{5 \cdot 2t}$

$$= \dfrac{r^2 - s^2}{10t}$$

EXAMPLE 2. $\dfrac{y^2 - 4}{14} \cdot \dfrac{7}{y-2} = \dfrac{(y+2)(y-2)7}{14(y-2)}$

$$= \dfrac{(y+2)7}{2 \cdot 7} = \dfrac{y+2}{2}$$

EXAMPLE 3. $\dfrac{3a + 3b}{a - b} \cdot \dfrac{2a - 2b}{12} = \dfrac{3(a + b)}{a - b} \cdot \dfrac{2(a - b)}{12}$

$$= \dfrac{(3)(2)(a + b)(a - b)}{12(a - b)} = \dfrac{a + b}{2}$$

EXAMPLE 4. $\dfrac{a^2 + 2ab + b^2}{3} \cdot \dfrac{b}{a^2 - b^2} = \dfrac{(a + b)(a + b)b}{3(a - b)(a + b)}$

$$= \dfrac{(a + b)b}{3(a - b)} = \dfrac{ab + b^2}{3a - 3b}$$

ORAL EXERCISES

Express each of the following in lowest terms.

SAMPLE: $\dfrac{a + b}{3} \cdot \dfrac{a - b}{a + b}$ *What you say:* $\dfrac{(a + b)(a - b)}{3(a + b)} = \dfrac{a - b}{3}$

1. $\dfrac{b - c}{3} \cdot \dfrac{2}{b + c}$ **5.** $\dfrac{-5}{8} \cdot \dfrac{a + b}{c^2}$

2. $\dfrac{m + n}{6} \cdot \dfrac{6}{m - n}$ **6.** $\dfrac{1}{m - n} \cdot \dfrac{m - n}{5}$

3. $\dfrac{2}{5} \cdot \dfrac{r^2 + t}{3}$ **7.** $\dfrac{(x - y)}{3} \cdot \dfrac{(x + y)}{2}$

4. $\dfrac{2}{3x} \cdot \dfrac{a^2 + b}{1}$ **8.** $\dfrac{-2(r + s)}{3} \cdot \dfrac{1}{r + s}$

WRITTEN EXERCISES

Write each product as a single fraction in lowest terms.

A   **1.** $\dfrac{a - b}{a} \cdot (a + b)$ **7.** $\dfrac{2}{1 - x^2} \cdot \dfrac{1 - x}{3}$

2. $\dfrac{t - w}{t + 2w} \cdot \dfrac{t + w}{t - 2w}$ **8.** $\dfrac{4 - y^2}{14} \cdot \dfrac{7}{2 + y}$

3. $\dfrac{2}{t + 2} \cdot \dfrac{3}{t + 2}$ **9.** $\dfrac{3}{m + n} \cdot \dfrac{m^2 - n^2}{-5}$

4. $\dfrac{k + 4}{5} \cdot \dfrac{k + 4}{5}$ **10.** $\dfrac{2y + 2z}{5} \cdot \dfrac{10}{y + z}$

5. $\dfrac{x + y}{15} \cdot \dfrac{9}{x + y}$ **11.** $\dfrac{3x + 15}{2x} \cdot \dfrac{4x}{4x + 20}$

6. $\dfrac{a + b}{5} \cdot \dfrac{2}{b + a}$ **12.** $\dfrac{2t + 14}{6t} \cdot \dfrac{9t^2}{t^2 + 7t}$

13. $\dfrac{1}{x^2 + 1} \cdot \dfrac{1}{x^2 + 1}$

19. $\dfrac{y - 3}{8y - 4} \cdot \dfrac{10y - 5}{5y - 15}$

14. $\dfrac{(m + 3)^2}{mn} \cdot \dfrac{1}{(m + 3)}$

20. $\dfrac{2z - 4}{3z + 6} \cdot \dfrac{2z + 3}{z - 2}$

15. $\dfrac{(a + b)^2}{a^2 + b^2}$

21. $\left(\dfrac{a - b}{3}\right)^2 \cdot \dfrac{-1}{a + b}$

16. $\dfrac{s}{s - r} \cdot \dfrac{r + s}{s}$

22. $\dfrac{7m + 7n}{10} \cdot \dfrac{2}{m + n}$

17. $\dfrac{3x + y}{x - y} \cdot \dfrac{3x - y}{x + y}$

23. $\dfrac{1}{x^2 - 2} \cdot \dfrac{1}{x^2 - 2}$

18. $\dfrac{c^2 - d^2}{4} \cdot \dfrac{12}{c + d}$

24. $\dfrac{n - 2}{n - 1} \cdot \dfrac{n + 2}{n + 1}$

Write each product as a single fraction in lowest terms. Then show that each indicated product equals the final single fraction when $a = 3$, $b = 2$, $x = 5$, and $y = 1$.

SAMPLE: $\dfrac{a^2 - b^2}{3} \cdot \dfrac{1}{a - b}$

Solution: $\dfrac{a^2 - b^2}{3} \cdot \dfrac{1}{a - b} = \dfrac{a + b}{3}$

$$\dfrac{3^2 - 2^2}{3} \cdot \dfrac{1}{3 - 2} \quad \Big| \quad \dfrac{3 + 2}{3}$$

$$\dfrac{5}{3} \quad \Big| \quad \dfrac{5}{3}$$

25. $\dfrac{x^2 - y^2}{5} \cdot \dfrac{1}{x + y}$

28. $\dfrac{x^2 - 1}{2} \cdot \dfrac{1}{(x + 1)^2}$

26. $\dfrac{2y - 3}{3y + 5} \cdot \dfrac{9y^2 - 25}{2y^2 + y - 6}$

29. $\dfrac{a^2 - b^2}{ab} \cdot \dfrac{1}{a - b}$

27. $\dfrac{2a + b}{3} \cdot \dfrac{2a - b}{5}$

30. $\dfrac{x}{x^2 - 4x + 4} \cdot \dfrac{x - 2}{1}$

Express each product as a single fraction in lowest terms.

SAMPLE: $\dfrac{m^2 + 3m + 2}{2(m + 1)} \cdot \dfrac{m + 3}{m^2 + 5m + 6}$

Solution: $\dfrac{(m + 2)(m + 1)}{2(m + 1)} \cdot \dfrac{m + 3}{(m + 2)(m + 3)}$

$$= \dfrac{(m + 2)(m + 1)(m + 3)}{2(m + 1)(m + 2)(m + 3)} = \dfrac{1}{2}$$

B **31.** $\dfrac{b^2 + 2b + 1}{ab^2} \cdot \dfrac{a}{b + 1}$

34. $\dfrac{9x^2 - 1}{6x + 2} \cdot \dfrac{2}{3x - 1}$

32. $\dfrac{m^2 + m}{m^2} \cdot \dfrac{3m - 3}{m^2 - 1}$

35. $\dfrac{2a + b}{3} \cdot \dfrac{6a - 3b}{4a^2 - b^2}$

33. $\dfrac{6a + 6b}{a^2 - b^2} \cdot \dfrac{a^2 - ab}{2a}$

36. $\dfrac{a^2 + 5a + 4}{a + 4} \cdot \dfrac{a + 5}{a^2 + 6a + 5}$

C **37.** $\dfrac{c^2 - 5c - 6}{c^2 + 3c} \cdot \dfrac{c + 3}{6 - c}$

38. $\dfrac{b^2 + 5bc + 4c^2}{bc + 4c^2} \cdot \dfrac{b^2 + 5bc}{b^2 + 6bc + 5c^2}$

39. $\dfrac{x - y}{x^2 + xy} \cdot \dfrac{x^2 - y^2}{x^2 - xy}$

40. $\dfrac{t^2 - 2t - 3}{t^2 - 9} \cdot \dfrac{t^2 + 5t + 6}{t^2 - 1}$

Division

7–3 Basic Ideas about Division with Fractions

The equation $3 \div \frac{3}{2} = ?$ can be thought of as asking the question "How many $\frac{3}{2}$'s are in 3?" We can show a model of this by using a

number line. Notice that we have begun at **3** and drawn arrows, each $\frac{3}{2}$ units long, to the left. Since **two** arrows are needed to finish at the origin, we can write

$$3 \div \frac{3}{2} = 2.$$

The **3** is called the **dividend**; the number by which it is divided, $\frac{3}{2}$, is the **divisor**; the result of the division, **2**, is the **quotient**.

$$\text{dividend} \longrightarrow 3 \div \underset{\underset{\text{divisor}}{\uparrow}}{\tfrac{3}{2}} = 2 \longleftarrow \text{quotient}$$

Now, recall that the **quotient** of two numbers can be expressed as the **product** of the dividend and the **reciprocal** of the divisor. That is, we can write $3 \div \frac{3}{2} = ?$ as $3 \cdot \frac{2}{3} = ?$ Then, multiplying the fractions $\frac{3}{1}$ and $\frac{2}{3}$, we have

$$\frac{3}{1} \cdot \frac{2}{3} = \frac{6}{3} = 2.$$

So, $3 \div \frac{3}{2} = 2$.

In a similar way we can verify the meaning of the equation $\frac{2}{3} \div \frac{1}{6} = ?$, which asks the question "How many $\frac{1}{6}$'s are in $\frac{2}{3}$?"

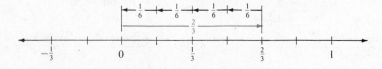

Do you see that our number line model shows that $\frac{2}{3} \div \frac{1}{6} = 4$? If we compute by multiplying the dividend by the reciprocal of the divisor, we have

$$\frac{2}{3} \div \frac{1}{6} = \frac{2}{3} \cdot \frac{6}{1}$$
$$= \frac{12}{3} = 4.$$

So, $\frac{2}{3} \div \frac{1}{6} = 4$.

The equation $\frac{1}{4} \div \frac{1}{2} = ?$ asks the question "How many $\frac{1}{2}$'s are in $\frac{1}{4}$?" Using the method of computing by multiplying the dividend by the reciprocal of the divisor, we have

$$\frac{1}{4} \div \frac{1}{2} = \frac{1}{4} \cdot \frac{2}{1}$$
$$= \frac{2}{4} = \frac{1}{2}.$$

So, $\frac{1}{4} \div \frac{1}{2} = \frac{1}{2}$.

So far, we have shown only divisions involving positive numbers. However, the method for division with fractions that represent negative numbers is similar. Of course, we must observe the usual rules for working with directed numbers.

EXAMPLE 1. $\frac{3}{4} \div \left(-\frac{2}{3}\right) = \frac{3}{4} \cdot \left(-\frac{3}{2}\right) = -\frac{9}{8}$

EXAMPLE 2. $\dfrac{-5}{8} \div \dfrac{3}{2} = -\dfrac{5}{8} \cdot \dfrac{2}{3} = -\dfrac{10}{24} = -\dfrac{5}{12}$

Notice that we have used the fact that $\dfrac{-5}{8} = -\dfrac{5}{8}$; recall that it also equals $\dfrac{5}{-8}$.

We have seen that an indicated division can be represented by a fraction.

$$4 \div 5 = \frac{4}{5} \qquad 6 \div 2 = \frac{6}{2} \qquad 12 \div 7 = \frac{12}{7}$$

In a similar way we can write

$$\frac{\frac{1}{2}}{\frac{1}{3}} = \frac{1}{2} \div \frac{1}{3}.$$

An expression in fraction form is called a **complex fraction** when its numerator or its denominator (or both) is expressed as a fraction. So we can **simplify** a complex fraction by performing the indicated division. For example:

$$\frac{\frac{7}{8}}{\frac{1}{5}} = \frac{7}{8} \div \frac{1}{5} \qquad \frac{\frac{9}{5}}{10} = \frac{9}{5} \div 10 \qquad \frac{7}{\frac{2}{5}} = 7 \div \frac{2}{5}$$

ORAL EXERCISES

Name the reciprocal of each of the following.

1. $\frac{5}{8}$ **5.** $\frac{17}{8}$ **9.** -8

2. $\frac{7}{2}$ **6.** $\frac{13}{3}$ **10.** $-\frac{3}{8}$

3. $\frac{-3}{5}$ **7.** $-\frac{7}{2}$ **11.** $\frac{2}{-7}$

4. $\frac{5}{2}$ **8.** 6 **12.** $\frac{11}{2}$

Tell whether the quotient of each indicated division is a positive or a negative number. Do not compute the quotient.

13. $\frac{1}{2} \div \left(-\frac{2}{3}\right)$ **16.** $\frac{7}{2} \div \frac{1}{8}$ **19.** $\frac{2}{5} \div (-6)$

14. $\left(-\frac{3}{5}\right) \div \frac{7}{8}$ **17.** $\left(-\frac{1}{3}\right) \div \left(-\frac{1}{4}\right)$ **20.** $\left(-4\frac{1}{3}\right) \div 3$

15. $\dfrac{\frac{-1}{5}}{\frac{4}{3}}$ **18.** $\dfrac{-5}{\frac{1}{10}}$ **21.** $\dfrac{-6\frac{1}{2}}{-\frac{1}{4}}$

WRITTEN EXERCISES

Match each question in Column 1 with the related model in Column 2. Then answer the question.

COLUMN 1   COLUMN 2

 1. How many $\frac{3}{4}$'s are in 3?   **A.**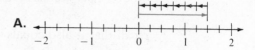

2. How many $\frac{1}{3}$'s are in 2?   **B.**

3. How many $\frac{1}{4}$'s are in $1\frac{1}{2}$?   **C.**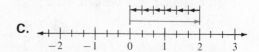

4. How many $-\frac{2}{3}$'s are in $-2\frac{2}{3}$? **D.**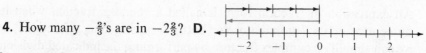

Express each quotient as a single fraction in lowest terms.

SAMPLE: $\frac{3}{8} \div \frac{6}{5}$ *Solution:* $\frac{3}{8} \div \frac{6}{5} = \frac{3}{8} \cdot \frac{5}{6}$

$$= \frac{15}{48} = \frac{5}{16}$$

5. $\frac{2}{5} \div \frac{7}{10}$ **6.** $\frac{3}{7} \div 63$ **7.** $\left(-\frac{3}{4}\right) \div \frac{1}{5}$

8. $\frac{3}{5} \div 6$ **11.** $\frac{1}{5} \div \frac{5}{3}$ **14.** $\left(-\frac{5}{10}\right) \div \left(-\frac{5}{8}\right)$

9. $\frac{5}{8} \div 10$ **12.** $(-6) \div \frac{4}{5}$ **15.** $\left(-\frac{7}{16}\right) \div \left(-\frac{3}{2}\right)$

10. $\frac{3}{2} \div 5$ **13.** $12 \div \frac{7}{8}$ **16.** $\frac{15}{4} \div \frac{16}{3}$

Replace the variables in each equation with integers so that a true statement results. Check your answers.

SAMPLE: $\quad \dfrac{2}{3} \div \dfrac{x}{y} = \dfrac{10}{21}$ *Solution:* $\dfrac{2}{3} \div \dfrac{x}{y} = \dfrac{10}{21}$ *Check:* $\dfrac{2}{3} \div \dfrac{7}{5} = \dfrac{10}{21}$

$$\dfrac{2}{3} \cdot \dfrac{y}{x} = \dfrac{10}{21}$$

$$\begin{array}{c|c} \frac{2}{3} \cdot \frac{5}{7} & \frac{10}{21} \\[4pt] \frac{10}{21} & \frac{10}{21} \end{array}$$

$$y = 5$$

$$x = 7$$

17. $\dfrac{5}{7} \div \dfrac{m}{n} = \dfrac{15}{14}$ **21.** $\dfrac{b}{d} \div \dfrac{12}{5} = \dfrac{35}{96}$

18. $\dfrac{3}{5} \div \dfrac{a}{b} = \dfrac{3}{40}$ **22.** $\dfrac{3}{5} \div \dfrac{b}{c} = \dfrac{6}{5}$

19. $\dfrac{-3}{8} \div \dfrac{x}{y} = -\dfrac{15}{56}$ **23.** $\left(-\dfrac{7}{8}\right) \div \dfrac{r}{t} = -\dfrac{21}{8}$

20. $\dfrac{r}{s} \div \dfrac{3}{10} = \dfrac{50}{27}$ **24.** $\dfrac{12}{25} = \dfrac{m}{n} \div \dfrac{5}{3}$

Show whether each statement is true or false.

SAMPLE: $\quad \frac{2}{5} \div \frac{3}{4} = \frac{3}{4} \div \frac{2}{5}$ *Solution:* $\dfrac{2}{5} \div \dfrac{3}{4} \overset{?}{=} \dfrac{3}{4} \div \dfrac{2}{5}$

$$\begin{array}{c|c} \frac{2}{5} \cdot \frac{4}{3} & \frac{3}{4} \cdot \frac{5}{2} \\[4pt] \frac{8}{15} & \frac{15}{8} \end{array}$$

$\frac{2}{5} \div \frac{3}{4} = \frac{3}{4} \div \frac{2}{5}$ is a false statement.

25. $\frac{1}{2} \div \frac{5}{8} = \frac{5}{10} \div \frac{5}{8}$ **29.** $\frac{6}{10} \div \left(-\frac{8}{4}\right) = \frac{3}{5} \div (-2)$

26. $\left(-\frac{3}{4}\right) \div \frac{6}{7} = \frac{3}{4} \div \left(-\frac{6}{7}\right)$ **30.** $\frac{12}{2} \div 2 = \frac{30}{5} \div \frac{10}{5}$

27. $\frac{4}{5} \div \frac{4}{3} = \frac{4}{3} \div \frac{4}{5}$ **31.** $\left(-\frac{5}{16}\right) \div \frac{8}{5} = -\left(\frac{5}{16} \div \frac{8}{5}\right)$

28. $\left(-\frac{5}{8}\right) \div \left(-\frac{1}{4}\right) = \frac{5}{8} \div \frac{1}{4}$ **32.** $\frac{5}{2} \div \frac{5}{3} = \left(-\frac{5}{2}\right) \div \left(-\frac{5}{3}\right)$

Express each indicated quotient as a single fraction in lowest terms.

SAMPLE: $\quad \dfrac{\frac{5}{8}}{\frac{3}{4}}$ *Solution:* $\dfrac{\frac{5}{8}}{\frac{3}{4}} = \dfrac{5}{8} \div \dfrac{3}{4}$

$$= \dfrac{5}{8} \cdot \dfrac{4}{3} = \dfrac{5}{6}$$

33. $\dfrac{\frac{1}{2}}{\frac{2}{9}}$ **35.** $\dfrac{\frac{4}{5}}{\frac{4}{5}}$ **37.** $\dfrac{-\frac{10}{7}}{\frac{7}{10}}$

34. $\dfrac{\frac{2}{3}}{\frac{9}{10}}$ **36.** $\dfrac{\frac{3}{10}}{-\frac{3}{10}}$ **38.** $\dfrac{\frac{3}{4}}{\frac{1}{4}}$

B **39.** $\dfrac{\frac{4}{3}}{\frac{7}{8}}$ **41.** $\dfrac{-\frac{9}{4}}{\frac{3}{2}}$ **43.** $\dfrac{\frac{7}{8}}{\frac{9}{16}}$

40. $\dfrac{\frac{5}{2}}{-\frac{16}{5}}$ **42.** $\dfrac{-\frac{9}{10}}{-\frac{4}{3}}$ **44.** $\dfrac{-\frac{25}{2}}{\frac{1}{8}}$

7–4 Division with Fractions Having Monomial Numerators and Denominators

We have been using the idea that division by a number gives the same result as multiplication by the reciprocal of the number. This rule for division with fractions can be stated as follows:

> For any directed numbers *a*, *b*, *c*, and *d*, where *b*, *c*, and *d* are not zero,
>
> $$\frac{a}{b} \div \frac{c}{d} = \frac{a}{b} \cdot \frac{d}{c}.$$

In the following examples, we apply this rule to express each quotient as a single fraction. Of course, no denominator may equal zero. Since that is always true, we shall assume that it is understood from now on, without stating it specifically each time that a variable occurs in a denominator.

EXAMPLE 1. $\dfrac{a^2}{b^3} \div \dfrac{a}{b} = \dfrac{a^2}{b^3} \cdot \dfrac{b}{a}$

$$= \frac{a^2 b}{ab^3} = \frac{a}{b^2}$$

EXAMPLE 2. $25x^2 \div \dfrac{15x}{2} = \dfrac{25x^2}{1} \cdot \dfrac{2}{15x}$

$$= \frac{10x}{3}$$

EXAMPLE 3. $(-18x^2 y) \div \dfrac{10}{3}x = (-18x^2 y) \div \dfrac{10x}{3}$

$$= (-18x^2 y) \cdot \frac{3}{10x} = -\frac{27xy}{5}$$

Note in Example 3 that, since $\dfrac{10}{3}x = \dfrac{10x}{3}$, we have used $\dfrac{3}{10x}$ as the reciprocal of $\dfrac{10}{3}x$. This idea is further illustrated in the following statements.

The reciprocal of $\dfrac{1}{2}x$ is $\dfrac{2}{x}$.

The reciprocal of $-\dfrac{5}{8}t$ is $-\dfrac{8}{5t}$.

The reciprocal of $\dfrac{-4}{3}m$ is $-\dfrac{3}{4m}$.

ORAL EXERCISES

Name the reciprocal of each of the following.

SAMPLE: $\dfrac{5xyz}{8m}$ *What you say:* $\dfrac{8m}{5xyz}$

1. $\dfrac{3s^2}{2t}$

2. $\dfrac{2m^2}{7n^2}$

3. $\dfrac{10rst}{7}$

4. $\dfrac{-3xy}{4z}$

5. $\dfrac{m^3}{n^2}$

6. $-\dfrac{ab}{3}$

7. $-\dfrac{3k}{2}$

8. $\dfrac{a^2b}{2}$

9. $\frac{1}{5}t$

10. $-\frac{5}{2}s^2t$

11. $12b^2$

12. $-3mn$

WRITTEN EXERCISES

Express each quotient as a single fraction in lowest terms.

SAMPLE: $\dfrac{2b^2}{3} \div \dfrac{4b}{5}$ *Solution:* $\dfrac{2b^2}{3} \div \dfrac{4b}{5} = \dfrac{2b^2}{3} \cdot \dfrac{5}{4b}$

$= \dfrac{5b}{6}$

1. $\left(-\dfrac{5}{8}\right) \div \dfrac{x}{y}$

2. $\dfrac{2n^2}{5} \div \dfrac{3n}{2}$

3. $\dfrac{3mn}{5} \div \dfrac{2n}{5}$

4. $\dfrac{4}{5}x^2 \div \dfrac{2x}{3}$

5. $\left(-\dfrac{2}{3}\right) \div (-3m)$

6. $3k \div \frac{3}{2}m$

7. $\dfrac{3x}{4} \div \dfrac{x^2}{4}$

10. $\dfrac{27x^5y^3}{-8} \div \dfrac{-3x^2y^5}{16}$

13. $\dfrac{7}{3}b^3 \div \dfrac{14}{c}$

8. $3t^2 \div \dfrac{2t}{3}$

11. $\dfrac{15}{14ab} \div \dfrac{ab}{2}$

14. $\dfrac{-7d}{10c^2} \div \dfrac{4d}{3}$

9. $\left(-\dfrac{a}{b}\right) \div \dfrac{7}{3}$

12. $\dfrac{10a}{3b} \div \dfrac{5c}{12d}$

15. $-14xy \div \dfrac{3x}{2y}$

Express each complex fraction as a single fraction in lowest terms.

SAMPLE: $\dfrac{\dfrac{x}{y^2}}{\dfrac{x^2}{y}}$

Solution: $\dfrac{\dfrac{x}{y^2}}{\dfrac{x^2}{y}} = \dfrac{x}{y^2} \div \dfrac{x^2}{y}$

$$= \dfrac{x}{y^2} \cdot \dfrac{y}{x^2} = \dfrac{1}{xy}$$

16. $\dfrac{\dfrac{r^2}{s^2}}{\dfrac{r}{s^3}}$

19. $\dfrac{\dfrac{-3t}{8s^2}}{\dfrac{12t^2}{4s^3}}$

22. $(-10z^2) \div \dfrac{5z}{3}$

17. $\dfrac{\dfrac{p^2}{2q}}{\dfrac{p^4}{4q^3}}$

20. $\dfrac{\dfrac{81k^2}{28k}}{\dfrac{9k}{7k^3}}$

23. $\dfrac{\dfrac{3a^2}{b}}{-9}$

18. $\dfrac{\dfrac{n^2}{m^3}}{\dfrac{3n}{m^4}}$

21. $\dfrac{20a^2}{\dfrac{4a}{3}}$

24. $\dfrac{\dfrac{-8x^2}{10}}{-\dfrac{3y}{10}}$

Show that each of the following is true when $a = 5$, $b = 2$, $c = 3$, and $d = -2$.

SAMPLE: $\dfrac{ab}{c} \div \dfrac{b^2}{c^2} = \dfrac{a}{b} \cdot c$

Solution: $\dfrac{ab}{c} \div \dfrac{b^2}{c^2} = \dfrac{a}{b} \cdot c$

$$\begin{array}{c|c} \dfrac{5 \cdot 2}{3} \div \dfrac{2^2}{3^2} & \dfrac{5}{2} \cdot 3 \\[2ex] \dfrac{15}{2} & \dfrac{15}{2} \end{array}$$

B **25.** $\dfrac{ab}{c} \div \dfrac{ac}{d} = \dfrac{b}{c} \cdot \dfrac{d}{c}$

28. $\dfrac{ad^2}{14} \div \dfrac{bd^2}{10} = \dfrac{a}{b} \div \dfrac{7}{5}$

26. $\dfrac{10b}{c} \div \dfrac{ab^2}{c^2} = 10\dfrac{c}{ab}$

29. $\dfrac{ab^3}{d} \div (b + c) = 2d$

27. $\dfrac{3a^2}{b^2} \div \dfrac{18a}{b^3} = \dfrac{a}{6} \cdot b$

30. $\dfrac{4b^2c}{3a^2} \div \dfrac{8b^2c^3}{15a} = \dfrac{1}{bc^2}$

Find the missing numerator or denominator in each equation.

SAMPLE: $\dfrac{2m^4}{6n} \div \dfrac{m^2}{(?)} = \dfrac{2m^2}{3}$

Solution: $\dfrac{2m^4}{6n} \div \dfrac{m^2}{(?)} = \dfrac{2m^4}{6n} \cdot \dfrac{(?)}{m^2}$

$$= \dfrac{2m^4 \cdot (?)}{6m^2n}$$

$$= \dfrac{m^2 \cdot (?)}{3n}$$

$$\dfrac{2m^2}{3} = \dfrac{2m^2 \cdot n}{3n} = \dfrac{m^2 \cdot (2n)}{3n}$$

The missing denominator is $2n$.

[C] **31.** $\dfrac{3mn^2}{20a} \div \dfrac{(?)}{5a^2} = \dfrac{an^2}{8}$

33. $\dfrac{4a^2}{(?)} \div \dfrac{5a}{b^2} = \dfrac{4a}{45}$

32. $\dfrac{(?)}{4} \div \dfrac{12b^2}{5} = \dfrac{5a}{16b}$

34. $\dfrac{m^5}{n} \div \dfrac{(?)}{3} = \dfrac{3m^2}{7n}$

PROBLEMS

1. The circumference, in inches, of a circle is represented by the fraction $\dfrac{110k^2}{63}$. What is the diameter of the circle? Use $\pi = \frac{22}{7}$.

   Hint: Since circumference $= \pi \cdot$ diameter, we know circumference $\div$ $\pi =$ diameter.

2. The distance, in miles, traveled by an ICBM is given by the expression $\dfrac{3s^2g^3}{19m}$. The speed of the missile, in miles per hour, is represented by $\dfrac{21sg^2}{57m}$. Find an expression to represent the number of hours required by the missile to travel the distance given. Hint: distance $=$ rate $\times$ time, so $\dfrac{\text{distance}}{\text{rate}} =$ time.

3. Find the area of the larger square region in the diagram at the left below. Then decide how many of the smaller squares will fit into the larger one.

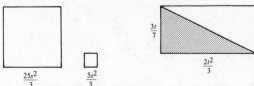

$\dfrac{25s^2}{3}$ $\dfrac{5s^2}{3}$ $\dfrac{3t}{7}$ $\dfrac{2t^2}{3}$

4. Find the area of the shaded part of the rectangular region in the figure at the right above.

5. The quotient of two numbers is $\frac{15}{4}$. Find the dividend if the divisor is $\frac{2}{3}$. Hint: $(?) \div \frac{2}{3} = \frac{15}{4}$.

6. What number must be divided by $\frac{2}{5}$ to give the quotient $\frac{35}{16}$? Hint: $(?) \div \frac{2}{5} = \frac{35}{16}$.

7–5 More about Division with Fractions

Now, let us see how we can combine the basic ideas of division with your understanding of factoring polynomials.

EXAMPLE 1.
$$\frac{2x - 2y}{10} \div \frac{x^2 - y^2}{5} = \frac{2x - 2y}{10} \cdot \frac{5}{x^2 - y^2}$$
$$= \frac{2(x - y)}{10} \cdot \frac{5}{(x + y)(x - y)}$$
$$= \frac{10(x - y)}{10(x + y)(x - y)} = \frac{1}{x + y}$$

EXAMPLE 2.
$$\frac{n + 3}{3n + 3} \div \frac{n^2 - n - 12}{n^2 - 1} = \frac{n + 3}{3n + 3} \cdot \frac{n^2 - 1}{n^2 - n - 12}$$
$$= \frac{(n + 3)}{3(n + 1)} \cdot \frac{(n + 1)(n - 1)}{(n + 3)(n - 4)}$$
$$= \frac{(n + 3)(n + 1)(n - 1)}{3(n + 1)(n + 3)(n - 4)}$$
$$= \frac{(n - 1)}{3(n - 4)}, \text{ or } \frac{n - 1}{3n - 12}$$

In Examples 1 and 2, we have assumed, of course, that no value of the variable results in a zero denominator. Did you notice how the reciprocals of the divisors were written?

Divisor	Reciprocal
$\dfrac{x^2 - y^2}{5}$	$\dfrac{5}{x^2 - y^2}$
$\dfrac{n^2 - n - 12}{n^2 - 1}$	$\dfrac{n^2 - 1}{n^2 - n - 12}$

In general, we use the following procedure for division with fractions whose numerators and denominators include polynomials of two or more terms:

(1) Restate the problem as the **product** of the dividend and the **reciprocal** of the divisor.
(2) **Factor** all polynomials completely.
(3) Identify any factors that are common to both the numerator and the denominator of the product; use the **multiplication property** of **one** to simplify the product.
(4) Write the final result in simplest form.

WRITTEN EXERCISES

Simplify each indicated quotient.

SAMPLE: $\dfrac{x+2}{x+3} \div \dfrac{x+2}{2}$

Solution: $\dfrac{x+2}{x+3} \div \dfrac{x+2}{2} = \dfrac{x+2}{x+3} \cdot \dfrac{2}{x+2}$

$$= \dfrac{2(x+2)}{(x+3)(x+2)} = \dfrac{2}{x+3}$$

A

1. $\dfrac{2}{5-t} \div \dfrac{3}{5-t}$

2. $\dfrac{a+b}{5} \div \dfrac{a-b}{5}$

3. $\dfrac{r}{s-t} \div \dfrac{r}{r-s}$

4. $\dfrac{5s}{s+6} \div \dfrac{-2}{s+6}$

5. $\dfrac{1}{(2x+1)(x-2)} \div \dfrac{3}{x-2}$

6. $\dfrac{(x+2)(x+1)}{x+3} \div (x+2)$

7. $(a+b) \div \dfrac{(a+b)(a-b)}{3a}$

8. $\dfrac{3k-1}{28} \div \dfrac{3k-1}{7}$

9. $\dfrac{(2m+5)(m-3)}{m+2} \div \dfrac{3(m-3)}{2}$

10. $\dfrac{3a+b+c}{2a-b} \div \dfrac{2a-b+c}{2a-b}$

11. $\dfrac{a^3}{(x-y)^2} \div \dfrac{2a}{(x-y)^2}$

12. $\dfrac{3r-s}{5} \div \dfrac{(r+3)}{10}$

Show that each of the following is correct.

SAMPLE: $\dfrac{4-x^2}{3x} \div (2+x) = \dfrac{2-x}{3x}$

Solution: $\dfrac{4-x^2}{3x} \div (2+x) = \dfrac{4-x^2}{3x} \cdot \dfrac{1}{(2+x)}$

$$= \dfrac{(2-x)(2+x)}{3x(2+x)} = \dfrac{2-x}{3x}$$

13. $\dfrac{ab+b^2}{a^3+2a^2b} \div \dfrac{2ab+b^2}{a^2+2ab} = \dfrac{a+b}{2a^2+ab}$

14. $\dfrac{x^2 + 2x + 1}{x^2} \div (x + 1) = \dfrac{x + 1}{x^2}$

15. $\dfrac{m^2 - 9}{2m} \div (m + 3) = \dfrac{m - 3}{2m}$

16. $\dfrac{t + 5}{t^2 - 25} \div \dfrac{1}{t - 5} = 1$

17. $\dfrac{x^2 - 4x + 4}{x^3} \div \dfrac{x - 2}{x} = \dfrac{x - 2}{x^2}$

18. $\dfrac{y^2 - 4}{y^2 - 4y + 4} \div \dfrac{3y + 6}{7y - 14} = \dfrac{7}{3}$

19. $\dfrac{4r + 2}{2r^2 + 2r} \div \dfrac{4r^2 - 1}{4r^2 - 4} = \dfrac{4r - 4}{2r^2 - r}$

20. $\dfrac{a^2 - 4a + 4}{a^2 - 4} \div \dfrac{7a - 14}{3a + 6} = \dfrac{3}{7}$

Simplify each indicated quotient.

21. $\dfrac{3a - b}{4a^2} \div \dfrac{3a - b}{10b^2}$

22. $\dfrac{6z - 3}{36} \div \dfrac{3z - 1}{9}$

23. $\dfrac{s + 5}{s^2 - 9} \div \dfrac{1}{s - 3}$

24. $\dfrac{y^3}{y^2 + 4y + 4} \div \dfrac{y}{y + 2}$

25. $\dfrac{3y + 3z}{4y^2} \div \dfrac{y^2 - z^2}{2y^2}$

26. $\dfrac{y^2 - 4}{2y} \div (y + 2)$

27. $\dfrac{m^2 - 2m + 1}{m^2} \div (m - 1)$

28. $\dfrac{x^2 + 2x + 1}{3} \div \dfrac{x + 1}{7}$

29. $\dfrac{r^2 + 2rs}{2rs + s^2} \div \dfrac{r^3 + 2r^2s}{rs + s^2}$

30. $\dfrac{x^2 - 4}{x^3} \div \dfrac{x^2 - 4x + 4}{x^2}$

B 31. $\dfrac{n^2 - m^2}{n^2 - 3n - 4} \div \dfrac{n - m}{n^2 + n}$

32. $\dfrac{4z^2 + 8z + 3}{2z^2 - 5z + 3} \div \dfrac{4z^2 - 1}{6z^2 - 9z}$

33. $\dfrac{r^2 - r - 20}{r^2 + 7r + 12} \div \dfrac{(r - 5)^2}{(r + 3)^2}$

34. $\dfrac{3s^2 - 14s + 8}{2s^2 - 3s - 20} \div \dfrac{24s^2 - 25s + 6}{16s^2 + 34s - 15}$

CHAPTER SUMMARY

Inventory of Structure and Concepts

1. The **basic rule** for **multiplication** with fractions states that for any directed numbers a, b, c, and d, where neither b nor d is zero, $\dfrac{a}{b} \cdot \dfrac{c}{d} = \dfrac{a \cdot c}{b \cdot d}$.

2. Multiplication with fractions is **commutative**: for any directed numbers a, b, c, and d, where neither b nor d is zero, $\dfrac{a}{b} \cdot \dfrac{c}{d} = \dfrac{c}{d} \cdot \dfrac{a}{b}$.

3. Multiplication with fractions is **associative**: for any directed numbers a, b, c, d, e, and f, where b, d, and f are not zero,

$$\left(\frac{a}{b} \cdot \frac{c}{d}\right) \cdot \frac{e}{f} = \frac{a}{b} \cdot \left(\frac{c}{d} \cdot \frac{e}{f}\right).$$

4. The **multiplicative property** of **one** states that for directed numbers a and b, where b is not zero, $\dfrac{a}{b} \cdot 1 = 1 \cdot \dfrac{a}{b} = \dfrac{a}{b}$.

5. In the division sentence $a \div b = c$, a is called the **dividend**, b is called the **divisor**, and c is called the **quotient**.

6. A quotient can be expressed as the **product** of the dividend and the **reciprocal** of the divisor. Thus the **basic rule** for **division** with fractions states that for any directed numbers a, b, c, and d, where b, c, and d are not zero, $\dfrac{a}{b} \div \dfrac{c}{d} = \dfrac{a}{b} \cdot \dfrac{d}{c}$.

7. An expression in fraction form is called a **complex fraction** when its numerator or its denominator (or both) is expressed as a fraction.

Vocabulary and Spelling

commutative property (*p. 221*)

associative property (*p. 222*)

multiplicative property of one (*p. 222*)

dividend (*p. 228*)

divisor (*p. 228*)

quotient (*p. 228*)

reciprocal (*p. 228*)

complex fraction (*p. 229*)

Chapter Test

Write each indicated product as a single fraction in lowest terms.

1. $\dfrac{n}{4} \cdot \dfrac{3}{5}$

2. $\dfrac{7k}{3n} \cdot \dfrac{4k^2}{11m^2 n^2}$

3. $-\left(\tfrac{3}{8} \cdot \tfrac{2}{5}\right) \cdot 10$

4. $\dfrac{2a^2}{5} \cdot \left(\dfrac{7a}{2b} \cdot \dfrac{4}{3b}\right)$

5. $\dfrac{a+b}{7} \cdot \dfrac{a-b}{2c}$

6. $\dfrac{x^2 - 9}{10} \cdot \dfrac{5}{x-3}$

7. $\left(-\dfrac{4}{a}\cdot\dfrac{1}{2a}\right)\cdot\left(-\dfrac{1}{2}\right)$

9. $\dfrac{7a+7b}{a-b}\cdot\dfrac{3a-3b}{-21}$

8. $\dfrac{-12t^2}{3}\cdot\dfrac{2s}{5}$

Express each complex fraction as a single fraction in lowest terms.

10. $\dfrac{\frac{3}{5}}{\frac{2}{3}}$

11. $\dfrac{\frac{-5}{8}}{\frac{3}{4}}$

12. $\dfrac{\frac{5x^2}{y}}{-\frac{2x}{10y}}$

Write each indicated quotient as a single fraction in lowest terms.

13. $\frac{3}{5}\div\frac{4}{3}$

15. $(-18r^2s)\div\dfrac{9rs}{5}$

14. $(-5)\div\frac{1}{4}$

16. $\dfrac{24x^3y^4}{-5}\div\dfrac{-8xy^2}{2}$

Simplify each indicated product or quotient.

17. $\dfrac{m^2-2mn+n^2}{m^2}\div(m-n)$

20. $\dfrac{k^2}{k^2+6k+9}\div\dfrac{k}{k+3}$

18. $\dfrac{3}{r^2-s^2}\cdot\dfrac{r+s}{7}$

21. $\dfrac{p+3}{p^2-4}\cdot\dfrac{3p+6}{p^2+p-6}$

19. $\dfrac{x^2-9}{3x^2}\div\dfrac{x^2+5x+6}{x^3}$

22. $\dfrac{m^2+4m+3}{2m^2-3m-5}\cdot\dfrac{2m-5}{3m+3}$

Chapter Review

7–1 Basic Ideas about Multiplication with Fractions

Complete each statement.

1. $\frac{1}{10}$ of $\frac{2}{3}$ is ___?___.

3. $\frac{5}{2}$ of $\frac{3}{10}$ is ___?___.

5. $\frac{3}{8}$ of -6 is ___?___.

2. $\frac{1}{3}$ of $\frac{5}{8}$ is ___?___.

4. $\frac{7}{8}\cdot12=$ ___?___.

6. $\left(-\frac{3}{4}\right)\cdot\frac{4}{5}=$ ___?___.

Write each of the following as a single fraction in lowest terms.

7. $\dfrac{5a}{3b}\cdot\dfrac{2a}{12b}$

9. $\dfrac{45st}{7s}\cdot\dfrac{st}{15t}$

11. $\dfrac{-10ac}{5}\cdot\dfrac{-4bc}{25b^2}$

8. $12x^2y^2\cdot\dfrac{2}{8x}$

10. $\left(\dfrac{-2x}{3}\right)\cdot\dfrac{1}{4x}\cdot\dfrac{7x}{2}$

12. $\dfrac{15yz}{6y}\cdot\dfrac{-8y^2z}{2z}$

7–2   Using Factoring in Multiplication with Fractions

Write each of the following as a single fraction in lowest terms.

13. $\dfrac{(a+b)^2}{(a+b)} \cdot \dfrac{a-b}{3}$

15. $\dfrac{2x^2 + x - 6}{x^2 - 25} \cdot \dfrac{x+5}{2x-3}$

14. $\dfrac{4m-n}{m+n} \cdot \dfrac{4m+n}{m-n}$

16. $\dfrac{x^2 + 3x + 2}{x+1} \cdot \dfrac{x-5}{3x+6}$

7–3   Basic Ideas about Division with Fractions

Name the reciprocal for each of the following.

17. $\frac{3}{8}$ **18.** $-\frac{4}{5}$ **19.** $-\frac{16}{3}$ **20.** $\frac{7}{4}$

Write each quotient as a single fraction in lowest terms.

21. $\frac{6}{35} \div \frac{3}{14}$ **23.** $\left(\dfrac{-13}{15}\right) \div \dfrac{39}{20}$ **25.** $\frac{7}{12} \div \frac{7}{12}$

22. $\frac{22}{49} \div \frac{55}{14}$ **24.** $\frac{9}{5} \div \left(-\frac{3}{5}\right)$ **26.** $\frac{7}{48} \div \frac{35}{12}$

7–4   Division with Fractions Having Monomial Numerators and Denominators

Write each quotient as a single fraction in lowest terms.

27. $\dfrac{3}{10x^2} \div \dfrac{4}{15x}$

29. $\dfrac{9z^2}{5} \div 3z$

28. $\dfrac{26a^2}{15c^2} \div \dfrac{39a^2}{20c}$

30. $\dfrac{-22x^3}{35y^4} \div \dfrac{11x}{7y^5}$

Solve each problem.

31. The number of square feet in the area of a rectangle is represented by the fraction $\dfrac{9x^2y}{15}$. If the fraction $\dfrac{3xy}{5}$ represents the number of feet in the width, how would you represent the number of feet in the length?

32. A certain number divided by $\frac{2}{3}$ gives the quotient $\frac{9}{10}$. What is the number?

7–5   More about Division with Fractions

Simplify each quotient.

33. $\dfrac{b-2}{a^2+a} \div \dfrac{b^2-4}{a^2+3a+2}$

34. $\dfrac{1-c}{d+d^2} \div \dfrac{1-c^2}{1-d^2}$

35. $\dfrac{2x + x^2}{4x - 5} \div \dfrac{4x^2 + 2x^3}{16x - 20}$

38. $\dfrac{x^2 + 13xy + 12y^2}{3xy^2} \div (x + y)$

36. $\dfrac{m^2 - n^2}{mn^2} \div \dfrac{mn + n^2}{m}$

39. $\dfrac{(x + y)^2(x + y)}{7} \div (x + y)^2$

37. $\dfrac{8a - 32}{a + b} \div \dfrac{16}{3a + 3b}$

40. $\dfrac{2xy}{x^2 - 4xy + 3y^2} \div \dfrac{4xy^2}{x^2 + xy - 2y^2}$

Review of Skills

Write each number as the product of primes.

1. 42   **3.** 66   **5.** 120   **7.** 90

2. 70   **4.** 12   **6.** 16   **8.** 28

Evaluate each of the following when $a = 10$ and $b = 2$.

9. $\dfrac{-a}{-b}$ **11.** $-\left(\dfrac{-a}{b}\right)$ **13.** $-\left(\dfrac{-b}{a}\right)$

10. $-\left(\dfrac{a}{-b}\right)$ **12.** $\dfrac{-b}{-a}$ **14.** $-\left(\dfrac{b}{-a}\right)$

Simplify each sum or difference.

15. $\frac{1}{3} + \frac{1}{4}$ **17.** $\frac{5}{6} - \frac{1}{3}$ **19.** $(\frac{5}{2} - \frac{3}{4}) + \frac{1}{4}$

16. $\frac{3}{8} + \frac{1}{2}$ **18.** $\frac{1}{2} + \frac{1}{3} + \frac{1}{4}$ **20.** $1\frac{1}{3} + \frac{5}{6}$

Write each percent as a fraction whose denominator is 100.

21. 3%   **22.** 6%   **23.** 12%   **24.** $7\frac{1}{2}$%

Copy and complete each sentence.

25. $\dfrac{5m}{8} \cdot \dfrac{8}{5} = \underline{\ ?\ }$ **27.** $\dfrac{7x}{6} \cdot \underline{\ ?\ } = x$

26. $\dfrac{3}{4} \cdot \dfrac{4k}{3} = \underline{\ ?\ }$ **28.** $\dfrac{4m^2}{5} \cdot \underline{\ ?\ } = m^2$

Make a number line graph of each set of directed numbers.

29. {the directed numbers greater than 1}

30. {the directed numbers less than $-\frac{1}{2}$}

31. {the directed numbers greater than or equal to -2}

32. {the directed numbers less than or equal to 4}

Solve each open sentence and write the solution set. The domain of the variable is {the directed numbers}.

33. $2b + 7 = 19$ **37.** $7w \geq 21$

34. $9m - 11 = 25$ **38.** $-6b \leq 30$

35. $-4(n + 5) = 0$ **39.** $3m + 5 < m + 9$

36. $k(5 + k) - k^2 = 35$ **40.** $3t + t - 6 > -18$

Match each statement in Column 1 with the property it illustrates in Column 2.

COLUMN 1

41. If $a = b$, then $ac = bc$.

42. If $a > b$, then $a + c > b + c$.

43. If $a = b$, then $a + c = b + c$.

44. If $a = b$ and $b = c$, then $a = c$.

45. If $a < b$ and $c > 0$, then $ac < bc$.

COLUMN 2

A. Addition property for equality

B. Multiplication property for inequality

C. Transitive property for equality

D. Addition property for inequality

E. Multiplication property for equality

■ ■

CHECK POINT
FOR EXPERTS

Logic and Venn Diagrams

A Venn diagram can often be used to represent a simple logical statement involving one of the adjectives **all**, **some**, or **no**.

EXAMPLE 1.   All dogs are animals.

In the Venn diagram, the closed curve representing the set of all dogs lies wholly within the curve that represents the set of animals, indicating that every dog is also an animal.

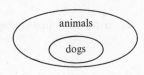

EXAMPLE 2. No dogs are horses.

This time the Venn diagram consists of two closed curves that have no points in common, indicating that there is *no* dog that is also a horse. The two sets, of dogs and of horses, are called disjoint sets.

As we use it in logic, the word **some** has the meaning **at least one**. For example, consider the sentence "Some fish can fly." This sentence is true if

a. there is just *one* fish that can fly, or

b. there are *two or more* fish that can fly, or

c. *all* fish fly.

EXAMPLE 3. Some prime numbers are even numbers.

This Venn diagram consists of two overlapping curves, to indicate that there is at least one number that is both an even number and a prime number. Can you name such a number?

Questions

Match each statement in Column 1 with its Venn diagram in Column 2.

COLUMN 1   COLUMN 2

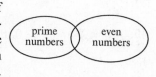

1. All squares are rectangles.   A.

2. No boys are strong.   B.

3. Some boys are strong.   C.

4. Some rectangles are squares.   D.

For each statement draw an appropriate Venn diagram.

5. All tigers are cats.

6. Some quadrilaterals are squares.

7. Some angles of a triangle are acute angles.

8. No whole numbers are negative numbers.

9. No tigers are friendly.

10. All multiples of 10 are divisible by 2.

Write a statement for each diagram:

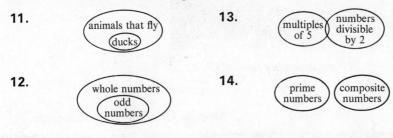

11.   animals that fly / ducks

13.   multiples of 5 / numbers divisible by 2

12.   whole numbers / odd numbers

14.   prime numbers / composite numbers

Ford assembly line of 1913 . . .

Modern assembly-line production . . .

Addition and Subtraction with Fractions

Assembly-line production, for which men groped in the workshops of the eighteenth and nineteenth centuries, was finally achieved by Henry Ford early in the twentieth century. Elements required by mass production include division of labor, standardization of parts, precision-tooling, and the assembly line. The Ford assembly line of 1913 ended outside the plant; a "Model T" body was skidded down a ramp and dropped onto the complete chassis, which was driven out from under the ramp. This operation, primitive though it seems today, helped change the automobile from a luxury to a common mode of transportation. Over the ensuing half-century, assembly-line production has developed steadily by means of scientific advances.

Combining Fractions with Equal Denominators

8–1   Addition with Fractions Having Equal Monomial Denominators

We have defined a fraction as a symbol for a number, rather than as a number. That is why we have been careful to talk about operations *with* fractions, rather than operations *on* fractions. For example, you cannot add two symbols, but you *can* learn to add the **numbers** that the symbols represent. From here on, let us agree to use the simpler language and say, for instance, "addition of fractions" when we mean "addition of numbers represented by fractions."

You already know how to add simple fractions. For example, you know that

$$\tfrac{2}{7} + \tfrac{3}{7} = \tfrac{5}{7}.$$

We can justify this conclusion in two ways: by a number line model, and by applying the familiar distributive property.

Number Line:

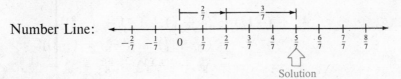

Solution

247

Distributive Property: $\frac{2}{7} + \frac{3}{7} = (2 \cdot \frac{1}{7}) + (3 \cdot \frac{1}{7})$
$$= (2 + 3)\frac{1}{7}$$
$$= 5 \cdot \frac{1}{7} = \frac{5}{7}$$

In general, we say:

For any numbers **a**, **b**, and **c**, where **b** is not zero,

$$\frac{a}{b} + \frac{c}{b} = \frac{a + c}{b}.$$

Study the following examples which apply this idea to the addition of directed numbers represented by fractions.

EXAMPLE 1. $(-\frac{9}{10}) + \frac{5}{10} = (-9 \cdot \frac{1}{10}) + (5 \cdot \frac{1}{10})$
$$= (-9 + 5)\frac{1}{10}$$
$$= (-4)\frac{1}{10} \quad = -\frac{4}{10} = -\frac{2}{5}$$

$$\underset{\text{Solution}}{\Uparrow}$$

EXAMPLE 2. $(-\frac{5}{8}) + \frac{3}{8} + \frac{1}{8} = (-5 \cdot \frac{1}{8}) + (3 \cdot \frac{1}{8}) + (1 \cdot \frac{1}{8})$
$$= (-5 + 3 + 1)\frac{1}{8}$$
$$= (-1)\frac{1}{8} = -\frac{1}{8}$$

Now consider the sum $3\frac{1}{5} + 6\frac{3}{5}$. Recall that a symbol like $3\frac{1}{5}$ is called a **mixed numeral,** and represents the sum of an integer and the number that the fraction represents; that is, $3\frac{1}{5} = 3 + \frac{1}{5}$.

EXAMPLE 3. $3\frac{1}{5} + 6\frac{3}{5} = (3 + \frac{1}{5}) + (6 + \frac{3}{5})$
$$= (3 + 6) + (\frac{1}{5} + \frac{3}{5})$$
$$= 9 + \frac{4}{5} = 9\frac{4}{5}$$

Remember also that in arithmetic you learned that a mixed numeral can be written as a single fraction. For example $4\frac{7}{8} = 4 + \frac{7}{8} = \frac{32}{8} + \frac{7}{8} = \frac{39}{8}$.

EXAMPLE 4. $4\frac{7}{8} + (-1\frac{3}{8}) = (4 + \frac{7}{8}) + [-1 + (-\frac{3}{8})]$
$$= (\frac{32}{8} + \frac{7}{8}) + [(-\frac{8}{8}) + (-\frac{3}{8})]$$
$$= \frac{39}{8} + (-\frac{11}{8}) = \frac{28}{8} = 3\frac{4}{8} = 3\frac{1}{2}$$

Compare the two ways of dealing with a mixed numeral used in Examples 3 and 4. In Example 5 we find the sum $(-5\frac{3}{10}) + 1\frac{9}{10}$ by both methods. Do you find that one of them is easier for you than the other?

EXAMPLE 5.
$$(-5\tfrac{3}{10}) + 1\tfrac{9}{10} = [-5 + (-\tfrac{3}{10})] + (1 + \tfrac{9}{10})$$
$$= [(-5) + 1] + [(-\tfrac{3}{10}) + \tfrac{9}{10}]$$
$$= (-4) + \tfrac{6}{10} = -4 + \tfrac{3}{5} = -3\tfrac{2}{5}$$
$$(-5\tfrac{3}{10}) + 1\tfrac{9}{10} = [-5 + (-\tfrac{3}{10})] + (1 + \tfrac{9}{10})]$$
$$= [(-\tfrac{50}{10}) + (-\tfrac{3}{10})] + (\tfrac{10}{10} + \tfrac{9}{10})$$
$$= (-\tfrac{53}{10}) + \tfrac{19}{10} = -\tfrac{34}{10} = -3\tfrac{2}{5}$$

ORAL EXERCISES

Tell how to express each mixed numeral both as the sum of an integer and a fraction and as a single fraction.

SAMPLE 1: $-5\frac{1}{7}$ *What you say:* $(-5) + (-\frac{1}{7}); -\frac{36}{7}$

1. $2\frac{4}{5}$ **4.** $-8\frac{1}{4}$ **7.** $1\frac{1}{3}$

2. $10\frac{1}{2}$ **5.** $-10\frac{2}{3}$ **8.** $5\frac{1}{9}$

3. $-3\frac{1}{4}$ **6.** $25\frac{1}{8}$ **9.** $-2\frac{1}{5}$

Express each of the following as a single fraction in lowest terms.

10. $\dfrac{3+4}{8}$ **12.** $\dfrac{3+2+6}{15}$ **14.** $\dfrac{(-5)+(-1)}{7}$

11. $\dfrac{5+4}{10}$ **13.** $\dfrac{6+3+5}{10}$ **15.** $\dfrac{8-3-2}{4}$

Name the integer represented by each numeral.

16. $\frac{8}{2}$ **18.** $-\frac{50}{10}$ **20.** $\dfrac{-5}{5}$

17. $\dfrac{-20}{5}$ **19.** $\dfrac{30}{-6}$ **21.** $\frac{47}{47}$

WRITTEN EXERCISES

In each of the following, replace the question mark by a numeral so that the resulting statement is true.

   1. $5 + (?) = 5\frac{1}{4}$ **2.** $-\frac{7}{8} = -7(?)$

3. $3\frac{1}{8} = 3 + (?)$

4. $\frac{4}{5} = 4(?)$

5. $\frac{1}{3} + (?) = 8\frac{1}{3}$

6. $-(5 + \frac{1}{7}) = (?)$

7. $-\frac{9}{10} = (?)\frac{1}{10}$

8. $-6\frac{1}{2} = (?) + (-\frac{1}{2})$

9. $-3\frac{3}{4} = (-3) + (?)$

10. $\frac{1}{5} + (?) = 2\frac{1}{5}$

11. $-\frac{5}{3} = (-5)(?)$

12. $(-\frac{1}{10}) + (-3) = (?)$

13. $-6\frac{5}{8} = (?) + (-\frac{5}{8})$

14. $(-4)(\frac{1}{9}) = (?)$

15. $10\frac{5}{6} = 10 + (?)$

Express each sum as a single fraction in lowest terms, or as a mixed numeral with the fractional part in lowest terms.

16. $\frac{1}{8} + \frac{3}{8} + \frac{2}{8}$

17. $\frac{3}{10} + \frac{1}{10} + \frac{4}{10}$

18. $\frac{4}{15} + \frac{8}{15} + \frac{-7}{15}$

19. $\frac{3}{20} + \frac{5}{20} + \frac{-7}{20}$

20. $4\frac{1}{12} + 6\frac{5}{12}$

21. $(-3\frac{1}{8}) + 9\frac{7}{8}$

22. $\frac{-3}{10} + \frac{8}{10} + \frac{1}{10}$

23. $\frac{-3}{8} + \frac{5}{8} + 3$

Show that each of the following results in a true statement when $r = 3$, $s = -2$, $t = 5$, and $q = -4$.

SAMPLE: $\dfrac{r}{t} + \dfrac{q}{t} = \dfrac{r + q}{t}$

Solution: $\dfrac{r}{t} + \dfrac{q}{t} = \dfrac{r + q}{t}$

$$\dfrac{3}{5} + \dfrac{-4}{5} \quad \Big| \quad \dfrac{3 + (-4)}{5}$$

$$-\frac{1}{5} \quad \Big| \quad -\frac{1}{5}$$

24. $\dfrac{t}{r} + \dfrac{s}{r} = \dfrac{t + s}{r}$

25. $\dfrac{r}{t} + \dfrac{r}{t} = \dfrac{2r}{t}$

26. $\dfrac{r}{s} + \dfrac{t}{s} = \dfrac{r + t}{s}$

27. $\dfrac{t}{s} + \dfrac{r}{s} = \dfrac{t + r}{s}$

Complete each of the following. Remember that no denominator can equal zero.

SAMPLE: $\dfrac{4}{m} + \dfrac{5}{m} = \dfrac{? + ?}{m} = \dfrac{?}{m}$

Solution: $\dfrac{4}{m} + \dfrac{5}{m} = \dfrac{4 + 5}{m} = \dfrac{9}{m}$

28. $\dfrac{5}{t} + \dfrac{3}{t} = \dfrac{? + ?}{t} = \dfrac{?}{t}$

29. $\dfrac{2}{b} + \dfrac{3}{b} = \dfrac{? + ?}{b} = \dfrac{?}{b}$

30. $\dfrac{x}{9} + \dfrac{3x}{9} = \dfrac{? + ?}{9} = \dfrac{?}{9}$

31. $\dfrac{7}{y} + \dfrac{2}{y} + \dfrac{1}{y} = \dfrac{? + ? + ?}{y} = \dfrac{?}{y}$

32. $\dfrac{4}{6x} + \dfrac{8}{6x} + \dfrac{1}{6x} = \dfrac{? + ? + ?}{6x} = \dfrac{?}{6x}$

33. $\dfrac{12}{m} + \dfrac{-3}{m} + \dfrac{4}{m} = \dfrac{? + ? + ?}{m} = \dfrac{?}{m}$

Express each sum as a fraction in lowest terms. Of course, no denominator can equal zero.

SAMPLE: $\dfrac{-5}{k} + \dfrac{9}{k}$ *Solution:* $\dfrac{-5}{k} + \dfrac{9}{k} = \dfrac{(-5) + 9}{k} = \dfrac{4}{k}$

34. $\dfrac{3m}{15} + \dfrac{2m}{15}$ **38.** $\dfrac{ax}{b} + \dfrac{ax}{b}$ **42.** $\dfrac{b}{9} + \dfrac{5b}{9} + \dfrac{6b}{9}$

35. $\dfrac{6}{x} + \dfrac{3}{x}$ **39.** $\dfrac{m}{5} + \dfrac{n}{5}$ **43.** $\dfrac{2}{x^2} + \dfrac{7}{x^2} + \dfrac{-3}{x^2}$

36. $\dfrac{12}{mn} + \dfrac{2}{mn}$ **40.** $\dfrac{3}{r} + \dfrac{t}{r}$ **44.** $\dfrac{13}{m} + \dfrac{-6}{m} + \dfrac{2}{m}$

37. $\dfrac{3a}{7} + \dfrac{-a}{7}$ **41.** $\dfrac{t}{a} + \dfrac{2s}{a}$ **45.** $\dfrac{-5x}{12k} + \dfrac{9x}{12k} + \dfrac{6x}{12k}$

B   **46.** $\dfrac{-3x}{4y} + \dfrac{10x}{4y} + \dfrac{1}{4y}$ **48.** $\dfrac{a}{4a} + \dfrac{-3}{4a} + \dfrac{x^2}{4a}$

47. $\dfrac{t}{13m} + \dfrac{3t}{13m} + \dfrac{-5}{13m}$ **49.** $\dfrac{-3}{z} + \dfrac{-5}{z} + \dfrac{-2}{z}$

8–2   Addition with Fractions Having Equal Polynomial Denominators

The same ideas that we explored for adding fractions with monomial denominators can be applied to adding fractions that have equal polynomial denominators.

EXAMPLE 1. $\dfrac{3}{m+n} + \dfrac{6}{m+n} = 3 \cdot \dfrac{1}{m+n} + 6 \cdot \dfrac{1}{m+n}$

$$= (3 + 6) \cdot \dfrac{1}{m+n}$$

$$= 9 \cdot \dfrac{1}{m+n} = \dfrac{9}{m+n}$$

EXAMPLE 2.

$$\dfrac{4a}{x+y-z} + \dfrac{10a}{x+y-z} = 4a \cdot \dfrac{1}{x+y-z} + 10a \cdot \dfrac{1}{x+y-z}$$

$$= (4a + 10a) \cdot \dfrac{1}{x+y-z}$$

$$= 14a \cdot \dfrac{1}{x+y-z} = \dfrac{14a}{x+y-z}$$

The fractions in the sum $\frac{1}{5} + \frac{6}{15}$ have different denominators. It is not easy to add fifths and fifteenths directly. Sometimes, however, reducing a fraction to lowest terms can help. In this case, $\frac{6}{15} = \frac{2}{5}$, so we can write

$$\frac{1}{5} + \frac{6}{15} = \frac{1}{5} + \frac{2}{5} = \frac{3}{5}.$$

Similarly, we can find the sum $\dfrac{5}{x + 3} + \dfrac{2x - 6}{x^2 - 9}$ by reducing the fraction $\dfrac{2x - 6}{x^2 - 9}$ to lowest terms.

$$\frac{5}{x + 3} + \frac{2x - 6}{x^2 - 9} = \frac{5}{x + 3} + \frac{2(x - 3)}{(x + 3)(x - 3)}$$

$$= \frac{5}{x + 3} + \frac{2}{x + 3} = \frac{7}{x + 3}$$

ORAL EXERCISES

Tell how to simplify each of the following expressions.

1. $\dfrac{4 + 9}{a + b}$

2. $\dfrac{10 - 6}{r + s}$

3. $\dfrac{3 - 8}{m + n}$

4. $\dfrac{2 - 15}{2x + y}$

5. $\dfrac{3m + 8m}{m - n}$

6. $\dfrac{3k + (-k)}{s - t}$

7. $\dfrac{3a + 4a + a}{b - c}$

8. $\dfrac{3 - 5 - 7}{2m - 9n}$

9. $\dfrac{2}{y + z} + \dfrac{8}{y + z}$

10. $\dfrac{a^2}{m - n} + \dfrac{4a^2}{m - n}$

11. $\dfrac{-5}{c - d} + \dfrac{2}{c - d}$

12. $\dfrac{8}{a + r} + \dfrac{-7}{a + r}$

13. $\dfrac{2}{x^2 - 3y^2} + \dfrac{m}{x^2 - 3y^2}$

14. $\dfrac{x^2}{3 + b} + \dfrac{y^2}{b + 3}$

15. $\dfrac{3}{a + b} + \dfrac{2k}{a + b} + \dfrac{4}{a + b}$

WRITTEN EXERCISES

Complete each of the following. Remember that no denominator can equal zero.

SAMPLE: $\dfrac{5c}{3a + b} + \dfrac{-c}{3a + b} = \dfrac{? + ?}{3a + b} = \dfrac{?}{3a + b}$

Solution: $\dfrac{5c}{3a + b} + \dfrac{-c}{3a + b} = \dfrac{5c + (-c)}{3a + b} = \dfrac{4c}{3a + b}$

A 1. $\dfrac{2m}{m-n} + \dfrac{5m}{m-n} + \dfrac{m}{m-n} = \dfrac{?+?+?}{m-n} = \dfrac{?}{m-n}$

2. $\dfrac{4}{2a+c} + \dfrac{3}{2a+c} + \dfrac{5}{2a+c} = \dfrac{?+?+?}{2a+c} = \dfrac{?}{2a+c}$

3. $\dfrac{3a}{3a+5} + \dfrac{5}{3a+5} = \dfrac{?+?}{3a+5} = ?$

4. $\dfrac{2x}{2(x-y)} + \dfrac{y}{x-y} = \dfrac{x}{x-y} + \dfrac{y}{x-y} = \dfrac{?+?}{x-y}$

5. $\dfrac{x^2}{x-y} + \dfrac{-y^2}{x-y} = \dfrac{?+?}{x-y} = \dfrac{(?+?)(?-?)}{x-y} = ?$

6. $\dfrac{a^2}{a-3} + \dfrac{-9}{a-3} = \dfrac{?+?}{a-3} = \dfrac{(?+?)(?-?)}{a-3} = ?$

Express each sum in lowest terms.

SAMPLE: $\dfrac{2x}{x-y} - \dfrac{2y}{x-y}$ *Solution:* $\dfrac{2x}{x-y} - \dfrac{2y}{x-y} = \dfrac{2x-2y}{x-y}$

$$= \dfrac{2(x-y)}{x-y} = 2$$

7. $\dfrac{x}{x-3} + \dfrac{3y}{x-3}$ 12. $\dfrac{6}{3x+3y} + \dfrac{10}{5x+5y}$

8. $\dfrac{a}{a-5} + \dfrac{-5}{a-5}$ 13. $\dfrac{5m}{x^2-3x+9} + \dfrac{t}{x^2-3x+9}$

9. $\dfrac{4m}{n+k} + \dfrac{m}{n+k} + \dfrac{3}{n+k}$ 14. $\dfrac{3(x+y)}{(x+y)^2} + \dfrac{5}{(x+y)}$

10. $\dfrac{c^2}{3a-4} + \dfrac{7c^2}{3a-4} + \dfrac{-d}{3a-4}$ 15. $\dfrac{1}{y^2+3} + \dfrac{3x}{xy^2+3x}$

11. $\dfrac{m-n}{m^2-n^2} + \dfrac{4}{m+n}$ 16. $\dfrac{2r}{2(r+s)} + \dfrac{t}{(r+s)}$

Show that each statement is true when $a = 3$, $b = 2$, $c = 5$, and $d = -4$.

SAMPLE: $\dfrac{2b}{b^2+c} + \dfrac{b}{b^2+c} = \dfrac{3b}{b^2+c}$

Solution: $\dfrac{2b}{b^2+c} + \dfrac{b}{b^2+c} = \dfrac{3b}{b^2+c}$

$$\dfrac{2\cdot2}{2^2+5} + \dfrac{2}{2^2+5} \quad \bigg| \quad \dfrac{3\cdot2}{2^2+5}$$

$$\dfrac{4}{9} + \dfrac{2}{9} \quad \bigg| \quad \dfrac{6}{9}$$

$$\dfrac{6}{9} \quad \bigg| \quad \dfrac{6}{9}$$

17. $\dfrac{2bc}{b + c} + \dfrac{b^2}{b + c} = \dfrac{2bc + b^2}{b + c}$

18. $\dfrac{5c}{d^2 - 10} + \dfrac{-c}{d^2 - 10} = \dfrac{4c}{d^2 - 10}$

19. $\dfrac{-2d}{b^2 + bc + c^2} + \dfrac{-3d}{b^2 + bc + c^2} = \dfrac{-5d}{b^2 + bc + c^2}$

20. $\dfrac{5 - b}{16 - b^2} + \dfrac{10}{16 - b^2} = \dfrac{15 - b}{16 - b^2}$

21. $\dfrac{1 + a}{a^2 + 3a - 4} + \dfrac{2a + a^2}{a^2 + 3a - 4} = \dfrac{1 + 3a + a^2}{a^2 + 3a - 4}$

Express each sum in lowest terms.

SAMPLE: $\dfrac{2ab}{a + b} + \dfrac{a^2 + b^2}{a + b}$

Solution: $\dfrac{2ab}{a + b} + \dfrac{a^2 + b^2}{a + b} = \dfrac{a^2 + 2ab + b^2}{a + b} = \dfrac{(a + b)^2}{a + b} = a + b$

B **22.** $\dfrac{x^2}{x + y} + \dfrac{2xy + y^2}{x + y}$ **24.** $\dfrac{3}{x^2 - 3x - 4} + \dfrac{x - 2}{x^2 - 3x - 4}$

23. $\dfrac{m^2 + n^2}{m - n} + \dfrac{-2mn}{m - n}$ **25.** $\dfrac{2y}{y^2 - y - 2} + \dfrac{-(y + 2)}{y^2 - y - 2}$

C **26.** $\dfrac{7a}{a^2 - b^2} + \dfrac{5a + 4b}{a^2 - b^2}$ **28.** $\dfrac{x^2}{x - 3} + \dfrac{9}{x - 3} + \dfrac{-6}{x - 3}$

27. $\dfrac{5 - b}{b^2 - 16} + \dfrac{-(b^2 - 3)}{b^2 - 16}$ **29.** $\dfrac{4t + 10}{2t^2 + t - 3} + \dfrac{-(2t - 7)}{2t^2 + t - 3}$

8–3   Subtraction with Fractions: The Inverse of Addition

Until now we have been working only with **sums** of fractions, such as

$$\frac{3a}{b} + \frac{5}{b} \; ; \; \frac{4}{m + n} + \frac{-3}{m + n} \; ; \; \frac{a}{a^2 - b^2} + \frac{-b}{a^2 - b^2} \cdot$$

As you may have guessed, when we need to find the **difference** of two fractions we can use the fact that addition and subtractions are **inverse operations.** Suppose that we wish to simplify expressions like the following:

$$\frac{4n}{m} - \frac{3n}{m} \; ; \; \frac{10}{x - y} - \frac{t}{x - y} \cdot$$

Recall that, to subtract one number from another, we add the **opposite (additive inverse)** of the number that is to be subtracted.

EXAMPLE 1. $\dfrac{4n}{m} - \dfrac{3n}{m} = \dfrac{4n}{m} + \left(-\dfrac{3n}{m}\right)$

$$= \dfrac{4n}{m} + \dfrac{-3n}{m} = \dfrac{4n - 3n}{m} = \dfrac{n}{m}$$

EXAMPLE 2. $\dfrac{10}{x - y} - \dfrac{t}{x - y} = \dfrac{10}{x - y} + \left(-\dfrac{t}{x - y}\right)$

$$= \dfrac{10}{x - y} + \dfrac{-t}{x - y} = \dfrac{10 - t}{x - y}$$

We can summarize this idea for simplifying differences as follows:

For any numbers **a**, **b**, and **c**, where **b** is not zero,

$$\frac{a}{b} - \frac{c}{b} = \frac{a}{b} + \left(-\frac{c}{b}\right) = \frac{a}{b} + \frac{-c}{b} = \frac{a - c}{b}.$$

ORAL EXERCISES

Match each fraction in Column 1 with its opposite in Column 2.

COLUMN 1

1. $\dfrac{-3}{x + y}$

2. $\dfrac{5}{m - 3}$

3. $\dfrac{10}{ab^2}$

4. $\dfrac{7}{x - z}$

5. $\dfrac{10}{mn}$

6. $\dfrac{r - s}{st^2}$

COLUMN 2

A. $-\left(\dfrac{10}{ab^2}\right)$

B. $\dfrac{3}{x + y}$

C. $-\left(\dfrac{7}{x - z}\right)$

D. $\dfrac{-r + s}{st^2}$

E. $\dfrac{-5}{m - 3}$

F. $\dfrac{-10}{mn}$

State two different ways of naming the opposite of each of the following.

SAMPLE 1: $\dfrac{4}{x}$ *What you say:* $-\dfrac{4}{x} ; \dfrac{-4}{x}$

SAMPLE 2: $\dfrac{m}{n - 5}$ *What you say:* $-\left(\dfrac{m}{n - 5}\right) ; \dfrac{-m}{n - 5}$

7. $\dfrac{5}{2k}$ **11.** $\dfrac{b^2}{ac}$ **15.** $\dfrac{3}{8-x}$

8. $\dfrac{5}{r+5}$ **12.** $\dfrac{m-n}{10}$ **16.** $\dfrac{-10}{cd}$

9. $\dfrac{a}{b-c}$ **13.** $\dfrac{4}{x^2-y^2}$ **17.** $\dfrac{6}{-ab}$

10. $\dfrac{a+b}{3}$ **14.** $\dfrac{7r}{s^2+t^2}$ **18.** $\dfrac{3}{-x+y}$

WRITTEN EXERCISES

Show that each of the following results in a true statement when $q = 4$, $r = 3$, $s = 6$, and $t = 10$.

SAMPLE: $-\left(\dfrac{t}{s+t}\right) = \dfrac{-t}{s+t}$ *Solution:* $-\left(\dfrac{t}{s+t}\right) = \dfrac{-t}{s+t}$

$$-\left(\dfrac{10}{6+10}\right) \,\bigg|\, \dfrac{-10}{6+10}$$

$$-\left(\dfrac{10}{16}\right) \,\bigg|\, \dfrac{-10}{16}$$

$$-\tfrac{5}{8} \,\bigg|\, -\tfrac{5}{8}$$

A **1.** $\dfrac{-4}{r+s} = -\left(\dfrac{4}{r+s}\right)$ **5.** $-\left(\dfrac{r-q}{t}\right) = \dfrac{q-r}{t}$

2. $\dfrac{-r}{q-s} = -\left(\dfrac{r}{q-s}\right)$ **6.** $-\left(\dfrac{s-t}{5}\right) = \dfrac{t-s}{5}$

3. $-\left(\dfrac{qr}{t}\right) = \dfrac{-qr}{t}$ **7.** $\dfrac{-qr}{q^2-s} = -\left(\dfrac{qr}{q^2-s}\right)$

4. $\dfrac{-7}{st} = -\left(\dfrac{7}{st}\right)$ **8.** $\dfrac{t-r}{15} = -\left(\dfrac{r-t}{15}\right)$

Write each of the following as a single fraction in lowest terms.

SAMPLE: $\dfrac{7k}{4y} - \dfrac{3k}{4y}$ *Solution:* $\dfrac{7k}{4y} - \dfrac{3k}{4y} = \dfrac{7k-3k}{4y}$

$$= \dfrac{4k}{4y} = \dfrac{k}{y}$$

9. $\dfrac{9a}{15} - \dfrac{5a}{15}$ **11.** $\left(\dfrac{7k}{m^2} - \dfrac{k}{m^2}\right) + \dfrac{2k}{m^2}$

10. $\dfrac{x}{2a} - \dfrac{y}{2a}$ **12.** $\left(\dfrac{4mn}{ab} - \dfrac{-3mn}{ab}\right) - \dfrac{5mn}{ab}$

13. $\dfrac{4rs}{st^2} - \dfrac{3rs}{st^2}$

14. $\dfrac{8}{a+b} - \dfrac{5}{a+b}$

15. $\dfrac{10a}{x-y} - \dfrac{3}{x-y}$

16. $\left(\dfrac{7a-2}{b+c} + \dfrac{2}{b+c}\right) - \dfrac{3}{b+c}$

17. $\left(\dfrac{9bd}{xy^2} - \dfrac{4bd}{xy^2}\right) + \dfrac{6bd}{xy^2}$

18. $\left(\dfrac{7}{10x} - \dfrac{3}{10x}\right) - \dfrac{yz}{10x}$

SAMPLE: $\dfrac{x}{x^2-25} - \dfrac{5}{x^2-25}$

Solution: $\dfrac{x}{x^2-25} - \dfrac{5}{x^2-25} = \dfrac{x-5}{x^2-25} = \dfrac{x-5}{(x+5)(x-5)} = \dfrac{1}{x+5}$

19. $\dfrac{3y}{y-x} - \dfrac{3x}{y-x}$

20. $\dfrac{3x}{2x-4} - \dfrac{x}{2x-4}$

B **23.** $\dfrac{c^2}{c-d} - \dfrac{d^2}{c-d}$

24. $\dfrac{x^2+y^2}{x-y} - \dfrac{2xy}{x-y}$

21. $\dfrac{2x}{(2x-1)^2} - \dfrac{1}{(2x-1)^2}$

22. $\dfrac{x}{x^2-1} - \dfrac{1}{x^2-1}$

25. $\dfrac{x^2}{x+3} - \dfrac{9}{x+3}$

26. $\dfrac{4m+10}{2m^2+m-3} - \dfrac{2m+7}{2m^2+m-3}$

8–4 Simplifying Sums and Differences

Sometimes the simplifying of a sum or a difference is a little more tricky. For example, consider the difference $\dfrac{m}{3k} - \dfrac{n}{-3k}$ and the sum $\dfrac{9}{mn} + \dfrac{2}{-mn}$. In each, the two denominators are not quite alike, because the second denominator is the **opposite** of the first denominator. We can take care of this difficulty very easily by recognizing that

$$-\frac{x}{y} = \frac{x}{-y} = \frac{-x}{y}, \text{ and}$$

$$\frac{x}{y} = \frac{-x}{-y} = -\frac{-x}{y} = -\frac{x}{-y}.$$

EXAMPLE 1. $\dfrac{m}{3k} - \dfrac{n}{-3k} = \dfrac{m}{3k} + \left(-\dfrac{n}{-3k}\right)$

$$= \frac{m}{3k} + \frac{n}{3k} = \frac{m+n}{3k}$$

EXAMPLE 2. $\dfrac{9}{mn} + \dfrac{2}{-mn} = \dfrac{9}{mn} + \dfrac{-2}{mn}$

$$= \dfrac{9-2}{mn} = \dfrac{7}{mn}$$

In Example 3, we consider the difference $\dfrac{3}{a-b} - \dfrac{5}{b-a}$, and show how the fact that $-\dfrac{x}{y} = \dfrac{x}{-y}$ can be used to rewrite the difference as the sum of two fractions whose denominators are alike.

EXAMPLE 3. $\dfrac{3}{a-b} - \dfrac{5}{b-a} = \dfrac{3}{a-b} + \left(-\dfrac{5}{b-a}\right)$

$$= \dfrac{3}{a-b} + \dfrac{5}{-(b-a)}$$

$$= \dfrac{3}{a-b} + \dfrac{5}{-b+a}$$

$$= \dfrac{3}{a-b} + \dfrac{5}{a-b} = \dfrac{8}{a-b}$$

Notice that the original difference is first written as a sum. This is done by expressing the denominator of the second fraction, $\dfrac{5}{b-a}$, as its opposite, $\dfrac{5}{-(b-a)}$, and finally as $\dfrac{5}{a-b}$.

Now consider the sum $\dfrac{8}{m-3} + \dfrac{5}{3-m}$. Again the two fractions making up the sum seem to have unlike denominators. But observe what happens when we apply the idea that $\dfrac{x}{y}$ is the same as $\dfrac{-x}{-y}$.

EXAMPLE 4. $\dfrac{8}{m-3} + \dfrac{5}{3-m} = \dfrac{8}{m-3} + \dfrac{-5}{-(3-m)}$

$$= \dfrac{8}{m-3} + \dfrac{-5}{-3+m}$$

$$= \dfrac{8}{m-3} + \dfrac{-5}{m-3}$$

$$= \dfrac{8-5}{m-3} = \dfrac{3}{m-3}$$

ORAL EXERCISES

Tell whether each sentence is true for all values of the variable for which the denominators are not zero.

1. $\dfrac{3}{y} = \dfrac{-3}{-y}$

2. $-\dfrac{8}{xy} = \dfrac{-8}{xy}$

3. $\dfrac{2}{-ab} = \dfrac{-2}{ab}$

4. $\dfrac{-m}{-n} = \dfrac{m}{n}$

5. $\dfrac{-t}{10} = \dfrac{t}{-10}$

6. $\dfrac{-5}{d} = -\dfrac{5}{-d}$

7. $-\dfrac{a^2b}{30} = \dfrac{-a^2b}{30}$

8. $-\dfrac{12}{rs} = \dfrac{12}{-rs}$

9. $-\dfrac{4}{ab} = \dfrac{4}{ab}$

10. $-\dfrac{5}{b-a} = \dfrac{5}{a-b}$

11. $-\dfrac{10}{3-x^2} = \dfrac{10}{x^2-3}$

12. $-\dfrac{5}{y-x} = \dfrac{-5}{x-y}$

13. $\dfrac{d-c}{3} = -\dfrac{c-d}{3}$

14. $\dfrac{x^2-1}{-3} = \dfrac{1-x^2}{3}$

15. $\dfrac{-15ab}{c^2+1} = \dfrac{15ab}{c^2+1}$

WRITTEN EXERCISES

Show that each of the following results in a true statement when $r = 2$, $s = 18$, $d = -3$, and $z = 8$.

SAMPLE: $\dfrac{r}{s} = \dfrac{-r}{-s} = -\dfrac{r}{-s} = -\dfrac{-r}{s}$

Solution: $\dfrac{r}{s} = \dfrac{-r}{-s} = -\dfrac{r}{-s} = -\dfrac{-r}{s}$

$\dfrac{2}{18}$	$\dfrac{-2}{-18}$	$-\dfrac{2}{-18}$	$-\dfrac{-2}{18}$
$\frac{1}{9}$	$\frac{1}{9}$	$-(-\frac{1}{9})$	$-(-\frac{1}{9})$
		$\frac{1}{9}$	$\frac{1}{9}$

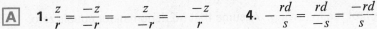

A **1.** $\dfrac{z}{r} = \dfrac{-z}{-r} = -\dfrac{z}{-r} = -\dfrac{-z}{r}$

2. $-\dfrac{z}{s} = \dfrac{-z}{s} = \dfrac{z}{-s}$

3. $\dfrac{r}{z} = \dfrac{-r}{-\cdot z} = -\dfrac{-r}{z} = -\dfrac{r}{-z}$

4. $-\dfrac{rd}{s} = \dfrac{rd}{-s} = \dfrac{-rd}{s}$

5. $\dfrac{5}{z-r} = -\dfrac{-5}{z-r} = -\dfrac{5}{r-z}$

6. $-\dfrac{20}{s-z} = \dfrac{-20}{s-z} = \dfrac{20}{z-s}$

Show that each of the following results in a true statement when $a = 5$, $b = 3$, $m = 2$, and $n = 8$.

SAMPLE: $-\left(\dfrac{a}{n - m}\right) = \dfrac{a}{m - n}$ Solution: $-\left(\dfrac{a}{n - m}\right) = \dfrac{a}{m - n}$

$$
\begin{array}{c|c}
-\left(\dfrac{5}{8 - 2}\right) & \dfrac{5}{2 - 8} \\[2ex]
-\left(\dfrac{5}{6}\right) & \dfrac{5}{-6} \\[2ex]
-\frac{5}{6} & -\frac{5}{6}
\end{array}
$$

7. $-\left(\dfrac{6}{ab}\right) = \dfrac{-6}{ab}$

8. $\dfrac{3m}{a^2 - n^2} = \dfrac{-3m}{n^2 - a^2}$

9. $\dfrac{-10}{m + n} = -\left(\dfrac{10}{m + n}\right)$

10. $\dfrac{b - a}{-a^2 + 2ab} = \dfrac{a - b}{a^2 - 2ab}$

11. $\dfrac{-m + n}{mn} = \dfrac{m - n}{-mn}$

12. $-\left(\dfrac{a}{a - b}\right) = \dfrac{-a}{a - b}$

13. $-\left(\dfrac{-3}{n - 3}\right) = \dfrac{3}{n - 3}$

14. $-\left(\dfrac{-5}{1 - 2b}\right) = \dfrac{5}{1 - 2b}$

15. $-\dfrac{2}{n - a} = \dfrac{-2}{n - a}$

16. $\dfrac{-3}{3 - a} = -\left(\dfrac{3}{3 - a}\right)$

17. $-\left(\dfrac{4}{a^2 - b^2}\right) = \dfrac{-4}{a^2 - b^2}$

18. $\dfrac{-10}{m^2 + n^2} = -\left(\dfrac{10}{m^2 + n^2}\right)$

Write each fraction in a form that has the indicated numerator or denominator.

SAMPLE: $-\left(\dfrac{a}{3 - b}\right) = \dfrac{?}{b - 3}$

Solution: $-\left(\dfrac{a}{3 - b}\right) = \dfrac{a}{-(3 - b)} = \dfrac{a}{-3 + b} = \dfrac{a}{b - 3}$

19. $-\dfrac{5}{6 - a} = \dfrac{?}{a - 6}$

20. $-\dfrac{3r}{t - s} = \dfrac{?}{s - t}$

21. $\dfrac{10}{k - 2} = \dfrac{?}{2 - k}$

22. $-\dfrac{3 - n}{mn} = \dfrac{n - 3}{?}$

23. $-\dfrac{2s - r}{5} = \dfrac{r - 2s}{?}$

24. $\dfrac{b - 3a}{b - a} = \dfrac{?}{a - b}$

Complete each of the following. Assume that no denominator equals zero.

SAMPLE 1: $\dfrac{7}{10x} - \dfrac{2}{-10x} = \dfrac{?}{10x} + \dfrac{?}{10x} = \dfrac{9}{10x}$

Solution: $\dfrac{7}{10x} - \dfrac{2}{-10x} = \dfrac{7}{10x} + \dfrac{2}{10x} = \dfrac{9}{10x}$

SAMPLE 2: $\dfrac{4}{x-y} - \dfrac{3a}{y-x} = \dfrac{?}{x-y} + \dfrac{?}{x-y} = \dfrac{4+3a}{x-y}$

Solution: $\dfrac{4}{x-y} - \dfrac{3a}{y-x} = \dfrac{4}{x-y} + \dfrac{3a}{x-y} = \dfrac{4+3a}{x-y}$

25. $\dfrac{t}{3y} - \dfrac{5}{-3y} = \dfrac{?}{3y} + \dfrac{?}{3y} = \dfrac{t+5}{3y}$

26. $\dfrac{4m}{xy} + \dfrac{n}{-xy} = \dfrac{?}{xy} + \dfrac{?}{xy} = \dfrac{4m-n}{xy}$

27. $\dfrac{10}{r^2 s} + \dfrac{3}{-r^2 s} = \dfrac{?}{r^2 s} + \dfrac{?}{r^2 s} = \dfrac{7}{r^2 s}$

28. $\dfrac{9}{4k} - \dfrac{2}{-4k} = \dfrac{?}{4k} + \dfrac{?}{4k} = \dfrac{11}{4k}$

29. $\dfrac{4t}{r-s} - \dfrac{t}{s-r} = \dfrac{?}{r-s} + \dfrac{?}{r-s} = \dfrac{5t}{r-s}$

30. $\dfrac{8}{x-y} + \dfrac{5}{y-x} = \dfrac{?}{x-y} + \dfrac{?}{x-y} = \dfrac{3}{x-y}$

31. $\dfrac{a+b}{a-b} + \dfrac{3b}{b-a} = \dfrac{?}{a-b} + \dfrac{?}{a-b} = \dfrac{a-2b}{a-b}$

32. $\dfrac{m^2 n^2}{3-x} - \dfrac{5}{x-3} = \dfrac{?}{3-x} + \dfrac{?}{3-x} = \dfrac{m^2 n^2 + 5}{3-x}$

Simplify each indicated sum or difference.

SAMPLE: $\dfrac{3x^2}{10k} - \dfrac{y}{10k}$ *Solution:* $\dfrac{3x^2}{10k} - \dfrac{y}{10k} = \dfrac{3x^2 - y}{10k}$

33. $\dfrac{9k}{yz} + \dfrac{k}{-yz}$

34. $\dfrac{10ab}{rs} + \dfrac{6ab}{-rs}$

35. $\dfrac{3n}{m-n} - \dfrac{6n}{n-m}$

36. $\dfrac{3}{10b} - \dfrac{2}{-10b}$

37. $\dfrac{5x}{r-s} + \dfrac{2x}{s-r}$

38. $\dfrac{5a^2 b}{y-2} + \dfrac{3a^2 b}{2-y}$

B **39.** $\dfrac{3a}{2x-y} - \dfrac{8a}{y-2x}$

40. $\dfrac{4}{2x-6y} + \dfrac{3}{3y-x}$

41. $\dfrac{a^2}{a-b} + \dfrac{b^2}{b-a}$

42. $\dfrac{9}{3-x} + \dfrac{x^2}{x-3}$

C **43.** $\dfrac{x^2}{x-3} + \dfrac{6x}{3-x} + \dfrac{9}{x-3}$

44. $\dfrac{7a-2a}{ab-ac} - \dfrac{5a}{c-b}$

45. $\dfrac{4x+10}{2x^2 + x - 3} + \dfrac{2x+7}{3 - 2x^2 - x}$

46. $\dfrac{x^2 + y^2}{x-y} - \dfrac{-2xy}{y-x}$

Combining Fractions with Unlike Denominators

8–5   Sums and Differences with Unlike Monomial Denominators

Simplifying the sum $\frac{7}{15} + \frac{4}{15}$ is easy, because the two denominators are the same. That is, the two fractions have a **common denominator**.

To simplify the sum $\frac{1}{12} + \frac{2}{15}$ we need to rewrite each fraction in an equivalent form so that the two fractions will have the same denominator. The common denominator of the two fractions we are considering might be any positive integer that has both **12** and **15** as factors. However, it is usually most satisfactory to use the **lowest common denominator** (abbreviated **L.C.D.**).

For the two fractions $\frac{1}{12}$ and $\frac{2}{15}$, you might recognize at a glance that their L.C.D. is **60**. However, a systematic way to determine it is to write each denominator as the product of its prime factors:

$$12 = 2 \cdot 2 \cdot 3 = 2^2 \cdot 3 \quad \text{and} \quad 15 = 3 \cdot 5$$

The L.C.D. must contain 2^2, **3**, and **5** as factors, so it is $2^2 \cdot 3 \cdot 5 = 60$. Remember, the L.C.D. of two fractions contains each factor the *greatest number* of times that it appears in either denominator.

To rewrite $\frac{1}{12}$ and $\frac{2}{15}$ so that each has the denominator **60**, we must be able to complete the following sentences:

$$12 \cdot (?) = 60 \quad \text{and} \quad 15 \cdot (?) = 60.$$

Since we know that

$$12 \cdot 5 = 60 \quad \text{and} \quad 15 \cdot 4 = 60$$

we can express each fraction as an **equivalent fraction** with the denominator **60** as follows:

$$\frac{1}{12} \cdot \frac{5}{5} = \frac{5}{60} \qquad \frac{2}{15} \cdot \frac{4}{4} = \frac{8}{60}$$

Do you agree that $\frac{1}{12}$ and $\frac{5}{60}$ are equivalent fractions, and also that the fractions $\frac{2}{15}$ and $\frac{8}{60}$ are equivalent? So we find the sum $\frac{1}{12} + \frac{2}{15}$ as follows:

$$\frac{1}{12} + \frac{2}{15} = \frac{5}{60} + \frac{8}{60} = \frac{5+8}{60} = \frac{13}{60}$$

We can apply similar methods in simplifying sums and differences whose denominators contain variables. To simplify $\dfrac{5}{x^3} + \dfrac{3}{x^2}$, we consider the denominators, x^3 and x^2, and see that the greatest number of times x appears as a factor is **three**.

$$x^3 = x \cdot x \cdot x \quad \text{and} \quad x^2 = x \cdot x$$

So the **L.C.D.** is $x \cdot x \cdot x$ or x^3, and we simplify $\dfrac{5}{x^3} + \dfrac{3}{x^2}$ as follows:

$$\frac{5}{x^3} + \frac{3}{x^2} = \frac{5}{x^3} + \left(\frac{3}{x^2} \cdot \frac{x}{x}\right) = \frac{5}{x^3} + \frac{3x}{x^3} = \frac{5 + 3x}{x^3}$$

Follow each step in Examples 1 and 2 to be certain that you understand the methods used.

EXAMPLE 1. Simplify $\dfrac{5k}{3x} - \dfrac{4}{x^2}$.

$3x = 3 \cdot x$ and $x^2 = x \cdot x$, so the **L.C.D.** is $3x^2$.

$$\frac{5k}{3x} - \frac{4}{x^2} = \left(\frac{5k}{3x} \cdot \frac{x}{x}\right) - \left(\frac{4}{x^2} \cdot \frac{3}{3}\right)$$

$$= \frac{5kx}{3x^2} - \frac{12}{3x^2} = \frac{5kx - 12}{3x^2}$$

EXAMPLE 2. Simplify $\dfrac{3m}{6t} + \dfrac{n}{9s}$.

$6t = 2 \cdot 3 \cdot t$ and $9s = 3 \cdot 3 \cdot s$,

so the **L.C.D.** is $2 \cdot 3 \cdot 3 \cdot s \cdot t$, or **18st**.

$$\frac{3m}{6t} + \frac{n}{9s} = \left(\frac{3m}{6t} \cdot \frac{3s}{3s}\right) + \left(\frac{n}{9s} \cdot \frac{2t}{2t}\right)$$

$$= \frac{9ms}{18st} + \frac{2nt}{18st} = \frac{9ms + 2nt}{18st}$$

ORAL EXERCISES

Tell whether or not the fractions in each pair are equivalent. Use the cross-product method if necessary.

SAMPLE: $\dfrac{3}{5a}, \dfrac{21}{35a}$ *What you say:* Equivalent, because $3(35a) = 21(5a)$.

1. $\dfrac{4}{m^2}, \dfrac{12}{3m^2}$ **2.** $\dfrac{3}{8m}, \dfrac{3m}{8m^2}$ **3.** $\dfrac{3a^2bc}{15m^2n}, \dfrac{a^2bc}{5}$

4. $\dfrac{3}{x^3}, \dfrac{6}{x^6}$ **7.** $\dfrac{xb}{ab}, \dfrac{x}{a}$ **10.** $\dfrac{4xy}{18x^2y}, \dfrac{2xy}{9x^2y}$

5. $\dfrac{12}{4x}, \dfrac{6}{2x}$ **8.** $\dfrac{at}{tr}, \dfrac{a}{r}$ **11.** $\dfrac{14a^3}{35b^3}, \dfrac{2a^3}{5b^3}$

6. $\dfrac{3}{10a}, \dfrac{45}{150a}$ **9.** $\dfrac{-10bc}{5nc}, \dfrac{-2b}{n}$ **12.** $\dfrac{3}{5x}, \dfrac{24x^2y}{40x^3y}$

Name the L.C.D. of the denominators in each of the following. Do not simplify.

13. $\dfrac{x}{9} + \dfrac{x}{6}$ **16.** $\dfrac{x}{2} + \dfrac{x}{3} + \dfrac{x}{4}$ **19.** $\dfrac{m}{2} + \dfrac{m}{4} + \dfrac{m}{6}$

14. $\dfrac{x}{4} - \dfrac{y}{10}$ **17.** $\dfrac{x}{3} + \dfrac{x}{a} + \dfrac{x}{6}$ **20.** $\dfrac{3}{t^4} + \dfrac{8}{t^2} + \dfrac{10}{t}$

15. $\dfrac{x}{6} + \dfrac{x}{14}$ **18.** $\dfrac{x}{y^2} + \dfrac{x}{y} - \dfrac{x}{y^5}$ **21.** $\dfrac{5}{ax} + \dfrac{3}{ay} + \dfrac{2}{a}$

WRITTEN EXERCISES

Copy and complete each of the following.

SAMPLE 1: $\dfrac{3x}{15y} \cdot \dfrac{y^2}{y^2} = ?$ *Solution:* $\dfrac{3x}{15y} \cdot \dfrac{y^2}{y^2} = \dfrac{3xy^2}{15y^3}$

SAMPLE 2: $\dfrac{4m}{3st} \cdot \dfrac{?}{?} = \dfrac{20mst}{15s^2t^2}$ *Solution:* $\dfrac{4m}{3st} \cdot \dfrac{5st}{5st} = \dfrac{20mst}{15s^2t^2}$

A

1. $\dfrac{3}{xy^2} \cdot \dfrac{x^3}{x^3} = \dfrac{?}{?}$ **5.** $\dfrac{-5n}{8d} \cdot \dfrac{?}{?} = \dfrac{-30an}{48ad}$

2. $\dfrac{10a}{14cd^2} \cdot \dfrac{ac}{ac} = \dfrac{?}{?}$ **6.** $-\dfrac{k}{3vw^2} \cdot \dfrac{?}{?} = -\dfrac{3k}{9vw^2}$

3. $\dfrac{6yz^2}{5rs} \cdot \dfrac{?}{?} = \dfrac{42ryz^2}{35r^2s}$ **7.** $\dfrac{?}{?} \cdot \dfrac{8a^2}{7b} = \dfrac{48a^2c^2}{42bc^2}$

4. $\dfrac{1}{x^2y^3} \cdot \dfrac{?}{?} = \dfrac{19x}{19x^3y^3}$ **8.** $\dfrac{a^3b^2}{10a^2b^4} = \dfrac{?}{?} \cdot \dfrac{a}{10b^2}$

Write a fraction equivalent to the given fraction and having the indicated denominator.

SAMPLE: $\dfrac{3m}{7rs} = \dfrac{?}{42r^3s}$ *Solution:* $\dfrac{3m}{7rs} \cdot \dfrac{6r^2}{6r^2} = \dfrac{18mr^2}{42r^3s}$

9. $\dfrac{2b}{a} = \dfrac{?}{6a^2b}$ **11.** $\dfrac{19x^3y^2}{3} = \dfrac{?}{15}$

10. $\dfrac{12x^3}{8y^2} = \dfrac{?}{32x^2y^2}$ **12.** $\dfrac{-a}{x} = \dfrac{?}{43xy^2z^3}$

13. $\dfrac{2m^2}{7n^2} = \dfrac{?}{56m^3n^3}$ **15.** $\dfrac{5}{3c^2} = \dfrac{?}{45a^3b^3c^3}$

14. $\dfrac{ax}{any} = \dfrac{?}{3a^2ny}$ **16.** $\dfrac{6a^7}{7b^6} = \dfrac{?}{63ab^6c^7}$

Simplify each of the following, using the L.C.D. given.

SAMPLE: $\dfrac{4}{3mn} - \dfrac{2}{mr}$; L.C.D., $3mnr$

Solution: $\dfrac{4}{3mn} - \dfrac{2}{mr} = \left(\dfrac{4}{3mn} \cdot \dfrac{r}{r}\right) - \left(\dfrac{2}{mr} \cdot \dfrac{3n}{3n}\right)$

$$= \dfrac{4r}{3mnr} - \dfrac{6n}{3mnr} = \dfrac{4r - 6n}{3mnr}$$

17. $\dfrac{3}{xy^2} + \dfrac{1}{x^2}$; L.C.D., x^2y^2 **22.** $\dfrac{5}{3x} - \dfrac{7}{4x}$; L.C.D., $12x$

18. $\dfrac{4}{r^2s} - \dfrac{2}{rs}$; L.C.D., r^2s **23.** $\dfrac{7}{15y} + \dfrac{5}{6y^2}$; L.C.D., $30y^2$

19. $\dfrac{a}{yz} + \dfrac{x}{xz}$; L.C.D., xyz **24.** $\dfrac{6}{7x} + \dfrac{3}{14x^2} + \dfrac{5}{2x}$; L.C.D., $14x^2$

20. $\dfrac{1}{6ab} + \dfrac{5}{21ac}$; L.C.D., $42abc$ **25.** $\dfrac{5}{3y^2} - \dfrac{6}{7y}$; L.C.D., $21y^2$

21. $\dfrac{10}{a^3} + \dfrac{2}{a^2} + \dfrac{1}{a}$; L.C.D., a^3 **26.** $\dfrac{x}{3y} + \dfrac{3y}{x}$; L.C.D., $3xy$

Name the L.C.D. for the fractions in each exercise, and then simplify.

SAMPLE: $\dfrac{3}{4ab^2} + \dfrac{1}{6a}$

Solution: L.C.D., $12ab^2$

$\dfrac{3}{4ab^2} + \dfrac{1}{6a} = \left(\dfrac{3}{4ab^2} \cdot \dfrac{3}{3}\right) + \left(\dfrac{1}{6a} \cdot \dfrac{2b^2}{2b^2}\right) = \dfrac{9}{12ab^2} + \dfrac{2b^2}{12ab^2} = \dfrac{9 + 2b^2}{12ab^2}$

27. $\dfrac{3n}{6} + \dfrac{m}{9}$ **30.** $\dfrac{2}{x^2y} + \dfrac{3}{x^2}$

28. $\dfrac{5}{a} + \dfrac{1}{2}$ **31.** $\dfrac{2}{rs^2} - \dfrac{4}{rs^2}$

29. $\dfrac{2}{3} + \dfrac{7}{b}$ **32.** $\dfrac{m}{ab} + \dfrac{n}{3bc} + \dfrac{m}{ac}$

B **33.** $\dfrac{2x}{3y} + \dfrac{9}{4y} - \dfrac{2}{y}$ **35.** $\dfrac{4}{m^2n} - \dfrac{2 - m}{mn^2}$

34. $\dfrac{3}{xy^2} + \dfrac{2 - x}{x^2y}$ **36.** $\dfrac{t}{bc} + \dfrac{t + c}{ac} - \dfrac{t + b}{ab}$

8–6 Sums and Differences with Unlike Polynomial Denominators

The same ideas that we have used to simplify sums and differences involving fractions with monomial denominators can be applied in simplifying an expression like $\dfrac{3}{2x + 2y} + \dfrac{y}{x^2 - y^2}$, where the denominators are unlike polynomials of two or more terms.

Factoring each of the denominators will help us find the L.C.D. so that we can write equivalent fractions with like denominators and then simplify.

EXAMPLE 1. Simplify $\dfrac{3}{2x + 2y} + \dfrac{y}{x^2 - y^2}$.

Since the factored forms of the denominators are

$$2x + 2y = 2(x + y) \quad \text{and} \quad x^2 - y^2 = (x + y)(x - y),$$

the **L.C.D.** is $2(x + y)(x - y)$.

$$\frac{3}{2x + 2y} + \frac{y}{x^2 - y^2} = \frac{3}{2(x + y)} \cdot \frac{x - y}{x - y} + \frac{y}{(x^2 - y^2)} \cdot \frac{2}{2}$$

$$= \frac{3x - 3y}{2(x^2 - y^2)} + \frac{2y}{2(x^2 - y^2)}$$

$$= \frac{3x - 3y + 2y}{2(x^2 - y^2)} = \frac{3x - y}{2(x^2 - y^2)}$$

Follow each step that is used in combining the fractions in Examples 2 and 3. Do you see why the **L.C.D.** of the fractions in Example 2 is $3(b + 2)$, and in Example 3 is $5(r + s)$?

EXAMPLE 2.

$$\frac{5c}{3b + 6} + \frac{c - 1}{b + 2} = \frac{5c}{3(b + 2)} + \frac{c - 1}{b + 2}$$

$$= \frac{5c}{3(b + 2)} + \frac{c - 1}{b + 2} \cdot \frac{3}{3}$$

$$= \frac{5c}{3(b + 2)} + \frac{3c - 3}{3(b + 2)}$$

$$= \frac{5c + 3c - 3}{3(b + 2)} = \frac{8c - 3}{3(b + 2)}$$

EXAMPLE 3.

$$\frac{3}{5} - \frac{4s}{r+s} = \left(\frac{3}{5} \cdot \frac{r+s}{r+s}\right) - \left(\frac{4s}{r+s} \cdot \frac{5}{5}\right)$$

$$= \frac{3(r+s)}{5(r+s)} - \frac{4s \cdot 5}{5(r+s)}$$

$$= \frac{3r+3s-20s}{5(r+s)} = \frac{3r-17s}{5(r+s)}$$

ORAL EXERCISES

Name the L.C.D. of the denominator in each sum or difference.

SAMPLE: $\dfrac{3}{a+2} + \dfrac{5}{a-2}$ *What you say:* $(a+2)(a-2)$, or $a^2 - 4$.

1. $\dfrac{n}{3} + \dfrac{n}{m+1}$

2. $\dfrac{5}{b} + \dfrac{2}{a+c}$

3. $\dfrac{3}{t} - \dfrac{10}{s-t}$

4. $\dfrac{xy}{a+z} + \dfrac{xz}{a}$

5. $\dfrac{mn}{d+4} + \dfrac{mn}{d-4}$

6. $\dfrac{x}{r+3} + \dfrac{y}{r-3}$

7. $\dfrac{5}{a+b} - \dfrac{2}{a-b}$

8. $\dfrac{3x}{4n} + \dfrac{8y}{m+n}$

9. $\dfrac{4}{d+1} + \dfrac{5}{3d+1}$

10. $\dfrac{1}{x^2-y^2} - \dfrac{3}{x+y}$

WRITTEN EXERCISES

Complete each of the following.

SAMPLE 1: $\dfrac{a}{a-b} \cdot \dfrac{a+b}{a+b} = ?$ *Solution:* $\dfrac{a}{a-b} \cdot \dfrac{a+b}{a+b} = \dfrac{a^2+ab}{a^2-b^2}$

SAMPLE 2: $\dfrac{3}{x+5} \cdot \dfrac{?}{?} = \dfrac{12}{4x+20}$ *Solution:* $\dfrac{3}{x+5} \cdot \dfrac{4}{4} = \dfrac{12}{4x+20}$

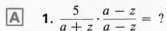

1. $\dfrac{5}{a+z} \cdot \dfrac{a-z}{a-z} = ?$

2. $\dfrac{m}{3a} \cdot \dfrac{a-b}{a-b} = ?$

3. $\dfrac{3t}{5s} \cdot \dfrac{2t+1}{2t+1} = ?$

4. $\dfrac{m^2}{x+y} \cdot \dfrac{?}{?} = \dfrac{2m^2n}{2nx+2ny}$

5. $\dfrac{4}{k+1} \cdot \dfrac{?}{?} = \dfrac{4k-4}{k^2-1}$

6. $\dfrac{5}{w-5} \cdot \dfrac{w+2}{w+2} = ?$

7. $\dfrac{10}{b + c} \cdot \dfrac{?}{?} = \dfrac{30}{3b + 3c}$ **8.** $\dfrac{4}{2a + 3} \cdot \dfrac{a - 5}{a - 5} = ?$

For each fraction write an equivalent fraction having the indicated denominator.

SAMPLE: $\dfrac{7}{3m} = \dfrac{?}{3m^2 + 3mn}$ *Solution:* $\dfrac{7}{3m} \cdot \dfrac{m + n}{m + n} = \dfrac{7m + 7n}{3m^2 + 3mn}$

9. $\dfrac{7}{c} = \dfrac{?}{c^2 - 3c}$ **13.** $\dfrac{m + n}{m - n} = \dfrac{?}{m^2 - n^2}$

10. $\dfrac{3}{x + y} = \dfrac{?}{8x + 8y}$ **14.** $\dfrac{5}{x + y} = \dfrac{?}{(x + y)^2}$

11. $\dfrac{3z}{5} = \dfrac{?}{5x^2 - 5y^2}$ **15.** $\dfrac{8a}{a + 3} = \dfrac{?}{2a + 6}$

12. $\dfrac{4}{a + c} = \dfrac{?}{3a^2 + 3ac}$ **16.** $\dfrac{7}{m + 4} = \dfrac{?}{m^2 + 6m + 8}$

Simplify each sum or difference, using the L.C.D. given.

SAMPLE: $\dfrac{5}{4m} + \dfrac{8}{n - 3}$; L.C.D., $4m(n - 3)$

Solution: $\dfrac{5}{4m} + \dfrac{8}{n - 3} = \left(\dfrac{5}{4m} \cdot \dfrac{n - 3}{n - 3}\right) + \left(\dfrac{8}{n - 3} \cdot \dfrac{4m}{4m}\right)$

$= \dfrac{5n - 15}{4mn - 12m} + \dfrac{32m}{4mn - 12m}$

$= \dfrac{32m + 5n - 15}{4mn - 12m}$

17. $\dfrac{3x}{2} + \dfrac{y}{x - y}$; L.C.D., $2(x - y)$

18. $\dfrac{2}{a} - \dfrac{1}{a - b}$; L.C.D., $a(a - b)$

19. $\dfrac{3}{n + 1} + \dfrac{5}{n + 2}$; L.C.D., $(n + 1)(n + 2)$

20. $\dfrac{4n}{n + 5} + \dfrac{2}{n - 5}$; L.C.D., $(n + 5)(n - 5)$

21. $\dfrac{4}{p - q} - \dfrac{1}{2p - 2q}$; L.C.D., $2(p - q)$

22. $\dfrac{2}{b - 1} + \dfrac{3}{b + 1}$; L.C.D., $(b + 1)(b - 1)$

23. $\dfrac{y}{x^2 - 1} + \dfrac{y}{x + 1}$; L.C.D., $(x - 1)(x + 1)$

24. $\dfrac{4}{5} - \dfrac{rs}{r - s}$; L.C.D., $5(r - s)$

25. $\dfrac{xy}{(x+y)^2} + \dfrac{yz}{(x+y)}$; L.C.D., $(x+y)^2$

26. $\dfrac{2}{3} + \dfrac{1}{2} + \dfrac{d}{c+d}$; L.C.D., $6(c+d)$

Find the L.C.D. for each of the following, and then simplify.

SAMPLE: $\dfrac{3a}{2a+6} - \dfrac{a-1}{a+3}$

Solution: L.C.D. is $2(a+3)$, or $2a+6$

$$\frac{3a}{2a+6} - \frac{a-1}{a+3} = \frac{3a}{2a+6} - \left(\frac{a-1}{a+3} \cdot \frac{2}{2}\right)$$

$$= \frac{3a}{2a+6} - \frac{2a-2}{2a+6} = \frac{a+2}{2a+6}$$

27. $\dfrac{1}{a+b} + \dfrac{2}{3}$

28. $\dfrac{1}{x-y} + \dfrac{x}{x^2-y^2}$

29. $\dfrac{4}{x+4} + \dfrac{2}{x+3}$

30. $\dfrac{3}{t+2} + \dfrac{5}{t+2} + \dfrac{1}{2}$

31. $\dfrac{3}{x} + \dfrac{6}{y} + \dfrac{1}{x+y}$

32. $\dfrac{1}{r^2-s^2} + \dfrac{1}{r+s}$

33. $\dfrac{3b}{a-b} + \dfrac{a+b}{b}$

34. $\dfrac{2}{xy} - \dfrac{1}{x-y}$

SAMPLE: $\dfrac{3a}{a^2-9} - \dfrac{a-1}{3a+9}$

Solution: $a^2 - 9 = (a+3)(a-3)$ and $3a + 9 = 3(a+3)$

L.C.D. is $3(a+3)(a-3)$, or $3(a^2-9)$

$$\frac{3a}{a^2-9} - \frac{a-1}{3a+9} = \left(\frac{3a}{a^2-9} \cdot \frac{3}{3}\right) - \left(\frac{a-1}{3a+9} \cdot \frac{a-3}{a-3}\right)$$

$$= \frac{9a}{3(a^2-9)} - \frac{a^2-4a+3}{3(a^2-9)}$$

$$= \frac{9a-a^2+4a-3}{3(a^2-9)} = \frac{-a^2+13a-3}{3(a^2-9)}$$

B **35.** $\dfrac{1}{p^2+pq} + \dfrac{1}{p^2-q^2}$

36. $\dfrac{4r-2}{2r-s} + \dfrac{3a}{8r+4s}$

37. $\dfrac{4a-b}{9a^2-b^2} - \dfrac{5c}{3a+b}$

38. $\dfrac{m+3}{m^2-4} + \dfrac{3m-1}{m^2+m-6}$

39. $\dfrac{4x-7}{x^2-3x+2} - \dfrac{3}{x-1}$

40. $\dfrac{n}{n^2-25} - \dfrac{1}{2n+10}$

41. $\dfrac{27}{x^2-81} + \dfrac{3}{2x+18}$

42. $\dfrac{a+b}{3r^2+rs} - \dfrac{a-b}{r(3r-s)}$

C 43. $\dfrac{2}{x-1} - \dfrac{3}{1+x} - \dfrac{x-5}{1-x^2}$ 46. $\dfrac{3}{y^2-25} - \dfrac{1}{5+y} - \dfrac{y+1}{5-y}$

44. $\dfrac{3}{2+b} + \dfrac{5b-2}{4-b^2} + \dfrac{2}{b-2}$ 47. $\dfrac{6m-13}{m^2-5m+6} - \dfrac{5}{m-3}$

45. $\dfrac{2}{3+y} + \dfrac{5}{y^2-9} + \dfrac{2y-1}{3-y}$ 48. $\dfrac{4x-7}{x^2-3x+2} - \dfrac{3}{x-1}$

8–7 Mixed Expressions

You will recall that in the first section of this chapter we worked with **mixed numerals** like $3\frac{1}{4}$ and $2\frac{5}{8}$, each of which represents the sum of an integer and a fraction. We often need to write such a mixed numeral as a single fraction. The procedure for doing this is illustrated in Examples 1 and 2.

EXAMPLE 1. $3\frac{1}{4} = 3 + \frac{1}{4}$ **EXAMPLE 2.** $2\frac{5}{8} = 2 + \frac{5}{8}$

$\qquad\qquad\quad = \frac{12}{4} + \frac{1}{4} \qquad\qquad\qquad\qquad\qquad = \frac{16}{8} + \frac{5}{8}$

$\qquad\qquad\quad = \frac{13}{4} \qquad\qquad\qquad\qquad\qquad\qquad\quad = \frac{21}{8}$

An expression such as $2 + \dfrac{3d}{c}$, which is a sum or difference of a polynomial and a fraction, is called a **mixed expression**. Examples 3 and 4 show how we can write a mixed expression as a single fraction.

EXAMPLE 3. $3 + \dfrac{c}{b} = \dfrac{3}{1} + \dfrac{c}{b}$

$\qquad\qquad\qquad\quad = \left(\dfrac{3}{1} \cdot \dfrac{b}{b}\right) + \dfrac{c}{b}$

$\qquad\qquad\qquad\quad = \dfrac{3b}{b} + \dfrac{c}{b} = \dfrac{3b+c}{b}$

EXAMPLE 4. $5 - \dfrac{3b}{a+b}$

$\qquad\qquad\quad = \dfrac{5}{1} - \dfrac{3b}{a+b}$

$\qquad\qquad\quad = \left(\dfrac{5}{1} \cdot \dfrac{a+b}{a+b}\right) - \dfrac{3b}{a+b}$

$\qquad\qquad\quad = \dfrac{5a+5b}{a+b} - \dfrac{3b}{a+b} = \dfrac{5a+2b}{a+b}$

By reversing the procedure, a fraction such as $\dfrac{5x^3 - 4}{5x}$ can be written as a mixed expression.

EXAMPLE 5.

$$\frac{5x^3 - 4}{5x} = \frac{5x^3}{5x} - \frac{4}{5x}$$

$$= \left(\frac{x^2}{1} \cdot \frac{5x}{5x}\right) - \frac{4}{5x} = x^2 - \frac{4}{5x}$$

ORAL EXERCISES

Match each fraction in Column 1 with the corresponding mixed expression in Column 2.

COLUMN 1

1. $\dfrac{ab + 3}{b}$

2. $\dfrac{2b^2 - 3}{2b}$

3. $\dfrac{3 - ab}{b}$

4. $\dfrac{b^2 + 5}{b}$

5. $\dfrac{a - b + 3}{a - b}$

COLUMN 2

A. $\dfrac{3}{b} - a$

B. $b + \dfrac{5}{b}$

C. $b - \dfrac{3}{2b}$

D. $1 + \dfrac{3}{a - b}$

E. $a + \dfrac{3}{b}$

Tell how to express each of the following as a sum or a difference of two fractions. Do not reduce the resulting fractions.

6. $\dfrac{m^2 + 2}{m}$

7. $\dfrac{x^2 + 2}{x}$

8. $\dfrac{5y^2 + 6}{5y}$

9. $\dfrac{x - y + 6}{x - y}$

10. $\dfrac{3t^2 - st}{t^2}$

11. $\dfrac{3 + a + b}{a + b}$

WRITTEN EXERCISES

Write each mixed expression as a single fraction.

 1. $4 + \dfrac{3}{y}$

2. $8 - \dfrac{s}{t + 1}$

3. $m + \dfrac{1}{m + 1}$

4. $a - \dfrac{5}{b}$ **7.** $6 + \dfrac{xy}{x - y}$ **10.** $1 + \dfrac{x + y}{x - y}$

5. $x - \dfrac{3}{2x}$ **8.** $9 + \dfrac{a}{b - c}$ **11.** $a + 1 + \dfrac{b}{3}$

6. $y + \dfrac{6}{7y}$ **9.** $1 + \dfrac{n}{m + 3}$ **12.** $x + 1 + \dfrac{y}{x - 1}$

Write each of the following as a mixed expression.

SAMPLE: $\dfrac{15t^3 + 9}{3t}$ $Solution:$ $\dfrac{15t^3 + 9}{3t} = \dfrac{15t^3}{3t} + \dfrac{9}{3t}$

$$= 5t^2 + \dfrac{3}{t}$$

13. $\dfrac{12x^3 + 6}{3x}$ **17.** $\dfrac{3a^2b^2 + 9ab}{3a^2b^2}$ **21.** $\dfrac{z^2 + 3z + 7}{z}$

14. $\dfrac{10 - 2y^2}{2y}$ **18.** $\dfrac{8hk - 4h^2k^2}{4h^2k^2}$ **22.** $\dfrac{2y^2 + 4y + 7}{2y}$

15. $\dfrac{1 - 6b^3}{3b^3}$ **19.** $\dfrac{20r^2 + 5r}{4r^2}$ **23.** $\dfrac{b^2 + 2b - 2}{b}$

16. $\dfrac{6 - 20c^8}{4c^4}$ **20.** $\dfrac{ab + b + c}{b}$ **24.** $\dfrac{18x^2 + 3x + 9}{3x}$

Express each of the following as a mixed expression by completing the indicated division.

SAMPLE $\dfrac{a^2 + 5a + 6}{a + 1}$

$Solution:$ $a + 1 \overline{)a^2 + 5a + 6}$ with quotient $a + 4$

$$\begin{array}{r} a + 4 \\ a+1\overline{)a^2 + 5a + 6} \\ \underline{a^2 + a} \\ 4a + 6 \\ \underline{4a + 4} \\ 2 \end{array}$$

$$\dfrac{a^2 + 5a + 6}{a + 1} = a + 4 + \dfrac{2}{a + 1}$$

B **25.** $\dfrac{2x^2 + 5x - 6}{x - 1}$ **27.** $\dfrac{12x^2 - 8x - 17}{2x - 3}$

26. $\dfrac{r^2 + 7r + 8}{r + 1}$ **28.** $\dfrac{12k^2 + 14k - 17}{4k + 2}$

8–8   Solving Open Sentences Containing Fractions

Earlier in this book, in Chapter 2, we considered the various properties of equality and inequality that were useful in solving open sentences. Let us see now how the same ideas, together with the skill of working with fractions, can be applied in solving open sentences that involve fractions.

The two solutions given for Example 1 are very similar. Study both methods carefully. Notice that, in each solution, the **L.C.D.** is used to write an equivalent sentence that is easily simplified.

EXAMPLE 1. $\dfrac{x}{2} + \dfrac{2x}{3} = 21$

Solution (1)

$$6\left(\frac{x}{2} + \frac{2x}{3}\right) = 6 \cdot 21$$

$$\left(6 \cdot \frac{x}{2}\right) + \left(6 \cdot \frac{2x}{3}\right) = 6 \cdot 21$$

$$3x + 4x = 126$$

$$7x = 126$$

$$x = 18$$

Solution (2)

$$\frac{3x + 4x}{6} = 21$$

$$\frac{7x}{6} = 21$$

$$\frac{6}{7} \cdot \frac{7x}{6} = \frac{6}{7} \cdot 21$$

$$x = 18$$

The solution set is $\{18\}$.

In Example 2, similar methods are used to solve an **inequality** that contains fractions.

EXAMPLE 2. $t - \dfrac{t}{3} > \dfrac{2}{9}$

Solution (1)

$$9\left(t - \frac{t}{3}\right) > 9 \cdot \frac{2}{9}$$

$$(9 \cdot t) - \left(9 \cdot \frac{t}{3}\right) > 9 \cdot \frac{2}{9}$$

$$9t - 3t > 2$$

$$6t > 2$$

$$t > \tfrac{1}{3}$$

Solution (2)

$$\frac{9t}{9} - \frac{3t}{9} > \frac{2}{9}$$

$$\frac{6t}{9} > \frac{2}{9}$$

$$9 \cdot \frac{6t}{9} > 9 \cdot \frac{2}{9}$$

$$6t > 2$$

$$t > \tfrac{1}{3}$$

Thus the solution set is $\{$**the directed numbers greater than $\tfrac{1}{3}$**$\}$. The graph of the solution set is:

ORAL EXERCISES

Name the L.C.D. for each open sentence.

SAMPLE: $\dfrac{4p}{6} + \dfrac{p}{10} = 2$ *What you say:* The L.C.D. is 30.

1. $\dfrac{2x}{3} + \dfrac{x}{5} = 8$

6. $\tfrac{1}{2}b + \tfrac{2}{3}b = -2$

2. $\dfrac{k}{4} - \dfrac{3k}{6} = 6$

7. $\dfrac{s}{8} - s < \dfrac{1}{3}$

3. $\dfrac{n^2}{2} - \dfrac{n}{6} + \dfrac{2}{3} = 0$

8. $\dfrac{s}{3} - s = -\dfrac{7}{5}$

4. $\dfrac{b}{5} \geq \dfrac{4b}{7} + 3$

9. $\tfrac{1}{5}x + \tfrac{1}{4}x = \tfrac{1}{2}$

5. $\dfrac{x^2}{2} + \dfrac{x}{3} \geq \dfrac{1}{6}$

10. $\dfrac{x}{5} - \dfrac{x}{4} < \dfrac{5}{3}$

WRITTEN EXERCISES

Write a simpler open sentence that is equivalent to the given sentence by multiplying each term by the given L.C.D. Do not solve the open sentence.

SAMPLE: $\dfrac{x}{4} + \dfrac{2x}{3} = 3$; L.C.D., 12   *Solution:* $\dfrac{x}{4} + \dfrac{2x}{3} = 3$

$$12\left(\dfrac{x}{4} + \dfrac{2x}{3}\right) = 12 \cdot 3$$

$$\dfrac{12x}{4} + \dfrac{24x}{3} = 36$$

$$3x + 8x = 36$$

A

1. $\dfrac{n}{2} + \dfrac{5n}{6} = 10$; L.C.D., 6

7. $\dfrac{3c}{2} + \dfrac{8c}{7} < 5$; L.C.D., 14

2. $\dfrac{3t^2}{5} - \dfrac{t}{7} = 2$; L.C.D., 35

8. $\tfrac{1}{3}y + \tfrac{1}{2}y = y + 1$; L.C.D., 6

3. $\dfrac{a}{2} + \dfrac{a}{3} = \dfrac{1}{4}$; L.C.D., 12

9. $\dfrac{x^2}{2} + \dfrac{x}{6} - \dfrac{1}{4} = 0$; L.C.D., 12

4. $\dfrac{x}{3} + \dfrac{x}{4} + 2 = 0$; L.C.D., 12

10. $\dfrac{t}{4} - t \leq \dfrac{3}{5}$; L.C.D., 20

5. $\dfrac{n}{8} - \dfrac{n}{6} = 1$; L.C.D., 24

11. $\dfrac{b^2}{13} + 3b > \dfrac{5}{39}$; L.C.D., 39

6. $\dfrac{s}{5} - s > \dfrac{2}{3}$; L.C.D., 15

12. $\dfrac{w^2}{5} - \dfrac{w}{2} + \dfrac{7}{10} = -3$; L.C.D., 10

Solve each equation and check.

SAMPLE: $\dfrac{x}{5} - \dfrac{x}{10} = \dfrac{3}{10}$

Solution: $10\left(\dfrac{x}{5} - \dfrac{x}{10}\right) = 10 \cdot \dfrac{3}{10}$ *Check:* $\dfrac{x}{5} - \dfrac{x}{10} = \dfrac{3}{10}$

$$\dfrac{10x}{5} - \dfrac{10x}{10} = \dfrac{30}{10}$$

$$2x - x = 3$$

$$x = 3$$

Check column:

$$\dfrac{3}{5} - \dfrac{3}{10} \;\Big|\; \dfrac{3}{10}$$

$$\dfrac{6}{10} - \dfrac{3}{10} \;\Big|\; \dfrac{3}{10}$$

$$\dfrac{3}{10} \;\Big|\; \dfrac{3}{10}$$

13. $\dfrac{k}{4} - \dfrac{k}{8} = \dfrac{3}{8}$

14. $\frac{1}{3}n + \frac{1}{2}n = n - 2$

15. $\dfrac{2x}{3} - \dfrac{3x}{5} = 1$

16. $\dfrac{3t}{7} - \dfrac{t}{3} = 4$

17. $3a - \dfrac{7a}{3} = 1$

18. $\dfrac{k}{2} + 45 = \dfrac{4k}{3}$

19. $\dfrac{3m}{4} + \dfrac{m}{3} = 26$

20. $\frac{2}{3}z = \frac{3}{5}z + 1$

21. $\dfrac{7y}{3} = 3y - 1$

22. $\dfrac{5x}{4} + \dfrac{x + 3}{10} = 3$

Solve each inequality and graph its solution set.

SAMPLE: $\dfrac{a}{3} + \dfrac{a}{4} > \dfrac{7}{2}$

Solution: $12\left(\dfrac{a}{3} + \dfrac{a}{4}\right) > 12 \cdot \dfrac{7}{2}$

$$\dfrac{12a}{3} + \dfrac{12a}{4} > \dfrac{84}{2}$$

$$4a + 3a > 42$$

$$7a > 42$$

$$a > 6$$

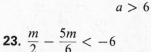

23. $\dfrac{m}{2} - \dfrac{5m}{6} < -6$

24. $\dfrac{s}{4} + s > \dfrac{7}{8}$

25. $\frac{1}{3}x + \frac{1}{4}x \geq \frac{7}{2}$

26. $\frac{1}{4}m + \frac{1}{5}m < \frac{9}{2}$

27. $\dfrac{2d}{3} + 1 \leq \dfrac{d}{2}$

28. $\dfrac{y}{5} - \dfrac{y}{3} < \dfrac{6}{5}$

29. $\dfrac{x}{7} - \dfrac{x}{4} > \dfrac{6}{7}$

30. $\dfrac{s}{3} - s < \dfrac{14}{7}$

Solve each sentence:

B **31.** $0.02k \geq 0.01k - 0.1$

32. $\dfrac{n + 3}{2} \geq \dfrac{n - 8}{5} + 1$

33. $0.5s - 1.4s = 0.9$

34. $\frac{3}{4}n = 26 - \frac{1}{3}n$

35. $\frac{1}{2}x - \frac{4}{5}x = -45$

36. $\dfrac{2b - 5}{5} + 1 \leq \dfrac{b - 3}{4}$

C **37.** $0.04x + 0.06(20{,}000 - x) = 960$

38. $1 + \frac{5}{8}(3s - 1) = \frac{3}{4}(2s + 5)$

39. $\dfrac{n - 3}{4} - \dfrac{2n - 5}{5} \leq 1$

40. $0.03k + 0.05(1000 - k) = 34$

PROLEMS

1. Mr. Carson invested $2500 at 7% interest for a period of two years. How much interest did he receive?
   Hint: Interest = principal × rate × time
   $= 2500 \cdot \frac{7}{100} \cdot 2$

2. Mr. McFarland has an investment of $900.00 that earns interest at the rate of 8% a year. How much interest will he earn over a three year period?
   Hint: Use $I = prt$.

3. An investment at 10% simple interest earned $750 in five years. What was the amount of the investment?
   Hint: Use $I = prt$.

4. Mr. Thompson invested a sum of money that earned 6% simple interest per year. After six months (half a year) he was paid $45 interest. How much money did Mr. Thompson have invested?

5. An investment of $1500 earned 9% simple interest per year. What was the total value of the investment after 5 years?

The area of a trapezoid is given by the formula
$$\text{Area} = \dfrac{B + b}{2} \cdot h.$$

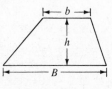

6. Find the area of the trapezoid when $B = 12\frac{1}{4}$ inches, $b = 9\frac{3}{4}$ inches, and $h = 7$ inches.

7. If the area of the trapezoid pictured here is 270 square inches, find the height, h, of the trapezoid.

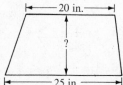

The formula for the volume of a sphere is $V = \frac{4}{3}\pi r^3$. In Problems 8 and 9, use $\pi = \frac{22}{7}$.

8. A large tank in the shape of a sphere is used for storing natural gas. If the radius, r, of the tank is 15 feet, how many cubic feet of gas can be stored in the tank?

9. A hemisphere is half of a sphere. Find the volume of this hemisphere, whose diameter is 21 feet, as shown.

10. A hopper for sand, used in a cement plant, is shaped like a cone. The volume of a cone is given by the formula $V = \frac{1}{3}\pi r^2 h$. If the height, h, of the hopper is 15 feet and its base is a circle with a radius, r, of 6 feet, how many cubic yards of sand will it hold? (1 cubic yard = 27 cubic feet; use $\pi = \frac{22}{7}$.)

11. The pyramid shown here is 8 inches high and has a square base. Find its volume, using the formula $V = \frac{1}{3}Bh$, where B is the area of the base and h is the height of the pyramid.

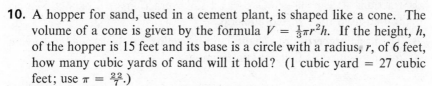

CHAPTER SUMMARY

Inventory of Structure and Concepts

1. The **sum** of two fractions $\frac{a}{b}$ and $\frac{c}{b}$, where a, b, and c represent any numbers, except that b is not zero, is given by the equation

$$\frac{a}{b} + \frac{c}{b} = \frac{a + c}{b}.$$

2. A symbol such as $8\frac{1}{3}$ is called a **mixed numeral**. It can be expressed either as the sum of an integer and a fraction or as a single fraction; thus $8\frac{1}{3} = 8 + \frac{1}{3}$ and $8\frac{1}{3} = \frac{25}{3}$.

3. The operations of addition and subtraction are **inverse operations**. To subtract one number from another is equivalent to adding the opposite of the number that is to be subtracted. Thus the **difference** of two fractions $\frac{a}{b}$ and $\frac{c}{b}$, where a, b, and c represent any numbers, except that b is not zero, is given by the equation

$$\frac{a}{b} - \frac{c}{b} = \frac{a}{b} + \left(-\frac{c}{b}\right).$$

4. For any numbers a and b, except that b is not zero,
$$-\frac{a}{b} = \frac{-a}{b} = \frac{a}{-b}.$$

5. Two fractions with unequal denominators can be added if the fractions are first replaced by equivalent fractions having a **common denominator**.

6. The **lowest common denominator** for two or more fractions is the expression that contains each factor of the denominators the greatest number of times that it appears in any denominator.

7. A **mixed expression** is the sum or difference of a polynomial and a fraction. It can be expressed as a single fraction by a method similar to that used for a mixed numeral.

8. The **basic properties** of **equality** and **inequality** can be applied in solving number sentences that contain fractions.

Vocabulary and Spelling

mixed numerals (*p. 248*)
inverse operations (*p. 254*)
opposite (*p. 254*)
additive inverse (*p. 254*)

lowest common denominator
  (L.C.D.) (*p. 262*)
equivalent fraction (*p. 262*)
mixed expression (*p. 270*)

Chapter Test

Express each of the following as a mixed numeral or as a mixed expression.

1. $\frac{15}{4}$

2. $-\frac{19}{7}$

3. $\dfrac{m^2 + 2n}{m}$

4. $\dfrac{a + b + c}{a + b}$

Express each sum or difference as a single fraction in lowest terms.

5. $\dfrac{4(a - b)}{(a - b)^2} + \dfrac{5}{a - b}$

6. $\left(\dfrac{9m}{4a} + \dfrac{7m}{4a}\right) - \dfrac{3n}{a}$

7. $\dfrac{a}{c - 3} + \dfrac{d}{c - 3}$

8. $\dfrac{7x}{8y} - \dfrac{3}{-8y}$

9. $\dfrac{3r^2 s}{y - 2} - \dfrac{r^2 s}{2 - y}$

10. $\dfrac{3}{ab} + \dfrac{4}{bc} - \dfrac{2}{ac}$

11. $\dfrac{5}{r + 3} + \dfrac{7}{r + 2}$

12. $\dfrac{5p}{3q + 6} + \dfrac{p - 1}{q + 2}$

Solve each inequality and graph its solution set.

13. $\dfrac{t}{3} - \dfrac{t}{4} < \dfrac{1}{6}$

15. $\dfrac{n}{2} + \dfrac{n}{3} + \dfrac{2n}{3} \geq \dfrac{3}{2}$

14. $\dfrac{m}{5} > \dfrac{6}{5} + \dfrac{m}{3}$

16. $\dfrac{2c}{3} + 1 < \dfrac{c}{2}$

Solve each equation and check the solution.

17. $\dfrac{3b}{2} + \dfrac{b}{6} = 20$

19. $\dfrac{m+2}{10} + \dfrac{2m}{5} = -\dfrac{4}{5}$

18. $\dfrac{t}{4} - \dfrac{t}{5} = \dfrac{3}{10}$

20. $8 = 3n - \dfrac{5n}{3}$

Solve each problem.

21. A cone-shaped pile of sand is about 6 feet high. Its base is about 9 feet in diameter. What is the approximate number of cubic yards in the pile? Recall that the volume of a cone is given by the formula $V = \frac{1}{3}Bh$, where B is the area of the base and h is the height of the cone.

22. An investment of $10,000 held by Mr. Johnson pays interest at the rate of $9\frac{1}{2}\%$ per year. What is the total value of the investment at the end of one year?

Chapter Review

8–1 Addition with Fractions Having Equal Monomial Denominators

Express each sum as a single fraction in lowest terms.

1. $\frac{1}{7} + \frac{3}{7} + \frac{2}{7}$

3. $\dfrac{4t}{15} + \dfrac{t}{15}$

5. $\dfrac{2n}{15} + \dfrac{n}{15} + \dfrac{3n}{15}$

2. $\dfrac{1}{5} + \dfrac{3}{5} + \dfrac{-2}{5}$

4. $\dfrac{6}{rs} + \dfrac{2}{rs} + \dfrac{1}{rs}$

6. $\dfrac{2t}{a} + \dfrac{r}{a} + \dfrac{x}{a}$

8–2 Addition with Fractions Having Equal Polynomial Denominators.

Simplify each expression.

7. $\dfrac{4n + 7n}{(a+b)^2}$

8. $\dfrac{m}{m-n} + \dfrac{n}{m-n}$

9. $\dfrac{a^2}{y+2} + \dfrac{b^2}{2+y}$

10. $\dfrac{2(r+s)}{(r+s)^2} + \dfrac{3}{r+s}$

11. $\dfrac{a-b}{a^2-b^2} + \dfrac{2}{a+b}$

12. $\dfrac{2}{b^2+3} + \dfrac{5a}{ab^2+3a}$

8–3 Subtraction with Fractions: The Inverse of Addition

Write each difference as a single fraction in lowest terms.

13. $\dfrac{7mn}{n^2} - \dfrac{2mn}{n^2}$

14. $\dfrac{3xy}{2ab} - \dfrac{xy}{2ab}$

15. $\dfrac{5a}{x+y} - \dfrac{5}{x+y}$

16. $\dfrac{3t}{2ab} - \dfrac{t}{2ab}$

17. $\dfrac{m}{m-n} - \dfrac{n}{m-n}$

18. $\dfrac{x}{x^2-4} - \dfrac{2}{x^2-4}$

8–4 Simplifying Sums and Differences

Write each sum or difference as a single fraction in lowest terms.

19. $\dfrac{6}{5w} - \dfrac{2}{-5w}$

20. $\dfrac{3}{x-y} + \dfrac{1}{y-x}$

21. $\dfrac{5}{a} - \dfrac{2}{-a}$

22. $\dfrac{a^2b^2}{4-d} - \dfrac{c}{d-4}$

23. $\dfrac{9z}{x-y} + \dfrac{3z}{y-x}$

24. $\dfrac{15}{3x-6y} + \dfrac{4}{2y-x}$

8–5 Sums and Differences with Unlike Monomial Denominators

Simplify each of the following:

25. $\dfrac{5}{ax} + \dfrac{2}{ay}$

26. $\dfrac{3}{a^2b} - \dfrac{2}{a^2}$

27. $\dfrac{r}{xy} + \dfrac{s}{yz} - \dfrac{1}{3}$

8–6 Sums and Differences with Unlike Polynomial Denominators

Write each fraction as an equivalent fraction having the indicated denominator.

28. $\dfrac{3}{b} = \dfrac{?}{3ab+b^2}$

29. $\dfrac{2}{m+n} = \dfrac{?}{m^2-n^2}$

30. $\dfrac{2b}{k+2} = \dfrac{?}{3k+6}$

Simplify each sum or difference.

31. $\dfrac{3}{5} - \dfrac{1}{r+s}$

32. $\dfrac{b}{a^2-b^2} + \dfrac{1}{a+b}$

33. $\dfrac{5n}{m-n} + \dfrac{m+n}{m}$

8–7 Mixed Expressions

Write each fraction as a mixed expression.

34. $\dfrac{15n^2 + 9}{3n}$ **35.** $\dfrac{15 - 21z^3}{7z}$ **36.** $\dfrac{x^2 - 5x + 4}{x}$

Write each mixed expression as a single fraction.

37. $2 + \dfrac{5}{a}$ **38.** $10 - \dfrac{x}{y + 1}$ **39.** $n - 1 + \dfrac{t}{n + 1}$

8–8 Solving Open Sentences Containing Fractions

Solve each equation and check.

40. $\dfrac{3}{8} + \dfrac{x}{8} = \dfrac{x}{4}$ **41.** $\frac{2}{3}m - 1 = \frac{3}{5}m$ **42.** $\dfrac{5x}{2} + \dfrac{x + 3}{5} = 6$

Solve each inequality and graph its solution set.

43. $\dfrac{x}{2} + 6 \geq -\dfrac{5}{2}$ **44.** $\dfrac{3n}{2} - \dfrac{4n}{3} < -\dfrac{1}{2}$

Use $I = prt$ to find the unknown quantity.

45. $I = \$486$, $r = 6\%$, $p = \$2700$, $t = ?$

Review of Skills

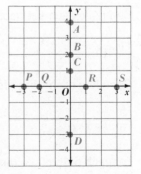

Refer to the figure at the right to answer Questions 1–4.

1. Write the ordered number pair that corresponds to each labeled point on the horizontal axis.

2. Write the ordered number pair that corresponds to each labeled point on the vertical axis.

3. If the first number in an ordered pair of numbers is 0 and the second number is *not* 0, then the ordered pair corresponds to a point on the __?__ axis.

4. If the first number in an ordered pair of numbers is *not* 0 and the second number is 0, then the ordered pair corresponds to a point on the __?__ axis.

Use a number plane to graph each point that is described, and label the point with the indicated letter.

5. Point R: first coordinate is 3; second coordinate is 2.

6. Point M: first coordinate is -2; second coordinate is 1.

7. Point Q: first coordinate is 1; second coordinate is -1.

Complete each table by using the given function machine or function equation. Then write the resulting function as a set of ordered pairs.

8.

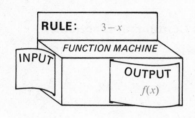

x	$f(x)$	$(x, f(x))$
-2	5	$(-2, 5)$
-1	?	?
0	?	?
1	?	?
2	?	?

9. $f(x) = 3x - 4$

x	$f(x)$	$(x, f(x))$
2	2	$(2, 2)$
1	?	?
0	?	?
-1	?	?

10. $f(x) = \dfrac{x}{2} - 3$

x	$f(x)$	$(x, f(x))$
10	2	$(10, 2)$
8	?	?
6	?	?
4	?	?

Complete each subtraction.

11. $\dfrac{1}{10} - \dfrac{1}{15} = \dfrac{1}{?}$　　　**12.** $\dfrac{1}{4} - \dfrac{1}{6} = \dfrac{1}{?}$　　　**13.** $\dfrac{2}{3} - \dfrac{1}{2} = \dfrac{1}{?}$

Complete each of the following to make a true statement.

14. $12 \cdot 1 = ?$　　　**16.** $(1.5)(?) = 0$　　　**18.** $0 = 8 \cdot 3 \cdot (?)$

15. $6 \cdot \frac{1}{2} \cdot 0 = ?$　　　**17.** $(1.5)(?) = 1.5$　　　**19.** $19 + (?) = 19$

For each of the following, write an equivalent equation whose left member is x.

SAMPLE:　$x + 2y = 5$　　　　*Solution:* $x = 5 - 2y$

20. $x - 5y = 1$　　　**21.** $2x + z = 3$　　　**22.** $-x + 3 = y$

Write each fraction as a percent.

23. $\frac{3}{20}$　　　**24.** $\frac{9}{100}$　　　**25.** $\frac{2}{40}$　　　**26.** $\frac{7}{10}$

Albert Einstein

One of the greatest scientists of all time, Albert Einstein, was born in Ulm, Württemberg, Germany, on March 14, 1879. When, at the age of five, he was shown a pocket compass, he was deeply impressed by the mysterious behavior of the compass needle. He later said that he felt then that "something deeply hidden had to be behind things." Much of his lifetime was to be spent in the search for what it was that was hidden.

After his graduation from the Swiss Polytechnic Institute in Zurich, Switzerland, Einstein worked as an examiner at the Swiss Patent Office in Bern, a position that left him a great deal of free time for scientific investigation. It was during this time that he made some of his greatest contributions to scientific knowledge, recorded in papers published in a German scientific periodical. Included were a paper using the quantum theory to explain the photoelectric effect, which is the basis of the "electric eye," and one discussing the *Brownian movement* of particles in a liquid or gas, which confirmed the atomic theory of matter.

Another paper related mass to energy, through the famous equation

$$E \quad = \quad m \quad \cdot \quad c^2$$

$$\text{(energy)} = \text{(mass)} \text{(velocity of light)}^2$$

which was a foundation stone in the development of atomic energy. Still another set forth the theory of relativity with which the name of Einstein is especially associated.

Albert Einstein supported the concept of world government. He felt strongly that peace among nations could be maintained in the atomic age only by bringing all men together under a system of world law. In 1933 the Nazi government confiscated his property and deprived him of his position as director of the Kaiser Wilhelm Physical Institute in Berlin. However, he had already accepted the position of director of the Institute for Advanced Study in Princeton, N.J., a post which he filled until his death in 1955.

"Puffing Billy," an early steam locomotive . . .

A modern high-speed TurboTrain . . .

Solving Equations and Graphing

The first great advance in transportation brought about by the Machine Age was the railroad, introduced to America early in the nineteenth century. The oldest steam locomotive in existence today is the wood-burning "Puffing Billy." The rapid expansion of the country in the decades that followed, aided by the development of railroads, saw wood as fuel for trains give way to coal, to oil, and to electricity. The TurboTrain is a modern high-speed train whose light weight and streamlined design allow it to reach speeds as great as 170 miles an hour. With its improved acceleration and deceleration, it has been possible to cut a full hour from the time previously required for a 230-mile trip. The TurboTrain, designed by aerospace engineers using the technology of flight, is truly a product of modern science.

Equations

9–1   Factors and Zero Products

Earlier you learned that if any factor of a product is zero, then the product is zero. To illustrate this idea consider these sentences:

$$4 \cdot 0 = ? \qquad 0 \cdot (-6) = ?$$
$$\tfrac{5}{8} \cdot 0 = ? \qquad 15 \cdot 9 \cdot 0 = ?$$

Do you see that the product is zero in each case?

Similarly, you know that if any product is zero, then at least one of the factors is zero. For example:

$$8 \cdot (?) = 0 \qquad (-2) \cdot (?) = 0$$
$$\tfrac{9}{5} \cdot (?) = 0 \qquad \tfrac{1}{2} \cdot \tfrac{3}{5} \cdot (?) = 0$$

Do you agree that the **missing factor** is **zero** in each of the sentences above? This idea is called the **principle of zero products**.

For any numbers **r** and **s**,

$$r \cdot s = 0 \quad \text{if and only if} \quad r = 0 \quad \text{or} \quad s = 0.$$

How do you suppose we can apply the principle of zero products to solve an equation like $(x - 5)(x + 2) = 0$? We know for sure that, since the **product** is **0**, either the factor $(x - 5)$ or the factor $(x + 2)$ must equal **0**.

$$\underbrace{(x - 5)}\underbrace{(x + 2)} = 0$$

factor   factor   product

Suppose that $(x - 5)$ is zero. Clearly then the correct replacement for *x* is **5**. If $(x + 2)$ is zero, then the correct replacement for *x* is **−2**. It seems safe to conclude that the equation $(x - 5)(x + 2) = 0$ results in a true statement when *x* is replaced either by **5** or by **−2**. Thus the solution set is $\{5, -2\}$.

The following examples further illustrate how the zero products principle can be applied in solving equations.

EXAMPLE 1. $3(x - 9) = 0$

$x - 9 = 0$

$x = 9$ The solution set is $\{9\}$.

EXAMPLE 2. $(m + 10)(m - 7) = 0$

$m + 10 = 0$ or $m - 7 = 0$

$m = -10$ or $m = 7$

The solution set is $\{-10, 7\}$.

ORAL EXERCISES

Name the replacement for each variable that will give the expression the value zero.

1. $(x - 1)$ **5.** $(12 + k)$ **9.** $(2 - x)$

2. $(y + 4)$ **6.** $(2x + 1)$ **10.** $(3n + 1)$

3. $(x - 2)$ **7.** $3m$ **11.** $(5b + 2)$

4. $(c + 9)$ **8.** m^2 **12.** $(3n - 1)$

WRITTEN EXERCISES

Complete each of the following to make a true statement.

A **1.** $3 \cdot (?) = 0$ **2.** $0(3 + 4) = ?$

3. $\frac{5}{10} \cdot (?) = 0$

4. $\frac{1}{2} \cdot \frac{3}{5} \cdot (?) = 0$

5. $0 \cdot (-\frac{1}{3})(\frac{1}{7}) = ?$

6. $0 = (-5)(-2)(?)$

7. $(1.8)(3.2)(?) = 0$

8. $(?)(\frac{2}{5})(-\frac{7}{8}) = 0$

9. $(17)(9)(?)(-6) = 0$

10. $(5)(0)(-3)(0) = ?$

Solve each equation and write the solution set.

SAMPLE: $3(a - 2) = 0$

Solution: $3(a - 2) = 0$
$$a - 2 = 0$$
$$a = 2; \quad \{2\}$$

11. $5(x - 3) = 0$

12. $2(a - 8) = 0$

13. $13(b + 2) = 0$

14. $-4(5 + c) = 0$

15. $3(y + 9) = 0$

16. $-6(x + 4) = 0$

17. $(n - \frac{2}{5})3 = 0$

18. $\frac{2}{3}(t + \frac{1}{2}) = 0$

19. $0 = \frac{5}{8}(\frac{1}{3} + n)$

20. $0 = -\frac{1}{2}(-\frac{1}{3} + k)$

SAMPLE: $(x + 2)(x - 3) = 0$ *Solution:* $(x + 2)(x - 3) = 0$
$$x + 2 = 0 \quad \text{or} \quad x - 3 = 0$$
$$x = -2 \quad \text{or} \quad x = 3$$

The solution set is $\{-2, 3\}$.

21. $(x - 3)(x - 5) = 0$

22. $(x + 4)(x + 7) = 0$

23. $(y - 8)(y + 6) = 0$

24. $t(t - 1) = 0$

25. $n(2n - 5) = 0$

26. $0 = (x + 10)(x - 1)$

27. $0 = (a + 3)(a - 3)$

28. $(b + 5)(b + 5) = 0$

29. $k(k + 2) = 0$

30. $y(3y + 7) = 0$

Write the solution set for each sentence.

SAMPLE 1: $0(x - 3) = 0$ *Solution:* {the directed numbers}

SAMPLE 2: $0\left(\frac{2}{x} - \frac{1}{3}\right) = 0$ *Solution:* {the nonzero directed numbers}

B **31.** $0(z + 9) = 0$

32. $0(y - 3) = 0$

33. $0\left(\frac{2}{m} + \frac{5}{8}\right) = 0$

34. $0\left(\frac{5}{2} - \frac{3}{w}\right) = 0$

35. $0 = (12 - m)0$

36. $0 = 0\left(18 - \frac{9}{b}\right)$

C **37.** $29\left(\frac{1}{a} + \frac{2}{5}\right) = 0$

38. $-15\left(\frac{1}{a} + \frac{3}{5}\right) = 0$

39. $(5k + 1)(k - 3) = 0$

40. $(6r + 3)(7r + 14) = 0$

9–2   Solving Polynomial Equations

An equation whose left and right members are polynomials is called a **polynomial equation**. For example, the sentence $t^2 - 2t = 48$ is a polynomial equation, since both $t^2 - 2t$ and **48** are polynomials. When solving such a polynomial equation, we usually write it in **standard form**, with one member zero and the other a simplified polynomial. In standard form, the equation $t^2 - 2t = 48$ becomes

$$t^2 - 2t - 48 = 0.$$

Recall that such an equation, of degree **two**, is called a **quadratic equation**. An equation of degree **one**, such as $3x + 2 = 2x$, is called a **linear equation**; an equation like $x^3 - 3x^2 = 4x$, which is of degree **three**, is called a **cubic equation**.

As you may have suspected, if it is possible to factor one member of a polynomial equation in standard form, the **principle of zero products** can be used to solve the equation.

EXAMPLE 1.

$t^2 - 2t = 48$	Given equation.
$t^2 - 2t - 48 = 0$	Write the equation in standard form.
$(t + 6)(t - 8) = 0$	Factor the left member.
$t + 6 = 0$ or $t - 8 = 0$	Set each factor equal to zero.
$t = -6$ or $t = 8$	Solve each equation.

Check: For $t = -6$ For $t = 8$

$$\begin{array}{c|c} t^2 - 2t & = 48 \\ \hline 36 + 12 & 48 \\ 48 & 48 \end{array} \qquad \begin{array}{c|c} t^2 - 2t & = 48 \\ \hline 64 - 16 & 48 \\ 48 & 48 \end{array}$$

Therefore, the solution set is $\{-6, 8\}$.

The following example illustrates the solution of a cubic equation by factoring and applying the principle of zero products.

EXAMPLE 2.

$x^3 - 3x^2 = 4x$	Given equation.
$x^3 - 3x^2 - 4x = 0$	Write the equation in standard form.
$x(x^2 - 3x - 4) = 0$	Factor the left member
$x(x - 4)(x + 1) = 0$	completely.

$x = 0$ or $x - 4 = 0$ or $x + 1 = 0$ **Set each factor equal to zero.**

$x = 0$ or $x = 4$ or $x = -1$ **Solve each equation.**

Check:

For $x = 0$		For $x = 4$		For $x = -1$	
$x^3 - 3x^2 = 4x$		$x^3 - 3x^2 = 4x$		$x^3 - 3x^2 = 4x$	
$0 - 0$	0	$64 - 48$	16	$(-1) - (3 \cdot 1)$	-4
0	0		16	16	-4	-4

Therefore, the solution set is $\{0, 4, -1\}$.

ORAL EXERCISES

Give the degree of each equation and tell whether it is linear, quadratic, or cubic.

SAMPLE: $4n - 3 = 5n^2$ *What you say:* degree two; quadratic

1. $5x + 3 = 8x$

2. $4x^3 + x^2 = 1 + x$

3. $10 + y = 3y - 1$

4. $r^2 + 2 = 3r$

5. $n^2 - 1 = 0$

6. $4 - z^3 = z$

7. $\frac{1}{2} + 3k = 0$

8. $x - 3x^2 = 1 + x^3$

9. $3 + 10a = 4 + a$

10. $3x^2 + 7x - 4 = 0$

Express each equation in standard form.

11. $x^3 + 5x = x^2$

12. $9k^2 = 16$

13. $3n + 4 = n + 1$

14. $5 = 3x - 2x^2$

15. $2m = m^2 - 7m^3$

16. $8 - 3 = n - 5$

WRITTEN EXERCISES

Factor each polynomial completely.

1. $k + 3k^2$.

2. $x^2 + 9x + 14$

3. $t^2 - 5t - 24$

4. $2x^2 + x$

5. $n^2 - 8n + 15$

6. $3y^2 + 7y$

7. $y^2 - 16y$

8. $x^2 - 6x + 9$

9. $2z^2 - 5z$

10. $2n^2 - 11n + 5$

11. $a^2 + a - 90$

12. $c^3 - 6c^2 - 40c$

Find the solution set of each equation.

13. $n^2 + 2n = 0$

14. $2a^2 - 7a = 0$

15. $3y^2 = 5y$

16. $w^2 + 5w - 14 = 0$

17. $z^2 - 2z = 15$

18. $r^2 + 5r - 50 = 0$

19. $s^2 = 3s + 18$

20. $x^2 + 8x = -15$

21. $t^2 + 11t = -18$

22. $y^2 + 3 = 4y$

23. $d^2 + 5 = 6d$

24. $x^2 = 108 + 3x$

25. $s^2 - 66 = 5s$

26. $25y^2 - 100 = 0$

27. $b^2 - 225 = 0$

28. $4z^2 = 25$

B **29.** $2t^2 + 9t = -10$

30. $3r^2 + 13r + 14 = 0$

31. $2b^2 + 5 = 11b$

32. $3y^2 + 9y = 0$

33. $2s^2 - 17s = -21$

34. $2x^3 - 8x = 0$

35. $3k^2 + 10 = 17k$

36. $4x^2 + 8x = 140$

C **37.** $m^3 - 6m^2 - 40m = 0$

38. $t^3 + 8t^2 - 84t = 0$

39. $9s^3 - 12s^2 + 4s = 0$

40. $x^4 - 17x^2 + 16 = 0$

PROBLEMS

Use a quadratic equation to solve each of the following problems.

SAMPLE: A fence encloses a yard in the shape of a rectangle. The area of the yard is 9000 square feet. If the width of the yard is 10 feet less than the length, what are the dimensions of the yard?

9000 sq. ft.

$x - 10$

x

Solution: If x represents the number of feet in the length, then $x - 10$ represents the number of feet in the width. The area of a rectangle is given by the formula $A = lw$.

$$x(x - 10) = 9000$$
$$x^2 - 10x - 9000 = 0$$
$$(x + 90)(x - 100) = 0$$
$$x + 90 = 0 \quad \text{or} \quad x - 100 = 0$$
$$x = -90 \quad \text{or} \quad x = 100$$

Therefore the length, x, is 100 feet and the width, $x - 10$, is 90 feet. Note that we reject the solution $x = -90$ because a negative number is not meaningful as the measure of a side of a rectangle.

1. A rectangle is 4 feet longer than it is wide. The area of the rectangle is 77 square inches. Find the dimensions.

> 77 sq. in. | x
>
> $x+4$

2. A rectangle is 2 feet longer than it is wide. The area of the rectangle is 99 square feet. Find its dimensions.

> 99 sq. ft. | x
>
> $x+2$

3. Find two consecutive odd integers the sum of whose squares is 202. Hint: $x^2 + (x + 2)^2 = 202$.

4. Find the base and the height of a triangle whose area is 40 square inches, if the sum of the base and the height is 18 inches. Use $A = \frac{1}{2}bh$.

> x
>
> $18-x$

5. Find two consecutive even integers the sum of whose squares is 100. Hint: $x^2 + (x + 2)^2 = 100$.

9–3 Solving Fractional Equations

The equation $\dfrac{2}{3} = \dfrac{6}{x - 2}$ has a variable in the denominator of one member, while the equation $\dfrac{12}{x + 2} = \dfrac{4}{x - 2}$ has a variable in both denominators. An equation that has a variable in at least one denominator is called a **fractional equation**. In solving a fractional equation, the L.C.D. of the fractions is used to simplify the work.

EXAMPLE 1. Solve $\dfrac{12}{x + 2} = \dfrac{4}{x - 2}$

The L.C.D. is $(x + 2)(x - 2)$, or $x^2 - 4$.   *Check:*

$$(x^2 - 4) \cdot \frac{12}{x + 2} = (x^2 - 4) \cdot \frac{4}{x - 2}$$

$$(x - 2) \cdot 12 = (x + 2) \cdot 4$$

$$12x - 24 = 4x + 8$$

$$8x = 32$$

$$x = 4$$

$$\frac{12}{x + 2} = \frac{4}{x - 2}$$

$$\frac{12}{4 + 2} \quad \Big| \quad \frac{4}{4 - 2}$$

$$\frac{12}{6} \quad \Big| \quad \frac{4}{2}$$

$$2 \quad \Big| \quad 2$$

The solution set is $\{4\}$.

EXAMPLE 2. Solve $\dfrac{6}{x^2 - 4} + 1 = \dfrac{3}{x - 2}$.

The L.C.D. is $x^2 - 4$.

$$(x^2 - 4) \cdot \dfrac{6}{x^2 - 4} + (x^2 - 4) \cdot 1 = (x^2 - 4) \cdot \dfrac{3}{x - 2}$$

$$6 + x^2 - 4 = 3x + 6$$

$$x^2 - 3x - 4 = 0$$

$$(x - 4)(x + 1) = 0$$

$$x - 4 = 0 \quad \text{or} \quad x + 1 = 0$$

$$x = 4 \quad \text{or} \quad x = -1$$

Check:

For $x = 4$

$$\dfrac{6}{x^2 - 4} + 1 = \dfrac{3}{x - 2}$$

$\dfrac{6}{16 - 4} + 1$	$\dfrac{3}{4 - 2}$
$\dfrac{1}{2} + 1$	$\dfrac{3}{2}$
$1\frac{1}{2}$	$1\frac{1}{2}$

For $x = -1$

$$\dfrac{6}{x^2 - 4} + 1 = \dfrac{3}{x - 2}$$

$\dfrac{6}{1 - 4} + 1$	$\dfrac{3}{-1 - 2}$
$-2 + 1$	$\dfrac{3}{-3}$
-1	-1

The solution set is $\{4, -1\}$.

ORAL EXERCISES

Name the L.C.D. for each fractional equation. Do not solve.

SAMPLE: $\dfrac{5}{2x} = \dfrac{3}{4}$ *What you say:* $4x$

1. $\dfrac{10}{x} = \dfrac{1}{2}$

2. $\dfrac{-2}{3} = \dfrac{5}{a}$

3. $\dfrac{3}{4x} = \dfrac{x}{1}$

4. $\dfrac{2}{n} = \dfrac{n + 1}{3}$

5. $\dfrac{3}{2x} + \dfrac{1}{x} = \dfrac{4}{5}$

6. $\dfrac{1}{5z} + \dfrac{3}{z} = \dfrac{1}{3}$

7. $\dfrac{3}{4x} - \dfrac{7}{8} = \dfrac{2}{3x}$

8. $2 + \dfrac{1}{a - 1} = \dfrac{2}{a + 1}$

WRITTEN EXERCISES

Solve each equation.

A   1. $\dfrac{9}{2x} + 1 = \dfrac{1}{2}$

7. $\dfrac{6k}{k-1} = \dfrac{5}{2}$

2. $\dfrac{3}{x} + \dfrac{1}{2x} = 3$

8. $\dfrac{3}{a-4} = \dfrac{1}{a+4}$

3. $\dfrac{12}{s+2} = \dfrac{3}{s}$

9. $\dfrac{3}{4x} + \dfrac{1}{x} = \dfrac{7}{8}$

4. $\dfrac{4}{n-2} = \dfrac{12}{n+2}$

10. $\dfrac{1}{w} + \dfrac{2}{3w} = \dfrac{5}{9}$

5. $\dfrac{2}{y+2} = \dfrac{7}{y-3}$

11. $\dfrac{5}{2n} - \dfrac{7}{3n} = \dfrac{5}{12}$

6. $\dfrac{5}{x} = \dfrac{2}{x-3}$

12. $\dfrac{5}{4k} + \dfrac{4}{3k-1} - \dfrac{2}{k} = 0$

Name the L.C.D. for each equation and solve.

13. $\dfrac{b+4}{3} = \dfrac{3}{b-4}$

17. $\dfrac{n+5}{2n} - \dfrac{7}{3n} = \dfrac{5}{12}$

14. $\dfrac{5}{x} = \dfrac{x-3}{2}$

18. $\dfrac{4}{3b} - \dfrac{b+4}{6b} = 2$

15. $\dfrac{6}{z-1} = \dfrac{z}{2}$

19. $\dfrac{4}{3t-2} + \dfrac{7}{3t} - \dfrac{1}{t} = 0$

16. $\dfrac{5}{c+6} = \dfrac{c-6}{c}$

20. $\dfrac{3}{4k} + \dfrac{4}{3k-1} = \dfrac{2}{k}$

B   21. $a - \dfrac{2}{a-3} = \dfrac{a-1}{3-a}$

23. $\dfrac{2x}{x+2} - 2 = \dfrac{x-8}{x-2}$

22. $c - \dfrac{c}{1-c} = \dfrac{2-c}{c-1}$

24. $\dfrac{y-7}{y} = \dfrac{21}{y^2} + 1$

C   25. $\dfrac{28}{x^2-9} - \dfrac{x}{x-3} + \dfrac{7}{x+3} = 1$

27. $\dfrac{y}{y-1} + \dfrac{2}{y^2-1} = \dfrac{8}{y+1}$

26. $\dfrac{2}{n+2} + \dfrac{n}{n-2} = \dfrac{n^2+4}{n^2-4}$

28. $\dfrac{t+2}{2t-6} - \dfrac{3}{t-3} = \dfrac{t}{2}$

9–4   Problems and Fractional Equations

Suppose that a painter, working steadily, can paint a room in two hours. At this rate it is clear that he should complete $\frac{1}{2}$ of the job in one hour. If another painter would require 3 hours to paint the same room he should complete $\frac{1}{3}$ of the job in one hour. Do you see that, in general, if a job requires x hours of working time to complete, then the part of the job completed in one hour can be represented by the fraction $\frac{1}{x}$? The following example illustrates how we apply these ideas.

EXAMPLE. Payroll checks of the Amex Company are prepared by computer. The faster of two available computers can complete the payroll checks in **10** hours; the slower computer requires **15** hours for the same task. How long might it take to complete the payroll if both computers could be used?

Solution: The faster computer can do $\frac{1}{10}$ of the job in **1** hour. The slower computer can do $\frac{1}{15}$ of the job in **1** hour. If x represents the number of hours required when both computers are used, then the part of the job done in **1** hour by both is represented by $\frac{1}{x}$.

The part of the job completed in one hour is the sum of the parts done by the two computers, so

$$\frac{1}{10} + \frac{1}{15} = \frac{1}{x}$$
$$3x + 2x = 30$$
$$5x = 30$$
$$x = 6$$

The two computers together could complete the payroll in **6** hours.

PROBLEMS

1. **a.** An electronics technician can overhaul a color T.V. in 10 hours. At this rate what part of the job should he complete in 1 hour? in 2 hours? in 8 hours? in 10 hours?
   b. Another technician could overhaul the same T.V. in 7 hours. What part of the job could he complete in 1 hour? 3 hours? 7 hours?
   c. If both technicians work together, what fraction sum gives the part of the overhaul that they should complete in 1 hour? in 2 hours? in 3 hours? in 7 hours?

   d. Suppose that n represents the number of hours it would take both men working together to overhaul the T.V. What does $\frac{1}{n}$ represent?

   e. What does the equation $\frac{1}{10} + \frac{1}{7} = \frac{1}{n}$ state? Solve the equation.

   f. How long should it take the two men to complete the overhaul if they work together?

2. a. Tom can mow a large lawn in 3 hours. Ken can do the same job in 4 hours. What part of the job will Tom complete in 1 hour? What part of the job will Ken complete in 1 hour?

   b. Write a fraction sum for the part of the job that Tom and Ken could complete in one hour if they worked together.

   c. If x represents the number of hours it would take both boys working together to mow the lawn, what does $\frac{1}{x}$ represent?

   d. What does the equation $\frac{1}{3} + \frac{1}{4} = \frac{1}{x}$ state? Solve the equation.

   e. How long will it take the two boys, working together, to mow the entire lawn?

3. A water tank has two inlet pipes that can be used. If only pipe A is used, the time required to fill the tank is 4 hours. If pipe B is used alone, the time needed is 5 hours.

$$\text{Solve: } \frac{1}{4} + \frac{1}{5} = \frac{1}{x}.$$

If water flows into the tank through both inlet pipes at the same time, how long will it take to fill the tank?

4. A tank has both an inlet pipe and an outlet pipe. Inlet pipe A can fill the tank in 3 hours if no water flows out of the tank. Outlet pipe B can empty the tank in 5 hours if no water comes in. To find out how long it would take to fill the tank with both pipes operating, an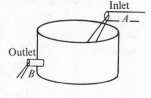

appropriate equation is $\frac{1}{3} - \frac{1}{5} = \frac{1}{x}$. Solve

the equation and tell how long it would take to fill the tank under those conditions.

 5. A medium-speed printing press can complete a job in 4 hours. The time required is cut in half when the job is done on a high-speed press. If both presses can be used together, how long will it take to complete the job?

6. The framing of a garage is completed by two carpenters in 12 hours. The faster of the two carpenters could have done the job by himself in 20 hours. How long would it have taken the slower carpenter to frame the garage by himself?

9–5 Equations in Two Variables

Suppose you were asked to write 5 as the sum of two whole numbers. You might respond in one of these ways:

$$4 + 1 \qquad 2 + 3 \qquad 0 + 5$$
$$1 + 4 \qquad 3 + 2 \qquad 5 + 0$$

Do you agree that we have named every possibility? We can express the fact that the sum of two numbers is 5 by writing the equation $x + y = 5$. This equation is called an equation in two variables, since it contains both the variable x and the variable y. We can arrange the replacements for the variables in a table, as shown below. In the last column we have recorded the values of x and y as ordered pairs of the form (x, y).

x	y	$x + y = 5$	*True/False*	*Solutions*
0	5	$0 + 5 = 5$	T	$(0, 5)$
1	4	$1 + 4 = 5$	T	$(1, 4)$
2	3	$2 + 3 = 5$	T	$(2, 3)$
3	2	$3 + 2 = 5$	T	$(3, 2)$
4	1	$4 + 1 = 5$	T	$(4, 1)$
5	0	$5 + 0 = 5$	T	$(5, 0)$

Each ordered pair that results in a true statement is called a solution, or root, of the equation; such ordered pairs are said to satisfy the equation. All the ordered pairs that satisfy the equation make up its solution set.

$$\{(0, 5), (1, 4), (2, 3), (3, 2), (4, 1), (5, 0)\}$$

This set of ordered pairs is a function, because corresponding to each **first** number, or value of x, there is *exactly one* **second** number, or value of y. The set of first numbers is called the domain of the function. The set of second numbers is called its range.

Domain: $\{0, 1, 2, 3, 4, 5\}$

Range: $\{5, 4, 3, 2, 1, 0\}$

EXAMPLE. Find the solution set of $2x + y = 9$, if the replacement set for each variable is {the whole numbers}.

Solution: Replacing x in the equation by the whole numbers from 0 to 6, inclusive, and finding the corresponding values of y, we get the set of ordered pairs shown in the last column of this table:

x	$2x + y = 9$	y	(x, y)
0	$(2 \cdot 0) + y = 9$	9	$(0, 9)$
1	$(2 \cdot 1) + y = 9$	7	$(1, 7)$
2	$(2 \cdot 2) + y = 9$	5	$(2, 5)$
3	$(2 \cdot 3) + y = 9$	3	$(3, 3)$
4	$(2 \cdot 4) + y = 9$	1	$(4, 1)$
5	$(2 \cdot 5) + (y) = 9$	-1	$(5, -1)$
6	$(2 \cdot 6) + (y) = 9$	-3	$(6, -3)$

Note that the entries below the red line contain values of *y* that are not members of the specified replacement set, since they are not *whole* numbers. Thus **4** is the greatest replacement for *x* that results in a solution, and the solution set of $2x + y = 9$, where the replacement set for each variable is {**the whole numbers**}, is

$$\{(0, 9), (1, 7), (2, 5), (3, 3), (4, 1)\}.$$

This set of ordered pairs is a function. Do you see that its **domain** is {**0, 1, 2, 3, 4**} and its **range** is {**9, 7, 5, 3, 1**}?

ORAL EXERCISES

For each of the following, tell whether the given number pair is a root of the equation. Assume that the replacement set for each variable is {the directed numbers}.

SAMPLE 1: $2x + y = 7; (3, 1)$

What you say: $(2 \cdot 3) + 1 = 7$, so $(3, 1)$ is a solution.

SAMPLE 2: $4x - y = 10; (2, 2)$

What you say: $(4 \cdot 2) - 2 \neq 10$, so $(2, 2)$ is *not* a solution.

1. $3x - y = 0; (3, 9)$

2. $x - y = 8; (12, 4)$

3. $x + 3y = 10; (4, 2)$

4. $2x - y = 8; (3, 2)$

5. $x + 2y = 1; (-5, 2)$

6. $-x + y = 5; (-3, 2)$

7. $x - 5y = 4; (-1, -1)$

8. $x^2 + y = 1; (-2, 3)$

9. $xy + y = 3; (-2, -3)$

10. $xy - x = 12; (4, 4)$

Give the domain and range of the function indicated in each table of values.

SAMPLE:

x	0	−1	−2	−3
y	0	2	4	6

What you say: Domain: $\{0, -1, -2, -3\}$; Range: $\{0, 2, 4, 6\}$

11.

x	0	2	4	6	8
y	1	3	5	7	9

13.

x	0	−1	−2	−3	−4	−5
y	0	1	2	3	4	5

12.

x	1	2	3	4	5
y	5	4	3	2	1

14.

x	1	2	3	4	5
y	−3	−4	−5	−6	−7

WRITTEN EXERCISES

Complete the table of values that accompanies each equation.

SAMPLE: $y = x - 2$

x	1	2	3	4	5
y	−1	?	?	?	?

Solution:

x	1	2	3	4	5
y	−1	0	1	2	3

A

1. $x + y = 10$

x	0	2	4	6	8
y	10	?	?	4	?

4. $x = y + 5$

x	5	?	?	2	?
y	0	−1	−2	−3	−4

2. $x - y = 5$

x	5	10	15	20	25
y	?	5	?	?	?

5. $y = x - 2$

x	1	2	3	4	5
y	−1	?	?	2	?

3. $x + 2y = 7$

x	0	1	2	3	4
y	$3\frac{1}{2}$	?	?	?	?

6. $x - 2y = 5$

x	15	13	11	9	7
y	?	?	?	?	?

7. $2x - y = 6$

x	4	8	10	11	12
y	?	?	?	?	?

8. $2x = y + 1$

x	$\frac{1}{2}$	$1\frac{1}{2}$	2	$2\frac{1}{2}$	3
y	?	?	?	?	?

Complete each table according to the given equation. Then write the solution set.

SAMPLE: $3x + y = 10$

x	$3x + y = 10$	y	(x, y)
0	$(3 \cdot 0) + y = 10$	10	$(0, 10)$
1	$(3 \cdot 1) + y = 10$	?	?
2	?	?	?
3	?	?	?

Solution:

x	$3x + y = 10$	y	(x, y)
0	$(3 \cdot 0) + y = 10$	10	$(0, 10)$
1	$(3 \cdot 1) + y = 10$	7	$(1, 7)$
2	$(3 \cdot 2) + y = 10$	4	$(2, 4)$
3	$(3 \cdot 3) + y = 10$	1	$(3, 1)$

Solution set: $\{(0, 10), (1, 7), (2, 4), (3, 1)\}$

9. $2x + y = 5$

x	$2x + y = 5$	y	(x, y)
0	$(2 \cdot 0) + y = 5$	5	$(0, 5)$
1	$(2 \cdot 1) + y = 5$	3	$(1, 3)$
2	?	?	?
3	?	?	?

10. $x = y + 3$

x	$x = y + 3$	y	(x, y)
1	$1 = y + 3$	-2	$(1, -2)$
2	$2 = y + 3$	-1	$(2, -1)$
3	?	?	?
4	?	?	?
5	?	?	?

11. $x + 2y = 1$

x	$x + 2y = 1$	y	(x, y)
0	$0 + 2y = 1$	$\frac{1}{2}$	$(0, \frac{1}{2})$
2	$2 + 2y = 1$	$-\frac{1}{2}$	$(2, -\frac{1}{2})$
4	___?___	___?___	___?___
-2	___?___	___?___	___?___
-4	___?___	___?___	___?___

B **12.** $3x + 4y = 36$

x	$3x + 4y = 36$	y	(x, y)
0	$(3 \cdot 0) + 4y = 36$	9	$(0, 9)$
4	___?___	?	?
8	___?___	?	?
12	___?___	?	?

13. $x^2 + y = 11$

x	$x^2 + y = 11$	y	(x, y)
2	___?___	___?___	?
4	___?___	___?___	?
-2	___?___	___?___	?
-4	___?___	___?___	?

C **14.** $x - 2y = 3$

x	$x - 2y = 3$	y	(x, y)
-2	___?___	___?___	?
-1	___?___	___?___	?
0	___?___	___?___	?
1	___?___	___?___	?

15. $xy + y = 9$

x	$xy + y = 9$	y	(x, y)
2	$2y + y = 9$	3	$(2, 3)$
1	___?___	?	?
0	___?___	?	?
-2	___?___	?	?

Graphs of Equations

9–6   Graphing Linear Equations in Two Variables

Earlier in this book, in Chapters 2 and 3, we worked with functions and the graphing of ordered pairs on the number plane. These ideas can help us to graph linear equations in two variables, since number pairs that are solutions of a linear equation can be used to determine the graph of the equation.

For a simple equation such as $x + y = 9$, it is rather easy to find the set of values for y (the **range**) that correspond to a specified set of replacements for x (the **domain**). The task is more difficult in the case of an equation like $-4x + y = 1$, but much of the difficulty can be avoided if we begin by writing an equivalent equation in which the variable y stands alone as one member.

$$-4x + y = 1 \quad \text{is equivalent to} \quad y = 1 + 4x$$

The following table contains several roots of the equation, represented as number pairs in the (x, y) column. The graph of each root is shown in Figure 9–1. The **horizontal axis** is the x-axis and the **vertical axis** is the y-axis.

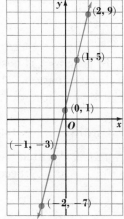

x	$y = 1 + 4x$	y	(x, y)
-2	$y = 1 + (-8)$	-7	$(-2, -7)$
-1	$y = 1 + (-4)$	-3	$(-1, -3)$
0	$y = 1 + (0)$	1	$(0, 1)$
1	$y = 1 + (4)$	5	$(1, 5)$
2	$y = 1 + (8)$	9	$(2, 9)$

Figure 9–1

You probably noticed in Figure 9–1 that each point corresponding to a root of the **linear** equation $-4x + y = 1$ falls on a straight-line path. This is suggested by the line joining these points in the figure.

If you choose for x some value not in the table and find the corresponding value of y, the resulting number pair is a root of the equation. The number pair also gives the coordinates of a point that falls somewhere on the straight-line path.

For Figure 9–1, then:

The line is the **graph** of the equation $-4x + y = 1$.
The equation $-4x + y = 1$ is the **equation** of the **line**.

> In the number plane, the graph of any equation of the form
> $ax + by = c$, with a and b not *both* zero, is a **straight line**.

EXAMPLE 1.   Graph $x + 2y = 4$ in the number plane.

Solution:

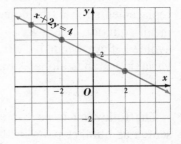

x	$y = \dfrac{4 - x}{2}$	y	(x, y)
2	$y = \dfrac{4 - 2}{2}$	1	$(2, 1)$
0	$y = \dfrac{4 - 0}{2}$	2	$(0, 2)$
-2	$y = \dfrac{4 - (-2)}{2}$	3	$(-2, 3)$
-4	$y = \dfrac{4 - (-4)}{2}$	4	$(-4, 4)$

In general it is necessary to locate only two points in order to graph a linear equation. However, it is a good idea to locate a third point to check your accuracy.

EXAMPLE 2.   Graph $y = 3$ in the number plane.

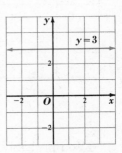

Solution: Written as an equation in two variables, $y = 3$ becomes

$$0x + y = 3.$$

Thus *every* number pair that has 3 as its second number is a root of $y = 3$. Its graph is the horizontal line shown.

ORAL EXERCISES

For each ordered pair of numbers, name the corresponding labeled point on the graph.

SAMPLE: (3, 1)

What you say: C

1. (2, 4)   5. (−3, 2)
2. (1, 0)   6. (2, −5)
3. (0, 3)   7. (−3, 0)
4. (0, −2)   8. (−4, −4)

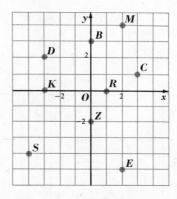

Use the graph of the linear equation $x + 1 = y$ to decide which of the following ordered pairs are roots of the equation.

SAMPLE: (3, 2)

What you say: (3, 2) is not a root, since it does not correspond to a point on the line.

9. (3, 4)   14. (−3, 2)
10. (4, 3)   15. (−4, 3)
11. (0, 1)   16. (−1, 0)
12. (−2, −1)   17. (0, −1)
13. (0, 0)   18. (2, −3)

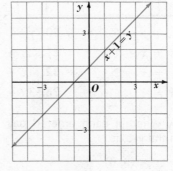

WRITTEN EXERCISES

For each of the following, write an equivalent equation in which y stands alone as the left member.

SAMPLE: $x + 5y = 1$ *Solution:* $5y = 1 - x$

$$y = \frac{1 - x}{5}$$

1. $x + y = 5$ 6. $5y + 1 = x$ 11. $4y = x - 9$
2. $3x + y = 9$ 7. $3x - 2y = 10$ 12. $y - x = -2$
3. $3x + 2y = 7$ 8. $2x + 3y = 0$ 13. $-x + 3y = 1$
4. $x - y = 8$ 9. $3x - 2y = 0$ 14. $4x - y = 2$
5. $2x - y = 5$ 10. $2x - 3y = 5$ 15. $5x - y = -2$

Make a table of values for each equation. Then draw its graph in the number plane.

SAMPLE: $x + 3y = 9$

Solution:

x	$y = \dfrac{9 - x}{3}$	y	(x, y)
3	$y = \dfrac{9 - 3}{3}$	2	$(3, 2)$
0	$y = \dfrac{9 - 0}{3}$	3	$(0, 3)$
-3	$y = \dfrac{9 - (-3)}{3}$	4	$(-3, 4)$
-6	$y = \dfrac{9 - (-6)}{3}$	5	$(-6, 5)$

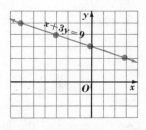

16. $x + y = 6$ **20.** $y = -2$ **24.** $x = 2$

17. $y = x + 1$ **21.** $2x + y = 6$ **25.** $x = -3$

18. $y = x - 2$ **22.** $4x - y = 2$ **26.** $y + 3x = 10$

19. $y = 4$ **23.** $3x - y = 6$ **27.** $-2x + y = 1$

Show whether each ordered pair corresponds to a point on the x-axis or on the y-axis.

SAMPLE: $(3, 0)$ *Solution:*

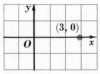

$(3, 0)$ is on the x-axis.

28. $(-1, 0)$ **30.** $(-2, 0)$ **32.** $(0, 1)$

29. $(0, 3)$ **31.** $(0, -2)$ **33.** $(4, 0)$

Use "x-axis" or "y-axis" to complete each statement.

34. If the first number in an ordered pair of numbers is zero and the second number is *not* zero, then the graph of the corresponding point is on the __?__.

35. If the first number in an ordered pair of numbers is *not* zero and the second number is zero, then the graph of the corresponding point is on the __?__.

Locate only the two points where the graph of the equation crosses the
x-axis and the *y*-axis. Then draw the graph.

SAMPLE: $2x + 4y = 8$

Solution: If $x = 0$, then $y = 2$.
If $y = 0$, then $x = 4$.
So the graph crosses the *x*-axis at $(4, 0)$
and the *y*-axis at $(0, 2)$.

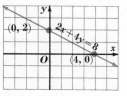

B   **36.** $2x - 3y = 6$ **38.** $5x - 2y = 3x + 8$
37. $3x + 4y = 12$ **39.** $y + 5x = 10 - y$

C   **40.** $x - 3y = -9$ **43.** $x + \frac{1}{3}y = -1$
41. $2x - y = -4$ **44.** $x - \frac{1}{5}y = 1$
42. $\dfrac{3x}{4} + \dfrac{y}{2} = -\dfrac{3}{2}$ **45.** $0.25x - 0.50y = -2$

9–7   Slope

The highway from Millville to Casper **slopes** downward.

The railroad train is
going up the **grade**.

The roof of a house has a **pitch** so that water will drain from it.

For miles through the desert the roadway is **flat**.

All of these statements deal with the idea known as **slope** in
mathematics.

EXAMPLE.   The roof of the building pictured
here has a certain slope. Notice
that the drawing indicates a **vertical rise** of 9 feet over a **horizontal
run** of 30 feet. Thus the pitch of
the roof can be expressed by the

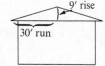

ratio $\dfrac{\text{rise}}{\text{run}}$, which in this case is $\frac{9}{30}$,

or $\frac{3}{10}$. Since $\frac{3}{10} = 30\%$, we can say that the roof has
a 30% pitch, or slope.

Slope is expressed by the ratio of vertical change to horizontal
change:

$$\text{slope} = \frac{\text{rise}}{\text{run}} = \frac{\text{vertical change}}{\text{horizontal change}}.$$

WRITTEN EXERCISES

For each of the following, express the slope both as a ratio in lowest terms and as a percent.

SAMPLE: Find the slope of the sidewalk.

$6'$ rise

$40'$ run

Solution: Slope $= \dfrac{\text{rise}}{\text{run}} = \dfrac{6}{40} = \dfrac{3}{20}$

$\dfrac{3}{20} = 15\%$

A **1.** Find the slope (pitch) of the roof.

2. Find the slope (grade) of the railroad tracks.

3. Find the slope of the sidewalk.

4. What is the slope of the highway?

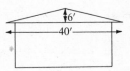

5. What is the slope of this loading ramp?

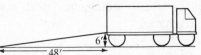

Express the slope for each of the following as a fraction in lowest terms.

SAMPLE: rise = 95 feet
run = 190 feet

Solution: slope $= \dfrac{\text{rise}}{\text{run}}$

$= \dfrac{95}{190} = \dfrac{1}{2}$

6. rise = 3 inches
run = 15 inches

7. rise = 1 mile
run = 40 miles

8. rise = 0 feet
run = 90 feet

9. rise = 70 meters
run = 1000 meters

10. rise = 6000 feet
run = 6000 feet

11. rise = 70 inches
run = 35 inches

12. rise = $\frac{1}{4}$ mile
run = 5 miles

13. rise = 20 feet
run = 2 feet

Find the measure of the unknown vertical or horizontal change for each of the following.

SAMPLE: slope $= \frac{1}{10}$ *Solution:* $\frac{1}{10} = \frac{8}{x}$

vertical change $= 8$ feet $x = 80$
horizontal change $= ?$ feet   The horizontal change is
                                       80 feet.

B **14.** slope $= \frac{1}{5}$ **16.** slope $= 3$
vertical change $= 10$ yards   vertical change $= ?$ meters
horizontal change $= ?$ yards   horizontal change $= 2000$ meters

15. slope $= \frac{3}{5}$ **17.** slope $= \frac{1}{2}$
vertical change $= 54$ feet   vertical change $= 4$ feet
horizontal change $= ?$ feet   horizontal change $= ?$ feet

Complete each of the following statements.

C **18.** When the vertical change and the horizontal change are the same, the slope is ___?___.

19. When the vertical change is half as great as the horizontal change, the slope is ___?___.

20. When the horizontal change is ten times as great as the vertical change, the slope is ___?___.

9–8 Slope of a Line

The slope of a line in the number plane can be computed by choosing two points on the line and noting both the vertical change and the horizontal change in moving from one point to the other. Then the slope can be written as a ratio, using

$$\textbf{slope} = \frac{\textbf{rise}}{\textbf{run}} = \frac{\textbf{vertical change}}{\textbf{horizontal change}}.$$

For example, in the figure at the right, by counting squares we can determine that the **rise** is **3** and the **run** is **1**, so we have

$$\textbf{slope} = \frac{\textbf{rise}}{\textbf{run}} = \frac{3}{1} = 3.$$

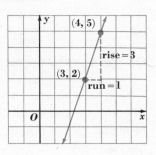

Notice that, instead of counting squares, we could have found the **rise** by finding the difference of the **second** numbers (*y*-coordinates) in the number pairs (**4, 5**) and (**3, 2**);

5 − 2 = 3, which is the same vertical change, or rise, that we found before. Similarly, the **run** is the difference of the **first** numbers (*x*-coordinates); **4 − 3 = 1**. Thus we can write

$$\textbf{slope} = \frac{\text{difference in } y\text{-coordinates}}{\text{difference in } x\text{-coordinates}} = \frac{3}{1} = \textbf{3.}$$

Thus far in discussing slope, we have not said anything about the fact that a line that is not horizontal may slope either **upward** or **downward**. Let us agree that when a **left-to-right** movement on a line is combined with an **upward** movement we say the line has positive slope. In this case, the value of the *y*-coordinate is **increasing** as we move from left to right, and the line slopes upward. When the **left-to-right** movement is combined with a **downward** movement, the line slopes downward, and we say it has negative slope; the value of the *y*-coordinate **decreases** as we move from left to right.

The following examples show lines with positive and negative slope.

EXAMPLE 1.

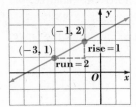

Positive slope: $\frac{1}{2}$

EXAMPLE 2.

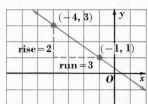

Negative slope: $-\frac{2}{3}$

What do you think is the slope of a **horizontal** line, like that shown here? Since it contains the points **(4, 2)** and **(1, 2)**, we find the slope as follows:

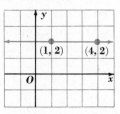

$$\textbf{slope} = \frac{\textbf{difference in } y\textbf{-coordinates}}{\textbf{difference in } x\textbf{-coordinates}}$$

$$= \frac{2 - 2}{4 - 1} = \frac{0}{3} = \textbf{0.}$$

Do you see why the slope of any horizontal line must be zero?

Next we consider the slope of a **vertical** line, like the one shown on the right. Using the coordinates of two points, **(2, 4)** and **(2, 1)**, on the line, we have

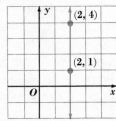

$$\text{slope} = \frac{\text{difference in } y\text{-coordinates}}{\text{difference in } x\text{-coordinates}}$$

$$= \frac{4-1}{2-2} = \frac{3}{0}.$$

Since division by zero is not possible, we say that this line has *no* slope. Do you see that any **vertical** line would be said to have **no slope**?

ORAL EXERCISES

Tell whether the slope of each line is positive or negative.

1.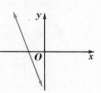

2.

3.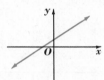

4.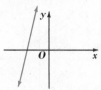

5.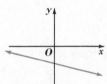

6.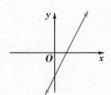

WRITTEN EXERCISES

Decide whether each line has positive or negative slope; then use either slope = $\dfrac{\text{rise}}{\text{run}}$ or slope = $-\dfrac{\text{rise}}{\text{run}}$ to compute the slope.

SAMPLE: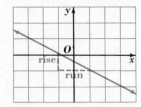

Solution: The slope is negative;

$$\text{slope} = -\frac{\text{rise}}{\text{run}} = -\frac{1}{2}$$

1.

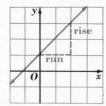

2.

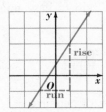

3.

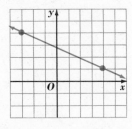

4.

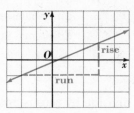

5.

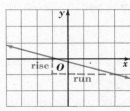

6.

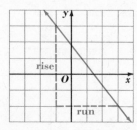

Find the slope of each line.

7.

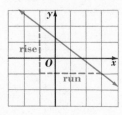

8.

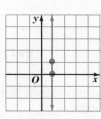

9.

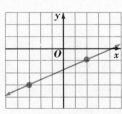

10.

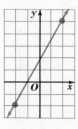

11.

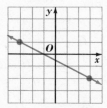

12.

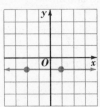

Locate each pair of points on the number plane and draw the line that contains the points. Then determine the slope of the line.

SAMPLE: $(3, 0), (0, 2)$ *Solution:*

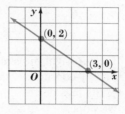

The slope is $-\frac{2}{3}$.

B **13.** $(3, 1), (1, 4)$ **15.** $(-2, 3), (0, 2)$ **17.** $(4, 2), (-3, 2)$

14. $(1, 3), (4, 5)$ **16.** $(3, -1), (3, 3)$ **18.** $(-2, 4), (-1, 0)$

CHAPTER SUMMARY

Inventory of Structure and Concepts

1. The **principle** of **zero products** states that, for any numbers r and s, $r \cdot s = 0$ if and only if $r = 0$ or $s = 0$.

2. A **polynomial equation** is an equation whose left and right members are polynomials.

3. Equations can be classified and named according to the highest degree of the variable involved.
   a. A **linear** equation is an equation of degree **one**.
   b. A **quadratic** equation is an equation of degree **two**.
   c. A **cubic** equation is an equation of degree **three**.

4. Solutions of equations in two variables take the form of **ordered** number pairs. The **solution set** of an equation in two variables is the set of all ordered pairs that satisfy the equation.

5. The **domain** of a function is the set of first elements in the set of ordered pairs that make up the function. The **range** of a function is the set of second elements in the set of ordered pairs that make up the function.

6. In the number plane, the horizontal axis is the **x-axis** and the vertical axis is the **y-axis**.

7. Each point in the number plane that corresponds to a root of a given linear equation in two variables falls on a straight-line path.

8. In the number plane, the **graph** of any equation of the form $ax + by = c$, where a and b are not *both* zero, is a straight line.

9. The **slope** of a line is the ratio of "rise" to "run," or **vertical** change to **horizontal** change:

$$\text{slope} = \frac{\text{rise}}{\text{run}} = \frac{\text{vertical change}}{\text{horizontal change}}.$$

10. If left-to-right movement along a line results in an increase in the value of the y-coordinate, the line has **positive** slope; if left-to-right movement results in a decrease in the value of the y-coordinate, the line has **negative** slope.

11. The slope of every **horizontal** line is **0**; a **vertical** line has **no slope**.

Vocabulary and Spelling

zero products (*p. 285*)
standard form of a polynomial
   equation (*p. 288*)
quadratic equation (*p. 288*)
linear equation (*p. 288*)
cubic equation (*p. 288*)
fractional equation (*p. 291*)
equations in two variables (*p. 296*)
domain (of a function) (*p. 296*)
range (of a function) (*p. 296*)

x-axis (*p. 301*)
y-axis (*p. 301*)
graph (of a linear equation) (*p. 301*)
equation of a line (*p. 302*)
slope (*p. 305*)
slope (of a line) (*p. 307*)
positive slope (*p. 308*)
negative slope (*p. 308*)
zero slope (*p. 308*)
no slope (*p. 309*)

Chapter Test

Solve each polynomial equation and write the solution set.

1. $x(x - 2) = 0$

2. $0(m - 6) = 0$

3. $x^2 + 2x - 48 = 0$

4. $n^2 - 3n = 0$

5. $5t^2 = 3t$

6. $x^2 = 11x + 42$

7. $m^3 - 4m = 3m^2$

8. $n^2 - 81 = 0$

Solve each fractional equation.

9. $\dfrac{4}{x} + \dfrac{2}{3x} = 2$

10. $\dfrac{5x}{3} + 2 = \dfrac{1}{2}$

11. $\dfrac{2}{3k} + \dfrac{1}{k + 2} - \dfrac{3}{k} = 0$

12. $\dfrac{3}{x - 2} = \dfrac{5}{x - 3}$

13. Mr. Carlson can complete a painting job in 6 hours if he works alone. Mr. Washington can do the same job in 4 hours.

   a. What part of the job can Mr. Carlson complete in 1 hour?

   b. What part of the job can Mr. Washington complete in 1 hour?

   c. If the two men work together on the painting job how long will it take to complete it?

Write the domain and the range for each function.

14. $\{(1, -3), (2, -2), (3, -1), (4, 0)\}$

15. $\{(0, -8), (1, -6), (2, -4), (3, -2)\}$

Graph each equation in the number plane.

16. $3x + y = 5$ **18.** $y = 6 - 2x$ **20.** $y = 1$

17. $x - 2y = 2$ **19.** $2x = 1 - y$ **21.** $x = -5$

Give the slope of each line shown on the number plane.

22. 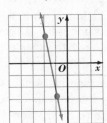   **23.** 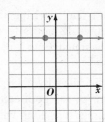   **24.**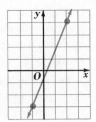

Chapter Review

9–1 Factors and Zero Products

Complete each of the following to make a true statement.

1. $(\frac{3}{4})(6)(?) = 0$ **2.** $0 = (7.1)(-1.5)(?)$ **3.** $(9)(0)(4)(0) = ?$

Solve each equation and write its solution set.

4. $\frac{3}{4}(m + \frac{1}{2}) = 0$ **6.** $t(t - 5) = 0$

5. $(x - 3)(x + 9) = 0$

9–2   Solving Polynomial Equations

Solve each equation and write its solution set.

7. $3r^2 + 5r = 0$ **8.** $a^2 - 6a = -5$ **9.** $x^2 - 5x - 14 = 0$

10. A rectangle is 5 feet longer than it is wide. Find its length and width if its area is 150 square feet.

150 sq. ft. x

$x+5$

9–3   Solving Fractional Equations

Solve each equation.

11. $\dfrac{1}{t} + \dfrac{7}{4t} = \dfrac{5}{8}$ **13.** $\dfrac{5}{12} + \dfrac{7}{3y} = \dfrac{5}{2y}$ **15.** $\dfrac{1}{a} + \dfrac{2}{3a} = \dfrac{5}{9}$

12. $\dfrac{b - 3}{2} = \dfrac{5}{b}$ **14.** $\dfrac{n - 6}{n} = \dfrac{5}{n + 6}$ **16.** $\dfrac{r}{2} = \dfrac{6}{r - 1}$

9–4   Problems and Fractional Equations

17. One electrician can complete a wiring job in 12 hours while an apprentice electrician requires 18 hours to do the same job. If the two men work together how much time will be required to complete the wiring job?

18. A swimming pool can be filled by a large input pipe in 24 hours. A drain pipe in the bottom of the pool can empty the pool in 72 hours. If both pipes are operating, how long will it take to fill the pool?

9–5   Equations in Two Variables

Complete the table of values for each equation.

19. $y = 3 + 2x$

x	-2	-1	0	1	2
y	-1	?	?	?	?

21. $x = 2y - 1$

x	?	?	?	?	?
y	-1	0	1	2	3

20. $2x + y = 12$

x	$2x + y = 12$	y	(x, y)
-4	$2(-4) + y = 12$	?	?
-2	?	?	?
0	?	?	?
2	?	?	?

22. $y = 3 - x$

x	$y = 3 - x$	y	(x, y)
1	?	?	?
2	?	?	?
3	?	?	?
4	?	?	?

9–6 Graphing Linear Equations in Two Variables

Match each number pair with its corresponding point on the graph.

23. $(2, 1)$ **26.** $(0, -1)$

24. $(-3, -3)$ **27.** $(1, -4)$

25. $(-2, 4)$ **28.** $(-4, 1)$

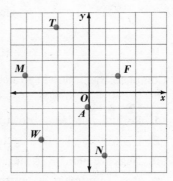

Draw a graph for each equation.

29. $3x + y = 5$ **30.** $-x + 2y = 1$

9–7 Slope

31. Use the words "rise" and "run" to complete: Slope $= \dfrac{?}{?}$.

32. Use the words "vertical change" and "horizontal change" to complete:
Slope $= \dfrac{?}{?}$.

33. The elevation of a roadway changes 20 feet over a horizontal distance
of 1000 feet. Express the slope of the roadway as a percent.

9–8 Slope of a Line

Tell whether the slope of each line is positive or negative.

34. 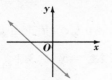   **35.** 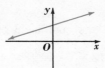   **36.**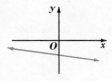

Find the slope of each line.

37. 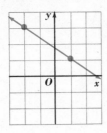 **38.** 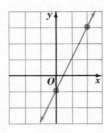 **39.**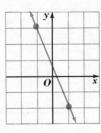

Review of Skills

Complete the following rules for multiplication and division of positive and negative numbers.

1. Positive number $\times$ positive number = __?__ number.

2. Positive number $\times$ negative number = __?__ number.

3. Negative number $\times$ negative number = __?__ number.

4. Positive number $\div$ positive number = __?__ number.

5. Positive number $\div$ negative number = __?__ number.

6. Negative number $\div$ negative number = __?__ number.

Match each open sentence in Column 1 with an equivalent sentence in Column 2.

COLUMN 1

7. $3x + y = 5$

8. $x - y = 5$

9. $3x + 2y > 10$

10. $3y - 2x > 15$

COLUMN 2

A. $y > 5 - \dfrac{3x}{2}$

B. $x = \dfrac{5}{3} - \dfrac{y}{3}$

C. $y > 5 + \dfrac{2x}{3}$

D. $y = x - 5$

In each expression name the coefficient of *x* and the coefficient of *y*.

11. $3x + 4y$ **12.** $\dfrac{x}{5} - y$ **13.** $-5y + 3 + \dfrac{x}{4}$

14. $\frac{1}{2}y + x$ **16.** $-\frac{x}{4} + 10y$ **18.** $1.6x + 3.5y$

15. $\frac{2x}{3} + \frac{y}{2}$ **17.** $6x - \frac{1}{3}y$ **19.** $-x + (3)^2 y$

State the solution set for each equation if the domain of the variable is {the integers}.

20. $m^2 = 36$ **22.** $y^2 = 144$ **24.** $4b^2 = 64$

21. $r^2 = 49$ **23.** $3x^2 = 27$ **25.** $\frac{n^2}{2} = 4.5$

State the solution set for each equation if the domain of the variable is {the whole numbers}.

26. $m^2 = 36$ **28.** $t^2 = -25$ **30.** $x^2 + 2 = 51$

27. $x^2 = 144$ **29.** $k^2 = 25$ **31.** $z^2 - 3 = 97$

Find the solution set for each equation by using the method of zero products.

32. $x^2 - 4x - 45 = 0$ **34.** $x^2 + 21 = -10x$

33. $2x^2 + x - 6 = 0$ **35.** $x^2 + 14x = -48$

Write each product as a single fraction in lowest terms.

36. $\frac{4x^2}{5} \cdot \frac{1}{2x}$ **38.** $\frac{9}{10} \cdot \frac{r^2 + k}{3}$ **40.** $\frac{n^2 - 9}{1} \cdot \frac{n + 3}{n - 3}$

37. $\frac{a + b}{5} \cdot \frac{-2}{a + b}$ **39.** $\frac{x^2 - y^2}{7} \cdot \frac{2}{x - y}$ **41.** $\frac{6ab^2}{14} \cdot \frac{7b}{3a}$

Write each quotient as a single fraction in lowest terms.

42. $\frac{9}{10} \div \frac{3}{5}$ **43.** $\frac{2n^2}{5} \div \frac{4n}{5}$ **44.** $\frac{(x + y)^2}{3} \div \frac{x + y}{2}$

Name the percent equivalent for each of the following.

45. $\frac{1}{4}$ **47.** $\frac{1}{2}$ **49.** $\frac{4}{5}$ **51.** $\frac{53}{100}$ **53.** $\frac{3}{8}$

46. $\frac{3}{5}$ **48.** $\frac{3}{4}$ **50.** $\frac{9}{10}$ **52.** 1.5 **54.** $\frac{1}{5}$

■ ■

CHECK POINT
FOR EXPERTS

Logical Arguments and Validity

Logical arguments are based on **deductive reasoning**. This is a sort of reasoning which proceeds from beginning information, called the **hypothesis**, to arrive at a result called the **conclusion**. If the information given as the basis for the argument is accepted as true, then the conclusion arrived at by reasoning from that hypothesis must be logically acceptable, and the argument is **valid**.

In an informal study of logic, Venn diagrams can be used to help us decide when the conclusion is a logical result and thus assure us that the argument is valid. As an example, consider the following simple argument, and the accompanying Venn diagram.

Hypothesis: All sophomores are students.
　　　　　All students are people.

Conclusion: All sophomores are people.

Do you see that this is the only way that a Venn diagram can be drawn to represent the conditions stated? Also notice that, since the curve which represents the set of all sophomores lies entirely within the outer curve, representing the set of all people, the diagram satisfies the conditions of the conclusion, "All sophomores are people." Therefore, the conclusion is a logical result, and we see that the argument is **valid**.

When you are working with logical arguments, it is important for you to understand that the words **truth** and **validity** have somewhat different meanings. For example, consider the following argument and its Venn diagram representation.

Hypothesis: All dogs are birds.
　　　　　All birds can fly.

Conclusion: All dogs can fly.

The Venn diagram completely satisfies the conditions of the argument. Moreover, it is not possible to draw a different diagram that also satisfies the conditions. Therefore, the conclusion is **valid** even though none of the three statements is true.

Questions

1. What is the difference in meaning between the expression "true statement" and the expression "valid statement"?

Copy and complete each of the following valid arguments and their related Venn diagrams.

2. Hypothesis: All squares are quadrilaterals.
   All quadrilaterals are polygons.
   ___?___ : All squares are polygons.

3. ___?___ : No snakes are mammals.
   All fish are mammals.
   Conclusion: No fish are ___?___ .

4. Hypothesis: All A's are B's.
   All B's are C's.
   Conclusion: All ___?___ are C's.

For each argument, draw a Venn diagram to show that it is valid.

5. Hypothesis: All R's are S's.
   All S's are T's.
   Conclusion: All R's are T's.

6. Hypothesis: All girls are students.
   All students are pretty.
   Conclusion: All girls are pretty.

7. Hypothesis: All squares are circles.
   No polygon is a circle.
   Conclusion: No polygon is a square.

8. Hypothesis: No criminals are honest.
   All lawyers are honest.
   Conclusion: No lawyers are criminals.

A spinning wheel from a colonial home . . .

A modern factory spinning room . . .

Solving Inequalities
and Graphing

Spinning is the process of making threads by twisting fibers together. The spinning wheel, which was common household equipment in colonial times, could make only one thread at a time, with the fineness depending upon the speed with which the twisting thread was drawn off the distaff. An hour's output of the most skillful spinner was very limited compared to the output of the modern spinning room, with a long row, called a "frame," of bobbins and spindles, tended by one woman on an electric cart. From the upper row of bobbins, yarn passes through a succession of rollers and onto the spindles at the bottom. Each spindle spins 900 yards of size 30 thread an hour. The output of the frame, which contains about 320 spindles, is over 270,000 yards per hour. The yarn being spun in the picture is a blend of 40% cotton and 60% polyester.

Inequalities and Their Graphs

10–1 Inequalities in Two Variables

An inequality may involve two variables, such as x and y. In solving an **inequality in two variables**, we look for all of the ordered pairs that will make the inequality a true statement. Just as was the case with equations in two variables, each such ordered pair is called a **solution**, or **root**, and is said to **satisfy** the inequality. The set of all possible solutions of an inequality in two variables is called its **solution set**. Unless replacement sets are stated for the variables, we assume each to be {**the directed numbers**}.

Consider the inequality $x + y \geq 3$, where the domain (replacement set) is $\{-2, -1, 0\}$ for x and is $\{1, 2, 3, 4, 5\}$ for y. As a matter of convenience, we begin by writing an equivalent inequality which has y as the left member.

$$x + y \geq 3 \quad \text{is equivalent to} \quad y \geq 3 - x.$$

Now we can organize our work in a table. As each replacement is

321

made for x, we record in the y-column each member of the replacement set for y that makes the statement true. The last column of the table lists all possible solutions of the given inequality for the stated replacement sets.

x	$3 - x$	$y \geq 3 - x$	y	*Possible Solutions*
-2	$3 - (-2)$	$y \geq 5$	5	$(-2, 5)$
-1	$3 - (-1)$	$y \geq 4$	4, 5	$(-1, 4), (-1, 5)$
0	$3 - 0$	$y \geq 3$	3, 4, 5	$(0, 3), (0, 4), (0, 5)$

From the last column we can write the solution set:

$$\{(-2, 5), (-1, 4), (-1, 5), (0, 3), (0, 4), (0, 5)\}.$$

Do you see that this set of ordered pairs is *not* a function? For example, two pairs have -1 as the first number, but their second numbers are different.

ORAL EXERCISES

For each inequality, tell whether the given number pair is a solution. The replacement set for both x and y is {the directed numbers}.

1. $x + y > 3$; (4, 0)
2. $x + y < 0$; $(-3, -1)$
3. $2x + y \geq 5$; (2, 2)
4. $x - y \leq 4$; (5, 0)
5. $x - y > 3$; (8, 4)

6. $2x - y < 10$; (8, 6)
7. $x + 2y \geq -3$; $(4, -4)$
8. $y > 1 + x$; (0, 2)
9. $x < y - 3$; $(-1, 3)$
10. $x + xy < 1$; (0, 0)

WRITTEN EXERCISES

Transform each of the following into an equivalent inequality with y as the left member.

SAMPLE 1: $3x + 2y < 2$ *Solution:* $3x + 2y < 2$
$$2y < 2 - 3x$$
$$y < \frac{2 - 3x}{2}$$

SAMPLE 2: $x - y > -2$ *Solution:* $x - y > -2$
$$-y > -2 - x$$
$$y < 2 + x$$

A **1.** $x + y \leq 3$

2. $x + y > -5$

3. $2x + y \geq 3$

4. $-x + y < 10$

5. $y - 3x \leq 5$

6. $x - y < 4$

7. $2x - y > -9$

8. $x + 2y > 15$

Show that each number pair is a solution for the given inequality.

SAMPLE: $y > 2x - 2$;
  $(0, 0)$ and $(-1, 3)$

Solution:

For $(0, 0)$:

y	$>$	$2x - 2$
0		$2(0) - 2$
0		$0 - 2$
0		-2

$0 > -2$, so $(0, 0)$ is a solution.

For $(-1, 3)$:

y	$>$	$2x - 2$
3		$2(-1) - 2$
3		$-2 - 2$
3		-4

$3 > -4$, so $(-1, 3)$ is a solution.

9. $y \leq -x + 4$;
  $(-3, 5)$ and $(1, 0)$

10. $y > x - 1$;
  $(1, 1)$ and $(1, 2)$

11. $y \geq 3 - 2x$;
  $(-1, 5)$ and $(1, 2)$

12. $2x + y > 7$;
  $(0, 8)$ and $(-3, 15)$

13. $y \geq x$;
  $(-1, -1)$ and $(-3, -1)$

14. $2x + y < -3$;
  $(-4, 4)$ and $(-4, 0)$

15. $1 - x > y$;
  $(2, -3)$ and $(10, -10)$

16. $x - y < x$;
  $(-1, 1)$ and $(1, 2)$

17. $x + 3y \leq -8$;
  $(3, -4)$ and $(-5, -1)$

18. $x + xy \geq 0$;
  $(0, 1)$ and $(1, 0)$

For each inequality, name four ordered pairs that satisfy the open sentence.

19. $y > 3x + 1$

20. $y < 2x$

21. $y < \dfrac{x}{2} + 1$

22. $y \leq x - 2$

23. $y < 4 + x$

24. $y > -3x$

25. $x > -4 + y$

26. $3x - y \geq 7$

27. $2y < -5x$

Complete each table of values for the given inequality when the replacement set for *x* is $\{-2, 0, 2\}$ and for *y* is $\{1, 2, 3\}$. Write the solution set.

SAMPLE: $y > 2x + 1$

x	$2x + 1$	$y > 2x + 1$	y
-2	?	?	?
0	?	?	?
2	?	?	?

Solution: $y > 2x + 1$

x	$2x + 1$	$y > 2x + 1$	y
-2	$-4 + 1$	$y > -3$	1, 2, 3
0	$0 + 1$	$y > 1$	2, 3
2	$4 + 1$	$y > 5$	none

$\{(-2, 1), (-2, 2), (-2, 3), (0, 2), (0, 3)\}$

28. $y \le 2x + 1$

x	$2x + 1$	$y \le 2x + 1$	y
-2	?	?	?
0	?	?	?
2	?	?	?

29. $y > \dfrac{x - 2}{2}$

x	$\dfrac{x - 2}{2}$	$y > \dfrac{x - 2}{2}$	y
-2	?	?	?
0	?	?	?
2	?	?	?

30. $y \le -2x + 1$

x	$-2x + 1$	$y \le -2x + 1$	y
-2	?	?	?
0	?	?	?
2	?	?	?

Find the solution set for each inequality when the replacement set for *x* is $\{-1, 0, 1\}$ and for *y* is $\{-2, -1, 0, 1, 2\}$.

B **31.** $y > 2x$ **34.** $y \le 2x - 1$

32. $y < x$ **35.** $y - 3x \le 1$

33. $y > x$ **36.** $2y < x$

C **37.** $x + y > x - y$ **38.** $2x + 1 < 1 - x$

10–2 Inequalities and Half-Planes

If you draw a line across a sheet of paper, the paper is divided into two pieces. Similarly, the graph of the equation $y = 2$ divides the number plane into two pieces, each called a half-plane. One half-plane is *above* the graph of $y = 2$ and the other is *below* it.

Do you agree that every point above the graph of $y = 2$ must have a *y*-coordinate that is *greater* than 2? Therefore, every point in the shaded portion of the number plane shown in Figure 10–1 has a **y-coordinate greater than 2**. Verify this fact by checking the coordinates of the two sample points marked in the figure. We call this shaded region the **graph of the inequality** $y > 2$. Do you see why points on the line $y = 2$ are not included in the graph of $y > 2$? We indicate this fact by using a dashed line for the graph of $y = 2$.

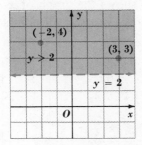

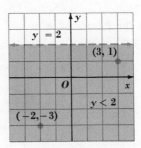

Figure 10–1   **Figure 10–2**

Applying the same thinking to Figure 10–2, notice that every point *below* the graph of $y = 2$ has a y-coordinate that is *less* than **2**. Therefore, the shaded portion of the number plane in Figure 10–2 is the **graph of the inequality** $y < 2$. Again note that a dashed line has been used to show that points *on* the graph of $y = 2$ are *not* included in the graph of $y < 2$.

It is of special importance to note that the graph of the linear equation $y = 2$ serves as the common **boundary** of the graphs of the two inequalities, $y > 2$ and $y < 2$. However, points *on* the line are not included in the graph of *either* inequality.

The graph of the linear equation $x = 1$ divides the number plane into two half-planes. The region to the *right* of the vertical line is the graph of the inequality $x > 1$, while the region to the *left* is the graph of $x < 1$. The graph of $x = 1$ is shown by a dashed line, of course. Check the sample points to verify the fact that the x-coordinate of each point on the **left** of the line is *less* than **1** and the x-coordinate of each point on the **right** is *greater* than **1**.

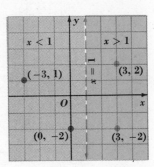

In general:

A line in a plane divides the plane into three distinct sets of points:

the set of points on one side of the line;
the set of points on the other side of the line;
the set of points that is the line itself.

Now consider the graph of the inequality $y \geq 1$, shown in Figure 10–3. In this case, the line that is the graph of $y = 1$ is a **solid** line. We use a solid line to indicate that the points *on* the line are included in the graph of $y \geq 1$. (Recall that "$y \geq 1$" is read "y is greater than or equal to **1**.") Similarly, Figure 10–4 shows the graph of $x \leq -2$, with the graph of $x = -2$ a solid line. As you see, all points *on* the line are included in the graph of $x \leq -2$.

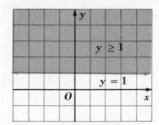

Figure 10–3

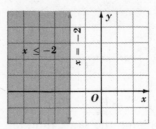

Figure 10–4

ORAL EXERCISES

Give an equation for each line drawn on the number plane.

SAMPLE:

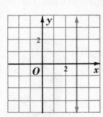

What you say: $x = 3$

1.

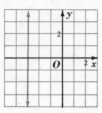

3.

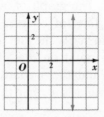

2.

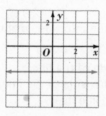

4.

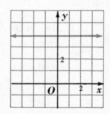

Name an inequality suggested by the graph in each of the following.

5.

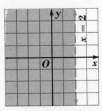

7.

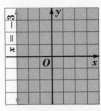

6.

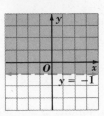

8.

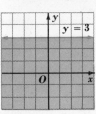

WRITTEN EXERCISES

Draw a number-plane graph for each inequality.

SAMPLE: $x \geq -3\frac{1}{2}$ *Solution:*

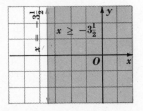

1. $x > 2$	**5.** $y \geq 2\frac{1}{2}$	**9.** $x > 0$
2. $y < 4$	**6.** $x < -1$	**10.** $2x > -8$
3. $x \geq 2$	**7.** $y > 2\frac{1}{2}$	**11.** $3y < -6$
4. $y \leq 4$	**8.** $x \leq -1$	**12.** $y \leq 0$

For each ordered pair, tell whether its graph is or is not included in the graph shown here. Copy the graph and check each answer by indicating the point corresponding to the ordered pair.

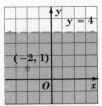

SAMPLE: $(-2, 1)$

Solution: The y-coordinate, 1, is less than 4, so the point $(-2, 1)$ is in the graph.

Check: See the graph.

13. $(4, 2)$ **14.** $(0, -4)$ **15.** $(5, 3)$

16. $(3, -3)$ **17.** $(2, 5)$ **18.** $(-3, 7)$

For each ordered pair, tell why its graph is or is not included in the graph shown here.

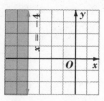

SAMPLE: $(3, -3)$

Solution: Since the *x*-coordinate, 3, is greater than -4, it is neither less than nor equal to -4, so the point $(3, -3)$ is not in the graph.

19. $(-1, 5)$ **21.** $(-5, -3)$ **23.** $(-6, 2)$
20. $(2, 1)$ **22.** $(-4, 4)$ **24.** $(0, -4)$

For each of the following inequalities, draw a number-plane graph; name three points included in the graph.

SAMPLE: .   *Solution:* $x + 1.5 < 0$
$x + 1.5 < 0$ $x < -1.5$

Points: $(-2, 2)$; $(-3, 5)$; $(-2, -2)$

$\boxed{\text{B}}$ **25.** $y - 3 \leq \frac{1}{2}$ **28.** $y + 9 \geq 4$
    26. $x - 2 < 0$ **29.** $y - 2 > -3$
    27. $x + 5 < 7.5$ **30.** $x - 1 \leq \frac{1}{2}$

$\boxed{\text{C}}$ **31.** $\frac{y}{3} + 1 < \frac{1}{2}$ **32.** $4x - 2 \geq 6$

10–3   Lines and Half-Planes

In Section 10–2 just completed we worked with half-planes that were formed by either **horizontal** lines or **vertical** lines.

Now let us explore the idea of half-planes formed by lines that are neither horizontal nor vertical. That is, we will work on each side of the graph of a linear equation such as $2x + y = 4$. It will help if we transform the equation to a form in which the variable *y* stands alone as the left member, so we write the equivalent equation $y = -2x + 4$.

The line that is the graph of $y = -2x + 4$ divides the number plane into two half-planes, as shown here. Suppose you found several solutions of the inequality $y > -2x + 4$, such as the number pairs $(1, 4)$, $(3, -1)$, and $(2, 1)$. The points that correspond to these pairs are shown

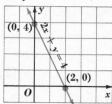

in Figure 10–5. Notice that all three of the points lie in the same half-plane, which has the graph of $y = -2x + 4$ as boundary. The line $y = -2x + 4$ is a dashed line to indicate that points *on* the line are *not* solutions of $y > -2x + 4$.

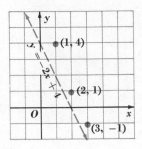

Figure 10–5

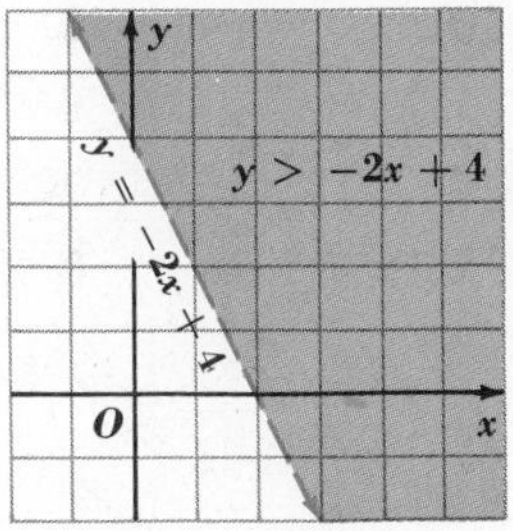

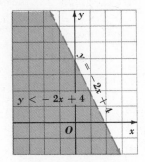

Figure 10–6

Try some other number-pair solutions of the inequality $y > -2x + 4$ and note that each corresponds to a point in the same half-plane. Therefore we see that the shaded half-plane in Figure 10–6 is the graph of $y > -2x + 4$. If you test the number pairs $(1, 1)$ and $(-1, 3)$ to see if they satisfy the inequality, of course you will find that they do not, since they are the coordinates of points that are *not* in the shaded half-plane. They are *not* solutions of $y > -2x + 4$.

What do you suppose the graph of the inequality $y < -2x + 4$ is like? Some of the ordered pairs that satisfy the inequality are $(0, 1)$, $(-1, 4)$, and $(1, -2)$. The graphs of these pairs are shown in Figure 10–7. Do they all lie on the same side of the line that is the graph of the linear equation $y = -2x + 4$? Will *all* solutions of $y < -2x + 4$ lie in that same half-plane? If you are thinking correctly, your answer to each question is "Yes." Figure 10–8 shows the graph of the inequality. Note that again the dashed line is used to indicate that points *on* the line are *not* part of the graph.

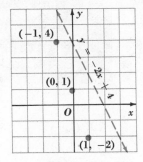

Figure 10–7

Figure 10–8

ORAL EXERCISES

Tell whether each point is located in the half-plane labeled *R* or in the half-plane labeled *T*.

1. $(0, 0)$	**5.** $(4, -1)$
2. $(1, 3)$	**6.** $(3, 0)$
3. $(-1, -2)$	**7.** $(0, -5)$
4. $(-3, 1)$	**8.** $(0, 2)$

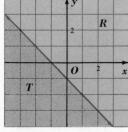

Tell whether each pair of numbers corresponds to a point included in the graph of $y > 2x + 1$, in the graph of $y < 2x + 1$, or in neither graph.

9. $(1, 1)$	**15.** $(4, 4)$
10. $(1, -1)$	**16.** $(0, 0)$
11. $(0, 3)$	**17.** $(-1, -2)$
12. $(3, 0)$	**18.** $(-1, -1)$
13. $(0, 1)$	**19.** $(0, -8)$
14. $(-2, 1)$	**20.** $(6, 3)$

WRITTEN EXERCISES

Make a copy of the number plane shown here. Tell whether each number pair is a solution of $y > -x + 1$ or of $y < -x + 1$ and check your answer by plotting the point.

SAMPLE: $(-2, 1)$

Solution: The graph of the number pair $(-2, 1)$ is included in the graph of $y < -x + 1$.

Check: See the number plane.

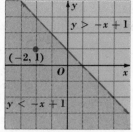

A	**1.** $(2, 0)$	**5.** $(1, -1)$		**9.** $(0, -3)$
	2. $(0, 3)$	**6.** $(4, 1)$		**10.** $(1, -3)$
	3. $(0, 0)$	**7.** $(4, -1)$		**11.** $(1, 4)$
	4. $(-1, 1)$	**8.** $(-2, 0)$		**12.** $(0, 1\frac{1}{2})$

Tell whether each ordered pair satisfies $y > 2x - 1$ or $y < 2x - 1$. Then give the inequality for which Region A is the graph and the inequality for which Region B is the graph.

13. $(1, 3)$ **18.** $(0, -3)$

14. $(0, 0)$ **19.** $(0, 3)$

15. $(-1, 1)$ **20.** $(4, 4)$

16. $(3, 1)$ **21.** $(2, 0)$

17. $(-1, -4)$ **22.** $(2, -4)$

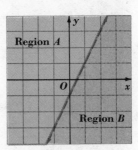

23. Region A is the graph of __?__.

24. Region B is the graph of __?__.

Refer to the number plane shown here, and complete each statement with either $x + y > 2$ or $x + y < 2$.

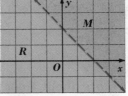

25. The number pair $(0, 0)$ satisfies the inequality __?__.

26. The graph of the number pair $(0, 3)$ is included in the graph of the inequality __?__.

27. Region M is the graph of the inequality __?__, and Region R is the graph of __?__.

For each of the following figures, write an inequality for which Region A is the graph and an inequality for which the graph is Region B.

SAMPLE:

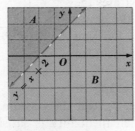

Solution: Region A: $y > x + 2$
           Region B: $y < x + 2$

28.

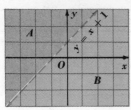

29.

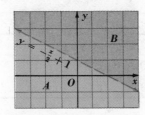

30.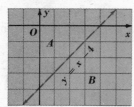

31.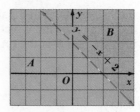

B **32.**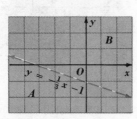

33.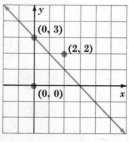

Make a number plane graph of each pair of inequalities.

C **34.** $y > x$ and $y < x$ **35.** $y < 3x - 2$ and $y > 3x - 2$

10–4   More about Lines and Half-Planes

In the preceding section we considered only inequalities that contained the $>$ or $<$ relationship symbol. For the boundary of the graph of such an inequality we used a dashed line to indicate that points on the boundary line were not included in the graph.

We shall now consider the graphs of the inequalities $x + y \geq 3$ and $x + y \leq 3$, which make use of the symbols $\geq$ and $\leq$. In either case, do you see that the line that separates the number plane into two half-planes is the graph of the linear equation $x + y = 3$? Do you agree that this time the line must be included in the graph?

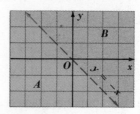

To decide in which direction the graph of each inequality extends from the line, we test the coordinates of the sample points indicated and see which inequality is satisfied.

Point	$x + y \geq 3$	True/False	$x + y \leq 3$	True/False
(2, 2)	$2 + 2 \geq 3$	true	$2 + 2 \leq 3$	false
(0, 0)	$0 + 0 \geq 3$	false	$0 + 0 \leq 3$	true
(0, 3)	$0 + 3 \geq 3$	true	$0 + 3 \leq 3$	true

Since the number pair $(0, 3)$ satisfies *both* open sentences, we find that the line which is the graph of $x + y = 3$ should be included in both graphs, a fact which will be indicated by using a **solid** line.

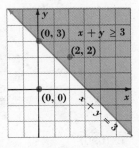

The number pair $(2, 2)$ satisfies the inequality $x + y \geq 3$, while the pair $(0, 0)$ does not, so we see that the graph of $x + y \geq 3$ is on the side that includes the point $(2, 2)$, as shown here.

The number pair $(2, 2)$ does *not* satisfy the inequality $x + y \leq 3$, while the pair $(0, 0)$ does satisfy it. So we see that the graph of $x + y \leq 3$ is on the side of the line $x + y = 3$ that includes the point $(0, 0)$.

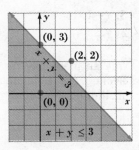

ORAL EXERCISES

Tell which of the following pairs correspond to points which lie in the graph indicated.

SAMPLE: $(-2, 4)$ *What you say:* $(-2, 4)$ does *not* name a point in the indicated graph.

1. $(0, 0)$ **6.** $(0, 2)$

2. $(0, -2)$ **7.** $(2, 5)$

3. $(1, 4)$ **8.** $(-2, 0)$

4. $(-2, 2)$ **9.** $(1, 3)$

5. $(-2, -2)$ **10.** $(-4, 1)$

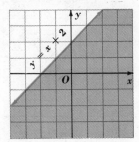

WRITTEN EXERCISES

Copy the two number planes shown and tell whether each number pair is a solution of $y \leq x + 1$, of $y \geq x + 1$, or of both. Check each answer by plotting the point on both number planes.

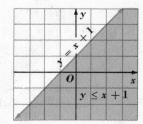

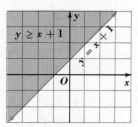

A

1. $(0, 0)$ **5.** $(0, 1)$ **9.** $(-2, -1)$

2. $(1, 0)$ **6.** $(-1, \frac{1}{2})$ **10.** $(-2, -1\frac{1}{2})$

3. $(-1, 1)$ **7.** $(3, 3)$ **11.** $(0, -10)$

4. $(-2, 0)$ **8.** $(-1, 0)$ **12.** $(-4, -3)$

Write an inequality for each number-plane graph. Check your work by selecting one point that is in the graph and one point that is not, and substituting the coordinates in the equality you have written.

SAMPLE:

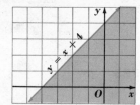

Solution: $y \leq x + 4$

Check: $(0, 0)$ names a point in the graph; $0 \leq 0 + 4$ is true.
$(-4, 1)$ names a point not in the graph; $1 \leq -4 + 4$ is false.

13.

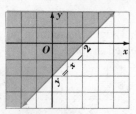

16.

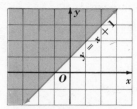

14.

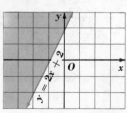

17.

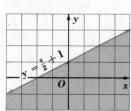

15.

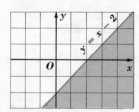

18.

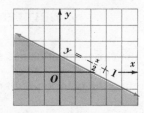

For each of the following, show the graphs of the linear equation and the related inequality on the same number plane.

19. $y = 2x - 3$
$y \geq 2x - 3$

21. $y = 1 - 2x$
$y \leq 1 - 2x$

23. $y = 2x + 1$
$y \geq 2x + 1$

20. $y = x + 1$
$y \leq x + 1$

22. $y = 3x$
$y \leq 3x$

24. $y = \dfrac{x}{2} - 1$
$y \leq \dfrac{x}{2} - 1$

B **25.** $y - \dfrac{x}{2} - 1 = 0$
$y - \dfrac{x}{2} - 1 \geq 0$

26. $y - \dfrac{x}{3} = 1$
$y - \dfrac{x}{3} \leq 1$

27. $2x + 2y = 4$
$2x + 2y \leq 4$

C **28.** $y - \dfrac{x}{4} = -2$
$y - \dfrac{x}{4} \geq -2$

29. $x = -y - 5$
$x \leq -y - 5$

30. $y = -2\frac{1}{2} + x$
$y \leq -2\frac{1}{2} + x$

Intercepts and Slopes

10–5 Lines and y-Intercepts

If a line in the number plane is not a vertical line, it will have at least one point in common with the *y*-axis. For example, the graph of the equation $y + 3 = 2x$, shown here, has the point $(0, -3)$ in common with the *y*-axis. For this reason, the number -3 is called the *y*-intercept of the graph of $y + 3 = 2x$.

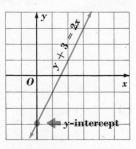

As you might guess, since every point on the *y*-axis has a first co-ordinate of **0**, we can find the *y*-intercept of the graph of an equation by letting *x* equal **0** and solving for the corresponding value of *y*. For the equation $y + 3 = 2x$, when $x = 0$ we have:

$$y + 3 = 2 \cdot 0$$
$$y + 3 = 0$$
$$y = -3$$

So we see that the *y*-intercept is -3.

In the figure at the right are the graphs of the three equations:

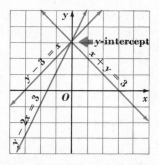

$$y - 2x = 3$$
$$y - 3 = x$$
$$x + y = 3$$

Now, a very interesting thing appears when we write these equations in the equivalent form in which **y** stands alone as the left member. See if you can find something that is common to all three equations.

$y - 2x = 3$ is equivalent to $y = 2x + 3$.
$y - 3 = x$ is equivalent to $y = x + 3$.
$x + y = 3$ is equivalent to $y = -x + 3$.

Do you see that when each equation is rewritten its constant term is **3**? Look at the graph and check that **3** is also the common *y*-intercept of the three lines.

In general we can say:

For any equation of the form **y = mx + b**, where **m** and **b** are directed numbers, the number-plane graph is a line whose *y*-intercept is **b**.

ORAL EXERCISES

Name the common *y*-intercept of the three graphs shown in each figure.

1.

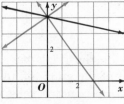

3.

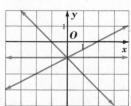

2.

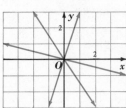

4.

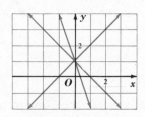

Tell how to complete each statement.

5. The y-intercept of the graph of $y = -2x + 4$ is __?__.

6. The y-intercept of the graph of $y = \dfrac{x}{5} - 1$ is __?__.

7. The y-intercept of the graph of $y = -3x$ is __?__.

8. The y-intercept of the graph of $y = 2$ is __?__.

WRITTEN EXERCISES

For each of the following, name the common y-intercept of the graphs of the two equations given; check by drawing their number-plane graphs.

SAMPLE: $y = x + 1$
$y = 1$

Check:

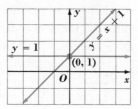

Solution: The common y-intercept is 1.

A

1. $y = x + 5$
$y = -2x + 5$

2. $y = 2$
$y = x + 2$

3. $y = x - 3$
$y = 2x - 3$

4. $y = \dfrac{x}{2} + 4$
$y = -x + 4$

5. $y = -1$
$y = 3x - 1$

6. $y = x + 1$
$y = -x + 1$

7. $y = 3x - 6$
$y = x - 6$

8. $y = 2x + 3$
$y = \dfrac{x}{3} + 3$

Write each equation in the form $y = mx + b$ and name the y-intercept of its graph.

SAMPLE: $2y - x = 4$ *Solution:* $2y = x + 4$
$y = \dfrac{x}{2} + 2$; the y-intercept is 2.

9. $y - x = 3$

10. $y + 2x + 8 = 0$

11. $y + 3 = x$

12. $2x = y - 3$

13. $5 = 2x + y$

14. $x + y = 2$

15. $2y + 3 = 0$

16. $2y = 4x + 1$

17. $x + y + 1 = 0$

18. $3y = x - 6$

B **19.** $x - 3y + 6 = 0$ **21.** $4x - 2y - 4 = 0$
   20. $4y = 3 - 2x$ **22.** $2y + 8x = 3$

C **23.** $y - 1.5x = 0.75$ **25.** $7x + 3y = -10$
   24. $\dfrac{y}{2} + \dfrac{x}{4} = \dfrac{1}{3}$ **26.** $1.5x - 2y = 3$

10–6   The Slope-Intercept Form of a Linear Equation

When the idea of slope was discussed in Chapter 9, recall that we said

$$\text{slope} = \frac{\text{rise}}{\text{run}} = \frac{\text{vertical change}}{\text{horizontal change}}.$$

We also said that the slope of a line in the number plane is positive if a left-to-right movement along the line results in an **increase** in the value of the y-coordinate; it is negative when the left-to-right movement results in a **decrease** in the value of the y-coordinate.

The number plane pictured here shows the graphs of $y = 2x + 1$ and $y = 2x - 4$. Do you see that the slope of each line is 2? Do you agree that different lines with the same slope must be parallel? Note that each equation is in the form $y = mx + b$. In each equation the value of m is 2, the same number as the slope of the line. If you were to draw the graphs of other equations of the $y = mx + b$ form, you would 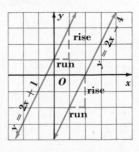 find that the value of m, the coefficient of x, is always the same number as the slope of the line. The equation $y = mx + b$ is called the slope-intercept form of the equation of a line, because it shows at a glance both the **slope** and the **y-intercept** of the line.

 For any equation of the form $y = mx + b$, where m and b are directed numbers, the number-plane graph is a line whose slope is m and whose y-intercept is b.

Equation	Equivalent equation of the form $y = mx + b$	Slope m	y-intercept b
$x + 2y = 4$	$y = -\dfrac{x}{2} + 2$	$-\dfrac{1}{2}$	2
$y + 3 = 2x$	$y = 2x - 3$	2	-3
$2y - 2 = 0$	$y = 0x + 1$	0	1

ORAL EXERCISES

For each equation, name the numbers that correspond to m and b in the slope-intercept form $y = mx + b$.

SAMPLE: $y = \frac{3}{5}x - 2$ *What you say:* $\frac{3}{5}$ corresponds to m;
-2 corresponds to b.

1. $y = -3x + 5$ **5.** $y = \dfrac{2x}{3} - 3$

2. $y = -2x + 6$ **6.** $y = -\dfrac{3x}{5} + 2$

3. $y = x + 2$ **7.** $y = 1.5x - 3.75$

4. $y = \dfrac{x}{2} - 1$ **8.** $y = -0.5x - 1.5$

Complete each statement.

9. For the line that is the graph of $y = 2x + 1$, the slope is __?__ and the y-intercept is __?__.

10. For the line that is the graph of $y = -2x + 1$, the slope is __?__ and the y-intercept is __?__.

11. For the line that is the graph of $y = (?)x + (?)$, the slope is 3 and the y-intercept is -2.

12. For the line that is the graph of $2y = x + 6$, the slope is __?__ and the y-intercept is __?__.

WRITTEN EXERCISES

Write each equation in the form $y = mx + b$; then give the slope and the y-intercept of the graph of the equation.

SAMPLE: $y - 1 = 2x$

Solution: $y = 2x + 1$; the slope is 2 and the y-intercept is 1.

1. $3x + y = 4$ **7.** $y - 4 = 0$

2. $5 + y = 3x$ **8.** $3y = -15$

3. $-2x + y = 3$ **9.** $y + 2 = \frac{3}{4}x$

4. $2y = x - 2$ **10.** $y + 2 = 5x$

5. $5y = 3x + 10$ **11.** $2y = -\frac{1}{2}x + 3$

6. $y + \frac{1}{2}x = 1$ **12.** $7 - y = 8x$

Write a linear equation whose graph has the given slope and *y*-intercept.

SAMPLE: $m = 3$; $b = -2$ *Solution:* $y = mx + b$
                                              $y = 3x - 2$

13. $m = 2$; $b = 5$ **18.** $m = 7$; $b = \frac{1}{2}$

14. $m = -4$; $b = 2$ **19.** $m = -\frac{1}{3}$; $b = 2$

15. $m = -3$; $b = 0$ **20.** $m = 0$; $b = 3$

16. $m = 5$; $b = -4$ **21.** $m = 0$; $b = -3$

17. $m = \frac{1}{3}$; $b = 8$ **22.** $m = -\frac{2}{3}$; $b = -\frac{1}{6}$

For each graph on the number plane, write a linear equation in the form $y = mx + b$.

SAMPLE:

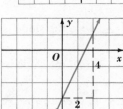

Solution: Slope $= \frac{2}{3}$; *y*-intercept $= 1$
             $y = mx + b$
             $y = \frac{2}{3}x + 1$

B **23.**

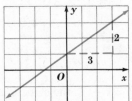

25.

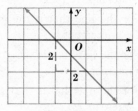

24.

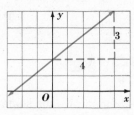

26.

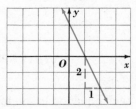

Use only the *y*-intercept and the slope to graph each equation.

SAMPLE: $y - 2x = 3$

Solution: The slope is 2;   The graph is:
           the *y*-intercept is 3.

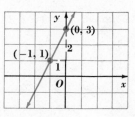

C **27.** $y - 2x = -2$ **29.** $2x + y = 0$

28. $3x + y = 1$ **30.** $6x + 2y + 1 = 0$

Special Graphs

10–7 Quadratic Equations and Graphs

So far we have considered only equations whose graphs are lines. Our work in graphing would not be complete without some consideration of equations whose graphs are other geometric curves. The illustrations below show a circular cone cut by a plane in three different ways. In each, the curve shown in red is called a **section** of the cone.

Case I   Case II   Case III

In Case I, the plane that cuts the cone is parallel to the base, and the section is a **circle** When the plane cuts the cone obliquely, as in Case II, the section is an **ellipse**. Case III shows a cone cut by a plane that is parallel to a line connecting the vertex of the cone to any point in its base; the resulting section is called a **parabola**.

To draw the graph called for in each of the following examples, we begin by finding several ordered pairs that satisfy the equation. Then we locate the corresponding points in the number plane, and draw a smooth curve through the points.

EXAMPLE 1. Draw the graph of $x^2 + 4y^2 = 64$.

Notice that, in this table, we get two values for y for each replacement for x, except **8** and **−8**.

x	$x^2 + 4y^2 = 64$	y	(x, y)
−8	$64 + 4y^2 = 64$	0	$(-8, 0)$
−4	$16 + 4y^2 = 64$	3.5 and −3.5	$(-4, 3.5), (-4, -3.5)$
0	$0 + 4y^2 = 64$	4 and −4	$(0, 4), (0, -4)$
4	$16 + 4y^2 = 64$	3.5 and −3.5	$(4, 3.5), (4, -3.5)$
8	$64 + 4y^2 = 64$	0	$(8, 0)$

In the table we show values **3.5** and **−3.5** for y. These are not exact, but are very close approximations. When **x** is either **−4** or **4**, the equation becomes

$$16 + 4y^2 = 64$$
$$4y^2 = 48$$
$$y^2 = 12.$$

If **y** is replaced by either **3.5** or **−3.5**, the value of y^2 is very close to **12**, so we find that these approximate values are satisfactory for our purpose.

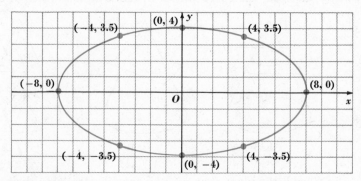

The curve is an **ellipse**.

EXAMPLE 2.   Draw the graph of $y = x^2$.

x	$y = x^2$	y	(x, y)
0	$y = 0$	0	$(0, 0)$
1	$y = 1$	1	$(1, 1)$
2	$y = 4$	4	$(2, 4)$
3	$y = 9$	9	$(3, 9)$
−1	$y = 1$	1	$(−1, 1)$
−2	$y = 4$	4	$(−2, 4)$
−3	$y = 9$	9	$(−3, 9)$

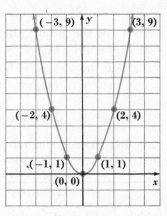

The curve is a **parabola**.

EXAMPLE 3.   Draw the graph of $x^2 + y^2 = 25$.

In the following table, notice that, for each replacement for **x** except **5** and **−5**, there are **two** values for **y**.

x	$x^2 + y^2 = 25$	y	(x, y)
-5	$25 + y^2 = 25$	0	$(-5, 0)$
-4	$16 + y^2 = 25$	3 and -3	$(-4, 3), (-4, -3)$
-3	$9 + y^2 = 25$	4 and -4	$(-3, 4), (-3, -4)$
0	$0 + y^2 = 25$	5 and -5	$(0, 5), (0, -5)$
3	$9 + y^2 = 25$	4 and -4	$(3, 4), (3, -4)$
4	$16 + y^2 = 25$	3 and -3	$(4, 3), (4, -3)$
5	$25 + y^2 = 25$	0	$(5, 0)$

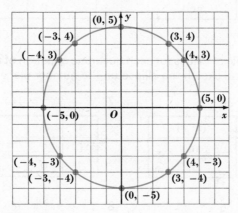

The curve is a circle.

WRITTEN EXERCISES

Complete the table of values for each quadratic equation of a circle. Then plot the points and sketch the circle on the number plane.

SAMPLE: $x^2 + y^2 = 4$

x	y	(x, y)
0	$?$	$?$ and $?$
$?$	0	$?$ and $?$

Solution:

x	y	(x, y)
0	2 and -2	$(0, 2)$ and $(0, -2)$
2 and -2	0	$(2, 0)$ and $(-2, 0)$

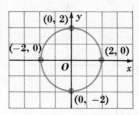

A **1.** $x^2 + y^2 = 16$

x	y	(x, y)
0	?	? and ?
?	0	? and ?

3. $x^2 + y^2 = 9$

x	y	(x, y)
0	?	? and ?
?	0	? and ?

2. $x^2 + y^2 = 36$

x	y	(x, y)
0	?	? and ?
?	0	? and ?

4. $x^2 + y^2 = 49$

x	y	(x, y)
0	?	? and ?
?	0	? and ?

Complete the table of values for each quadratic equation of an ellipse. Then plot the points and sketch the ellipse on the number plane.

5. $x^2 + 4y^2 = 36$

x	y	(x, y)
0	?	? and ?
?	0	? and ?

7. $x^2 + 9y^2 = 144$

x	y	(x, y)
0	?	? and ?
?	0	? and ?

6. $4x^2 + y^2 = 36$

x	y	(x, y)
0	?	? and ?
?	0	? and ?

8. $x^2 + 9y^2 = 36$

x	y	(x, y)
0	?	? and ?
?	0	? and ?

Complete the table of values for each quadratic equation of a parabola. Then plot the points and sketch the graph on the number plane.

SAMPLE: $2y = x^2$ *Solution:*

x	y	(x, y)
0	?	?
2	?	?
4	?	?
-2	?	?
-4	?	?

x	y	(x, y)
0	0	$(0, 0)$
2	2	$(2, 2)$
4	8	$(4, 8)$
-2	2	$(-2, 2)$
-4	8	$(-4, 8)$

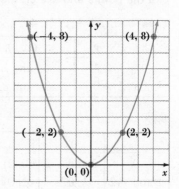

9. $y = 2x^2$

x	y	(x, y)
0	?	?
1	?	?
2	?	?
−1	?	?
−2	?	?

11. $y = \dfrac{x^2}{2}$

x	y	(x, y)
0	?	?
1	?	?
2	?	?
−1	?	?
−2	?	?

10. $x^2 = 4y$

x	y	(x, y)
0	?	?
1	?	?
2	?	?
−1	?	?
−2	?	?

12. $y = -2x^2$

x	y	(x, y)
0	?	?
1	?	?
2	?	?
−1	?	?
−2	?	?

10–8 Bar and Line Graphs

The table below provides a record of snowfall measured in a certain midwestern city over a period of seven years. From the table we learn that the least snowfall was 16.2 inches, which occurred during the winter of 1963–64. The most snow fell during the winter of 1969–70, when a fall of 48.2 inches was recorded. The accompanying graph, called a bar graph, shows the same information as the table, but in a form that helps us to see certain facts more clearly and quickly. Can you easily decide from the graph which were the three winters having the greatest snowfall? The three having the least?

Winter	Snowfall (in inches)
1963–64	16.2
1964–65	45.7
1965–66	18.1
1966–67	16.3
1967–68	40.4
1968–69	24.4
1969–70	48.2

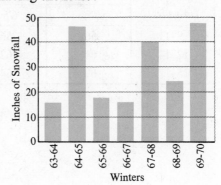

Often a broken-line graph can be used to convey information effectively. For example, in the broken-line graph shown, time is paired with temperature. The dots joined by line segments are the graphs of the ordered pairs in the table, which shows temperature readings recorded each hour over a six-hour period.

Time	Temperature (in degrees F.)	Ordered Pair
1 P.M.	60	(1 P.M., 60)
2 P.M.	40	(2 P.M., 40)
3 P.M.	30	(3 P.M., 30)
4 P.M.	25	(4 P.M., 25)
5 P.M.	20	(5 P.M., 20)
6 P.M.	15	(6 P.M., 15)

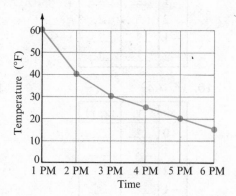

Do you see that such a graph is actually the graph of a function? Use the graph to help you answer the following questions:

1. Did the temperature drop each hour during the observations?
2. What was the coldest recorded temperature? When did it occur?
3. During which one-hour period did the sharpest temperature drop occur?

A comparison bar graph provides an effective way to show how corresponding measures of two groups compare. The one shown here is based on the accompanying table which records the average heights of boys and of girls in three different age groups.

Age Group (in years)	Average Height (in inches)	
	Boys	Girls
9–11	56	56
12–14	61	62
15–17	69	64

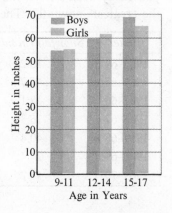

WRITTEN EXERCISES

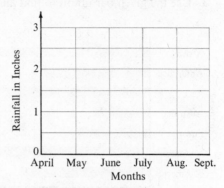

A **1.** The table gives the average monthly rainfall in Seattle, Washington, over a period of six months. Make a broken-line graph showing the same information; use horizontal and vertical axes as suggested.

Month	Rainfall (in inches)
April	2.7
May	2.2
June	1.7
July	0.5
August	0.7
September	1.9

Use the graph to find the answers to the following questions:

a. During which month was the least rainfall recorded?

b. Did more rainfall occur during the first three months or during the last three months?

c. During which two months was the rainfall less than 1 inch?

d. During which two months was the rainfall in excess of 2 inches?

e. Does the graph represent a function?

2. Make a comparison bar graph to show the average snowfall in a certain city for a four-month period and the actual snowfall for the same four-month period of a given year.

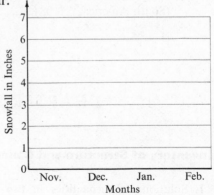

Month	Snowfall (in inches)	
	Average	Actual
Nov.	6.8	5.3
Dec.	6.1	1.5
Jan.	7.4	8.1
Feb.	5.0	7.2

a. In which month were the average snowfall and the actual snowfall most nearly the same?

b. In which month did the average snowfall differ most from the actual snowfall?

c. In which month was the actual snowfall greater than the average snowfall?

d. What was the total actual snowfall over the four-month period?

3. Use the given bar graph to find answers to the following questions.

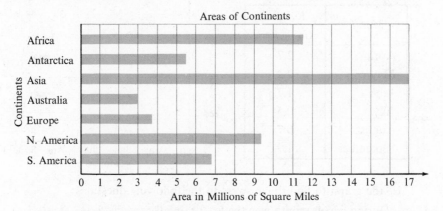

Areas of Continents

Area in Millions of Square Miles

a. What is the approximate area of each continent?

b. Which is the smallest continent? Which is the largest?

c. Which continent has an area that is about one-third the area of North America?

d. List the names of the continents in order of size, beginning with the smallest.

e. Complete the set of ordered pairs relating continent to size in millions of square miles: {(Asia, 17.0), (Africa, 11.5), (North America, __?__), (South America, __?__), (__?__, 3.7), (Australia, __?__), (__?__, 5.5)}.

CHAPTER SUMMARY

Inventory of Structure and Concepts

1. Solutions of **inequalities** in **two variables** take the form of ordered number pairs. The **solution set** of an inequality in two variables is the set of all ordered pairs of numbers that satisfy the inequality.

2. A line in a number plane divides the plane into two **half-planes**. The line is the common boundary of the two half-planes.

3. A line in a plane divides the plane into **three sets of points**: The set of points making up the half-plane on one side of the line; the set of points making up the half-plane on the other side of the line; the set of points that make up the line itself.

4. The **y-intercept** of the graph of a linear equation in x and y can be found by replacing x in the equation by 0 and solving for y; if the equation is in the form $y = mx + b$, its y-intercept is b.

5. For a linear equation in the form $y = mx + b$, the **slope** of its graph is m.

6. The intersection of a circular cone with a plane is called a **section** of the cone. If the plane is parallel to the base of the cone, the section is a **circle**; if the plane is oblique to the base and the section is a closed curve, it is an **ellipse**; if the plane is parallel to a line connecting the vertex of the cone to a point in its base, the section is a **parabola**.

7. Information listed in a table can often be presented effectively by means of a **bar graph**, a **broken-line graph**, or a **comparison bar graph**.

Vocabulary and Spelling

inequality in two variables (*p. 321*) circle (*p. 341*)
half-plane (*p. 324*) ellipse (*p. 341*)
boundary of a graph (*p. 325*) parabola (*p. 341*)
y-intercept (*p. 335*) bar graphs (*p. 345*)
slope-intercept form (*p. 338*) broken-line graphs (*p. 346*)
section of a cone (*p. 341*) comparison bar graphs (*p. 346*)

Chapter Test

For each of the following, write an equivalent equation or inequality in the slope-intercept form.

1. $2x + y > 1$ **3.** $2x + y \geq 3$ **5.** $x - y = 0$
2. $4y - 3 = 8x$ **4.** $x + 2y \leq 6$ **6.** $x + y - 10 < 0$

For each inequality, name two number pairs that are in its solution set.

7. $2x + 1 < y$ **9.** $x + y \geq 0$ **11.** $y > \frac{1}{2}x + 2$
8. $2y < x$ **10.** $y \leq 3x + 4$ **12.** $3x + 2y \geq 4$

Make a number plane graph for each inequality.

13. $x \leq 5$ **15.** $y \geq -2x + 4$ **17.** $x \geq -y - 3$

14. $y > 0$ **16.** $y > x + 2$ **18.** $y \leq 1 - 3x$

Write each equation in the form $y = mx + b$ and give the slope and the y-intercept of its graph.

19. $2x + y = 5$ **20.** $y = -x + 4$ **21.** $2y = 3x + 6$

Make a number plane graph for each quadratic equation.

22. $x^2 + y^2 = 49$ **23.** $y = 4x^2$

Make a graph for each table of information.

24. Estimated World Population

Year	Population (in millions)
1750	750
1800	880
1850	1200
1900	1650
1950	2500

25. One Week's Daily High Temperatures

Day	Temperature (in degrees F.)
Mon.	74
Tues.	68
Wed.	61
Thurs.	79
Fri.	80
Sat.	80
Sun.	76

Chapter Review

10–1 **Inequalities in Two Variables**

Write an equivalent inequality having y as the left member.

1. $8x + y > 10$ **3.** $-3x + y \geq 6$

2. $\frac{1}{2}x + y < 5$ **4.** $5x + 3y \leq 9$

For each of the following, name three ordered pairs of numbers that satisfy the inequality.

5. $y > 4x - 3$ **7.** $x < -5y + 1$

6. $3x + y \geq 5$ **8.** $2y \leq x + 4$

10–2 Inequalities and Half-Planes

Make a number-plane graph for each of the following:

9. $y \geq -4$ **10.** $y \leq 3\frac{1}{2}$ **11.** $2x < -5$

Make a number-plane graph for each inequality and show which of the accompanying ordered pairs represent points included in the graph.

12. $y \geq -1.5$; $(0, 0)$, $(3, -4)$, $(-6, 2)$, $(-3, -2)$.
13. $y - 2 < 0$; $(0, 0)$, $(4, 0)$, $(0, 4)$, $(1, -3)$, $(-1, 3)$.
14. $x + 1 > 0$; $(0, 0)$, $(-2, 3)$, $(0, 4)$, $(1, -2)$, $(-2, -2)$.

10–3 Lines and Half-Planes

Write an inequality that corresponds to each graph.

15.
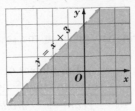

16.
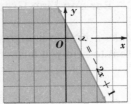

10–4 More about Lines and Half-Planes

Write an inequality that corresponds to each graph.

17.
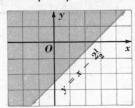

18.
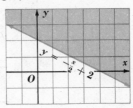

10–5 Lines and y-Intercepts

Write each equation in the form $y = mx + b$ and give the y-intercept of its number-plane graph.

19. $2y - 3x = 4$ **20.** $y - x = -1$ **21.** $x + 3y - 9 = 0$

10–6   The Slope-Intercept Form of a Linear Equation

Write each equation in the form $y = mx + b$ and give the slope and the y-intercept of its number-plane graph.   Graph each equation to check your work.

22. $3x + y = 4$ **23.** $4 + y = \dfrac{x}{2}$ **24.** $y + \dfrac{5x}{2} = 1$

10–7   Quadratic Equations and Graphs

Make a number-plane graph for each equation by plotting at least four points and joining them with a smooth curve.

25. $x^2 + 9y^2 = 81$ (ellipse)   **27.** $6y = x^2$ (parabola)
26. $x^2 + y^2 = 81$ (circle)

10–8   Bar and Line Graphs

28. Make a broken-line graph for the information given in the table and use it to help you answer the questions.

a. Over which two-year period did the enrollment remain the same?
b. How much difference is there between the smallest and the largest enrollments given?

Enrollment of
Lincoln High School

Year	Enrollment
1966–67	2800
1967–68	2950
1968–69	2950
1969–70	3100
1970–71	3000

Review of Skills

Add.

1. $x + 3y$
$\underline{x + 5y}$

2. $x + 4z$
$\underline{x -\ z}$

3. $3a +\ b$
$\underline{a - 3b}$

4. $-2m + 5n$
$\underline{\ m -\ n}$

5. $x - 2$
$\underline{x + 5}$

6. $-2r - 6s$
$\underline{-\ r -\ s}$

Subtract each lower polynomial from the one above.

7. $2x - y$
    $\underline{x + y}$

9. $-m + 3n$
    $\underline{-m - n}$

11. $9a - 6b$
    $\underline{a - 6b}$

8. $4c + d$
    $\underline{3c + d}$

10. $4w + 2z$
    $\underline{w + 2z}$

12. $2x - 9y$
    $\underline{2x - 3y}$

Translate each word statement into an open number sentence and solve.

13. Some number increased by -3 is 10. Find the number.

14. Twice some number, increased by 6 is 0. Find the number.

15. One-half some number, increased by 3 is 8. What is the number?

16. Three times a number, decreased by 12 is 9. What is the number?

For each figure, tell which line segments are parallel.

17.
Square

18.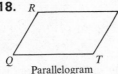
Parallelogram

19.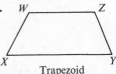
Trapezoid

Complete each of the following to make a true statement.

20. If lines in a plane are extended indefinitely and do not intersect they are __?__ lines.

21. If lines in a plane are not parallel they __?__ in exactly one point.

22. Equivalent sentences are sentences that have the same __?__.

Find the value of each expression if the first number in the ordered pair is the replacement for *x* and the second number is the replacement for *y*.

23. $5x - y$; $(4, 0)$

26. $3x - 3y$; $(0, 3)$

24. $-x + y$; $(3, 6)$

27. $x + 3y + 0$; $(4, -1)$

25. $2x + y$; $(-1, 1)$

28. $-x + 4y + 1$; $(-2, 2)$

Give a reason to justify each statement.

SAMPLE: If $3x - y = 6$, then $2(3x - y) = 2(6)$.

Solution: Multiplication property of equality.

29. If $2m + n = -8$, then $(2m + n) + 8 = (-8) + 8$

30. If $x + 3y = 1$, then $5(x + 3y) = 5(1)$.

31. If $\frac{x}{3} = -4$, then $3\left(\frac{x}{3}\right) = 3(-4)$

■ ■

CHECK POINT
FOR EXPERTS

Valid and Invalid Logical Arguments

In the discussion on page 318 we showed how a Venn diagram can be used to determine the validity of an argument. For example, consider the following argument:

Hypothesis: All squares are rectangles.
All rectangles are polygons.
Conclusion: All squares are polygons.

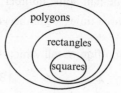

The Venn diagram completely satisfies the conditions of the argument, and is the only diagram that will do so. Thus we see that the argument is **valid**. If we accept the information in the hypothesis as true, then the logical conclusion is also true.

Now consider the following argument:

Hypothesis: All males play baseball.
All boys play baseball.
Conclusion: All boys are male.

Do you see that each of the following Venn diagrams correctly represents the conditions of the hypothesis?

Figure 1

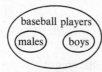

Figure 2

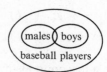

Figure 3

However, do you see that only the diagram in Figure 1 also satisfies the conditions of the conclusion? In Figure 2 the diagram shows that a possible conclusion is, "No boys are males." The conclusion illustrated in Figure 3 is, "Some boys are males." Since more than one conclusion is logically possible, we say that the argument is **invalid**, even though the statement for the conclusion shown in Figure 1 is a true statement.

Questions

Complete the diagram that accompanies each argument, then decide whether the argument is valid or invalid by noting whether or not the diagram satisfies the conditions of the conclusion.

1. Hypothesis: Some polygons are triangles. Some polygons are quadrilaterals.

   Conclusion: Some triangles are quadrilaterals.

   The argument is __?__.

2. Hypothesis: All X's are Y's. All Z's are Y's.

   Conclusion: All X's are Z's.

   The argument is __?__.

3. Hypothesis: All turtles are amphibians. All amphibians have tails.

   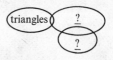

   Conclusion: All turtles have tails.

   The argument is __?__.

For each *valid* argument, draw its Venn diagram; indicate each *invalid* argument by drawing at least two *different* Venn diagrams that satisfy the conditions of the hypothesis.

4. Hypothesis: All juniors are wise people. All wise people are clever.

   Conclusion: All juniors are clever.

5. Hypothesis: Some rectangles are squares. Some rectangles are trapezoids.

   Conclusion: Some squares are trapezoids.

6. Hypothesis: All K's are M's. All J's are M's.

   Conclusion: No K's are J's.

7. Hypothesis: All squares are cubes. No circle is a cube.

   Conclusion: No circle is a square.

The "Water Monster" . . .

A modern hydrofoil . . .

Systems of Open Sentences

The Bell-Baldwin hydrofoil, designed and built by Alexander Graham Bell and F. W. "Casey" Baldwin in the early twentieth century, was called the "Water Monster" because of its unusual size and shape. Its speed-boat record of 70.86 miles an hour, set in 1919, was to be unequalled for over 40 years. A hydrofoil skims over the water acting on the same principle as the airplane wing. Its foils, with propellors attached, extend beneath the boat; as the speed increases, the difference in water pressure on the submerged foils lifts the craft out of the water. Although modern hydrofoils can travel at far higher speeds, their chief use today is for commercial service, at a speed of 35–45 miles an hour, with the comfort of passengers controlled by the automatic pilot acting on the movement of the foils.

Graphical Methods for Solving Systems of Equations

11–1   Graphs of Systems of Linear Equations

We have spent some time working with linear equations in two variables and their number-plane graphs. Such linear equations have the general form $ax + by = c$; however, much more information for graphing is available when a linear equation is written as an equivalent equation in the slope-intercept form.

$$y = \underbrace{mx}_{\text{slope}} + \underbrace{b}_{y\text{-intercept}}$$

The number m, which is the coefficient of x, tells us the slope of the graph, while the number b is the y-intercept, or the value of y at the point where the graph crosses the y-axis.

If we have two equations in two variables, we say that we have a system of equations. Because the two equations impose two conditions on the variables *at the same time*, we often refer to the system as a set of simultaneous **equations** in two variables. The solution set of such a system is the set of all ordered pairs that satisfy *both* equations of the system.

EXAMPLE 1. Solve the system $y = 2x + 1$

$$y = 2x - 2$$

Both equations are in the **slope-intercept** form. Since each has a slope of **2**, do you see that their graphs are parallel lines? Thus there is *no* point which lies on *both* lines, so there is no ordered pair which satisfies both equations. The solution set is ∅.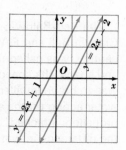

Since solving a set of **simultaneous equations** consists of finding the ordered pairs which make both equations true *simultaneously* (that is, at the same time), do you see that in the case of two equations whose graphs are parallel lines there is no such pair? For this reason, we say that such a system is an inconsistent system. It is not consistent with our wish to find a common solution.

 If the graphs of the two equations in a simultaneous system are different lines having the **same slope**, the lines are parallel and the equations have no common solution; such equations are **inconsistent**.

EXAMPLE 2. Solve the system $y - x = 2$

$$2y = 2x + 4$$

The graphs of the two equations in this system are the same line; we say that the lines coincide. Since every solution of one equation is also a solution of the other, do you agree that this is a consistent system? Do you also see that the equations in the system are equivalent, since their solution sets are the same?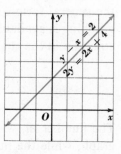

To determine whether or not the two equations in a set of simultaneous linear equations in two variables are equivalent, we can write them in slope-intercept form:

$$y - x = 2 \qquad\qquad 2y = 2x + 4$$
$$y = x + 2 \qquad\qquad y = x + 2$$

Written in this form, the two equations are identical, so we see that their graphs have the same slope and the same *y*-intercept.

If the graphs of the two equations in a simultaneous system are the **same line**, then the equations are **equivalent**, and every solution of one equation is a solution of the other.

ORAL EXERCISES

Tell how to complete each statement.

1. The equation $y = 3x - 1$ is written in the __?__ form.
2. When two lines in a plane are __?__ they have no point in common.
3. The slope of the graph of a linear equation in slope-intercept form is the __?__ of *x*.
4. If two different lines in a plane have the same slope, the lines are __?__ and their equations are __?__.
5. If the graph of a system of equations is two parallel lines, the lines must have the same __?__.
6. If the slope-intercept forms of two linear equations are the same, the equations are __?__.

Tell whether the two lines in each plane are parallel.

7.

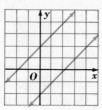

9.

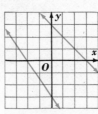

8.

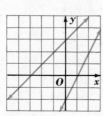

10.

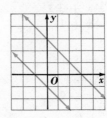

WRITTEN EXERCISES

For the two equations in each system, write the slope-intercept form; then tell whether the graphs of the equations coincide or are parallel lines.

SAMPLE: $y + 3 = x$ *Solution:* $y = x - 3$

$y = 2 + x$ $y = x + 2$

Since the slope of each graph is 1, but the y-intercepts are different, the graphs are parallel lines.

A

1. $x - y = -1$
$3y + 3 = 3x$

2. $y + 1 = 3x$
$2y = 6x - 2$

3. $x + 2y = 8$
$\frac{x}{2} + y = 4$

4. $2x + y = -10$
$x + \frac{y}{2} = -5$

5. $y + \frac{3}{4}x = \frac{1}{2}$
$y - \frac{1}{2} = -\frac{3}{4}x$

6. $2x + y = 4$
$y - 3 = -2x$

7. $y - 6x = 4$
$2y = 12x + 8$

8. $y + 2 = 2x$
$\frac{y}{2} = x - 2$

9. $2y = 4 - 9x$
$y + \frac{9x}{2} + 4 = 0$

10. $4y - 1 = 2x$
$4x + 2 = 8y$

Graph each system of simultaneous equations and tell whether the equations in the system are inconsistent or equivalent.

SAMPLE: $y = 2x - 2$ *Solution:*
$2y + 4 = 4x$

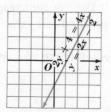

Since the same line is the graph of both equations, the equations are equivalent.

11. $y = -x + 3$
$y = -x + 1$

12. $y - 2x = 6$
$y + 3 = 2x$

13. $y = 2x + \frac{1}{2}$
$4y = 8x + 2$

14. $x + 4 = y$
$y - x = 4$

15. $2y = -2x + 3$
$2y + 2x = 3$

16. $5y = 10x + 5$
$y - 5 = 2x$

B **17.** $\dfrac{5y}{2} = 5x + 10$

$y - 2x = -4$

18. $2x + 3y = -2$

$y + \dfrac{2x}{3} + 2 = 0$

11–2 More about Graphs of Systems of Linear Equations

Usually the graphs of a set of simultaneous linear equations in two variables intersect in *exactly one* point. The graphs of the equations $y = x + 2$ and $y = -x - 4$, shown here, have the point of intersection $(-3, -1)$. From this fact, we conclude that the number pair $(-3, -1)$ is a common solution of the two equations. We can verify this conclusion by replacing x by -3 and y by -1 in both of the original equations.

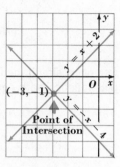

$y =$	$x + 2$
-1	$-3 + 2$
-1	-1

$y =$	$-x - 4$
-1	$-(-3) - 4$
-1	$3 - 4$
-1	-1

Since the two lines intersect in a single point, do you agree that $(-3, -1)$ is the *only* common solution of the two equations? Thus the solution set of the system is $\{(-3, -1)\}$. Since the solution set is *not empty*, the equations in the system are consistent.

Thus we can solve a system of linear equations in two variables by graphing the two equations in the same number plane and determining the coordinates of all points that are common to both graphs.

ORAL EXERCISES

Name the coordinates of the point of intersection of each pair of lines.

1.

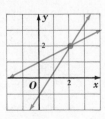

2.

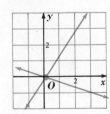

3. 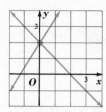 **4.**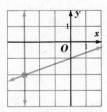

WRITTEN EXERCISES

For each simultaneous system, show whether or not the given number pair satisfies both equations.

SAMPLE: $x + y = 7$
$x - y = 5$; (6, 1)

Solution:

$x + y = 7$		$x - y = 5$	
$6 + 1$	7	$6 - 1$	5
7	7	5	5

(6, 1) satisfies both equations.

A

1. $x + y = 2$
$x - 3 = y$; (1, 1)

2. $2x = y$
$x + 2y = 0$; (0, 0)

3. $x + y = 1$
$x + 1 = y$; (2, −1)

4. $2x + 3y = 2$
$2x - 3y = -2$; $(0, \frac{2}{3})$

5. $x + y = 10$
$x - y = 0$; (5, 5)

6. $x - 2y = 0$
$x + 2y = 3$; $(1, \frac{1}{2})$

Determine the coordinates of the point of intersection of each pair of lines and show that the number pair is a solution of both equations.

SAMPLE: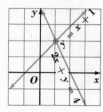

Solution: The lines intersect at (1, 2).

$y = x + 1$		$2x + y = 4$	
2	$1 + 1$	$(2 \cdot 1) + 2$	4
2	2	4	4

7. 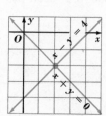 **8.**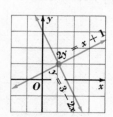

9.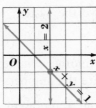

10.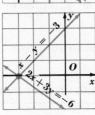

11.

12.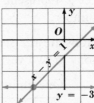

Graph each system of simultaneous equations and name the solution set.

SAMPLE: $x + 2y = 0$
$\quad\quad\quad 2x - y = 0$

Solution: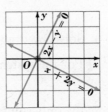

The solution set is $\{(0, 0)\}$.

13. $y - x = 0$
$\quad\ y + x = 2$

14. $y - 2x = 0$
$\quad\ y = 6 - x$

15. $x + y = 3$
$\quad\ x - y = 1$

16. $2x + y = 3$
$\quad\ x + 2y = 0$

17. $x + y = 5$
$\quad\ x + y = 3$

18. $x + y = 0$
$\quad\ x + 2y = 2$

B **19.** $2x - 2y = 4$
$\quad\quad y = x - 2$

20. $y = 2x + 1$
$\quad\ x + y = -2$

21. $y = \frac{2}{3}x + 5$
$\quad\ y = -\frac{2}{3}x + 5$

22. $x = y - 1$
$\quad\ y = x - 1$

23. $x - 3y - 1 = 0$
$\quad\ 2x + 3y + 4 = 0$

24. $-x + y = -2$
$\quad\ 5x - 6 = 2y$

11–3   Problems with Two Variables

We can use a set of simultaneous equations in solving any problem
for which we can translate word sentences into a system of linear

equations in two variables. When we solve the system, we find the answer to the problem.

EXAMPLE: One number is **4** greater than another number. The sum of the numbers is **10**. What are the numbers?

Step 1. Let x represent the first number and y represent the second number.

Step 2. Translate the sentences in the problem into two linear equations in two variables.

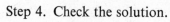

One number is 4 greater than another number.

$$x \qquad = \qquad y + 4$$

The sum of the numbers is 10.

$$x + y \qquad = \quad 10$$

Step 3. Solve by drawing the graph of the system.

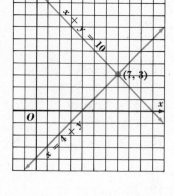

For the system $x = y + 4$
$$x + y = 10$$

the only solution is represented by the intersection of the graphs of the equations in the system. Thus we see that the solution is **(7, 3)**.

Step 4. Check the solution.

$x = y + 4$			$x + y = 10$	
7	3 + 4		7 + 3	10
7	7		10	10

The solution set is $\{(7, 3)\}$.

Step 5. Answer the question. The numbers are 7 and 3.

PROBLEMS

Solve each problem by writing a system of simultaneous equations and determining the intersection of their graphs.

A   **1.** One number is 3 more than another. The sum of the two numbers is 27. What are the numbers?

2. The sum of two numbers is 12. One of the numbers is three times the other. Find the numbers.

3. The sum of two numbers is 14. The difference of the numbers is 8. Find the numbers.

4. A 17 foot length of rope is cut into two pieces. One piece is 3 feet longer than the other. What is the length of each piece of rope?

5. An amount of $11 is divided into two parts. One part contains $5 less than the other. What are the two amounts?

6. Find two numbers having a sum of 8 if one of the numbers is 2 more than the other.

7. The perimeter of a rectangle is 16 feet. It is 4 feet longer than it is wide. What are the dimensions of the rectangle?

B 8. Half the perimeter of a rectangle is 15 inches. Also, the rectangle is 3 inches longer than it is wide. What are the dimensions of the rectangle?

9. Half the perimeter of a house foundation is 20 yards. The house is 4 yards longer than it is wide. Find the dimensions of the house foundation.

10. Mr. Carson owns a piece of property that contains 3 acres more than Mr. Peterson's property. Altogether they own 8 acres. How large is each piece of property?

11. The difference between twice a certain number and a smaller number is 13. The sum of the smaller number and twice the larger is 17. What are the numbers?

12. The difference between twice some number and a smaller number is 11. The sum of the larger number and twice the smaller is 7. What are the numbers?

Algebraic Methods for Solving Systems of Equations

11-4 Addition and Subtraction Methods of Solving Simultaneous Equations

In solving the last three exercises of the set of problems in the last section, you may have had difficulty in determining the solution set of the system of equations because it was not a pair of integers.

For example, in Problem 12 you had to solve the system

$$2x - y = 11$$
$$x + 2y = 7.$$

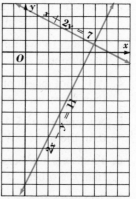

The graphs of the two equations intersect at a point for which x is between **5** and **6**, and y is between **0** and **1**. The only way you can determine the *exact* values is by trial and error. The solution actually is $(5\frac{4}{5}, \frac{3}{5})$.

This experience indicates that the graphical method is not always satisfactory, and that some algebraic method might be more useful. In Example 1 we show a set of simultaneous equations solved both by graphs and by an algebraic method in which we use the addition and subtraction properties of equality to obtain a system equivalent to the original system. We do this in such a way that each equation contains only *one* of the two variables.

EXAMPLE 1. Solve the system $x + y = 3$
$$x - y = 5$$

Graphical Method: The graphs of the two equations appear to intersect at the point $(4, -1)$. Checking in the two equations:

$x +$	$y = 3$	$x -$	$y = 5$
$4 + (-1)$	3	$4 - (-1)$	5
$4 -\ \ 1$	3	$4 +\ \ 1$	5
3	3	5	5

Thus the solution set is $\{(4, -1)\}$.

Algebraic Method: Adding the left members and the right members:

$$x + y = 3$$
$$\underline{x - y = 5}$$
$$2x\qquad\ = 8$$
$$x = 4$$

Subtracting the members of the second equation from the corresponding members of the first:

$$x + y = 3$$
$$\underline{x - y = 5}$$
$$2y = -2$$
$$y = -1$$

We can see on the graph shown here that the system

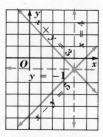

$$x = 4$$
$$y = -1$$

is equivalent to the original system, since it has the same solution set $\{(4, -1)\}$.

The Addition and Subtraction Method illustrated in Example 1 makes use of previously assumed properties of equality to change the simultaneous system into an equivalent system whose solution is obvious. Once we arrived at the equation $x = 4$, we could have shortened the work by noting that this equation assures us that the point of intersection will have **4** as its first coordinate. Then, replacing x in one of the original equations by **4**, we have

$$x + y = 3$$
$$4 + y = 3$$
$$y = -1.$$

Thus we see that when x is **4**, y must be -1 to make the first equation of the original system a true statement. As we have already seen, the ordered pair $(4, -1)$ is also a solution of the second equation, and the solution set is $\{(4, -1)\}$.

EXAMPLE 2. Use the algebraic method in solving the system

$$x + 3y = 15$$
$$x + y = 7$$

Subtracting the members of the second equation from the corresponding members of the first, we have

$$x + 3y = 15$$
$$\underline{x + y = 7}$$
$$2y = 8$$
$$y = 4$$

Replacing *y* by **4** in the second equation:

$$x + 4 = 7$$
$$x = 3$$

Checking the pair **(3, 4)** in both equations:

$x +$ $3y = 15$	
$3 + 3(4)$	15
15	15

$x + y = 7$	
$3 + 4$	7
7	7

The solution set is $\{(3, 4)\}$.

ORAL EXERCISES

Tell whether you would add or subtract to get an equivalent equation in which only one variable appears. Give a reason for your answer.

1. $x + y = 7$
    $x - y = 1$

2. $x - y = 3$
    $x + y = -3$

3. $x + 3y = 6$
    $2x + 3y = 8$

4. $4x - 4y = 2$
    $x - 4y = 11$

5. $r + s = 45$
    $r - s = 21$

6. $3p - q = 10$
    $3p + 2q = 8$

7. $11s - t = 0$
    $3s + t = 42$

8. $2 = a - 3b$
    $-4 = a - b$

WRITTEN EXERCISES

Solve each system of equations by the algebraic method. Check each solution set by substituting in both equations.

SAMPLE: $x + y = 14$
         $2x - y = 10$

Solution: $x + y = 14$
           $2x - y = 10$ Replace *x* by 8 in the first equation:
Add: $3x = 24$ $8 + y = 14$
         $x = 8$ $y = 6$

Check:

$x + y = 14$	
$8 + 6$	14
14	14

$2x - y = 10$	
$16 - 6$	10
10	10

A

1. $x + y = 5$
$x - y = 1$

2. $x + y = 3$
$x - y = 1$

3. $m + n = 4$
$m - n = 2$

4. $r + 2s = 2$
$r + s = 0$

5. $c + d = 74$
$c - d = 16$

6. $3s - t = 18$
$3s + t = 60$

7. $5b - c = 7$
$3b - c = 5$

8. $3s + 2t = 17$
$s + 2t = 5$

9. $4k - 5n = 10$
$2k + 5n = -10$

10. $5m - 3n = 19$
$2m + 3n = -5$

11. $x + 2y = -4$
$-7x + 2y = 4$

12. $2a + b = 2$
$a - b = -5$

13. $r + s - 4 = 0$
$r - s + 2 = 0$

14. $2w - 3z = -4$
$4w - 3z = -6$

15. $2x + y = -2$
$2x + 3y = 6$

16. $2x + 3y = -1$
$2x - y = -9$

B

17. $x - 3y = 0$
$2x + 3y + 4 = 0$

18. $5x - 2y = 6$
$2y = -4 + 2x$

19. $2m - 265 = -11n$
$5m + 11n = 316$

20. $8c = 158 - 3d$
$8c = 230 - 7d$

C

21. $\dfrac{x}{2} + \dfrac{y}{4} = 5$
$\dfrac{x}{2} - \dfrac{y}{2} = 1$

22. $0.25x + 0.87y = 1.50$
$0.25x + 0.27y = 0.50$

23. $\frac{3}{4}x + y = 1$

$\frac{1}{4}x - y = 1$

24. $0.7(a - b) = 7$
$0.5(a + b) = 10$

PROBLEMS

Translate each problem into a system of simultaneous equations. Do not solve.

SAMPLE: One number is three times another. Their sum is 24.

Solution: $x = 3y$ and $x + y = 24$

A

1. One number is nine times another. Their sum is 75.

2. One number is one-half of another. Their sum is $6\frac{3}{4}$.

3. The sum of two numbers is 24. One number is six times the other.

4. The difference of two numbers is 17. One number is five times the other.

5. The sum of the measures of two angles is 90 degrees. The measure of the larger angle is 30 degrees greater than the smaller angle.

6. The length of a rectangle is six times its width. The perimeter of the rectangle is 120 feet.

For each problem write a system of equations in two variables; then solve the system and give the answer to the problem.

SAMPLE: Half the distance around the foundation of a house is 84 feet. The foundation is 14 feet longer than it is wide. Find the dimensions of the foundation.

Solution:

$$
\begin{array}{lll}
x + y = 84 & x + y = 84 & 49 + y = 84 \\
x = y + 14 & \underline{x - y = 14} & y = 84 - 49 \\
& 2x = 98 & y = 35 \\
& x = 49 &
\end{array}
$$

The length is 49 feet and the width is 35 feet.

[B] 7. Half the perimeter of a building is 72 feet. The length of the building is 12 feet more than the width. What are the dimensions of the building?

8. Mr. Norton's farm is 64 acres larger than Mr. Kenton's farm. Together the farms contain 288 acres. How many acres are in each farm?

9. The difference between twice some number and a smaller number is 21. The sum of twice the larger number and the smaller number is 27. Find the numbers.

10. If Carol were twice as old she would be 18 years older than William. In that case their combined ages would be 38. Find the ages of Carol and William.

11–5 Using Multiplication in Solving Simultaneous Equations

For many systems of equations, neither adding nor subtracting leads to an equivalent equation in which only one variable appears. For these, it is necessary to use the multiplication property of equality first.

EXAMPLE 1. Solve the system $3x + 4y = 45$
$$6x - 2y = 30$$

If we add the two equations of this system, we have the equation $9x + 2y = 75$; if we subtract the second equation from the first, we have $-3x + 6y = 15$. Neither equation is what we want: an equation in which a single variable appears.

Now, what happens when we use the multiplication property of equality to multiply both members of the **second equation** by 2? We have the equivalent system

$$3x + 4y = 45$$
$$12x - 4y = 60.$$

Adding the members of the two equations:

$$15x = 105$$
$$x = 7$$

If we replace x by 7 in the first equation of the original system, we have

$$3(7) + 4y = 45$$
$$4y = 24$$
$$y = 6.$$

It appears that $(7, 6)$ is a solution, which we check by substituting in both of the original equations.

$3x$	$+$	$4y$	$= 45$
$3(7)$	$+$	$4(6)$	45
21	$+$	24	45
		45	45

$6x$	$-$	$2y$	$= 30$
$6(7)$	$-$	$2(6)$	30
42	$-$	12	30
		30	30

The solution set is $\{(7, 6)\}$.

EXAMPLE 2. Solve the system $2x + 5y = 28$
$$3x + 2y = 31$$

This time we need to apply the multiplication property of equality to *both* equations. Suppose that we multiply the first equation by 3 and the second equation by 2. We then have the equivalent system

$$6x + 15y = 84$$
$$6x + 4y = 62.$$

Subtracting the second equation from the first:

$$11y = 22$$
$$y = 2$$

Replacing *y* by **2** in the second equation of the original system:

$$3x + 2(2) = 31$$
$$3x = 27$$
$$x = 9$$

Checking the apparent solution, **(9, 2)**, in each of the original equations:

$2x$ + $5y$ = 28	
$2(9) + 5(2)$	28
$18 + 10$	28
28	28

$3x$ + $2y$ = 31	
$3(9) + 2(2)$	31
$27 + 4$	31
31	31

The solution set is $\{(9, 2)\}$.

ORAL EXERCISES

For each system, name the number by which you might multiply one equation so that addition or subtraction of the equations will give an equivalent equation in which only one variable appears.

SAMPLE: $2x + y = 10$
$x + 3y = 16$

What you say: Either multiply the first equation by 3 or the second equation by 2.

1. $m + n = 10$
$2m + 3n = 21$

2. $x - 5y = 16$
$2x + 3y = 6$

3. $4a - 5b = -1$
$a + b = 7$

4. $3r + 2s = 8$
$6r - s = 10$

5. $5x - 7y = -5$
$2x - y = 7$

6. $7a + 10b = 0$
$3a + b = 15$

7. $4p - 9q = 12$
$8p - 15q = 24$

8. $2w - 5z = 6$
$6w + 3z = -4$

For each system, tell how to multiply each equation in order to have an equivalent system which can be solved by either addition or subtraction.

SAMPLE: $6x - 5y = 8$
$4x + 2y = 10$

What you say: Either multiply the the first equation by 2 and the second by 3, or multiply the first by 2 and the second by 5.

9. $3m - 6n = -3$
$2m - 9n = 0$

12. $5a + 12b = 31$
$7a + 8b = 50$

10. $6x - 5y = -8$
$4x + 3y = 7$

13. $4c - 7d = 8$
$5c + 9d = 45$

11. $9s - 14t = 8$
$6s - 5t = 3$

14. $3x + 6y = 24$
$5x + 4y = 22$

WRITTEN EXERCISES

Solve each system of equations; check the solution set by substituting in both equations.

SAMPLE: $2x + y = 12$
$x - 2y = 1$

Solution:
$2x + y = 12$ $4x + 2y = 24$ Replacing x by 5,
$x - 2y = 1$ $\underline{x - 2y = 1}$ $4(5) + 2y = 24$
$5x = 25$ $2y = 4$
$x = 5$ $y = 2$

The solution set is $\{(5, 2)\}$.

1. $2a + 3b = 12$
$3a - b = 7$

8. $-4c - d = 5$
$3c + 3d = 0$

2. $m - n = 73$
$2m - 7n = 21$

9. $4x + 3y = 6$
$2x - y = -2$

3. $3x + y = 8$
$x + 3y = 8$

10. $2r - s = 5$
$r + 2s = 25$

4. $5w + z = 4$
$w - 2z = 3$

11. $3a + b - 3 = 0$
$2a - 3b - 13 = 0$

5. $c - 2d = 5$
$-5c + 4d = -22$

12. $4x - y = 7$
$3x + y = 7$

6. $3x - 8y = 6$
$x - y = 52$

13. $2a + 5b = 18$
$3a + 4b = 27$

7. $2b - 3c = 1$
$3b - 4c = 7$

14. $6q + 12r = 5$
$9q - 8r = 1$

B **15.** $\dfrac{2x}{3} + 2y = 1$

$\dfrac{4x}{9} - \dfrac{y}{3} = \dfrac{1}{9}$

17. $\dfrac{m}{3} + \dfrac{n}{9} = 1$

$\dfrac{m}{2} + \dfrac{n}{3} = 2$

16. $\dfrac{c}{5} + \dfrac{d}{2} = -1$

$\dfrac{d}{4} - \dfrac{c}{3} = -\dfrac{1}{2}$

18. $\dfrac{x}{4} - \dfrac{y}{6} = 0$

$\dfrac{3x}{8} + \dfrac{5y}{12} = -4$

PROBLEMS

For each problem, write a system of equations in two variables; then solve
the system and give the answer to the problem.

1. The sum of two numbers is 30. Twice the first number, reduced by
   three times the second number is 5. Find the numbers.

2. The ages of Tim's father and mother total 68 years. If his father's age
   were doubled the difference between their ages would be 40 years.
   What are the ages of Tim's father and mother?

3. Tom bought 3 erasers and 2 pencils for 34¢ at the store; Karen bought
   4 erasers and 5 pencils for 57¢ at the same store. What is the price of
   an eraser? a pencil?

4. An auto dealer has a total of 30 cars and trucks. When 2 more cars
   are delivered he will have 3 times as many cars as trucks. How many
   of each does he have now?

5. Tom buys 2 six-pack cartons of cola and 3 bags of potato chips for
   $3.10. He later buys another carton of cola and 2 bags of potato chips
   for $1.85. What is the price of a carton of cola? What is the price of
   a bag of potato chips?

11–6   The Substitution Method of Solving Simultaneous Equations

Some systems of equations can be solved readily by another algebraic
method called the Substitution Method. This method uses the fact that
both equations of a simultaneous system in two variables must be true
at the same time. It consists of transforming one equation so that we
have an expression for one of the two variables in terms of the other.
This expression is then substituted in the other equation, as illustrated
in the following examples.

EXAMPLE 1.   Solve the system $x + 2y = 5$

$$x = 3y$$

In this system, the second equation tells us at once
that x is the same as $3y$, so we replace x by $3y$ in the
first equation:

$$3y + 2y = 5$$
$$5y = 5$$
$$y = 1$$

Replacing y by **1** in the second equation:

$$x = 3(1) = 3$$

We leave it for you to check the solution **(3, 1)** by substituting **3** for x and **1** for y in *both* of the original equations, thus verifying that the solution set is $\{(3, 1)\}$.

EXAMPLE 2. Solve the system $3x + 2y = 5$
$$x + y = 2$$

Transforming the second equation, we get

$$x + y = 2$$
$$y = 2 - x.$$

Replacing y by $2 - x$ in the first equation:

$$3x + 2(2 - x) = 5$$
$$3x + 4 - 2x = 5$$
$$x = 1$$

Replacing x by **1** in the transformed second equation:

$$y = 2 - x$$
$$y = 2 - 1 = 1$$

Now *you* check the solution **(1, 1)** by substituting in both original equations, and verify that the solution set is $\{(1, 1)\}$.

WRITTEN EXERCISES

Solve each system of equations by using the Substitution Method. Check your answers in both equations of the system.

1. $3x + y = 5$
$\quad\quad\ y = 2x$

2. $\quad\quad r = -3s$
$\quad r + 5s = 2$

3. $3a + 2b = 5$
$\quad\ a + b = 2$

4. $m + n = -5$
$\quad\quad n = 1 + m$

5. $\quad\quad q = 5p$
$\quad 2p + q = 7$

6. $2c - d = 7$
$\quad\ c - d = 1$

7. $3r - s = 20$
$\quad\ r - s = 2$

8. $2b + 3c = 19$
$\quad\ b - c = 12$

9. $5x - 3y = -1$
$x + y = 3$

10. $x + 3y = 2$
$2x + 3y = 7$

11. $3w - 2z = 5$
$w + 2z = 15$

12. $m - 2n = 0$
$4m - 3n = 15$

13. $m - 3n = -4$
$2m + 6n = 5$

14. $3c - 2d = 3$
$2c - d = 2$

15. $x + 7y = 10$
$3x - 4y = 5$

16. $2p + 3q = 22$
$-2p + q = -6$

B **17.** $3r + 3s = 33$
$2r - 3s = 0$

18. $3a - 4b = 0$
$2a + b = 33$

19. $x + y = 9$
$x - \frac{1}{3}y = 5$

20. $m + n = 9$
$m - \frac{1}{4}n = 4$

C **21.** $a - b = 8$
$\frac{a}{3} - \frac{b}{2} = 1$

22. $\frac{s}{3} - t = 2$
$s - t = 20$

23. $x - \frac{y}{2} = 4$
$x + y = 7$

24. $3a - 2b = 11$
$a - \frac{b}{2} = 4$

PROBLEMS

Translate each problem into a system of simultaneous equations and solve by using the Substitution Method.

1. Half the sum of two numbers is $\frac{5}{2}$ and half their difference is $-\frac{5}{2}$. What are the numbers?

2. Half the sum of two numbers is $\frac{3}{2}$ and half their difference is $\frac{1}{2}$. What are the numbers?

3. The average of two numbers is $\frac{5}{6}$. One half their difference is $-\frac{1}{2}$. What are the numbers?

4. The perimeter of a rectangle is 92 inches. The length is 6 inches more than the width. Find the dimensions of the rectangle.

5. The sum of two numbers is 28. The sum of twice the first number and three times the second number is 72. What are the numbers?

6. The difference of two numbers is -5. The sum of three times the first number and five times the second number is -31. What are the numbers?

Systems of Inequalities

11–7 Graphs of Systems of Linear Inequalities Involving < and >

You will recall that the graph of the inequality $x + y < 6$ is a **half-plane**. To draw its graph, we begin by graphing the related equation $x + y = 6$ as a **dashed line**. Then we decide on which side of the line the graph of the inequality lies by selecting a sample point from one of the half-planes and testing its coordinates in the inequality. For example, consider the point $(0, 0)$. Since the statement $0 + 0 < 6$ is *true*, we see that the half-plane that is the graph of $x + y < 6$ must contain this point. The graph is shown in Figure 11–1.

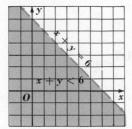

Figure 11–1

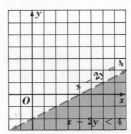

Figure 11–2

Similarly, to draw the graph of the inequality $x - 2y > 4$, we draw the graph of $x - 2y = 4$ as a dashed line. Using $(0, 0)$ again as a sample point, we find that $0 - 2(0) > 4$ is *false*, so we know that the half-plane that is the graph of $x - 2y > 4$ must *not* contain this point, as is shown in Figure 11–2.

The graph of the simultaneous system consisting of the same two inequalities

$$x + y < 6$$
$$x - 2y > 4$$

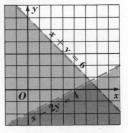

is shown here. Both inequalities have been graphed on the same number plane. The region that the two graphs have in common (the intersection of the two graphs) is the graph of the system. Remember that the points on the dashed lines are *not* included in the graph.

ORAL EXERCISES

Tell which of the following ordered pairs correspond to points in the graph shown here of the system

$$x + y > 2$$
$$x < y.$$

1. $(0, 0)$

2. $(3, 1)$

3. $(-2, 2)$

4. $(1, 2)$

5. $(0, 3)$

6. $(3, 0)$

7. $(-1, 4)$

8. $(0, 2)$

9. $(1, 1\frac{1}{2})$

10. $(0, 2\frac{1}{2})$

11. $(1, 1)$

12. $(-3, 3)$

13. $(-2, 1)$

14. $(1, 0)$

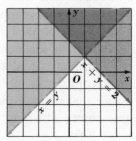

WRITTEN EXERCISES

For each system of inequalities, write three ordered pairs that are in the solution set and three that are *not;* the graph of each system is shown to help you with your selection.

1. $x + y > 3$
   $x - y < 3$

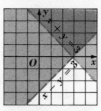

3. $x + y < 2$
   $x - y < 2$

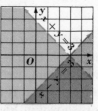

2. $x + y < 3$
   $x - y > 3$

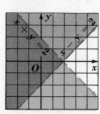

4. $x + y > 2$
   $x - y > 2$

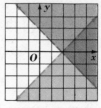

Graph each system of simultaneous inequalities.

5. $x + y < 3$
   $x - y < 3$

6. $y < 2x$
   $x > 1$

7. $y > 2x$
   $y > 1$

8. $x + y > 4$
   $x - y < 4$

9. $y > x$
   $y > x - 4$

10. $x + y < 2$
   $x - y < 2$

11. $y > x$
     $y > x + 2$

12. $x + y > 5$
     $x + y > 4$

13. $y < 2x + 1$
     $y > x - 2$

14. $y > 3x - 6$
     $y < 2x + 4$

15. $y < x - 1$
     $y > 1 - x$

16. $-y > 2$
     $-x < y$

17. $-y < 3$
     $-x > y$

18. $y < 3x + 1$
     $x + y < 7$

Write the system of inequalities whose graph is the shaded region. Hint: Use the slope-intercept formula $y = mx + b$.

C   **19.**

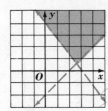

20.

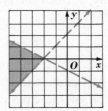

11–8 Graphs of Systems of Linear Inequalities Involving $\leq$ and $\geq$

It is no doubt apparent that the same procedures that were used in the last section can be applied in graphing the solution set of a system of inequalities such as $y \geq 3x - 2$ and $x + y \leq 5$.

We begin by drawing the graphs of the related equations $y = 3x - 2$ and $x + y = 5$, as shown in Figures 11–3 and 11–4. Note that this time solid lines are used, since points *on* the lines must be included in the graphs of the inequalities. Using $(0, 0)$ as a sample point, we check that $0 > 3(0) - 2$ and $0 + 0 < 5$ are both *true* statements. This tells us that each graph must include the half-plane that contains the point $(0, 0)$.

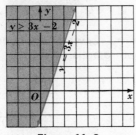

Figure 11–3

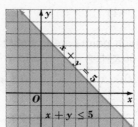

Figure 11–4

Verify that the graph of the inequality $y \geq 3x - 2$ is shown in Figure 11–3 and that Figure 11–4 shows the graph of $x + y \leq 5$.

The intersection of the two graphs is the graph of the simultaneous system
$$y \geq 3x - 2$$
$$x + y \leq 5.$$

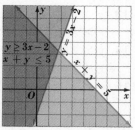

In the figure at the right, the graph of the solution set of the system is the darkly shaded region. Note that this time the point of intersection of the two lines is included, as well as the portions of the lines that lie in the shaded areas.

Sometimes a simultaneous system consists of an equation and an inequality, such as the system
$$x + y \geq 4$$
$$x - y = 0.$$

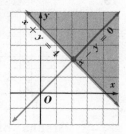

The graph of the inequality $x + y \geq 4$ is the shaded half-plane and its boundary, shown here. The graph of the equation, of course, is a line, as indicated. Do you agree that the heavy red portion of the line in the figure, including the point $(2, 2)$, is the graph of the system?

ORAL EXERCISES

Tell which points are in only the graph of $x - y \geq 2$, which are in only the graph of $y \geq -x + 2$, and which are in both graphs.

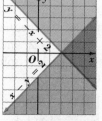

1. $(3, 0)$ **7.** $(-2, 0)$

2. $(0, 0)$ **8.** $(-2, 4)$

3. $(1, 2)$ **9.** $(-1, -6)$

4. $(2, -1)$ **10.** $(2, 0)$

5. $(4, 1)$ **11.** $(2, \frac{1}{2})$

6. $(4, -1)$ **12.** $(2\frac{1}{2}, 0)$

Tell which points are in only the graph of $x = -2$, which are in only the graph of $x + y < -1$, and which are in both graphs.

13. $(0, 0)$ **18.** $(-2, 0)$

14. $(-2, -1)$ **19.** $(-2, -2)$

15. $(1, 3)$ **20.** $(-3, -1)$

16. $(-1, 5)$ **21.** $(0, 4)$

17. $(-1, -5)$ **22.** $(-2, -10)$

WRITTEN EXERCISES

Graph each simultaneous system.

A

1. $y \leq x + 4$
$\quad y \geq x - 3$

2. $y \leq x - 1$
$\quad y \geq 2x + 2$

3. $y \geq 3x$
$\quad y \leq 3$

4. $y \geq x$
$\quad y \geq -1$

5. $y \leq 2x - 1$
$\quad y \geq x - 2$

6. $y \geq 2x + 1$
$\quad y \leq -x + 2$

7. $y \leq -x + 1$
$\quad y \geq 2x$

8. $y \leq -x + 3$
$\quad y \geq -1$

9. $y \leq -x - 2$
$\quad y \leq -1$

10. $x = 3$
$\quad x \geq y$

Graph each simultaneous system; then write three ordered pairs that are in the solution set and three pairs that are not.

B

11. $y \geq -x + 1$
$\quad y > x - 1$

12. $y > -2$
$\quad x \leq -3$

13. $y < 3x - 1$
$\quad y \leq \frac{x}{2} + 2$

14. $x + y \geq 3$
$\quad x = 4$

15. $x + y \leq 2$
$\quad x = -1$

16. $y \leq 3x + 1$
$\quad x + y = 7$

17. $x + 3y \geq 2$
$\quad x + 3y < 5$

18. $2x - 3y = 5$
$\quad x + 4y < 2$

Write the system of inequalities whose graph is shown.

C

19.

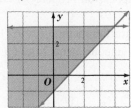

20.

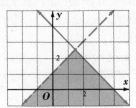

CHAPTER SUMMARY

Inventory of Structure and Concepts

1. A system of equations in two variables imposes two conditions on the variables at the same time; such a system is called a set of **simultaneous equations.**

2. If the graphs of the two equations in a simultaneous system are different lines having the same slope, the lines are parallel; the equations are called **inconsistent** because they have no common solution.

3. If the equations in a simultaneous system have at least one common solution, they are **consistent**; if their graphs coincide, the equations are **equivalent** and every solution of one equation is a solution of the other.

4. If the equations in a simultaneous system are consistent but not equivalent, their graphs intersect in one point, their **point of intersection**.

5. The solution set of a system of simultaneous equations in two variables is the set of all ordered pairs that correspond to points common to the graphs of the two equations.

6. A system of equations in two variables can be solved algebraically by **addition** or **subtraction** if either operation leads to an equivalent equation in which only one of the variables appears.

7. The multiplication property of equality can be applied to one or both equations of a system in order to transform it into an equivalent system to which the Addition or Subtraction Method can be applied.

8. An alternate method for solving a system of equations in two variables is the Substitution Method.

9. The graph of the solution set of a system of linear inequalities in two variables is the intersection of the graphs of the two inequalities.

Vocabulary and Spelling

simultaneous equations (*p. 358*)
parallel lines (*p. 358*)
inconsistent equations (*p. 358*)
equivalent equations (*p. 358*)
coincide (*p. 358*)
consistent equations (*p. 358*)
point of intersection (*p. 361*)

addition or subtraction method (*p. 365*)
multiplication property of equality (*p. 370*)
substitution method (*p. 374*)
simultaneous inequalities (*p. 377*)

Chapter Test

Graph each system of equations and determine its solution set.

1. $2x + y = 0$
$x + 2y = 6$

2. $y = x + 3$
$y = -2x$

Solve each system of equations by using an algebraic method.

3. $x + 2y = 6$
$\quad x - y = -9$

5. $5a - 4b = 14$
$\quad 5a + 2b = 8$

4. $2m + 3n = 122$
$\quad 2m + \ n = 78$

6. $5t - 3s = -4$
$\quad 4t + 7s = 25$

Complete each statement.

7. The graph of a linear equation is a __?__ .

8. If the graphs of two different equations are parallel lines, they have the same __?__ .

9. If the graphs of two equations coincide, the equations are __?__ .

10. The graph of a linear equation in two variables separates the number plane into two __?__ .

Complete the following statements about the graph shown here.

11. The slope–intercept form of the equation $y - x = 2$ is __?__ .

12. The point of intersection of the graphs of $y - x = 2$ and $y - 2x = 0$ is __?__ .

13. The y-intercept of the graph of $y - x = 2$ is __?__ .

14. The solution set of the simultaneous system represented is __?__ .

Questions 15–18 refer to the graph of the system of inequalities $x + y > 3$ and $2x + y < 4$, shown here.

15. Name two points in the graph of $x + y > 3$ that are *not* in the graph of $2x + y < 4$.

16. Which of the inequalities in the system is satisfied by the solution $(0, 0)$?

17. Name three ordered pairs that satisfy *both* inequalities in the system.

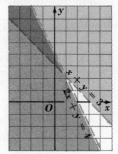

18. What is the point of intersection of the graphs of the equations $x + y = 3$ and $2x + y = 4$? Is this point the graph of a solution of the system of inequalities shown?

Chapter Review

11–1 Graphs of Systems of Linear Equations

For each simultaneous system tell whether the graphs of the equations coincide or are parallel lines. (Do not draw the graphs.)

1. $y = 3x - 2$
$y = 3x + 1$

2. $4y - 4x = 8$
$y = x - 2$

3. $y = -x + 4$
$y = -x - 1$

By making a number-plane graph, show whether the equations in each simultaneous system are equivalent or inconsistent.

4. $y = 2x + 6$
$y = 2x - 3$

5. $y - 2 = 2x$
$3y = 6x + 6$

6. $y - x = 0$
$x = y$

11–2 More about Graphs of Systems of Linear Equations

Show whether or not each number pair is a solution of the system.

7. $x + 2y = 10$
$3y - x = 0$; $(6, 2)$

8. $y = -x$
$5y = -x + 2$; $(\frac{1}{3}, -\frac{1}{3})$

Graph each simultaneous system and find its solution set.

9. $y - 2x = 3$
$2y = x$

10. $2y - x = 2$
$y + 2x = 2$

11. $x - y = 4$
$y = -4$

11–3 Problems with Two Variables

Find the solution of each problem by writing a system of simultaneous equations and determining the intersection of their graphs.

12. One of two numbers is 5 more than the other. The sum of the numbers is -1. What are the numbers?

13. A carpenter saws a 16-foot wooden plank into two pieces such that one is $2\frac{1}{2}$ feet longer than the other. How long is each piece of the plank?

11–4 Addition and Subtraction Methods of Solving Simultaneous Equations

Solve each system of equations by addition or subtraction.

14. $3x + 2y = 17$
$x + 2y = -9$

15. $x + y = 8$
$x - y = 3$

16. $2a + 5b = -12$
$4a - 5b = 0$

11–5   Using Multiplication in Solving Simultaneous Equations

Solve each system of equations, and check your answers.

17. $x + 3y = 25$ **18.** $2x + y = 2$ **19.** $6x - 3y = 18$
        $2x - y = 8$ $4x + 3y = 0$ $5x + 2y = 6$

Write a system of equations and solve it to complete this problem.

20. Three times some number, increased by seven times a second number is 5. The sum of the numbers is 3. Find the numbers.

11–6   The Substitution Method of Solving Simultaneous Equations

Solve each system of equations by the Substitution Method.

21. $x + y = 2$ **22.** $2x - y = 9$ **23.** $m + n = 2$
        $3x + 2y = 10$ $x + y = 0$ $3m + 2n = 5$

11–7   Graphs of Systems of Linear Inequalities Involving < and >

Graph each system of inequalities.

24. $x - y < 5$ **25.** $2x + y > 4$ **26.** $x + y > 1$
        $x + y < 2$ $x - y > 4$ $x - y < 3$

11–8   Graphs of Systems of Linear Inequalities Involving ≤ and ≥

Graph each system of inequalities.

27. $y \leq x + 3$ **28.** $y \leq x - 3$ **29.** $x + y = 1$
        $y \geq x - 2$ $y \geq 2x + 2$ $x - y < 2$

Review of Skills

Express each of the following as a terminating or a repeating decimal.

1. $\frac{1}{3}$ **3.** $3 \div 8$ **5.** $1\frac{3}{4}$ **7.** $\frac{39}{100}$

2. $\frac{4}{5}$ **4.** $\frac{1}{12}$ **6.** $\frac{8}{3}$ **8.** $37 \div 1000$

Round off each decimal to the nearest tenth.

9. 73.146   **11.** 5.333   **13.** 15.006

10. 0.496   **12.** 0.099   **14.** 3.995

Simplify each expression.

15. $n \cdot n \cdot n = $?   **17.** $(-2)^2 = $?   **19.** $\frac{1}{2} \cdot \frac{1}{2} \cdot \frac{1}{2} = $?

16. $x^2 \cdot x^2 \cdot x^2 = $?   **18.** $-(5)^3 = $?   **20.** $(-3)(-3)(-3) = $?

Express each number as the quotient of two integers.

21. $5\frac{1}{2}$ **23.** 0.05   **25.** 9

22. -3.5 **24.** 4.1   **26.** -6

Find the area of each square or circle. (Use $\pi = 3.14$.)

27.   **28.** 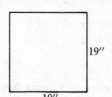   **29.**

Find the total surface area and the volume of each cube.

30.   **31.** 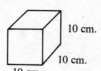   **32.**

Name the legs and the hypotenuse in each right triangle.

33.   **34.**   **35.**

Use the Pythagorean Theorem to find the third side of each right triangle.

36.   **37.**   **38.**

Simplify each expression by factoring.

39. $\dfrac{x^2 - 1}{x + 1}$ **40.** $\dfrac{a + b}{a^2 - b^2}$

41. $\dfrac{x^2 + 7x + 12}{x + 3}$

42. $\dfrac{n - 3}{n + 3} \cdot \dfrac{5n + 15}{1}$

Find the solution set for each equation if the domain of the variable is {the directed numbers}.

43. $m^2 + 7m + 10 = 0$ **45.** $2m^2 - 5m = 3$

44. $t^2 - 4 = 0$ **46.** $4x - 12 = 0$

■ ■

CHECK POINT
FOR EXPERTS

Modular Mathematics: Addition and Subtraction

The sets of numbers that we ordinarily use in mathematics are **infinite** sets, such as {the integers}, {the rational numbers}, and {the real numbers}. Now we are going to investigate some mathematics, called **modular mathematics,** which will use a **finite** set of numbers.

Figure 1

A clock face like that shown in Figure 1 will help us to interpret operations in what we shall call the **Mod 5 system.** Note that the set of numbers for the system is {0, 1, 2, 3, 4}, which, as you see, is a **finite** set. Do you see why we call it **Mod 5?**

Let us agree that the single hand on the clock can move either in the same direction as on an ordinary clock, which we call the **clockwise** direction, or in the opposite, or **counterclockwise**, direction. In modular systems, **addition** is indicated by the symbol $\oplus$; on the clock, addition is represented by a **clockwise** motion of the hand.

Figure 2

To find the sum represented by **2 $\oplus$ 4**, we begin at zero and move the clock hand **2** units in the **clockwise** direction, and then **4** units more, also **clockwise**, as is shown by the arrows in Figure 2. We finish at **1**, so in the Mod 5 system we find that

$$2 \oplus 4 = 1.$$

Subtraction in modular systems is indicated by the symbol $\ominus$; as you might expect, we represent subtraction on the clock by a **counterclockwise** motion of the hand.

We use the clock to find the result of $2 \ominus 3$ by starting at zero, moving **2** units in the **clockwise** direction, and then **3** units in the **counterclockwise** direction. See how this is shown by the arrows in Figure 3. Do you agree that in the Mod 5 system

$$2 \ominus 3 = 4?$$

Figure 3

As you may have guessed, another way to find the meaning of $2 \ominus 3$ would be to apply the idea of equivalent sentences.

$$2 \ominus 3 = ? \quad \text{is equivalent to} \quad 3 \oplus ? = 2.$$

Look at the clock and see that for the hand to move from **3** to **2** in the **clockwise** direction, a move of **4** units is needed. So $3 \oplus 4 = 2$, and the question mark should be replaced by **4**.

Questions

For each of the following, find the number that will make the statement true in the Mod 5 system.

1. $4 \oplus 3 = ?$ **4.** $(0 \oplus 3) \oplus 1 = ?$ **7.** $4 \ominus 3 = ?$

2. $2 \oplus 2 = ?$ **5.** $3 \oplus 4 = ?$ **8.** $1 \ominus 3 = ?$

3. $3 \oplus 2 = ?$ **6.** $4 \oplus (4 \oplus 3) = ?$ **9.** $0 \ominus 3 = ?$

10. Complete the table at the right, showing addition in the Mod 5 system.

$\oplus$	0	1	2	3	4
0		1			
1			3		
2				0	
3					
4		1			

11. Is there an identity element for addition in the Mod 5 system? If so, what is it?

12. Is addition a commutative operation in the Mod 5 system? Explain your answer.

13. Is addition an associative operation in the Mod 5 system? Explain your answer.

Write each subtraction sentence as an equivalent addition sentence, then use the table completed in Question 10 to solve the sentence for Mod 5.

14. $4 \ominus 3 = ?$ **16.** $1 \ominus 3 = ?$ **18.** $2 \ominus 4 = ?$

15. $3 \ominus 4 = ?$ **17.** $3 \ominus 3 = ?$ **19.** $3 \ominus 2 = ?$

20. The clock shown here represents a Mod 7 system.

Mod 7

    a. Construct an addition table for the system.

    b. Does the system have an identity element? If so, what is it?

    c. Is the operation of addition both commutative and associative in this system? Explain your answer.

The Hughes Electric Cookstove, 1909 . . .

A modern electric Counterange . . .

The Real Number System

Although the World's Columbian Exposition in Chicago in 1893 featured an electric kitchen, it was not until the early part of the twentieth century that electric ranges were generally available. About 1909, the Hughes Electric Heating Company, a pioneer in the industry, baked the first loaf of bread to be cooked with electricity; the stove pictured is now owned by the Henry Ford Museum. By 1915 the idea of electric cooking had definitely taken hold. Contrast the open-wire heating elements of the early range with the modern "Counterange" and its flat glass-ceramic rangetop that shows no heating units or burner openings. Only the area marked by a sunburst heats up when the unit is turned on; adjacent areas remain cool. With its self-cleaning oven, it represents a contribution of mathematics-based technology in making housework easier and more pleasant.

Rational Numbers

12–1   Fractional Representations of Rational Numbers

You are familiar with the set of whole numbers, the basic operations performed on them, and the properties of those operations. The whole number system is the set containing zero and the positive integers, together with the operations and their properties.

Early in the study of arithmetic the number system which you used was extended to include fractional numbers, the numbers that can be represented by numerals like $\frac{5}{8}$ and $\frac{7}{2}$, called "fractions." Including the fractions allowed you to solve problems like $3 \div 5 = ?$, which has no solution in the set of whole numbers. The set of all positive numbers that can be written in fractional form is called the set of positive rational numbers. The positive integers belong to this set, because any integer can be written in fractional form. For example

$$9 = \frac{9}{1} = \frac{18}{2} = \frac{27}{3} = \frac{36}{4}, \text{ and so on.}$$

Notice that zero is not included in the set of positive rational numbers, since it is not positive. Zero is *neither* positive *nor* negative.

We further extended our number system to include all **negative** numbers that can be expressed in fractional form. This extension allows us to solve such problems as $4 - 7 = ?$ and $-3 \div 4 = ?$. The negative numbers, which are the opposites of the positive numbers, make up the set of negative rational numbers.

The complete set of rational numbers includes:

1. the set of positive rational numbers;
2. zero;
3. the set of negative rational numbers.

In set language, it is the union of the three sets, and we can write

{**the rational numbers**} =

{the positive rationals} ∪ {0} ∪ {the negative rationals}.

A basic property of a rational number, which distinguishes it from every non-rational number, is the fact that it can be expressed in the fractional form $\frac{r}{s}$ where r and s are integers, with $s \neq 0$. For example, some ways of writing the numbers **3, −2, 0,** and **4** in fractional form are as follows:

$$3 = \frac{12}{4}; \qquad -2 = \frac{-4}{2}; \qquad 0 = \frac{0}{8}; \qquad 4\frac{1}{5} = \frac{21}{5}.$$

Any number that can be expressed in the form $\frac{r}{s}$, where r is an integer and s is a nonzero integer, is a rational number.

Suppose that you were to select two rational numbers like $\frac{1}{4}$ and $\frac{1}{5}$ that appear to be very close to each other on the number line, as pictured here. Are there other rational num- bers between $\frac{1}{4}$ and $\frac{1}{5}$? If your answer is "yes," you are correct. For example, $\frac{1}{4} = \frac{10}{40}$ and $\frac{1}{5} = \frac{8}{40}$, and $\frac{8}{40} < \frac{9}{40} < \frac{10}{40}$, so $\frac{9}{40}$ is a rational number between $\frac{1}{4}$ and $\frac{1}{5}$. Do you see that between any pair of rational numbers you can find as many more rational numbers as you please? For example, you could rename $\frac{1}{5}$ as $\frac{200}{1000}$ and $\frac{1}{4}$ as $\frac{250}{1000}$. Then you could name the rational numbers

$$\frac{201}{1000}, \quad \frac{202}{1000}, \quad \cdots, \quad \frac{248}{1000}, \quad \frac{249}{1000},$$

all of which are between $\frac{1}{5}$ and $\frac{1}{4}$.

By renaming the fractions $\frac{1}{5}$ and $\frac{1}{4}$ in other ways, many more numbers between $\frac{1}{5}$ and $\frac{1}{4}$ could be easily identified. We say that the set of rational numbers is **dense** or that it has the **property of density**.

Between any two rational numbers there is another rational number.

ORAL EXERCISES

For each number given, tell to which of the sets listed it belongs.

	Given number	{the whole numbers}	{the integers}	{the positive rationals}	{the negative rationals}	{the rationals}
SAMPLE:	-6	no	yes	no	yes	yes
1.	-4	?	?	?	?	?
2.	$1\frac{1}{2}$	?	?	?	?	?
3.	$\frac{3}{8}$	?	?	?	?	?
4.	$-\frac{2}{5}$	?	?	?	?	?
5.	0	?	?	?	?	?
6.	35	?	?	?	?	?

WRITTEN EXERCISES

Show what integer should replace each variable to make the statement true.

SAMPLE: $2\frac{3}{4} = \frac{x}{4}$ *Solution:* $2\frac{3}{4} = \frac{11}{4}$; replace x by 11.

1. $3 = \frac{t}{5}$ **5.** $1\frac{1}{3} = \frac{b}{9}$ **9.** $-2\frac{1}{5} = -\frac{a}{5}$

2. $7 = \frac{70}{m}$ **6.** $\frac{4}{r} = 4$ **10.** $\frac{3+2}{7} = \frac{5}{x}$

3. $-2 = \frac{-8}{x}$ **7.** $\frac{-10}{s} = 5$ **11.** $\left(\frac{1}{2}\right)^2 = \frac{m}{4}$

4. $-5 = \frac{y}{2}$ **8.** $\frac{0}{-9} = \frac{x}{7}$ **12.** $\frac{2}{3} = \frac{10}{z}$

Show that each of the following represents a rational number by expressing it as the quotient of two integers.

SAMPLE: 7   *Solution:* $7 = \frac{14}{2}$ (Many other answers are possible.)

13. 5   **17.** 50%   **21.** $\left(\frac{2}{3}\right)^2$

14. -10 **18.** 30%   **22.** $\left(-\frac{1}{4}\right)^2$

15. $1\frac{1}{4}$ **19.** 3^2 **23.** $-\left(\frac{1}{2}\right)^2$

16. 0   **20.** $(-2)^2$ **24.** $-4\frac{1}{5}$

Name three rational numbers between each given pair of rational numbers.

SAMPLE 1: $-3, -4$ *Solution:* $-3\frac{1}{5}, -3\frac{2}{5}, -3\frac{3}{5}$
                                    (Other answers are possible.)

SAMPLE 2: $\frac{1}{2}, \frac{1}{4}$ *Solution:* Since $\frac{1}{2} = \frac{10}{20}$ and $\frac{1}{4} = \frac{5}{20}$, some
                                    possible answers are $\frac{6}{20}, \frac{7}{20}, \frac{8}{20}$.

25. $\frac{3}{10}, \frac{4}{10}$ **28.** $-7, -8$ **31.** $\frac{1}{2}, \frac{3}{4}$

26. $-\frac{1}{5}, -\frac{2}{5}$ **29.** $43, 44$ **32.** $\frac{1}{25}, \frac{2}{25}$

27. $8, 9$ **30.** $\frac{1}{8}, \frac{1}{4}$ **33.** $1, \frac{1}{2}$

B **34.** $\frac{1}{19}, \frac{1}{20}$ **36.** $\frac{3}{2}, \frac{4}{2}$ **38.** $0, -\frac{1}{10}$

35. $-\frac{3}{8}, -\frac{1}{4}$ **37.** $\frac{7}{8}, \frac{8}{7}$ **39.** $0, \frac{1}{100}$

Use *all, some,* or *no* to complete each statement.

40. __?__ whole numbers are integers.

41. __?__ integers are negative rational numbers.

42. __?__ whole numbers are rational numbers.

43. __?__ whole numbers are positive rational numbers.

44. __?__ whole numbers are positive integers.

For each variable, name three replacements that will make the statement true. The domain of the variable is {the rational numbers}.

C **45.** $\frac{2}{5} < x < \frac{3}{5}$ **47.** $\frac{7}{100} < k < \frac{8}{100}$

46. $-\frac{6}{13} < y < -\frac{5}{13}$ **48.** $\frac{9}{1000} < w < \frac{10}{1000}$

12–2 Decimal Representations of Rational Numbers

In an earlier chapter, we explored the idea that every fraction can be expressed as either a **terminating decimal** or a **repeating decimal**. For example, when we calculate the quotient indicated by the fraction $\frac{3}{4}$, we find that it "comes out even"; that is, we end up with a remainder of **0**. The quotient indicated by the fraction $\frac{1}{12}$ does not "come out even," but after a time the remainder **4** repeats.

EXAMPLE 1. $\frac{3}{4}$

$$
\begin{array}{r}
0.75 \\
4)\overline{3.00} \\
\underline{2.8} \\
20 \\
\underline{20} \\
0
\end{array}
$$

EXAMPLE 2. $\frac{1}{12}$

$$
\begin{array}{r}
0.0833 \\
12)\overline{1.0000} \\
\underline{96} \\
40 \\
\underline{36} \\
40 \\
\underline{36} \\
4
\end{array}
$$

$\frac{3}{4} = 0.75$, a terminating decimal $\frac{1}{12} = 0.0833 \ldots$, a repeating decimal

In writing a repeating decimal, recall that we often use a bar above a group of digits to show that they repeat.

> $0.0833 \ldots$ can be written $0.08\overline{3}$.
>
> $-0.\overline{13}$ is a short way to write $-0.131313 \ldots$.

The decimal representation of any rational number $\dfrac{r}{s}$ either terminates or is a repeating decimal.

Similarly, any terminating or repeating decimal represents a number that can be expressed in the form $\dfrac{r}{s}$, with r and s integers, and s not **0**. This is a basic property of rational numbers.

Any terminating or repeating decimal numeral represents a rational number.

ORAL EXERCISES

Tell what integer should replace each variable to make the statement true.

1. $0.4 = \dfrac{x}{10}$ **3.** $-0.8 = \dfrac{r}{10}$ **5.** $-3.1 = \dfrac{w}{10}$

2. $-0.1 = \dfrac{-1}{m}$ **4.** $0.003 = \dfrac{3}{n}$ **6.** $-0.\overline{6} = \dfrac{-2}{x}$

Match each terminating or repeating decimal in Column 1 with its fractional equivalent in Column 2.

COLUMN 1

7. $0.\overline{3}$

8. 0.375

9. 0.60

10. -0.50

11. $0.\overline{6}$

12. -0.0009

COLUMN 2

A. $\frac{3}{8}$

B. $-\frac{1}{2}$

C. $\frac{2}{3}$

D. $-\frac{9}{10,000}$

E. $\frac{1}{3}$

F. $\frac{3}{5}$

WRITTEN EXERCISES

Show that the left member of each equation represents a rational number by replacing each variable with an integer.

SAMPLE: $1.8 = \dfrac{a}{b}$ *Solution:* $1.8 = \dfrac{18}{10}$

A

1. $0.7 = \dfrac{x}{y}$ **5.** $-0.\overline{6} = \dfrac{m}{s}$ **9.** $0.005 = \dfrac{n}{s}$

2. $0.13 = \dfrac{m}{n}$ **6.** $-0.19 = \dfrac{b}{c}$ **10.** $-0.0003 = \dfrac{y}{z}$

3. $1.5 = \dfrac{a}{c}$ **7.** $0 = \dfrac{d}{n}$ **11.** $(0.03)^2 = \dfrac{a}{c}$

4. $5.0 = \dfrac{a}{t}$ **8.** $30\% = \dfrac{p}{q}$ **12.** $(-0.1)^2 = \dfrac{x}{y}$

Find the terminating or repeating decimal equivalent for each number.

13. $\frac{4}{5}$ **16.** $\frac{1}{9}$ **19.** $-\frac{5}{1000}$

14. $\frac{10}{3}$ **17.** $-\frac{2}{5}$ **20.** $10\frac{1}{2}\%$

15. $-\frac{7}{8}$ **18.** $\frac{13}{1000}$ **21.** $-\frac{27}{10,000}$

Name three rational numbers between each given pair of rational numbers.

SAMPLE: $0.5, 0.6$ *Solution:* $0.51, 0.52, 0.53$
                    (Many other answers are possible.)

B

22. $0.1, 0.2$ **24.** $0.25, 0.26$ **26.** $-0.0011, -0.0010$

23. $0.9, 1.0$ **25.** $0.153, 0.154$ **27.** $0.\overline{3}, 0.\overline{4}$

Use *all, some,* or *no* to complete each of the following statements.

C

28. __?__ negative rational numbers can be expressed as terminating decimals.

29. __?__ positive rational numbers have opposites that are negative rational numbers.

30. __?__ rational numbers can be expressed in the form $\dfrac{a}{b}$ where $a = 0$ and $b \neq 0$.

31. __?__ rational numbers can be expressed in the form $\dfrac{a}{b}$ where a is an integer and $b \neq 0$.

Roots of Numbers

12–3   Square Roots of Numbers

You will recall that **squaring** a number means raising it to the **second** power, or multiplying it by itself. For example, in $7^2 = \mathbf{49}$, we say that the number **7** is **squared**, and that the result, **49**, is the **square** of **7**.

The opposite of squaring a number is called finding its square root. To find the square root of **81**, for example, we are looking for the answer to the question, "What numbers are there whose squares equal **81**?" Do you agree that, since $(-9)^2 = 81$ and $(9)^2 = 81$, the number **81** has **two** square roots, one positive and the other negative? As you may have concluded already, every positive number has both a **positive square root** and a **negative square root**. The number zero has only one square root, **zero**.

A number **r** is a square root of a number **s** if $r^2 = s$.

Do you think that a negative number such as **−81** has square roots? Can you name a replacement for **n** in the sentence $-\mathbf{81} = (\mathbf{n})(\mathbf{n})$ that will make the statement true? Do you agree that *no* negative number has square roots in the system of directed numbers?

To indicate the **positive** square root of a number, we use the symbol $\sqrt{}$, called a radical sign. The expression $\sqrt{81}$ is called a radical, and indicates the **positive square root** of the number **81**, generally called its principal square root. If $\sqrt{81}$ indicates the **positive** square root, **9**, then the **negative** square root, **−9**, is indicated by $-\sqrt{81}$. When we wish to indicate *both* the positive and the negative square roots, we can write $\pm\sqrt{81}$.

EXAMPLE 1. $\sqrt{49} = 7$ and $-\sqrt{49} = -7$; $\pm\sqrt{49} = \pm7$.

EXAMPLE 2. $\sqrt{121} = 11$ and $-\sqrt{121} = -11$; $\pm\sqrt{121} = \pm11$.

Every positive number has exactly two different square roots; one root is a positive number and the other is a negative number, the opposite of the positive root.

ORAL EXERCISES

Tell how to complete each of the following to make a true statement.

1. If $n = 10$, the value of n^2 is __?__ .
2. If $n = -10$, the value of n^2 is __?__ .
3. If $k = 8$, the value of k^2 is __?__ .
4. If $a = -3$, the value of a^2 is __?__ .
5. If $x = \frac{1}{5}$, the value of x^2 is __?__ .
6. If $x = -\frac{1}{5}$, the value of x^2 is __?__ .
7. If $y^2 = 144$, the positive value of y is __?__ .
8. If $m^2 = 36$, the negative value of m is __?__ .

WRITTEN EXERCISES

Give the principal square root of each number.

SAMPLE: 0.64   *Solution:* 0.8

A

1. 25   **6.** 64   **11.** 0.36
2. 36   **7.** 400   **12.** 0.04
3. 144   **8.** $\frac{4}{25}$ **13.** $\frac{25}{81}$
4. 100   **9.** $\frac{9}{49}$ **14.** $\frac{9}{1}$
5. 81   **10.** 0.25   **15.** $\frac{49}{36}$

Find the solution set for each equation, if the domain of the variable is {the rational numbers}.

SAMPLE: $n^2 = \frac{1}{9}$ *Solution:* $\{\frac{1}{3}, -\frac{1}{3}\}$

16. $x^2 = 4$ **20.** $r^2 = 0.25$ **24.** $m^2 = 1$
17. $t^2 = \frac{1}{16}$ **21.** $a^2 = 0.09$ **25.** $c^2 = (4)(9)$
18. $m^2 = 900$ **22.** $s^2 = \frac{9}{100}$ **26.** $r^2 = 0.0004$
19. $y^2 = \frac{100}{169}$ **23.** $k^2 = \frac{1}{81}$ **27.** $z^2 = \frac{64}{81}$

Simplify each expression.

28. $\sqrt{100}$ **29.** $\sqrt{\dfrac{25}{9}}$ **30.** $-\sqrt{4^2 + 3^2}$

31. $\sqrt{225}$ **34.** $-\sqrt{\dfrac{36}{49}}$ **37.** $\sqrt{6^2 + 8^2}$

32. $-\sqrt{81}$ **35.** $\sqrt{5^2}$ **38.** $\pm\sqrt{\dfrac{t^2}{64}}$

33. $\sqrt{8^2}$ **36.** $\pm\sqrt{\dfrac{1}{49}}$ **39.** $\pm\sqrt{\dfrac{n^2}{100}}$

B   **40.** $(\sqrt{49})^2$ **42.** $-\sqrt{13^2 - 12^2}$ **44.** $\sqrt{(-3)^2}$

    41. $(\sqrt{16})^2$ **43.** $\pm\sqrt{10^2 - 8^2}$ **45.** $\sqrt{(-7)^2}$

C   **46.** $\pm\sqrt{\dfrac{x^2}{64}}$ **48.** $-\sqrt{49n^4}$ **50.** $\pm\sqrt{\dfrac{t^2}{81}}$

    47. $\pm\sqrt{\dfrac{m^2}{144}}$ **49.** $-\sqrt{36y^6}$ **51.** $\pm\sqrt{\dfrac{9m^8}{25}}$

12–4   Product and Quotient Properties of Square Roots

It is a simple matter to find the principal square root of 144, since you know that $12 \cdot 12 = 144$. Therefore, $\sqrt{144} = 12$. It is also possible to find a square root by factoring, as is illustrated in the following examples.

EXAMPLE 1. $\sqrt{144} = ?$ **EXAMPLE 2.** $-\sqrt{196} = ?$

$$\sqrt{144} = \sqrt{9 \cdot 16} \qquad\qquad -\sqrt{196} = -\sqrt{4 \cdot 49}$$
$$= \sqrt{9} \cdot \sqrt{16} \qquad\qquad\qquad = -(\sqrt{4} \cdot \sqrt{49})$$
$$= 3 \cdot 4 = 12 \qquad\qquad\qquad = -(2 \cdot 7) = -14$$

Check: $(12)(12) = 144$ Check: $(-14)(-14) = 196$

Each example makes use of the **product property** of square roots, which is summarized as follows:

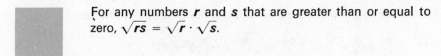

For any numbers **r** and **s** that are greater than or equal to zero, $\sqrt{rs} = \sqrt{r} \cdot \sqrt{s}$.

You can no doubt name $\sqrt{\dfrac{16}{49}}$ as $\dfrac{4}{7}$ without doing any written cal-culations. You can also find $\sqrt{\dfrac{16}{49}}$ by expressing it as $\dfrac{\sqrt{16}}{\sqrt{49}}$ and sim-plifying the numerator and the denominator.

EXAMPLE 3. $\sqrt{\dfrac{16}{49}} = ?$ EXAMPLE 4. $-\sqrt{\dfrac{64}{25}} = ?$

$\sqrt{\dfrac{16}{49}} = \dfrac{\sqrt{16}}{\sqrt{49}}$ $-\sqrt{\dfrac{64}{25}} = -\dfrac{\sqrt{64}}{\sqrt{25}}$

$\phantom{\sqrt{\dfrac{16}{49}}} = \dfrac{4}{7}$ $\phantom{-\sqrt{\dfrac{64}{25}}} = -\dfrac{8}{5}$

Check: $\left(\dfrac{4}{7}\right)\left(\dfrac{4}{7}\right) = \dfrac{16}{49}$ Check: $\left(-\dfrac{8}{5}\right)\left(-\dfrac{8}{5}\right) = \dfrac{64}{25}$

In Examples 3 and 4, we have used the **quotient property** of square roots:

For any numbers **r** and **s**, where **r** is greater than or equal to zero and **s** is greater than **0**,

$$\sqrt{\dfrac{r}{s}} = \dfrac{\sqrt{r}}{\sqrt{s}}.$$

ORAL EXERCISES

Tell how to complete each of the following to make a true statement.

1. $\sqrt{100} = \sqrt{4 \cdot (?)}$ **6.** $\sqrt{25} \cdot \sqrt{49} = \sqrt{(?) \cdot (?)}$

2. $\sqrt{81} = \sqrt{9 \cdot (?)}$ **7.** $\sqrt{64} \cdot \sqrt{4} = \sqrt{(?)}$

3. $\sqrt{\dfrac{16}{100}} = \dfrac{\sqrt{(?)}}{\sqrt{(?)}}$ **8.** $\sqrt{\dfrac{36}{25}} = \dfrac{\sqrt{?}}{\sqrt{?}}$

4. $\sqrt{(?)} = \sqrt{25 \cdot 9}$ **9.** $\sqrt{(?)} = \sqrt{4} \cdot \sqrt{225}$

5. $\dfrac{\sqrt{5^2}}{\sqrt{9^2}} = \sqrt{\dfrac{?}{?}}$ **10.** $\sqrt{81 \cdot 4} = \sqrt{(?)}$

Tell how to complete the pairs of statements in each exercise.

11. $\dfrac{\sqrt{64}}{\sqrt{4}} = \dfrac{8}{2} = ?; \quad \dfrac{\sqrt{64}}{\sqrt{4}} = \sqrt{\dfrac{64}{4}} = \sqrt{16} = ?$

12. $\dfrac{\sqrt{36}}{\sqrt{9}} = \dfrac{6}{3} = ?; \quad \dfrac{\sqrt{36}}{\sqrt{9}} = \sqrt{\dfrac{36}{9}} = \sqrt{4} = ?$

13. $\dfrac{\sqrt{4}}{\sqrt{36}} = \dfrac{2}{6} = ?; \quad \dfrac{\sqrt{4}}{\sqrt{36}} = \sqrt{\dfrac{4}{36}} = \dfrac{2}{6} = ?$

WRITTEN EXERCISES

Show that each of the following is a true statement.

SAMPLE 1: $\sqrt{9} \cdot \sqrt{100} = \sqrt{900}$

Solution: $\underline{\sqrt{9} \cdot \sqrt{100} = \sqrt{900}}$

$3 \cdot 10$	30
30	30

SAMPLE 2: $\sqrt{\dfrac{144}{9}} = \dfrac{\sqrt{144}}{\sqrt{9}}$

Solution: $\sqrt{\dfrac{144}{9}} = \dfrac{\sqrt{144}}{\sqrt{9}}$

$\sqrt{16}$	$\dfrac{12}{3}$
4	4

A 1. $\sqrt{16} \cdot \sqrt{4} = \sqrt{64}$

2. $\sqrt{36} \cdot \sqrt{4} = \sqrt{36 \cdot 4}$

3. $\sqrt{100} \cdot \sqrt{16} = \sqrt{1600}$

4. $\sqrt{\dfrac{100}{4}} = \dfrac{\sqrt{100}}{\sqrt{4}}$

5. $\sqrt{\dfrac{36}{4}} = \dfrac{\sqrt{36}}{\sqrt{4}}$

6. $\sqrt{\dfrac{81}{9}} = \dfrac{\sqrt{81}}{\sqrt{9}}$

7. $\sqrt{400} \cdot \sqrt{9} = \sqrt{3600}$

8. $\sqrt{25} \cdot \sqrt{100} = \sqrt{2500}$

9. $\sqrt{16} \cdot \sqrt{25} = \sqrt{400}$

10. $\sqrt{1} \cdot \sqrt{81} = \sqrt{1 \cdot 81}$

11. $\sqrt{\dfrac{1}{4}} \cdot \sqrt{\dfrac{1}{9}} = \sqrt{\dfrac{1}{36}}$

12. $\dfrac{\sqrt{25}}{\sqrt{144}} = \sqrt{\dfrac{25}{144}}$

13. $\sqrt{\dfrac{400}{100}} = \dfrac{\sqrt{400}}{\sqrt{100}}$

14. $\sqrt{\dfrac{2500}{100}} = \dfrac{\sqrt{2500}}{\sqrt{100}}$

Find the integer named by each expression if $a = 3$, $b = 5$, $c = 6$, and $d = 8$.

15. $\sqrt{a^2} + \sqrt{b^2}$

16. $\sqrt{a + b + d}$

17. $\sqrt{c^2} + \sqrt{d^2}$

18. $\sqrt{a^2} + \sqrt{b^2} + \sqrt{c^2}$

19. $\sqrt{4} \cdot \sqrt{c^2}$

20. $\sqrt{9} \cdot \sqrt{a^2}$

21. $\sqrt{\dfrac{2d}{4}}$

22. $\dfrac{\sqrt{c^2}}{\sqrt{a^2}}$

Express each of the following products as a single radical, assuming that the value of each variable is greater than or equal to zero.

SAMPLE: $\sqrt{x} \cdot \sqrt{y}$

Solution: $\sqrt{xy}$

B 23. $\sqrt{m} \cdot \sqrt{n}$

24. $\sqrt{k} \cdot \sqrt{t}$

25. $\sqrt{10} \cdot \sqrt{y}$

26. $\sqrt{r} \cdot \sqrt{2}$

27. $\sqrt{135} \cdot \sqrt{c}$

28. $\sqrt{s} \cdot \sqrt{t}$

12–5 Roots Other than Square Roots

Suppose that you wish to find a replacement for n in the sentence $n^3 = 27$ which will make the statement true. Since $3 \cdot 3 \cdot 3 = 27$, do you agree that the replacement should be **3**? 3^3 represents **3** to the third power, and is usually read "3 cubed," so we call **3** the cube root of **27**. Do you see why **27** has no *negative* cube root?

Do you have an idea what number should replace n in $n^3 = -8$? Since $(-2)(-2)(-2) = -8$, we can say that the **cube root** of -8 is -2. Do you agree that there could not be a *positive* cube root of -8?

A number r is a cube root of a number s if $r^3 = s$.

We can give definitions for **fourth roots, fifth roots**, and so on, that correspond to those we have given for square roots and cube roots. To indicate a root other than a square root, a root index is assigned to the radical. The root index is named by a small numeral attached to the radical sign, as illustrated in the following examples.

EXAMPLE 1.   Find $\sqrt[3]{64}$.
The root index **3** means that we are to find the **cube root** of **64**.
$$4 \cdot 4 \cdot 4 = 64, \quad \text{so} \quad \sqrt[3]{64} = 4.$$

EXAMPLE 2.   Find $\sqrt[4]{81}$.
The root index **4** means that we are to find the **fourth** root of **81**.
$$3 \cdot 3 \cdot 3 \cdot 3 = 81, \quad \text{so} \quad \sqrt[4]{81} = 3.$$

EXAMPLE 3.   Find $\sqrt[5]{32}$.
The root index **5** means that we are to find the **fifth** root of **32**.
$$2 \cdot 2 \cdot 2 \cdot 2 \cdot 2 = 32, \quad \text{so} \quad \sqrt[5]{32} = 2.$$

Study the following examples to see whether you should look for a **positive** root of a number, or a **negative** root, or for **two** roots, one **positive** and one **negative**.

EXAMPLE 4. When the **root index** is an odd number:

$$2 \cdot 2 \cdot 2 = 8, \quad \text{so} \quad \sqrt[3]{8} = 2.$$
$$(-2)(-2)(-2) = -8, \quad \text{so} \quad \sqrt[3]{-8} = -2.$$
$$3 \cdot 3 \cdot 3 \cdot 3 \cdot 3 = 243, \quad \text{so} \quad \sqrt[5]{243} = 3.$$
$$(-3)(-3)(-3)(-3)(-3) = -243,$$
$$\text{so} \quad \sqrt[5]{-243} = -3.$$

Do you agree that when the root index is an **odd** number there will be **one** root which will be either positive or negative, according to the sign of the number of which we are finding the root?

EXAMPLE 5. When the **root index** is an even number:

$$2 \cdot 2 \cdot 2 \cdot 2 = 16 \quad \text{and} \quad (-2)(-2)(-2)(-2) = 16,$$
$$\text{so} \quad \sqrt[4]{16} = 2 \quad \text{and} \quad -\sqrt[4]{16} = -2.$$
$$3 \cdot 3 \cdot 3 \cdot 3 \cdot 3 \cdot 3 = 729, \quad \text{and}$$
$$(-3)(-3)(-3)(-3)(-3)(-3) = 729,$$
$$\text{so} \quad \sqrt[6]{729} = 3 \quad \text{and} \quad -\sqrt[6]{729} = -3.$$

Thus, when the root index is **even,** there will be one **positive** root and one **negative** root.

For the nth root of r, where n is a positive integer greater than **1**:

if n is even and $r > 0$, r has both a positive and a negative nth root; the positive root is called the **principal root;**

if n is odd and $r > 0$, r has a **positive** nth root;

if n is odd and $r < 0$, r has a **negative** nth root;

if $r = 0$, its nth root is **0.**

ORAL EXERCISES

For each of the following radicals, tell the root index and state the meaning of the symbol.

SAMPLE: $\sqrt[5]{-32}$ *What you say:* The root index is 5; the fifth root of -32.

1. $\sqrt[4]{16}$ **3.** $\sqrt[3]{-125}$ **5.** $\sqrt[3]{\frac{27}{1000}}$

2. $\sqrt[3]{64}$ **4.** $\sqrt[3]{125}$ **6.** $\sqrt[7]{128}$

7. $\sqrt[6]{1}$ **9.** $\sqrt[5]{\frac{1}{32}}$ **11.** $\sqrt[7]{-128}$

8. $\sqrt[5]{-1}$ **10.** $\sqrt[4]{\frac{1}{16}}$ **12.** $\sqrt[6]{64}$

For each of the following, tell whether you would look for one positive root, or one negative root, or one positive and one negative root. Do *not* find the roots.

13. The fifth root of 1

14. The fifth root of -1

15. The fourth root of 256

16. The cube root of 216

17. The cube root of -216

18. The cube root of -0.001

19. The fourth root of 10,000

20. The sixth root of 729

21. The square root of 0.01

22. The seventh root of 128

WRITTEN EXERCISES

Copy and complete the following tables of powers.

 1.

n	n^3	n^4	n^5
1			
2			
3			
4			
5			

2.

n	n^3	n^4	n^5
6			
7			
8			
9			
10			

Complete each of these statements.

SAMPLE: Since $5 \cdot 5 \cdot 5 = 125$, we know $\sqrt[3]{125} = $ ___?___ .

Solution: Since $5 \cdot 5 \cdot 5 = 125$, we know $\sqrt[3]{125} = 5$.

3. Since $2 \cdot 2 \cdot 2 \cdot 2 = 16$, we know $\sqrt[4]{16} = $ ___?___ .

4. Since $8 \cdot 8 \cdot 8 = 512$, we know $\sqrt[3]{512} = $ ___?___ .

5. Since $10 \cdot 10 \cdot 10 \cdot 10 \cdot 10 = 100,000$, we know $\sqrt[5]{100,000} = $ ___?___ .

6. Since $1 \cdot 1 \cdot 1 \cdot 1 \cdot 1 \cdot 1 = 1$, we know $\sqrt[6]{1} = $ ___?___ .

7. Since $(-3)(-3)(-3) = -27$, we know $\sqrt[3]{-27} = $ ___?___ .

8. Since $(-2)(-2)(-2)(-2)(-2) = -32$, we know $\sqrt[5]{-32} = $ ___?___ .

9. Since $4 \cdot 4 \cdot 4 \cdot 4 = 256$ and $(-4)(-4)(-4)(-4) = 256$, we know $\pm\sqrt[4]{256} = $ ___?___ .

10. Since $2 \cdot 2 \cdot 2 \cdot 2 \cdot 2 \cdot 2 = 64$ and $(-2)(-2)(-2)(-2)(-2)(-2) = 64$, we know $\pm\sqrt[6]{64} = $ ___?___ .

Evaluate each radical. Use the tables completed in Exercises 1 and 2.

11. $\sqrt[3]{729}$ **16.** $\sqrt[5]{243}$ **21.** $\pm\sqrt[4]{10,000}$

12. $\sqrt[4]{625}$ **17.** $\sqrt[5]{-3125}$ **22.** $-\sqrt[5]{100,000}$

13. $-\sqrt[4]{1296}$ **18.** $\pm\sqrt[4]{6561}$ **23.** $\sqrt[5]{7776}$

14. $\sqrt[3]{-512}$ **19.** $-\sqrt[4]{16}$ **24.** $\sqrt[3]{-1000}$

15. $\sqrt[5]{1024}$ **20.** $\sqrt[5]{-1}$ **25.** $\sqrt[3]{27}$

Use the appropriate symbol, $>$, $<$, or $=$, to make each statement true.

SAMPLE: $\sqrt[3]{216}$? $\sqrt[4]{4096}$ *Solution:* $\sqrt[3]{216}$? $\sqrt[4]{4096}$

$$\begin{array}{c|c} \sqrt[3]{6^3} & \sqrt[4]{8^4} \\ 6 & 8 \end{array}$$

$$6 < 8, \text{ so } \sqrt[3]{216} < \sqrt[4]{4096}.$$

B   **26.** $\sqrt{64}$? $\sqrt[3]{512}$ **29.** $\sqrt[3]{-1000}$? $-\sqrt{144}$

27. $\sqrt[3]{27}$? $\sqrt[4]{16}$ **30.** $\sqrt[5]{1024}$? $\sqrt[3]{125}$

28. $\sqrt[3]{-512}$? $\sqrt[3]{512}$ **31.** $\sqrt[3]{625}$? $\sqrt[3]{1}$

12–6 Product and Quotient Properties of Roots Other than Square Roots

In our work with square roots we applied the product property and found that $\sqrt{400} = \sqrt{4 \cdot 100} = \sqrt{4} \cdot \sqrt{100} = 2 \cdot 10 = 20$. The following examples show how we apply the same property in finding other roots.

EXAMPLE 1. $\sqrt[3]{1000} = ?$ EXAMPLE 2. $\sqrt[4]{1296} = ?$

$$\sqrt[3]{1000} = \sqrt[3]{8 \cdot 125} \qquad\qquad \sqrt[4]{1296} = \sqrt[4]{16 \cdot 81}$$

$$= \sqrt[3]{8} \cdot \sqrt[3]{125} \qquad\qquad = \sqrt[4]{16} \cdot \sqrt[4]{81}$$

$$= 2 \cdot 5 = 10 \qquad\qquad\quad = 2 \cdot 3 = 6$$

We can summarize the **product property of roots** as follows:

For any positive integer **n** greater than **1**:

if **r** and **s** are **positive** numbers or **zero**, and **n** is even, or if **r** and **s** are any directed numbers and **n** is odd, then $\sqrt[n]{rs} = \sqrt[n]{r} \cdot \sqrt[n]{s}$.

We can also extend the quotient property, used earlier with square roots, to apply to other roots.

EXAMPLE 3. $\sqrt[4]{\dfrac{81}{625}} = ?$ **EXAMPLE 4.** $\sqrt[5]{\dfrac{32}{243}} = ?$

$$\sqrt[4]{\frac{81}{625}} = \frac{\sqrt[4]{81}}{\sqrt[4]{625}}$$

$$\sqrt[5]{\frac{32}{243}} = \frac{\sqrt[5]{32}}{\sqrt[5]{243}}$$

$$= \frac{3}{5}$$

$$= \frac{2}{3}$$

The following statement summarizes the quotient property of roots:

For any positive integer **n** greater than **1**:

if **r** $\geq$ **0** and **s** > **0**, with **n** even, or
if **r** is any directed number and **s** $\neq$ **0**, with **n** odd, then

$$\sqrt[n]{\frac{r}{s}} = \frac{\sqrt[n]{r}}{\sqrt[n]{s}}.$$

ORAL EXERCISES

Tell how to complete the two statements in each exercise.

SAMPLE: $\frac{1}{2} \cdot \frac{1}{2} \cdot \frac{1}{2} = ?$; $\sqrt[3]{\frac{1}{8}} = ?$

What you say: $\frac{1}{2} \cdot \frac{1}{2} \cdot \frac{1}{2} = \frac{1}{8}$; $\sqrt[3]{\frac{1}{8}} = \frac{1}{2}$.

1. $\frac{3}{4} \cdot \frac{3}{4} \cdot \frac{3}{4} = ?$; $\sqrt[3]{\frac{27}{64}} = ?$
2. $\frac{2}{3} \cdot \frac{2}{3} \cdot \frac{2}{3} \cdot \frac{2}{3} = ?$; $\sqrt[4]{\frac{16}{81}} = ?$
3. $\frac{1}{5} \cdot \frac{1}{5} \cdot \frac{1}{5} = ?$; $\sqrt[3]{\frac{1}{125}} = ?$
4. $\sqrt[3]{27 \cdot 8} = \sqrt[3]{?} \cdot \sqrt[3]{?} = ?$
5. $\sqrt[4]{256 \cdot 16} = \sqrt[4]{?} \cdot \sqrt[4]{?} = ?$

WRITTEN EXERCISES

Complete the pairs of statements in each exercise.

A **1.** $\dfrac{\sqrt[3]{8}}{\sqrt[3]{125}} = ?$; $\dfrac{\sqrt[3]{8}}{\sqrt[3]{125}} = \sqrt[3]{\dfrac{8}{125}} = ?$

2. $\dfrac{\sqrt[5]{243}}{\sqrt[5]{100,000}} = ?$; $\dfrac{\sqrt[5]{243}}{\sqrt[5]{100,000}} = \sqrt[5]{\dfrac{243}{100,000}} = ?$

3. $\dfrac{\sqrt[4]{625}}{\sqrt[4]{1296}} = ?$; $\dfrac{\sqrt[4]{625}}{\sqrt[4]{1296}} = \sqrt[4]{\dfrac{625}{1296}} = ?$

4. $\dfrac{\sqrt[3]{-64}}{\sqrt[3]{-27}} = ? \; ; \; \dfrac{\sqrt[3]{-64}}{\sqrt[3]{-27}} = \sqrt[3]{\dfrac{-64}{-27}} = ?$

5. $\dfrac{\sqrt[5]{1}}{\sqrt[5]{32}} = ? \; ; \; \dfrac{\sqrt[5]{1}}{\sqrt[5]{32}} = \sqrt[5]{\dfrac{1}{32}} = ?$

6. $\dfrac{\sqrt[4]{16}}{\sqrt[4]{625}} = ? \; ; \; \dfrac{\sqrt[4]{16}}{\sqrt[4]{625}} = \sqrt[4]{\dfrac{16}{625}} = ?$

Show that each of the following is a true statement.

SAMPLE: $\sqrt[3]{64} \cdot \sqrt[3]{8} = \sqrt[3]{512}$ *Solution:* $\underline{\sqrt[3]{64} \cdot \sqrt[3]{8} = \sqrt[3]{512}}$

$$\begin{array}{c|c} 4 \cdot 2 & 8 \\ 8 & 8 \end{array}$$

7. $\sqrt[3]{8} \cdot \sqrt[3]{125} = \sqrt[3]{1000}$

8. $\sqrt[5]{1} \cdot \sqrt[5]{32} = \sqrt[5]{32}$

9. $\sqrt[3]{1000} \cdot \sqrt[3]{27} = \sqrt[3]{27,000}$

10. $\sqrt[4]{16} \cdot \sqrt[4]{1} = \sqrt[4]{16}$

11. $\sqrt[4]{81} \cdot \sqrt[4]{16} \cdot \sqrt[4]{1} = 6$

12. $\sqrt[3]{1000} \cdot \sqrt[3]{125} \cdot \sqrt[3]{27} = 150$

13. $\sqrt[3]{64} \cdot \sqrt[3]{729} = 36$

14. $\sqrt[3]{16} \cdot \sqrt[3]{64} = \sqrt[3]{512}$

Irrational Roots

12–7 Irrational Numbers

If the rational number **5** is squared, the result is **25**, which is called a **perfect square**. On the other hand, the **square root** of **16** is obviously **4**, because **16** is the square of **4**; **16** is also a perfect square. Do you see how the squares in Figures 12–1 and 12–2 give us a geometric interpretation of these two ideas?

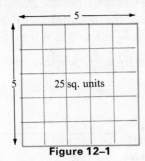

Figure 12–1

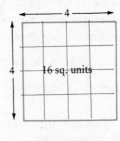

Figure 12–2

That is, the area enclosed by the red square in Figure 12–1 represents the number **25**, and the square root of **25** is **5**, the length of one side. Similarly, in Figure 12–2 the length of one side is **4**, which is the square root of **16**, and **16** is the area enclosed by the red square in this figure.

Now consider the red square shown here. If you count the small squares and half-squares inside the large square, you will find that its area is **8** square units, and so the length of each side must be $\sqrt{8}$ units. Does $\sqrt{8}$ name an integer? What would you guess is the length of each side? Since $2 \cdot 2 = 4$, and $4 < 8$, it is clear that the length of each side is *more* than **2** units. However, $3 \cdot 3 = 9$, and $8 < 9$, so we also see that each side must be *less* than **3** units long. Do you agree that the length of each side is *between* **2** and **3** units? Thus $\sqrt{8}$ is not an integer, but is a number between **2** and **3**.

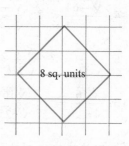

For the side of the square, we might now guess a length of **2.5** units, since the number **2.5** is halfway between **2** and **3**.

$$(2.5)^2 = 6.25 \quad \text{and} \quad 6.25 < 8$$

The guess of **2.5** units is too small, so we next try the number **2.75**, which is halfway between **2.5** and **3**.

$$(2.75)^2 = 7.5625 \quad \text{and} \quad 7.5625 < 8$$

So **2.75** is still too small, but we are getting closer. Thus you see that we are getting a better and better estimate of the length of a side of a square whose area is **8** square units. If we continued the process, we would find that the length of the side, rounded off to six decimal places, is 2.828427 units. Thus we write

$$\sqrt{8} \doteq 2.828427$$

using the symbol $\doteq$ to mean "is approximately equal to."

If we were to compute $\sqrt{8}$ to more decimal places, perhaps by utilizing a computer, we would find that the decimal form of $\sqrt{8}$ neither terminates nor repeats. This means that $\sqrt{8}$ is not a rational number, and cannot be expressed in the form $\frac{r}{s}$, where r and s are integers, $s \neq 0$. The symbol $\sqrt{8}$ represents what is called an irrational number.

If you were to investigate further, you could find many other irrational numbers. For example, the only integers whose **square roots** are **rational** are those integers which are **squares** of **integers**. Thus the symbols $\sqrt{2}$, $\sqrt{3}$, $\sqrt{5}$, $\sqrt{7}$, and $\sqrt{10}$ must represent irrational numbers, since **2**, **3**, **5**, **7**, and **10**

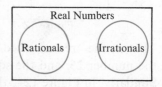

Figure 12–3

are not squares of integers. The Venn diagram in Figure 12–3 shows how the sets of rational numbers, of irrational numbers, and of real numbers are related.

The set of rational numbers and the set of irrational numbers combine to form the set of real numbers.

To perform computations that require the square roots and cube roots of numbers that are not perfect squares and perfect cubes, we often use a table of powers and roots. In the table on page 411, the values of irrational roots have been rounded off to three decimal places.

ORAL EXERCISES

Name the value of each expression as given in the table of Powers and Roots on page 411. Indicate whether the value is exact or approximate.

SAMPLE 1: $\sqrt{68}$ *What you say:* 8.246; approximate

SAMPLE 2: $\sqrt[3]{25}$ *What you say:* 2.924; approximate

SAMPLE 3: $\sqrt{676}$ *What you say:* 26; exact

1. $\sqrt{10}$ 7. $(65)^2$ 13. $\sqrt[3]{64}$

2. $\sqrt{20}$ 8. $(65)^3$ 14. $\sqrt{96}$

3. $\sqrt{2}$ 9. $\sqrt{80}$ 15. $\sqrt{42}$

4. $\sqrt[3]{45}$ 10. $\sqrt{65}$ 16. $\sqrt{8836}$

5. $(47)^2$ 11. $(-34)^2$ 17. $\sqrt{2401}$

6. $(28)^2$ 12. $(-19)^3$ 18. $\sqrt[3]{95}$

Use the table of Powers and Roots to decide which symbols represent rational numbers and which represent irrational numbers.

SAMPLE 1: $\sqrt{5329}$ *What you say:* $5329 = 73^2$, so $\sqrt{5329}$ represents a rational number.

SAMPLE 2: $\sqrt{15}$ *What you say:* $\sqrt{15} \doteq 3.873$, so $\sqrt{15}$ represents an irrational number.

19. $\sqrt{7}$ 22. $-\sqrt{36}$ 25. $\sqrt{200}$

20. $\sqrt{25}$ 23. $\sqrt[3]{64}$ 26. $-\sqrt{15}$

21. $\sqrt{100}$ 24. $\sqrt{18}$ 27. $\sqrt{9}$

WRITTEN EXERCISES

Use the table of Powers and Roots to complete each statement.

SAMPLE: 3.072 is the approximate cube root of __?__.

Solution: 3.072 is the approximate cube root of 29.

A
1. 2.410 is the approximate cube root of __?__.
2. 3.476 is the approximate cube root of __?__.
3. 5.196 is the approximate square root of __?__.
4. 8.718 is the approximate square root of __?__.
5. −2.759 is the approximate cube root of __?__.
6. __?__ is the square of 33.
7. __?__ is the square of 37.
8. __?__ is the cube of 21.
9. __?__ is the cube of 85.
10. 5329 is the square of __?__.
11. 2304 is the square of __?__.
12. 1728 is the cube of __?__.
13. 132,651 is the cube of __?__.

Find the approximate value of each radical expression, rounding off your answer to two decimal places.

SAMPLE 1: $\sqrt{71}$ *Solution:* $\sqrt{71} \doteq 8.43$

SAMPLE 2: $\sqrt{\dfrac{13}{100}}$ *Solution:* $\sqrt{\dfrac{13}{100}} = \dfrac{\sqrt{13}}{\sqrt{100}} = \dfrac{\sqrt{13}}{10} \doteq \dfrac{3.606}{10}$

$$\doteq 0.36$$

14. $\sqrt{19}$ 18. $\sqrt{35}$ 22. $\sqrt[3]{-62}$
15. $\sqrt{38}$ 19. $\sqrt{61}$ 23. $\sqrt[3]{79} + \sqrt[3]{69}$
16. $\sqrt{78}$ 20. $\sqrt[3]{13}$ 24. $\sqrt{2} + \sqrt{52}$
17. $\sqrt{99}$ 21. $\sqrt[3]{28}$ 25. $\sqrt{11} + \sqrt{83}$

B
26. $\sqrt[3]{4} + \sqrt[3]{10} + \sqrt{15}$ 29. $3(\sqrt{8} + \sqrt{10})$
27. $\sqrt{12} - \sqrt[3]{15}$ 30. $(2 \cdot \sqrt{20}) + \sqrt{5}$
28. $\sqrt{20} - \sqrt[3]{29}$ 31. $4(\sqrt[3]{72} - \sqrt{50})$

C
32. $\sqrt[3]{\dfrac{8}{125}} + \sqrt{\dfrac{81}{100}}$ 33. $\sqrt[3]{\dfrac{27}{64}} + \sqrt[3]{-\dfrac{27}{64}}$

POWERS AND ROOTS

No.	Squares	Cubes	Square Roots	Cube Roots	No.	Squares	Cubes	Square Roots	Cube Roots
1	1	1	1.000	1.000	51	2 601	132 651	7.141	3.708
2	4	8	1.414	1.260	52	2 704	140 608	7.211	3.733
3	9	27	1.732	1.442	53	2 809	148 877	7.280	3.756
4	16	64	2.000	1.587	54	2 916	157 464	7.348	3.780
5	25	125	2.236	1.710	55	3 025	166 375	7.416	3.803
6	36	216	2.449	1.817	56	3 136	175 616	7:483	3.826
7	49	343	2.646	1.913	57	3 249	185 193	7.550	3.849
8	64	512	2.828	2.000	58	3 364	195 112	7.616	3.871
9	81	729	3.000	2.080	59	3 481	205 379	7.681	3.893
10	100	1 000	3.162	2.154	60	3 600	216 000	7.746	3.915
11	121	1 331	3.317	2.224	61	3 721	226 981	7.810	3.936
12	144	1 728	3.464	2.289	62	3 844	238 328	7.874	3.958
13	169	2 197	3.606	2.351	63	3 969	250 047	7.937	3.979
14	196	2 744	3.742	2.410	64	4 096	262 144	8.000	4.000
15	225	3 375	3.873	2.466	65	4 225	274 625	8.062	4.021
16	256	4 096	4.000	2.520	66	4 356	287 496	8.124	4.041
17	289	4 913	4.123	2.571	67	4 489	300 763	8.185	4.062
18	324	5 832	4.243	2.621	68	4 624	314 432	8.246	4.082
19	361	6 859	4.359	2.668	69	4 761	328 509	8.307	4.102
20	400	8 000	4.472	2.714	70	4 900	343 000	8.367	4.121
21	441	9 261	4.583	2.759	71	5 041	357 911	8.426	4.141
22	484	10 648	4.690	2.802	72	5 184	373 248	8.485	4.160
23	529	12 167	4.796	2.844	73	5 329	389 017	8.544	4.179
24	576	13 824	4.899	2.884	74	5 476	405 224	8.602	4.198
25	625	15 625	5.000	2.924	75	5 625	421 875	8.660	4.217
26	676	17 576	5.099	2.962	76	5 776	438 976	8.718	4.236
27	729	19 683	5.196	3.000	77	5 929	456 533	8.775	4.254
28	784	21 952	5.292	3.037	78	6 084	474 552	8.832	4.273
29	841	24 389	5.385	3.072	79	6 241	493 039	8.888	4.291
30	900	27 000	5.477	3.107	80	6 400	512 000	8.944	4.309
31	961	29 791	5.568	3.141	81	6 561	531 441	9.000	4.327
32	1 024	32 768	5.657	3.175	82	6 724	551 368	9.055	4.344
33	1 089	35 937	5.745	3.208	83	6 889	571 787	9.110	4.362
34	1 156	39 304	5.831	3.240	84	7 056	592 704	9.165	4.380
35	1 225	42 875	5.916	3.271	85	7 225	614 125	9.220	4.397
36	1 296	46 656	6.000	3.302	86	7 396	636 056	9.274	4.414
37	1 369	50 653	6.083	3.332	87	7 569	658 503	9.327	4.431
38	1 444	54 872	6.164	3.362	88	7 744	681 472	9.381	4.448
39	1 521	59 319	6.245	3.391	89	7 921	704 969	9.434	4.465
40	1 600	64 000	6.325	3.420	90	8 100	729 000	9.487	4.481
41	1 681	68 921	6.403	3.448	91	8 281	753 571	9.539	4.498
42	1 764	74 088	6.481	3.476	92	8 464	778 688	9.592	4.514
43	1 849	79 507	6.557	3.503	93	8 649	804 357	9.644	4.531
44	1 936	85 184	6.633	3.530	94	8 836	830 584	9.695	4.547
45	2 025	91 125	6.708	3.557	95	9 025	857 375	9.747	4.563
46	2 116	97 336	6.782	3.583	96	9 216	884 736	9.798	4.579
47	2 209	103 823	6.856	3.609	97	9 409	912 673	9.849	4.595
48	2 304	110 592	6.928	3.634	98	9 604	941 192	9.899	4.610
49	2 401	117 649	7.000	3.659	99	9 801	970 299	9.950	4.626
50	2 500	125 000	7.071	3.684	100	10 000	1 000 000	10.000	4.642

12–8   Geometric Applications of Square and Cube Roots

In the last section, we used the relationship between the area of a square and the length of one of its sides to introduce the idea of square root. We saw that, if the area of a square is known, then the length of one side is equal to the square root of the area.

EXAMPLE 1.   Using the table of Powers and Roots on p. 411, find the length of one side of a square whose area is **18** square inches.

$$A = s^2$$
$$18 = s^2$$
$$s = \sqrt{18} \doteq 4.243$$

The length of one side is approximately **4.243** inches.

Can we use a similar method to find the edge of a cube? Recall that the formula $V = e^3$ is used to find the volume of a cube of edge e. So if the volume of a cube is known, the length of an edge is equal to the cube root of the volume.

EXAMPLE 2.   Find the length of an edge of a cube whose volume is **30** cubic inches.

$$V = e^3$$
$$30 = e^3$$
$$e = \sqrt[3]{30} \doteq 3.107$$

The length of an edge is approximately **3.107** inches.

You will find many other opportunities to use your knowledge of powers and roots of numbers. For example, the area of a circle of radius r is given by the formula $A = \pi r^2$.

EXAMPLE 3.   Find the radius of a circle whose area is **31.416** square feet. Use $\pi = 3.1416$.

$$A = \pi r^2$$
$$31.416 = 3.1416 r^2$$
$$r^2 = \frac{31.416}{3.1416} = 10$$
$$r = \sqrt{10} \doteq 3.162$$

The length of the radius is approximately **3.162** feet.

PROBLEMS

Use the table of Powers and Roots on page 411 in solving each of the following problems. Make a sketch if one is not given.

1. The area of a square room is 98 square feet. How long is each side of the room?

2. Sixteen square floor tiles, of two colors, are arranged as shown here. The tiles cover a total area of 1296 square inches. What are the dimensions of each tile?

3. A cube has a total surface area of 90 square inches. How many faces does a cube have? What is the area of each face of the cube described? What is the length of each edge of the cube?

4. The floor of a square room is partially covered by a square rug, indicated by the shaded area in the figure. If the part of the floor not covered by the rug has an area of 65 square feet, what is the area of the rug? Find its dimensions to the nearest whole foot.

5. A cube-shaped packing box has a volume of 30 cubic feet. Find the length of each edge of the box to the nearest whole foot.

6. Two cube-shaped boxes just fit into a larger box, as shown here. If the volume of the larger box is 128 cubic inches, how long is the edge of each of the smaller boxes?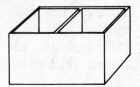

7. When completely filled, a food freezer that has the shape of a cube holds 14 cubic feet of frozen foods. Find the inside dimensions of the freezer to the nearest tenth of a foot.

8. The large box pictured here has a volume of 38 cubic feet. When a small cube-shaped box is placed inside of the larger box, the unfilled portion of the large box amounts to 11 cubic feet. What are the dimensions of the small box?

9. The area of a circle is 47.10 square feet. Find the radius of the circle. (Use $\pi = 3.14$.)

B **10.** The figure shows a circle inscribed in a square. The area of the circle is 28.26 square inches. What is the radius of the circle? (Use $\pi = 3.14$.) What are the dimensions of the square? What is its area? What is the area of the shaded portion of the figure?

11. In a circle whose area is 78.50 square feet a square is inscribed, as shown in the figure. What is the radius of the circle? How long is a diagonal of the square?

12–9 The Pythagorean Theorem

Do you remember the **Pythagorean Theorem**, which states the relationship of the legs of a right triangle to its hypotenuse? Recall that the hypotenuse of a right triangle is the side opposite the right angle, and that the other two sides are called the legs of the triangle.

Figure 12–4 gives a geometric interpretation of the theorem. It shows that for the triangle given, the **sum** of the **areas** of the **squares** drawn on the two **legs** is equal to the **area** of the **square** on the **hypotenuse**. The lengths of the legs are **3** inches and **4** inches, and the length of the hypotenuse is **5** inches. So the areas of the squares are **9, 16,** and **25** square inches, and **9 + 16 = 25**.

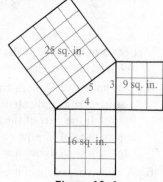

Figure 12–4

An algebraic generalization of the Pythagorean Theorem is based on the triangle shown in Figure 12–5. The variables *a* and *b* represent the lengths of the legs of **any** right triangle, and *c* represents the length of the hypotenuse. The formula which states the Pythagorean relation,

$$a^2 + b^2 = c^2,$$

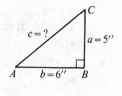

$a^2+b^2=c^2$

Figure 12–5

is useful in solving problems concerning right triangles.

In the following examples applying the Pythagorean Theorem, the table of Powers and Roots is used to find approximate roots.

EXAMPLE 1. Find the length of the **hypotenuse** of $\triangle ABC$.

$$a^2 + b^2 = c^2$$
$$5^2 + 6^2 = c^2$$
$$c^2 = 25 + 36 = 61$$
$$c = \sqrt{61} \doteq 7.810$$

The length of the **hypotenuse** is approximately **7.810** inches.

EXAMPLE 2. Find the length of side *BC* of
$\triangle ABC$.

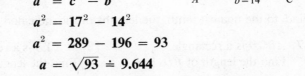

$$a^2 + b^2 = c^2$$
$$a^2 = c^2 - b^2$$
$$a^2 = 17^2 - 14^2$$
$$a^2 = 289 - 196 = 93$$
$$a = \sqrt{93} \doteq 9.644$$

The length of side *BC* is approximately 9.644 feet.

WRITTEN EXERCISES

Show whether or not the given dimensions in each exercise could represent the lengths of the sides of a right triangle.

SAMPLE: $a = 9''$; $b = 12''$; $c = 15''$

Solution:

$a^2 + b^2$	$\stackrel{?}{=}$ c^2
$9^2 + 12^2$	15^2
$81 + 144$	225
225	225

Since $225 = 225$, the dimensions could represent the sides of a right triangle.

A

1. $a = 30''$; $b = 40''$; $c = 50''$
2. $a = 3$ cm.; $b = 5$ cm.; $c = 6$ cm.
3. $a = 15'$; $b = 8'$; $c = 17'$
4. $a = 4$ yd.; $b = 6$ yd.; $c = 7$ yd.
5. $a = 9''$; $b = 12''$; $c = 15''$
6. $a = 12$ mi.; $b = 5$ mi.; $c = 13$ mi.
7. $a = 11$ cm.; $b = 60$ cm.; $c = 61$ cm.
8. $a = 24''$; $b = 7''$; $c = 25''$
9. $a = 9$ yd.; $b = 30$ yd.; $c = 41$ yd.
10. $a = 6''$; $b = 8''$; $c = 10''$

In each right triangle, find the missing dimension to the nearest tenth.

11.

12.

13.

14. 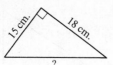   **15.** 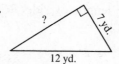   **16.**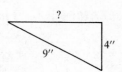

Find, to the nearest tenth, the lengths of the indicated segments.

17. *ABCD* is a rectangle. Find the length of $\overline{BD}$.

18. *EFGH* is a square. Find the length of $\overline{EG}$.

19. *WXYZ* is a rectangle. Find the length of $\overline{XY}$.

20. *QRST* is a square. Find the length of $\overline{QS}$.

21. *CDEF* is a square. Find the length of $\overline{DE}$. Find the length of $\overline{FE}$.

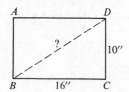

22. *JKLM* is a trapezoid. Find the length of $\overline{JK}$. Find the length of $\overline{KM}$.

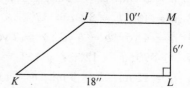

PROBLEMS

1. The distance from the foot of a 20-foot ladder to the base of a wall against which the ladder is leaning is 6 feet. How far above the ground does the ladder touch the wall?

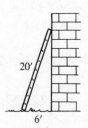

2. A room in the shape of a rectangle is 12 feet long and 8 feet wide. How far is it from one corner of the room to the corner diagonally opposite to it?

3. A utility pole is supported by a guy wire 30 feet long. The point at which the wire is anchored in the ground is 24 feet from the foot of the pole. How high up on the pole is the wire attached?

4. After a man drives his car 8 miles west and then 6 miles north, how far is he from his starting point?

5. The top of an 18-foot ladder touches a building at a point 14 feet above ground. How far is the foot of the ladder from the base of the building?

Radical Expressions

12–10   Multiplication, Division, and Simplification of Radicals

In the study of algebra it is often necessary to multiply, divide, or simplify radical expressions. To accomplish this we can use the familiar commutative and associative properties along with the product and quotient properties of square roots.

EXAMPLES.

$$\sqrt{5} \cdot \sqrt{7} = \sqrt{35}$$

$$\sqrt{12} \cdot \sqrt{3} = \sqrt{36} = 6$$

$$3\sqrt{5} \cdot 2\sqrt{7} = (3 \cdot 2)(\sqrt{5} \cdot \sqrt{7}) = 6\sqrt{35}$$

$$\frac{\sqrt{15}}{\sqrt{3}} = \sqrt{\frac{15}{3}} = \sqrt{5}$$

$$\sqrt{45} = \sqrt{9} \cdot \sqrt{5} = 3\sqrt{5}$$

To simplify the expression $\dfrac{\sqrt{5}}{\sqrt{2}}$, we wish to write a form which will not have an irrational denominator. We can accomplish this by using the multiplicative property of one, as follows:

$$\frac{\sqrt{5}}{\sqrt{2}} = \frac{\sqrt{5}}{\sqrt{2}} \cdot \frac{\sqrt{2}}{\sqrt{2}} = \frac{\sqrt{10}}{\sqrt{4}} = \frac{\sqrt{10}}{2}.$$

Since the final form gives us a fraction equivalent to the original one, but with a **rational** denominator, the process is called rationalizing the denominator.

ORAL EXERCISES

Name a simpler form for each expression.

SAMPLE: $\sqrt{7} \cdot \sqrt{5}$ *What you say:* $\sqrt{35}$

1. $\sqrt{5} \cdot \sqrt{3}$ **5.** $\dfrac{\sqrt{18}}{\sqrt{6}}$ **9.** $\sqrt{6} \cdot \sqrt{\frac{1}{2}}$

2. $\sqrt{6} \cdot \sqrt{7}$ **6.** $\dfrac{\sqrt{40}}{\sqrt{8}}$ **10.** $\sqrt{\frac{1}{3}} \cdot \sqrt{12}$

3. $\sqrt{19} \cdot \sqrt{2}$ **7.** $\dfrac{\sqrt{5}}{\sqrt{15}}$ **11.** $\sqrt{15} \cdot \sqrt{2}$

4. $\dfrac{\sqrt{15}}{\sqrt{3}}$ **8.** $\sqrt{\frac{1}{2}} \cdot \sqrt{\frac{2}{3}}$ **12.** $2\sqrt{3} \cdot \sqrt{5}$

Tell how to complete each statement.

13. $\dfrac{\sqrt{27}}{\sqrt{3}} = \sqrt{\dfrac{27}{3}} = \sqrt{?} = ?$ **15.** $\sqrt{3} \cdot \sqrt{3} = \sqrt{?} = ?$

14. $\sqrt{12} \cdot \sqrt{3} = \sqrt{?} = ?$ **16.** $\sqrt{7} \cdot \sqrt{7} = \sqrt{?} = ?$

WRITTEN EXERCISES

Simplify each expression.

SAMPLE 1: $\sqrt{32}$ *Solution:* $\sqrt{32} = \sqrt{16} \cdot \sqrt{2} = 4\sqrt{2}$

SAMPLE 2: $(5\sqrt{3})^2$ *Solution:* $(5\sqrt{3})^2 = 5\sqrt{3} \cdot 5\sqrt{3}$
$$= (5 \cdot 5)(\sqrt{3} \cdot \sqrt{3}) = 25\sqrt{9}$$
$$= 25 \cdot 3 = 75$$

1. $(4\sqrt{\frac{1}{2}})^2$ **7.** $(3\sqrt{10})^2$ **13.** $\frac{1}{3}\sqrt{45}$

2. $\dfrac{\sqrt{80}}{\sqrt{5}}$ **8.** $\dfrac{\sqrt{50}}{\sqrt{2}}$ **14.** $\frac{1}{2}\sqrt{80}$

3. $3\sqrt{2} \cdot \sqrt{8}$ **9.** $\sqrt{75}$ **15.** $\sqrt{48}$

4. $4\sqrt{12} \cdot \sqrt{3}$ **10.** $\sqrt{72}$ **16.** $\sqrt{28}$

5. $(2\sqrt{3})^2$ **11.** $\sqrt{300}$ **17.** $3\sqrt{24}$

6. $\dfrac{15\sqrt{10}}{5\sqrt{2}}$ **12.** $\dfrac{\sqrt{2}}{\sqrt{98}}$ **18.** $\dfrac{\sqrt{75}}{\sqrt{3}}$

Simplify each of the following, then express its approximate value as a decimal numeral, using the table of Powers and Roots on page 411.

SAMPLE: $2\sqrt{3} \cdot \sqrt{6}$ *Solution:* $2\sqrt{3} \cdot \sqrt{6} = 2\sqrt{18}$
$$= 2\sqrt{9} \cdot \sqrt{2} = 2 \cdot 3\sqrt{2}$$
$$= 6\sqrt{2} \doteq 6(1.414) \doteq 8.484$$

19. $\sqrt{6} \cdot \sqrt{5}$

20. $\dfrac{\sqrt{20}}{\sqrt{2}} \cdot \sqrt{2}$

21. $(2\sqrt{5} \cdot \sqrt{5}) \cdot \sqrt{2}$

22. $5\sqrt{3} \cdot \sqrt{2} \cdot \sqrt{5}$

23. $2\sqrt{3} \cdot (3\sqrt{2} \cdot \sqrt{8})$

24. $\sqrt{10} \cdot \sqrt{3}$

25. $\dfrac{\sqrt{15}}{\sqrt{3}} \cdot \sqrt{4}$

26. $(3\sqrt{2})^2 \cdot (\sqrt{3})^2$

27. $\sqrt{15} \cdot \sqrt{\tfrac{1}{3}} \cdot \sqrt{3}$

28. $2\sqrt{20} \cdot (3\sqrt{18} \cdot \sqrt{2})$

Simplify each expression.

SAMPLE 1: $\sqrt{\dfrac{3}{5}}$ *Solution:* $\sqrt{\dfrac{3}{5}} = \dfrac{\sqrt{3}}{\sqrt{5}}$
$$= \dfrac{\sqrt{3}}{\sqrt{5}} \cdot \dfrac{\sqrt{5}}{\sqrt{5}} = \dfrac{\sqrt{15}}{\sqrt{25}}$$
$$= \dfrac{\sqrt{15}}{5} = \dfrac{1}{5}\sqrt{15}$$

SAMPLE 2: $\dfrac{\sqrt{8}}{\sqrt{3}}$ *Solution:* $\dfrac{\sqrt{8}}{\sqrt{3}} = \dfrac{\sqrt{8}}{\sqrt{3}} \cdot \dfrac{\sqrt{3}}{\sqrt{3}}$
$$= \tfrac{1}{3}\sqrt{24} = \tfrac{1}{3}\sqrt{4} \cdot \sqrt{6}$$
$$= \tfrac{1}{3} \cdot 2 \cdot \sqrt{6} = \tfrac{2}{3}\sqrt{6}$$

B **29.** $\sqrt{\tfrac{2}{3}}$

30. $\sqrt{\tfrac{5}{8}}$

31. $3\sqrt{\tfrac{3}{5}}$

32. $6\sqrt{\tfrac{20}{9}}$

33. $\dfrac{\sqrt{10}}{\sqrt{6}}$

34. $4\sqrt{\tfrac{11}{12}}$

35. $\sqrt{72c^2}$

36. $\dfrac{\sqrt{60}}{3\sqrt{6}}$

37. $\tfrac{3}{4}\sqrt{12}$

C **38.** $\sqrt{x}(\sqrt{x} - 5)$

39. $(5\sqrt{ab^2})(3\sqrt{a})$

40. $\dfrac{2\sqrt{7} + \sqrt{14}}{\sqrt{7}}$

12–11 Addition and Subtraction of Radicals

If a radical expression contains two or more terms having the same radical factor, the familiar distributive property can be used in simplifying the expression.

EXAMPLE 1. $5\sqrt{3} + 2\sqrt{3} = (5 + 2)\sqrt{3} = 7\sqrt{3}$

EXAMPLE 2. $3\sqrt{7} + 6\sqrt{5} + 2\sqrt{7} - 2\sqrt{5}$
$$= (3 + 2)\sqrt{7} + (6 - 2)\sqrt{5}$$
$$= 5\sqrt{7} + 4\sqrt{5}$$

EXAMPLE 3. $2\sqrt{18} + 3\sqrt{2} = 2\sqrt{9} \cdot \sqrt{2} + 3\sqrt{2}$
$$= 2 \cdot 3\sqrt{2} + 3\sqrt{2}$$
$$= 6\sqrt{2} + 3\sqrt{2}$$
$$= (6 + 3)\sqrt{2} = 9\sqrt{2}$$

Did you notice, in Example 3, that $2\sqrt{18}$ had to be simplified first, so that you could see that each term has $\sqrt{2}$ as a common radical factor?

ORAL EXERCISES

Tell how to complete each of the following so the result is a true statement.

1. $5\sqrt{2} + 8\sqrt{2} = (? + ?)\sqrt{2} = (?)\sqrt{2}$
2. $2\sqrt{3} - 5\sqrt{3} = (? - ?)\sqrt{3} = (?)\sqrt{3}$
3. $5\sqrt{7} - 2\sqrt{7} = (? - ?)\sqrt{7} = (?)\sqrt{7}$
4. $7\sqrt{6} + 2\sqrt{6} = (? + ?)\sqrt{6} = (?)\sqrt{6}$
5. $\sqrt{5} + 4\sqrt{5} = (? + ?)\sqrt{5} = (?)\sqrt{5}$
6. $3\sqrt{2} - 5\sqrt{2} + 2\sqrt{2} = (? - ? + ?)\sqrt{2} = (?)\sqrt{2} = ?$

WRITTEN EXERCISES

Simplify each expression by combining like radicals.

A

1. $2\sqrt{10} + 7\sqrt{10} + 10\sqrt{10}$ **7.** $2\sqrt{13} + 4\sqrt{13} - 9\sqrt{13}$
2. $3\sqrt{7} - 2\sqrt{7} + 5\sqrt{11}$ **8.** $3\sqrt{x} + \sqrt{x} - 3\sqrt{x}, x \geq 0$
3. $-2\sqrt{5} - 6\sqrt{5} - 3\sqrt{5}$ **9.** $\sqrt{y} - 5\sqrt{y} + \sqrt{y}, y \geq 0$
4. $6\sqrt{3} - 3\sqrt{3} + 4\sqrt{3}$ **10.** $3\sqrt{2} + \sqrt{3} + 5\sqrt{2}$
5. $5\sqrt{2} - 6\sqrt{2} - 2\sqrt{2}$ **11.** $6\sqrt{5} + \sqrt{2} - 3\sqrt{5}$
6. $10\sqrt{5} - \sqrt{5} - 3\sqrt{5}$ **12.** $\sqrt{6} + \sqrt{3} - 3\sqrt{6} + 2\sqrt{3}$

13. $\sqrt{2} + \sqrt{8}$ **16.** $\sqrt{8} + \sqrt{18}$ **19.** $5\sqrt{48} - \sqrt{32}$
14. $\sqrt{12} + \sqrt{3}$ **17.** $\sqrt{8} - \sqrt{2}$ **20.** $6\sqrt{300} + \sqrt{75}$
15. $\sqrt{18} + \sqrt{2}$ **18.** $3\sqrt{3} + \sqrt{27}$ **21.** $\sqrt{50} - \sqrt{98}$

B **22.** $\sqrt{2} + \sqrt{\frac{1}{2}}$

23. $\sqrt{6} + \sqrt{\frac{2}{3}}$

24. $3\sqrt{63} + \frac{1}{4}\sqrt{28}$

25. $2\sqrt{150} - \frac{3}{8}\sqrt{96}$

26. $4\sqrt{\frac{5}{2}} - 10\sqrt{\frac{1}{10}}$

27. $10\sqrt{\frac{3}{5}} + 30\sqrt{\frac{5}{3}}$

C **28.** $\sqrt{3} + 2\sqrt{27} - 6\sqrt{\frac{1}{3}}$

29. $3\sqrt{10} - 4\sqrt{90} + 5\sqrt{\frac{1}{10}}$

30. $12\sqrt{\frac{2}{3}} - 2\sqrt{1\frac{1}{2}}$

31. $10\sqrt{\frac{2}{5}} - \frac{1}{4}\sqrt{40}$

CHAPTER SUMMARY

Inventory of Structure and Concepts

1. A number that can be expressed in the form $\frac{r}{s}$, where r and s are any integers, $s \neq 0$, is a **rational number**.

2. The **set** of **rational numbers** is made up of all the positive rationals, all the negative rationals, and zero.

3. Between any two rational numbers, there is another rational number; thus you can find as many rational numbers as you wish between two given rationals; this is the **density** property.

4. A rational number represented in decimal form is either a **terminating decimal** or a **repeating decimal**; conversely, each terminating decimal and each repeating decimal represents a rational number.

5. A number r is a **square root** of a number s if $r^2 = s$.

6. Every positive number has **two square roots**, a **positive** root, and a **negative** root that is the opposite of the positive root; the positive root is called the **principal root**.

7. The **product property** of square roots states that for any numbers r and s, equal to or greater than zero, $\sqrt{rs} = \sqrt{r} \cdot \sqrt{s}$.

8. The **quotient property** of square roots states that for any numbers r and s, $r \geq 0$ and $s > 0$, $\sqrt{\frac{r}{s}} = \frac{\sqrt{r}}{\sqrt{s}}$.

9. A number r is a **cube root** of a number s if $r^3 = s$.

10. Concerning the nth **root** of the number r, where n is a positive integer greater than 1:

if n is even and $r > 0$, then r has both a positive and a negative nth root;

if n is odd and $r > 0$, then r has a positive nth root;

if n is odd and $r < 0$, then r has a negative nth root;

if $r = 0$, then its nth root is 0.

11. In general the **product property** and **quotient property** of roots state:

    For all positive numbers r and s, if n is a positive integer greater than 1, then $\sqrt[n]{rs} = \sqrt[n]{r} \cdot \sqrt[n]{s}$ and $\sqrt[n]{\dfrac{r}{s}} = \dfrac{\sqrt[n]{r}}{\sqrt[n]{s}}$.

12. If r is a positive number that is not a **perfect square**, the symbol $\sqrt{r}$ represents an **irrational number**, and cannot be expressed as either a terminating or a repeating decimal.

13. The **set of real numbers** is the union of the set of rational numbers and the set of irrational numbers.

14. The **Pythagorean Theorem** states that the sum of the squares on the legs of a right triangle is equal to the square on the hypotenuse; if a and b represent the lengths of the **legs**, and c represents the length of the **hypotenuse**, then $a^2 + b^2 = c^2$.

Vocabulary and Spelling

positive rational numbers (*p. 391*)

negative rational numbers (*p. 392*)

set of rational numbers (*p. 392*)

property of density (*p. 393*)

terminating decimal (*p. 394*)

repeating decimal (*p. 394*)

square root (*p. 397*)

radical (*p. 397*)

principal root (*p. 397*)

product property of square roots (*p. 399*)

quotient property of square roots (*p. 400*)

cube root (*p. 402*)

root index (*p. 402*)

product property of roots (*p. 405*)

quotient property of roots (*p. 406*)

perfect square (*p. 407*)

irrational number (*p. 408*)

set of real numbers (*p. 409*)

Pythagorean Theorem (*p. 414*)

leg of a right triangle (*p. 414*)

hypotenuse (*p. 414*)

rationalizing denominators (*p. 417*)

Chapter Test

Tell which of the following represent rational numbers and which represent irrational numbers.

1. 0.0025

2. $\sqrt{6}$

3. $\sqrt{2} \cdot \sqrt{8}$

4. $\frac{17}{19}$

5. $2.3\overline{7}$

6. 35%

Find the solution set for each equation.

7. $n^2 = 900$

8. $5x = 180$

9. $x = \sqrt[3]{-27}$

10. $y^4 = \sqrt{256}$

Use the symbol $=$ or $\doteq$ to complete each statement.

11. $\sqrt{2}$? 1.414

12. $\frac{4}{3}$? $1.\overline{3}$

13. $\sqrt{12}$? 3.4641

Simplify each radical expression.

14. $\sqrt{6.4} \cdot \sqrt{10}$

15. $\sqrt{400}$

16. $-\sqrt{\frac{9}{121}}$

17. $4\sqrt{15} \cdot 2\sqrt{15}$

18. $3\sqrt{7} \cdot 3\sqrt{2}$

19. $\dfrac{3\sqrt{49}}{3\sqrt{40}}$

20. $5\sqrt{3} \cdot \sqrt{5} \cdot \sqrt{6}$

21. $3\sqrt{5} + 2\sqrt{5}$

22. $3\sqrt{27} \cdot \sqrt{\frac{1}{3}}$

Name three rational numbers between each given pair of rational numbers.

23. 0.06 and 0.07

24. $-\frac{1}{4}$ and $-\frac{1}{3}$

25. -8 and -9

26. $\frac{1}{10}$ and $\frac{2}{10}$

Complete each statement.

27. The set of real numbers is made up of the set of __?__ numbers and the set of __?__ numbers.

28. Every positive number has __?__ square root(s).

29. Every negative number has __?__ square root(s).

30. An irrational number cannot be expressed as either a __?__ decimal or a __?__ decimal.

Find the third side of right triangle QRS if $\overline{QR}$ is the hypotenuse and the lengths of two sides are as given.

31. $\overline{RS}$, 20 in.; $\overline{QR}$, 25 in.

32. $\overline{QS}$, 16 cm.; $\overline{RS}$, 12 cm.

Chapter Review

12-1 Fractional Representations of Rational Numbers

Express each of the following as the quotient of two integers.

1. -8

2. $1\frac{1}{2}$

3. $(-5)^2$

4. 25%

Name two rational numbers between the numbers in each pair.

5. 9, 10 **6.** 2.3, 2.4 **7.** $\frac{1}{8}, \frac{1}{10}$ **8.** $-3, -4$

12–2 Decimal Representations of Rational Numbers

Express each fraction as a repeating or a terminating decimal.

9. $\frac{9}{10}$ **10.** $-\frac{2}{3}$ **11.** $\frac{3}{5}$ **12.** $\frac{4}{7}$

Express each of the following as a fraction.

13. 0.0327 **14.** 0.025 **15.** -0.0009 **16.** $0.\overline{3}$

12–3 Square Roots of Numbers

Name the principal square root of each number.

17. 256 **18.** 576 **19.** $\frac{16}{81}$ **20.** 0.09

Simplify each radical expression.

21. $-\sqrt{16}$ **23.** $\pm\sqrt{\frac{144}{169}}$ **25.** $\sqrt{3^2 + 4^2}$ **27.** $\pm\sqrt{\frac{x^2}{25}}$

22. $\sqrt{10,000}$ **24.** $-\sqrt{121}$ **26.** $\pm\sqrt{\frac{49}{25}}$ **28.** $\pm\sqrt{\frac{36k^2}{289}}$

12–4 Product and Quotient Properties of Square Roots

Write each expression as a single radical and then simplify.

29. $\sqrt{5} \cdot \sqrt{49}$ **31.** $\frac{\sqrt{36}}{\sqrt{4}}$ **33.** $\sqrt{4s} \cdot \sqrt{s}$, $s \geq 0$

30. $\sqrt{3} \cdot \sqrt{27}$ **32.** $\frac{\sqrt{64}}{\sqrt{16}}$ **34.** $\sqrt{3} \cdot \sqrt{4} \cdot \sqrt{3}$

12–5 Roots Other than Square Roots

Find each indicated root.

35. $\sqrt[3]{125}$ **37.** $\sqrt[4]{256}$ **39.** $\pm\sqrt[4]{625}$

36. $\sqrt[4]{81}$ **38.** $\sqrt[3]{-27}$ **40.** $\sqrt[5]{-1024}$

12-6 Product and Quotient Properties of Roots Other than Square Roots

Simplify each radical expression.

41. $\dfrac{\sqrt[3]{27}}{\sqrt[3]{125}}$ **43.** $\sqrt[4]{\dfrac{81}{10,000}}$ **45.** $\sqrt[3]{8} \cdot \sqrt[3]{27}$

42. $\sqrt[5]{\dfrac{32}{243}}$ **44.** $\sqrt[4]{\dfrac{256}{16}}$ **46.** $\sqrt[4]{81} \cdot \sqrt[3]{27}$

12-7 Irrational Numbers

Use the table of Powers and Roots on page 411 to complete each statement.

47. $\sqrt[3]{61} \doteq ?$ **49.** $4 \cdot \sqrt{5} \doteq ?$ **51.** $\pm \sqrt{68} \doteq ?$

48. $\sqrt[3]{47} \doteq ?$ **50.** $- \sqrt[3]{84} \doteq ?$ **52.** $\sqrt{5} + \sqrt{10} \doteq ?$

12-8 Geometric Applications of Square and Cube Roots

53. The area of a square is 86 square feet. What are the approximate dimensions of the square?

54. A cube-shaped packing box has a volume of 43 cubic feet. Find the length of an edge of the box to the nearest tenth of a foot.

12-9 The Pythagorean Theorem

Find the length of the indicated leg or hypotenuse of each right triangle. If the length is represented by an irrational number, round it off to the nearest tenth.

55.   **56.**   **57.**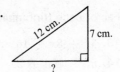

58. The guy wire attached to the mast of a sailboat is 19 feet long. It is fastened to the deck of the boat at a point 13 feet from the base of the mast. How far above the deck is the guy wire fastened to the mast?

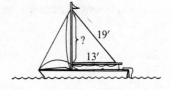

12–10 Multiplication, Division, and Simplification of Radicals

Simplify each of the following.

59. $\sqrt{75}$ **61.** $5\sqrt{20}$ **63.** $\sqrt{21} \cdot \sqrt{\frac{1}{3}}$

60. $\dfrac{\sqrt{180}}{\sqrt{5}}$ **62.** $\dfrac{\sqrt{4}}{\sqrt{25}}$ **64.** $\dfrac{\sqrt{15}}{\sqrt{3}} \cdot \sqrt{5}$

12–11 Addition and Subtraction of Radicals

Simplify each expression. Use the distributive property.

65. $4\sqrt{3} + 10\sqrt{3}$ **67.** $\sqrt{50} + \sqrt{2}$

66. $\sqrt{6} + 3\sqrt{6} - 2\sqrt{6}$ **68.** $5\sqrt{27} - \sqrt{18}$

Review of Skills

Name the two integers that form the solution set for each sentence.

1. $64 = n \cdot n$ **3.** $x^2 + 1 = 26$ **5.** $k^2 = 400$

2. $x \cdot x = 169$ **4.** $t^2 - 3 = 46$ **6.** $r^2 = 196$

Find each indicated product.

7. $(x + y)(x + y)$ **9.** $(s - 3)(s + 3)$ **11.** $(m + 3)^2$

8. $(n + 1)(n + 1)$ **10.** $(a + b)(a - b)$ **12.** $(3s + 2)^2$

Factor each trinomial.

13. $x^2 + 8x + 16$ **16.** $y^2 + y + \frac{1}{4}$

14. $n^2 - 10n + 25$ **17.** $t^2 - t + \frac{1}{4}$

15. $a^2 + 2ax + x^2$ **18.** $k^2 + \frac{1}{2}k + \frac{1}{16}$

Use exponential notation to express each of the following.

19. $x \cdot x \cdot x$ **22.** $3s \cdot 3t \cdot 3s \cdot 3t$

20. $3t \cdot 3t$ **23.** $(-2)(-2)(-2)$

21. $(x + 2)(x + 2)$ **24.** $(y + 1)(y + 1)(y + 1)$

Express the area of each rectangle as a polynomial.

25. 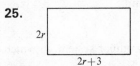   **26.** 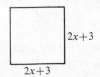   **27.**

Write each quadratic expression in standard form and then factor the polynomial completely.

28. $3x^2 + 9 + 12x$ **30.** $5n - 4 + 6n^2$

29. $-10 + x^2 + 3x$ **31.** $8t^2 - 2$

Express each equation in the slope-intercept form $y = mx + b$ and draw its number-plane graph.

32. $x - y = -1$ **34.** $x + y = 3$ **36.** $y - 3x = 1$

33. $y = -2$ **35.** $2x + y = 4$ **37.** $2y - 5x = 4$

■ ■

CHECK POINT
FOR EXPERTS

Modular Mathematics: Multiplication and Division

In the discussion of modular mathematics on page 387 we considered finite mathematical systems and found that they had operations similar to those in ordinary mathematics.

We especially considered the **Mod 5** system represented on the clock face shown here. Using a clockwise movement of the hand for addition and a counterclockwise movement for subtraction, we were able to verify such statements as $4 \oplus 3 = 2$ and $2 \ominus 3 = 4$, where $\oplus$ indicates addition and $\ominus$ indicates subtraction.

In ordinary arithmetic you found that multiplication of whole numbers could be thought of as repeated addition. For example

$$3 \times 7 \quad \text{means} \quad 7 + 7 + 7.$$

The same idea can be used for multiplication in a modular system, in which the symbol $\otimes$ is used to indicate multiplication.

$$3 \otimes 2 \quad \text{means} \quad 2 \oplus 2 \oplus 2.$$

Check the clock diagram shown here and verify that

$$2 \oplus 2 \oplus 2 = 1,$$

so we know that

$$3 \otimes 2 = 1$$

in Mod 5.

Division in a modular system is indicated by the symbol $\ominus$. The easiest way to do division in modular mathematics is to apply the idea of equivalent sentences. Thus,

$$1 \ominus 3 = ? \quad \text{is equivalent to} \quad 3 \otimes ? = 1.$$

We have just found that $3 \otimes 2 = 1$ in Mod 5, so we know that in the same system $1 \ominus 3 = 2$.

Questions

Write each multiplication expression as a repeated addition.

1. $2 \otimes 3$ **3.** $4 \otimes 2$ **5.** $4 \otimes 1$

2. $3 \otimes 1$ **4.** $3 \otimes 4$ **6.** $3 \otimes 3$

7. Complete the table at the right, showing multiplication in the Mod 5 system.

$\otimes$	0	1	2	3	4
0		0			
1					4
2			4		
3	0				
4				2	

Use the multiplication table completed in Question 7 to find the correct solution in the Mod 5 system for each multiplication sentence.

8. $3 \otimes 4 = ?$ **10.** $3 \otimes (2 \otimes 3) = ?$

9. $2 \otimes 3 = ?$ **11.** $(4 \otimes 3) \otimes 1 = ?$

12. $2 \otimes 4 = ?$

13. $(2 \otimes 2) \otimes 2 = ?$

14. $4 \otimes 4 = ?$

15. $3 \otimes 2 = ?$

Write each division sentence as an equivalent multiplication sentence, then use the multiplication table completed in Question 7 to solve the sentence for Mod 5.

16. $4 \oplus 3 = ?$

17. $1 \oplus 2 = ?$

18. $2 \oplus 1 = ?$

19. $0 \oplus 3 = ?$

20. $3 \oplus 2 = ?$

21. $2 \oplus 3 = ?$

Answer each question and justify your answer.

22. Is multiplication a commutative operation in the Mod 5 system?

23. Is multiplication an associative operation in the Mod 5 system?

24. Is there an identity element for multiplication in the Mod 5 system? If so, what is it?

25. The clock shown here represents a Mod 7 mathematical system.

Mod 7

   a. Construct a multiplication table for the system.
   b. What is the identity element in the system?
   c. Is the operation of multiplication both commutative and associative in this system? Explain your answer.

Horse-drawn steamer for extinguishing fires . . .

Modern fire-fighting equipment . . .

Products, Roots, and Quadratic Equations

The effectiveness of equipment in extinguishing a fire and the speed with which the fire can be reached have always been of great concern to fire fighters. In the 1800's, bucket brigades and hand-operated pumps were replaced by horse-drawn, steam-operated pumpers. With the development of internal combustion engines, vast improvements became possible in fire-fighting apparatus with respect to both maneuverability and the capability of the pumps. The aerial elevating platform shown is an example of very modern fire equipment. It allows the accurate placement of a water stream of 1000 gallons per minute, and can lift a load of as much as 1200 pounds from ground level to an elevation of 85 feet in the air. Thus it is useful for rescuing stranded persons, as well as for pouring large amounts of water on a blaze.

Radical Expressions

13–1 Products of Binomials Containing Radicals

In this chapter, in which we shall be finding roots of quadratic equations, it is important for you to be able to deal with multiplication of binomials of the sort in which one term is an integer and the other is an indicated square root. Here is where your previous experience in multiplying binomials like $x + y$ and $x - y$ will help you.

EXAMPLE 1. Multiply $(5 + \sqrt{3})(5 - \sqrt{3})$.

For all values of x and y, $\qquad (x + y)(x - y) = x^2 - y^2$,

$$\text{so } (5 + \sqrt{3})(5 - \sqrt{3}) = 5^2 - (\sqrt{3})^2$$
$$= 25 - 3 = 22.$$

EXAMPLE 2. Multiply $(2 + \sqrt{7})(2 + \sqrt{7})$.

For all x and y, $\qquad (x + y)(x + y) = x^2 + 2xy + y^2$,

$$\text{so } (2 + \sqrt{7})(2 + \sqrt{7}) = 2^2 + 2(2)(\sqrt{7}) + (\sqrt{7})^2$$
$$= 4 + 4\sqrt{7} + 7 = 11 + 4\sqrt{7}.$$

These skills in multiplying binomials can be applied in **rationalizing the denominators** of certain fractions. Recall that if we wish to rationalize the denominator of the fraction $\dfrac{3}{\sqrt{5}}$, we use the multiplication property of **1** to multiply the fraction by $\dfrac{\sqrt{5}}{\sqrt{5}}$:

$$\frac{3}{\sqrt{5}} = \frac{3}{\sqrt{5}} \cdot \frac{\sqrt{5}}{\sqrt{5}} = \frac{3\sqrt{5}}{5}$$

Now suppose that you have the fraction $\dfrac{1}{2\sqrt{5}+1}$. Do you see that to multiply by $\dfrac{\sqrt{5}}{\sqrt{5}}$ will not rationalize the denominator in this case?

That is, $\quad \dfrac{1}{2\sqrt{5}+1} = \dfrac{1}{2\sqrt{5}+1} \cdot \dfrac{\sqrt{5}}{\sqrt{5}} = \dfrac{\sqrt{5}}{10+\sqrt{5}}.$

However, since $(2\sqrt{5}+1)(2\sqrt{5}-1) = 20 - 1 = 19$, we can rationalize the denominator as shown in the following example.

EXAMPLE 3. Rationalize the denominator of $\dfrac{1}{2\sqrt{5}+1}$.

$$\frac{1}{2\sqrt{5}+1} = \frac{1}{2\sqrt{5}+1} \cdot \frac{2\sqrt{5}-1}{2\sqrt{5}-1}$$

$$= \frac{2\sqrt{5}-1}{(2\sqrt{5})^2 - (1)^2}$$

$$= \frac{2\sqrt{5}-1}{20-1} = \frac{2\sqrt{5}-1}{19}$$

ORAL EXERCISES

Tell how to complete each chain of equations.

1. $(3+\sqrt{2})(3-\sqrt{2}) = 9 - (\sqrt{2})^2$
$\qquad\qquad\qquad\quad = 9 - (?) = (?)$

2. $(7+\sqrt{6})(7-\sqrt{6}) = 49 - (\sqrt{6})^2$
$\qquad\qquad\qquad\quad = 49 - (?) = (?)$

3. $(7+\sqrt{3})(7+\sqrt{3}) = 49 + 2(7\sqrt{3}) + (\sqrt{3})^2$
$\qquad\qquad\qquad\quad = 49 + (?) + (?)$
$\qquad\qquad\qquad\quad = (?) + (?)$

4. $(2\sqrt{3}+5)(2\sqrt{3}-5) = (?)^2 - 25 = (?)$

WRITTEN EXERCISES

Match each indicated product in Column 1 with an equivalent expression in Column 2.

COLUMN 1	COLUMN 2
1. $(1 + \sqrt{5})(1 - \sqrt{5})$	**A.** $(4 + \sqrt{2})^2$
2. $(2 + \sqrt{3})(2 - \sqrt{3})$	**B.** $(\sqrt{3})^2 + 2(3\sqrt{3}) + 3^2$
3. $(4 + \sqrt{2})(4 + \sqrt{2})$	**C.** $1 - (\sqrt{5})^2$
4. $(2 + \sqrt{6})(2 + \sqrt{6})$	**D.** $4 + 2(2\sqrt{6}) + (\sqrt{6})^2$
5. $(\sqrt{3} + 3)^2$	**E.** $16 - (\sqrt{7})^2$
6. $(4 + \sqrt{7})(4 - \sqrt{7})$	**F.** $4 - (\sqrt{3})^2$

Simplify each indicated product.

7. $(2 + \sqrt{5})(2 - \sqrt{5})$

8. $(7 + \sqrt{2})(7 - \sqrt{2})$

9. $(3 + \sqrt{2})(3 + \sqrt{2})$

10. $(\sqrt{6} + 2)(\sqrt{6} - 2)$

11. $(\sqrt{3} + 2)(\sqrt{3} - 2)$

12. $(\sqrt{3} - \sqrt{2})(\sqrt{3} + \sqrt{2})$

13. $(\sqrt{3} + 1)(\sqrt{3} - 1)$

14. $(1 - \sqrt{8})(1 + \sqrt{8})$

15. $(5 + \sqrt{7})(5 + \sqrt{7})$

16. $(\sqrt{2} + \sqrt{5})(\sqrt{2} - \sqrt{5})$

17. $(2\sqrt{3} - 5)(2\sqrt{3} - 3)$

18. $\sqrt{3}\,(\sqrt{7} + 2\sqrt{3})$

19. $(4\sqrt{3} + 1)(2\sqrt{3} - 3)$

20. $(5\sqrt{7} + 3)(5\sqrt{7} - 3)$

21. $(2\sqrt{5} + 7)(2\sqrt{5} - 7)$

22. $(\sqrt{2} + \pi)(\sqrt{2} - \pi)$

23. $(5 - \sqrt{10})^2$

24. $(5\sqrt{3} - 4)^2$

25. $2\sqrt{6}\,(3\sqrt{2} + \sqrt{3})$

26. $5\sqrt{10}\,(2\sqrt{5} - \sqrt{15})$

27. $(\sqrt{6} - \sqrt{3})(\sqrt{6} + 3\sqrt{3})$

28. $(6\sqrt{15} + \sqrt{5})(2\sqrt{15} - 3\sqrt{5})$

Rationalize the denominator of each of the following.

SAMPLE: $\dfrac{1}{\sqrt{5} - 3}$ *Solution:* $\dfrac{1}{\sqrt{5} - 3} \cdot \dfrac{\sqrt{5} + 3}{\sqrt{5} + 3} = \dfrac{\sqrt{5} + 3}{(\sqrt{5})^2 - 9}$

$$= \dfrac{\sqrt{5} + 3}{5 - 9} = \dfrac{\sqrt{5} + 3}{-4}$$

$$= -\dfrac{\sqrt{5} + 3}{4}$$

29. $\dfrac{1}{\sqrt{7} + 2}$

31. $\dfrac{3}{\sqrt{3} - 1}$

33. $\dfrac{\sqrt{6}}{5 - \sqrt{6}}$

30. $\dfrac{2}{\sqrt{2} + 3}$

32. $\dfrac{\sqrt{2}}{\sqrt{2} + 3}$

34. $\dfrac{3 - \sqrt{5}}{2 - \sqrt{5}}$

13-2 Roots of Radical Equations

When an equation has a variable under a radical sign, it is called a **radical equation.** For example, the equation $\sqrt{x} = 7$ is a radical equation. Do you see that if we square both members of the equation we shall have an equation that does *not* contain a radical?

EXAMPLE 1. Solve $\sqrt{x} = 7$.

Squaring both members: $(\sqrt{x})^2 = 7^2$

$$x = 49$$

The solution set is $\{49\}$.

Check:

$\sqrt{x} = 7$	
$\sqrt{49}$	7
7	7

EXAMPLE 2. Solve $2\sqrt{x} + 1 = 5$.

$$2\sqrt{x} = 4$$
$$(2\sqrt{x})^2 = 4^2$$
$$4x = 16$$
$$x = 4$$

Check:

$2\sqrt{x} + 1 = 5$	
$2\sqrt{4} + 1$	5
$2(2) + 1$	5
5	5

The solution set is $\{4\}$.

The next example shows why it is important to check the solutions that result from the squaring process.

EXAMPLE 3. Solve $3 = 2\sqrt{x} + x$.

An equivalent equation is $3 - x = 2\sqrt{x}$.
$$(3 - x)^2 = (2\sqrt{x})^2$$
$$9 - 6x + x^2 = 4x$$
$$x^2 - 10x + 9 = 0$$
$$(x - 9)(x - 1) = 0$$
$$x - 9 = 0 \text{ or } x - 1 = 0$$
$$x = 9 \text{ or } x = 1$$

Check:

For $x = 9$

$3 = 2\sqrt{x} + x$	
3	$2\sqrt{9} + 9$
3	$6 + 9$
3	15

For $x = 1$

$3 = 2\sqrt{x} + x$	
3	$2\sqrt{1} + 1$
3	$2 + 1$
3	3

$3 \neq 15$, so 9 is not a root. $3 = 3$, so 1 is a root.
The solution set is $\{1\}$.

Do you wonder why it is that **9** turns out *not* to be a root? Think about the step where we squared both members of the equation. Now, if two numbers a and b are equal, it is true that $a^2 = b^2$, but it is *not necessarily true* that if $a^2 = b^2$, then $a = b$. For example:

$$3^2 = (-3)^2 \text{ is true, but}$$
$$3 = -3 \text{ is false.}$$

WRITTEN EXERCISES

Transform each equation so that the radical term containing the variable stands alone as one member of the equation. Do not solve the equations.

1. $\sqrt{x} + 1 = 5$ **4.** $\sqrt{x} + 36 = 0$

2. $\sqrt{\dfrac{x}{2}} + 2 = 5$ **5.** $\sqrt{3z} + \frac{1}{2} = \frac{3}{2}$

3. $\sqrt{2a} - 2 = 0$ **6.** $3 + \sqrt{m} = 10$

Solve each equation by squaring both members; check your solution.

SAMPLE: $\sqrt{3t} = 6$

Solution: $(\sqrt{3t})^2 = (6)^2$ *Check:*

$$3t = 36$$
$$t = 12$$

The solution set is $\{12\}$.

$\sqrt{3t} =$	6
$\sqrt{3(12)}$	6
$\sqrt{36}$	6
6	6

7. $\sqrt{x} = 4$ **9.** $9 = \sqrt{y}$ **11.** $\sqrt{2x} = 1$

8. $\sqrt{m} = 12$ **10.** $\sqrt{a} = (3 + 4)$ **12.** $\sqrt{y} = 0.1$

Transform each radical equation so that the radical term stands alone as one member; then solve the equation and check your solution.

13. $\sqrt{7z} + 1 = \frac{9}{2}$ **15.** $\sqrt{r} - \frac{1}{2} = \frac{3}{2}$ **17.** $\sqrt{\dfrac{m}{3}} + 2 = 3$

14. $\sqrt{m} + 4 = 7$ **16.** $2\sqrt{x} - 1 = 7$ **18.** $\sqrt{y} + 5 = 13$

19. $\sqrt{x + 10} = 5$ **22.** $3 = \sqrt{r + 5}$ **25.** $\sqrt{5n - 1} - 8 = -1$

20. $\sqrt{m - 4} = 9$ **23.** $\sqrt{y + 7} = 2$ **26.** $\sqrt{4m - 3} + 7 = 10$

21. $\sqrt{\dfrac{9x}{2}} - 2 = 7$ **24.** $\frac{1}{2}\sqrt{10x} = \frac{5}{2}$ **27.** $\sqrt{\dfrac{4x}{3}} - 2 = 2$

28. $\sqrt{3t} = 4\sqrt{3}$ **30.** $2\sqrt{5} = \sqrt{x}$ **32.** $\sqrt{a^2 + 9} = a + 3$

29. $\sqrt{\dfrac{1 + 5b}{6}} = 1$ **31.** $\sqrt{\dfrac{3x - 5}{4}} = 2$ **33.** $\sqrt{x^2 - 16} = x - 4$

PROBLEMS 🔲

Solve each problem.

SAMPLE: Five times the square root of a number is 25. Find the number.

Solution: $5\sqrt{x} = 10$
$(5\sqrt{x})^2 = (10)^2$
$25x = 100$
$x = 4$

Check: $\dfrac{5\sqrt{x} = 10}{\begin{array}{c|c} 5\sqrt{4} & 10 \\ 5 \cdot 2 & 10 \\ 10 & 10 \end{array}}$

The number is 4.

1. Two times the square root of a number is 8. What is the number?
2. Seven times the square root of a number is 14. Find the number.
3. One-half the square root of some number is 6. Find the number.
4. One-third the square root of some number is 9. What is the number?
5. If the square root of a number is increased by 5, the result is 11. Find the number.
6. The square root of five times a number is equal to 20. What is the number?
7. The rectangle shown here has a perimeter of 32 inches. Find its dimensions.

$$\boxed{} \sqrt{x}$$
$$10+\sqrt{x}$$

8. When 9 is added to the square root of five times a number, the result is 29. What is the number?

Solution of Quadratic Equations

13–3   Solving Quadratic Equations of Type $ax^2 + c = 0$

An equation that can be put into the standard quadratic form

$$ax^2 + bx + c = 0,$$

where a, b, and c are real numbers with $a \neq 0$, is called a **quadratic equation**. When $b = 0$, the equation becomes

$$ax^2 + c = 0.$$

An equation of this type is called a **pure quadratic equation**, and is easily solved. For example, when $a = 1$ and $c = -16$, the equation is $x^2 - 16 = 0$. It then follows that $x^2 = 16$, and, if x is a real number, then $x = 4$ or $x = -4$.

EXAMPLE 1. Solve $x^2 - 16 = 0$.

$$x^2 = 16$$
$$x = 4 \text{ or } x = -4$$

Check: For $x = 4$

$x^2 - 16 = 0$	
$4^2 - 16$	0
$16 - 16$	0
0	0

For $x = -4$

$x^2 - 16 = 0$	
$(-4)^2 - 16$	0
$16 - 16$	0
0	0

The solution set is $\{4, -4\}$.

EXAMPLE 2. Solve $x^2 - 18 = 0$.

$$x^2 = 18$$
$$x = \sqrt{18} \text{ or } x = -\sqrt{18}$$
$$x = 3\sqrt{2} \text{ or } x = -3\sqrt{2}$$

Check: For $x = 3\sqrt{2}$

$x^2 - 18 = 0$	
$(3\sqrt{2})^2 - 18$	0
$18 - 18$	0
0	0

For $x = -3\sqrt{2}$

$x^2 - 18 = 0$	
$(-3\sqrt{2})^2 - 18$	0
$18 - 18$	0
0	0

The solution set is $\{3\sqrt{2}, -3\sqrt{2}\}$.

The property used in Examples 1 and 2 is called the **property of square roots of equal numbers**, and can be stated in general as follows:

> For any real numbers **r** and **s**, it is true that $r^2 = s^2$ only when $r = s$ or when $r = -s$.

Do you suppose that there are quadratic equations which have *no* roots in the set of real numbers? Study Examples 3 and 4 and you will see that not every quadratic equation can be solved using real numbers.

EXAMPLE 3. Solve $x^2 + 5 = 2$.

$$x^2 = -3$$

Since there is *no* real number whose square is -3, the solution set is $\emptyset$.

EXAMPLE 4. Solve $4y^2 + 12 = 11$.
$$4y^2 = -1$$
$$y^2 = -\tfrac{1}{4}$$

Since there is *no* real number whose square is $-\tfrac{1}{4}$, the solution set is $\emptyset$.

ORAL EXERCISES

Name the roots of each quadratic equation if the domain of the variable is {the real numbers}.

SAMPLE: $m^2 = 4$ *What you say:* 2 and -2

SAMPLE: $x^2 = -81$ *What you say:* No real roots

1. $t^2 = 9$ **4.** $z^2 = \tfrac{1}{4}$ **7.** $x^2 = 0.09$

2. $s^2 = 64$ **5.** $n^2 = \tfrac{4}{9}$ **8.** $d^2 = 0.25$

3. $k^2 = -49$ **6.** $144 = a^2$ **9.** $y^2 = -\tfrac{1}{100}$

WRITTEN EXERCISES

Simplify each radical expression.

 1. $\sqrt{12}$ **6.** $-\sqrt{20}$ **11.** $\sqrt{48}$

2. $(2\sqrt{5})^2$ **7.** $(-3\sqrt{6})^2$ **12.** $(-2\sqrt{13})^2$

3. $(3\sqrt{2})^2$ **8.** $(10\sqrt{5})^2$ **13.** $(-3\sqrt{7})^2$

4. $\sqrt{27}$ **9.** $(-10\sqrt{5})^2$ **14.** $(-2\sqrt{15})^2$

5. $(-2\sqrt{5})^2$ **10.** $\sqrt{45}$ **15.** $-\sqrt{500}$

Solve each quadratic equation and check your answers.

SAMPLE: $x^2 - 64 = 0$ *Solution:* $x^2 = 64$
$$x = 8 \quad \text{or} \quad x = -8$$

Check: For $x = 8$ For $x = -8$

$x^2 - 64 = 0$		$x^2 - 64 = 0$	
$8^2 - 64$	0	$(-8)^2 - 64$	0
$64 - 64$	0	$64 - 64$	0
0	0	0	0

The solution set is $\{8, -8\}$.

16. $t^2 - 49 = 0$ **18.** $a^2 - 5 = 0$ **20.** $4c^2 = 1$

17. $r^2 - 81 = 0$ **19.** $x^2 + 81 = 0$ **21.** $25n^2 = 1$

22. $z^2 - 10 = 0$ **25.** $k^2 - 15 = 0$ **28.** $81x^2 = 16$

23. $x^2 - 0.25 = 0$ **26.** $8b^2 - 2 = 0$ **29.** $9y^2 = 4$

24. $y^2 - 0.04 = 0$ **27.** $9y^2 - 4 = 0$ **30.** $16x^2 = -1$

Solve each equation. The domain of the variable is {the real numbers}.

31. $9x^2 - 140 = 4$ **34.** $27k^2 - 3 = 0$ **37.** $2x^2 + 4 = 0$

32. $3y^2 - 65 = 10$ **35.** $64y^2 - 1 = 0$ **38.** $9a^2 + 25 = 50$

33. $9y^2 - \frac{1}{4} = 0$ **36.** $8t^2 - \frac{1}{2} = 0$ **39.** $18z^2 - \frac{1}{2} = 0$

B   **40.** $2y^2 - 121 = 0$ **43.** $125 - d^2 = 0$ **46.** $27 - t^2 = 0$

41. $\dfrac{s^2}{3} - 7 = 0$ **44.** $\dfrac{r^2}{2} - 18 = 0$ **47.** $\dfrac{2x^2}{3} + 4 = 0$

42. $4n^2 - \frac{1}{25} = 0$ **45.** $\dfrac{t^2}{4} - 25 = 0$ **48.** $\dfrac{3r^2}{5} - 1 = 0$

13–4   Solving Quadratic Equations of Type $ax^2 + bx + c = 0$

The property of square roots of equal numbers can be extended to help in solving quadratic equations in general. For example, consider the equation

$$x^2 - 8x + 16 = 49,$$

which can be written in the $ax^2 + bx + c = 0$ form as

$$x^2 - 8x - 33 = 0.$$

In its original form note that the left member, $x^2 - 8x + 16$, is a perfect square trinomial, so we apply the property of square roots, as shown in the example.

EXAMPLE.   Solve $x^2 - 8x + 16 = 49$.

$$(x - 4)^2 = 49$$

$$x - 4 = 7 \text{ or } x - 4 = -7$$

$$x = 11 \text{ or } \qquad x = -3$$

Check:

For $x = 11$		For $x = -3$	
$x^2 - 8x + 16 = 49$		$x^2 - 8x + 16 = 49$	
$11^2 - (8)(11) + 16$	49	$(-3)^2 - (8)(-3) + 16$	49
$121 - 88 + 16$	49	$9 - (-24) + 16$	49
49	49	49	49

The solution set is {11, −3}.

In this example, we have applied the property of square roots of equal numbers by recognizing that, if $(x - 4)^2 = 49$ and x is a real number, then $x - 4 = 7$ or $x - 4 = -7$.

ORAL EXERCISES

Tell how to complete each equation.

SAMPLE: $m^2 + 10m + 25 = (? + ?)^2$

What you say: $m^2 + 10m + 25 = (m + 5)^2$

1. $x^2 - 14x + 49 = (? - ?)^2$ 5. $k^2 - 10k + 25 = (? - ?)^2$
2. $y^2 + 20y + 100 = (? + ?)^2$ 6. $s^2 - 24s + 144 = (? - ?)^2$
3. $t^2 - 2t + 1 = (? - ?)^2$ 7. $r^2 - 6r + 9 = (? - ?)^2$
4. $n^2 + 6n + 9 = (? + ?)^2$ 8. $a^2 + a + \frac{1}{4} = (? + ?)^2$

WRITTEN EXERCISES

Solve each equation and check your solution.

SAMPLE: $(x - 1)^2 = 9$

Solution:

$$(x - 1)^2 = 9$$
$$x - 1 = \pm\sqrt{9}$$
$$x - 1 = 3 \text{ or } x - 1 = -3$$
$$x = 4 \text{ or } x = -2$$

The solution set is $\{4, -2\}$.

Check:

For $x = 4$		For $x = -2$	
$(x - 1)^2 = 9$		$(x - 1)^2 = 9$	
$(4 - 1)^2$	9	$(-2) - 1^2$	9
3^2	9	$(-3)^2$	9
9	9	9	9

1. $(x - 2)^2 = 25$ 4. $(k + \frac{3}{4})^2 = 4$ 7. $3(n + 2)^2 = 27$
2. $(y + 1)^2 = 9$ 5. $(s - \frac{3}{5})^2 = 1$ 8. $9(x - 5)^2 = 144$
3. $(a + 3)^2 = 100$ 6. $(y + 2)^2 = 1$ 9. $(b - \frac{1}{3})^2 = 36$

Solve each equation.

SAMPLE 1: $x^2 + 8x + 16 = 9$ *Solution:* $x^2 + 8x + 16 = 9$
$$(x + 4)^2 = 9$$
$$x + 4 = 3 \quad \text{or } x + 4 = -3$$
$$x = -1 \text{ or } \qquad x = -7$$
The solution set is $\{-1, -7\}$.

10. $x^2 + 10x + 25 = 9$ 13. $c^2 + 14c + 49 = 81$
11. $y^2 - 12y + 36 = 16$ 14. $y^2 - 20y + 100 = 25$
12. $n^2 - 6n + 9 = 25$ 15. $x^2 - x + \frac{1}{4} = 1$

16. $z^2 - 14z + 49 = 4$ **17.** $b^2 + 24b + 144 = 36$

SAMPLE 2: $x^2 - 6x + 9 = 5$ *Solution:* $x^2 - 6x + 9 = 5$
$$(x - 3)^2 = 5$$
$$x - 3 = \pm\sqrt{5}$$

$x - 3 = \sqrt{5}$ or $x - 3 = -\sqrt{5}$
$x = 3 + \sqrt{5}$ or $x = 3 - \sqrt{5}$

The solution set is $\{3 + \sqrt{5}, 3 - \sqrt{5}\}$.

B
18. $(x + 1)^2 = 3$ **22.** $y^2 - 24y + 144 = 188$
19. $(t - 6)^2 = 5$ **23.** $t^2 - 8t + 16 = 24$
20. $(x - 4)^2 = 12$ **24.** $r^2 - r + \frac{1}{4} = 1$
21. $x^2 + \frac{2}{3}x + \frac{1}{9} = 4$ **25.** $y^2 + \frac{2}{9}y + \frac{1}{81} = 1$

C
26. $y^3 - 4y = 0$ **28.** $9t - t^3 = 0$
27. $\frac{1}{5}n^3 - 5n = 0$ **29.** $4x - \frac{1}{4}x^3 = 0$

13–5 Solving Quadratic Equations by Completing Trinomial Squares

In the section just completed you found that it is possible to solve a quadratic equation when one of its members is a trinomial square. It is always possible to transform a quadratic equation that does not have a trinomial square as one member into an equivalent equation that does, and then solve the resulting equation. This is called the method of **completing the square.**

EXAMPLE: Solve $x^2 + 6x - 27 = 0$.
$$x^2 + 6x \qquad = 27$$
$$x^2 + 6x + 9 \; = 27 + 9$$
$$(x + 3)^2 = 36$$
$$x + 3 = 6 \text{ or } x + 3 = -6$$
$$x = 3 \text{ or } x = -9$$

Check: For $x = 3$ For $x = -9$

$x^2 + 6x - 27 = 0$		$x^2 + 6x - 27 = 0$	
$(3)^2 + 6(3) - 27$	0	$(-9)^2 + 6(-9) - 27$	0
$9 + 18 - 27$	0	$81 - 54 - 27$	0
0	0	0	0

The solution set is $\{3, -9\}$.

ORAL EXERCISES

Name the third term that will make each expression a trinomial square.

SAMPLE: $x^2 + 8x + \underline{\quad?\quad}$ *What you say:* $x^2 + 8x + 16$

1. $x^2 + 2x + \underline{\quad?\quad}$ **6.** $k^2 - 10k + \underline{\quad?\quad}$

2. $r^2 - 4r + \underline{\quad?\quad}$ **7.** $a^2 + 14a + \underline{\quad?\quad}$

3. $s^2 - 2s + \underline{\quad?\quad}$ **8.** $m^2 - 18m + \underline{\quad?\quad}$

4. $y^2 + 6y + \underline{\quad?\quad}$ **9.** $n^2 + 18n + \underline{\quad?\quad}$

5. $t^2 + 10t + \underline{\quad?\quad}$ **10.** $b^2 + 40b + \underline{\quad?\quad}$

WRITTEN EXERCISES

Tell what number you add to each member of the equation so that one member becomes a trinomial square; then solve the equation and check.

A

1. $x^2 - 2x + \underline{\quad?\quad} = 24 + \underline{\quad?\quad}$ **6.** $n^2 - 14n + \underline{\quad?\quad} = 15 + \underline{\quad?\quad}$

2. $m^2 + 2m + \underline{\quad?\quad} = 15 + \underline{\quad?\quad}$ **7.** $x^2 - 8x + \underline{\quad?\quad} = 20 + \underline{\quad?\quad}$

3. $y^2 + 4y + \underline{\quad?\quad} = 5 + \underline{\quad?\quad}$ **8.** $\underline{\quad?\quad} + 9 = y^2 - 8y + \underline{\quad?\quad}$

4. $t^2 - 6t + \underline{\quad?\quad} = 27 + \underline{\quad?\quad}$ **9.** $r^2 + 10r + \underline{\quad?\quad} = -9 + \underline{\quad?\quad}$

5. $a^2 + 8a + \underline{\quad?\quad} = 33 + \underline{\quad?\quad}$ **10.** $x^2 + 12x + \underline{\quad?\quad} = 13 + \underline{\quad?\quad}$

In each of the following, replace the variable k by a number that makes the trinomial a perfect square, then express the trinomial as the square of a binomial.

11. $n^2 + 8n + k$ **16.** $c^2 + 6c + k$

12. $r^2 - 12r + k$ **17.** $x^2 - 6x + k$

13. $y^2 + y + k$ **18.** $s^2 - 0.6s + k$

14. $x^2 + 20x + k$ **19.** $z^2 + 1.2z + k$

15. $m^2 - 10m + k$ **20.** $x^2 - x + k$

Solve each quadratic equation by completing the square.

B

21. $n^2 + 2n = 7$ **25.** $s^2 - 18s = -17$

22. $t^2 + 4t = 14$ **26.** $x^2 - 10x = 75$

23. $m^2 - 8m = -2$ **27.** $y^2 - 10y = 5$

24. $n^2 + 6n = -4$ **28.** $t^2 - 5 = 2t$

C

29. $s^2 + \frac{2}{3}s = 0$ **31.** $k^2 + \frac{3}{2}k = 0$

30. $z^2 + \frac{5z}{2} = 25$ **32.** $x^2 + \frac{2x}{5} = 3$

PROStemsBLEMS

Solve each problem, using a quadratic equation. Reject any solutions of the equation that do not give sensible answers to the problem.

SAMPLE: The width and the length of a rectangle are represented by consecutive even integers. If the area is 120 square feet, find the dimensions of the rectangle.

Solution:

If x represents the width, then $x + 2$ represents the length.

$$x(x + 2) = 120$$
$$x^2 + 2x = 120$$
$$x^2 + 2x + 1 = 120 + 1$$
$$(x + 1)^2 = 121$$
$$x + 1 = \pm\sqrt{121}$$
$$x + 1 = 11 \text{ or } x + 1 = -11$$
$$x = 10 \text{ or } \qquad x = -12$$

Since the width must be a positive number, we reject the root -12. The rectangle is 10 feet wide and 12 feet long.

1. The dimensions of a rectangle are represented by consecutive even integers. The area of the rectangle is 80 square inches. Find its dimensions.

2. The dimensions of a rectangle are represented by consecutive odd integers. The area of the rectangle is 35 square inches. Find its dimensions.

3. If the square of a certain number is increased by 12 times the original number, the result is 108. What is the number?

4. If the square of a given number is decreased by 16 times the given number, the result is 161. What is the number?

13–6   The Quadratic Formula

You will recall that earlier we gave the standard form for a quadratic equation as

$$ax^2 + bx + c = 0,$$

where the coefficients a, b, and c are real numbers with $a \neq 0$. We found that it is always possible to rewrite this equation in a form in which the **left** member is a **trinomial square** and the **right** member is a **real number**. This suggests that we ought to be able to develop a formula for the **roots** of the equation in terms of the numbers a, b, and c.

It turns out that it is possible to do this by the method of completing the square. However, the calculations are rather complicated, so for our purposes in this book it is sufficient to summarize the outcome as follows:

For the quadratic equation $ax^2 + bx + c = 0$, where a, b, and c are real numbers and $a \neq 0$, the real number solutions are given by

$$x = \frac{-b \pm \sqrt{b^2 - 4ac}}{2a},$$

provided that $b^2 - 4ac \geq 0$.

The formula $x = \dfrac{-b \pm \sqrt{b^2 - 4ac}}{2a}$ is called the **quadratic formula**. Do you see why $b^2 - 4ac$ must represent a number greater than or equal to zero for real number solutions to exist?

In applying the formula, we must first identify the values of the coefficients a, b, and c. A quadratic equation should always be written in standard form before naming the coefficients.

For $3x^2 + 8x - 3 = 0$, the equation is in standard form, so
$$a = 3, \quad b = 8, \quad \text{and} \quad c = -3.$$

For $2y^2 = 7y + 3$, the standard form is $2y^2 - 7y - 3 = 0$, so
$$a = 2, \quad b = -7, \quad \text{and} \quad c = -3.$$

EXAMPLE: Use the quadratic formula to solve $5x^2 + 8x + 1 = 0$.
The coefficients are: $a = 5$, $b = 8$, and $c = 1$.

$$x = \frac{-b + \sqrt{b^2 - 4ac}}{2a} \qquad \text{or} \qquad x = \frac{-b - \sqrt{b^2 - 4ac}}{2a}$$

$$= \frac{-8 + \sqrt{8^2 - 4(5)}}{2(5)} \qquad\qquad = \frac{-8 - \sqrt{8^2 - 4(5)}}{2(5)}$$

$$= \frac{-8 + \sqrt{64 - 20}}{10} \qquad\qquad = \frac{-8 - \sqrt{64 - 20}}{10}$$

$$= \frac{-8 + \sqrt{44}}{10} \qquad\qquad\quad = \frac{-8 - \sqrt{44}}{10}$$

$$= \frac{-8 + 2\sqrt{11}}{10} \qquad\qquad\quad = \frac{-8 - 2\sqrt{11}}{10}$$

$$= \frac{-4 + \sqrt{11}}{5} \qquad\qquad\quad = \frac{-4 - \sqrt{11}}{5}$$

The solution set is $\left\{ \dfrac{-4 + \sqrt{11}}{5}, \dfrac{-4 - \sqrt{11}}{5} \right\}$.

ORAL EXERCISES

For each equation, state the values of the coefficients *a*, *b*, and *c* in the standard form $ax^2 + bx + c = 0$.

SAMPLE: $x^2 - 3x = -2$

What you say: The standard form is $x^2 - 3x + 2 = 0$, so $a = 1$, $b = -3$, $c = 2$.

1. $x^2 + 12x - 9 = 0$
2. $x^2 - 14x + 1 = 0$
3. $m^2 + 3m - 2 = 0$
4. $2y^2 + 4y + 1 = 0$
5. $2r^2 + 6r + 4 = 0$
6. $3t^2 - 7t - 3 = 0$
7. $17x - 8x^2 = 1$

8. $7y^2 = 12y - 3$
9. $x^2 - 7x = 0$
10. $3x^2 = 7$
11. $3y^2 - 10y = -8$
12. $6x^2 = 3x + 5$
13. $3n^2 - 17 = 0$
14. $x^2 + 9x = 0$

WRITTEN EXERCISES

Simplify each expression.

SAMPLE: $\dfrac{8 - \sqrt{25 - 13}}{4}$

Solution: $\dfrac{8 - \sqrt{12}}{4} = \dfrac{8 - 2\sqrt{3}}{4}$

$\qquad\qquad = \dfrac{2(4 - \sqrt{3})}{4}$

$\qquad\qquad = \dfrac{4 - \sqrt{3}}{2}$

 A

1. $\dfrac{7 + \sqrt{25 - 24}}{12}$
2. $\dfrac{3 + \sqrt{9 + 0}}{4}$
3. $\dfrac{8 - \sqrt{54 - 10}}{6}$
4. $\dfrac{1 - \sqrt{9 + 18}}{5}$

5. $\dfrac{8 + \sqrt{64 - 40}}{10}$
6. $\dfrac{2 - \sqrt{4 + 12}}{2}$
7. $\dfrac{15 + \sqrt{36 + 14}}{5}$
8. $\dfrac{9 + \sqrt{16 + 38}}{3}$

Solve each equation by using the quadratic formula $x = \dfrac{-b \pm \sqrt{b^2 - 4ac}}{2a}$.

9. $x^2 + 6x - 7 = 0$
10. $x^2 + 2x - 8 = 0$
11. $x^2 - 7x + 10 = 0$
12. $x^2 - 4x - 12 = 0$

13. $x^2 + 2x = 8$
14. $x^2 = 7x - 12$
15. $10x - 25 = x^2$
16. $6x^2 + x = 2$

17. $x^2 + 3x - 10 = 0$ **18.** $3x^2 - x = 0$

B   **19.** $x^2 - 5 = 0$ **21.** $3x^2 + 5x + 1 = 0$
    20. $x^2 + 4x = -1$ **22.** $4x^2 + 7x + 2 = 0$

C   **23.** $20x^2 = 17x - 3$ **25.** $2x^2 - 3x - 1 = 0$
    24. $5x^2 - 17 = 0$ **26.** $x + 1 = 5x^2$

CHAPTER SUMMARY

Inventory of Structure and Concepts

1. An equation in which a variable occurs under a radical sign is called a **radical equation**.

2. The **standard form** for a quadratic equation is $ax^2 + bx + c = 0$, where a, b, and c are real numbers, with $a \neq 0$.

3. A **pure quadratic equation** is of the form $ax^2 + c = 0$, where a and c are real numbers, with $a \neq 0$.

4. The **property of square roots of equal numbers** states that, for any real numbers r and s, it is true that $r^2 = s^2$ only when $r = s$ or when $r = -s$.

5. A quadratic equation of the form $ax^2 + bx + c = 0$ can be solved by the method of **completing the square**; this consists of transforming it so that one member is a trinomial square and then applying the property of square roots of equal numbers.

6. The real roots of a quadratic equation of the form $ax^2 + bx + c = 0$ can be determined by applying the quadratic formula
$$x = \frac{-b \pm \sqrt{b^2 - 4ac}}{2a},$$
provided that $b^2 - 4ac$ represents a real number equal to or greater than zero.

Vocabulary and Spelling

radical equation (*p. 434*)
standard form of a quadratic
   equation (*p. 436*)
pure quadratic equation (*p. 436*)

property of square roots of equal
   numbers (*p. 437*)
completing the square (*p. 441*)
trinomial square (*p. 443*)
quadratic formula (*p. 444*)

Chapter Test

Simplify each of the following.

1. $(5 + \sqrt{10})(5 - \sqrt{10})$ **3.** $(\sqrt{5} + 2\sqrt{3})\sqrt{3}$

2. $(4 + \sqrt{5})^2$ **4.** $\dfrac{1}{\sqrt{3} - 5}$

Find the solution set for each equation.

5. $2\sqrt{y} = 20$ **8.** $3t^2 - 108 = 0$

6. $\sqrt{x} + 8 = 15$ **9.** $n^2 - 12 = 0$

7. $\sqrt{\dfrac{y}{2}} + 3 = 5$ **10.** $81x^2 - 16 = 0$

Solve and check each equation.

11. $(x + 5)^2 = 169$ **13.** $2(x - 2)^2 = 200$

12. $(y - \frac{1}{2})^2 = \frac{1}{4}$ **14.** $(t + \frac{1}{3})^2 = \frac{1}{9}$

Complete each of the following to make a perfect trinomial square; then write the trinomial as the square of a binomial.

15. $x^2 + 22x + \underline{\quad?\quad}$ **17.** $m^2 - 2m + \underline{\quad?\quad}$

16. $x^2 - 6x + \underline{\quad?\quad}$ **18.** $y^2 + \frac{1}{2}y + \underline{\quad?\quad}$

19. Write the standard form for any quadratic equation, and the special form for a pure quadratic equation.

Use the method of completing the square to solve each equation.

20. $y^2 - 6y = 55$ **22.** $x^2 + 20x = 125$

21. $x^2 + 12x + 20 = 0$ **23.** $x^2 = 20x + 10$

Use the quadratic formula to solve each equation.

24. $2x^2 - 3x + 1 = 0$ **26.** $x^2 + 5x = -4$

25. $3x^2 - 4x - 2 = 0$ **27.** $y^2 - 3 = -y$

Solve each problem, using a quadratic equation.

28. One-fourth the square root of a certain number is 10. What is the number?

29. Seven times the square of a number is 28. What is the number?

30. The length of a rectangle is 3 feet more than the width. If the area is 70 square feet, find the dimensions of the rectangle.

Chapter Review

13–1   Products of Binomials Containing Radicals

Complete each indicated multiplication.

1. $(7 + \sqrt{5})(7 - \sqrt{5})$ **3.** $(2\sqrt{5} + 3)(2\sqrt{5} - 3)$

2. $(3 + \sqrt{6})(3 + \sqrt{6})$ **4.** $\sqrt{7}(\sqrt{5} + 2\sqrt{3})$

13–2   Roots of Radical Equations

Solve each equation and check.

5. $\sqrt{n} = 9$ **7.** $\sqrt{3x} = 12$ **9.** $\sqrt{b} + 3 = 8$

6. $\sqrt{y} = \frac{3}{5}$ **8.** $\sqrt{2x} = 1.6$ **10.** $\sqrt{\dfrac{x}{2}} - 5 = 7$

11. Five times the square root of a certain number is 15. What is the number?

12. The square root of six times a number is 18. What is the number?

13–3   Solving Quadratic Equations of Type $ax^2 + c = 0$

Solve each equation and check.

13. $k^2 - 400 = 0$ **15.** $-x^2 + 49 = 0$ **17.** $4x^2 - 54 = 10$

14. $m^2 - 225 = 0$ **16.** $12y^2 - 3 = 0$ **18.** $2x^2 - \frac{1}{32} = 0$

13–4   Solving Quadratic Equations of Type $ax^2 + bx + c = 0$

Solve each equation and check.

19. $(y - 6)^2 = 25$ **22.** $(n - \frac{1}{2})^2 = 4$

20. $(x - 3)^2 = 0$ **23.** $2(a - 2)^2 = 18$

21. $x^2 - 16x + 64 = 81$ **24.** $k^2 + 30k + 225 = 49$

13–5   Solving Quadratic Equations by Completing Trinomial Squares

Supply the missing term to make each of the following a trinomial square.

25. $x^2 + 12x + \underline{\ ?\ }$ **27.** $b^2 + 24b + \underline{\ ?\ }$

26. $y^2 - 20y + \underline{\ ?\ }$ **28.** $18m + m^2 + \underline{\ ?\ }$

Tell what number you add to each member of the equation so that one member becomes a trinomial square; then solve the equation.

29. $x^2 + 6x + \underline{\ ?\ } = 40 + \underline{\ ?\ }$ **32.** $-17 + \underline{\ ?\ } = k^2 - 18k + \underline{\ ?\ }$

30. $y^2 - 4y + \underline{\ ?\ } = 45 + \underline{\ ?\ }$ **33.** $25 + \underline{\ ?\ } = n^2 + 24n + \underline{\ ?\ }$

31. $t^2 + 8t + \underline{\ ?\ } = -7 + \underline{\ ?\ }$ **34.** $16x + x^2 + \underline{\ ?\ } = 17 + \underline{\ ?\ }$

35. The width and the length of a rectangle are represented by consecutive even integers. The area of the rectangle is 360 square feet. What are the dimensions of the rectangle?

36. If the square of a given number is decreased by 6 times the given number, the result is 135. What is the number?

13–6   The Quadratic Formula

Use the quadratic formula $x = \dfrac{-b \pm \sqrt{b^2 - 4ac}}{2a}$ to solve each equation.

37. $x^2 - 3x - 5 = 0$ **39.** $x^2 + 6x - 3 = 0$

38. $x^2 + 6x + 3 = 0$ **40.** $x^2 + 8x + 5 = 0$

Review of Skills

Indicate whether or not each figure is a polygon.

1.   **3.**   **5.**

2.   **4.**    **6.**

Name the line segments that form each polygon.

7.   **8.** 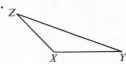   **9.**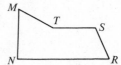

Complete each statement.

10. Angles are usually measured in units called __?__.

11. The sum of the measures of the angles of a triangle is __?__.

12. The sum of the measures of the angles of a quadrilateral is __?__.

13. The measure of any right angle is __?__.

Write a fractional name for each percent.

14. 60% **16.** 75% **18.** 55%

15. 10% **17.** 40% **19.** 80%

Write a percent name for each fraction.

20. $\frac{3}{8}$ **22.** $\frac{1}{3}$ **24.** $\frac{1}{6}$ **26.** $\frac{1}{4}$

21. $\frac{1}{20}$ **23.** $\frac{1}{5}$ **25.** $\frac{1}{8}$ **27.** $\frac{5}{8}$

Name the line segment that is the hypotenuse in each right triangle.

28.   **29.**   **30.**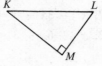

Factor each expression completely.

31. $4x^3 + 6x$ **34.** $x^2y + xy^2$ **37.** $4n + 12m$

32. $15ab^2 - 10ab$ **35.** $2x^2 + 8x + 6$ **38.** $6r^2s + 180s^2$

33. $x^2 - 9$ **36.** $5n^2 - 80$ **39.** $2x^2y - 8y$

Express each fraction in lowest terms, assuming that no denominator equals zero.

40. $\dfrac{24m^2n}{40mn}$ **41.** $\dfrac{-8xy^2}{56xy}$ **42.** $\dfrac{19r^2s^2}{114r^2s}$

Vieta

François Viète (1540–1603), better known as Vieta, was one of those whose work made possible the expansion of mathematical knowledge which took place in Western Europe during the 16th century.

Vieta, a lawyer by profession, was a member of the King's council during the rule of Henry III and Henry IV of France. When France was at war with Spain, Vieta used his mathematical skill to break the Spanish secret codes. He was so successful that Spain accused him of being in partnership with the devil.

Vieta exerted a strong influence in the European movement to adopt the decimal system of numeration, based on tens. He opposed the use of a system based on sixties, such as that used by the Babylonians. The adoption of the decimal system made computation much simpler.

Vieta made a number of contributions in the field of algebra. One of the most important of these was the introduction of symbols. The improvement of notation greatly furthered the development of algebra by later mathematicians.

He produced the first actual formula for finding the value of π when he reduced the problem of squaring the circle to that of evaluating the expression:

$$\frac{2}{\pi} = \sqrt{\frac{1}{2}} \times \sqrt{\frac{1}{2} + \frac{1}{2}\sqrt{\frac{1}{2}}} \times \sqrt{\frac{1}{2} + \frac{1}{2}\sqrt{\frac{1}{2} + \frac{1}{2}\sqrt{\frac{1}{2}}}} \times \cdots$$

From this, he computed the value of π to ten decimal places.

451

An African tribal hall . . .

New City Hall, Boston . . .

Polygons and Circles

The striking geometric similarity of the two buildings pictured shows the use of the rectangle in architecture in two widely separated areas. The African building, the home of a Dogon priest, the oldest man of the village, is a rectangular structure with a flat roof and an interior courtyard, a style well adapted to defense. The modern city hall is planned for three chief functions of city government. On its easily reached lower floors, are the offices frequently visited by the public for errands such as payment of taxes, licensing, and registration. City departments needing flexible office space rather than accessibility to the public are housed on the upper four floors. In between are the office of the mayor and the chambers in which the city council meets, located where they are visible and directly accessible to everyone.

Polygons

14–1   Polygons and Polygonal Regions

A **triangle** is defined as the **union** of three line segments determined by three points not on the same line. Recall that earlier we classified triangles as among the simple closed plane curves, so that a triangle does not include its interior. The **union** of a **triangle** and its **interior** is called a **triangular region**. Figure 14–1 shows a triangle, while Figure 14–2 pictures a triangular region.

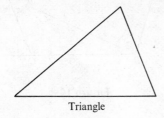

Triangle

Figure 14–1

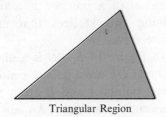

Triangular Region

Figure 14–2

453

Of course, you are familiar with other simple closed plane curves formed by the union of line segments. All such figures are called polygons, and the terms **side, vertex, interior,** and **exterior** are used in the same way as for triangles. The simple closed plane curves in Figure 14–3 are samples of convex polygons.

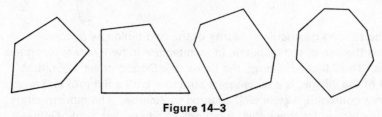

Figure 14–3

Each of the closed curves in Figure 14–4 fits the description of a polygon, because each is the union of line segments. Do you see how they differ from the polygons in Figure 14–3? The curves in Figure 14–4 are called concave polygons.

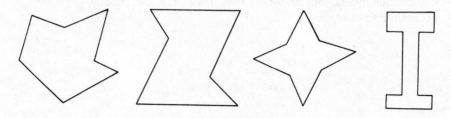

Figure 14–4

For our purposes let us agree that when we use the word "polygon" alone, we mean a convex polygon.

In Figure 14–5, capital letters are used to name the vertices of the polygon; the numbered angles are called interior angles of the polygon. The two endpoints of any side of a polygon are called consecutive vertices; two sides with a common endpoint are called consecutive sides; a diagonal of a polygon is a segment joining two vertices that are not consecutive.

In Figure 14–5, $\overline{BD}$ is a **diagonal**; $\overline{CD}$ and $\overline{DE}$ are a pair of **consecutive sides**; points A and B are a pair of **consecutive vertices.** An angle like

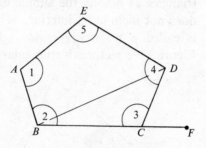

Figure 14–5

$\angle DCF$, formed by extending one side of the polygon, is called an exterior angle of the polygon.

Since a polygon is defined as a union of line segments, it follows that the **union** of a **polygon** and its **interior** is a polygonal region.

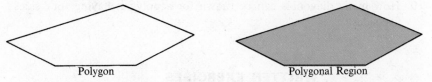

Polygon   Polygonal Region

In Figure 14–6 note how a polygonal region can be thought of as the result of piecing together a number of triangular regions.

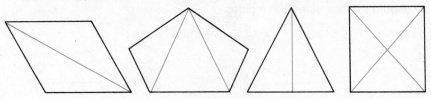

Figure 14–6

As a matter of fact, we can be certain that a figure represents a polygonal region if we can show a way of dividing it into triangular regions.

ORAL EXERCISES

Tell which of the following figures are polygons and which are not.

1. **3.** **5.**

2. **4.** **6.**

Refer to the following figures to answer each question.

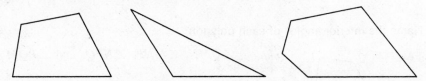

7. What is the least number of sides a polygon may have? the least number of vertices? the least number of interior angles?

8. How many diagonals can be drawn for a polygon having three sides?

9. If a polygon has four sides, how many vertices does it have? how many interior angles?

10. How many diagonals can be drawn for a polygon having four sides? five sides?

WRITTEN EXERCISES

Make a copy of each figure below, and show that it is a polygonal region by dividing it into triangular regions.

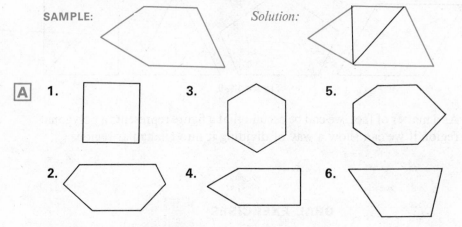

SAMPLE: *Solution:*

A **1.**   **3.**   **5.**

2.   **4.**   **6.**

Name the diagonals drawn in each polygon.

SAMPLE: *Solution:* $\overline{BD}$ and $\overline{AC}$

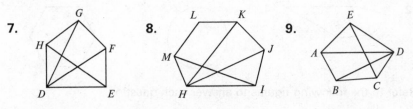

7.   **8.**   **9.**

Name the interior angles of each polygon.

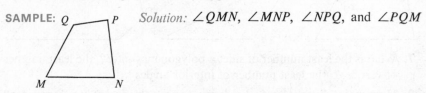

SAMPLE: Q   P   *Solution:* $\angle QMN$, $\angle MNP$, $\angle NPQ$, and $\angle PQM$

10.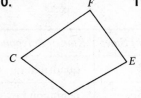

11.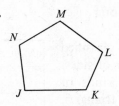

12.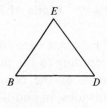

Complete each of the following with reference to the figure below.

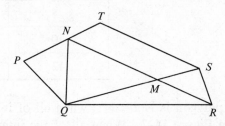

B **13.** Name a line segment that is a diagonal of polygon *PQRST*.

14. Name a line segment that is neither a diagonal nor a side of *PQRST*.

15. Name two consecutive sides of *PQRST*.

16. Name two consecutive vertices of *PQRST*.

17. Name a point in the interior of polygon *PQRST*.

18. Name a point on polygon *PQRST*, but not one of its vertices.

Copy each figure and use *exactly four* line segments to divide it into triangular regions.

SAMPLE:  *Solution:*

C **19.** **21.**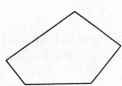

20. 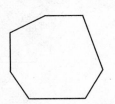 **22.**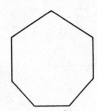

14–2   Kinds of Polygons

Polygons are often classified according to the number of sides. Some of the common kinds of polygons, in addition to triangles, are shown in the table.

Number of Sides	Kind of Polygon
4	quadrilateral
5	pentagon
6	hexagon
8	octagon
10	decagon
12	dodecagon

We say that a polygon is equilateral when all of its sides have the same length, as in Figure 14–7. When all of the interior angles of a polygon have the same measure, as in Figure 14–8, we call the polygon equiangular.

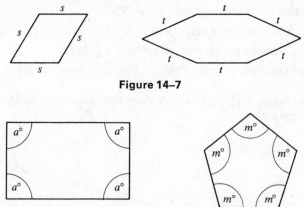

Figure 14–7

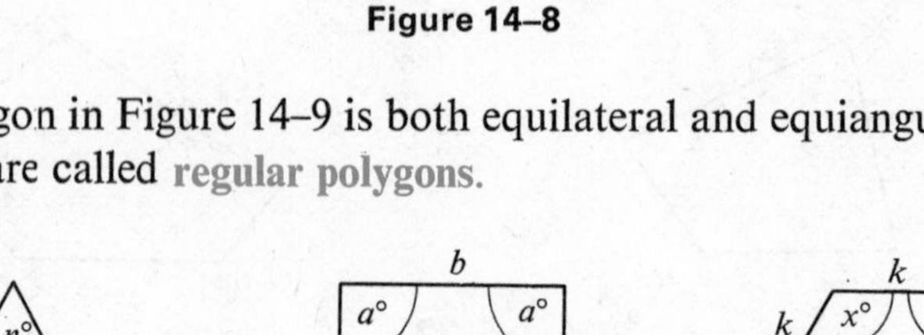

Figure 14–8

Each polygon in Figure 14–9 is both equilateral and equiangular. Such polygons are called regular polygons.

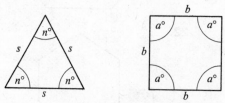

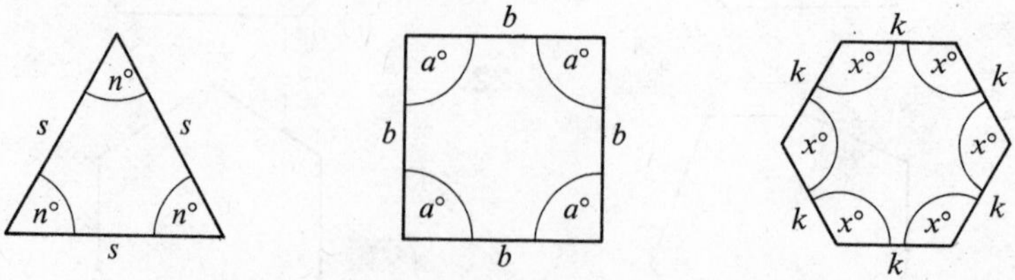

Figure 14–9

In our previous work we found that the **sum of the measures** of the interior angles of a **triangle** is 180°. Do you also recall that the **sum of the measures** of the interior angles of a **quadrilateral** is 360°? To find the sum of the measures of the interior angles of any polygon of more than three sides, we can draw all of the diagonals from one fixed vertex, thus dividing the polygon into triangles. Since we know the sum of the measures of the interior angles of a triangle, do you see that the sum of the measures of the interior angles of the polygon is equal to **180°** times the number of triangles?

The polygons in Figure 14–10 illustrate this. The first is a quadrilateral, which is divided into **two** triangles. The sum of the measures of its angles is 2(180) = **360°**. The second is a hexagon, which is divided into **four** triangles, so the sum of the measures of its angles is 4(180) = **720**.

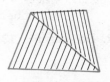
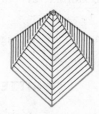

Figure 14–10

Try this method for finding the sum of the measures of the angles of various polygons. Do you see that there is a pattern? When you draw the diagonals from a single vertex of a polygon, the result is a number of triangles that is two less than the number of sides. Thus we can state, in general, that

> For a polygon of *n* sides, the sum of the degree measures of the interior angles is (*n* − 2)180.

ORAL EXERCISES

Give the correct name for each polygon.

1.   **2.** 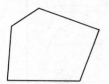   **3.**

4. 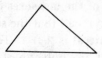 **5.** 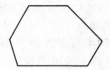 **6.**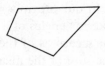

Tell how many diagonals can be drawn from vertex *A* in each figure.

7. 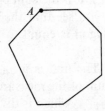 **8.** 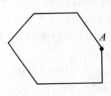 **9.**

For each polygon named below, give the number of sides, of interior angles, and of vertices.

SAMPLE: Quadrilateral   *What you say:* 4 sides, 4 vertices,
4 interior angles

10. Octagon   **11.** Hexagon   **12.** Dodecagon   **13.** Decagon

WRITTEN EXERCISES

Supply the information required to fill in each blank.

	Polygon	Figure	Number of Triangles × 180	Sum of Measures of Interior Angles
1.	Pentagon (5 sides)		3 · 180	?
2.	Hexagon (6 sides)		4 · 180	?
3.	Quadrilateral (4 sides)		__?__ · 180	?
4.	Octagon (8 sides)		__?__ · 180	?

Find the sum of the measures of the angles for each polygon. Use sum = (*n* − 2)180.

SAMPLE:

Solution: sum = (*n* − 2)180
= (7 − 2)180
= 5 · 180 = 900 (degrees)

5.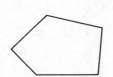

7.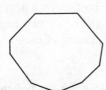

9. A dodecagon

10. A nonagon (9 sides)

6.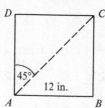

8.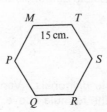

11. A decagon

Assume that each figure is a regular polygon. Supply the missing information to make true statements.

12.

Perimeter = ?
m∠*BAC* = ?
m$\overline{AB}$ = ?

m∠*ADC* = ?
m$\overline{CD}$ = ?

13.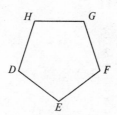

Perimeter = ?
m$\overline{QR}$ = ?
m∠*QPM* = ?

m$\overline{MT}$ = ?
m∠*STM* = ?

14.

Perimeter = 105 ft.
m$\overline{HG}$ = ?
m∠*DHG* = ?

m$\overline{EF}$ = ?
m∠*DEF* = ?

[B] **15.** The measures of three angles of a quadrilateral are 65°, 70°, and 85°. What is the measure of the fourth angle?

16. When certain diagonals of a regular hexagon are drawn as shown in the figure, six equilateral triangles are formed. Supply the missing information.

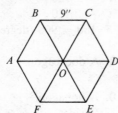

Perimeter of $\triangle BOC$ = ?
$m\overline{OC}$ = ? $m\overline{OE}$ = ? $m\overline{AD}$ = ?
Perimeter of hexagon $ABCDEF$ = ?
$m\angle OBC$ = ? $m\angle BOC$ = ? $m\angle ABC$ = ?

17. In baseball, home plate is officially a pentagon, with right angles as pictured. If the other two angles have equal measures, what is the measure of each?

Find the number of sides in a regular polygon where the measure of one angle is as given.

SAMPLE: 90°   *Solution:* $(n - 2)180 = 90 \cdot n$
$$180n - 360 = 90n$$
$$90n = 360$$
$$n = 4 \quad \text{There are 4 sides.}$$

C **18.** 108°   **19.** 144°   **20.** 60°   **21.** 120°   **22.** 150°

The following formula gives the number of all possible diagonals that can be drawn in a polygon of *n* sides:

$$\text{Number of diagonals} = \frac{n}{2}(n - 3)$$

Draw each polygon named and all of its possible diagonals. Verify the number of diagonals in your drawing by use of the formula above.

SAMPLE: Pentagon

Solution:

5 diagonals

Check: $d = \frac{n}{2}(n - 3)$
$$= \frac{5}{2}(5 - 3)$$
$$= \frac{5}{2} \cdot 2 = 5$$

23. Hexagon   **24.** Quadrilateral   **25.** Octagon

Circles

14–3 Circles and Circular Regions

A circle is a figure that is familiar to everyone. We define it as follows:

A circle is the set of all points in a plane that are at a given distance from a given point called the center.

The distance of the points from the center is called the radius of the circle. The word **radius** is also used to refer to a line segment of which one endpoint is the center of the circle and the other endpoint is on the circle. The plural of "radius" is "radii." Since all points of the circle are the same distance from the center, do you see that all radii of a given circle are equal in length? This property makes it possible for you to draw a circle of radius r, with a given point P as center, by using a compass, as shown in Figure 14–11.

Figure 14–11

If two circles in the same plane have the same center but different radii, as shown in Figure 14–12, they are called concentric circles. Figure 14–13 pictures a circular region which is the union of a circle and its interior.

Figure 14–12

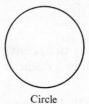

Circle

Circular Region

Figure 14–13

A chord of a circle is a line segment whose endpoints are on the circle. A diameter is a chord that passes through the center. The word "diameter" is also used to refer to the length of a chord through the center of the circle. Thus we can see that the diameter of a circle is twice as long as the radius, and that all diameters of a given circle have the same length.

A **central angle** of a circle is an angle whose vertex is the center of the circle. The rays which are the sides of a central angle thus contain radii of the circle.

A circle is usually named by naming its center. In circle *O* shown here,

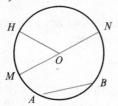

O is the **center**;
$\overline{MN}$ is a **diameter**;
$\overline{AB}$ is a **chord,** but not a diameter;
$\overline{OH}$, $\overline{OM}$, and $\overline{ON}$ are **radii**;
∠*HON* and ∠*HOM* are **central angles.**

ORAL EXERCISES

Name the items called for, with respect to circle *C* shown here.

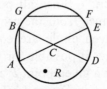

1. Two diameters
2. Two chords that are not diameters
3. Four central angles
4. Four radii
5. Two points inside the circle

6. Five points on the circle
7. Six points equally distant from point *C*
8. One point that is equally distant from both point *G* and point *F*

WRITTEN EXERCISES

1. Draw a circle and label the center *P*. Mark any two points on the circle and label them *R* and *S*. Draw chord *RS*. Draw a diameter *AB*. Draw a radius *PQ*.

2. Draw a line and a circle that intersect in exactly two points.

3. Draw a line and a circle that intersect in exactly one point.

4. Draw a circle of any convenient radius. Label any point *C* on the circle and lay off chords *CD*, *DE*, and so on as illustrated, each having a length equal to the length of the radius. How many such chords were you able to draw? Did they form a closed curve? What is the name of the simple closed curve formed by the chords?

14–4   Arcs and Central Angles

We have defined a central angle as an angle whose vertex is the center of a circle. We pointed out that this means that each side of a central angle is a ray which includes a radius of the circle. In Figure 14–14, central angle *ACB* cuts off, or intercepts, the portion of the circle shown in red. Such a part of a circle is called an arc. The arc in the figure can be named **arc *ADB*** (in symbols, $\overset{\frown}{ADB}$), since points *A* and *B* are endpoints of the arc, while *D* is a point on the arc between *A* and *B*.

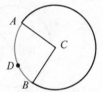

Figure 14–14

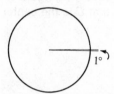

Figure 14–15

Imagine drawing as many central angles of measure 1°, as indicated in Figure 14–15, as can be fitted around the center of a circle, with the center as common vertex, and with none of the angles overlapping. When all the space has been used up, how many angles will have been drawn? If your answer is **360**, you are correct. Thus each 1° angle intercepts an arc that is $\frac{1}{360}$ of the circle, so it is logical to use the word "degree" to name this unit arc which corresponds to the unit central angle of one degree. We express this by saying: "The measure of a circle is 360°." Of course, later we may want to measure the distance around a given circle in some unit of length, such as inches, but for the present we shall use this sort of measure, which we might call the angular measure of a circle because of its relation to the central angles.

Thus we see that if the measure of a central angle is 1°, the angular measure of the intercepted arc is 1°; a central angle whose measure is 15° intercepts an arc of measure 15°; in general, a central angle with a measure of *n*° will intercept an arc with an angular measure of *n*°. So we can conclude that

In a given circle, if two central angles have equal measures, then the measures of their intercepted arcs are equal.

In circle *C* shown here,

If $m\angle RCT = 80°$, then $m\overset{\frown}{RST} = 80°$.
If $m\overset{\frown}{PQN} = 35°$, then $m\angle PCN = 35°$.

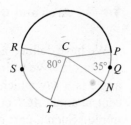

ORAL EXERCISES

Use the following figure to complete each exercise;
assume that *C* is the center of the circle.

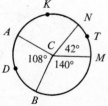

1. Name the arc intercepted by $\angle ACB$; by $\angle ACN$; by $\angle NCM$.
2. Give the measure of $\angle NCM$.
3. Give the measure of $\overset{\frown}{NTM}$.
4. $m\overset{\frown}{ADB} + m\overset{\frown}{AKN} + m\overset{\frown}{NTM} = ?$
5. Give the measure of $\overset{\frown}{AKN}$.
6. Give the measure of $\angle ACN$.
7. $m\overset{\frown}{ADB} + m\overset{\frown}{AKN} = ?$
8. $m\overset{\frown}{NTM} + m\overset{\frown}{AKN} = ?$
9. Name two acute central angles.
10. Name two obtuse central angles.

WRITTEN EXERCISES

 1. A circle is divided into five equal arcs. What is the measure of each arc?
2. A circle is divided into twelve equal arcs. What is the measure of each arc?
3. What is the measure of the angle formed by the hands of a clock at 3 o'clock?
4. In circle *O* pictured at the right, name an arc intercepted by a central angle; name an arc cut off by a chord; name an acute central angle; name an obtuse central angle.

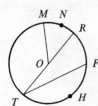

Use the given circles and protractor scales to complete each statement.

In circle O:

5. $m\angle QOS = ?$

6. $m\overarc{QRS} = ?$

7. $m\angle TOS = ?$

8. $m\overarc{SPT} = ?$

9. $m\overarc{QRS} + m\overarc{SPT} = ?$

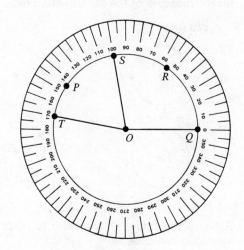

In circle P:

10. $m\overarc{ABC} = ?$

11. $m\overarc{BCD} = ?$

12. $m\overarc{EAB} = ?$

13. What is the measure of the arc which contains point K and is cut off by chord ED?

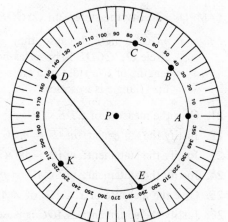

For these concentric circles, with common center at C:

14. $m\angle XCZ = ?$

15. $m\overarc{XYZ} = ?$

16. $m\overarc{GHK} = ?$

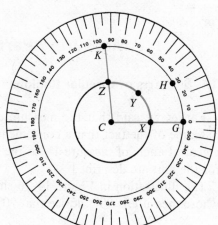

Match each figure in Column 1 with the best estimate from Column 2 for the measure of the arc shown in red.

COLUMN 1

COLUMN 2

17.

19.

A. 168°

B. 85°

C. 50°

D. 14°

E. 115°

18.

20.

Refer to the figure shown here to respond to the following exercises.

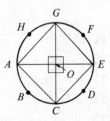

SAMPLE: Justify the statement: △*GOE* is isosceles.

Solution: $m\overline{GO} = m\overline{OE}$ because they are radii of circle *O*; △*GOE* is isosceles because if the lengths of two sides of a triangle are equal, the triangle is isosceles.

B   21. Give the measure of $\overset{\frown}{CDE}$.

22. Justify the statement: $m\overline{AE} = m\overline{CG}$.

23. Justify the statement: $m\overline{AO} = m\overline{OC}$.

24. Justify the statement: $m\angle CAO = m\angle ACO$.

25. Give the measure of $\angle CAO$; of $\angle ACO$.

26. Justify the statement: △*AOC* is isosceles.

27. Justify the statement: $m\overset{\frown}{ABC} = m\overset{\frown}{CDE}$

Measuring Parts of a Circle

14–5 Parts of Circular Regions

Earlier we said that the measure of a circle is 360°. This was an outcome of the fact that a convenient unit arc was one intercepted by a central angle of measure 1°, so the name "degree" is a logical name for the unit arc described.

The illustration in Figure 14–16 shows a circle with a central angle whose measure is 90°; notice that 90° is $\frac{90}{360}$, or $\frac{1}{4}$, of the total degree measure around point C. The angle intercepts an arc whose measure is 90°. Do you see that the length of the arc is $\frac{90}{360}$, or $\frac{1}{4}$, of the distance around the circle?

Figure 14–16

Figure 14–17

Figure 14–17 shows a circular region with an angle of measure 90° intercepting an arc. The "pie-shaped" region that is bounded by the 90° arc and the two radii is called a **sector** of the circle. Do you see that the sector is **one-fourth** of the entire circular region?

Our knowledge about central angles and arcs can help us to decide what part of a **circular region** is included in a given **sector**. For example:

In Figure 14–18, $m\angle QOR = 60°$, so the sector is $\frac{60}{360}$, or $\frac{1}{6}$ of the circular region.

In Figure 14–19, $m\overset{\frown}{ABC} = 120°$, so the sector is $\frac{120}{360}$, or $\frac{1}{3}$ of the circular region.

Figure 14–18

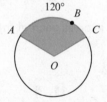

Figure 14–19

Moreover, if we know what part of a circular region a given sector represents, we can name the measure of the corresponding central angle and of its intercepted arc. For example, in the figure shown here, P is the center of the circle and the red sector is $\frac{1}{5}$ of the circular region, therefore:

$\frac{1}{5}$ of **360** is **72**,

$m\angle RPT = 72°$, and $m\overset{\frown}{RST} = 72°$.

As you probably know, an arc that is half of a circle is called a

semicircle.   In Figure 14–20, $\overset{\frown}{ABC}$ is a semicircle and has a measure of
180°; the remaining arc is also a semicircle with a measure of 180°.
Figure 14–21 shows two semicircular regions.

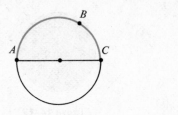
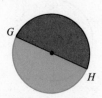

Figure 14–20   **Figure 14–21**

Notice that diameter GH is a common boundary for the **two semicircular
regions**.

ORAL EXERCISES

Give the simplest name for each fraction.

SAMPLE: $\frac{10}{360}$ *What you say:* $\frac{1}{36}$

1. $\frac{36}{360}$ 3. $\frac{12}{360}$ 5. $\frac{240}{360}$ 7. $\frac{50}{360}$

2. $\frac{5}{360}$ 4. $\frac{180}{360}$ 6. $\frac{10}{360}$ 8. $\frac{100}{360}$

Tell how to express each of the following as a fraction whose denominator
is 360.

SAMPLE: $\frac{1}{2}$ *What you say:* $\frac{1}{2} = \frac{180}{360}$

9. $\frac{1}{5}$ 11. $\frac{2}{3}$ 13. $\frac{3}{10}$ 15. $\frac{2}{10}$

10. $\frac{1}{3}$ 12. $\frac{1}{4}$ 14. $\frac{9}{10}$ 16. $\frac{3}{5}$

WRITTEN EXERCISES

State what part each red sector is of the given circular region.   Give each
fraction in simplest form.

SAMPLE: *Solution:* $\frac{72}{360} = \frac{1}{5}$ The sector is $\frac{1}{5}$ of the
                                                                                circular region.

A

1.

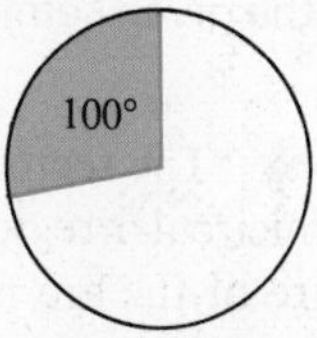

3.

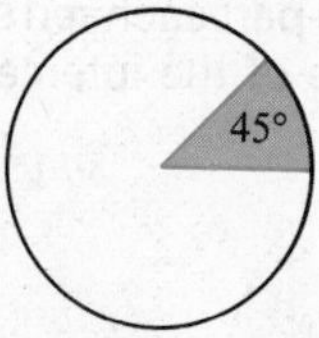

5.

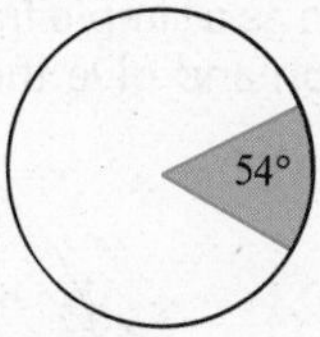

2.

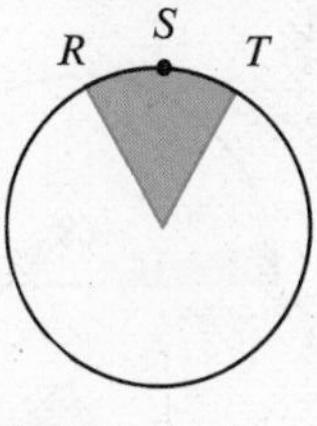

$m\widehat{RST} = 60°$

4.

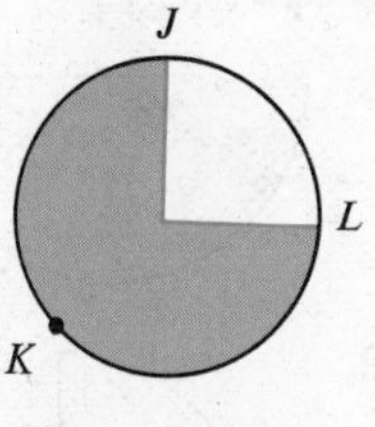

$m\widehat{JKL} = 270°$

6.

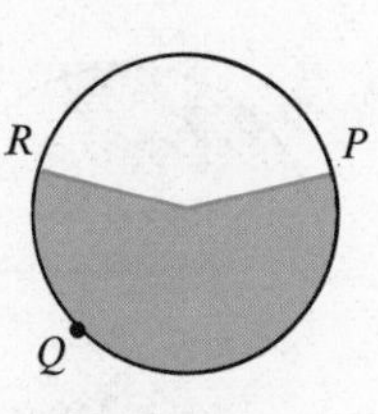

$m\widehat{PQR} = 208°$

For each circle *P*, find the measure of the central angle of the indicated sector, and the measure of the arc of the sector. The numeral in the sector indicates what part the sector is of the circular region.

SAMPLE:

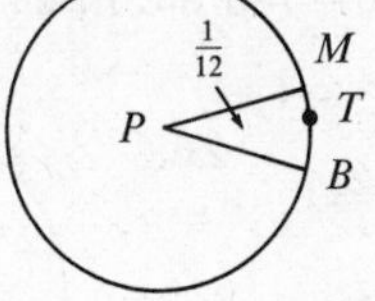

Solution: $\frac{1}{12} \cdot 360 = 30$
$m\angle MPB = 30°$
$m\widehat{MTB} = 30°$

7.

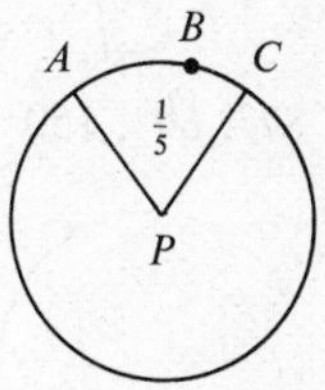

10.

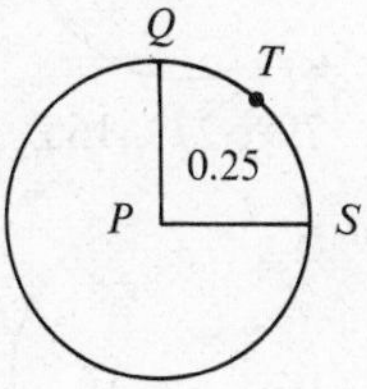

13.

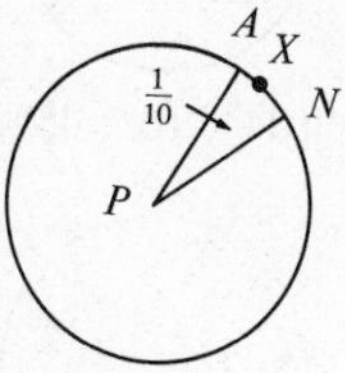

8.

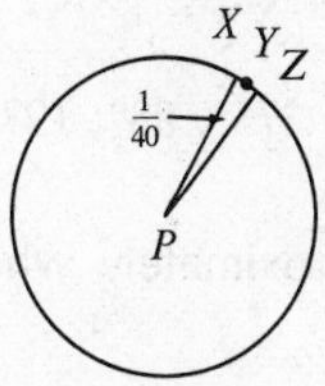

11.

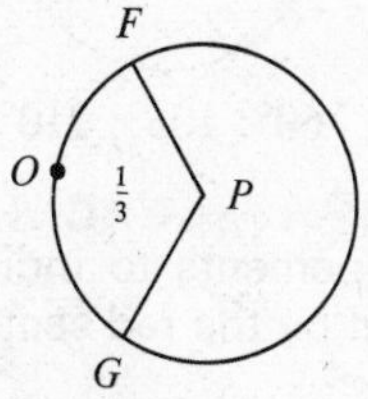

14.

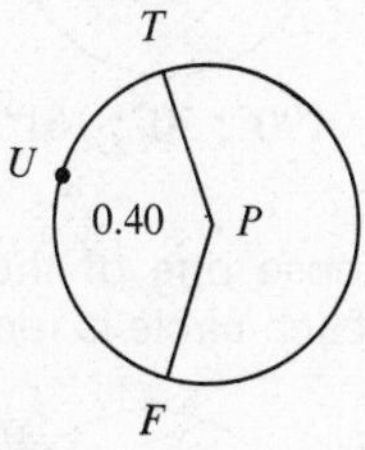

9.

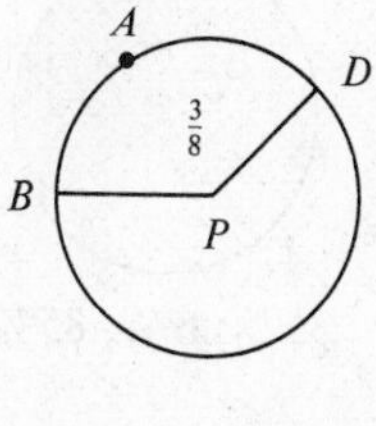

12.

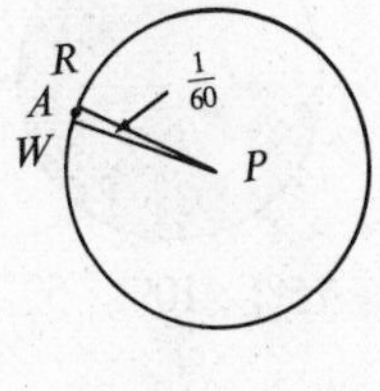

15.

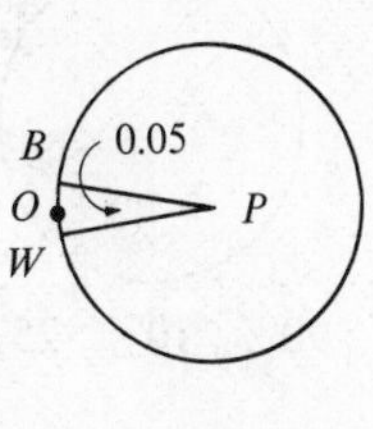

State as a simple fraction the part each red sector is of the given semicircular region and give the measure of the intercepted arc.

SAMPLE:

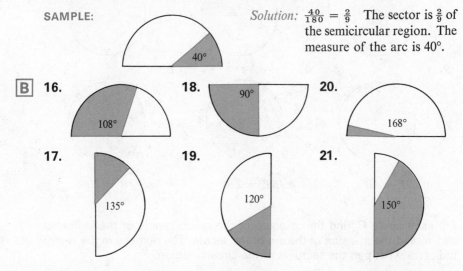

Solution: $\frac{40}{180} = \frac{2}{9}$ The sector is $\frac{2}{9}$ of the semicircular region. The measure of the arc is 40°.

B **16.**   **18.**   **20.**

17.   **19.**   **21.**

Three degree measures are suggested for the red arc in each figure. Tell which one is correct.

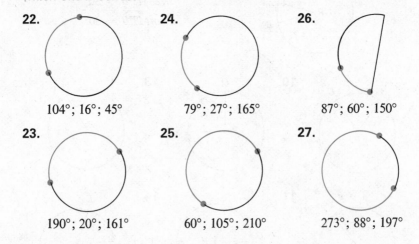

22.

104°; 16°; 45°

24.

79°; 27°; 165°

26.

87°; 60°; 150°

23.

190°; 20°; 161°

25.

60°; 105°; 210°

27.

273°; 88°; 197°

Choose one of the given percents to indicate approximately what part of each circle is represented by the red sector.

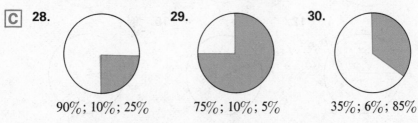

C **28.**

90%; 10%; 25%

29.

75%; 10%; 5%

30.

35%; 6%; 85%

31.

32.

33.

40%; 55%; 95%   12%; 40%; 70%   2%; 18%; 98%

14–6   Sectors and Circle Graphs

We often make use of graphs of various kinds to picture information. You have probably seen many graphs like the one shown here. This kind of diagram is called a **circle graph**, since it consists of a circular region divided into sectors which represent the information. This particular graph shows how a family might budget its income. Each sector represents the **percent** of income spent for the purpose indicated. For example, **25%** of the income is spent for "shelter" and that sector is 25% (or $\frac{1}{4}$) of the whole circular region. Do you see that since 25% of 360°, or $\frac{1}{4}$ of 360°, is 90°, the "shelter" sector must have a central angle whose measure is **90°**? Of course the sum of the percents represented by the sectors of the graph must total 100%. Can you explain why?

PROBLEMS

 1. Al made a circle graph to illustrate how he used his time on school days. Use the graph to determine the answer to each question.

    a. What is the sum of all the percents shown in the graph?

    b. Compute the measure of the central angle of the "School" sector; of the "Sleep" sector; of the "Homework" sector.

    c. According to the graph, about how many hours does Al devote to "Sleep"? to "School"? to "Recreation and other activities?" Give each answer to the nearest hour.

2. Use this circle graph of a family budget to determine the answer to each of the following questions.

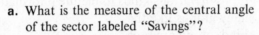

SAMPLE: What is the measure of the central angle of the sector labeled "Food"?

Solution: $25\% \cdot 360 = ?$
$\frac{1}{4} \cdot 360 = 90$

The measure of the angle is 90°.

a. What is the measure of the central angle of the sector labeled "Savings"?

b. What is the measure of the central angle of the sector labeled "Housing"?

c. What percent of the family budget is used for "Miscellaneous" purposes? What is the measure of the central angle of this sector?

3. A petroleum company refinery produces 40,000 barrels of petroleum products weekly, divided according to the circle graph shown here. Use the graph to complete the following exercises.

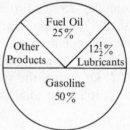

a. What is the measure of the central angle for the "Lubricants" sector? the "Fuel Oil" sector? the "Other Products" sector?

b. How many barrels of fuel oil are produced weekly? of lubricants?

Use a compass and a protractor to make a circle graph to illustrate the given information.

B **4.** Kinds of books in the school library:
$12\frac{1}{2}\%$ References
$37\frac{1}{2}\%$ Nonfiction
50% Fiction

5. Uses of natural gas:
10% Homes (heat and cooking)
$33\frac{1}{3}\%$ Industries
40% Generating electricity
$16\frac{2}{3}\%$ Miscellaneous

6. Uses of wood products:
80% Construction
10% Paper
5% Fuel
5% Miscellaneous

7. Students on the honor roll:
30% Grade nine
20% Grade ten
35% Grade eleven
15% Grade twelve

14–7 Arcs and Inscribed Angles

You will recall that a central angle of a circle has the center of the
circle as its vertex, and that its sides **intercept** an arc
of the circle. Let us next consider an angle formed
by two **chords** that have a **common endpoint**. This
kind of angle is called an **inscribed angle**. In Figure
14–22, chords *AB* and *BC* of circle *O* form **inscribed
angle *ABC*.** Notice that the vertex *B* lies on the
circle. $\overset{\frown}{AGC}$ is called the **intercepted arc** for $\angle ABC$.

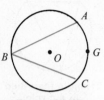

Figure 14–22

Now let us explore some ideas concerning the **measure** of an angle
inscribed in a circle. In the illustrations below, a circle and protractor
scale are provided. Figure 14–23 shows inscribed $\angle PQR$, whose
measure is **50°**. It intercepts $\overset{\frown}{PSR}$, whose measure, according to the
protractor scale, is **100°**.

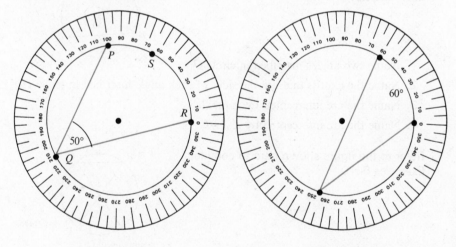

Figure 14–23   Figure 14–24

In Figure 14–24 the protractor scale shows that the inscribed angle
intercepts an arc whose measure is **60°**. Use your protractor to measure
the inscribed angle. Do you agree that it is **30°**?

The foregoing discussion suggests these basic ideas about circles and
inscribed angles.

(1) The measure of an **angle inscribed in a circle** is equal to **one-half**
the measure of the **intercepted arc**.

(2) The measure of an **arc of a circle** is equal to **twice** the measure of
an **inscribed angle** which intercepts the arc.

A polygon is said to be **inscribed in a circle** when each of its vertices is a point of the circle.

Triangle inscribed in a circle

Quadrilateral inscribed in a circle

Hexagon inscribed in a circle

ORAL EXERCISES

Refer to circle *O*, shown here, to complete each exercise.

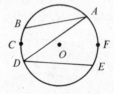

1. Name two angles inscribed in circle *O*.

2. Name the chords that are the sides of each angle inscribed in circle *O*.

3. Name the arc intercepted by $\angle BAD$.

4. Name the arc intercepted by $\angle ADE$.

Refer to the figure shown here to complete Exercises 5–10.

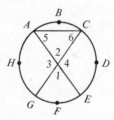

5. Name each angle inscribed in the circle; name the arc that the angle intercepts.

6. Name each central angle in the circle and its intercepted arc.

7. Name the arc intercepted by both $\angle 4$ and $\angle 5$.

9. Name the arc intercepted by both $\angle 3$ and $\angle 6$.

8. Justify each step:

$$m\angle 5 = \tfrac{1}{2}m\overset{\frown}{CDE}$$
$$m\overset{\frown}{CDE} = m\angle 4$$
$$\tfrac{1}{2}m\overset{\frown}{CDE} = \tfrac{1}{2}m\angle 4$$
$$m\angle 5 = \tfrac{1}{2}m\angle 4$$

10. Justify each step:

$$m\angle 6 = \tfrac{1}{2}m\overset{\frown}{AHG}$$
$$2m\angle 6 = m\overset{\frown}{AHG}$$
$$m\overset{\frown}{AHG} = m\angle 3$$
$$2m\angle 6 = m\angle 3$$

WRITTEN EXERCISES

Find the measure of each inscribed angle, if the measure of the intercepted arc is as indicated.

A **1.**

3.

5.

2.

4.

6.

Find the measure of each arc intercepted by an inscribed angle.

7.

9.

11.

8.

10.

12.

Refer to the figure and the given information to complete each exercise.

B **13.** $m\overset{\frown}{RQP} = 70°$
$m\angle 1 = ?$
$m\angle 2 = ?$

14. $m\angle 3 = 42°$
$m\overset{\frown}{MSN} = ?$
$m\angle 4 = ?$

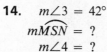

15. $m\overset{\frown}{BCD} = 30°$
$m\overset{\frown}{DEF} = 68°$
$m\angle 1 = ?$ $m\angle 2 = ?$
$m\overset{\frown}{BDF} = ?$ $m\overset{\frown}{BAF} = ?$

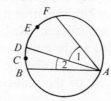

16. Square *ABCD* is inscribed in a circle as shown.
    m∠1 = ?   m∠2 = ?
    m$\overset{\frown}{BCD}$ = ?   m$\overset{\frown}{ADC}$ = ?

17. Triangle *AEC* is inscribed in circle *P* as shown. Use the protractor scale to complete these exercises.
    m$\overset{\frown}{CDE}$ = ?   m∠1 = ?
    m$\overset{\frown}{ABC}$ = ?   m∠3 = ?
    m$\overset{\frown}{AFE}$ = ?   m∠2 = ?
    m∠1 + m∠2 + m∠3 = ?
    m$\overset{\frown}{CDE}$ + m$\overset{\frown}{ABC}$ + m$\overset{\frown}{AFE}$ = ?

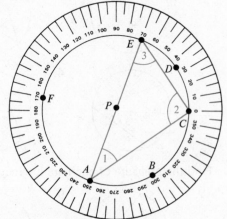

C 18. In this figure, equilateral triangle *XYZ* is inscribed in circle *O*.
    m$\overset{\frown}{XBY}$ = ?
    m$\overset{\frown}{YCZ}$ = ?
    m$\overset{\frown}{XAZ}$ = ?
    m∠1 + m∠2 + m∠3 = ?
    m∠*XOY* = ?   m∠*OXY* = ?

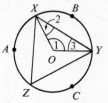

19. Draw a regular pentagon inscribed in a circle. What is the measure of each inscribed angle? What is the measure of each arc intercepted by an inscribed angle?

20. Draw a circle in which a central angle and an inscribed angle intercept the same arc. How do the measures of these two angles compare?

14–8 Triangles Inscribed in Semicircles

The drawing in Figure 14–25 shows a circle drawn on a piece of wood. A diameter has been drawn, dividing the circle into two semicircles. Notice that tacks have been placed at the endpoints of the diameter, as well as at three other points chosen at random on one of the semicircles. By using a

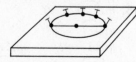

Figure 14–25

rubber band, we can make three models of triangles, as shown in Figure 14–26. In each case, two of the vertices are endpoints of the diameter, while the third vertex of the triangle is a point on the semicircle. Such a triangle is said to be inscribed in the semicircle.

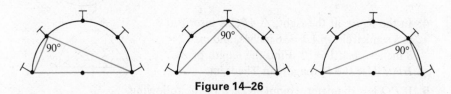

Figure 14–26

How do we know that each of the angles inscribed in a semicircle is a right angle? Do you see that in each case the intercepted arc is also a semicircle? Thus we know that the **measure** of the **inscribed angle** is **one-half** the **measure** of the **semicircle**, or $\frac{1}{2}(180°)$. Hence **any triangle inscribed in a semicircle is a right triangle**.

WRITTEN EXERCISES

A 1. Use circle O and the protractor scale to complete these statements.
$m\angle 1 = ?$ $m\angle 2 = ?$ $m\angle 3 = ?$
$\angle 3$ is a __?__ angle.
$\triangle PQR$ is a __?__ triangle.
The hypotenuse of $\triangle PQR$ is
a __?__ of circle P.
$m\overset{\frown}{PQR} = ?$ $m\overset{\frown}{PSR} = ?$

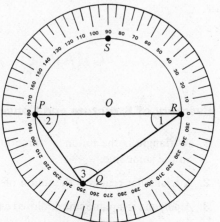

2. Use the given figure to complete each statement about circle P.
$\overline{AB}$ is a __?__ of circle P.
$\triangle ABC$ is inscribed in a __?__.
$m\overset{\frown}{AEC} = ?$ $m\overset{\frown}{CDB} = ?$
$m\angle 1 = ?$ $m\angle 2 = ?$

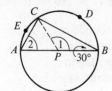

3. In the figure at the right, $\overline{EH}$ is a diameter of the circle and $m\widehat{ETG} = m\widehat{GRH}$.

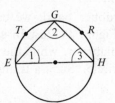

$m\widehat{ETG} = ?$ $m\widehat{GRH} = ?$
$m\angle 1 = ?$ $m\angle 2 = ?$ $m\angle 3 = ?$

B **4.** In the figure at the right, $\triangle ABC$ is inscribed in a semicircle, $m\overline{AB} = 6$ inches, and $m\overline{BC} = 8$ inches. $m\angle 1 = ?$ Find the length of $\overline{AC}$. *Hint:* Use the Pythagorean Theorem.

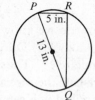

5. If $\overline{PQ}$ is a diameter, complete each of the following.
$m\angle PRQ = ?$
$m\overline{QR} = ?$
Perimeter of $\triangle PQR = ?$
Area of $\triangle PQR = ?$

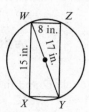

6. Quadrilateral $WXYZ$ is inscribed in circle C, and $\overline{WY}$ is a diameter of the circle.
$m\angle WZY = ?$ $m\angle WXY = ?$
$m\overline{ZY} = ?$ $m\overline{XY} = ?$
The perimeter of quadrilateral $WXYZ = ?$
The area of quadrilateral $WXYZ = ?$

CHAPTER SUMMARY

Inventory of Structure and Concepts

1. A **triangle** is the union of three line segments joining three points not on the same line.

2. A **triangular region** is the union of a triangle and its interior.

3. A **polygon** is a plane simple closed curve that is the union of line segments.

4. A **polygonal region** is the union of a polygon and its interior.

5. Polygons may be classified according to the number of sides:

3 sides — triangle	8 sides — octagon
4 sides — quadrilateral	10 sides — decagon
5 sides — pentagon	12 sides — dodecagon
6 sides — hexagon	

6. An **equilateral polygon** is a polygon all of whose sides have the same length.

7. An **equiangular polygon** is a polygon all of whose angles have the same measure.

8. A **regular polygon** is a polygon that is both equilateral and equiangular.

9. The **sum of the measures of the interior angles** of a polygon of n sides is $(n - 2)180$ degrees.

10. A **circle** is the set of all points in a plane that are a given distance from a point called the center of the circle.

11. A **circular region** is the union of a circle and its interior.

12. A **radius** of a circle is a line segment one of whose endpoints is the center of the circle and the other endpoint is on the circle.

13. A **chord** of a circle is a line segment whose endpoints are on the circle.

14. A **diameter** of a circle is a chord that passes through the center.

15. A **central angle** of a circle is an angle whose vertex is the center.

16. An **arc** of a circle is the set of all points of the circle between two specified endpoints.

17. The **angular measure of an arc** of a circle is equal to the measure of the central angle that intercepts the arc.

18. In a given circle, if two central angles have equal measures, then the measures of their intercepted arcs are equal.

19. A **sector** of a circular region is a region bounded by two radii and an arc.

20. A **semicircle** is an arc that is one-half of a circle.

21. An **inscribed angle** of a circle is an angle formed by two chords that have a common endpoint.

22. The **measure of an inscribed angle** is equal to one-half the measure of the intercepted arc.

23. The **measure of an arc intercepted by an inscribed angle** is equal to twice the measure of the angle.

24. A **polygon inscribed in a circle** has each of its vertices on the circle.

25. An **angle inscribed in a semicircle** is a right angle.

26. A **triangle** is **inscribed in a semicircle** if two of its vertices are endpoints of the diameter of the semicircle, and its third vertex is on the semicircle.

27. A **triangle inscribed in a semicircle** is a right triangle.

Vocabulary and Spelling

triangle (*p. 453*)

triangular region (*p. 453*)

polygon (*p. 454*)

convex polygon (*p. 454*)

concave polygon (*p. 454*)

interior angle (*p. 454*)

exterior angle (*p. 454*)

diagonal (*p. 454*)

polygonal region (*p. 455*)

quadrilateral (*p. 458*)

pentagon (*p. 458*)

hexagon (*p. 458*)

octagon (*p. 458*)

decagon (*p. 458*)

dodecagon (*p. 458*)

equilateral (*p. 458*)

equiangular (*p. 458*)

regular polygon (*p. 458*)

circle (*p. 463*)

circular region (*p. 463*)

concentric circles (*p. 463*)

radius (*p. 463*)

diameter (*p. 463*)

chord (*p. 463*)

central angle (*p. 464*)

arc (*p. 465*)

sector (*p. 469*)

semicircle (*p. 470*)

semicircular region (*p. 470*)

circle graph (*p. 473*)

inscribed angle (*p. 475*)

inscribed polygon (*p. 476*)

Chapter Test

---

1. Find the sum of the measures of the interior angles of a hexagon.

2. What is the number of diagonals that can be drawn from a single vertex of a quadrilateral?

3. Find the perimeter of a regular pentagon, one of whose sides measures 7 inches.

4. The longest chord of a circle is called the ___?___.

Given the circle in the adjacent diagram with its center at *O*, diameter *AD*, and quadrilateral *ACDE* inscribed in the circle,

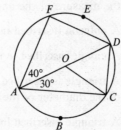

5. $m\widehat{DEF} = ?$

6. $m\angle AFD = ?$

7. $m\widehat{ABC} = ?$

8. $m\angle DOC = ?$

9. If the measure of the central angle of a sector of a given circle is 40°, what part of the circular region is the sector?

10. Triangle ABC is inscribed in circle O, with $\overline{AC}$ a diameter of the circle. If $m\overline{AB} = 4''$ and $m\overline{BC} = 3''$, what is the radius of the circle?

11. Two concentric circles with common center at P are shown in the adjacent diagram. If the measure of $\overset{\frown}{ABC} = 150°$, then the $m\overset{\frown}{DEF} = ?$

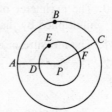

12. Equilateral triangle ADC is inscribed in circle O, as shown in the adjacent diagram. Find the measure of $\overset{\frown}{ABC}$.

13. For the figure used for Question 12, find the measure of $\angle DOC$.

Chapter Review

14–1 **Polygons and Polygonal Regions**

Refer to polygon *ABCDE* to answer the following questions.

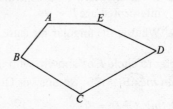

1. How many diagonals of polygon $ABCDE$ contain point E?

2. Which is the longest diagonal?

3. Into how many triangular regions can polygon $ABCDE$ be divided by segments containing point A?

4. Name a line segment that is not a diagonal.

5. Name two consecutive sides.

6. Name two consecutive vertices.

14–2 Kinds of Polygons

Tell whether each statement is true or false.

7. All angles of a regular polygon have the same measure.

8. Exactly three diagonals can be drawn from any one vertex of a hexagon.

9. {quadrilaterals} ⊂ {squares}.

10. The perimeter of a regular polygon is equal to the length of one side multiplied by the number of sides.

11. The measure of an interior angle of a regular pentagon is 72°.

12. The sum of the measures of the interior angles of an octagon is 1080°.

14–3 Circles and Circular Regions

Given circle *G* as shown. Match each expression in Column 1 with an appropriate choice from Column 2.

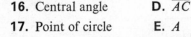

COLUMN 1	COLUMN 2	
13. Diameter	**A.** $\overline{GE}$	**F.** *F*
14. Radius	**B.** $\overline{BA}$	**G.** ∠*ABD*
15. Shortest chord	**C.** $\overline{BD}$	**H.** ∠*BFC*
16. Central angle	**D.** $\overline{AC}$	**I.** ∠*EGD*
17. Point of circle	**E.** *A*	

14–4 Arcs and Central Angles

18. If the measure of a central angle is 40°, what is the measure of the intercepted arc?

19. What is the angular measure of a circle?

Refer to circle *F* as shown, with diameter *BD*, and with $m\widehat{EAB} = 85°$, to answer Questions 20–24.

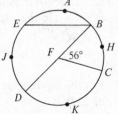

20. $m∠CFD = ?$

21. $m\widehat{BHC} = ?$

22. $m\widehat{DKC} = ?$

23. $m\widehat{DJE} = ?$

24. $m∠FBE = ?$

25. If the measure of a central angle of two concentric circles is 45°, what is the measure of the intercepted arc of the smaller circle? of the larger circle?

14–5 Parts of Circular Regions

26. If the central angle of a sector of a circle is 30°, what part of the circular region is the sector?

27. Find the measure of the central angle of a sector if the sector is two-fifths of the circular region.

28. The angular measure of the arc of a semicircle is __?__ degrees.

Use circle *O* shown here in answering Questions 29 and 30.

29. If $\overset{\frown}{ADC}$ is two-thirds of the circle, find $m\overset{\frown}{ABC}$.

30. What percent of the circular region is shaded?

14–6 Sectors and Circle Graphs

Use the circle graph showing the cost of operating a car to answer the following questions.

31. What is the measure of the central angle of the sector labeled "Repair"?

32. What is the measure of the central angle of the sector labeled "Car License"?

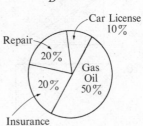

14–7 Arcs and Inscribed Angles

33. The measure of an inscribed angle that intercepts an arc of 30° is __?__.

34. An inscribed angle of 30° intercepts an arc of __?__.

35. A right angle inscribed in a circle intercepts an arc of __?__.

Given the circle shown, with inscribed △*ACE*, $m\angle CAE = 40°$, and $m\overset{\frown}{ABC} = 100°$.

36. $m\angle CEA = ?$

37. $m\angle ACE = ?$

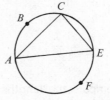

14–8 Triangles Inscribed in Semicircles

In circle *O*, diameter *AD* is 10 inches long and $\overline{CD}$ is 6 inches long.

38. $m\angle ACD = ?$

39. $m\overline{AC} = ?$

40. $m\overline{OC} = ?$

Review of Skills

Express each of the following as a decimal correct to four decimal places.

1. $\frac{5}{12}$ **3.** $\frac{35.3}{50}$ **5.** $\frac{26.5}{100}$ **7.** $\frac{\sqrt{14}}{\sqrt{7}}$

2. $\frac{9}{40}$ **4.** $\frac{5.6}{8.4}$ **6.** $\frac{8}{17.4}$ **8.** $\frac{2}{\sqrt{3}}$

Find the value of the variable in each of the following triangles; express your answer to the nearest tenth.

9. 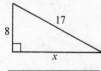   **11.** 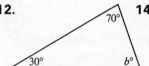   **13.**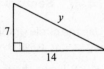

10. 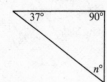   **12.**   **14.**

Find the value of the variable in each of the following proportions; express your answer to the nearest tenth.

15. $\frac{5}{8} = \frac{t}{16}$ **18.** $\frac{3.6}{5.4} = \frac{s}{10.8}$ **21.** $\frac{x}{4} = \frac{54}{36}$

16. $\frac{6}{b} = \frac{16}{24}$ **19.** $\frac{27}{21} = \frac{72}{r}$ **22.** $\frac{4}{15} = \frac{t}{35}$

17. $\frac{a}{24} = \frac{7}{28}$ **20.** $\frac{21}{49} = \frac{3}{n}$ **23.** $\frac{y}{15} = \frac{4}{10}$

Compare the lengths of pairs of line segments by completing the indicated ratios.

24. 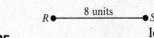 $\dfrac{\text{length of } \overline{MN}}{\text{length of } \overline{RS}} = \dfrac{?}{?}$

25. 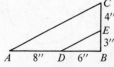 $\dfrac{\text{length of } \overline{AB}}{\text{length of } \overline{DB}} = \dfrac{?}{3}$ $\dfrac{\text{length of } \overline{AB}}{\text{length of } \overline{BC}} = \dfrac{?}{?}$

$\dfrac{\text{length of } \overline{BC}}{\text{length of } \overline{EC}} = \dfrac{?}{?}$

A Beautiful Rectangle

Certain geometric shapes seem more satisfying than others to the person viewing them. Of these, one of the most pleasing is called the Golden Rectangle, a rectangle in which the fraction $\frac{\text{length}}{\text{width}}$ is equal to the fraction $\frac{\text{length} + \text{width}}{\text{length}}$. The value of each fraction is about 1.6. Such a rectangle is pictured in Figure 1 below.

Figure 1

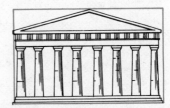

Figure 2

The drawing of the Parthenon in Figure 2 shows how its front fits almost exactly into the Golden Rectangle once the missing part is supplied. Although its builders in the Fifth Century B.C. probably had no knowledge of the mathematics of the Golden Rectangle, the design incorporates many geometrical balances.

A Golden Rectangle can be constructed as follows:

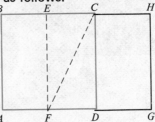

(1) Draw a square *ABCD*.
(2) Divide the square into two equal parts (segment *EF* in the figure).
(3) Extend $\overline{AD}$ to point *G*, so that $\overline{FG}$ is the same length as $\overline{FC}$.
(4) Complete rectangle *AGHB*, which is a Golden Rectangle.

An interesting property of the Golden Rectangle is that, if the original square is removed, the part that remains is another Golden Rectangle. Thus *CDGH* in the drawing is also a Golden Rectangle.

487

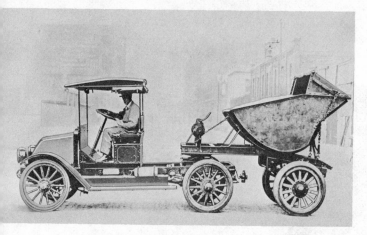

1915 model of a truck with a concrete mixer . . .

A modern concrete mixer truck . . .

Ratios and Similar
Right Triangles

Mathematics has played its part in technological advances in the building trades. Until the early 1900's, concrete, a mixture of cement, water, and other materials, had to be mixed at the site as needed. The development of mixers mounted on trucks made for more efficient use of this important building material. The early model shown had a capacity of about 1 cubic yard of concrete. In contrast, a modern mixer truck usually has a capacity of from 9 to 12 cubic yards, while some very large models can mix and transport as many as 16 cubic yards of concrete. It is usual for the architect of a large building to specify the exact proportions of cement, water, sand, and coarser materials to be used. Modern trucks make it possible for the concrete to be mixed to specifications at the plant and then delivered to any building site, however distant.

Similar Triangles

15–1   Congruence and Similarity

Plane geometric figures that have the same size and shape are called **congruent figures**. For two figures to be congruent, their corresponding angles must have equal measures and the lengths of corresponding sides must be equal.

In the following figure, we have used a symbol called a "prime" to show the corresponding parts of the two triangles. Thus point A' (read "A-prime") corresponds to point A, point B' to point B, and point C' to point C.

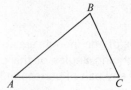 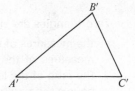

To simplify our notation, let us agree that when there is only one angle in a figure that has a given point as vertex, we can name the angle by using only that letter, instead of using three letters, as we have done before. For example, in the figure showing congruent triangles *ABC* and *A'B'C'*, when we talk about $\angle A$ we are referring to $\angle BAC$.

The symbol $\cong$ is used to indicate the congruence relationship. Thus

$$\triangle ABC \cong \triangle A'B'C'$$

is read "triangle *ABC* is congruent to triangle *A'B'C'*." From our definition of the congruence relationship for geometric figures, do you see that when we write $\triangle ABC \cong \triangle A'B'C'$ we are saying that six things are true? They are:

$$m\angle A = m\angle A' \qquad \text{length of } \overline{AB} = \text{length of } \overline{A'B'}$$
$$m\angle B = m\angle B' \qquad \text{length of } \overline{BC} = \text{length of } \overline{B'C'}$$
$$m\angle C = m\angle C' \qquad \text{length of } \overline{AC} = \text{length of } \overline{A'C'}$$

If two triangles have the same shape but not necessarily the same size, they are called **similar triangles**. The symbol $\sim$ is used to mean "is similar to." If two triangles are similar, the measures of their corresponding angles are equal and the lengths of their pairs of corresponding sides have the same ratio.

Thus for triangles *RST* and *R'S'T'* shown here, if $\triangle RST \sim \triangle R'S'T'$, we know that

$$m\angle R = m\angle R'$$
$$m\angle S = m\angle S'$$
$$m\angle T = m\angle T'$$
$$\frac{m\overline{RS}}{m\overline{R'S'}} = \frac{m\overline{ST}}{m\overline{S'T'}} = \frac{m\overline{RT}}{m\overline{R'T'}}$$

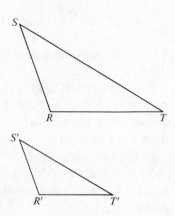

Did you notice that, in order to simplify our notation still further, we have used $m\overline{RS}$ as an abbreviation for "the length of $\overline{RS}$," and similar notations for the other lengths?

In general:

Two triangles are similar if:

a. the measures of the angles of one triangle are equal to the measures of the corresponding angles of the other, and
b. the ratio of the lengths of any pair of corresponding sides equals the ratio of the lengths of any other pair of corresponding sides.

As a matter of fact, it can be shown that if *one* of the conditions stated is true, then the other condition is also true. Thus we know that two triangles are similar if *either* the measures of their corresponding angles are equal *or* the ratios of the lengths of the corresponding sides are equal.

EXAMPLE. $\triangle XYZ \sim \triangle X'Y'Z'$; find the lengths of $\overline{Y'Z'}$ and $\overline{X'Z'}$.

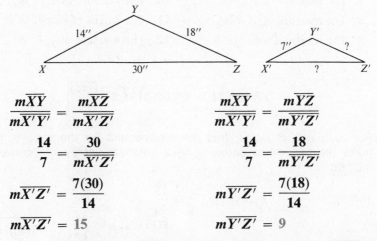

$$\frac{m\overline{XY}}{m\overline{X'Y'}} = \frac{m\overline{XZ}}{m\overline{X'Z'}} \qquad \frac{m\overline{XY}}{m\overline{X'Y'}} = \frac{m\overline{YZ}}{m\overline{Y'Z'}}$$

$$\frac{14}{7} = \frac{30}{m\overline{X'Z'}} \qquad \frac{14}{7} = \frac{18}{m\overline{Y'Z'}}$$

$$m\overline{X'Z'} = \frac{7(30)}{14} \qquad m\overline{Y'Z'} = \frac{7(18)}{14}$$

$$m\overline{X'Z'} = 15 \qquad m\overline{Y'Z'} = 9$$

The length of $\overline{X'Z'}$ is **15** inches; the length of $\overline{Y'Z'}$ is **9** inches.

ORAL EXERCISES

Complete each of the following statements about sides and angles of the similar triangles *JKH* and *J'K'H'*.

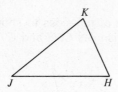
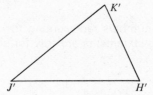

1. $\overline{JH}$ corresponds to __?__.

2. $\angle J$ corresponds to __?__.

3. $\overline{J'K'}$ corresponds to __?__.

4. $\angle H'$ corresponds to __?__.

5. $\overline{KH}$ corresponds to __?__.

6. $\angle K$ corresponds to __?__.

Complete each of the following statements by referring to congruent triangles *PQR* and *P'Q'R'*.

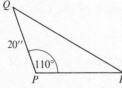 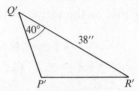

7. The measure of ∠*Q* is ___?___.   **10.** The measure of ∠*P'* is ___?___.

8. The measure of ∠*R* is ___?___.   **11.** The length of side *P'Q'* is ___?___.

9. The length of side *QR* is ___?___.   **12.** The measure of ∠*R'* is ___?___.

WRITTEN EXERCISES

For each pair of ratios, find the replacement for the variable that will make the two ratios equal. Check your answer by the cross-product method.

SAMPLE: $\dfrac{x}{8}, \dfrac{15}{40}$ *Solution:* $\dfrac{x}{8} = \dfrac{15}{40}$

$$x = \dfrac{8(15)}{40} = 3$$

Replace *x* by 3.

Check:

$$\dfrac{3}{8} \bowtie \dfrac{15}{40}$$

| 3(40) | 8(15) |
| 120 | 120 |

A

1. $\dfrac{9}{10}, \dfrac{x}{20}$ **5.** $\dfrac{10}{3}, \dfrac{25}{k}$ **9.** $\dfrac{70}{35}, \dfrac{x}{4}$

2. $\dfrac{12}{y}, \dfrac{4}{5}$ **6.** $\dfrac{10}{14}, \dfrac{s}{35}$ **10.** $\dfrac{42}{n}, \dfrac{18}{21}$

3. $\dfrac{15}{15}, \dfrac{47}{m}$ **7.** $\dfrac{45}{20}, \dfrac{9}{a}$ **11.** $\dfrac{\sqrt{3}}{x}, \dfrac{3\sqrt{3}}{15}$

4. $\dfrac{1.5}{1.8}, \dfrac{0.5}{z}$ **8.** $\dfrac{t}{9}, \dfrac{12}{108}$ **12.** $\dfrac{\sqrt{2}}{5}, \dfrac{y}{10}$

Use the numbers representing the lengths of the sides to show that the following statements are true for similar triangles *CDE* and *C'D'E'*.

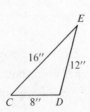 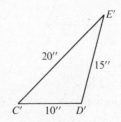

13. $\dfrac{m\overline{CE}}{m\overline{C'E'}} = \dfrac{m\overline{DE}}{m\overline{D'E'}}$

16. $\dfrac{m\overline{D'E'}}{m\overline{DE}} = \dfrac{m\overline{C'E'}}{m\overline{CE}}$

14. $\dfrac{m\overline{CD}}{m\overline{C'D'}} = \dfrac{m\overline{CE}}{m\overline{C'E'}}$

17. $\dfrac{m\overline{C'D'}}{m\overline{CD}} = \dfrac{m\overline{C'E'}}{m\overline{CE}}$

15. $\dfrac{m\overline{CD}}{m\overline{C'D'}} = \dfrac{m\overline{CE}}{m\overline{C'E'}} = \dfrac{m\overline{DE}}{m\overline{D'E'}}$

For each exercise, find the measures indicated.

B 18.

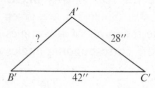

$\triangle ABC \sim \triangle A'B'C'$.
What is the length of $\overline{AC}$?
What is the length of $\overline{A'B'}$?

19.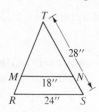

$\triangle RST \sim \triangle MNT$ and $m\overline{MR} = m\overline{NS}$.
What is the length of $\overline{NT}$?
What is the length of $\overline{NS}$?
What is the length of $\overline{MR}$?

20.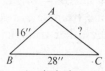

$\triangle DEF \sim \triangle GHF$.
What is the length of $\overline{FG}$?
What is the length of $\overline{EF}$?

21.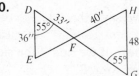

$\triangle BTH \sim \triangle BGK$.
What is the measure of $\angle BHT$?
What is the measure of $\angle BTH$?
What is the measure of $\angle BGK$?

15–2 Similar Right Triangles

We have already defined the **hypotenuse** of a right triangle as the side opposite the right angle. The other two sides are called the **legs** of the triangle. Look at the right triangle shown in the figure and observe the two angles marked in red.

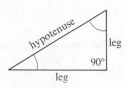

Do you see that every right triangle has just one right angle, and that the other two angles are both **acute** angles?

How can we verify that the two right triangles pictured here are a pair of **similar** triangles?

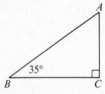

Can you give the reason why $m\angle C = m\angle F$? Why is it true that $m\angle A = m\angle D$? Since we are given that $m\angle B = m\angle E = 35°$, we know that the measures of the angles of one triangle are equal to the measures of the corresponding angles of the other triangle, so we can write

$$\triangle ABC \sim \triangle DEF.$$

Note that, in naming the two triangles, we have been careful to name corresponding vertices in the same order.

The basic property of similar right triangles that appears here can be stated as follows:

 Two right triangles are similar if the measure of an acute angle of one triangle is equal to the measure of an acute angle of the other.

In the following figure, notice that when we say "the side opposite $\angle A$" we mean **leg** BC, and by "the side adjacent to $\angle A$" we mean **leg** AC. Which leg do you think we would mean if we said, "the side opposite $\angle B$"? Which leg is "the side **adjacent** to $\angle B$"?

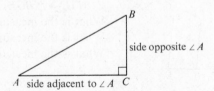

side opposite $\angle A$

A side adjacent to $\angle A$ C

ORAL EXERCISES

Name the hypotenuse and the two legs of each right triangle.

SAMPLE:

What you say: Side PR is the hypotenuse; sides PQ and QR are the legs.

1.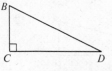

3.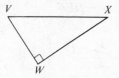

2.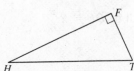

4.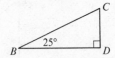

WRITTEN EXERCISES

Complete each of the following statements about similar right triangles *BCD* and *B'C'D'*.

 1. The measure of ∠*BCD* is __?__ .

2. The measure of ∠*B'C'D'* is __?__ .

3. Side *BD* corresponds to side __?__ .

4. Side *C'D'* corresponds to side __?__ .

5. ∠*BCD* corresponds to ∠__?__ .

6. ∠*C'B'D'* corresponds to ∠__?__ .

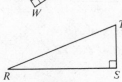

Complete each of the following statements about right triangles *ABC* and *A'B'C'*. Express each ratio in lowest terms.

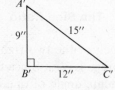

7. $\dfrac{m\overline{AB}}{m\overline{A'B'}} = \dfrac{?}{?}$

8. $\dfrac{m\overline{BC}}{m\overline{B'C'}} = \dfrac{?}{?}$

9. $\dfrac{m\overline{AC}}{m\overline{A'C'}} = \dfrac{?}{?}$

10. $\dfrac{m\overline{AB}}{m\overline{A'B'}} = \dfrac{m\overline{AC}}{m(?)} = \dfrac{m(?)}{m\overline{B'C'}}$

11. △*ABC* ~ △__?__ because the __?__ of the lengths of corresponding sides are equal.

For each pair of similar right triangles, find the lengths indicated.

12. △*RST* ~ △*R'S'T'*

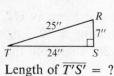

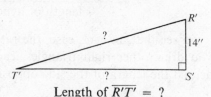

Length of $\overline{T'S'}$ = ?   Length of $\overline{R'T'}$ = ?

B **13.** △*ABC* ~ △*DEF*

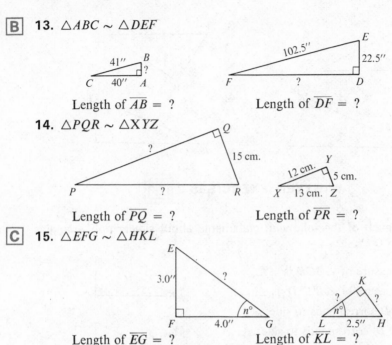

Length of $\overline{AB}$ = ?   Length of $\overline{DF}$ = ?

14. △*PQR* ~ △*XYZ*

Length of $\overline{PQ}$ = ?   Length of $\overline{PR}$ = ?

C **15.** △*EFG* ~ △*HKL*

Length of $\overline{EG}$ = ?   Length of $\overline{KL}$ = ?
Length of $\overline{HK}$ = ?

The Trigonometric Ratios

15–3   The Sine Ratio

In each of the two right triangles shown below, the measure of one acute angle is **30°**. Since they are right triangles for which the measure of an acute angle of one is equal to the measure of an acute angle of the other, we know that the triangles are **similar.**

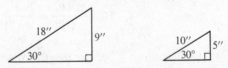

For each triangle, consider the ratio

$$\frac{\text{length of side opposite the 30° angle}}{\text{length of hypotenuse}}.$$

Do you see that, in each case, the ratio in lowest terms is **1:2**, or $\frac{1}{2}$? If you drew other right triangles, each containing a **30°** angle, and measured the length of the side opposite the **30°** angle and the length of the hypotenuse, you would find each time that

$$\frac{\text{length of side opposite}}{\text{length of hypotenuse}} = \frac{1}{2}.$$

This ratio has the special name **sine ratio**. The word **sine** is often shortened to the three-letter form **sin**, although both forms are pronounced like the word "sign." Thus we write

$$\sin 30° = \tfrac{1}{2}, \quad \text{or} \quad \sin 30° = 0.50.$$

In general, we define the **sine** of an acute angle of a right triangle as

$$\frac{\textbf{length of side opposite}}{\textbf{length of hypotenuse}}.$$

For each right triangle in Examples 1 and 2, which follow, note that the measure of one acute angle is **20°**. For each triangle the length of the **hypotenuse** is given, as well as the approximate length of the **leg opposite** the **20°** angle.

EXAMPLE 1.

Find **sin 20°**, using the given lengths of the sides of △*ABC*.

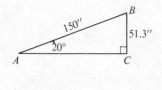

$$\textbf{sin 20°} = \frac{\text{length of side opposite}}{\text{length of hypotenuse}}$$

$$= \frac{m\overline{BC}}{m\overline{AB}} = \frac{\textbf{51.3}}{\textbf{150}} = 0.342$$

EXAMPLE 2.

Find **sin 20°**, using the given lengths of the sides of △*DEF*.

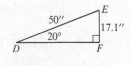

$$\textbf{sin 20°} = \frac{m\overline{EF}}{m\overline{DE}} = \frac{\textbf{17.1}}{\textbf{50}} = 0.342$$

Do you see that in each example the value of **sin 20°** is the same number, although the sides of △*ABC* are given as three times as long as the sides of △*DEF*? This gives us the basic fact about the sine ratio: for an acute angle of a given measure, the sine ratio always has the same value.

For any right triangle **RST**, if **r°** is the measure of ∠**R** and **t°** is the measure of ∠**T**, then

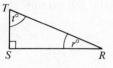

$$\sin r° = \frac{m\overline{ST}}{m\overline{TR}}; \quad \sin t° = \frac{m\overline{RS}}{m\overline{TR}}.$$

To use this fact in solving problems about right triangles, we need to know the values of the sine ratio for acute angles, so tables of these values have been developed. In the table on page 499, the first and the fifth columns give measures of angles in degrees, while the second and sixth columns, headed Sine, give values of the corresponding sine ratio, rounded off to four decimal places. In the table, most of the values given are only approximate; in fact the only *exact* values given for sine ratios are those for **sin 30°** and **sin 90°**. When we use approximate values we must realize that the answers to the problems will also be approximations.

The following examples illustrate the use of the table in solving problems about right triangles.

EXAMPLE 1. Find the length of side **BC**.

$$\sin A = \frac{m\overline{BC}}{m\overline{AB}}$$

$$\sin 43° = \frac{x}{5}$$

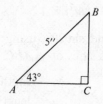

In the table, we find that **sin 43° ≐ 0.6820**, so we have:

$$\frac{x}{5} ≐ 0.6820$$

$$x ≐ 5(0.6820) = 3.4100$$

The length of side **BC** is about 3.4 inches.

EXAMPLE 2. Find the measure of ∠R to the nearest degree.

$$\sin R = \frac{m\overline{ST}}{m\overline{RT}}$$

$$\sin r° = \tfrac{12}{20} = 0.6000$$

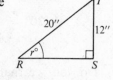

In the table on p. 499, the value in the **Sine** column that is nearest to 0.6000 is **0.6018**, which is the sine of **37°**. Therefore, the measure of ∠R is about 37°.

FOUR-PLACE VALUES OF TRIGONOMETRIC RATIOS

Angle	Sine	Cosine	Tangent	Angle	Sine	Cosine	Tangent
1°	.0175	.9998	.0175	46°	.7193	.6947	1.0355
2°	.0349	.9994	.0349	47°	.7314	.6820	1.0724
3°	.0523	.9986	.0524	48°	.7431	.6691	1.1106
4°	.0698	.9976	.0699	49°	.7547	.6561	1.1504
5°	.0872	.9962	.0875	50°	.7660	.6428	1.1918
6°	.1045	.9945	.1051	51°	.7771	.6293	1.2349
7°	.1219	.9925	.1228	52°	.7880	.6157	1.2799
8°	.1392	.9903	.1405	53°	.7986	.6018	1.3270
9°	.1564	.9877	.1584	54°	.8090	.5878	1.3764
10°	.1736	.9848	.1763	55°	.8192	.5736	1.4281
11°	.1908	.9816	.1944	56°	.8290	.5592	1.4826
12°	.2079	.9781	.2126	57°	.8387	.5446	1.5399
13°	.2250	.9744	.2309	58°	.8480	.5299	1.6003
14°	.2419	.9703	.2493	59°	.8572	.5150	1.6643
15°	.2588	.9659	.2679	60°	.8660	.5000	1.7321
16°	.2756	.9613	.2867	61°	.8746	.4848	1.8040
17°	.2924	.9563	.3057	62°	.8829	.4695	1.8807
18°	.3090	.9511	.3249	63°	.8910	.4540	1.9626
19°	.3256	.9455	.3443	64°	.8988	.4384	2.0503
20°	.3420	.9397	.3640	65°	.9063	.4226	2.1445
21°	.3584	.9336	.3839	66°	.9135	.4067	2.2460
22°	.3746	.9272	.4040	67°	.9205	.3907	2.3559
23°	.3907	.9205	.4245	68°	.9272	.3746	2.4751
24°	.4067	.9135	.4452	69°	.9336	.3584	2.6051
25°	.4226	.9063	.4663	70°	.9397	.3420	2.7475
26°	.4384	.8988	.4877	71°	.9455	.3256	2.9042
27°	.4540	.8910	.5095	72°	.9511	.3090	3.0777
28°	.4695	.8829	.5317	73°	.9563	.2924	3.2709
29°	.4848	.8746	.5543	74°	.9613	.2756	3.4874
30°	.5000	.8660	.5774	75°	.9659	.2588	3.7321
31°	.5150	.8572	.6009	76°	.9703	.2419	4.0108
32°	.5299	.8480	.6249	77°	.9744	.2250	4.3315
33°	.5446	.8387	.6494	78°	.9781	.2079	4.7046
34°	.5592	.8290	.6745	79°	.9816	.1908	5.1446
35°	.5736	.8192	.7002	80°	.9848	.1736	5.6713
36°	.5878	.8090	.7265	81°	.9877	.1564	6.3138
37°	.6018	.7986	.7536	82°	.9903	.1392	7.1154
38°	.6157	.7880	.7813	83°	.9925	.1219	8.1443
39°	.6293	.7771	.8098	84°	.9945	.1045	9.5144
40°	.6428	.7660	.8391	85°	.9962	.0872	11.4301
41°	.6561	.7547	.8693	86°	.9976	.0698	14.3007
42°	.6691	.7431	.9004	87°	.9986	.0523	19.0811
43°	.6820	.7314	.9325	88°	.9994	.0349	28.6363
44°	.6947	.7193	.9657	89°	.9998	.0175	57.2900
45°	.7071	.7071	1.0000	90°	1.0000	.0000	

ORAL EXERCISES

Use the table on page 499 to complete each statement.

1. sin 15° ≐ __?__

2. sin 36° ≐ __?__

3. sin 30° = __?__

4. sin __?__ ≐ 0.4540

5. sin 1° ≐ __?__

6. sin 45° ≐ __?__

7. sin 60° ≐ __?__

8. sin __?__ ≐ 0.7660

9. sin __?__ ≐ 0.1045

10. sin 23° ≐ __?__

WRITTEN EXERCISES

Find the measure of each indicated angle to the nearest degree.

SAMPLE:

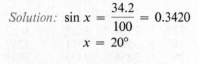

$x = $ __?__ degrees

Solution: $\sin x = \dfrac{34.2}{100} = 0.3420$

$x = 20°$

 1.

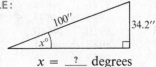

$n = $ __?__ degrees

3.

$a = $ __?__ degrees

2.

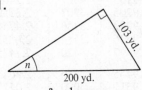

$t = $ __?__ degrees

4.

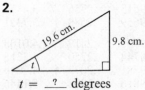

$m = $ __?__ degrees

For each right triangle, find the length of the side indicated; round off your answer to the nearest tenth of a unit.

5.

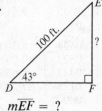

$m\overline{EF} = ?$

6.

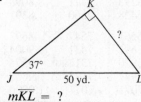

$m\overline{KL} = ?$

7.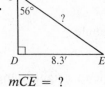

$m\overline{CE} = ?$

8.

$m\overline{RT} = ?$

Find the values of the variables in each figure.

B **9.**

11.

10.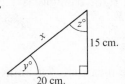

12.

For each of the following, use the dimensions given to determine the sine of the indicated angle; express any answers that involve radicals in simplest radical form.

C **13.**

$\sin 45° = \underline{\ ?\ }$ **15.**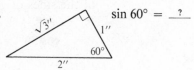

$\sin 60° = \underline{\ ?\ }$

14.

$\sin 60° = \underline{\ ?\ }$ **16.**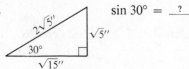

$\sin 30° = \underline{\ ?\ }$

15–4 The Cosine Ratio

In the last section we investigated the ratio of two sides of a right triangle, the side **opposite** an acute angle and the **hypotenuse**. Now let us consider the ratio of the side **adjacent** to the acute angle and the **hypotenuse**. For the two right triangles shown here, the measure of one acute angle of each triangle is **60°**. Note that this tells us that the two triangles are similar.

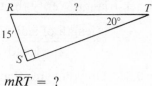

For each triangle, verify the fact that the ratio

$$\frac{\text{length of side adjacent to the 60° angle}}{\text{length of hypotenuse}}$$

is $\frac{1}{2}$, or **0.50**. Do you agree that, for *every* 60° angle in a right triangle,

$$\frac{\text{length of side adjacent}}{\text{length of hypotenuse}} = \frac{1}{2} ?$$

We call this ratio the **cosine ratio**. Using the three-letter abbreviation **cos**, we write

$$\cos 60° = \tfrac{1}{2}, \quad \text{or} \quad \cos 60° = \textbf{0.50,}$$

and define the cosine of any acute angle of a right triangle as

$$\frac{\textbf{length of side adjacent}}{\textbf{length of hypotenuse}} .$$

The following examples further illustrate the idea that, for an acute angle of a given measure in a right triangle, the cosine ratio has a **constant** value.

EXAMPLE 1.   Find **cos 36°**, using the given lengths of the sides of $\triangle ABC$.

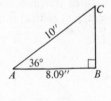

$$\cos 36° = \frac{m\overline{AB}}{m\overline{AC}}$$

$$= \frac{8.09}{10} = 0.809$$

EXAMPLE 2.   Find **cos 36°**, using the given lengths of the sides of $\triangle KLM$.

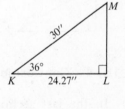

$$\cos 36° = \frac{m\overline{KL}}{m\overline{KM}}$$

$$= \frac{24.27}{30} = 0.809$$

In general, we can say:

 For any right triangle **RST**, if **r°** is the measure of $\angle R$ and **t°** is the measure of $\angle T$, then

$$\cos r° = \frac{m\overline{RS}}{m\overline{RT}}; \quad \cos t° = \frac{m\overline{ST}}{m\overline{RT}} .$$

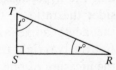

In the table on page 499, the third and the seventh columns, which are headed **Cosine,** give values for the cosines of the angle measures listed. Again, we must realize that most of the values in the table are approximations.

ORAL EXERCISES

Complete the following statements with ratios in terms of x, y, and z.

SAMPLE: *What you say:* $\cos 15° = \dfrac{x}{z}$

$$\cos 15° = ?$$

1.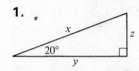

$$\cos 20° = ?$$

3.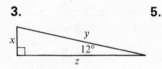

$$\cos 12° = ?$$

5.

$$\cos 40° = ?$$

2.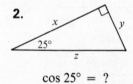

$$\cos 25° = ?$$

4.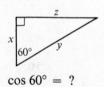

$$\cos 60° = ?$$

6.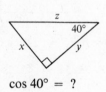

$$\cos 40° = ?$$

Use the table on page 499 to complete each of the following.

7. $\cos 31° \doteq$ ___?___

8. $\cos 49° \doteq$ ___?___

9. $\cos$ ___?___ $\doteq 0.8090$

10. $\cos$ ___?___ $\doteq \frac{9}{40}$

11. $\cos$ ___?___ $\doteq 0.6157$

12. $\cos 24° \doteq$ ___?___

13. $\cos$ ___?___ $\doteq \frac{7}{400}$

14. $\cos 10° \doteq$ ___?___

WRITTEN EXERCISES

Find each indicated angle measure to the nearest degree by using the cosine ratio.

SAMPLE:

$$x = \underline{\ ?\ } \text{ degrees}$$

Solution: $\cos x = \dfrac{86.6}{100} = 0.866$

$$x = 30°$$

A **1.**

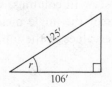

$r = $ __?__ degrees

3.

$n = $ __?__ degrees

5.

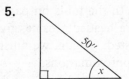

$x = $ __?__ degrees

2.

$a = $ __?__ degrees

4.

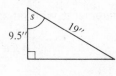

$s = $ __?__ degrees

6.

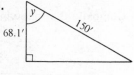

$y = $ __?__ degrees

For each right triangle, find the length of the side indicated; round off your answer to the nearest tenth of a unit.

7.

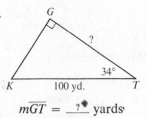

$m\overline{BC} = $ __?__ inches

9.

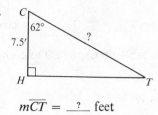

$m\overline{BZ} = $ __?__ inches

8.

$m\overline{GT} = $ __?__ yards

10.

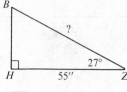

$m\overline{CT} = $ __?__ feet

Find the values of the variables in each figure.

B **11.**

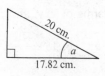

13.

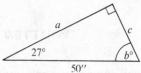

12.

14.

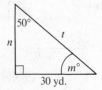

For each of the following, use the dimensions given to determine the cosine of the indicated angle; express any answer that involves a radical in simplest radical form.

15.

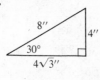

cos 30° = ?

16.

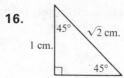

cos 45° = ?

15–5   Complementary Angles and Sine-Cosine Relationships

You know that the sum of the measures of the angles of a triangle is 180°. Thus in a right triangle the sum of the measures of the **two acute angles** must be **90°**. If the sum of the measures of two angles is 90°, the angles are said to be complementary. Each angle is called the complement of the other.

 For any right triangle **XYZ**, if ∠**X** is the right angle, then ∠**Y** and ∠**Z** are complementary;

$$m\angle Y + m\angle Z = 90°.$$

The sine and cosine ratios are called **trigonometric** ratios. For the right triangle shown here, we can write the following ratios:

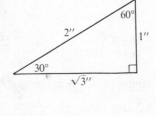

$$\sin 30° = \frac{1}{2} \qquad \sin 60° = \frac{\sqrt{3}}{2}$$

$$\cos 60° = \frac{1}{2} \qquad \cos 30° = \frac{\sqrt{3}}{2}$$

Do you agree that **sin 30° = cos 60°** and **cos 30° = sin 60°**? Notice that the word **cosine** is made up of the two syllables **co** and **sine**; now verify in the table on page 499 that the **cosine** of any acute angle is equal to the **sine** of the complementary angle.

 For any right triangle **XYZ**, if **y** is the measure of an acute angle, then **sin y = cos (90 − y)** and **cos y = sin (90 − y)**.

ORAL EXERCISES

For each pair of angle measures, tell whether or not two angles with those measures are complementary.

1. 15°, 49°	**5.** 45°, 45°	**9.** 81°, 9°
2. 70°, 20°	**6.** 1°, 89°	**10.** 36°, 54°
3. 10°, 80°	**7.** 63°, 27°	**11.** 56°, 24°
4. 40°, 40°	**8.** 18°, 72°	**12.** 17°, 73°

Find the degree measure that will make each statement true.

13. 38° + __?__ = 90°   **16.** 90° − 28° = __?__

14. 61° + __?__ = 90°   **17.** 90° − __?__ = 33°

15. __?__ + 25° = 90°   **18.** 90° − __?__ = 51°

WRITTEN EXERCISES

Use the table on page 499 to find each value.

SAMPLE: sin 10° = ?   *Solution:* sin 10° ≐ 0.1736
          cos 80° = ?   cos 80° ≐ 0.1736

1. sin 40° = ?	**4.** sin 85° = ?	**7.** sin 45° = ?
cos 50° = ?	cos 5° = ?	cos 45° = ?
2. sin 33° = ?	**5.** sin 25° = ?	**8.** sin 38° = ?
cos 57° = ?	cos 65° = ?	cos 52° = ?
3. sin 26° = ?	**6.** sin 66° = ?	**9.** sin 6° = ?
cos 64° = ?	cos 24° = ?	cos 84° = ?

Name the correct replacement for *x* in each of the following.

10. sin 36° = cos *x*°   **13.** sin 85° = cos (90 − *x*)°

11. sin 55° = cos *x*°   **14.** cos 70° = sin (90 − *x*)°

12. sin *x*° = cos 75°   **15.** cos 13° = sin (90 − *x*)°

Copy and complete each statement.

SAMPLE: sin 16° = cos (90 − ?)° = cos (?)° = __?__

Solution: sin 16° = cos (90 − 16)° = cos 74° ≐ 0.2756

16. sin 58° = cos (90 − ?)° = cos (?) = __?__

17. sin 77° = cos (90 − ?)° = cos (?)° = __?__

18. cos 34° = sin (90 − ?)° = sin (?)° = __?__

19. $\cos 13° = \sin (90 - ?)° = \sin (?)° = \underline{\ ?\ }$

20. $\sin 42° = \underline{\ ?\ } (90 - ?)° = \underline{\ ?\ } (?)° = \underline{\ ?\ }$

15–6 The Tangent Ratio

Another trigonometric ratio is called the **tangent ratio**. The **tangent** of an acute angle in a right triangle is the ratio of the length of the **side opposite** the angle to the length of the **side adjacent** to the angle. As was true of the sine and cosine ratios, the tangent ratio is also constant for an angle of a given measure. The three-letter abbreviation for the word **tangent** is **tan**.

For any right triangle **RST**, if $r°$ is the measure of $\angle R$ and $t°$ is the measure of $\angle T$, then

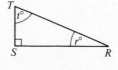

$$\tan r° = \frac{m\overline{TS}}{m\overline{SR}}; \quad \tan t° = \frac{m\overline{SR}}{m\overline{TS}}$$

In right triangle **RST**, remember that the two acute angles **R** and **T** are **complementary**. What do you notice about the tangents of these two angles? Do you see why the tangent of one of the two acute acute angles is the **reciprocal** of the tangent of the other?

In the table on page 499, the tangent ratios of the angles are listed in the columns headed **Tangent**.

ORAL EXERCISES

Complete the following statements with ratios in terms of x, y, and z.

SAMPLE:

What you say: $\tan 38° = \dfrac{x}{z}$

$\tan 38° = ?$

1.

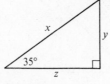

$\tan 35° = ?$

2.

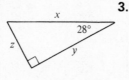

$\tan 28° = ?$

3.

$\tan 47° = ?$

4.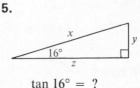

tan 27° = ?

5.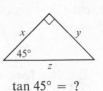

tan 16° = ?

6.

tan 45° = ?

Use the table on page 499 to evaluate each of the following:

7. tan 19° ≐ _?_   **10.** tan 30° ≐ _?_   **13.** tan 60° ≐ _?_

8. tan 45° = _?_   **11.** tan 24° ≐ _?_   **14.** tan 52° ≐ _?_

9. tan 57° ≐ _?_   **12.** tan 31° ≐ _?_   **15.** tan 28° ≐ _?_

WRITTEN EXERCISES

Find each indicated angle measure to the nearest degree by using the tangent ratio.

SAMPLE:

Solution: $\tan x = \frac{7}{10} = 0.7000$

$x \doteq 35°$

$x =$ _?_ degrees

A **1.**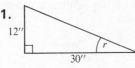

$r =$ _?_ degrees

3.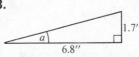

$a =$ _?_ degrees

5.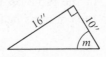

$m =$ _?_ degrees

2.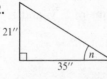

$n =$ _?_ degrees

4.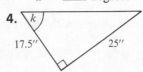

$k =$ _?_ degrees

6.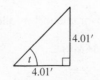

$t =$ _?_ degrees

Find the length of the side indicated in each right triangle. Round off each answer to the nearest tenth.

7.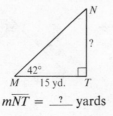

$m\overline{NT} =$ _?_ yards

8.

$m\overline{CD} =$ _?_ inches

9.

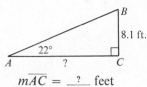

$m\overline{AC} = $ __?__ feet

10.

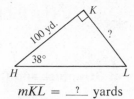

$m\overline{KL} = $ __?__ yards

Find the number represented by each variable.

B **11.**

13.

12.

14.

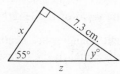

PROBLEMS

Use sine, cosine, and tangent ratios to solve the following problems.

1. A rocket maintains a 45° angle of climb. After covering a ground distance of 6 miles how high is it above the ground?

2. A ladder leaning against a wall forms an angle of 60° with the ground. If the foot of the ladder is 6 feet from the base of the wall, how far up the wall does the top of the ladder rest?

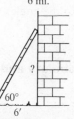

3. A guy wire supporting a radio antenna makes an angle of 55° with the ground. The wire is fastened to the antenna at a point 40 feet above the ground. How long is the guy wire?

4. A surveyor wants to find the distance across a lake. He lays out a right triangle as shown in the figure. He finds that the length of $\overline{AB}$ is 800 yards, and that the measure of angle BAC is 58°. What is the distance AC across the lake?

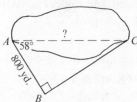

CHAPTER SUMMARY

Inventory of Structure and Concepts

1. Triangles are **congruent** if they have the same size and shape; if they are congruent, their corresponding angles have equal measures and their corresponding sides have equal lengths.

2. Two **similar** triangles have these properties:
   a. the measures of the angles of one are equal to the measures of the corresponding angles of the other, and
   b. the ratio of the lengths of any pair of corresponding sides is equal to the ratio of the lengths of any other pair of corresponding sides.

3. Two **right triangles** are **similar** if the measure of an acute angle of one triangle is equal to the measure of an acute angle of the other.

4. The **sine** of an acute angle in a right triangle is the ratio of the length of the side opposite the angle to the length of the hypotenuse.

5. The **cosine** of an acute angle in a right triangle is the ratio of the length of the side adjacent to the angle to the length of the hypotenuse.

6. Two angles are **complementary** if the sum of their measures is 90 degrees.

7. In any right triangle, if x represents the degree measure of an acute angle, then $\sin x = \cos (90 - x)$ and $\cos x = \sin (90 - x)$.

8. The **tangent** of an acute angle in a right triangle is the ratio of the length of the side opposite the angle to the length of the side adjacent to the angle.

Vocabulary and Spelling

congruent (*p. 489*)

corresponding angles (*p. 489*)

corresponding sides (*p. 489*)

similar triangles (*p. 490*)

hypotenuse (*p. 493*)

legs (*p. 493*)

opposite side (*p. 493*)

adjacent side (*p. 493*)

right triangle (*p. 493*)

right angle (*p. 493*)

acute angle (*p. 493*)

sine ratio (*p. 497*)

cosine ratio (*p. 502*)

constant (*p. 502*)

complementary angles (*p. 505*)

trigonometric ratios (*p. 505*)

tangent ratio (*p. 507*)

Chapter Test

Complete each of the following by referring to similar triangles *ABC* and *RST*.

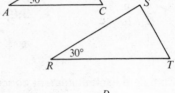

1. Side __?__ corresponds to side *ST*.
2. Angle *ABC* corresponds to angle __?__ .
3. Angle *ACB* corresponds to angle __?__ .
4. Side *AC* corresponds to side __?__ .
5. Side *RS* corresponds to side __?__ .

Complete each equation by naming a ratio of lengths of sides of right triangle *BDC*.

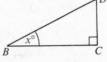

6. $\sin x = \dfrac{?}{?}$ **7.** $\tan x = \dfrac{?}{?}$ **8.** $\cos x = \dfrac{?}{?}$

Tell whether each statement is true or false.

9. $\sin 60° = \cos 30°$ and $\cos 60° = \sin 30°$.
10. $\sin 36° = \cos 54°$ and $\cos 36° = \sin 54°$.
11. $\sin 15° = \cos 85°$ and $\cos 15° = \sin 85°$.
12. $\sin 16° = \cos (90 - 16)°$ and $\cos 16° = \sin (90 - 16)°$.

For each of the following, use the table on page 499, to find the value of *x*.

13. $\sin x = \frac{32}{64}$ **14.** $\cos x = \frac{90}{400}$ **15.** $\tan x = \frac{35}{2000}$

Find the value of the variable for each right triangle.

16. 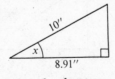   **17.**   **18.**

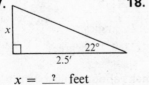

$x =$ __?__ degrees $x =$ __?__ feet $x =$ __?__ yards

△*ABC* ~ △*A'B'C'*. Find the lengths of the indicated sides of △*A'B'C'*.

19. $mB'C' =$ __?__ inches   **20.** $mA'B' =$ __?__ inches

Chapter Review

15–1   Congruence and Similarity

For each pair of ratios, find the replacement for the variable that will make the two ratios equal.

1. $\dfrac{n}{5}$, $\dfrac{6}{10}$ **3.** $\dfrac{3}{2}$, $\dfrac{x}{30}$ **5.** $\dfrac{12}{4}$, $\dfrac{3}{n}$

2. $\dfrac{4}{k}$, $\dfrac{18}{27}$ **4.** $\dfrac{b}{10}$, $\dfrac{(3)(2)}{(5)(2)}$ **6.** $\dfrac{18}{25}$, $\dfrac{a}{10}$

Complete each statement concerning similar triangles *PQR* and *P'Q'R'*.

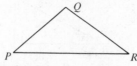 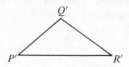

7. Side *PQ* corresponds to side __?__.

8. Side *P'R'* corresponds to side __?__.

9. Side *QR* corresponds to side __?__.

10. Angle *PRQ* corresponds to angle __?__.

11. Angle *P'Q'R'* corresponds to angle __?__.

15–2   Similar Right Triangles

Complete each of the following statements about right triangle *ABC*.

12. The hypotenuse of $\triangle ABC$ is side __?__.

13. The side adjacent to $\angle C$ is __?__.

14. The side opposite $\angle C$ is __?__.

15. $\angle A$ and $\angle C$ are __?__ angles.

16. The measure of $\angle C$ is __?__ degrees.

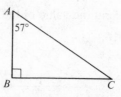

Complete each statement about similar right triangles *ABC* and *A'B'C'*.

17. $\dfrac{m\overline{AB}}{m\overline{A'B'}} = \dfrac{m\overline{AC}}{m\overline{A'C'}}$, so

   $m\overline{A'B'} = $ __?__

18. $\dfrac{m\overline{BC}}{m\overline{B'C'}} = \dfrac{m\overline{AC}}{m\overline{A'C'}}$, so

   $m\overline{BC} = $ __?__

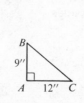 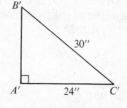

15-3 The Sine Ratio

Use the table on page 499 to find the measure of each indicated angle or side.

19.

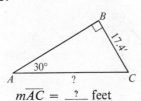

$r =$ ___?___ degrees

21.

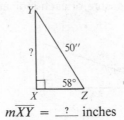

$x =$ ___?___ degrees

20.

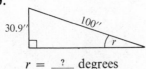

$m\overline{AC} =$ ___?___ feet

22.

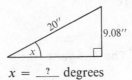

$m\overline{XY} =$ ___?___ inches

15-4 The Cosine Ratio

Find the measure of each indicated side or angle.

23.

$y =$ ___?___ degrees

25.

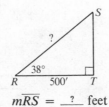

$m\overline{RS} =$ ___?___ feet

24.

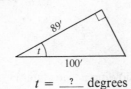

$t =$ ___?___ degrees

26.

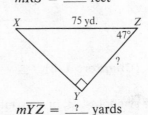

$m\overline{YZ} =$ ___?___ yards

15-5 Complementary Angles and Sine-Cosine Relationships

Replace each blank with the degree measure that will make the statement true.

27. $47° +$ ___?___ $= 90°$

28. ___?___ $+ 21° = 90°$

29. $90° -$ ___?___ $= 37°$

30. $90° -$ ___?___ $= 68°$

Show that each statement is true by replacing each member of the equation with its numerical value from the table on page 499.

31. $\sin 50° = \cos 40°$

33. $\sin 20° = \cos (90 - 20)°$

32. $\cos 31° = \sin 59°$

34. $\cos 22° = \sin (90 - 22)°$

15–6 The Tangent Ratio

Find the measure of each indicated angle or side.

35.

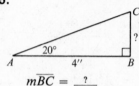

$m\overline{BC} = \underline{\ ?\ }$

37.

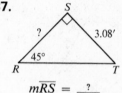

$m\overline{RS} = \underline{\ ?\ }$

36.

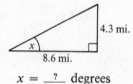

$x = \underline{\ ?\ }$ degrees

38.

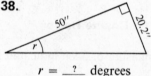

$r = \underline{\ ?\ }$ degrees

Cumulative Test

Part I (Chapters 1–8)

Use the symbol $>$, $<$, or $=$ to make each of the following a true statement.

1. $-10 \ ? \ -9$

4. $|\tfrac{1}{4}| \ ? \ |-\tfrac{1}{2}|$

7. $-|8| \ ? \ |-8|$

2. $3.01 \ ? \ 3.001$

5. $\tfrac{4}{5} \ ? \ 0.80$

8. $2^3 \ ? \ 3^2$

3. $|-8| \ ? \ |8|$

6. $-0.25 \ ? \ -0.155$

9. $\tfrac{1}{2} \ ? \ \tfrac{1}{10}$

Complete each statement with the word "positive" or the word "negative."

10. If n represents a number that is neither greater than nor equal to zero, we know that n is a $\underline{\ ?\ }$ number.

11. The absolute value of a directed number is never a __?__ number.

12. When n is a negative number, the opposite of n is a __?__ number.

Simplify each expression.

13. $10 + 13 + (-2)$

14. $4x + (-x) + 3x$

15. $-5.7 + 3.1 + 1.8 + (-2.9)$

16. $16 + (-10) + (-15) + 2$

Match each property listed in Column 1 with a related equation in Column 2.

COLUMN 1	COLUMN 2
17. Commutative property of multiplication	**A.** $a + 0 = 0 + a = a$
18. Associative property of addition	**B.** $a + b = b + a$
19. Multiplication property of 1	**C.** $a(b + c) = ab + ac$
20. Distributive property	**D.** $ab = ba$
21. Addition property of 0	**E.** $a \cdot 1 = 1 \cdot a = a$
22. Commutative property of addition.	**F.** $a + (b + c) = (a + b) + c$

Express each set in roster form.

23. {the integers between 0 and -8}

24. {the whole numbers less than 5}

25. {the whole numbers that are divisors of 12}

Graph the solution set of each sentence on the number line. The domain of the variable is {the directed numbers}.

26. $x > -3$

27. $n + 1 < 4$

28. $k \leq \frac{5}{2}$

29. $t \geq -\frac{2}{3}$

Solve each equation, check the solution, and write the solution set.

30. $b - 7 = 19$

31. $-n + 3 = 0$

32. $1.5x = 7.5$

33. $2t + 4 = 24$

34. $-x + 4x = -18$

35. $-2(y + 4) = 0$

Solve each inequality and graph the solution set.

36. $x + 1 > 3$

37. $y + 7 < 6$

38. $\frac{1}{2}n \leq -1$

39. $\frac{2b}{5} \geq \frac{3}{5}$

40. $4x - 1 \leq 7$

41. $-15 \leq 3y - 6$

In each of the following, complete the set of ordered pairs which is the function described by the given function equation for the given domain of the variable.

42. $2x - 1 = f(x)$;   domain: $\{0, 2, 4, 6, 8\}$
    $\{(0, -1), (2, 3), (4, \underline{\ \ ?\ \ }), (6, \underline{\ \ ?\ \ }), (8, \underline{\ \ ?\ \ })\}$

43. $r^2 + 2 = f(r)$;   domain: $\{-1, -2, -3, 1, 2, 3\}$
    $\{(-1, 3), (-2, 6), (-3, \underline{\ \ ?\ \ }), (1, \underline{\ \ ?\ \ }), (2, \underline{\ \ ?\ \ }), (3, \underline{\ \ ?\ \ })\}$

44. $f(n) = n + (-n)$;   domain: $\{-2, -1, 0, 1, 2\}$
    $\{(-2, 0), (-1, 0), (0, \underline{\ \ ?\ \ }), (1, \underline{\ \ ?\ \ }), (2, \underline{\ \ ?\ \ })\}$

Complete each of the following to make a true statement.

45. $10 + ? = 0$ **47.** $\frac{3}{7} \cdot ? = 1$ **49.** $(-\frac{5}{2}) \cdot ? = 1$

46. $? + (-3) = 0$ **48.** $0 = ? + \frac{1}{2}$ **50.** $1 = ? \cdot \frac{4}{1}$

Add.

51. $12y - 3x$ **52.** $5n^2 - 2n + 8$ **53.** $10x^2 + 2y$
    $\underline{\ \ 3y + \ \ x}$ $\underline{\ \ n^2 + \ \ n - 3}$ $-x^2 + 6y$
    $\underline{\ \ \ \ \ \ \ \ \ \ \ \ \ \ \ \ 4x^2 - \ \ y}$

Simplify each of the following.

54. $(7t - 5) + 3t$ **56.** $(xy - 2x) + (x^2 - xy - 5x)$
55. $-5x + (4 - 3x)$ **57.** $(1.2a^2 - 1.9) + (3.4a^2 - a)$

Subtract each lower polynomial from the one above it.

58. $5x + 3b$ **59.** $3mn + 5n$ **60.** $2x^2 - 4y + 3$
    $\underline{-x + 2b}$ $\underline{9mn - 2n}$ $\underline{-x^2 - 3y + 5}$

State the solution set of each equation if the domain of the variable is {the directed numbers}.

61. $8x + (4x - 3) = 69$ **63.** $4n - (n + 3) = 18$
62. $(5y - 7) - y = 41$ **64.** $-3x - (7 - 5x) = -1$

65. Write the set of ordered pairs of numbers that correspond to the points enclosed in the curve on the lattice at the right.

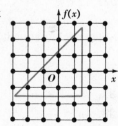

66. Write the set of ordered pairs that is the function represented by the points marked ✕ on the lattice at the right.

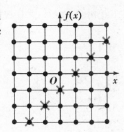

Complete each indicated multiplication or division.

67. $9x^3 - 3x - 2$
$ \times 4x$

70. $\dfrac{75x^4y^5 - 30x^2y^2}{-15x^2y}$

68. $-3rs(-r^2 + s^2)$

71. $(3y^2 - 6 - 7y) \div (3y + 2)$

69. $(3x + 2)^2$

72. $(3 - 2y)^3$

Factor each polynomial completely.

73. $t^2 - 25$

74. $x^2 + 5x - 6$

75. $m^3 - 6m^2 + 9m$

76. $t^2 - 17t - 60$

77. $b^2 + 13b + 30$

78. $21y + 10y^2 + y^3$

79. $9t^2 - 36$

80. $5n^2 - 3n - 2$

Write each of the following either as a repeating decimal or as a terminating decimal.

81. $\frac{3}{5}$

82. $\frac{2}{3}$

83. $\frac{1}{12}$

84. $\frac{7}{8}$

85. $\frac{49}{100}$

86. $\frac{1}{9}$

Complete each statement.

87. 15% of 140 is __?__.

88. 30 is 10% of __?__.

89. 19 is __?__% of 95.

90. 21% of 68 is __?__.

91. $5\frac{1}{2}$% of 2500 is __?__.

92. 500% of $2\frac{1}{5}$ is __?__.

Find each indicated product and express the answer in lowest terms. Remember that no divisor can have the value zero.

93. $\dfrac{18t}{7s} \cdot \dfrac{35st}{9s}$

94. $\dfrac{4}{3y} \cdot \left(\dfrac{2x^2}{7} \cdot \dfrac{3y}{x}\right)$

95. $\dfrac{2}{m + n} \cdot \dfrac{m - n}{3}$

96. $\dfrac{(a + b)}{4} \cdot \dfrac{(a - b)}{3}$

97. $\dfrac{x - 3}{8x - 4} \cdot \dfrac{10x - 5}{5x - 15}$

98. $\dfrac{1}{x + 3} \cdot \dfrac{x^2 - 9}{x - 3} \cdot 5$

99. $\dfrac{x}{x^2 - 6x + 9} \cdot \dfrac{x - 3}{1}$

100. $\dfrac{9a^2 - 25}{2a^2 + a - 6} \cdot \dfrac{2a - 3}{3a + 5}$

Express each of the following as a single fraction in lowest terms.

101. $\dfrac{\frac{1}{2}}{\frac{3}{5}}$

102. $\dfrac{3xy}{7} \div \dfrac{2y}{7}$

103. $\dfrac{\frac{36x^2}{4x}}{5}$

104. $-15ab \div \dfrac{3a}{2b}$

105. $\dfrac{ab}{c} \div \dfrac{b^2}{c^2}$

106. $\dfrac{9x}{x+5} \div \dfrac{-3}{x+5}$

107. $\dfrac{x+3}{x^2-9} \div \dfrac{1}{x-3}$

108. $\dfrac{y^2-16}{2y} \div (y+4)$

109. $(t-3) \div \dfrac{t^2-9}{t+1}$

Express each sum or difference as a single fraction in lowest terms.

110. $\dfrac{3a}{a+b} + \dfrac{b}{a+b}$

111. $\dfrac{x}{x^2-9} - \dfrac{3}{x^2-9}$

112. $\dfrac{14xy}{st} + \dfrac{9xy}{-st}$

113. $\dfrac{5y^2z}{a-2} + \dfrac{3y^2z}{2-a}$

114. $\dfrac{4t}{6} + \dfrac{r}{9}$

115. $\dfrac{9}{4y} - \dfrac{2}{y}$

116. $\dfrac{2}{m+3} + \dfrac{4}{m+4}$

117. $\dfrac{1}{k+m} + \dfrac{1}{k^2-m^2}$

Solve each open sentence.

118. $\dfrac{5x}{6} - \dfrac{x}{3} < -9$

119. $\dfrac{r}{2} - \dfrac{r}{8} = \dfrac{3}{4}$

120. $\dfrac{3k}{5} - \dfrac{k}{3} = -8$

121. $\dfrac{y}{3} - y < 2$

122. $\frac{1}{2}x + \frac{1}{4}x \geq 2\frac{1}{2}$

123. $4c - \dfrac{5c}{3} = 21$

Part II (Chapters 9–15)

Solve each equation and write the solution set.

1. $x^2 - 3x = 0$

2. $t^2 - 7t = 18$

3. $y^2 - 18 = 3y$

4. $\dfrac{1}{m+4} = \dfrac{3}{m-4}$

5. $\dfrac{1}{t} + \dfrac{2}{3t} = \dfrac{5}{9}$

6. $\dfrac{a-6}{a} = \dfrac{5}{a+6}$

7. One painter can completely paint a large room in 8 hours while a second painter requires only 6 hours to paint the same room. If both painters work together, how long will it take them to paint the room?

8. A high speed computer could process the payroll checks for a company in 10 hours. A slower computer would take 12 hours to complete the same payroll. If both computers could be put to work, how much time would be required to process the payroll checks?

9. Complete the table for the equation $5x - y = 3$. Tell whether or not the resulting set of ordered pairs is a function and if it is, give the domain and the range.

x	$5x - y = 3$	y	(x, y)
1	$5(1) - y = 3$	2	$(1, 2)$
2	?	?	?
0	?	?	?
-1	?	?	?

For each equation, write an equivalent equation in which the variable y stands alone as the left member.

10. $2x + y = 7$ **11.** $x - y = 19$ **12.** $2x + 3y = 0$

For each equation, give the coordinates of its intersections with the x-axis and the y-axis.

13. $x + y = 5$ **15.** $x = -2$

14. $2x + y = 3$ **16.** $4x - y = 2$

Find at least three ordered pairs that satisfy the given equation and draw its graph in the number plane.

17. $y = x + 2$ **19.** $y = -1.5$

18. $3x - y = 6$ **20.** $2x + 4y = 12$

Use the formula $slope = \dfrac{rise}{run}$ to complete the following:

21. rise = 8 inches   **22.** rise = 24 inches
      run = 20 inches   run = __?__ inches
      slope = __?__   slope = $\frac{2}{5}$

23. The sloping roof of a garage rises 4 feet over a horizontal distance of 12 feet. What is the slope of the roof?

24. The slope of a stretch of highway is $\frac{1}{25}$. Over a horizontal distance of 500 feet what is the amount of rise of the highway?

Find the slope of the line drawn in the number plane.

25.

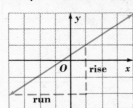

26.

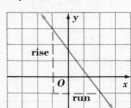

For each inequality write an equivalent inequality where *y* stands alone as the left member.

27. $x > y - 2$

28. $-x + y \geq 5$

29. $y - 9 < 2x$

30. $x + 2y \leq 8$

31. Name an inequality for which Region *A* is the graph and an inequality for which Region *B* is the graph.

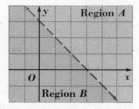

32. Name an inequality graphed on the number plane at the right.

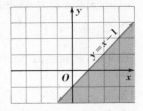

Draw a number plane graph of each inequality.

33. $x \geq -3\frac{1}{2}$

34. $2x + y > 1$

35. $y < 3$

36. $y \leq x - 1$

Write each equation in the slope–intercept form $y = mx + b$; give the slope and the *y*-intercept of the graph of the equation.

37. $y - 2x = 5$

38. $3y = x - 6$

39. $y + 2 = 4x$

40. $6x + 2y = 5$

For each quadratic equation, complete the table of values; then plot the points that correspond to each number pair and join them with a smooth curve.

41. circle: $x^2 + y^2 = 100$

x	y	(x, y)
0	10 and -10	(0, 10) and (0, -10)
6	?	?
8	?	?
-6	?	?
-8	?	?

42. parabola: $y = 2x^2$

x	y	(x, y)
0	0	(0, 0)
1	?	?
2	?	?
-1	?	?
-2	?	?

Make a number plane graph for each system of simultaneous equations and write the solution set of the system.

43. $3x - y = -4$

$x + y = 0$

44. $x + \dfrac{y}{2} = 2$

$x - y = -1$

Solve each system of simultaneous equations by using algebraic methods.

45. $x - y = 5$
$x + y = 3$

47. $2x + y = 5$
$x + y = 1$

46. $3x - y = 1$

$x + 2y = 5$

48. $\dfrac{x}{2} + 3y = 12$

$x = 2y$

Draw the graph of each simultaneous system.

49. $x + y > 1$
$x - y > 1$

50. $y \le \frac{1}{2}x + 2$
$y \le 3x - 1$

Name the principal square root of each number.

51. 64

52. $\frac{16}{25}$

53. 0.0016

54. 0.81

Simplify each expression.

55. $\sqrt[3]{64}$

57. $\sqrt{400}$

59. $-\sqrt{36}$

56. $\pm\sqrt{225}$

58. $\sqrt{179^2}$

60. $\sqrt[3]{-125}$

61. $\sqrt{4} \cdot \sqrt{5} \cdot \sqrt{5}$

63. $(\sqrt{5} + 2)(\sqrt{5} - 2)$

62. $\sqrt{8} \cdot \sqrt{2} \cdot \sqrt{4}$

64. $\sqrt{3} \cdot \sqrt{48}$

Use a table of powers and roots to find the missing dimension for each figure to the nearest tenth of a unit.

65. Right triangle

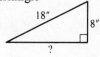

66. Rectangle

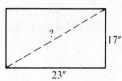

Solve each equation and check.

67. $1 + \sqrt{5x} = 11$

69. $3t^2 - 26 = 10$

68. $3\sqrt{5x} - 3 = 1$

70. $2x^2 - 5 = 3 - 6x$

Use the method of completing the square to solve each equation.

71. $x^2 + 10x - 3 = 0$

72. $r^2 - 16r = 3$

Use the quadratic formula to solve each equation.

73. $4x^2 + 3x - 1 = 0$ **75.** $n^2 - 7 = 2n$

74. $2x^2 - 3x = 5$ **76.** $3x^2 + 5x = 3 + x$

Use the given figure to complete each statement.

77. $m\angle POR = $ ___?___

78. $m\angle ROT = $ ___?___

79. $m\overarc{PQR} = $ ___?___

80. $m\overarc{RST} = $ ___?___

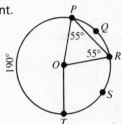

Use the given figure to complete each statement if square *ABCD* is inscribed in circle *O* and $\overline{AC}$ is a diameter. The length of $\overline{AC}$ is 10 inches.

81. $m\angle ABC = $ ___?___   **83.** $m\overarc{ADC} = $ ___?___   **85.** $m\overarc{AO} = $ ___?___

82. $m\angle ADC = $ ___?___   **84.** $m\overarc{ABD} = $ ___?___

86. The area of circle *O* is ___?___.

87. The area of $\triangle ABC$ is ___?___.

88. The area of $\triangle ADC$ is ___?___.

89. The circumference of circle *O* is ___?___.

90. The radius of circle *O* is ___?___.

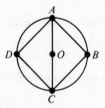

Find the measure of the indicated angle or side of each right triangle by using the indicated trigonometric function.

91.

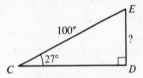

$m\overline{DE} = $ ___?___ inches
(Use the sine function.)

93.

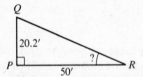

$m\angle PRQ = $ ___?___ degrees
(Use the tangent function.)

92.

$m\overline{RT} = $ ___?___ inches
(Use the cosine function.)

94.

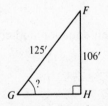

$m\angle FGH = $ ___?___ degrees
(Use the sine function.)

FORMULAS

Circle	$A = \pi r^2,\ C = 2\pi r$	Cube	$V = s^3$
Parallelogram	$A = bh$	Rectangular Box	$V = lwh$
Right Triangle	$A = \frac{1}{2}bh,\ c^2 = a^2 + b^2$	Cylinder	$V = \pi r^2 h$
Square	$A = s^2$	Pyramid	$V = \frac{1}{3}Bh$
Trapezoid	$A = \frac{1}{2}h(b + b')$	Cone	$V = \frac{1}{3}\pi r^2 h$
Triangle	$A = \frac{1}{2}bh$	Sphere	$V = \frac{4}{3}\pi r^3$
Sphere	$A = 4\pi r^2$		

TABLE OF WEIGHTS AND MEASURES

AMERICAN SYSTEM OF WEIGHTS AND MEASURES

LENGTH

12	inches	= 1 foot
3	feet	= 1 yard
$5\frac{1}{2}$	yards	= 1 rod
5280	feet	= 1 land mile
6076	feet	= 1 nautical mile

AREA

144	square inches	= 1 square foot
9	square feet	= 1 square yard
160	square rods	= 1 acre
640	acres	= 1 square mile

VOLUME

1728	cubic inches	= 1 cubic foot
27	cubic feet	= 1 cubic yard

WEIGHT

16	ounces	= 1 pound
2000	pounds	= 1 ton
2240	pounds	= 1 long ton

CAPACITY

Dry Measure

2	pints	= 1 quart
8	quarts	= 1 peck
4	pecks	= 1 bushel

Liquid Measure

16	fluid ounces	= 1 pint
2	pints	= 1 quart
4	quarts	= 1 gallon
231	cubic inches	= 1 gallon

METRIC SYSTEM OF WEIGHTS AND MEASURES

LENGTH	10 millimeters (mm)	= 1 centimeter (cm)	≐	0.3937	inch
	100 centimeters	= 1 meter (m)	≐	39.37	inches
	1000 meters	= 1 kilometer (km)	≐	0.6	mile
CAPACITY	1000 milliliters (ml)	= 1 liter (l)	≐	1.1	quart
	1000 liters (l)	= 1 kiloliter (kl)	≐	264.2	gallons
WEIGHT	1000 milligrams (mg)	= 1 gram (g)	≐	0.035	ounce
	1000 grams	= 1 kilogram (kg)	≐	2.2	pounds

Glossary

Absolute value of a number. Either the number or its opposite, whichever is positive. The absolute value of 0 is 0. (p. 9)

Acute angle. An angle with measure greater than 0° and less than 90°. (p. 493)

Addition property of equality. For all r, s, and t, if $r = s$, then $r + t = s + t$. (p. 47)

Addition property of inequality. For all r, s, and t: if $r < s$, then $r + t < s + t$; if $r > s$, then $r + t > s + t$. (p. 47)

Additive inverse. For every real number a, the real number $-a$ such that $a + (-a) = 0$ and $(-a) + a = 0$. (p. 7)

Additive property of opposites. For every number r, $(-r) + r = r + (-r) = 0$. (p. 12)

Additive property of zero. For every number r, $0 + r = r + 0 = r$. (p. 12)

Algebraic fraction. A fraction in which a variable occurs in the numerator or the denominator, or in both. (p. 184)

Arc. The set of all points of a circle between two specified endpoints. (p. 465)

Associative properties. For all numbers r, s, and t, $(r + s) + t = r + (s + t)$ (p. 12); $(r \cdot s)t = r(s \cdot t)$ (p. 21)

Base. In the expression 3^5, 3 is the base. (p. 82)

Binomial. A two-termed polynomial. (p. 74)

Central angle. An angle whose vertex is the center of a circle. (p. 464)

Chord of a circle. A line segment whose endpoints are on the circle. (p. 463)

Circle. The set of all points in a plane that are a given distance from a point called the center of the circle; the graph of an equation of the form $x^2 + y^2 = r^2$, where $r > 0$. (pp. 341, 463)

Circular region. The union of a circle and its interior. (p. 463)

Closure property. A set of numbers is closed under a given operation if each result of the operation is a unique element of the given set. (p. 12)

Coefficient. Any factor of a product is the coefficient of the product of the remaining factors; in general, the numerical factor of an algebraic product is called its coefficient. (p. 51)

Coincide. Two lines coincide if they have all their points in common. If the lines are graphs of equations, the equations are equivalent. (p. 358)

Commutative properties. For all r and s, $r + s = s + r$ (p. 12); $r \cdot s = s \cdot r$ (p. 21)

Complementary angles. Two angles the sum of whose measures is 90°. (p. 505)

Complex fraction. An expression in fraction form in which either the numerator or the denominator (or both) is expressed as a fraction. (p. 229)

Composite number. Any integer, other than 1, that is not prime; a number which is the product of prime numbers. (p. 117)

Concentric circles. Circles with the same center but with different radii. (p. 463)

Congruent triangles. Triangles having the same size and shape. (p. 489)

Consistent equations. In a simultaneous system, two equations with at least one common solution. (p. 358)

Constant. A monomial that does not contain a variable. (p. 74)

Cosine of an angle. In a right triangle, the length of the leg adjacent to an acute angle divided by the length of the hypotenuse. (p. 501)

Cube root. A number r is a cube root of a number s if $r^3 = s$. (p. 402)

Cubic equation. An equation of degree three. (p. 288)

Degree of a polynomial in one variable. The greatest degree of any term. (p. 144)

Degree of a variable. The number indicated by the exponent of the variable. (p. 123)

Diagonal. A line segment which joins two nonconsecutive vertices of a polygon. (p. 454)

Diameter of a circle. A chord that passes through the center of the circle. (p. 463)

Distributive property. For all numbers r, s, and t, $r(s + t) = rs + rt$ and $(s + t)r = sr + tr$ (p. 21)

Dividend. In the expression $a \div b = c$, a is the dividend. (p. 228)

Division. The inverse operation of multiplication; dividing by a number is the same as multiplying by its reciprocal. (p. 23)

Division by zero. The division of any number by zero is not defined. (p. 23)

Divisor. In the expression $a \div b = c$, b is the divisor. (p. 228)

Domain. The set of first numbers in the ordered pairs that form the function. (p. 296)

Domain of a variable. The set whose members may be used as replacements for the variable; also called *replacement set* (p. 38)

Ellipse. The section of a circular cone which results when a plane cuts the cone obliquely; the graph of the equation $ax^2 + by^2 = r^2$, where $a \neq b$, $a > 0$, and $b > 0$. (p. 341)

Empty set. The set containing no elements; the usual symbol is $\emptyset$. (p. 38)

Equiangular polygon. A polygon all of whose angles have the same measure. (p. 458)

Equilateral polygon. A polygon all of whose sides have the same length. (p. 458)

Equivalent fractions. Fractions which name the same number. (p. 186)

Equivalent open sentences. Open sentences which have the same solution set. (p. 18)

Exponent. In the expression 5^4, the 4 is the exponent of the base 5; the exponent 4 tells the number of times 5 is used as a factor. (p. 82)

Exterior angle. An angle, lying outside a polygonal region, determined by one side of the polygon and the extension of a consecutive side. (p. 454)

Factor. A number which is multiplied by another number to form a product. (p. 82)

Flow chart. A diagram showing the steps to be followed in solving a problem, and the order in which they are to be performed. (p. 69)

Fraction. An indicated quotient of two algebraic expressions; a fraction is defined only when its denominator is not zero. (p. 183)

Fractional equation. An equation which has a variable in the denominator of one or more terms. (p. 291)

Function. A set of ordered pairs in which no two pairs have the same first number. (p. 59)

Function equation. An equation which assigns to each value of x a unique value of $f(x)$ in the ordered pair $(x, f(x))$ (p. 60)

Graph of a number. The point on the number line that is paired with the number. (p. 2)

Graph of an ordered number pair. The point in the number plane which is paired with the ordered number pair. (pp. 86, 301)

Greater than. A number a is greater than a number b ($a > b$), if the point paired with a is to the right of the point paired with b on the number line. (p. 4)

Greatest Common Factor (G. C. F.). The largest factor common to two numbers. (p. 118)

Half-plane. The part of a plane into which the plane is separated by a line. (p. 324)

Hypotenuse. The side opposite the right angle of a right triangle. (p. 414)

Inconsistent equations. Simultaneous equations having no common solution; the graphs of inconsistent linear equations are parallel lines. (p. 358)

Inscribed angle. An angle formed by two chords of a circle at a common endpoint. (p. 475)

Inscribed polygon. A polygon whose vertices lie on a circle. (p. 476)

Integer. A member of the set $\{\ldots, -3, -2, -1, 0, 1, 2, 3, \ldots\}$. (p. 38)

Integral factor. An integer which divides evenly into another integer. (p. 113)

Intercepted arc. An arc of a circle cut off by the sides of a central angle or an inscribed angle. (pp. 465, 475)

Interior angle. An angle determined by two consecutive sides of a polygon and lying within the polygonal region. (p. 454)

Inverse operations. Operations which produce opposite effects, such as addition and subtraction. (p. 18)

Irrational number. A number that cannot be expressed as a quotient of two integers. (p. 408)

Lattice. An array of points used to graph ordered pairs of integers. (p. 86)

Legs of a right triangle. The two sides that are adjacent to the right angle. (p. 414)

Less than. A number a is less than a number b ($a < b$) if the point paired with a is to the left of the point paired with b on the number line. (p. 4)

Linear equation. An equation of degree one. The graph of an equation of the form $ax + by = c$, where a and b are not both 0, is a straight line. (pp. 288, 301)

Lowest Common Denominator (L. C. D.). The simplest expression that contains each denominator as a factor. (pp. 262, 266)

Magnitude of a number. The distance on the number line between the origin and the graph of the number. (p. 2)

Mixed expression. The sum or difference of a polynomial and a fraction. (p. 270)

Mixed numeral. A numeral that represents the sum of an integer and a number written as a fraction. (p. 248)

Modular mathematics. A mathematics system which uses a finite set of numbers. (p. 387)

Monomial. A one-termed polynomial. (p. 74)

Multiplication property of equality. For all numbers r, s, and t, if $r = s$, then $rt = st$. (p. 51)

Multiplication property of inequality. For all numbers r, s, and t, with $r < s$:
if $t > 0$, then $rt < st$; if $t = 0$, then $rt = st = 0$; if $t < 0$, then $rt > st$. (p. 52)

Multiplicative inverse. See **Reciprocal.**

Multiplicative property of one. For every number r, $r \cdot 1 = 1 \cdot r = r$. (p. 21)

Multiplicative property of zero. For every number r, $r \cdot 0 = 0 \cdot r = 0$. (p. 21)

Negative direction. On the number line, the direction from the origin to a point on the negative side of the line. (p. 2)

Negative number. A number less than zero. (p. 1)

Obtuse angle. An angle whose measure is between 90° and 180°. (p. 466)

Open sentence. A number sentence containing one or more variables. (p. 37)

Opposite of a number. The number whose graph is the same distance from the origin as the graph of the given number, but on the opposite side of the origin; the *additive inverse* of the number. Zero is its own opposite. (p. 6)

Ordered number pair. A pair of numbers in which order is important, used generally in functions. (p. 59)

Origin. The point that is paired with zero on the number line; in the number plane, the zero point of both of two number lines that intersect at right angles. (pp. 1, 86)

Parabola. The section of a circular cone which results when the cone is cut by a plane parallel to a line connecting the vertex of the cone to any point in its base; the graph of an equation of the form $ax^2 + b = y$, where $a \neq 0$. (pp. 341–342)

Parallel lines. Distinct lines having the same slope. (p. 358)

Percent. Hundredths; divided by 100. The symbol for "percent" is "%". (p. 203)

Polygon. A simple closed plane curve that is the union of line segments. (p. 454)

Polygonal region. The union of a polygon and its interior. (p. 455)

Polynomial. An expression which indicates the addition, subtraction, or multiplication of numbers, variables, or combinations of numbers and variables. (p. 73)

Polynomial equation. An equation whose left and right members are polynomials. (p. 288)

Polynomial factoring. Expressing a given polynomial as a product of factors. (p. 125)

Polynomial in one variable. A polynomial in which a single variable occurs. (p. 73)

Positive direction. On the number line, the direction from the origin to a point on the positive side of the line. (p. 2)

Positive number. A number greater than zero. (p. 1)

Prime number. An integer greater than 1 which has exactly two different integral factors, 1 and the number itself. (p. 116)

Principle of zero products. For any r and s, $r \cdot s = 0$ if and only if $r = 0$ or $s = 0$. (p. 285)

Principal square root. The positive square root of a number. (p. 397)

Product. The result of multiplying two or more numbers. (p. 113)

Property of density. Between any two rational numbers there is a rational number. (p. 393)

Property of the opposite of a sum. For all r and s, $-(r + s) = -r + (-s)$. (p. 12)

Property of square roots of equal numbers. For any real numbers r and s, it is true that $r^2 = s^2$ if and only if $r = s$ or $r = -s$. (p. 437)

Pure quadratic equation. An equation of the form $ax^2 + c = 0$, where a and c are real numbers, and $a \neq 0$. (p. 436)

Pythagorean Theorem. If a and b represent the lengths of the legs of a right triangle, and c represents the length of the hypotenuse, then $a^2 + b^2 = c^2$. (p. 414)

Quadrant. One of the four regions into which the number plane is separated by two number lines that intersect at right angles. (p. 86)

Quadratic equation. An equation of degree two. (p. 288)

Quadratic formula. The formula $x = \dfrac{-b \pm \sqrt{b^2 - 4ac}}{2a}$, which gives the roots for the quadratic equation $ax^2 + bx + c = 0$. (p. 444)

Quadratic polynomial. A polynomial of degree two. (p. 144)

Quadrilateral. A polygon having four sides. (p. 458)

Quotient. In the expression $a \div b = c$, c is the quotient. (p. 228)

Radical. An expression in the form $\sqrt[n]{r}$. (p. 397)

Radical equation. An equation in which a variable occurs under a radical sign. (p. 434)

Radical sign. The symbol, $\sqrt{}$, which designates a root of a number; for $a > 0$, $\sqrt{a}$ names the positive square root of a. (p. 397)

Radius. The distance of any point on a circle from the center; any line segment connecting a point of the circle with the center. (p. 463)

Range. The set of second numbers in the ordered pairs that form the function. (p. 296)

Ratio. A comparison of two numbers; if r and s are numbers, and $s \neq 0$, the ratio of r to s can be written $\dfrac{r}{s}$ or $r{:}s$. (p. 199)

Rational number. A number that can be written as the indicated quotient of two integers (the second integer not zero). (p. 392)

Rationalizing the denominator. The process of simplifying a fraction so that there are no irrational terms in the denominator. (p. 417)

Real number. Any number that belongs to either the set of rational numbers or the set of irrational numbers. (p. 409)

Reciprocal. Two numbers whose product is 1 are reciprocals (*multiplicative inverses*) of each other. 0 has *no* reciprocal. (p. 23)

Reflexive property of equality. For any number r, $r = r$. (p. 44)

Regular polygon. A polygon that is both equilateral and equiangular. (p. 458)

Relatively prime integers. Any pair of integers whose greatest common factor is 1. (p. 120)

Repeating decimal. A decimal in which the same block of digits repeats unendingly. (p. 192)

Root index. A number assigned to a radical to indicate a root other than a square root; in $\sqrt[3]{8}$, the root index is 3. (p. 402)

Root of a number. For any positive integer n, a number x is an nth root of the number a if $x^n = a$. (p. 402)

Root of an open sentence. A solution of the open sentence. (p. 296)

Roster. A list of the members of a set. (p. 38)

Section of a cone. The intersection of a cone with a plane. (p. 341)

Sector of a circular region. A region bounded by two radii and the intercepted arc. (p. 469)

Semicircle. An arc that is one-half of a circle. (p. 470)

Semicircular region. The union of a semicircle, its diameter and its interior. (p. 470)

Similar terms. Terms which contain the same variable(s) as factor(s). (p. 44)

Similar triangles. Two triangles which have the same shape, but not necessarily the same size. (p. 490)

Simultaneous equations. See **System of equations.**

Simultaneous inequalities. See **System of inequalities.**

Sine of an angle. In a right triangle, the length of the leg opposite an acute angle divided by the length of the hypotenuse. (p. 497)

Slope of a line. The steepness of a nonvertical line, as defined by the quotient: $\dfrac{\text{rise}}{\text{run}} = \dfrac{\text{vertical change}}{\text{horizontal change}} = \dfrac{\text{difference in } y\text{-coordinates}}{\text{difference in } x\text{-coordinates}}$. A horizontal line has slope 0; a vertical line has *no* slope. (pp. 305–308)

Slope-intercept form. An equation of the form $y = mx + b$ is in slope-intercept form; m gives the slope of its graph, and b names its y-intercept. (p. 338)

Solution of an open sentence. Any replacement for the variable which causes the open sentence to become a true statement; also called a **root.** (p. 38)

Solution set. The set of all solutions of an open sentence; also called **truth set.** (p. 38)

Square of a number. The number raised to the second power. (p. 151)

Square root. A number r is a square root of a number s if $r^2 = s$. (p. 397)

Standard form of a polynomial. A polynomial in one variable is in standard form if the terms are written from left to right in descending order of the exponents of the variable. A polynomial in more than one variable is written in standard form by ordering the terms according to the exponents of one variable. (p. 74)

Substitution principle. For any numbers m and n, if $m = n$, then either one may be used in place of the other. (p. 44)

Symmetric property of equality. For any numbers r and s, if $r = s$, then $s = r$. (p. 44)

System of equations. A set of equations that impose different conditions on the same variables; also referred to as a set of *simultaneous equations.* (p. 357)

System of inequalities. A set of inequalities that impose different conditions on the same variables; also referred to as *simultaneous inequalities.* (p. 377)

Tangent of an angle. In a right triangle, the length of the leg opposite an acute angle divided by the length of the leg adjacent to the angle. (p. 507)

Terminating decimal. A decimal with a finite number of places. (p. 191)

Transitive property of equality. For all numbers r, s, and t, if $r = s$ and $s = t$, then $r = t$. (p. 44)

Transitive property of inequality. For all numbers r, s, and t, if $r < s$ and $s < t$, then $r < t$. (p. 44)

Triangle. The union of three line segments determined by three points not on a line. (p. 453)

Triangular region. The union of a triangle and its interior. (p. 453)

Trinomial. A three-termed polynomial. (p. 74)

Trinomial square. The three-termed quadratic polynomial which results from squaring a binomial. (p. 150)

Variable. A symbol which may represent any of the members of a specified set. (p. 37)

Whole numbers. Zero and the positive integers. (p. 391)

x-axis. The horizontal axis on a lattice or number plane. (pp. 129, 301)

y-axis. The vertical axis on a lattice or number plane. (p. 301)

y-intercept. The value of y at the point where a graph intersects the y-axis. (p. 335)

Answers to Odd-Numbered Exercises

Chapter 1. Directed Numbers and Operations

Pages 3–4 Written Exercises A 1. $6\frac{1}{5}$; left **3.** $4\frac{1}{2}$; right **5.** -16 **7.** 1.6 **9.** $1\frac{1}{8}$; left **11.** 3 **13.** -8
B 15. distance, 10.3 units; magnitude, 10.3 **17.** distance, 30 units; magnitude, 30 **19.** distance, $6\frac{1}{2}$ units; magnitude, $6\frac{1}{2}$ **21.** distance, $\frac{5}{2}$ units, magnitude, $\frac{5}{2}$ **23.** distance, 0.005 units; magnitude, 0.005 **25.** distance, 36.25 units, magnitude, 36.25 **27.** 17 **29.** -96 **31.** $-8\frac{1}{4}$ **33.** $5\frac{1}{8}$

Pages 5–6 Written Exercises A 1. 8 is less than 15; 8 lies to the left of 15 on the number line. **3.** 10 is greater than 4; 10 lies to the right of 4 on the number line. **5.** 2 is less than or equal to 5; 2 names the same point as 5 or names a point to the left of 5. **7.** 9 is greater than or equal to -3; 9 names the same point as -3 or names a point to the right of -3. **9.** -3 is greater than or equal to -3; -3 names the same point as -3 or names a point to the right of -3. **11.** -1 is less than 0; -1 lies to the left of 0. **13.** true
15. true **17.** false **19.** true **21.** true **23.** true **B 25.** false **27.** true **29.** false **31.** true **33.** true
35. true **37.** false **39.** false **C 41.** positive **43.** negative **45.** positive; negative

Pages 8–9 Written Exercises A 1. 65 **3.** -8.5 **5.** 2 **7.** $-5x$ **9.** 6.1 **11.** -8.3 **13.** 2
15. true **17.** false **19.** true **21.** true **23.** true **25.** -11 **27.** -2 **29.** -6 **31.** $3\frac{1}{3}$ **C 39.** $<$
41. $<$ **43.** $<$

Pages 11–12 Written Exercises A 1. $|-9| = 9$ **3.** $|3\frac{1}{4}| = 3\frac{1}{4}$ **5.** $|9.4| = 9.4$ **7.** true **9.** true
11. false **13.** true **15.** true **17.** false **19.** 19 **21.** 37 **23.** 5.7 **25.** 24 **27.** 4 **29.** -35 **B 31.** 8
33. 0 **35.** 0 **37.** 40 **39.** -12.4 **C 41.** 6 **43.** 140 **45.** 21 **47.** 11

Page 13 Written Exercises B 19. 2 **21.** s **23.** w **25.** 0

Page 16 Written Exercises A 1. 16 **3.** -2 **5.** 3 **7.** 2.9 **9.** 7 **11.** -5 **13.** 7 **15.** 0 **17.** 1
B 19. 39 **21.** -1.9 **23.** 4.9 **25.** -14.3

Page 17 Problems 1. Mr. Dent had $36.00 left in his account. **3.** The club has $26.50 left. **5.** The fullback gained $7\frac{1}{2}$ yards. **7.** The top is 164 feet above the ground level.

Pages 19–20 Written Exercises A 1. 35 **3.** 96 **5.** $-32a$ **7.** $-43x$ **9.** 0 **11.** -61 **13.** $-107mn$
15. -7.59 **17.** 13 **19.** -19 **21.** $-4x$ **23.** 0.3 **25.** $-0.9a$ **27.** $-5.9ab$ **29.** 730 **31.** $-117t$
B 33. ? $= 9 - 10$; -1 **35.** ? $= (-3) - 6$; -9 **37.** ? $= 4 - (-10)$; 14 **39.** ? $= -(4 + 9) - (-7)$; -6

Pages 22–23 Written Exercises A 1. -90 **3.** -45 **5.** 72 **7.** 1392 **9.** 125 **11.** 90 **13.** 42
15. 84 **17.** -48 **19.** 90 **21.** 80 **23.** $-64x^3$ **B 25.** $(-9)(-4) = 36$ **27.** $(-7)(5) = -35$
29. $(-2)(-12) = 24$ **31.** $(-2b)(-3) = 6b$ **33.** $(-402)(1) = -402$ **35.** $(1)(-m) = -m$
C 37. $[5(-7)](-3) = 105$ **39.** $(-1)[(-4)(-15)] = -60$ **41.** $-[2(-2)(-2)](-2) = 16$ **43.** closed
45. closed

Pages 25–26 Written Exercises A 1. $10 \cdot 2$ **3.** $36 \cdot (-\frac{1}{6})$ **5.** $14 \cdot (-2)$ **7.** $(-10) \cdot \frac{1}{5}$ **9.** $(-12) \cdot (-2)$
11. $13 \cdot \frac{1}{b}$ **13.** $4 \cdot (-1)$ **15.** $0 \cdot (\frac{1}{4})$ **17.** $4 \cdot (\frac{1}{4}) = 1$ **19.** $(-5) \cdot (-\frac{1}{5}) = 1$ **21.** $\frac{6}{2} = 6(\frac{1}{2})$ **23.** $1 = -\frac{2}{3}(-\frac{3}{2})$ **25.** $1 = 3(\frac{1}{3})$ **27.** $1 = a\left(\frac{1}{a}\right)$ **29.** $-\frac{5}{2} = -5(\frac{1}{2})$ **31.** $(-2)\frac{1}{3} = -\frac{2}{3}$ **33.** $\frac{3}{20}$ **35.** 3 **37.** $\frac{1}{2}$
39. 4 **41.** 15 **43.** 15 **B 45.** 27 **47.** -15 **49.** -8 **51.** -9 **C 53.** -3 **55.** 2

Pages 28–29 Chapter Test 1. $-4\frac{1}{10}$ **3.** $-3\frac{1}{2}$ **5.** $<$ **7.** $<$ **9.** $=$ **11.** $<$ **13.** 17 **15.** 12
17. 27 **19.** 75 **21.** -12.21 **23.** -8.22 **25.** 90 **27.** -24 **29.** 0

Pages 29–32 Chapter Review 1. negative **3.** positive **5.** $19\frac{1}{2}$ **7.** 27 **9.** 3.8 **11.** is not equal to
13. is less than or equal to **15.** is greater than or equal to **17.** $0 > -9$ **19.** $3 \geq -8$ **21.** $-1.6 \neq 1.6$
23. 45 **25.** $-x$ **27.** $-3m$ **29.** 0 **31.** 68 **33.** -5 **35.** $|\frac{1}{3}| = \frac{1}{3}$ **37.** 0 **39.** 13 **41.** 11 **43.** -25
45. add. property of 0 **47.** commutative **49.** true **51.** false **53.** always **55.** sometimes **57.** 13
59. 188 **61.** -2 **63.** 3 **65.** $45k$ **67.** $-1.4t$ **69.** -8 **71.** $-10t$ **73.** positive **75.** C **77.** A
79. E **81.** 665 **83.** 72 **85.** $21b$ **87.** $-\frac{1}{5}$ **89.** $\frac{3}{m}$ **91.** 5 **93.** $-2k$ **95.** $(-\frac{2}{3})(-\frac{3}{2}) = 1$

1

Pages 32–33   Review of Skills   1. 2^5 **3.** $(-5)^3$ **5.** $(\frac{1}{3})^3$ **7.** C   **9.** B   **11.** A   **13.** $-1\frac{1}{2}$ **15.** 2
17. $\{-1, 0, 1\}$ **19.** {numbers between 0 and 1}   **21.** $8x$ **23.** $7x + 9y$ **25.** $4x$ **27.** E   **29.** A   **31.** B
33. F

Page 35   Check Point for Experts   1. $a = 1$ **3.** $a = 4$ **5.** $d = 3$ **7.** $d = 5$ **9.** $d = 3$ **11.** no; no
13. yes; yes   **15.** no; no

Chapter 2.   Solving Open Sentences

Pages 39–40   Written Exercises   A 1. $-7; 0; 7$ **3.** $3; 0; 3$ **5.** $95; 175; 255$ **7.** $11; 9; 7$ **9.** $-4; 0; 4$
11. $13; 3; -7$ **13.** $-5; -10; -15$ **15.** $\frac{1}{2}; 0; -\frac{1}{2}$ **17.** $\{8\}$ **19.** $\{-3\}$ **21.** $\{8, 9, 10, \ldots\}$ **23.** $\{17\}$
25. $\{13\}$ **27.** $\{-5\}$ **29.** $\{\frac{14}{3}\}$ **31.** $\{-15\}$ **33.** $\{10\}$ **35.** $\{-2, 2\}$ **B 37.** {the directed numbers}
39. {the directed numbers}   **41.** {the directed numbers greater than -3}   **43.** {all directed numbers
except 0}   **45.** { } or $\emptyset$ **C 47.** $\{-3\}$

Pages 40–41   Problems   1. 150 square inches; 300 square inches   **3.** 6 square units; 24 square units; 96
square units; 150 square units   **5.** 960 cubic feet; 1920 cubic feet; 3840 cubic feet

Page 43   Written Exercises   A 1. $x = -1$ **3.** $x \geq -1$ **5.** $x < -\frac{1}{2}$ **7.** $x > -\frac{2}{3}$

9. 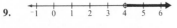   **11.**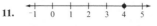

13.    **15.**

17. 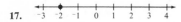   **19.**

B 21. C   **23.** D

C 25. 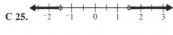   **27.**

29.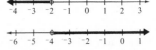

Pages 45–46   Written Exercises   A 1. $3(-8) = 12(-2)$ **3.** $-4 < 30$ **5.** $m + n = m - n$
7. $|-19| > |-2|$ **9.** $-3.2 \cdot 0 = 12 \cdot 0$ **11.** $16b + 7b$ **13.** $5xy + 4xy$ **15.** $2.5x^2 + 1.8x^2$
17. $12r^2s - 2r^2s$ **19.** $5n + 7n + 3n + 4n$ **21.** $18m + 20m + 36m$ **23.** $10.5x$ **25.** $7a$ **27.** $2y$ **29.** $7k$
31. $23a^2 + 6$ **B 33.** $16m$ **35.** $8t + 21$ **37.** $12k + 12$ **39.** $8a + 4c + 16$ **41.** $12a + 46$

Page 46   Problems   1. $P = 12m + 4n$ **3.** $P = 8m$ **5.** $A = 5n - 15$ square inches

Page 50   Written Exercises   A 1. $\{11\}$ **3.** $\{-9\}$ **5.** $\{5\}$ **7.** $\{18\}$ **9.** $\{4.5\}$ **11.** $\{-18\}$ **13.** $\{6\}$
15. $\{\frac{3}{4}\}$ **17.** $\{2, 3, 4, \ldots\}$ **19.** $\{-5, -6, -7, \ldots\}$ **21.** $\{-2, -1, 0, 1, \ldots\}$ **23.** $\{22, 21, 20, \ldots\}$
25. $\{5, 4, 3, \ldots\}$ **27.** $\{-5, -4, -3, \ldots\}$ **29.** $\{0, -1, -2, \ldots\}$ **B 31.** $x = a - m$ **33.** $x \geq m - t$
35. $x = -y - c$ **37.** $x = ab - 3$ **39.** $x = -h + c$

Pages 53–55   Written Exercises   A 1. $\{9\}$ **3.** $\{4\}$ **5.** {all directed numbers greater than 7}   **7.** {directed
numbers greater than or equal to -50}   **9.** $\{-5\}$ **11.** $\{-\frac{27}{4}\}$ **13.** {directed numbers less than -8}
15. $\{-9\}$ **17.** $\{-10\}$ **19.** {directed numbers less than -2}   **21.** {directed numbers less than or equal
to -6}   **23.** $\{17\}$

25. $t > \frac{3}{2}$    **27.** $y < -2$

29. $n > 0$    **31.** $r > -4$

33. $k \leq 4\frac{1}{3}$ **35.** $25 \leq n$

37. $\{-\frac{5}{2}\}$ **39.** $\{2\}$ **41.** $\{-\frac{4}{5}\}$ **B 43.** $\frac{v}{t} = a$ **45.** $\frac{V}{B} = h$ **47.** $\frac{P}{4} = s$ **49.** $\frac{V}{s^2} = h$ **51.** $\frac{V}{lw} = h$

Pages 57–58 Written Exercises A 1. $\{6\}$ **3.** $\{9\}$ **5.** $\{4\}$ **7.** $\{25\}$ **9.** $\{-4\}$ **11.** $\{-40\}$ **13.** $\{-\frac{2}{3}\}$
15. $\{6\}$ **17.** $\{-2\}$

19. $a \le 2$    **21.** $r < \frac{1}{3}$

23. $m \ge -2$ **25.** $1 < t$

27. $x < 4\frac{1}{2}$ **29.** $r \le -3$

31. $n < -5$ **33.** $1 \ge w$

B 35. {directed numbers less than or equal to -2}   **37.** $\{\frac{9}{2}\}$ **39.** {directed numbers}   **41.** $\{10\}$
C 43. $\{-1, 1\}$ **45.** $\{0\}$

Pages 58–59 Problems 1. $w + (w + 1) + (w + 2)$ **3.** 19, 21, 23   **5.** width is $7\frac{1}{2}$ feet   **7.** length is
25 feet   **9.** 59°, 60°, 61°

Pages 61–62 Written Exercises A 1. $\{(0, 1), (1, 2), (2, 3), (3, 4), (4, 5)\}$ **3.** $\{(5, 2), (7, 4), (9, 6), (11, 8),$
$(13, 10)\}$ **5.** $\{(6, 4), (8, 5\frac{1}{3}), (12, 8), (15, 10)\}$ **7.** $\{(1, -1), (2, -2), (-1, 1), (-2, 2)\}$ **9.** $\{(1, 2), (2, 5),$
$(3, 8), (4, 11), \ldots\}$ **11.** $\{(\frac{1}{2}, 4), (\frac{1}{3}, 2), (\frac{1}{4}, 1), (\frac{1}{6}, 0)\}$ **13.** $\{(-10, 100), (-8, 64), (-6, 36), (-4, 16), (-1, 1),$
$(0, 0)\}$ **15.** B   **17.** E   **19.** A   **B 21.** $\{(-1, \frac{3}{2}), (-2, 1), (-3, \frac{1}{2}), (-4, 0)\}$ **23.** $\{(-3, \frac{9}{2}), (-2, 2),$
$(-1, \frac{1}{2}), (0, 0), (1, \frac{1}{2}), (2, 2)\}$ **25.** $\{(\frac{1}{2}, 2\frac{1}{2}), (\frac{1}{3}, 2), (\frac{1}{4}, \frac{7}{4}), (-\frac{1}{2}, -\frac{1}{2}), (-\frac{1}{3}, 0), (-\frac{1}{4}, \frac{1}{4})\}$ **C 27.** $\{(-4, -1),$
$(-3, 0), (-2, 1), (-1, 2), (0, 3)\}$ **29.** $\{(0, 1), (1, 5), (2, 11), (-3, 1), (-5, 11), \ldots\}$

Pages 64–65 Chapter Test 1. $-15; \frac{1}{15}$ **3.** $-\frac{2}{5}; \frac{5}{2}$ **5.** $-x; \dfrac{1}{x}$ **7.** $\{12\}$ **9.** $\emptyset$ **11.** $\{9, 8, 7, \ldots, 1\}$
13. $\{3, 2, 1, 0, \ldots\}$ **15.** no; $21 \ne 3$ **17.** no; $144 \ne 36$ **19.** yes   **21.** neither   **23.** true   **25.** true
27. $-\frac{3}{5}, -\frac{3}{7}, -\frac{3}{8}, \frac{3}{8}, \frac{3}{7}, \frac{3}{5}$

29.   **31.**

33. $\{(-6, 78), (-4, 36), (-2, 10), (0, 0), (1, 1), (2, 6), (4, 28), (6, 66)\}$

Pages 65–67 Chapter Review 1. $\frac{1}{2}; 3; 5\frac{1}{2}; 8$ **3.** 18; 14; 10; 6; 2   **5.** $-1; 1; 3; 5; 7$ **7.** $\{4\}$
9. $\{-3, -4, -5, \ldots\}$ **11.** 110 miles; 165 miles; $247\frac{1}{2}$ miles; 275 miles; 330 miles
13.   **15.**   **17.**

19. A   **21.** $3k$ **23.** $9ab - 3a$ **25.** $-5b + 2$ **27.** $14z^2 + 3z$ **29.** 9   **31.** $5t$ **33.** $s < 10.5$ **35.** $m =$
$2b - a$ **37.** $m \le s - k$ **39.** -1 **41.** $\dfrac{5}{2a}$ **43.** $<; <$ **45.** $n \ge -15$

47. $s \ge -2$ **49.** $\{12\}$ **51.** $\{-5\}$ **53.** $\{10\}$

55. $t \le \frac{3}{2}$ **57.** $\{(-4, -13), (-2, -7), (0, -1), (2, 5), (4, 11)\}$

59. $\{\ldots, (-4, 18), (-2, 6), (0, 2), (2, 6), (4, 18), \ldots\}$

Pages 68–69 Review of Skills 1. $4x^2$ **3.** $8y^3$ **5.** $16ab$ **7.** $9t$ **9.** $3m^2$ **11.** $15x^2$ **13.** $-2t^2$
15. -7 **17.** $11x$ **19.** $-13t$ **21.** $62w^2$ **23.** $5y$ **25.** n **27.** $-3x^2$ **29.** $5ab$ **31.** 18.65   **33.** $25\frac{1}{2}$

35. $56\frac{7}{9}$ **37.** 22   **39.** 63   **41.**   **43.**

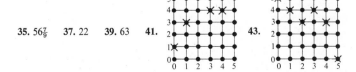

Page 70   Check Point for Experts   1.

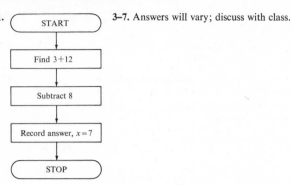

3–7. Answers will vary; discuss with class.

Chapter 3.   Operations with Polynomials

Pages 76–77   Written Exercises   A 1. $14n$ **3.** $3ab$ **5.** $9y^2 + 7y$ **7.** $4k + 8$ **9.** $-6c^2 + 10$
11. $12x + y$ **13.** $-2k + 3$ **15.** $5s^5 + 16t$ **17.** $-5x^2 + 8x + 5$ **19.** $3t^3 - 3t - 6$ **21.** $4w - 3$
23. correct   **25.** not correct; sum should be $2xy + 9z$ **27.** correct   **29.** $y = 5$ **31.** $m = 3$ **33.** $12b + 12$
35. $2x^2 + 4xy - 8x$ **B 37.** $y - 1$ **39.** $\frac{1}{3}k + 1$ **41.** $6a^4 + a^3 - 2a$ **C 43.** $5y^3 + y^2 - 2y + 5$
45. $w^4 - w^3 + 4w^2 - 6$

Pages 77–78   Problems   1. $8m + 2 + 10n$ **3.** $6x^2 + 2y^2$; $396\frac{1}{2}$ square inches   **5.** $4.8r^2s^2 + 5rs + 35$

Pages 80–81   Written Exercises   A 1. $3x^2$ **3.** $-5abc$ **5.** $-5r^2$ **7.** $9xy$ **9.** $-7.8k$ **11.** 0
13. $3.8xyz$ **15.** $7w - 1$ **17.** $3x^2 + 4y$ **19.** $-x + 5$ **21.** $2b^2 + 6b - 5$ **23.** $3y^2 - 5y + 3$
25. $7m - 9$ **27.** $5rs + 4s$ **29.** $-y + 2z$ **31.** $x = \frac{17}{3}$ **33.** $r = 9$ **35.** $k = 5$ **B 37.** $3t - 1$
39. $-6a + 14$ **C 41.** $-y - 6$ **43.** $4s^2$

Pages 81–82   Problems   1. $8m^2 + 6m - 4$; $4m^2 - 6m - 4$ **3.** $2.18g^2 + 5.3t + 1.02$ **5.** $0.08k^3 - 4.4k + 4.29$

Pages 84–86   Written Exercises   A 1. $a \cdot b \cdot b \cdot b$ **3.** $k \cdot k \cdot k \cdot k \cdot k$ **5.** $10 \cdot 10 \cdot 10 \cdot 10 \cdot n \cdot n \cdot n \cdot n$
7. $-3 \cdot -3 \cdot -3 \cdot n \cdot n \cdot n$ **9.** $3 \cdot x \cdot x \cdot x \cdot x \cdot y \cdot y \cdot y \cdot y \cdot y \cdot y$ **11.** $-1 \cdot r \cdot r \cdot r \cdot s \cdot s \cdot s \cdot s$
13. $(10)(m^{1+2})(n^{2+2})$; $10m^3n^4$ **15.** $(-42)(r^{1+1+3})(s^{1+2})$; $-42r^5s^3$ **17.** 243 **19.** $10{,}000$ **21.** -81
23. 16 **25.** -7200

B. 27.

a	b	$(ab)^2 \cdot (ab)^2$
-2	-1	16
-3	0	0
0	5	0
10	1	$10{,}000$

29.

m	n	$m(m^2 + 1) + (mn)^3$
3	0	30
4	0	68
-3	0	-30
-4	0	-68

C 31. $-20m^2n^2$ **33.** $2a^6r^7 + 30a^2r^5$

Pages 87–89   Written Exercises   A 1.–12.

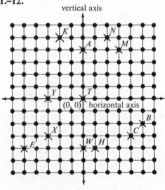

13. $\{(4, 5), (4, 4), (4, 3), (4, 2), (4, 1),$ $(4, 0), (4, -1), (4, -2), (4, -3),$ $(4, -4), (4, -5)\}$

15. $\{(5, 0), (4, 0), (3, 0), (2, 0),$ $(1, 0), (0, 0), (-1, 0),$ $(-2, 0), (-3, 0), (-4, 0),$ $(-5, 0)\}$

17. $\{(5, 2), (4, 2), (3, 2), (2, 2),$ $(1, 2), (0, 2), (-1, 2),$ $(-2, 2), (-3, 2), (-4, 2),$ $(-5, 2)\}$

19. triangle

21. pentagon

B 23. $\{(1, -1), (2, -2), (3, -3),$ $(4, -4), (5, -5)\}$

25. $\{(0, 0), (1, -1), (2, -2), (3, -3),$ $(4, -4), (5, -5)\}$

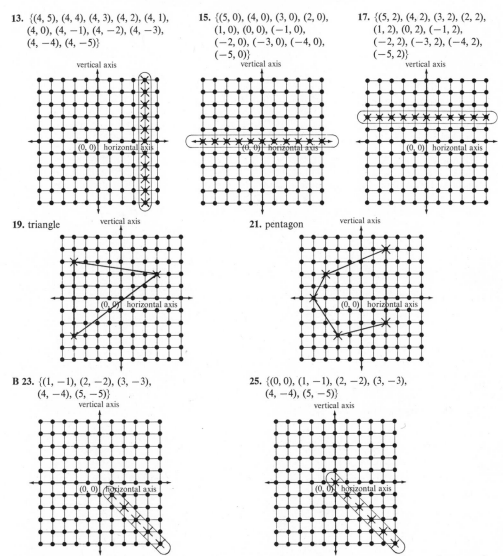

Page 91   Written Exercises   A 1. $24t^4 - 12t^2 + 6t$ **3.** $4a^2b + 2ab^3 - 3ab$ **5.** $-35a^3 - 15a^2b - 10ab^2$
7. $2a^3b + 2ab^3$ **9.** $-12 + 6x + 21x^2$ **11.** $-12m^3n + 8m^2n^2 - 6mn^3$ **13.** $r^2 + 3r + 2$ **15.** $a^2 - 4$
17. $t^2 - 10t + 25$ **19.** $3n^2 + 5n - 2$ **21.** $18d^2 - 3d - 15$ **23.** $14y^2 - 47y + 30$ **25.** $r = 9$ **27.** $x =$
-8 **29.** $y = 10$ **B 31.** $2x^2 + 5x - 3$ **33.** $2n^2 - 7n - 15$ **35.** $m^4 - n^4$ **37.** $4x^2 - 26xy + 30y^2$
C 39. $s^3 + 4s^2 - 2s - 5$ **41.** $5x^2 + 6x + 1$

Page 92   Problems   1. A $= 18ty$; B $= 3t$; C $= 12y$; D $= 2$; area $= 18ty + 3t + 12y + 2$ **3.** area $=$
$4.5b^2 - 8$ **5.** volume of large box $= 8x^2 + 12x - 8$; volume of small box $= 3x^2 - 3x - 6$; difference $=$
$5x^2 + 15x - 2$

Page 94   Written Exercises   A 1. $m^2 + 6m + 9$ **3.** $x^2 - 2x + 1$ **5.** $y^2 - 8y + 16$ **7.** $x^2 - 2xy + y^2$
9. $4x^2 + 12x + 9$ **11.** $9x^2 - 24xy + 16y^2$ **13.** $x^3 + 3x^2y + 3xy^2 + y^3$ **15.** $8x^3 - 24x^2 + 24x - 8$
17. $-3y^3 - 12y^2 - 12y$ **B 19.** $y^2 + y + \frac{1}{4}$ **21.** $2m^2 - 4m - 4$ **23.** $x^2 + \frac{2}{3}x + \frac{1}{9}$ **C 25.** $x^2 + y^2 +$
$m^2 + 2xm + 2ym + 2xy$ **27.** $m^2 + x^2 + y^2 - 2mx + 2my - 2xy$ **29.** $8x^3 - 36x^2y + 54xy^2 - 27y^3$
31. $x^4 + 4x^3y + 6x^2y^2 + 4xy^3 + y^4$ **33.** $4x^4 - 12x^3y + 13x^2y^2 - 6xy^3 + y^4$

Pages 94–95   Problems   1. A $= 4x^2 - 20x + 25$ **3.** V $= 9x^3 + 27x^2 - 36$

Pages 97–98   **Written Exercises**   **A 1.** x^7 **3.** $\dfrac{2}{y^3}$ **5.** $\dfrac{7}{5n^6}$ **7.** xy^3 **9.** $\dfrac{11m^3}{-3}$ **11.** $4m^5$ **13.** $\dfrac{1}{3m^3}$ **15.** $-4x^7$

17. c^2 **19.** $\dfrac{1}{x^4}$ **21.** $\dfrac{3x}{2y}$ **23.** $\dfrac{1}{7m^2}$ **25.** $3t$ **27.** -9 **B 29.** $4t^2s^5$ **31.** $-4s^5$ **33.** $\dfrac{8}{r^5s^3}$ **35.** $\dfrac{4a}{3b}$

C 37. $\dfrac{-2c^4}{d^2}$ **39.** $\dfrac{3m^4}{n^2}$

Pages 101–102   **Written Exercises**   **A 1.** $10x^4 - 8x^3 + 3x$ **3.** $7m^4 - 12m^2 + 5$ **5.** $8a^4b^3 - 9a^2b^3$
7. $-5a^4b^3 + 6a^2b$ **9.** $y + 4$ **11.** $8x + 1$ **13.** $x + 4$ **15.** $5x + 3$ **17.** $r - 8$, rem. $= 15$ **19.** $2s + 4$
21. $2z - 3$, rem. $= 1$ **23.** $x - 1$, rem. $= -1$ **B 25.** $2r - 1.2$ **27.** $a - 9b$ **29.** $2x + 3y$, rem. $= y^2$
31. $2x + 3$, rem. $= 1$ **C 33.** $x^2 + 5x + 6$, rem. $= -3$

Page 102   **Problems**   **1.** width $= 2m - 1$ **3.** area $= x^2 - 14$ **5.** speed $= 5x - 8$

Page 104   **Chapter Test**   **1.** $-3m^3 + m^2 + 4m + 10$ **3.** $-2y^5 + 12y^4 - 3y^2 + 5$ **5.** $4x^2 + 2x + 9$
7. $4w^2 - 11w + 2$ **9.** $24t^2 - 19t - 35$ **11.** $5m + 7$ **13.** $8a^3b^3$ **15.** $4x^2 - 12x + 9$ **17.** $\frac{1}{4}r^4s^4$
19. $a^3 + 3a^2c + 3ac^2 + c^3$ **21.** $9a^2 + 12ab + 4b^2$ **23.** $(1, 4)$; I   **25.** $(-2, -4)$; III   **27.** $x = 5$
29. $x = 5$

Pages 105–107   **Chapter Review**   **1.** $2 - 5m$ **3.** $10x^2 + x - 7$ **5.** $2x^2 + x + 1$ **7.** $4a^3 - 3a^2 -$
$3a + 3$ **9.** $3.2t^2 + 35.5t + 1$ **11.** $4r^2 - 10rs - 6$ **13.** $4c^2 + 7c - 13$ **15.** $4z^2 - 8y + 3$ **17.** $2r^2 -$
$18r - 1$ **19.** 3^3t^4 **21.** a^9 **23.** $5x^4y^5$ **25.** $-8c^6d^3$ **27.** $-6m^2n^8$ **29.** $(3, 0)$ **31.** $(0, 0)$ **33.** $(-1, -2)$
35. III   **37.** II   **39.** II   **41.** IV   **43.** $24k^4 - 8k^2 + 20k$ **45.** $2w^3 + 7w^2 + 17w + 7$ **47.** $2b^2 -$
$7ab - 15a^2$ **49.** $30m^2 - 34m - 8$ **51.** $t^2 + 10t + 25$ **53.** $16n^2 + 8nt + t^2$ **55.** $a^3 - a^2b - ab^2 + b^3$
57. $19m^3$ **59.** $25x^5$ **61.** $\dfrac{-2}{r^5s^3}$ **63.** $9m^7 - 6m^4$ **65.** $2x - 7$

Pages 108–109   **Review of Skills**   **1.** 3   **3.** 2   **5.** 3   **7.** 15   **9.** 4   **11.** E   **13.** C   **15.** $(12x)(y^2)$;
$(3x)(4y^2)$; $(6x)(2y^2)$ **17.** $(-10)(a)$; $(-1)(10a)$; $(-5)(2a)$ **19.** $(-3a)(2y)$; $(-6a)(y)$; $-6(ay)$ **21.** $(4a^2)(ab)$;
$(2ab)(2a^2)$; $(4a^3)(b)$ **23.** $\frac{3}{5}$ **25.** 4   **27.** $\frac{1}{2}$ **29.** $8\frac{5}{12}$ **31.** $43\frac{9}{16}$ **33.** $\{3, 5, 6, 9, 10, 12, 15, 20\}$; Ø
35. $\{1, 2, 3, 4, 5, 6, 7, 8, 9\}$; Ø

Page 111   **Check Point for Experts**
1. 487×26; answer, 12662

3.

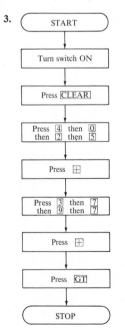

5.

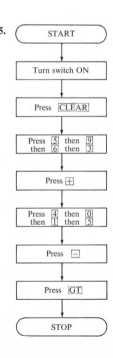

7.

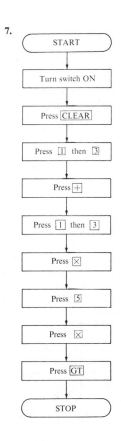

9.

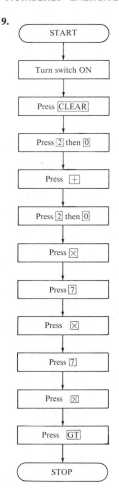

Chapter 4. Products and Factors

Page 115   Written Exercises   A 1. 900   **3.** 500   **5.** 800   **7.** 12   **9.** 450   **11.** 720   **13.** {1, 2, 3, 6, 9, 18}
15. {1, 3, 9, 27}   **17.** {1, 5, 7, 35}   **19.** {1, 3, 37, 111}   **21.** {1, 2, 3, 4, 6, 8, 9, 12, 18, 24, 36, 72}   **23.** 27 = $3 \cdot 1 \cdot 3 \cdot 3$ **25.** 42 = $3 \cdot 2 \cdot 7$ **27.** 24 = $2^2 \cdot 2 \cdot 3$ **29.** 30 = $5 \cdot 3 \cdot 2 \cdot 1$

Page 116   Problems   1. {2, 4, 6, 8, ...}   **3.** {17, 34, 51, 68, ...}   **5.** 119 = $17 \cdot 7$ **7.** 216 = $12 \cdot 18$

Pages 117–118   Written Exercises   A 1. $2 \cdot 5^2$ **3.** $2 \cdot 3 \cdot 7$ **5.** $2^4 \cdot 3$ **7.** $2^4 \cdot 3$ **9.** $2^3 \cdot 3 \cdot 5$ **11.** $2^3 \cdot 5$
13. $2^3 \cdot 3^2$ **15.** $2^2 \cdot 3 \cdot 5^2$ **17.** $2^4 \cdot 3^2$ **19.** $2 \cdot 3^3$ **21.** 2^5 **23.** 3 + 5   **25.** 5 + 13; 7 + 11   **27.** 3 + 23;
7 + 19   **29.** 3 + 29; 13 + 19   **31.** 7 + 23; 11 + 19; 13 + 17   **B 33.** {2, 3, 5, 7, 11, 13, 17, 19, 23, 29}
35. {2, 3, 5, 7, 11, 13, 17, 19, 23, 29, 31, 37, 41, 43, 47}   **C 37.** ∅

Pages 121–122   Written Exercises   A 1. 14: {1, 2, 7, 14}; 18: {1, 2, 3, 6, 9, 18}; G.C.F. = 2   **3.** 44: {1, 2, 4, 11, 22, 44}; 33: {1, 3, 11, 33}; G.C.F. = 11   **5.** 18: {1, 2, 3, 6, 9, 18}; 38: {1, 2, 19, 38}; G.C.F. = 2
7. 4: {1, 2, 4}; 11: {1, 11}; G.C.F. = 1   **9.** 42: {1, 2, 3, 6, 7, 14, 21, 42}; 54: {1, 2, 3, 6, 9, 18, 27, 54};
G.C.F. = 6   **11.** 15: {1, 3, 5, 15}; 28: {1, 2, 4, 7, 14, 28}; G.C.F. = 1   **13.** 2   **15.** 12   **17.** 1; relatively
prime   **19.** 14   **21.** 3   **B 23.** 35: {1, 3, 7, 35}; 26: {1, 2, 13, 26}   **25.** 15: {1, 3, 5, 15}; 16: {1, 2, 4, 8, 16}
27. 25: {1, 5, 25}; 27: {1, 3, 9, 27}   **29.** 15: {1, 3, 5, 15}; 28: {1, 2, 4, 7, 14, 28}   **C 31.** always
33. sometimes   **35.** never

Page 124　Written Exercises　A 1. $5r$　**3.** $4s$　**5.** $-7m^2n$　**7.** $7ab$　**9.** -7　**11.** $-3m^3nt^2$　**13.** $(24)(t)$; $8 \cdot 3t$; $(6t) \cdot 4$; $(12)(2t)$　**15.** $(10)(mn)$; $(5m)(2n)$; $(10m)n$　**17.** $(-15)(a^2b^2)$; $(-5a)(3ab^2)$; $(5b)(-3a^2b)$ **19.** $(19)(c^2d^2)$; $(19cd)(cd)$; $(-c^2)(-19d^2)$　**21.** $(-12)(c^2w^2)$; $(-6c^2)(2w^2)$; $(4cw)(-3cw)$　**23.** $3xy = 3 \cdot x \cdot y$; $10xy = 2 \cdot 5 \cdot x \cdot y$; G.C.F. $= xy$　**25.** $15x = 3 \cdot 5 \cdot x$; $10y = 2 \cdot 5 \cdot y$; G.C.F. $= 5$　**27.** $12abc^2 = 2 \cdot 2 \cdot 3 \cdot a \cdot b \cdot c \cdot c$; $10a^2b^2c = 2 \cdot 5 \cdot a \cdot a \cdot b \cdot b \cdot c$; G.C.F. $= 2abc$　**29.** $9st^3 = 3 \cdot 3 \cdot s \cdot t \cdot t \cdot t$; $9s^3t = 3 \cdot 3 \cdot s \cdot s \cdot s \cdot t$; G.C.F. $= 9st$　**31.** $4ax = 2 \cdot 2 \cdot a \cdot x$; $18ax^2y = 2 \cdot 3 \cdot 3 \cdot a \cdot x \cdot x \cdot y$; G.C.F. $= 2ax$ **33.** $-x^5y^4z^2 = -1 \cdot x \cdot x \cdot x \cdot x \cdot x \cdot y \cdot y \cdot y \cdot y \cdot z \cdot z$; $x^2y = x \cdot x \cdot y$; G.C.F. $= x^2y$　**B 35.** $12a^2$　**37.** $7rst$ **39.** x^2y^2

Page 127　Written Exercises　A 1. $15r^2 + 20r$　**3.** $-10n^2 - 2n$　**5.** $a^2b^2c - ab^2c^2$　**7.** $20m^3 - 15m^2$ **9.** $6a + 21a^2 + 3a^3$　**11.** $30r^4 - 5r^3 + 10r^2$　**13.** $2(2r + 3)$　**15.** $a(b^2 + 1)$　**17.** $2(2x^2 - 3)$ **19.** $b(6b + 7)$　**21.** $2(2x^2 + 4x - 3)$　**23.** $3ab(2a + b)$　**25.** $(x + 3)(y + 2)$　**27.** $(t^2 + 3)(t - 2)$ **B 29.** $(4r + 5s)(k - h)$　**31.** $(b + 4)(3b + 2)$　**C 33.** $(x + 2)(3x - 2)$　**35.** $(s + 2t)(2s + 1)$

Pages 127–128　Problems　1. $4x(7x - 5)$　**3.** $2(x - 1)(x - 6)$　**5.** $6x^2y$

Pages 130–132　Written Exercises　A 1. $\{(-1, -1), (0, 0), (1, 1), (2, 2), (3, 3), (4, 4), (5, 5)\}$　**3.** $\{(-4, 4),$ $(-2, 2), (0, 0), (2, -2), (4, -4)\}$　**5.** $\{(8, 39), (4, 19), (0, -1), (-4, -21), (-8, -41)\}$　**7.** $\{(-5, -2),$ $(-3, -1), (-1, 0), (0, \frac{1}{2}), (1, 1)\}$　**9.** $\{(-6, 104), (-4, 44), (-2, 8), (0, -4), (2, 8), (4, 44)\}$ **B 11.** $\{(0, 5), (1, 3), (2, 1),$ 　**13.** $\{(3, -5), (2, 0), (1, 3), (0, 4),$ 　**15.** $\{(-5, -1), (-3, 0), (-1, 1),$ 　　　　 $(3, -1), (4, -3), (5, -5)\}$ 　　　$(-1, 3), (-2, 0), (-3, 5)\}$ 　　　 $(1, 2), (3, 3), (5, 4)\}$

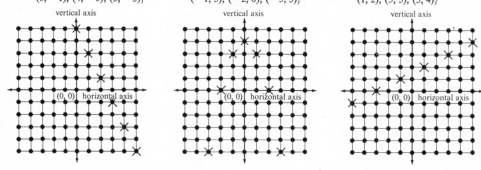

Pages 133–135　Chapter Test　1. $\{2, 3, 5, 7, 11, 13\}$　**3.** $\{1\}$　**5.** $70 \cdot 1$; $35 \cdot 2$; $5 \cdot 14$; $7 \cdot 10$　**7.** true **9.** true　**11.** true　**13.** 32; 24; 8　**15.** $\{(0, 7), (3, 9), (6, 11), (9, 13), (12, 15), (15, 17)\}$　**17.** $\{(-3, -2),$ $(-2, -2), (-1, -2), (0, -2), (1, 0), (2, 0), (3, 0)\}$　**19.** m^2　**21.** $\frac{1}{3}k^2t^3$　**23.** $7s^2t^4(-5s + t^3)$　**25.** $8x^2y^4$ **27.** $2 \cdot 2 \cdot 2 \cdot 3 \cdot 3$　**29.** $\{1, 3, 7, 9, 21, 63\}$

Pages 135–137　Chapter Review　1. $\{1, 3, 5, 15\}$　**3.** $\{1, 3, 7, 9, 21, 63\}$　**5.** $\{1, 2, 4, 11, 22, 44\}$ **7.** $\{1, 2, 4, 8, 16, 32, 64\}$　**9.** $\{1, 41\}$　**11.** 6 feet and 5 feet; 2 feet and 15 feet; 3 feet and 10 feet　**13.** $2 \cdot 13$ **15.** $1 \cdot 61$　**17.** $3 \cdot 37$　**19.** false　**21.** B　**23.** A　**25.** C　**27.** $\{1\}$; 7; 9; 1　**29.** 2　**31.** 20　**33.** 1 **35.** 1; are　**37.** 3; are not　**39.** 5　**41.** 5　**43.** 1　**45.** $9r^2$　**47.** $-6y^2z$　**49.** xy^2　**51.** $2a^2bc^2$ **53.** $6xy(5x + 3y)$　**55.** $6(a^2 + 5a - 3)$　**57.** $3ab(7abc^2 - 4b + 2ac)$ **59.** $\{(-8, -5), (-6, -4), (-4, -3), (-2, -2),$ 　**61.** $\{(-2, 3), (-1, 2), (-1, 1), (0, 1), (1, 1), (2, 1), (2, 2),$ 　　　$(0, -1), (2, 0)\}$ 　　　　 $(2, 3)\}$; not a function

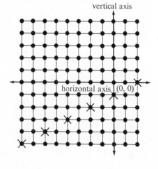

Pages 138–139 Review of Skills 1. -90 **3.** -30 **5.** $\frac{1}{15}$ **7.** -6 **9.** 49 **11.** $\{2, 3, 5, 7, 11, 13, 17,$
$19, 23, 29\}$ **13.** $\{4, 3, 2, 1, 0, -1, -2, -3, -4\}$ **15.** $x = 12$ **17.** $a = -\frac{19}{3}$ **19.** $\{\text{directed numbers}\}$

21. $x = 7$ **23.** $t > 2$ **25.** $k \geq -1.5$ **27.** $d = \frac{r}{t}$ **29.** $t = \frac{v}{a}$ **31.** $r = \frac{p}{i}$ **33.** $2t^2 + 19t + 35$

35. $a^3 + 4a^2b + 5ab^2 + 2b^3$ **37.** $4a - 5$ **39.** $7m^4 - 2m^3 + 3m^2 - 3$ **41.** $3x^2 - 4x + 10$
43. $6b^2 + 10b + 2$ **45.** $4x^2 + 2x$

Page 141 Check Point for Experts

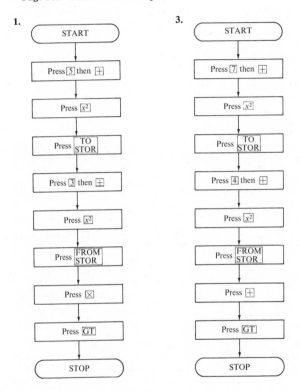

1.

START

Press 5 then +

Press x^2

Press TO STOR

Press 3 then +

Press x^2

Press FROM STOR

Press ×

Press GT

STOP

3.

START

Press 7 then +

Press x^2

Press TO STOR

Press 4 then +

Press x^2

Press FROM STOR

Press +

Press GT

STOP

Chapter 5. Quadratic Polynomials and Factoring

Pages 145–146 Written Exercises A 1. x^2 **3.** $2x^2$ **5.** $9m$ **7.** $-17k$ **9.** 10 **11.** -5 **13.** 8
15. $n^2 + 10n + 24$ **17.** $20 + 9t + t^2$ **19.** $8x^2 + 10x + 3$ **21.** $m^2 + 18m + 30$ **23.** $y^2 - 11y + 24$
25. $15k^2 - 60$ **27.** $2a^2 - a - 6$ **B 29.** $-2y^2 - y + 10$ **31.** $27m^2 - 60m - 7$ **33.** $-1 + 2r - r^2$
35. $35 - 19b + 2b^2$

Pages 147–148 Written Exercises **A 1.** $x^2 - 64$ **3.** 21 **5.** $16 - t^2$ **7.** $4c^2 - 16$ **9.** $25 - 9a^2$ **11.** $m^2 - 1$ **13.** $9 - t^2$ **15.** $x^2 - y^2$ **17.** $100 - 9s^2$ **19.** $36x^2 - 49$ **21.** $9t^2 - s^2$ **23.** $m^2 - \frac{1}{16}$ **25.** $a^2 - 9c^2$ **B 27.** $225x^2y^2 - 4$ **29.** $m^2 - 0.04$ **31.** $0.81 - d^2$ **33.** $\frac{1}{4}a^2b^2 - \frac{1}{25}c^2d^2$ **C 35.** $\frac{4a^2}{9} - \frac{b^2}{25}$ **37.** $\frac{-c^2}{4} + 9$

Pages 148–149 Problems **1.** $A = 16 - 81y$ **3.** $V = 256\pi^2 - 9$

Pages 150–151 Written Exercises **A 1.** $1 + 10b + 25b^2$ **3.** $225 - 30b + b^2$ **5.** $4m^2 - 12m + 9$ **7.** $49t^2 + 112t + 64$ **9.** $1 - 14d + 49d^2$ **11.** $9a^2 + 6ab + b^2$ **13.** $r^2 + 40r + 400$ **15.** $100k^2 - 240k + 144$ **B 17.** $r^2s^2 + 2rst + t^2$ **19.** $0.16c^2 - 0.4c + 0.25$ **21.** $x^4 - 30x^2 + 225$ **23.** $625 - 10r + \frac{1}{25}r^2$

Page 151 Problems **1.** $4b^2 - 36b + 81$ **3.** $400s^2 + 10s + \frac{1}{16}$ **5.** $144 + 216k + 81k^2$

Pages 153–154 Written Exercises **A 1.** 16, 25, 36, 49, 64, 81, 100, 121, 144, 169, 196, 225, 256, 289, 324, 361, 400, 441, 484, 529, 576, 625, 729, 784, 841, 900 **3.** $3m^2n^3$ **5.** $11x^5y^4z$ **7.** $8k^5m^4$ **9.** $12m^6n^5t^2$ **11.** 225 **13.** 26 **15.** 22 **17.** 289 **19.** 19 **21.** 27 **23.** $20r^2s^3$ **25.** $17km^7$ **27.** $529m^6z^{10}$ **29.** $256w^6x^4y^2$ **31.** $784x^2y^6z^2$ **B 33.** $6t^y$ **35.** $361a^2x^{4n}$ **37.** $17xy^n$

Pages 154–155 Problems **1.** $A = 256a^4b^6$ **3.** $A = a^4b^{10}c^6$ **5.** $s = 13r^4b$ **7.** $A = \pi \cdot 100x^4y^{10}$ **9.** $r = 27s^3t^2$

Page 157 Written Exercises **A 1.** $(r + 4)(r - 4)$ **3.** $(2m + 1)(2m - 1)$ **5.** $(5x + 1)(5x - 1)$ **7.** $(15 + n)(15 - n)$ **9.** $(5w + 7)(5w - 7)$ **11.** $(10 + 9s)(10 - 9s)$ **13.** $(7a + 10b)(7a - 10b)$ **15.** $(3 + 4t)(3 - 4t)$ **17.** $(11x + 20)(11x - 20)$ **19.** $2(n + 3)(n - 3)$ **21.** $2(4s + 1)(4s - 1)$ **23.** $10(y + 2)(y - 2)$ **B 25.** $3(x + 3)(x - 3)$ **27.** $3(r^3 + 1)(r^3 - 1)$ **29.** $(2a + 25)(2a - 25)$ **31.** $4x(y + 2)(y - 2)$ **33.** $2ab(c + 2)(c - 2)$ **35.** $5a(k + 4)(k - 4)$ **C 37.** $n(n^3 + 1)(n^3 - 1)$ **39.** $3(3 + b)(3 - b)$ **41.** $2y^4(y + 4)(y - 4)$

Pages 159–161 Written Exercises **A 11.** $n^2 + 14n + 49$ **13.** $y^2 + 20y + 100$ **15.** $4n^2 + 12n + 9$ **17.** $4x^2 + 4xy + y^2$ **19.** $9n^2 + 12mn + 4m^2$ **21.** $y^2 + 12y + 36$ **23.** $25 + 10y + y^2$ **25.** $4x^2 + 4x + 1$ **27.** $9n^2 + 6n + 1$ **29.** $4a^2 + 4ab + b^2$ **31.** $4x^2 + 12xy + 9y^2$ **33.** $(r + 4)^2$ **35.** $(n + 1)^2$ **37.** $(m + 1)^2$ **39.** $(3w + 1)^2$ **41.** $(5 + k)^2$ **B 43.** $(2t + 3)^2$ **45.** $(2xy + 3)^2$ **47.** $(4m + 5n)^2$ **C 49.** $6(m + 1)^2$ **51.** $x(x + 5)^2$

Pages 162–163 Written Exercises **A 9.** $16k^2 - 8k + 1$ **11.** $4y^2 - 12y + 9$ **13.** $9a^2 - 12ab + 4b^2$ **15.** $16 - 24m + 9m^2$ **17.** $c^2 - 4c + 4$ **19.** $y^2 - 10y + 25$ **21.** $9 - 6y + y^2$ **23.** $4n^2 - 12mn + 9m^2$ **25.** $t^2 - 16rt + 64r^2$ **27.** $16m^2 - 24mn + 9n^2$ **29.** $(r - 2)^2$ **31.** $(s - 4)^2$ **33.** $(r - 5)^2$ **35.** $(a - 6)^2$ **37.** $(2s - 1)^2$ **39.** $(5t - 1)^2$ **41.** $(1 - 2t)^2$ **43.** $(8x - y)^2$ **45.** $(6 - 5m)^2$ **B 47.** $(2xy - 3z)^2$ **49.** $(5x^2 - y)^2$ **51.** $(4t - 3xy)^2$ **C 53.** $2(3x - 1)^2$ **55.** $5r(2s - 3)^2$ **57.** $3a(1 - 7a)^2$

Pages 165–166 Written Exercises **A 1.** $1 \cdot 10$; $2 \cdot 5$; $-1 \cdot (-10)$; $-2 \cdot (-5)$ **3.** $15 \cdot 1$; $5 \cdot 3$; $-15 \cdot (-1)$; $-5 \cdot (-3)$ **5.** $16 \cdot 1$; $8 \cdot 2$; $4 \cdot 4$; $-16 \cdot (-1)$; $-8 \cdot (-2)$; $-4 \cdot (-4)$ **7.** $21 \cdot 1$; $7 \cdot 3$; $-21 \cdot (-1)$; $-7 \cdot (-3)$ **9.** $14 \cdot 1$; $7 \cdot 2$; $-14 \cdot (-1)$; $-7 \cdot (-2)$ **11.** $33 \cdot 1$; $11 \cdot 3$; $-33 \cdot (-1)$; $-11 \cdot (-3)$ **13.** $7 \cdot 1$; $-7 \cdot (-1)$ **15.** $1 \cdot 1$; $(-1) \cdot (-1)$ **17.** $(r + 8)(r + 3)$ **19.** $(t + 3)(t + 10)$ **21.** $(m + 10)(m + 2)$ **23.** $(w - 2) \times (w - 9)$ **25.** $(k + 4)(k + 3)$ **27.** $(s - 3)(s - 11)$ **29.** $(y + 7)(y + 1)$ **31.** $(b - 2)(b - 4)$ **33.** $(r - 1)(r - 7)$ **35.** $(b + 2)(b + 10)$ **37.** $(c + 5)(c + 6)$ **39.** $(k + 2)(k + 4)$ **41.** $(7 + c)(3 + c)$ **B 43.** $(8 - y)(6 - y)$ **45.** $(x - 16y)(x - 2y)$ **47.** $(s - 8t)(s - 3t)$

Page 168 Written Exercises **A 1.** $(s + 4)(s - 3)$ **3.** $(x + 3)(x - 1)$ **5.** $(b - 5)(b + 2)$ **7.** $(x + 3)(x - 2)$ **9.** $(n - 6)(n + 3)$ **11.** $(c + 5)(c - 4)$ **13.** $(y - 7)(y + 4)$ **15.** $(a - 8)(a + 4)$ **17.** $(w + 11)(w - 1)$ **19.** $(x + 13)(x - 2)$ **21.** $(a + 8)(a - 7)$ **23.** $(y - 9)(y + 7)$ **25.** $(r + 20)(r - 3)$ **27.** $(z + 10)(z - 5)$ **29.** $(k - 7)(k + 2)$ **31.** $(m - 8n)(m + 3n)$ **33.** $(a + 5b)(a - 2b)$ **35.** $(b + 12c)(b - 2c)$ **B 37.** $(x - 19z)(x + 3z)$ **39.** $(a - 27c)(a + 3c)$

Pages 171–172 Written Exercises **A 1.** $(2x + 1)(x + 1)$ **3.** $(5a - 2)(a - 1)$ **5.** $(4t + 3)(2t - 1)$ **7.** $(3x + 1)(x + 1)$ **9.** $(2y - 1)(y - 1)$ **11.** $(3m + 5)(m + 1)$ **13.** $(4c + 1)(c - 3)$ **15.** $(2y - 3) \times (2y + 5)$ **17.** $(2y + 1)(y - 5)$ **19.** $(2t - 1)(4t + 3)$ **21.** $(3a + 8)(a - 1)$ **23.** $(5r - 3)(r - s)$ **25.** $(7a - 4b)(a + b)$ **27.** $(2u + v)(u - 5v)$ **B 29.** $(2k + 7)(3k + 2)$ **31.** $(5x - 4)(3x + 2)$ **33.** $(3z + 4)(2z - 3)$ **C 35.** $(10t - 9s)(t + 2s)$ **37.** $(4c + 15d)(2c - d)$

Pages 173–174 Written Exercises A 1. $5(x + 1)(x - 1)$ **3.** $4(a + 1)(a - 1)$ **5.** $4(n + 3)(n - 3)$
7. $2(b + 5)(b - 5)$ **9.** $3(5 + 3x)(5 - 3x)$ **11.** $5(2 + n)(2 - n)$ **13.** $r(s + 6)(s - 6)$ **15.** $xy(z + 9) \times$
$(z - 9)$ **17.** $y(x - 2)^2$ **19.** $-1(t - 6)^2$ **21.** $ab(c - 3)^2$ **23.** $2a(2x - 1)^2$ **25.** $r(2n - 5)^2$
27. $-2(2b + 1)^2$ **29.** $2(5x + 6)(x + 3)$ **31.** $r(2s + 7)(2s + 1)$ **33.** $2(5a - 2)(2a + 3)$
35. $5(5w - 3)(w + 1)$ **37.** $2y(5x + 3)(x + 1)$ **39.** $2b^2(5c - 14)(c - 1)$ **B 41.** $n(n + 4)(n + 1)$
43. $(12a + 7b^2)(12a - 7b^2)$ **45.** $-1(y + 7)(y - 3)$ **47.** $12s^2(t - 1)^2$ **49.** $-3a(b + 7)(b + 2)$
51. $2(5h - k)(3h + k)$

Pages 175–176 Chapter Test 1. $x^2 + 8x + 15$ **3.** $b^2 - 9b + 20$ **5.** $25 - 16y^2$ **7.** $2x^2 - 21x + 27$
9. $4n^2 - 49$ **11.** $4b^2 - 12b + 9$ **13.** $\pm 6x$ **15.** m **17.** $18r^5s$ **19.** $(x + 2)(x + 5)$ **21.** $(r - 2)(r - 24)$
23. $(b + 14)(b - 3)$ **25.** $(6k - 7)(k - 1)$ **27.** $2(x - 3)^2$ **29.** $2s(5r - 1)(r - 3)$

Pages 176–178 Chapter Review 1. $10t$ **3.** 18 **5.** $45 - 4y - y^2$ **7.** $2a^2 - 9a + 10$ **9.** $-5 - x + 4x^2$
11. $x^2 - 144$ **13.** $49 - 9b^2$ **15.** $25y^2 - 30y + 9$ **17.** $9b^2 + 36b + 36$ **19.** $4a^2 + 4ab + b^2$ **21.** ± 14
23. ± 12 **25.** ± 13 **27.** $20a$ **29.** $24r^2s$ **31.** $784x^4y^2$ **33.** $(k + 7)(k - 7)$ **35.** $(8x + 1)(8x - 1)$
37. $(10 - m)(10 + m)$ **39.** $(x + 5)^2$ **41.** $(2r + 1)^2$ **43.** $(5n + 3)^2$ **45.** $(m - 8)^2$ **47.** $(1 - 6y)^2$
49. $(4 - 3m)^2$ **51.** $(x + 5)(x + 4)$ **53.** $(x - 6)(x - 3)$ **55.** $(z + 10)(z + 3)$ **57.** $(n - 6)(n + 4)$
59. $(t - 10)(t + 3)$ **61.** $(x - 5)(x + 4)$ **63.** $(y + 18)(y - 3)$ **65.** $(r - 7s)(r + 2s)$ **67.** $(7y + 1) \times$
$(y + 7)$ **69.** $(4z + 5)(2z - 3)$ **71.** $(4y - 3)(5y - 4)$ **73.** $(2n - 1)(3n + 7)$ **75.** $7(b + 3)(b - 3)$
77. $5(x + y)(x - y)$ **79.** $a(b - 8)^2$ **81.** $2(4x - 9)(x + 2)$ **83.** $5(t - 3)^2$

Pages 178–179 Review of Skills 1. $\frac{9}{16}$ **3.** $\frac{12}{16}$ **5.** $\frac{2}{4}$ **7.** $\frac{4}{16}; \frac{5}{20}; \frac{6}{24}; \frac{7}{28}$ **9.** $\frac{8}{20}; \frac{10}{25}; \frac{12}{30}; \frac{14}{35}; \frac{16}{40}$ **11.** $\frac{1}{5}$
13. $\frac{14}{21}$ **15.** $\frac{24}{80}$ **17.** $\frac{15}{6}$ **19.** $<$ **21.** $<$ **23.** $<$ **31.** $\frac{29}{100}; 0.29$ **33.** $\frac{45}{100}; 0.45$ **35.** $\frac{9}{100}; 0.09$
37. $\frac{15}{100}; 0.15$ **39.–46.**

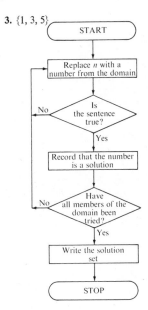

Page 181 Check Point for Experts

1.

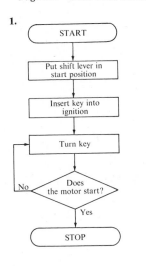

3. $\{1, 3, 5\}$

5.

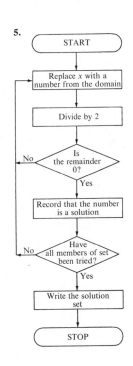

Chapter 6. Working with Fractions

Pages 185–186 Written Exercises A 1. $\dfrac{10}{y}$; $y \neq 0$ **3.** $\dfrac{-25}{b}$; $b \neq 0$ **5.** $\dfrac{10}{1}$; no restrictions **7.** $\dfrac{m}{m-2}$; $m \neq 2$ **9.** $\dfrac{a}{b}$; $b \neq 0$ **11.** $\dfrac{t}{3n+15}$; $n \neq -5$ **13.** 5 **15.** $5y$ **17.** $-8x$ **19.** $3x + 5y$ **21.** 3 **23.** 3 **25.** $\frac{6}{5}$ or 1.2 **27.** $\frac{19}{15}$ **29.** $\frac{1}{5}$ **31.** 1 **33.** $\frac{21}{5}$ **B 35.** $\dfrac{4b+3}{(b+2)(b+3)}$; $\{-3, -2\}$ **37.** $\dfrac{7t+8}{(t+6)(t+2)}$; $\{-6, -2\}$ **39.** $\dfrac{y+3}{(y+7)(y-2)}$; $\{-7, 2\}$ **41.** $\dfrac{-3k+10}{(k-3)(k-5)}$; $\{3, 5\}$

Pages 189–191 Written Exercises A 1. $\frac{4}{8}, \frac{5}{10}, \frac{6}{12}, \frac{7}{14}, \frac{8}{16}$ **3.** $\dfrac{4x}{12}, \dfrac{5x}{15}, \dfrac{6x}{18}, \dfrac{7x}{21}, \dfrac{8x}{24}$ **5.** $\dfrac{-15}{25}, \dfrac{-18}{30}, \dfrac{-21}{35}, \dfrac{-24}{40}, \dfrac{-27}{45}$ **7.** $\dfrac{8a}{-12}, \dfrac{10a}{-15}, \dfrac{12a}{-18}, \dfrac{14a}{-21}, \dfrac{16a}{-24}$ **9.** $\frac{6}{16}, \frac{3}{8}$; equivalent **11.** $\frac{5}{6}, \frac{15}{18}$; equivalent **13.** $\frac{9}{18}, \frac{2}{6}$; not equivalent **27.** $\dfrac{5x}{2} = \dfrac{20x}{8}$ **29.** $\dfrac{28k}{40} = \dfrac{7k}{10}$ **31.** $\dfrac{8xy}{16} = \dfrac{6xy}{12}$ **33.** $\dfrac{5r^2}{-8} = \dfrac{-15r^2}{24}$ **B 35.** $<$ **37.** $>$ **39.** $<$ **41.** $>$ **43.** $>$

Pages 193–195 Written Exercises A 1. $.375; \frac{3}{10} + \frac{7}{100} + \frac{5}{1000}; 0.3 + 0.07 + 0.005$ **3.** $.25; \frac{2}{10} + \frac{5}{100}; .2 + .05$ **5.** $.75; \frac{7}{10} + \frac{5}{100}; .7 + .05$ **7.** $.125; \frac{1}{10} + \frac{2}{100} + \frac{5}{1000}; .1 + .02 + .005$ **9.** $0.\overline{3}$ **11.** $-0.\overline{6}$ **13.** $0.\overline{1}$ **15.** $1.\overline{3}$ **17.** $0.\overline{142857}$ **19.** $\frac{386}{1000}; 0.386$ **21.** $\frac{5672}{10,000}; 0.5672$ **23.** $\frac{6074}{10,000}; 0.6074$ **25.** $\dfrac{-827}{1000}$; -0.827 **26.–37.**

39. $0.625r^2s^2$ **41.** $0.25a^2b^2$ **43.** $0.6\dfrac{ab}{c}$ **45.** $-0.039xy$ **B 47.** 0.257 **49.** -0.487

Pages 198–199 Written Exercises A 1. $\dfrac{5x}{2}$ **3.** $8a$ **5.** $\frac{4}{7}$ **7.** $\frac{1}{3}$ **9.** $\dfrac{2a}{3}$ **11.** $\dfrac{3(a-b)}{5(s+t)}$ **13.** $\dfrac{3x}{4}$ **15.** $\dfrac{3xy}{5}$ **17.** $\dfrac{a+c}{a-c}$ **19.** $\frac{2}{7}$ **21.** $\dfrac{2x+2y}{5x-5y}$ **23.** $2a - b$ **25.** $\dfrac{3(a+b)}{4(a-b)}$ **27.** $\dfrac{3(r+s)}{5(r-s)}$ **29.** $y - 3$ **31.** $\dfrac{1}{k+3}$ **33.** $\dfrac{2rs}{3s^2+5}$ **35.** $\dfrac{a}{b}$ **B 37.** $\dfrac{x}{x+1}$ **39.** $\dfrac{x+3}{x-2}$ **41.** $\dfrac{x+3y}{x-3y}$ **C 43.** $\dfrac{m-3}{m-2}$ **45.** $\dfrac{2x-5}{x-4}$

Pages 201–202 Written Exercises A 1. $1:2$ **3.** $1:10$ **5.** $5:7$ **7.** $x:y$ **9.** $9:4$ **11.** $1:3$ **13.** $\frac{25}{18}$ **15.** $\frac{9}{2}$ **17.** $\frac{3}{1}$ **19.** $\frac{3}{8}$ **21.** $\frac{4}{9}$ **23.** $x = 42$ **25.** $t = 15$ **27.** $x = 3$ **29.** $k = -33$ **B 31.** $\frac{7}{2}$ **33.** $\frac{1}{1}$ **35.** $\frac{2}{1}$ **37.** $\frac{5}{1}$ **39.** $\frac{12}{1}$ **C 41.** $\frac{4}{3}$ **43.** $\frac{7}{3}$

Page 203 Problems A 1. 29 miles; 116 miles; 72.5 miles **3.** $375.00 **5.** 3 seconds; 4.5 seconds **B 7.** 15 boys; 12 girls **9.** Judy is faster.

Pages 205–207 Written Exercises A 1. 40% **3.** 35% **5.** 75% **7.** $0.47; \frac{47}{100}; 47\%$ **9.** $0.95; \frac{95}{100}; 95\%$ **11.** $0.38; \frac{38}{100}; 38\%$ **13.** $0.375; \frac{37.5}{100}; 37.5\%$ **15.** $0.875; \frac{87.5}{100}; 87.5\%$ **17.** $0.46; \frac{46}{100}; 46\%$ **19.** $\frac{3}{10}$ **21.** $\frac{3}{4}$ **23.** $\frac{1}{20}$ **25.** $\frac{99}{100}$ **27.** 2 **29.** $\frac{1}{10}$ **31.**

33. $=$ **35.** $<$ **37.** $>$ **39.** $>$ **41.** $\frac{4}{10}$; 40% **43.** $\frac{5}{8}$; 62.5% **45.** $\frac{1}{5}$; 20% **47.** $\frac{2}{5}$; 40% **49.** $\frac{2}{4}$; 50% **B 51.** $\frac{1}{500}$; 0.002 **53.** $\frac{3}{400}$; 0.0075 **55.** $\frac{1}{2000}$; 0.0005

Pages 209–210 Written Exercises A 1. 45 **3.** 93.60 **5.** 600 **7.** 96.3 **9.** 52.50 **11.** 0.750 **13.** 1.23 **15.** 75 **17.** $m = 96$ **19.** $n = 75$ **21.** $b = 224$ **23.** $13 = y$ **25.** $64 = c$ **27.** $k = 63$ **29.** 70 **31.** 28 **33.** 67.3 **35.** 400 **37.** 700 **39.** 45% **41.** 69% **43.** 50% **45.** 1100% **B 47.** 2.6 **49.** $2266.\overline{6}$ **51.** $4791.\overline{6}$

Pages 210–211 **Problems** **1.** 66 boys have jobs. **3.** 38% are nonfiction; 4900 fiction; 3780 reference; 5320 nonfiction **5.** 182 students; 93% **7.** $69.75 **9.** 70%

Pages 212–213 **Chapter Test** **1.** $\frac{1}{2}, \frac{3}{5}, \frac{2}{3}, \frac{5}{3}$ **3.** 10%, 0.13, $\frac{1}{4}$, 100%, $\frac{10}{3}$, 42 **5.** 0.60; 60% **7.** 0.8$\overline{3}$; 83$\frac{1}{3}$% **9.** C **11.** D **13.** $\frac{28}{20k}, \frac{35}{25k}, \frac{42}{30k}, \frac{49}{35k}, \frac{56}{40k}$ **15.** = **17.** > **19.** $\frac{t^2}{3s}$ **21.** $\frac{m+n}{4(m-n)}$ **23.** $\frac{5}{9}$ **25.** 3060 pounds **27.** $80.40 **29.** 60%

Pages 214–215 **Chapter Review** **1.** $\frac{15}{3a-6}$; $a \neq 2$ **3.** $\frac{n+3}{n}$; $n \neq 0$ **5.** $\frac{10+y}{3y}$; $y \neq 0$ **7.** $\frac{3b}{b+8}$; $b \neq -8$ **9.** $\frac{7+9n}{n+10}$; $n \neq -10$ **11.** $\frac{-4x}{20}, \frac{-5x}{25}, \frac{-6x}{30}$ **13.** $\frac{8ab}{28}, \frac{10ab}{35}, \frac{12ab}{42}$ **15.** $\frac{5}{8}$ **17.** $\frac{7}{8}$ **19.** < **21.** 0.875 **23.** −0.60 **25.** 0.75 **27.** 2.50 **29.** 0.7195 **31.** 36.157 **33.** $\frac{a}{5}$ **35.** $\frac{1}{n+5}$ **37.** $\frac{-n}{19}$ **39.** $\frac{9}{5}$ **41.** $\frac{x+2}{x-2}$ **43.** $\frac{73}{32}$ **45.** $\frac{8}{5}$ **47.** $\frac{3}{17b}$ **49.** 7 **51.** 14 **53.** 30% **55.** 150% **57.** 0.25; 25% **59.** 0.95; 95% **61.** 1.20; 120% **63.** 1.52 **65.** 84 **67.** $14.80

Page 216 **Review of Skills** **1.** $15a^2b^3$ **3.** $-12bc^2d$ **5.** $-8st$ **7.** $9rt^2$ **9.** $-7xz$ **11.** $(x+7)(x-7)$ **13.** $(3+4r)(3-4r)$ **15.** $5m^2+4$ **17.** $(x-5)(x+2)$ **19.** $(2r+5)(r-4)$

Chapter 7. Multiplication and Division with Fractions

Pages 223–224 **Written Exercises** **A 1.** associative property **3.** associative property **5.** multiplicative property of one **7.** commutative property **9.** $\frac{1}{12}$ **11.** $\frac{1}{6}$ **13.** $\frac{1}{8}$ **15.** $\frac{7}{30}$ **17.** $\frac{5}{12}$ **19.** $\frac{5}{336}$ **21.** $\frac{b}{4}$ **23.** $4s$ **25.** $\frac{1}{8}$

Pages 224–225 **Problems** **A 1.** $\frac{5}{2}$ **3.** $\frac{11}{32}$ **5.** $\frac{27}{5}$ **7.** $\frac{5}{12}$ **B 9.** $x = 8$ **11.** $\frac{5\pi h}{3}$ gallons

Pages 226–228 **Written Exercises** **A 1.** $\frac{a^2-b^2}{a}$ **3.** $\frac{6}{(t+2)^2}$ **5.** $\frac{3}{5}$ **7.** $\frac{2}{3(1+x)}$ **9.** $\frac{3(m-n)}{-5}$ **11.** $\frac{3}{2}$ **13.** $\frac{1}{(x^2+1)^2}$ **15.** $\frac{(a+b)^2}{a^2+b^2}$ **17.** $\frac{9x^2-y^2}{x^2-y^2}$ **19.** $\frac{1}{4}$ **21.** $\frac{-(a-b)^2}{9(a+b)}$ **23.** $\frac{1}{(x^2-2)^2}$ **25.** $\frac{x-4}{5}$ **27.** $\frac{4a^2-b^2}{15}$ **29.** $\frac{a+b}{ab}$ **31.** $\frac{b+1}{b^2}$ **33.** 3 **35.** 1 **C 37.** $-\frac{c+1}{c}$ **39.** $\frac{x-y}{x^2}$

Pages 230–232 **Written Exercises** **A 1.** B **3.** A **5.** $\frac{4}{7}$ **7.** $\frac{-15}{4}$ **9.** $\frac{1}{16}$ **11.** $\frac{3}{25}$ **13.** $\frac{96}{7}$ **15.** $\frac{7}{24}$ **17.** $n = 3, m = 2$ **19.** $y = 5, x = 7$ **21.** $b = 7, a = 8$ **23.** $t = 3, r = 1$ **25.** true **27.** false **29.** true **31.** true **33.** $\frac{9}{4}$ **35.** 1 **37.** −1 **39.** $\frac{32}{21}$ **41.** $\frac{-3}{2}$ **43.** $\frac{14}{9}$

Pages 233–235 **Written Exercises** **A 1.** $\frac{-5y}{8x}$ **3.** $\frac{3m}{2}$ **5.** $\frac{2}{9m}$ **7.** $\frac{3}{x}$ **9.** $\frac{-3a}{7b}$ **11.** $\frac{15}{7a^2b^2}$ **13.** $\frac{b^3c}{6}$ **15.** $\frac{-28y^2}{3}$ **17.** $\frac{2q^2}{p^2}$ **19.** $\frac{-s}{8t}$ **21.** $15a$ **23.** $\frac{-a^2}{3b}$ **C 31.** $6m$ **33.** $9b^2$

Pages 235–236 **Problems** **1.** $\frac{5k^2}{9}$ inches **3.** $\frac{625s^4}{9}$; 25 **5.** $\frac{5}{2}$

Pages 237–238 **Written Exercises** **A 1.** $\frac{2}{3}$ **3.** $\frac{r-s}{s-t}$ **5.** $\frac{1}{3(2x+1)}$ **7.** $\frac{3a}{a-b}$ **9.** $\frac{2(2m+5)}{3(m+2)}$ **11.** $\frac{a^2}{2}$ **13.** $\frac{a+b}{2a^2+ab}$ **15.** $\frac{m-3}{2m}$ **17.** $\frac{x-2}{x^2}$ **19.** $\frac{4r-4}{2r^2-r}$ **21.** $\frac{5b^2}{2a^2}$ **23.** $\frac{s+5}{s+3}$ **25.** $\frac{3}{2(y-z)}$ **27.** $\frac{m-1}{m^2}$ **29.** $\frac{r+s}{r(2r+s)}$ **B 31.** $\frac{n(n+m)}{n-4}$ **33.** $\frac{r+3}{r-5}$

Pages 239–240 **Chapter Test** **1.** $\frac{3n}{20}$ **3.** $-\frac{3}{2}$ **5.** $\frac{a^2-b^2}{14c}$ **7.** $\frac{1}{a^2}$ **9.** $-(a+b)$ **11.** $\frac{-5}{6}$ **13.** $\frac{9}{20}$ **15.** $-10r$ **17.** $\frac{m-n}{m^2}$ **19.** $\frac{x(x-3)}{3(x+2)}$ **21.** $\frac{3}{(p-2)^2}$

Pages 240–241 Chapter Review 1. $\frac{1}{15}$ **3.** $\frac{3}{4}$ **5.** $-\frac{9}{4}$ **7.** $\frac{5a^2}{18b^2}$ **9.** $\frac{3st}{7}$ **11.** $\frac{8ac^2}{25b}$ **13.** $\frac{a^2-b^2}{3}$

15. $\frac{x+2}{x-5}$ **17.** $\frac{8}{3}$ **19.** $-\frac{3}{16}$ **21.** $\frac{4}{5}$ **23.** $\frac{-4}{9}$ **25.** 1 **27.** $\frac{9}{8x}$ **29.** $\frac{3z}{5}$ **31.** x **33.** $\frac{a+2}{a(b+2)}$ **35.** $\frac{2}{x}$

37. $\frac{3(a-4)}{2}$ **37.** $\frac{x+y}{7}$

Pages 242–243 Review of Skills 1. $2\cdot3\cdot7$ **3.** $2\cdot3\cdot11$ **5.** $2^3\cdot3\cdot5$ **7.** $2\cdot3^2\cdot5$ **9.** 5 **11.** 5
13. $\frac{1}{5}$ **15.** $\frac{7}{12}$ **17.** $\frac{1}{2}$ **19.** 2 **21.** $\frac{3}{100}$ **23.** $\frac{12}{100}$ **25.** m **27.** $\frac{6}{7}$

29.  **31.**

33. $\{6\}$ **35.** $\{-5\}$ **37.** {directed numbers greater than or equal to 3} **39.** {directed numbers less than 2}
41. E **43.** A **45.** B

Pages 244–245 Check Point for Experts 1. B **3.** A

5. **7.** **9.**

11. All ducks are animals that fly. **13.** Some multiples of 5 are divisible by 2.

Chapter 8. Addition and Subtraction with Fractions

Pages 249–251 Written Exercises A 1. $\frac{1}{4}$ **3.** $\frac{1}{8}$ **5.** 8 **7.** -9 **9.** $-\frac{3}{4}$ **11.** $\frac{1}{3}$ **13.** -6 **15.** $\frac{5}{6}$
17. $\frac{4}{5}$ **19.** $\frac{1}{20}$ **21.** $6\frac{3}{4}$ **23.** $3\frac{1}{4}$ **29.** $\frac{5}{b}$ **31.** $\frac{10}{y}$ **33.** $\frac{13}{m}$ **35.** $\frac{9}{x}$ **37.** $\frac{2a}{7}$ **39.** $\frac{m+n}{5}$ **41.** $\frac{t+2s}{a}$ **43.** $\frac{6}{x^2}$
45. $\frac{5x}{6k}$ **B 47.** $\frac{4t-5}{13m}$ **49.** $\frac{-10}{z}$

Pages 252–254 Written Exercises 1. $\frac{8m}{m-n}$ **3.** 1 **5.** $x+y$ **7.** $\frac{x+3y}{x-3}$ **9.** $\frac{5m+3}{n+k}$ **11.** $\frac{5}{m+n}$
13. $\frac{5m+t}{x^2-3x+9}$ **15.** $\frac{4}{y^2+3}$ **B 23.** $m-n$ **25.** $\frac{1}{y+1}$ **27.** $\frac{8-b-b^2}{b^2-16}$ **29.** $\frac{2t+17}{2t^2+t-3}$

Pages 256–257 Written Exercises A 9. $\frac{4a}{15}$ **11.** $\frac{8k}{m^2}$ **13.** $\frac{r}{t^2}$ **15.** $\frac{10a-3}{x-y}$ **17.** $\frac{11bd}{xy^2}$ **19.** 3 **21.** $\frac{1}{2x-1}$
23. $c+d$ **25.** $x-3$

Pages 259–261 Written Exercises A 19. $\frac{5}{a-6}$ **21.** $\frac{-10}{2-k}$ **23.** $\frac{r-2s}{5n}$ **25.** $\frac{t+5}{3y}$ **27.** $\frac{7}{r^2s}$ **29.** $\frac{5t}{r-s}$
31. $\frac{a-2b}{a-b}$ **33.** $\frac{8k}{yz}$ **35.** $\frac{9n}{m-n}$ **37.** $\frac{3x}{r-s}$ **B 39.** $\frac{11a}{2x-y}$ **41.** $a+b$ **C 43.** $x-3$ **45** $\frac{1}{x-1}$

Pages 264–265 Written Exercises A 1. $\frac{3x^3}{x^4y^2}$ **3.** $\frac{7r}{7r}$ **5.** $\frac{6a}{6a}$ **7.** $\frac{6c^2}{6c^2}$ **9.** $\frac{12ab^2}{6a^2b}$ **11.** $\frac{95x^3y^2}{15}$ **13.** $\frac{16m^5n}{56m^3n^3}$
15. $\frac{75a^3b^3c}{45a^3b^3c^3}$ **17.** $\frac{3x+y^2}{x^2y^2}$ **19.** $\frac{x(a+y)}{xyz}$ **21.** $\frac{a^2+2a+10}{a^3}$ **23.** $\frac{14y+25}{30y^2}$ **25.** $\frac{35-18y}{21y^2}$
27. L.C.D. $= 18$; $\frac{9n+2m}{18}$ **29.** L.C.D. $= 3b$; $\frac{2b+21}{3b}$ **31.** L.C.D. $= rs^2$; $\frac{-2}{rs^2}$ **B 33.** L.C.D. $= 12y$;
$\frac{8x+3}{12y}$ **35.** L.C.D. $= m^2n^2$; $\frac{4n-2m+m^2}{m^2n^2}$

Pages 267–270 Written Exercises A 1. $\frac{5a-5z}{a^2-z^2}$ **3.** $\frac{6t^2+3t}{10st+5s}$ **5.** $\frac{k-1}{k-1}$ **7.** $\frac{3}{3}$ **9.** $\frac{7c-21}{c^2-3c}$
11. $\frac{3x^2z-3y^2z}{5x^2-5y^2}$ **13.** $\frac{m^2+2mn+n^2}{m^2-n^2}$ **15.** $\frac{16a}{2a+6}$ **17.** $\frac{3x^2-3xy+2y}{2(x-y)}$ **19.** $\frac{8n+11}{(n+1)(n+2)}$ **21.** $\frac{7}{2(p-q)}$

23. $\dfrac{xy}{(x+y)(x-y)}$ **25.** $\dfrac{xyz + xy + y^2z}{(x+y)^2}$ **27.** L.C.D. $= 3(a+b)$; $\dfrac{3+2a+2b}{3(a+b)}$ **29.** L.C.D. $=$

$(x+4)(x+3)$; $\dfrac{6x+20}{(x+3)(x+4)}$ **31.** L.C.D. $= xy(x+y)$; $\dfrac{6x^2 + 10xy + 3y^2}{xy(x+y)}$ **33.** L.C.D. $= b(a-b)$;

$\dfrac{a^2 + 2b^2}{b(a-b)}$ **B 35.** L.C.D. $= p^3 - pq^2$; $\dfrac{2p-q}{p^3 - pq^2}$ **37.** L.C.D. $= (3a+b)(3a-b)$; $\dfrac{4a - b - 15ac + 5bc}{9a^2 - b^2}$

39. L.C.D. $= (x-2)(x-1)$; $\dfrac{1}{x-2}$ **41.** L.C.D. $= 2(x+9)(x-9)$; $\dfrac{3}{2(x-9)}$ **C 43.** L.C.D. $=$

$(x+1)(x-1)$; 0 **45.** L.C.D. $= (y+3)(y-3)$; $\dfrac{-2y^2 - 3y + 2}{(y+3)(y-3)}$ **47.** L.C.D. $= (m-2)(m-3)$; $\dfrac{1}{m-2}$

Pages 271–272 Written Exercises A 1. $\dfrac{4y+3}{y}$ **3.** $\dfrac{m^2 + m + 1}{m+1}$ **5.** $\dfrac{2x^2 - 3}{2x}$ **7.** $\dfrac{6x - 6y + xy}{x-y}$

9. $\dfrac{m+3+n}{m+3}$ **11.** $\dfrac{3a+3+b}{3}$ **13.** $4x^2 + \dfrac{2}{x}$ **15.** $\dfrac{1}{3b^3} - 2$ **17.** $1 + \dfrac{3}{ab}$ **19.** $5 + \dfrac{5}{4r}$ **21.** $z + 3 + \dfrac{7}{z}$

23. $b + 2 - \dfrac{2}{b}$ **B 25.** $2x + 7 + \dfrac{1}{x-1}$ **27.** $6x + 5 - \dfrac{2}{2x-3}$

Pages 274–276 Written Exercises A 1. $3n + 5n = 60$ **3.** $6a + 4a = 3$ **5.** $3n - 4n = 24$ **7.** $21c + 16c < 70$ **9.** $6x^2 - 2x - 3 = 0$ **11.** $3b^2 + 117b > 5$ **13.** $k = 3$ **15.** $x = 15$ **17.** $a = \frac{3}{2}$ **19.** $m = 24$ **21.** $y = \frac{3}{2}$

23. $m > 18$ 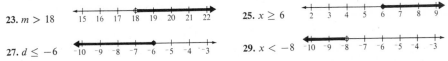 **25.** $x \geq 6$

27. $d \leq -6$ **29.** $x < -8$

B 31. $k \geq -10$ **33.** $s = -1$ **35.** $x = 150$ **C 37.** $x = 12{,}000$ **39.** $n \leq -5$

Pages 276–277 Problems 1. \$350 **3.** \$1500 **5.** \$2175 **7.** 12 inches **9.** 2425.5 cubic feet **11.** $80\frac{2}{3}$ cubic inches

Pages 278–279 Chapter Test 1. $3\frac{3}{4}$ **3.** $m + \dfrac{2n}{m}$ **5.** $\dfrac{9}{a-b}$ **7.** $\dfrac{a+d}{c-3}$ **9.** $\dfrac{4r^2s}{y-2}$ **11.** $\dfrac{12r+31}{(r+3)(r+2)}$

13. $t < 2$ **15.** $n \geq 1$

17. $b = 12$ **19.** $m = -2$ **21.** 5 cubic feet

Pages 279–281 Chapter Review 1. $\frac{6}{7}$ **3.** $\dfrac{t}{3}$ **5.** $\dfrac{2n}{5}$ **7.** $\dfrac{11n}{(a+b)^2}$ **9.** $\dfrac{a^2 + b^2}{y+2}$ **11.** $\dfrac{3}{a+b}$ **13.** $\dfrac{5m}{n}$

15. $\dfrac{5a-5}{x+y}$ **17.** 1 **19.** $\dfrac{8}{5w}$ **21.** $\dfrac{7}{a}$ **23.** $\dfrac{6z}{x-y}$ **25.** $\dfrac{5y+2x}{axy}$ **27.** $\dfrac{3rz + 3sx - xyz}{3xyz}$ **29.** $\dfrac{2m - 2n}{m^2 - n^2}$

31. $\dfrac{3r + 3s - 5}{5(r+s)}$ **33.** $\dfrac{m^2 + 5mn - n^2}{m(m-n)}$ **35.** $\dfrac{15}{7z} - 3z^2$ **37.** $\dfrac{2a+5}{a}$ **39.** $\dfrac{n^2 - 1 + t}{n+1}$ **41.** $m = 15$

43. $x \geq -17$ **45.** $t = 3$

Page 281 Review of Skills 1. P, $(-3, 0)$; Q, $(-2, 0)$; R, $(1, 0)$; S, $(3, 0)$ **3.** y-axis **5.–7.** **9.** $\{(2, 2), (1, -1), (0, -4), (-1, -7)\}$ **11.** $\frac{1}{30}$ **13.** $\frac{1}{6}$ **15.** 0 **17.** 1 **19.** 0 **21.** $x = -\dfrac{z}{2} + \dfrac{3}{2}$ **23.** 15% **25.** 5%

Chapter 9. Solving Equations and Graphing

Pages 286–287 Written Exercises A 1. 0 **3.** 0 **5.** 0 **7.** 0 **9.** 0 **11.** $x = 3$ **13.** $b = -2$
15. $y = -9$ **17.** $n = \frac{2}{5}$ **19.** $n = -\frac{1}{3}$ **21.** $\{3, 5\}$ **23.** $\{-6, 8\}$ **25.** $\{0, \frac{5}{2}\}$ **27.** $\{-3, 3\}$ **29.** $\{-2, 0\}$
B 31. {directed numbers} **33.** {the nonzero directed numbers} **35.** {directed numbers} **C 37.** $\{-\frac{5}{2}\}$
39. $\{-\frac{1}{5}, 3\}$

Pages 289–290 Written Exercises A 1. $k(1 + 3k)$ **3.** $(t - 8)(t + 3)$ **5.** $(n - 3)(n - 5)$ **7.** $y(y - 16)$
9. $z(2z - 5)$ **11.** $(a + 10)(a - 9)$ **13.** $\{-2, 0\}$ **15.** $\{0, \frac{5}{3}\}$ **17.** $\{-3, 5\}$ **19.** $\{-3, 6\}$ **21.** $\{-9, -2\}$
23. $\{1, 5\}$ **25.** $\{-6, 11\}$ **27.** $\{-15, 15\}$ **B 29.** $\{-\frac{5}{2}, -2\}$ **31.** $\{\frac{1}{2}, 5\}$ **33.** $\{\frac{3}{2}, 7\}$ **35.** $\{\frac{2}{3}, 5\}$
C 37. $\{-4, 0, 10\}$ **39.** $\{0, \frac{2}{3}\}$

Pages 290–291 Problems 1. width = 7 feet; length = 11 feet **3.** -11 and -9 or 9 and 11 **5.** -8 and
-6 or 6 and 10

Page 293 Written Exercises A 1. $\{-9\}$ **3.** $\{\frac{2}{3}\}$ **5.** $\{-4\}$ **7.** $\{-\frac{5}{7}\}$ **9.** $\{2\}$ **11.** $\{\frac{2}{5}\}$ **13.** L.C.D. =
$3b - 12$; $\{-5, 5\}$ **15.** L.C.D. = $2(z - 1)$; $\{-3, 4\}$ **17.** L.C.D. = $12n$; $\{-2\}$ **19.** L.C.D. = $3t(3t - 2)$;
$\{\frac{1}{3}\}$ **B 21.** L.C.D. = $3 - a$; $\{-1\}$ **23.** L.C.D. = $(x + 2)(x - 2)$; $\{-4, 6\}$ **C 25.** L.C.D. =
$(x + 3)(x - 3)$; $\{-2, 4\}$ **27.** L.C.D. = $(y + 1)(y - 1)$; $\{2, 5\}$

Pages 294–295 Problems 1. a. $\frac{1}{10}$; $\frac{1}{5}$; $\frac{4}{5}$; 1; (the whole job) **b.** $\frac{1}{7}$; $\frac{3}{7}$; 1, (the whole job) **c.** $\frac{17}{70}$; $\frac{34}{70}$; $\frac{51}{70}$;
$1\frac{7}{10}$ **d.** the part of the job done in 1 hour by both **e.** The part of the job completed in 1 hour is the sum
of the parts done by the two men; $4\frac{2}{7} = n$ **f.** $4\frac{2}{7}$ hours **3.** $2\frac{2}{9}$ hours **5.** $1\frac{1}{3}$ hours

Pages 298–300 Written Exercises A 1. 8; 6; 4; 2 **3.** $3\frac{1}{2}$; 3; $2\frac{1}{2}$; 2; $1\frac{1}{2}$ **5.** -1; 0; 1; 2; 3 **7.** 2; 10;
14; 16; 18 **9.** $\{(0, 5), (1, 3), (2, 1), (3, -1)\}$ **11.** $\{(0, \frac{1}{2}), (2, -\frac{1}{2}), (4, -1\frac{1}{2}), (-2, 1\frac{1}{2}), (-4, 2\frac{1}{2})\}$
B 13. $\{(2, 7), (4, -5), (-2, 7), (-4, -5)\}$ **C 15.** $\{(2, 3), (1, 4\frac{1}{2}), (0, 9), (-2, -9)\}$

Pages 303–305 Written Exercises A 1. $y = 5 - x$ **3.** $y = \dfrac{7 - x}{2}$ **5.** $y = 2x - 5$ **7.** $y = \dfrac{3x - 10}{2}$
9. $y = \dfrac{3x}{2}$ **11.** $y = \dfrac{x - 9}{4}$ **13.** $y = \dfrac{x + 1}{3}$ **15.** $y = 5x + 2$
17. $\{(-1, 0), (0, 1), (1, 2)\}$ **19.** $\{(-3, 4), (-1, 4), (1, 4)\}$ **21.** $\{(1, 4), (2, 2), (3, 0)\}$

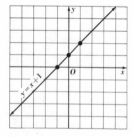
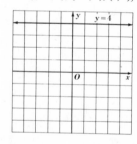
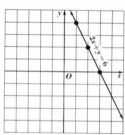

23. $\{(3, 3), (4, 6), (5, 9)\}$ **25.** $\{(-3, -2), (-3, -1), (-3, 0)\}$ **27.** $\{(-1, -1), (0, 1), (1, 3)\}$

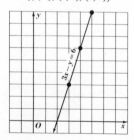
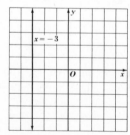
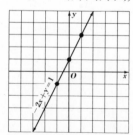

29. y-axis

31. y-axis

33. x-axis

35. x-axis

37. $\{(0, 3), (4, 0)\}$

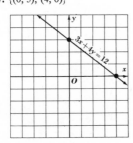

39. $\{(0, 5), (2, 0)\}$

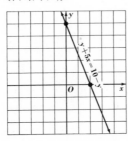

41. $\{(0, 4), (-2, 0)\}$

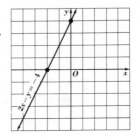

43. $\{(0, -3), (-1, 0)\}$

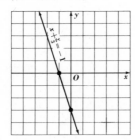

45. $\{(0, 4), (-8, 0)\}$

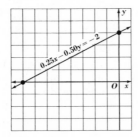

Pages 306–307   Written Exercises   A 1. $\frac{3}{10} = 30\%$ **3.** $\frac{3}{50} = 6\%$ **5.** $\frac{1}{8} = 12.5\%$ **7.** $\frac{1}{40}$ **9.** $\frac{7}{100}$ **11.** 2
13. 10   **15.** 90 feet   **17.** 8 feet   **19.** $\frac{1}{2}$

Pages 309–311   Written Exercises   A 1. 1   **3.** $-\frac{3}{4}$ **5.** $-\frac{1}{4}$ **7.** $-\frac{3}{7}$ **9.** 0   **11.** no slope

13. $-\frac{3}{2}$

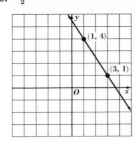

15. $-\frac{1}{2}$

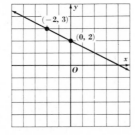

17. 0

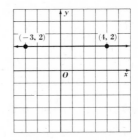

Pages 312–313   Chapter Test   1. $\{0, 2\}$ **3.** $\{-8, 6\}$ **5.** $\{0, \frac{3}{2}\}$ **7.** $\{-1, 0, 4\}$ **9.** $\{\frac{7}{3}\}$ **11.** $\{-\frac{7}{2}\}$
13. a. $\frac{1}{6}$ **b.** $\frac{1}{4}$ **c.** $2\frac{2}{5}$ hours   **15.** domain $= \{0, 1, 2, 3\}$; range $= \{-8, -6, -4, -2\}$

17.

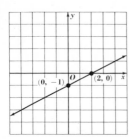

19.

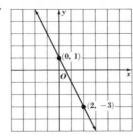

21.

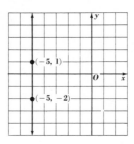

23. 0

Pages 313–315 Chapter Review 1. 0 **3.** 0 **5.** $\{-9, 3\}$ **7.** $\{-\frac{5}{3}, 0\}$ **9.** $\{-2, 7\}$ **11.** $\{\frac{5}{8}\}$ **13.** $\{\frac{2}{5}\}$
15. $\{3\}$ **17.** $7\frac{1}{5}$ hours **19.** $-1, 1, 3, 5, 7$ **21.** $-3, -1, 1, 3, 5$ **23.** F **25.** T **27.** N

29.

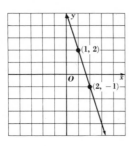

31. $\dfrac{\text{rise}}{\text{run}}$ **33.** 2% **35.** positive **37.** $-\frac{2}{3}$ **39.** $-\frac{5}{2}$

Pages 316–317 Review of Skills 1. positive **3.** positive **5.** negative **7.** B **9.** A **11.** coefficient of
$x = 3$; coefficient of $y = 4$ **13.** coefficient of $x = \frac{1}{4}$; coefficient of $y = -5$ **15.** coefficient of $x = \frac{2}{3}$;
coefficient of $y = \frac{1}{2}$ **17.** coefficient of $x = 6$; coefficient of $y = -\frac{1}{3}$ **19.** coefficient of $x = -1$; coefficient
of $y = 9$ **21.** $\{-7, 7\}$ **23.** $\{-3, 3\}$ **25.** $\{-3, 3\}$ **27.** $\{12\}$ **29.** $\{5\}$ **31.** $\{10\}$ **33.** $\{-2, \frac{3}{2}\}$
35. $\{-8, -6\}$ **37.** $-\frac{2}{5}$ **39.** $\dfrac{2(x + y)}{7}$ **41.** b^3 **43.** $\dfrac{n}{2}$ **45.** 25% **47.** 50% **49.** 80% **51.** 53%
53. 37.5%

Pages 318–319 Check Point for Experts 1. A statement is valid if its conclusion is a logical result of a deductive argument. A valid statement need not be true. A true statement is one which can be justified or proven
to hold in reality.
3. Hypothesis

5.

7.

Chapter 10. Solving Inequalities and Graphing

Pages 322–324 Written Exercises A 1. $y \le 3 - x$ **3.** $y \ge 3 - 2x$ **5.** $y \le 5 + 3x$ **7.** $y < 9 + 2x$
19.–27. Answers will vary. **19.** $(0, 2)$; $(-1, 1)$; $(1, 5)$; $(-2, -2)$ **21.** $(0, 0)$; $(2, 1)$; $(4, 2)$; $(6, 3)$ **23.** $(0, 3)$;
$(1, 4)$; $(2, 5)$; $(3, 6)$ **25.** $(-2, 1)$; $(-3, 0)$; $(-4, -1)$; $(-4, -2)$ **27.** $(0, -1)$; $(2, -6)$; $(4, -11)$; $(-2, 4)$
29. $\{(-2, 1), (-2, 2), (-2, 3), (0, 1), (0, 2), (0, 3), (2, 1), (2, 2), (2, 3)\}$ **B 31.** $\{(-1, -1), (-1, 0), (-1, 1),$
$(-1, 2), (0, 1), (0, 2)\}$ **33.** $\{(-1, 0), (-1, 1), (-1, 2), (0, 1), (0, 2), (1, 2)\}$ **35.** $\{(-1, -2), (0, 1), (0, 0),$
$(0, -1), (0, -2), (1, 2), (1, 1), (1, 0), (1, -1), (1, -2)\}$ **C 37.** $\{(-1, 1), (-1, 2), (0, 1), (0, 2), (1, 1), (1, 2)\}$

Pages 327–328   Written Exercises

A 1.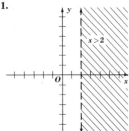

3.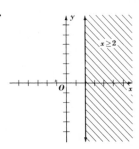

5.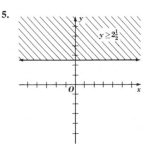

7.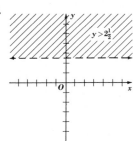

9.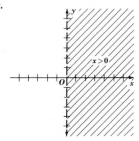

11.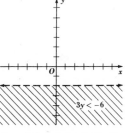

13. included   **15.** included   **17.** not included   **19.** not included   **21.** included   **23.** included   **B 25.–30.** Answers will vary.

25. $(1, 2)$; $(-1, 2)$; $(0, 0)$ **27.** $(2, 3)$; $(0, 0)$; $(-3, -1)$ **29.** $(0, 0)$; $(1, 3)$; $(-1, 4)$

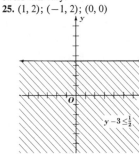
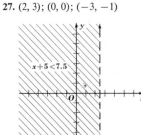
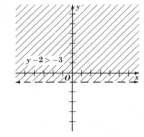

31. $(1, -3)$; $(0, -6)$; $(6, -3)$

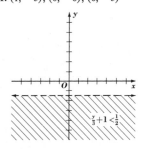

Pages 330–332   Written Exercises   **A 1.** $y > -x + 1$ **3.** $y < -x + 1$ **5.** $y < -x + 1$ **7.** $y > -x + 1$ **9.** $y < -x + 1$ **11.** $y > -x + 1$ **13.** $y > 2x - 1$ **15.** $y > 2x - 1$ **17.** $y < 2x - 1$ **19.** $y > 2x - 1$ **21.** $y < 2x - 1$ **23.** $y > 2x - 1$ **25.** $x + y < 2$ **27.** $x + y > 2$; $x + y < 2$ **29.** Region A: $y < \dfrac{-x}{2} + 1$; Region B: $y > \dfrac{-x}{2} + 1$ **31.** Region A: $x + y < 2$; Region B: $x + y > 2$ **B 33.** Region A: $x + y < 0$; Region B: $x + y > 0$

35.

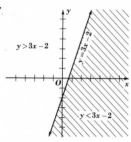

Pages 333–335   Written Exercises   A 1. $y \leq x + 1$ **3.** $y \geq x + 1$ **5.** both   **7.** $y \leq x + 1$ **9.** both

11. $y \leq x + 1$ **13.** $y \geq x + 1$ **15.** $y \leq x - 2$ **17.** $y \leq \dfrac{x}{2} + 1$

19.

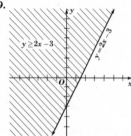

21.

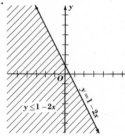

23.

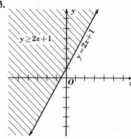

B 25.

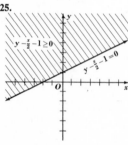

27.

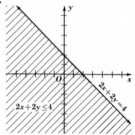

C 29.

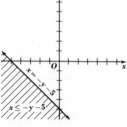

Pages 337–338   Written Exercises   A 1. 5   **3.** -3 **5.** -1 **7.** -6 **9.** $y = x + 3$; 3   **11.** $y = x - 3$; -3 **13.** $y = -2x + 5$; 5   **15.** $y = 0x - \frac{3}{2}$; $-\frac{3}{2}$ **17.** $y = -x - 1$; -1 **B 19.** $y = \dfrac{x}{3} + 2$; 2   **21.** $y = 2x - 2$; -2 **C 23.** $y = 1.5x + 0.75$; 0.75   **25.** $y = -\frac{7}{3}x - \frac{10}{3}$; $-\frac{10}{3}$

Pages 339–340   Written Exercises   A 1. $y = -3x + 4$; slope $= -3$; y-intercept $= 4$ **3.** $y = 2x + 3$; slope $= 2$; y-intercept $= 3$ **5.** $y = \frac{3}{2}x + 2$; slope $= \frac{3}{2}$; y-intercept $= 2$ **7.** $y = 0x + 4$; slope $= 0$; y-intercept $= 4$ **9.** $y = \frac{3}{4}x - 2$; slope $= \frac{3}{4}$; y-intercept $= -2$ **11.** $y = -\frac{1}{4}x + \frac{3}{2}$; slope $= -\frac{1}{4}$; y-intercept $= \frac{3}{2}$ **13.** $y = 2x + 5$ **15.** $y = -3x$ **17.** $y = \frac{1}{3}x + 8$ **19.** $y = -\frac{1}{3}x + 2$ **21.** $y = -3$ **B 23.** $y = 2x - 3$ **25.** $y = -x - 1$

C 27.

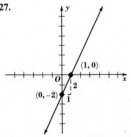

29.

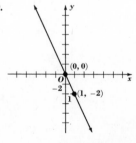

Pages 343–345

A 1. {(0, 4), (0, −4), (4, 0), (−4, 0)}

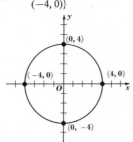

3. {(0, 3), (0, −3), (3, 0), (−3, 0)}

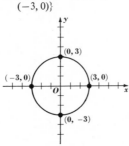

5. {(0, 3), (0, −3), (6, 0), (−6, 0)}

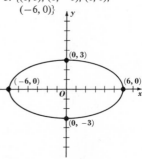

7. {(0, 4), (0, −4), (12, 0) (−12, 0)}

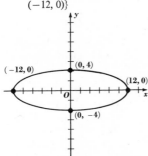

9. {(0, 0), (1, 2), (2, 8), (−1, 2), (−2, 8)}

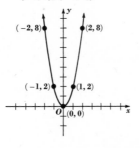

11. {(0, 0), (1, ½), (2, 2), (−1, ½), (−2, 2)}

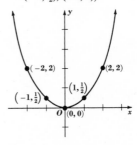

Pages 347–348 **Written Exercises** **1. a.** July **b.** first 3 months **c.** July and August **d.** April and May **e.** yes

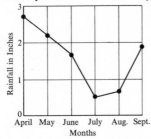

3. a. Africa, 11.5 million square miles; Antarctica, 5.5 million square miles; Asia; 17 million square miles; Australia, 3 million square miles; Europe, 3.7 million square miles; North America, 9.4 million square miles; South America, 6.8 million square miles **b.** Australia; Asia **c.** Australia **d.** Australia, Europe, Antarctica, South America, North America, Africa, Asia **e.** {(Asia, 17.0), (Africa, 11.5), (North America, 9.4), (South America, 6.8), (Europe, 3.7), (Australia, 3.0), (Antarctica, 5.5)}

Pages 349–350 **Chapter Test** **1.** $y > -2x + 1$ **3.** $y \geq -2x + 3$ **5.** $y = x$ **7.–12.** Answers will vary. **7.** (1, 4); (0, 2) **9.** (1, −1); (1, 1) **11.** (0, 3); (2, 4)

13.

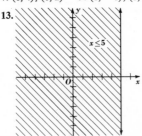

$x \leq 5$

15.

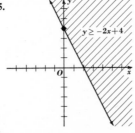

$y \geq -2x + 4$

17.

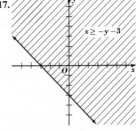

$x \geq -y - 3$

19. $y = -2x + 5$; slope $= -2$; y-intercept $= 5$ **21.** $y = \frac{3}{2}x + 3$; slope $= \frac{3}{2}$; y-intercept $= 3$

23.

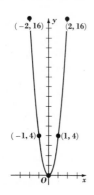

25.

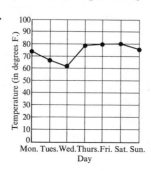

Pages 350–352   Chapter Review   1. $y > -8x + 10$ **3.** $y \geq 3x + 6$ **5.–8.** Answers will vary.
5. $(0, -2); (1, 2); (-1, 6)$ **7.** $(-5, 1); (0, 0); (5, -1)$

9.

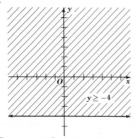

11.

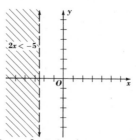

13. $(0, 0); (4, 0); (1, -3)$

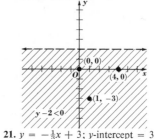

15. $y < x + 3$ **17.** $y \geq x - 2\frac{1}{2}$ **19.** $y = \frac{3}{2}x + 2$; y-intercept $= 2$ **21.** $y = -\frac{1}{3}x + 3$; y-intercept $= 3$
23. $y = \frac{1}{2}x - 4$; slope $= \frac{1}{2}$; y-intercept $= -4$

25.

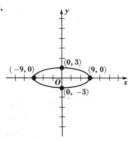

27.

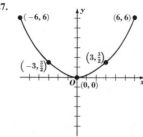

Pages 352–353   Review of Skills   1. $2x + 8y$ **3.** $4a - 2b$ **5.** $2x + 3$ **7.** $x - 2y$ **9.** $4n$ **11.** $8a$
13. $n = 13$ **15.** $n = 10$ **17.** $\overline{AB}$ and $\overline{CD}$; $\overline{BC}$ and $\overline{AD}$ **19.** $\overline{WZ}$ and $\overline{XY}$ **21.** sometimes intersect
23. 20   **25.** -1 **27.** 1   **29.** add. property of equality   **31.** mult. property of equality

Pages 354–355   Check Point for Experts

1. invalid   **3.** valid

5.

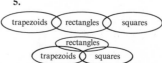

7.

Chapter 11.   Systems of Open Sentences

Pages 360–361   Written Exercises A 1. parallel   **3.** coincide   **5.** coincide   **7.** coincide   **9.** parallel
11. inconsistent   **13.** equivalent   **15.** equivalent

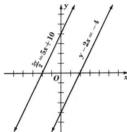   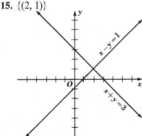   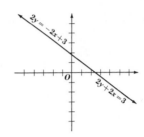

B 17. inconsistent

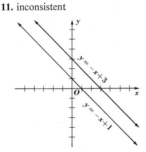

Pages 362–363   Written Exercises A 1. satisfies the first but not the second   **3.** satisfies the first but not
the second   **5.** satisfies both   **7.** $(2, -2)$ **9.** $(2, -1)$ **11.** $(-1, -1)$

13. $\{(1, 1)\}$ **15.** $\{(2, 1)\}$ **17.** $\emptyset$

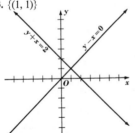   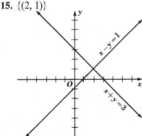   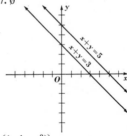

B 19. The set of all ordered pairs   **21.** $\{(0, 5)\}$ **23.** $\{(-1, -\frac{2}{3})\}$
(x, y) such that $y = x - 2$

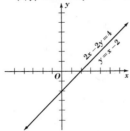   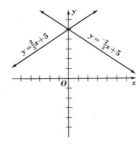   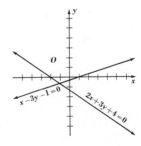

Pages 364–365   Problems

1. 15 and 12

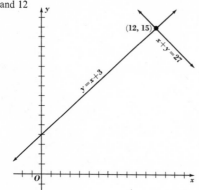

3. 11 and 3

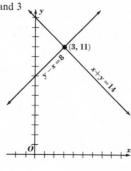

5. $8.00 and $3.00

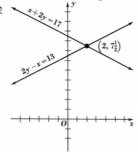

7. $5\frac{3}{4}$ feet and $1\frac{3}{4}$ feet

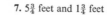

B 9. length = 12 yards
width = 8 yards

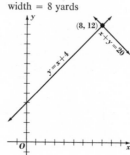

11. $7\frac{1}{2}$ and 2

Pages 368–369   Written Exercises A 1. $\{(3, 2)\}$ **3.** $\{(3, 1)\}$ **5.** $\{(45,29)\}$ **7.** $\{(1, -2)\}$ **9.** $\{(0, -2)\}$
11. $\{(-1, -\frac{3}{2})\}$ **13.** $\{(1, 3)\}$ **15.** $\{(-3, 4)\}$ **B 17.** $\{(-\frac{4}{3}, -\frac{4}{9})\}$ **19.** $\{(17, 21)\}$ **21.** $\{(\frac{22}{3}, \frac{16}{3})\}$
23. $\{(2, -\frac{1}{2})\}$

Pages 369–370   Problems A 1. $y = 9x$; $x + y = 75$ **3.** $x + y = 24$; $y = 6x$ **5.** $x + y = 90$;
$y = x + 30$ **B 7.** $l + w = 72$; $l = 12 + w$; length = 42 feet; width = 30 feet   **9.** $2x - y = 21$; $2y + x = 27$; 12 and 3

Page 373   Written Exercises A 1. $\{(3, 2)\}$ **3.** $\{(2, 2)\}$ **5.** $\{(4, -\frac{1}{2})\}$ **7.** $\{(17, 11)\}$ **9.** $\{(0, 2)\}$
11. $\{(2, -3)\}$ **13.** $\{(9, 0)\}$ **B 15.** $\{(\frac{1}{2}, \frac{1}{3})\}$ **17.** $\{(2, 3)\}$

Page 374   Problems   1. $f + s = 30$; $2f - 3s = 5$; 19 and 11   **3.** $3e + 2p = 34$; $4e + 5p = 57$: the erasers
cost $.08 and the pencils cost $.05.   **5.** $2c + 3b = 310$; $1c + 2b = 185$; the cola costs 65¢ per carton and the
potato chips cost 60¢.

Pages 375–376   Written Exercises   A 1. $\{(1, 2)\}$ **3.** $\{(1, 1)\}$ **5.** $\{(1, 5)\}$ **7.** $\{(9, 7)\}$ **9.** $\{(1, 2)\}$
11. $\{(5, 5)\}$ **13.** $\{(-\frac{3}{4}, \frac{13}{12})\}$ **15.** $\{(3, 1)\}$ **B 17.** $\{(\frac{33}{5}, \frac{22}{5})\}$ **19.** $\{(6, 3)\}$ **C 21.** $\{(18, 10)\}$ **23.** $\{(5, 2)\}$

Page 376   Problems   1. 0 and 5   **3.** $\frac{1}{3}$ and $\frac{4}{3}$ **5.** 12 and 16

Pages 378–379   Written Exercises   A 1.–4. Answers will vary.   **1.** (3, 1), (4, 3), (−1, 6) are in the solution set; (3, −1), (4, −3), (−1, −6) are not.   **3.** (0, 0), (−1, 1), (−1, −1) are in the solution set; (4, 1), (5, 2), and (6, 3) are not.

5.
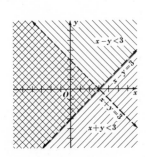

7.
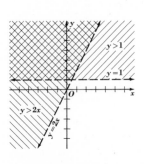

9.
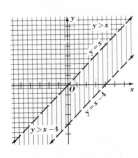

11.
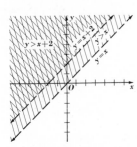

B 13.
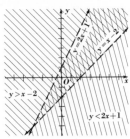

15.
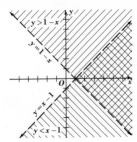

17.
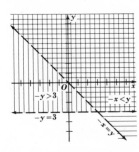

C 19. $y > x - 2$
$y > -\frac{4}{3}x + 4$

Page 381   Written Exercises

A 1.
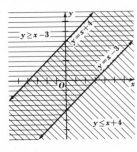

3.
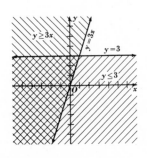

5.
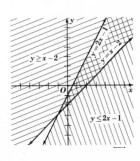

7.

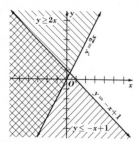

9.

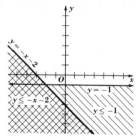

B 11.–18. Answers will vary.

11. (1, 1), (2, 2), (−1, 3) are in the solution set; (1, −1), (2, −2), and (−1, −3) are not.

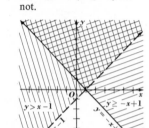

13. (1, −2), (4, 3), and (1, 1) are in the solution set; (0, 0), (0, 5), and (−1, 2) are not.

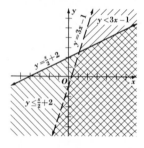

15. (−1, 2), (−1, 0) and (−1, −1) are in the solution set; (2, 1), (3, 2) and (1, 1) are not.

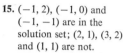
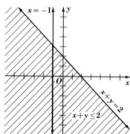

17. (1, 1), (0, 1) and (3, 0) are in the solution set; (0, 0), (1, −1), and (2, 3) are not.

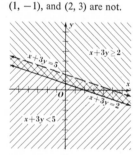

C 19. $y \le 3$
$y \ge x - 1$

Pages 382–383   Chapter Test

1. $\{(-2, 4)\}$

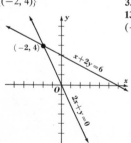

3. $\{(-4, 5)\}$ **5.** $\{(2, -1)\}$ **7.** line   **9.** equivalent   **11.** $y = x + 2$
13. 2   **15.** Answers will vary; (4, 0); (2, 3); (3, 1)   **17.** Answers will vary; (−1, 5); (−2, 6); (−3, 7)

Pages 384–385 **Chapter Review** **1.** parallel lines **3.** parallel lines
5. equivalent **7.** solution **9.** $\{(-2, -1)\}$ **11.** $\{(0, -4)\}$

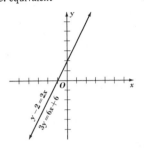
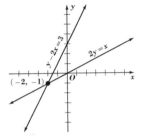
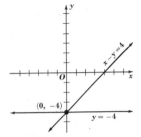

13. $9\frac{1}{4}$ feet; $6\frac{3}{4}$ feet **15.** $\{(5\frac{1}{2}, 2\frac{1}{2})\}$ **17.** $\{(7, 6)\}$ **19.** $\{(2, -2)\}$ **21.** $\{(6, -4)\}$ **23.** $\{(1, 1)\}$

25.

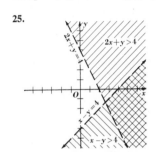

27.

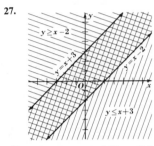

29.

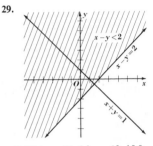

Pages 385–387 **Review of Skills** **1.** $0.\overline{3}$ **3.** 0.375 **5.** 1.75 **7.** 0.39 **9.** 73.1 **11.** 5.3 **13.** 15.0
15. n^3 **17.** 4 **19.** $\frac{1}{8}$ **21.** $\frac{11}{2}$ **23.** $\frac{5}{100}$ **25.** $\frac{18}{2}$ **27.** 6.25 square feet **29.** 314 square inches
31. surface area $= 600$ square centimeters; $V = 1000$ cubic centimeters **33.** legs: $\overline{AC}$ and $\overline{BC}$; hypotenuse is
$\overline{AB}$ **35.** legs: $\overline{DE}$ and $\overline{CE}$; hypotenuse is $\overline{CD}$ **37.** 18 centimeters **39.** $x - 1$ **41.** $x + 4$ **43.** $\{-5, -2\}$
45. $\{-\frac{1}{2}, 3\}$

Pages 387–389 **Check Point for Experts** **1.** 2 **3.** 0 **5.** 2 **7.** 1 **9.** 2 **11.** yes, 0 **13.** yes;
$a \oplus (b \oplus c) = (a \oplus b) \oplus c$ **15.** 4 **17.** 0 **19.** 1

Chapter 12. The Real Number System

Pages 393–394 **Written Exercises** **A 1.** $t = 15$ **3.** $x = 4$ **5.** $b = 12$ **7.** $s = -2$ **9.** $a = 11$
11. $m = 1$ **13.–24.** Answers will vary. **13.** $\frac{50}{10}$ **15.** $\frac{5}{4}$ **17.** $\frac{1}{2}$ **19.** $\frac{-18}{-2}$ **21.** $\frac{4}{9}$ **23.** $\frac{-8}{32}$
25.–39. Answers will vary. **25.** $\frac{13}{40}, \frac{14}{40}, \frac{15}{40}$ **27.** $8\frac{1}{6}, 8\frac{4}{6}, 8\frac{5}{6}$ **29.** $43\frac{1}{8}, 43\frac{3}{8}, 43\frac{5}{8}$ **31.** $\frac{9}{16}, \frac{10}{16}, \frac{11}{16}$ **33.** $\frac{5}{8}, \frac{6}{8},$
$\frac{7}{8}$ **B 35.** $\frac{-11}{40}, \frac{-12}{40}, \frac{-13}{40}$ **37.** $\frac{50}{56}, \frac{51}{56}, \frac{52}{56}$ **39.** $\frac{1}{400}, \frac{2}{400}, \frac{3}{400}$ **41.** some **43.** some **C 45.–48.** Answers
may vary. **45.** $\frac{9}{20}, \frac{10}{20}, \frac{11}{20}$ **47.** $\frac{29}{400}, \frac{30}{400}, \frac{31}{400}$

Pages 396–397 **Written Exercises** **A 1.–12.** Answers may vary. **1.** $\frac{7}{10}$ **3.** $\frac{15}{10}$ **5.** $\frac{-2}{3}$ **7.** $\frac{9}{5}$ **9.** $\frac{5}{1000}$
11. $\frac{9}{10,000}$ **13.** 0.8 **15.** -0.875 **17.** -0.4 **19.** -0.005 **21.** -0.0027 **B 22.–27.** Answers may vary.
23. $0.91, 0.92, 0.93$ **25.** $0.1531, 0.1532, 0.1533$ **27.** $0.34, 0.35, 0.36$ **C 29.** all **31.** some

Pages 398–399 **Written Exercises** **A 1.** 5 **3.** 12 **5.** 9 **7.** 20 **9.** $\frac{3}{7}$ **11.** 0.6 **13.** $\frac{5}{9}$ **15.** $\frac{7}{6}$
17. $\{-\frac{1}{4}, \frac{1}{4}\}$ **19.** $\{-\frac{10}{13}, \frac{10}{13}\}$ **21.** $\{-0.3, 0.3\}$ **23.** $\{-\frac{1}{9}, \frac{1}{9}\}$ **25.** $\{-6, 6\}$ **27.** $\{-\frac{8}{9}, \frac{8}{9}\}$ **29.** $\frac{5}{3}$
31. 15 **33.** 8 **35.** 5 **37.** 10 **39.** $\pm\dfrac{r}{10}$ **B 41.** 16 **43.** ± 6 **45.** 7 **47.** $\pm\dfrac{m}{12}$ **49.** $-6y^3$ **51.** $\pm\dfrac{3m^4}{5}$

Page 401 **Written Exercises** **A 15.** 8 **17.** 14 **19.** 12 **21.** 2 **B 23.** $\sqrt{mn}$ **25.** $\sqrt{10y}$ **27.** $\sqrt{135c}$

Pages 404–405   Written Exercises

A 1.

n	n^3	n^4	n^5
1	1	1	1
2	8	16	32
3	27	81	243
4	64	256	1024
5	125	625	3125

3. 2   **5.** 10   **7.** -3 **9.** ± 4 **11.** 9   **13.** -6 **15.** 4   **17.** -5 **19.** -2 **21.** ± 10 **23.** 6   **25.** 3   **B 27.** >   **29.** >   **31.** >

Pages 406–407   Written Exercises   A 1. $\frac{2}{5}$ **3.** $\frac{5}{6}$ **5.** $\frac{1}{2}$

Page 410   Written Exercises   A 1. 14   **3.** 27   **5.** -21 **7.** 1369   **9.** 614,125   **11.** 48   **13.** 51   **15.** 6.16   **17.** 9.95   **19.** 7.81   **21.** 3.04   **23.** 8.39   **25.** 12.43   **B 27.** 0.99   **29.** 17.97   **31.** -11.64 **C 33.** 0.0

Pages 413–414   Problems   A 1. approximately 9.899 feet   **3.** 6 faces; area of each face is 15 square inches; length of each edge is approximately 3.873 inches   **5.** 3 feet   **7.** 2.4 feet by 2.4 feet by 2.4 feet   **9.** radius = 3.873 feet   **B 11.** radius of circle = 5 feet; diagonal = 10 feet

Pages 415–416   Written Exercises   A 1. could   **3.** could   **5.** could   **7.** could   **9.** could not   **11.** 25 inches   **13.** 21 feet   **15.** approximately 9.7 yards   **B 17.** 18.9 inches   **19.** 9.8 feet   **C 21.** length $\overline{DE}$ = length $\overline{EF}$ $\doteq$ 5.7 centimeters

Pages 416–417   Problems   1. approximately 19.078 feet above the ground   **3.** 18 feet above the ground   **5.** approximately 11.314 feet

Pages 418–419   Written Exercises   A 1. 8   **3.** 12   **5.** 12   **7.** 90   **9.** $5\sqrt{3}$ **11.** $10\sqrt{3}$ **13.** $\sqrt{5}$ **15.** $4\sqrt{3}$ **17.** $6\sqrt{6}$ **19.** 5.477   **21.** 14.14   **23.** 41.568   **25.** 4.472   **27.** 3.873   **B 29.** $\frac{1}{3}\sqrt{6}$ **31.** $\frac{3}{5}\sqrt{15}$ **33.** $\frac{1}{3}\sqrt{15}$ **35.** $6c\sqrt{2}$ **37.** $\frac{3}{2}\sqrt{3}$ **39.** $15ab$

Pages 420–421   Written Exercises   A 1. $19\sqrt{10}$ **3.** $-11\sqrt{5}$ **5.** $-3\sqrt{2}$ **7.** $-3\sqrt{13}$ **9.** $-3\sqrt{y}$ **11.** $3\sqrt{5} + \sqrt{2}$ **13.** $3\sqrt{2}$ **16.** $4\sqrt{2}$ **17.** $\sqrt{2}$ **19.** $20\sqrt{3} - 4\sqrt{2}$ **21.** $-2\sqrt{2}$ **B 23.** $\frac{4}{3}\sqrt{6}$ **25.** $\frac{17}{2}\sqrt{6}$ **27.** $12\sqrt{15}$ **C 29.** $-\frac{17}{2}\sqrt{10}$ **31.** $\frac{3}{2}\sqrt{10}$

Pages 422–423   Chapter Test   1. rational   **3.** rational   **5.** rational   **7.** $\{-30, 30\}$ **9.** $\{-3\}$ **11.** $\doteq$ **13.** $\doteq$ **15.** 20   **17.** 120   **19.** $\frac{7}{20}\sqrt{10}$ **21.** $5\sqrt{5}$ **23.–26.** Answers may vary.   **23.** 0.061, 0.062, 0.063   **25.** $-8\frac{1}{4}, -8\frac{1}{2}, -8\frac{3}{4}$ **27.** rational; irrational   **29.** no   **31.** 15 inches

Pages 423–425   Chapter Review   1.–8. Answers may vary   **1.** $\dfrac{-16}{2}$ **3.** $\frac{25}{1}$ **5.** $9\frac{1}{2}, 9\frac{1}{4}$ **7.** $\frac{17}{160}, \frac{18}{160}$ **9.** 0.9   **11.** 0.6   **13.** $\dfrac{327}{10,000}$ **15.** $\dfrac{-9}{10,000}$ **17.** 16   **19.** $\frac{4}{9}$ **21.** -4 **23.** $\pm 1\frac{2}{13}$ **25.** 5   **27.** $\pm \dfrac{x}{5}$ **29.** $7\sqrt{5}$ **31.** 3   **33.** $2s, s \geq 0$ **35.** 5   **37.** 4   **39.** ± 5 **41.** $\frac{3}{5}$ **43.** $\frac{3}{10}$ **45.** 6   **47.** 3.936   **49.** 8.944   **51.** ± 8.246 **53.** 9.274 feet by 9.274 feet   **55.** 11.3 inches   **57.** 9.7 centimeters   **59.** $5\sqrt{3}$ **61.** $10\sqrt{5}$ **63.** $\sqrt{7}$ **65.** $14\sqrt{3}$ **67.** $6\sqrt{2}$

Pages 426–427   Review of Skills   1. $\{-8, 8\}$ **3.** $\{-5, 5\}$ **5.** $\{-20, 20\}$ **7.** $x^2 + 2xy + y^2$ **9.** $s^2 - 9$ **11.** $m^2 + 6m + 9$ **13.** $(x + 4)^2$ **15.** $(a + x)^2$ **17.** $(t - \frac{1}{2})^2$ **19.** x^3 **21.** $(x + 2)^2$ **23.** $(-2)^3$ **25.** $A = 4r^2 + 6r$ **27.** $A = 4x^2 + 12x + 9$ **29.** $x^2 + 3x - 10; (x + 5)(x - 2)$ **31.** $2(2t + 1)(2t - 1)$

33.

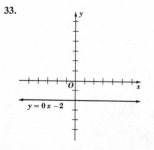

$y = 0x - 2$

35.

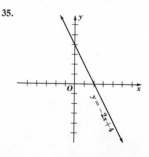

$y = -2x + 4$

37.

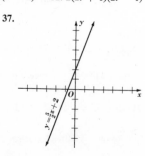

$y = \frac{5}{2}x + 2$

Pages 427–429 **Check Point for Experts** **1.** $3 \oplus 3$ **3.** $2 \oplus 2 \oplus 2 \oplus 2$ **5.** $1 \oplus 1 \oplus 1 \oplus 1$

7.

$\otimes$	0	1	2	3	4
0	0	0	0	0	0
1	0	1	2	3	4
2	0	2	4	1	3
3	0	3	1	4	2
4	0	4	3	2	1

25. a.

$\otimes$	0	1	2	3	4	5	6
0	0	0	0	0	0	0	0
1	0	1	2	3	4	5	6
2	0	2	4	6	1	3	5
3	0	3	6	2	5	1	4
4	0	4	1	5	2	6	3
5	0	5	3	1	6	4	2
6	0	6	5	4	3	2	1

9. 1   **11.** 2   **13.** 3   **15.** 1   **17.** $2 \otimes 3 = 1$
19. $3 \otimes 0 = 0$ **21.** $3 \otimes 4 = 2$ **23.** yes; $(a \otimes b) \otimes c = a \otimes (b \otimes c)$

b. identity element is 1   **c.** yes; yes; $a \otimes b = b \otimes a$; $(a \otimes b) \otimes c = a \otimes (b \otimes c)$

Chapter 13. Products, Roots and Quadratic Equations

Page 433 **Written Exercises** **A 1.** C   **3.** A   **5.** B   **7.** -1 **9.** $11 + 6\sqrt{2}$ **11.** -1 **13.** 2
15. $32 + 10\sqrt{7}$ **17.** $27 - 16\sqrt{3}$ **B 19.** $21 - 10\sqrt{3}$ **21.** -29 **23.** $35 - 10\sqrt{10}$ **25.** $12\sqrt{3} + 6\sqrt{2}$
C 27. $15 + 6\sqrt{2}$ **29.** $\dfrac{\sqrt{7} - 2}{3}$ **31.** $\dfrac{3\sqrt{3} + 3}{2}$ **33.** $\dfrac{5\sqrt{6} + 6}{19}$

Page 435 **Written Exercises** **A 1.** $\sqrt{x} = 4$ **3.** $\sqrt{2a} = 2$ **5.** $\sqrt{3z} = 1$ **7.** $\{16\}$ **9.** $\{81\}$ **11.** $\{\frac{1}{2}\}$
13. $\{\frac{7}{4}\}$ **15.** $\{4\}$ **17.** $\{3\}$ **19.** $\{15\}$ **21.** $\{18\}$ **23.** $\{-3\}$ **25.** $\{10\}$ **27.** $\{12\}$ **C 29.** $\{1\}$ **31.** $\{7\}$
33. $\{4\}$

Page 436 **Problems** **1.** 16   **3.** 144   **5.** 36   **7.** length = 13 inches; width = 3 inches

Pages 438–439 **Written Exercises** **A 1.** $2\sqrt{3}$ **3.** 18   **5.** 20   **7.** 54   **9.** 500   **11.** $4\sqrt{3}$ **13.** 63
15. $-10\sqrt{5}$ **17.** $\{-9, 9\}$ **19.** $\emptyset$ **21.** $\left\{\dfrac{-1}{5}, \dfrac{1}{5}\right\}$ **23.** $\{-0.5, 0.5\}$ **25.** $\{-\sqrt{15}, \sqrt{15}\}$ **27.** $\{-\frac{2}{3}, \frac{2}{3}\}$
29. $\{-\frac{2}{3}, \frac{2}{3}\}$ **31.** $\{-4, 4\}$ **33.** $\left\{\dfrac{-1}{6}, \dfrac{1}{6}\right\}$ **35.** $\left\{\dfrac{-1}{8}, \dfrac{1}{8}\right\}$ **37.** $\emptyset$ **39.** $\left\{\dfrac{-1}{6}, \dfrac{1}{6}\right\}$ **B 41.** $\{-\sqrt{21}, \sqrt{21}\}$
43. $\{-5\sqrt{5}, 5\sqrt{5}\}$ **45.** $\{-10, 10\}$ **47.** $\emptyset$

Pages 440–441 **Written Exercises** **A 1.** $\{-3, 7\}$ **3.** $\{7, -13\}$ **5.** $\left\{\dfrac{-2}{5}, \dfrac{8}{5}\right\}$ **7.** $\{-5, 1\}$ **9.** $\{-5\frac{2}{3}, 6\frac{1}{3}\}$
11. $\{2, 10\}$ **13.** $\{-16, 2\}$ **15.** $\{-\frac{1}{2}, 1\frac{1}{2}\}$ **17.** $\{-18, -6\}$ **B 19.** $\{6 - \sqrt{5}, 6 + \sqrt{5}\}$ **21.** $\{-2\frac{1}{3}, 1\frac{2}{3}\}$
23. $\{4 - 2\sqrt{6}, 4 + 2\sqrt{6}\}$ **25.** $\left\{\dfrac{-10}{9}, \dfrac{8}{9}\right\}$ **C 27.** $\{-5, 0, 5\}$ **29.** $\{-4, 0, 4\}$

Page 442 **Written Exercises** **A 1.** 1; $\{-4, 6\}$ **3.** 4; $\{-5, 1\}$ **5.** 16; $\{-11, 3\}$ **7.** 16; $\{-2, 10\}$
9. 25; $\{-9, -1\}$ **11.** 16; $(n + 4)^2$ **13.** $\frac{1}{4}$; $(y + \frac{1}{2})^2$ **15.** 25; $(m - 5)^2$ **17.** 9; $(x - 3)^2$ **19.** 0.36;
$(z + 0.6)^2$ **B 21.** $\{-2\sqrt{2} - 1, 2\sqrt{2} - 1\}$ **23.** $\{4 - \sqrt{14}, 4 + \sqrt{14}\}$ **25.** $\{1, 17\}$ **27.** $\{5 - \sqrt{30},$
$5 + \sqrt{30}\}$ **C 29.** $\left\{\dfrac{-2}{3}, 0\right\}$ **31.** $\left\{\dfrac{-3}{2}, 0\right\}$

Page 443 **Problems** **1.** width = 8 inches; length = 10 inches   **3.** 6 or -18

Pages 445–446 **Written Exercises** **A 1.** $\frac{2}{3}$ **3.** $\dfrac{4 - \sqrt{11}}{3}$ **5.** $\dfrac{4 + \sqrt{6}}{5}$ **7.** $3 + \sqrt{2}$ **9.** $\{1, -7\}$
11. $\{5, 2\}$ **13.** $\{2, -4\}$ **15.** $\{5\}$ **17.** $\{2, -5\}$ **B 19.** $\{\sqrt{5}, -\sqrt{5}\}$ **21.** $\left\{\dfrac{-5 + \sqrt{13}}{6}, \dfrac{-5 - \sqrt{13}}{6}\right\}$
C 23. $\{\frac{2}{5}, \frac{1}{4}\}$ **25.** $\left\{\dfrac{3 + \sqrt{17}}{4}, \dfrac{3 - \sqrt{17}}{4}\right\}$

Page 447   **Chapter Test**   **1.** 15   **3.** $\sqrt{15} + 6$ **5.** $\{100\}$ **7.** $\{8\}$ **9.** $\{-2\sqrt{3}, 2\sqrt{3}\}$ **11.** $\{-18, 8\}$
13. $\{-8, 12\}$ **15.** 121; $(x + 11)^2$ **17.** 1; $(m - 1)^2$ **19.** $ax^2 + bx + c = 0$; $ax^2 + c = 0$ **21.** $\{-10, -2\}$
23. $\{10 - \sqrt{110}, 10 + \sqrt{110}\}$ **25.** $\left\{\dfrac{2 + \sqrt{10}}{3}, \dfrac{2 - \sqrt{10}}{3}\right\}$ **27.** $\left\{\dfrac{-1 + \sqrt{13}}{2}, \dfrac{-1 - \sqrt{13}}{2}\right\}$ **29.** $\{2, -2\}$

Pages 448–449   **Chapter Review**   **1.** 44   **3.** 11   **5.** $\{81\}$ **7.** $\{48\}$ **9.** $\{25\}$ **11.** $\{9\}$ **13.** $\{-20, 20\}$
15. $\{-7, 7\}$ **17.** $\{-4, 4\}$ **19.** $\{1, 11\}$ **21.** $\{-1, 17\}$ **23.** $\{-1, 5\}$ **25.** 36   **27.** 144   **29.** 9; $\{-10, 4\}$
31. 16; $\{-7, -1\}$ **33.** 144; $\{-25, 1\}$ **35.** width = 18 feet; length = 20 feet   **37.** $\left\{\dfrac{3 + \sqrt{29}}{2}, \dfrac{3 - \sqrt{29}}{2}\right\}$
39. $\{-3 + 2\sqrt{3}, -3 - 2\sqrt{3}\}$

Pages 449–450   **Review of Skills**   **1.** yes   **3.** no   **5.** no   **7.** $\overline{AB}, \overline{BC}, \overline{CD}, \overline{AD}$ **9.** $\overline{MN}, \overline{NR}, \overline{RS}, \overline{ST}, \overline{MT}$
11. 180°   **13.** 90°   **15.** $\frac{1}{10}$ **17.** $\frac{2}{5}$ **19.** $\frac{4}{5}$ **21.** 5%   **23.** 20%   **25.** $12\frac{1}{2}$%   **27.** $62\frac{1}{2}$%   **29.** $\overline{RT}$
31. $2x(2x + 3)$ **33.** $(x + 3)(x - 3)$ **35.** $2(x + 3)(x + 1)$ **37.** $4(n + 3m)$ **39.** $2y(x + 2)(x - 2)$
41. $\dfrac{-y}{7}$

Chapter 14.   Polygons and Circles

Pages 456–457   **Written Exercises**   **A 1.**   **3.**   **5.**

7. $\overline{EH}, \overline{DF}$ **9.** $\overline{CE}, \overline{AD}, \overline{BD}$ **11.** $\angle JKL, \angle KLM, \angle LMN, \angle MNJ, \angle NJK$ **B 13.** $\overline{QS}$ **15.** $\overline{PQ}, \overline{QR}$;
$\overline{QR}, \overline{RS}$; $\overline{SR}, \overline{ST}$; $\overline{ST}, \overline{PT}$; $\overline{PT}, \overline{PQ}$ **17.** M

C 19.   **21.**

Pages 460–462   **Written Exercises**   **A 1.** 540°   **3.** 360°   **5.** 540°   **7.** 720°   **9.** 1800°   **11.** 1440°
13. Perimeter = 90 centimeters; $m\overline{QR}$ = 15 centimeters; $m\angle QPM$ = 120°; $m\overline{MT}$ = 15 centimeters; $m\angle STM$ =
120°   **B 15.** 140°   **17.** 135°   **C 19.** 10   **21.** 6   **23.** 9 diagonals   **25.** 20 diagonals

Page 464   **Written Exercises**   **1.–4.** Answers may vary.

1.   **3.**

Pages 466–468   **Written Exercises**   **A 1.** 72°   **3.** 90°   **5.** 100°   **7.** 70°   **9.** 170°   **11.** 110°   **13.** 140°
15. 95°   **17.** B   **19.** A   **B 21.** 90° since $m\angle COE$ = 90°   **23.** Radii of the same circle have equal lengths.
25. 45°; 45°; $\triangle AOC$ is an isosceles right triangle.   **27.** $m\angle AOC = m\angle COE$ since both are right angles; equal
central angles intercept arcs of equal measure.

Pages 470–473 Written Exercises A 1. $\frac{5}{18}$ **3.** $\frac{1}{8}$ **5.** $\frac{3}{20}$ **7.** 72° **9.** 135° **11.** 120° **13.** 36° **15.** 18°
B 17. $\frac{3}{4}$; 135° **19.** $\frac{2}{3}$; 120° **21.** $\frac{5}{6}$, 150° **23.** 161° **25.** 210° **27.** 273° **29.** 75% **31.** 55% **33.** 2%

Pages 473–474 Problems A 1. a. 100% **b.** 90°; 120°; 36° **c.** 8 hours; 6 hours; approximately 8 hours
3. a. 45°; 90°; 45° **b.** 10,000 barrels; 5000 barrels

B 5.

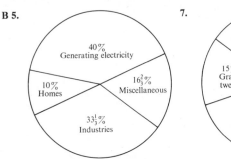

7.

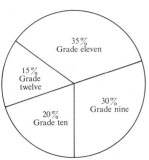

Pages 477–478 Written Exercises A 1. 31° **3.** 43° **5.** 15°; 32° **7.** 96° **9.** 220° **11.** 57°; 50°
B 13. $m\angle 1 = 35°$; $m\angle 2 = 35°$ **15.** $m\angle 1 = 15°$; $m\angle 2 = 34°$; $m\overset{\frown}{BDF} = 98°$; $m\overset{\frown}{BAF} = 262°$ **17.** $m\overset{\frown}{CDE} =$ 70°; $m\angle 1 = 35°$; $m\overset{\frown}{ABC} = 110°$; $m\angle 3 = 55°$; $m\overset{\frown}{AFE} = 180°$; $m\angle 2 = 90°$; $m\angle 1 + m\angle 2 + m\angle 3 = 180°$; $m\overset{\frown}{CDE} + m\overset{\frown}{ABC} + m\overset{\frown}{AFE} = 360°$ **C 19.** 108°; 216°

Pages 479–480 Written Exercises A 1. $m\angle 1 = 35°$; $m\angle 2 = 55°$; $m\angle 3 = 90°$; $\angle 3$ is a right angle. $\triangle PQR$ is a right triangle. The hypotenuse of $\triangle PQR$ is a diameter of circle P. $m\overset{\frown}{PQR} = 180°$; $m\overset{\frown}{PSR} = 180°$
3. $m\overset{\frown}{ETG} = 90°$; $m\overset{\frown}{GRH} = 90°$; $m\angle 1 = 45°$; $m\angle 2 = 90°$; $m\angle 3 = 45°$ **B 5.** $m\angle PRQ = 90°$; $m\overset{\frown}{QR} =$ 12 inches; perimeter of $\triangle PQR = 30$ inches; area of $\triangle PQR = 30$ square inches

Pages 482–483 Chapter Test 1. 720° **3.** 35 inches **5.** 80° **7.** 120° **9.** $\frac{1}{9}$ **11.** 150° **13.** 120°

Pages 483–485 Chapter Review 1. 2 **3.** 3 **5.** $\overline{AB}, \overline{BC}$; $\overline{BC}, \overline{CD}$; $\overline{CD}, \overline{DE}$; $\overline{DE}, \overline{AE}$; $\overline{AE}, \overline{AB}$ **7.** true
9. false **11.** false **13.** C **15.** B **17.** E **19.** 360° **21.** 50° **23.** 95° **25.** 45°; 45° **27.** 144°
29. 120° **31.** 72° **33.** 15° **35.** 180° **37.** 90° **39.** 8 inches

Page 486 Review of Skills 1. 0.4167 **3.** 0.7060 **5.** 0.2650 **7.** 0.1414 **9.** $x = 15$ **11.** $n = 12$
13. $y = 15.7$ **15.** $t = 10$ **17.** $a = 6$ **19.** $r = 56$ **21.** $x = 6$ **23.** $y = 6$ **25.** $\frac{7}{3}; \frac{7}{4}; \frac{2}{1}$

Chapter 15. Ratios and Similar Right Triangles

Pages 492–493 Written Exercises A 1. 18 **3.** 47 **5.** 7.5 **7.** 4 **9.** 8 **11.** 5 **B 19.** $m\overline{NT} = 21$
inches; $m\overline{NS} = 7$ inches; $m\overline{NR} = 7$ inches **21.** $m\angle BHT = 85°$; $m\angle BTH = 70°$; $m\angle BGK = 70°$

Pages 495–496 Written Exercises A 1. 65° **3.** $B'D'$ **5.** $B'C'D'$ **7.** $\frac{2}{3}$ **9.** $\frac{2}{3}$ **11.** $A'B'C'$; ratio
B 13. $m\overline{AB} = 9$ inches; $m\overline{DF} = 100$ inches **C 15.** $m\overline{EG} = 5$ inches; $m\overline{HK} = 1.5$ inches; $m\overline{KL} = 2$ inches

Pages 500–501 Written Exercises A 1. $n = 31°$ **3.** $a = 50°$ **5.** $m\overline{EF} = 68.2$ feet **7.** $m\overline{CE} = 10.0$ feet
B 9. $z = 55°$; $x = 5.7$ feet; $y = 8.2$ feet **11.** $s = 45°$; $t = 69.3$ feet **C 13.** $\dfrac{\sqrt{2}}{2}$ **15.** $\dfrac{\sqrt{3}}{2}$

Pages 503–505 Written Exercises A 1. $r = 32°$ **3.** $m = 86°$ **5.** $x = 38°$ **7.** $m\overline{BC} = 26.8$ inches
9. $m\overline{BZ} = 61.7$ inches **B 11.** $x = 60°$; $z = 21.7$ inches; $y = 12.5$ inches **13.** $b = 63°$; $a = 44.6$ inches; $c = 22.7$ inches **C 15.** $\cos 30° = \dfrac{\sqrt{3}}{2}$

Pages 506–507 Written Exercises A 1. 0.6428 **3.** 0.4384 **5.** 0.4226 **7.** 0.7071 **9.** 0.1045 **11.** $x = 35°$
13. $x = 85$ **15.** $x = 13$ **B 17.** $\cos 13° = 0.9744$ **19.** $\sin 77° = 0.9744$

Pages 508–509 Written Exercises A 1. $r = 22°$ **3.** $a = 14°$ **5.** $m = 58°$ **7.** $m\overline{NT} = 13.5$ yards
9. $m\overline{AC} = 20.0$ feet **B 11.** $x = 45°$; $y = 8$ cm.; $z = 11.3$ cm. **13.** $r = 53°$; $t = 12.0$ in.; $s = 20.0$ in.

Page 509 **Problems** **1.** 6 miles above the ground **3.** 48.8 feet

Page 511 **Chapter Test** **1.** BC **3.** RTS **5.** AB **7.** $\dfrac{m\overline{CD}}{m\overline{BC}}$ **9.** true **11.** false **13.** 30° **15.** 1° **17.** 1.010 ft. **19.** 28 in.

Pages 512–514 **Chapter Review** **1.** $n = 3$ **3.** $x = 45$ **5.** $n = 1$ **7.** $P'Q'$ **9.** $Q'R'$ **11.** PQR **13.** $\overline{BC}$ **15.** complementary **17.** $m\overline{AB} = 18$ inches **19.** $r = 18°$ **21.** $x = 27°$ **23.** $y = 60°$ **25.** $m\overline{RS} = 634.5$ feet **27.** 43° **29.** 53° **35.** $m\overline{BC} = 1.45$ inches **37.** $m\overline{RS} = 3.08$ feet

Pages 514–518 **Cumulative Test** **Part I** **(Chapters 1–8)** **1.** < **3.** = **5.** = **7.** < **9.** > **11.** negative **13.** 21 **15.** −3.7 **17.** D **19.** E **21.** A **23.** $\{-1, -2, -3, \ldots, -7\}$ **25.** $\{1, 2, 3, 4, 6, 12\}$

27. $n < 3$ 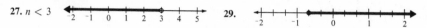 **29.**

31. $\{3\}$ **33.** $\{10\}$ **35.** $\{-4\}$ **37.** $y < -1$

39. $b \geq 1.5$ **41.** $y \geq -3$

43. $\{(-1, 3), (-2, 6), (-3, 11), (1, 3), (2, 6), (3, 11)\}$ **45.** −10 **47.** $\frac{7}{3}$ **49.** $-\frac{2}{5}$ **51.** $15y - 2x$ **53.** $13x^2 + 7y$ **55.** $4 - 8x$ **57.** $4.6a^2 - a - 1.9$ **59.** $-6mn + 7n$ **61.** $\{6\}$ **63.** $\{7\}$ **65.** $\{(1, 2), (1, 1), (1, -1), (0, 0), (0, -1), (0, 1), (1, 0), (-1, 0), (-1, -1), (-2, -1)\}$ **67.** $36x^4 - 12x^2 - 8x$ **69.** $9x^2 + 12x + 4$ **71.** $y - 3$ **73.** $(t + 5)(t - 5)$ **75.** $m(m - 3)^2$ **77.** $(b + 10)(b + 3)$ **79.** $9(t + 2)(t - 2)$ **81.** 0.6 **83.** $0.08\overline{3}$ **85.** 0.49 **87.** 21 **89.** 20% **91.** 137.5 **93.** $\dfrac{10t^2}{s}$ **95.** $\dfrac{2(m - n)}{3(m + n)}$ **97.** $\frac{1}{4}$ **99.** $\dfrac{x}{x - 3}$ **101.** $\frac{5}{6}$ **103.** $45x$ **105.** $\dfrac{ac}{b}$ **107.** 1 **109.** $\dfrac{t + 1}{t + 3}$ **111.** $\dfrac{1}{x + 3}$ **113.** $\dfrac{2y^2z}{a - 2}$ **115.** $\dfrac{1}{4y}$ **117.** $\dfrac{k - m + 1}{k^2 - m^2}$ **119.** $r = 2$ **121.** $y > -3$ **123.** $c = 9$

Pages 518–522 (1971 edition) **Cumulative Test** **Part II** **(Chapters 9–15)** **1.** $\{0, 3\}$ **3.** $\{-3, 6\}$ **5.** $\{3\}$ **7.** $3\frac{3}{7}$ hours **9.** $\{(1, 2), (2, 7), (0, -3), (-1, -8)\}$ **11.** $y = x - 19$ **13.** $(5, 0); (0, 5)$ **15.** $(-2, 0)$ **17.–19.** Answers may vary. **21.** $\frac{2}{5}$ **23.** $\frac{1}{3}$ **25.** $\frac{3}{5}$ **27.** $y < x + 2$ **29.** $y < 2x + 9$ **31.** $A: x + y > 3$; $B: x + y < 3$ **37.** $y = 2x + 5; 2; 5$ **39.** $y = 4x - 2; 4; -2$ **45.** $\{(-\frac{4}{3}, \frac{7}{3})\}$ **47.** $\{(0, 2)\}$ **51.** 6 **53.** $\frac{3}{4}$ **55.** 14 **57.** 3 **59.** ± 15 **61.** 2 **63.** 10 **65.** 8.6 inches **67.** $\{27\}$ **69.** $\{-5, 5\}$ **71.** $\{-2 + \sqrt{5}, -2 - \sqrt{5}\}$ **73.** $\{-2, \frac{1}{3}\}$ **75.** $\left\{\dfrac{7 + \sqrt{85}}{6}, \dfrac{7 - \sqrt{85}}{6}\right\}$ **77.** 112° **79.** 85° **81.** 55° **83.** $27\frac{1}{2}°$ **85.** 100° **87.** 50° **89.** 234.9 feet **91.** 58°

Pages 518–522 (1973 edition) **45.** $\{(4, -1)\}$ **47.** $\{(4, -3)\}$ **51.** 8 **53.** .04 **55.** 4 **57.** 20 **59.** −6 **61.** 10 **63.** 1 **65.** 16.1 inches **67.** $\{20\}$ **69.** $\{\pm 2\sqrt{3}\}$ **71.** $\{-5 + 2\sqrt{7}, -5 - 2\sqrt{7}\}$ **73.** $\{\frac{1}{4}, -1\}$ **75.** $\{1 + 2\sqrt{2}, 1 - 2\sqrt{2}\}$ **77.** 70° **79.** 70° **81.** 90° **83.** 180° **85.** 5 **87.** 25 sq. in. **89.** 10π in. **91.** $m(\overline{ED}) = 45.4$ in.